**Office Management
and Control**
*The Administrative
Managing of
Information*

Office Management and Control
The Administrative Managing of Information

GEORGE R. TERRY, Ph.D.

Ball State University

Seventh Edition   1975

60801

RICHARD D. IRWIN, INC.   *Homewood, Illinois   60430*

Irwin-Dorsey International   London, England   WC2H 9NJ
Irwin-Dorsey Limited   Georgetown, Ontario   L7G 4B3

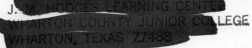

Seventh Edition

First Printing, May 1975

ISBN   0-256-01657-7
Library of Congress Catalog Card No. 74–27545
Printed in the United States of America

To the Memory of
My Mother

Preface

This seventh edition of *Office Management and Control* is a thoroughly modern volume placing its emphasis upon the management of paperwork and reflecting the tremendous change and constant improvement which continue to characterize nearly every facet of office management. Announcements of new office machines, new techniques, and new concepts of managing paperwork keep emerging at what seems to be a continuous rate. Describing how a given amount of office work was performed last year is commonly greeted by the statement, "We don't do it that way anymore." This dynamic quality of office management, however, is pointed toward very simple, yet significant goals. They are to (1) provide an essential service to the organization and (2) help all management members perform their work more effectively.

Featured in this seventh edition to support these goals are new patterns of office management thought, new and sharper tools with which to work, and a relating of the many fresh and specialized activities of the office into a coherent totality. In this book, to the tried and true past practices have been added the significant and most meaningful new developments in the office management area. Further, in the reworking, the adding, and the subtracting of material, careful attention was paid to suggestions and experiences shared by many users of the previous editions. The result is an updated, comprehensive, and practical office management book designed and written to meet the needs of the teacher, student, and practitioner, and a book about which they can be enthusiastic.

Several of the changes made in this seventh edition of *Office Management and Control* that reflect the dynamics of office management will be mentioned. First is the coverage of word processing systems that are revolutionizing the typing of all office materials. Without doubt, we are entering a new era in the performance of this most basic office work and in the discovery of how best to manage it. The human element in the office is receiving more and more managerial attention. Great forward strides in the management of this resource of resources are being made in the office, yet much more needs to be done. The most successful approaches, practices, and techniques in today's office management are included in this new seventh edition. Transactional analysis, for example, and its use in communication, in understanding human behavior, and in effective management are discussed in the light of the help this technique can provide the contemporary office manager. New material on the latest in office machines—improvements and developments in the centralized computer, the emphasis on computer networks with multiple terminal units equipped with screen and capability to input or output data, the minicomputer which brings computer processing within the economic reach of almost every enterprise—and the influence of many other developments such as OSHA's effect upon office safety practices are indicative of additional and specific improvements included in this new edition.

All of these changes, however, have not changed the real core of this book which deals basically with the management of creating, processing, retaining, and distributing information, whether manual or machine means are employed. Likewise, the key objective and the chief stabilizer of study in office management remains the same, namely, getting the necessary office work done in the best way. And it is interesting to observe that this was stated over 26 years ago in the first edition.

The terms *office management* and *information management* are used interchangeably in this book. The term information management is more representative, precise, and inclusive. Yet the original and older identification, office management, enjoys widespread acceptance and is, in fact, the common generic term. Hence, the interchangeability of the identifying terminology.

The material is presented in a logical and easy to follow sequence. First, an introduction and short review of office management is offered. Following this, the efforts included in planning *what office work* is to be done, are discussed. Conceptualization of the way in which the office work can best be accomplished is stressed. The analysis, design, and improvement of systems, the development of the best method for work accomplishment, and the creating and using of office forms, records, letters, and reports are representative of the key subject areas. Next, planning *how the office work* will be done, is discussed. This constitutes Part III which includes both the manual and the machine means. The latest developments in computer processing, computer information networks, and micrographics are included. Next, the area of office organizing is discussed in which the means for getting office employees to work together effectively are developed. The formal and informal office organizations, the importance of people in an organization, the bringing together and the arranging of office physical facilities to provide a coordinated and pleasing environment are presented in some depth. The current problems of office organization are fully covered. Following this, in Part V, the popular and vital area of actuating those who do the office work is discussed. The current concepts and latest activities in motivating office employees are thoroughly examined with suggestions offered as to their practical application in the office. Presented are contemporary thoughts on office supervision, development of office employees, salary administration, communication among office personnel, working with office unions, and office safety. Lastly, the office manager's task of controlling is discussed. These managerial efforts are performed to ensure that what is accomplished is in keeping with what was planned for. The need and use of office standards, the efficient use of time, and the achievement of adequate and proper quality and quantity of office work at an acceptable cost are among the important subject areas of this part.

This seventh edition features conciseness with broad coverage. The writing has been tightened, overlaps eliminated, and the presentations made more compact. However, no sacrifice of content is made. The number of chapters is reduced from 33 to 28, with 5 new chapters, a complete revising of 11 chapters, and updating of the remaining 12 chapters. It is believed that, in all, this new edition presents an attractive, complete, and interesting book on office management.

To encourage and facilitate study, nearly 400 review questions and 81 case problems are included. More than one-half of the questions and of the case problems are new. All questions and case problems appearing in the former edition were carefully screened and only those applicable to current office conditions or proven effective from usage of the previous edition were retained. Hence ample, appropriate, and selective material is provided for purposeful participation in studying office management.

A large number of practicing office managers, nonmanagers, friends, teachers, and students have assisted me, directly and indirectly, in preparing this seventh edition. To each of them I express my sincere appreciation. The suggestions of Warren C. Weber, California State Polytechnic University, and C. Joseph Basehore, Phoenix Community College, merit special acknowledgement. Their critical and detailed reviews included meaningful clues and important suggestions for improvement, and I hereby extend my special thanks for their timely helpfulness.

April 1975   GEORGE R. TERRY

Contents

fication. Applying Office Work Simplification. Obtain All the Facts about This Work. Devise Improvement. Apply the Derived Improved Means. Common Charts of Office Work Simplification: *Process Chart. Procedure Flow Chart. Movement Diagram. The Left- and Right-Hand Chart. Production Study Chart. Operator-Machine Activity Chart.*

Part I

Introduction

Let us start our study of office management with a discussion of what office work is, its reasons for being, its importance today, the vital changes it is undergoing, the brilliant opportunities it offers, and the essential concepts needed to manage it adequately. This introductory material provides a useful indoctrination to office management and consists of one chaper, "Information and Office Management."

Chapter 1

Information and Office Management

Talk that does not end in any kind of action is better suppressed altogether.

Thomas Carlyle

Our greatest resource is *information*. It is essential not only in modern living, but also in the administrating and the performing of most activities in every enterprise. It is basic, for example, to all efforts involving purchasing, sales, services, production, personnel, taxes, plans, programs, and controls. It is universal for it exists everywhere—in our stores, schools, businesses, churches, hospitals, military, and government.

Consider the production and sale of a television set. In order to follow a satisfactory plan of production, materials must be ordered and available when needed, a plan of manufacture designed, and shipping schedules developed. Likewise, bills, invoices, and correspondence must be written. In addition, records of transactions, accounting, cost figures, cost of services, and taxes will be required.

Since paper is often the medium used for information, the term "paperwork" is commonly used to identify information efforts, even when other media such as microfilm, tape, disc, or laser beam is involved. The term *information* is preferred and should be used. It is the more accurate and inclusive terminology.

Information is meaningful data—words, figures, or symbols—that convey usable knowledge. Data are the raw materials which by means of processing are converted into information. The processing, such as reading, writing, calculating, and sorting, puts the data in a form and relationship that reveals some significance pertinent to the event to which it applies. Much of this processing and handling of information is done

3

in a physical place called "the office", but by no means is all this work concentrated in such an area. Also, it should be noted that not all data are information and, from the user's viewpoint, some information has far greater value than other information.

The management of information is the direct thrust of this book. Among the important problems to be resolved are (1) to determine the nature of the information required, by whom, and in what format, and (2) to provide the necessary information at the time and place needed and at a cost compatible with an accepted value criteria. Basically information is to help; it should assist its recipient in performing a task. Management of information efforts is vital; it ranks as a major activity. To perform it satisfactorily necessitates an understanding of all the considerations comprising the activity of information administration.

The identity, *information management,* is gaining usage as is also *administrative management* in preference to that of the older term, *office management.* The latter, however, is the generic term and continues to enjoy wide acceptance especially by the layman. Therefore, in the title of this book, office management has been retained and with it the identities of information management and administrative management will be considered interchangeable.

Information Growth

Information has expanded very rapidly and along with this growth the need for more and better information management. Perphaps the best evidence of information growth is the number of people performing this type of work. Pertinent data are shown in Figure 1–1. Observe that from 1940 to 1973 the total population increased 58 percent, the total working force expanded 84 percent, and the number engaged in clerical occupations increased more than 211 percent. In 1940, about one employee in ten was a clerical employee; in 1973, about one in five.

Why this enormous growth? A number of factors seem responsible. First is the growth and complexity of our economy and the enterprises within it. As companies expand, merge, and diversify there is greater need for formal information. Greater product and service diversification, as well as geographical expansion—often to multinational dimensions, increase the demand for information. Further, communicating with remote subsidiaries and branches adds to the informational requirements. Extremely important is the increasing number of service industries. As of 1975 for the United States, nearly two-thirds of the private nonagricultural sector are clerical and service employees. By 1980, according to government forecasts, there will be two and one-half times more clerical

FIGURE 1-1
Total Population of the United States, Total Working Force, Number of
Clerical Workers, and Percentage of Clerical Workers to Total Working Force
for the Years 1870-1973

Year	Total Population of the United States	Total Working Force	Clerical Workers	Percentage– Clerical to Total Working Force
1973	208,824,000	83,299,000	14,372,000	17.3
1968	201,166,000	75,920,000	12,768,000	16.8
1965	194,700,000	70,169,242	10,963,761	15.6
1960	181,057,000	66,681,537	9,783,632	14.6
1950	151,230,000	55,835,340	6,866,374	12.3
1940	131,950,000	45,166,083	4,612,356	10.2
1930	123,080,000	48,829,920	4,025,324	8.2
1920	106,970,000	41,614,248	3,111,836	7.5
1910	92,410,000	38,167,336	1,718,458	4.5
1900	76,090,000	29,073,233	1,068,993	3.7
1890	63,056,438	22,735,661	801,505	3.5
1880	50,262,382	17,392,099	518,439	3.0
1870	39,904,593	12,505,923	305,502	2.4

Source: U.S. Government Printing Office publications authored by the following offices
of the U.S. Department of Commerce:
    Office of Business Economics, *Survey of Current Business* (May, 1973), pp. 7, 11–34;
and, Bureau of the Census, *Statistical Abstract*, 1973, pp. 5, 233, 245. *1955 Annual Report
on the Labor Force*, pp. 3–5. *1950 Census of Population*, vol. 1: *Population*, pp. 110–12.
Sixteenth Census of the United States, 1940, vol. 3: *Population*, p. 76. *Fifteenth Census of
the United States, 1930*, vol. 5: *Population*, pp. 10–22. *Twelfth Census of the United States,
1900*, Special Reports: "Occupations," pp. 1 and ii.

and service employees than manufacturing employees, or about 7 out
of every 10 employees will be in the clerical and service classification.
    Second, the trend toward more and more managers over specialized
areas has brought about the need for gathering, processing, and distributing information to a wide range of executives within relatively
short periods. Also, management members are becoming more and more
sophisticated in the use of information. They demand more information.
The problem of using information effectively centers mainly around
questions of the type and of the format in which the information should
come to managers. This is the reason for much of the college student's
and the management trainees work being focused on training for information use, which includes such subjects as systems information, financial data, accounting data, and new analytical techniques.
    A third major reason for the growth in information is the force of
competition, both domestic and foreign. The managers of a company,
for example, may have to decide where to locate a warehouse for maximum marketing impact. The information requirements necessary to reach
this decision are large and involve digestion of a considerable number

of facts. In turn, the increasing expenditures for research and development to gain a competitive edge have brought new processes and new products which, in turn, have accelerated the need for accurate information on production activities, financial needs, and other phases of a business. Likewise, many believe the emphasis upon quantitative techniques of management, the design of systems, and the increase in the number of computers are the basic causes for the growth of information.

Fourth, information of various types have come into existence because it is required by government. In this category is information relating to taxes and compliance with regulations and numerous legal requirements. Without proper information, managers are unable to comply with the law. And it is interesting to observe that there were in 1975 over 7 million office employees in public administration. The tidal wave of government paperwork evinces protests by business leaders swamped by official questionnaires and reports. Typical complaints: "we must keep information on 19 separate items about each employee," and "government red tape takes more than 180 hours of my time a year." The Federal Office of Management and Budget estimates that in 1971 about 6,500 different kinds of forms and inquiries, exclusive of tax and banking forms, were filled out by business, individuals, state and local officials. According to the National Archives and Records Service, cost of all paperwork in government approximates $8–10 billion each year. This is a lot of information and probably includes some nonessential data, a condition that poses opportunity for improvement via effective information management.

Last, some portion of the growth in information is undoubtedly due to inadequate efforts to manage it. Generally speaking, we have been lax in preparing essential information only, in adequate motivation of office employees, and in the development of proper systems, procedures, and methods.

Need for Information

Information is needed primarily for two major reasons (1) to serve as a discipline, and (2) to provide the basis for decisions. A course of action depends in great measure upon the information that an individual receives and the information returned. This two-way information flow is significant for it serves as an essential discipline. The flow of information to a person forms the basis for what is done; the flow of information away from a person includes the reporting of results achieved and the fulfilling of responsibility. These efforts stimulate the person to think and act in self-motivating terms. Gained is an understanding of what is being done and why, and in turn, this develops personal initiative in the performance of the work. The challenge is to design and achieve these informational flows so that all members of a group or of an entire enterprise behave and act in keeping with the master plan. In this sense, complete integration of efforts is won and there is a common bond among all members via the information linkage. In other words, information serves as the essential medium through which various effects of people of an enterprise are fused together. Thus, information can be called the "catalytic agent" of modern management.[1]

The second major reason, to provide the basis for decisions, deals with the fact that a manager's job is to achieve stated goals and the degree of success in this regard is directly dependent upon making the right decisions at the right time. The basis for right decisions is adequate, accurate, and timely information. Utilizing poor information for decision making can lead to deep troubles. But supplying the proper information is not an end in itself, rather it is a device by which the decision makers get information to help solve their problems. By selecting, rejecting, and coordinating the information, the decision maker converts the information into intelligence and action. Hence, some aptly refer to a manager as an "information converter."

The use of information in decision making implies that the decision maker, or operative manager, must be informed. Both the kind and amount of information supplied are important. And further, the recipient must understand the nature and type of information required to manage the activity under question. Quite often to meet this condition is a difficult task for the information manager to carry out. But being informed and understanding what is supplied is only half the story. The other half is that there is a need for the operating management member *not to know*. Commonly, more information is supplied than needed—a condition that stems from the erroneous belief that more and more information is desirable and will be good for the manager to know. Inevitably such a view results in supplying information that is nonessential. It is the responsibility of the information manager to refrain from providing information that does not inform or that is made up of details on which a management member is not required to reach a decision.

Further, there are two other considerations meriting inclusion here. First, much information required for decision making must be processed and distributed quickly if it is to be of value and a satisfactory level of service maintained. The timing of information is of significant importance in office management. Second, every decision, even if remote, eventually affects other decisions. This means that evaluation of informa-

---

[1] *Catalytic agent* is a term used in chemistry and means an element the presence of which is necessary to bring about a desired reaction between other elements but which does not itself enter into the reaction. In a similar manner, office work brings about a desired reaction of business elements but does not enter into the reaction itself.

tion in terms of operational results from use of that information must be performed with speed and accuracy, if the information is to provide maximum service. This requirement is eased somewhat by taking into account that within a given organization, all decisions and operations intertwine to some degree. Each activity is a part of a network of inter-related activities.

Classifications and Characteristics of Information

Information is heterogeneous. Different types are employed for different uses and each must be viewed in light of its own peculiar properties. The classifications of information are helpful in understanding and applying information management. One dichotomy of information is *internal and external information,* the names referring to the source of the information generated. Payrolls and products sold are representative of internal information; production plans of a competitor and the status of an order placed with a vendor represent external information. A second classification is *repetitive and nonrepetitive information.* The former is generated at intervals of not less than once a year such as inventory information; the latter includes special studies made to assist managers. Another classification is *compulsory and operational information.* Compulsory information is that required by government and other external agencies including auditing firms and insurance companies. It should be automated as much as possible and have minimum management engagement. In contrast, operational information is employed by managers to plan and to carry out their operations. Hence, operational information efforts should be designed to have maximum managerial utility and should be analyzed periodically to determine the benefits it delivers. Another classification is *active information* which requires its recipient to take some action, and *passive information* which does not, such as notification that a shipment has been made. A last and fifth classification is *past and future information.* Planning requires future information and projection based on past information.

From these classifications, the information manager normally employs generalizations helpful in analyzing the information requirements of an enterprise. To illustrate, the greater the number of management decisions at the higher levels, the greater is the importance of external and future information. Nonrepetitive information is a poor candidate for automation. In contrast, information that is repetitive and active usually offers good possibilities for automation. It is helpful to classify operational information by the stability of its input and the sensitivity of its output. Operational information of greatest managerial value has low input stability and high sensitivity output. It should be given priority in processing and normally merits careful analysis and interpretation.

Several outstanding characteristics of information help to provide a better comprehension of the thing being managed in information management. Quite important is the fact that information is *facilitating* in that it contributes and aids in accomplishing work considered essential. Information assists in efforts to increase output, lower costs, stimulate employees, pay wages, purchase materials, and ship orders. The individual work of practically every department in an enterprise is implemented by information. For example, a credit department cannot operate successfully without current records of creditors, amounts and dates due, lists of delinquent accounts, credit histories of customers, and a quantity of correspondence.

Closely allied with this facilitating characteristic is the feature of information having a *service* attribute. In and of itself, information serves little purpose. It is, for example, a service to the top executives, to the production department, to the sales department, and to the finance department. Information helps top executives by providing them with data which are necessary in order to manage the enterprise. By means of information, the production department is helped to improve its service and to lower costs, the sales department is aided in its work of selling the product, and the finance department is assisted in maintaining written evidence of the financial status of the enterprise.

Information is *dispersed;* it exists in every department of an enterprise. It is dispersed because it is required by people throughout an entire organization as well as by certain others outside the organization. The swing to office mechanization, and especially to large computers, has resulted in much information from a centralized area, but still more is created and used in other areas. For example, a milling machine operator in a factory brings into being information in the normal course of daily duty, and the amount is considerable if incentive and production control are used. Likewise the registered nurse in a hospital handles sizable amounts of information, and the same is true of the tax collector.

Further, it should be noted that to a significant degree the *volume* of information is determined by factors outside the control of those performing information management. Illustrative of these factors are the number of shipments, the amount of collections, the number of open accounts, the quantity of sales letters, the number of factory employees, and the number of items manufactured or sold. This unique characteristic makes for problems in information management. For example, provisions for fluctuations in the work load must be provided, even though the timing and extent of the variations usually cannot be accurately forecast. Also, decisions made by noninformation management members, and about which the information manager has little or nothing to say, affect the information volume.

In addition, information is generally characterized as being *an indirect contributor to profit,* since in private enterprises it acts through operative departments such as production, sales, and finance.[2] This means that those in information management are frequently on the defensive insofar as justifying expenditures is concerned. It is, for example, unlike sales, where by spending so much it is hoped to realize a resultant gain in sales and profits. The information manager normally must justify that department's work and its cost and point out wherein it is good management to make the expenditure.

Changes and Challenges

In an area such as office management that is so important and is growing so fast, it follows that there are within it an abundance of changes and challenges. This has been implied in the above discussion, but a brief elaboration of this condition appears warranted. The office has been in what might be described a constant state of flux during the past several decades. And there is nothing to indicate a letup in this constant change. Among the more important changes are those pertaining to technology, people, and demand. Technological change is evidenced by the seemingly endless line of new office machines and equipment being made available. Automation in the office is the classical example of what machines can do for humans, of how the mode of achieving work is altered, and of what managerial adjustments are thereby required.

People change is tremendous. The skills required, work environment, and philosophy of management are changing very significantly. Efforts are widespread to create an office conducive to greater personnel satisfaction, better concentration, and more productivity. And use of the relatively unskilled is modifying former concepts about the selecting and developing of office employees. There is a growing awareness of the social responsibility of the office manager and the need to alleviate social as well as economic problems of the office.

The demand change also is basic in modern office management. What was once described as a flood of paperwork was merely a dribble compared to the deluge of today. The demand for information and its proper handling seems insatiable. Month after month we are turning out more and more information; the peak is not yet in sight.

Fundamental changes such as these create new challenges to the office manager and some of the older challenges grow larger. Meeting these challenges confronts office managers because in the long run they can survive only if successful adaption to the new conditions is achieved.

---

[2] *Profit,* as used here, is the residual income accruing to the owner of an enterprise after paying all the economic aids of production—that is, rent on all land used, interest on all capital used, and wages to all labor used.

Those who do not recognize or adjust to change face limited success and in some instances almost certain failure.

Among the more exciting and important challenges are those in the following list which is intended to be suggestive rather than exhaustive:

1. *Developing a Greater Appreciation for Information among Management Members.* The need here is great. Many managers do not fully understand the vital contributions of the information manager.

2. *Applying Greater Creativity to Information Management.* While the track record in this area is reasonably good, it must not be forgotten that a new idea or a new concept may be the answer to a perplexing information management question.

3. *Coordinating All Activities via the Information Compiled and Distributed.* The desired unity of effort by all members of an organization can be greatly enhanced by means of well planned and executed information management. *is there a better way to do it?*

4. *Eliminating Unnecessary Paperwork Performed.* Information requirements should be defined more carefully. Information that is needed should be provided in the most efficient manner; information not needed should be eliminated.

5. *Increasing Office Productivity.* This challenge entails more than concentrating on lowering office costs. Productivity results from many different and related activities. Good utilization of equipment and machines and enlightened leadership are commonly and correctly pointed out as important contributors. However, in the office we are also concerned about the service provided and its improvement. In addition, the quality of information is important. An important secret of successful office productivity is quality, not quantity. Hence, the key consideration to attaining better office productivity is to gain effectiveness and economy with the best combination of price, service, and quality.

6. *Improving Information Systems.* Further progress is in order to develop plans of integrated systems which effectively link and coordinate the various subsystems, procedures, and methods.

7. *Using Effectively the "Automated Office."* Before transaction to automation, extreme care must be taken in evaluating the need for the changeover, the selection of machines, and the end results to be realized. Responding solely to what has been done in the past and automating past work or of following an "all purpose" approach encompassing all possible information for all levels of management, leads to built-in waste that defies eradication once it is in the computer.

8. *Developing an Improved Office Organization Structure.* Changes in the information management area are placing new demands upon the organization structure used. The present arrangements and practices must be modified to meet better the modern requirements.

9. Determining Better Means of Motivating Office Employees.
Benefits from using the best systems and office machines can easily
be offset unless the persons using them are capable, knowledgeable,
and highly motivated. Much more needs to be known about the behavior
of employees particularly with reference to what can the manager do
to insure that the work group members are satisfied, dedicated, and
enthusiastic employees.

must know your people

*10. Attracting and Acquiring the Better Graduates from Schools
for Information Work.* Badly needed are new and improved efforts
designed to make the desirable young person select information work
as a career. Information management is currently not as well known
as many of the other management areas.

11. Establishing More and Better Information Standards. There
is need for improved control based on better measurements and expectancy levels which stimulate the individual employee's initiative and
avoid excessive rigidity.

12. Reducing Cost of Supplying Needed Information. Wide adoption of improved office methods and machines along with extensive programs designed to improve personnel effectiveness demonstrate the
strong desire to reduce office costs. But this cost reduction must not
impair office services actually needed, otherwise the cost savings are
false and detrimental to the enterprise's total operations.

The Management of Information

Any enterprise incapable of managing its information requirements
is practically certain to find itself in difficulty. Managing information
covers the creation, collection, processing, storage, retrieval, transmission,
and ultimate destruction of information that appears in a variety of
shapes including office forms, reports, directives, and correspondence.
It involves the achievement of stated objectives and extends from the
inception of data at a remote point through its passage into the mainstream of the enterprise's processing and handling efforts to its final
terminus.

Analysis shows that the supplying of information requires the performance of certain fundamental activities upon data. We will term these
activities, basic elements. In any given individual case, a selected predetermined sequence or pattern of these elements is followed in order
to obtain information in a form and at a time and place desired. Figure
1–2 shows the ten basic elements along with the corresponding reason
each element is performed and the results obtained from it. For example,
sorting (number 6) is performed to classify the data and results in
the data being related to one or more bases. It would be difficult to
overstate the importance of these basic elements. They serve as the
nucleus around which all information work revolves.

FIGURE 1–2
The Basic Elements Performed on Data

Basic Element Performed	Why Performed	Results in:
1. Creating	To initiate and bring data into being	Data existence and availability
2. Collecting	To bring together the data for processing or storing	Identity of data location and volume
3. Reading	To interpret data by going over characters, words, and symbols	Awareness of data existence
4. Writing, typing, card punching, or papertape perforating (frequently called *input*)	To facilitate processing by putting data on or in medium, i.e., alphabetical or numerical marks on paper, holes in paper, magnetic areas on tape, and magnetic ink on paper	Start of data processing
5. Recording or printing (frequently called *output*)	To obtain results of processing, the data—in medium form for processing purposes—are converted to form easily read by a human being, if not already in that form	End of data processing
6. Sorting	To classify the data	Data being related to one or more bases
7. Transmitting	To disseminate, give or send out the data	Data availability for specific purpose and place
8. Calculating	To manipulate the data mathematically	Numerical data being added, subtracted, multiplied, or divided
9. Comparing	To check data for accuracy and completeness	Quantitative and qualitative inspection of data
10. Storing	To retain or set aside the data for future use	Data being available when needed

Note: The meaning of each of the following terms, frequently used in information management, is included in the above listing:

(a) Interpreting (usually associated with No. 4 or No. 5) is imprinting the meaning of the punched holes in a punched card on that card.

(b) Reproducing (usually associated with No. 4) is duplicating an exact copy of a punched card.

(c) Collating (usually associated with No. 6) is merging sets of related data into a single set.

(d) Segregating (usually associated with No. 6) is separating sets of related data into several sets.

(e) Verifying (usually associated with No. 9) is determining the accuracy of data.

Information management is, in essence, the application of management to the work associated with these basic elements. Management consists of four fundamental functions or activities including:

1. Planning. To determine mentally a course of action, giving consideration to the factors influencing the particular situation and attempting to indicate future conditions in order to accomplish a desired objective.

2. Organizing. To establish the work environment, divide the work into amounts suitable for efficient performance, appoint personnel to specific positions, provide the necessary materials and machines to perform designated activities, and establish proper work relationships among both the organization units and the personnel.

3. ***Actuating.*** To stimulate and maintain the desire of the members of the work group to perform their respective work enthusiastically in order to achieve the predetermined objective in accordance with the plan.

4. ***Controlling.*** To ascertain what is accomplished, evaluate it, determine the "feedback," and apply corrective measures, if needed, to insure results in keeping with the plan.

Tying together the concept of the basic elements and the fundamental functions of management, we have the illustration shown by Figure 1–3. Within the area of information represented by the large rectangle are the basic elements. Data are created and collected, then subjected to any or all of the six elements of read, write, record, sort, calculate, and compare. Frequently these six elements are called "processing" the data. Further, the data are either transmitted or stored. If stored, they are ultimately either retrieved or destroyed. Retrieved data are transmitted or reprocessed. Also, some data created and collected are not processed, but transmitted or stored for future use.

The work represented by these various elements is subjected to or constrained by the management forces of planning, organizing, actuating, and controlling. This is illustrated in the figure by the headings listing the major managerial work performed. Planning, for example, includes the manager taking actions to conceive, analyze, design, and forecast.

The four fundamental functions, planning, organizing, actuating, and controlling (POAC) are the distinguishing characteristics of management. They apply universally to management, be it production management, finance management, hospital management, or information management. This means that information management is an activity; it is not a person or a group of people. Management can be studied and proficiency in it can be attained. To qualify as a manager, one performs the activity of management. Hence, those who perform planning, organizing, actuating, and controlling in the information work area are information managers. The use of these four fundamental functions of management marks the essential difference between a clerk and information manager, or between an accountant and the manager of the accounting department. Knowing how to write letters, for example, is not sufficient to manage the correspondence department.

A schematic drawing of information management is shown in Figure 1–4. The objectives are shown on the right. They are accomplished by utilizing the basic resources available to an information manager, shown on the left of the figure. The information manager subjects these basic resources to planning, organizing, and controlling. The persons who are

FIGURE 1-3
Information Management in Diagrammatic Form

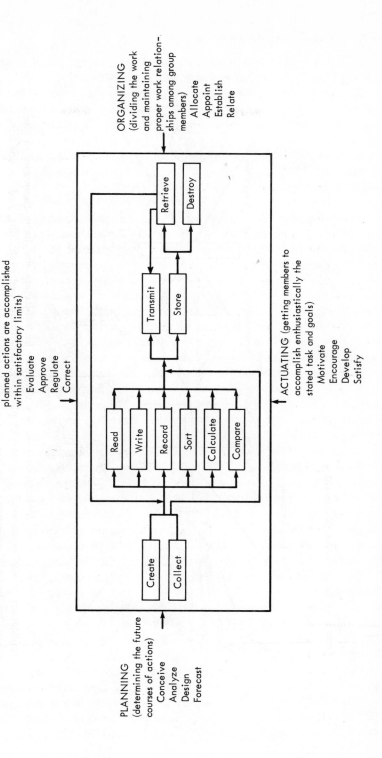

PLANNING (determining the future courses of actions)
Conceive
Analyze
Design
Forecast

CONTROLLING (seeing that planned actions are accomplished within satisfactory limits)
Evaluate
Approve
Regulate
Correct

ORGANIZING (dividing the work and maintaining proper work relation-ships among group members)
Allocate
Appoint
Establish
Relate

ACTUATING (getting members to accomplish enthusiastically the stated task and goals)
Motivate
Encourage
Develop
Satisfy

Create
Collect

Read
Write
Record
Sort
Calculate
Compare

Transmit
Store

Retrieve
Destroy

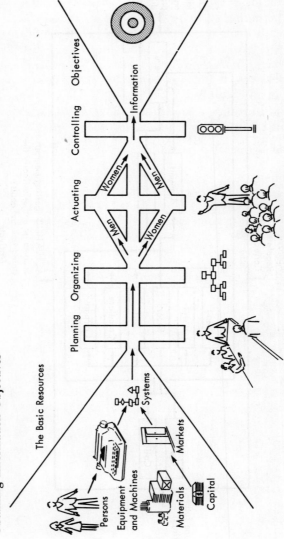

FIGURE 1-4
Obtaining Information Objectives

The Basic Resources

Persons
Equipment and Machines
Systems
Materials
Markets
Capital

Planning   Organizing   Actuating   Controlling   Objectives

Men   Women   Women   Men

Information

The objectives of the information work are obtained by subjecting the Basic Resources to the application of the managerial functions of planning, organizing, and controlling, and, in addition, subjecting the basic resources of persons to the activity of actuating.

members of the work group are subjected to actuating in order to get them to want to achieve the objectives and help insure that the end results will be the stated objectives.

From what has been stated, it follows that information management can be defined as *the planning, organizing, and controlling of information work, and actuating those performing it so as to achieve predetermined objectives.* It deals with the life cycle of business data and information from their creation through their processing, distributing, and ultimate destroying, if obsolete. This concept of information management is broad and inclusive; it includes managerial efforts over information work anywhere in an enterprise.

Among the well-known organizations active in the area of information management are:

Administrative Management Society, 1927 Old York Rd., Willow Grove, Pa. 19090

American Accounting Association, 653 S. Orange Ave., Sarasota, Florida. 33577

American Management Association, 135 W. 50th St., New York, N.Y. 10020

American Records Management Association, 24 N. Wabash Ave., Chicago, Illinois. 60602

American Society for Personnel Administration, 19 Church St., Berea, Ohio. 44017

Association for Computing Machinery, 1133 Avenue of Americas, New York, N.Y. 10036

Association for Systems Management, 24587 Bagley Rd., Cleveland, Ohio. 44138

Business Equipment Manufacturers' Association, 1828 L St. N.W., Washington, D.C. 20036

Conference of American Small Business Organizations, 407 S. Dearborn St., Chicago, Ill. 60605

The Conference Board, 845 Third Ave., New York, N.Y. 10022

Data Processing Management Association, 505 Busse Highway, Park Ridge, Ill. 60068

Financial Executives Institute, 633 Third Ave., New York, N.Y. 10017

National Microfilm Association, 8728 Colesville Road, Silver Spring, Maryland. 20910

National Records Management Council, 555 Fifth Ave., New York, N.Y. 10017

National Secretaries Association, 616 E. 63rd St., Kansas City, Mo. 64110

National Small Business Association, 1225 19th St. N.W., Washington, D.C. 20036

CURRENT VITAL CONSIDERATIONS OF INFORMATION MANAGEMENT

It is helpful to observe that in information management vital consideration must be given to the objectives being sought. Information management is purposive and all managers as well as management members engaged in information activity should be thoroughly familiar with what results are sought. There is a mission to perform, a project to initiate, a service to supply. Without objectives the meaning of management becomes nebulous and there is no satisfactory basis for evaluating the managerial efforts. Ideally, objectives should be specific, measurable, clearly defined, realistic, and readily understood by all affected by them.

Information objectives can be classified as pertaining primarily to (1) service, (2) social responsibilities, or (3) profit. Service is of great importance because information work is done to assist others in doing their work more effectively. Also of significance is the objective dealing with social responsibilities which stresses the attainment of the goal in accordance with certain moral and ethical codes as set forth by the industry and society in which the enterprise operates. Last, objectives emphasizing profit or gain assist in getting the work done effectively and for relatively low expenditures.[3] Objectives may be specific or general, written or unwritten, long- or short-term, temporary or permanent, or applicable to certain segments of the enterprise or to the office only.

Top management support is essential for information to be successful. Since the office manager is basically handling a service activity, the blessing and backing up of informational efforts undertaken is especially important. Personnel at all levels of the organization must understand what the office manager is trying to accomplish, the need for it, and how these efforts will benefit them. And preferably they should be given the opportunity to participate in such efforts.

Of all the basic resources utilized by the information manager, people are the most important. They can make or break the best of management's intentions and activities. Fortunately, the importance of people in information management is being given more and more emphasis. In this area, the key word to follow is *involvement*. People want a part in managerial activities that affect them. They want a chance to participate and they like to feel that in performing their daily work they are doing something important, and that what they do does make a difference. Basically from their job efforts they desire to gain job satisfactions important to them. At the present time there are tremendous efforts being expended in these directions. Job enrichment programs motivation plans, management by objectives, and employee participation of many different varieties are becoming commonplace both in contemporary literature and in the implementation of information management.

There is also the very important consideration of managerial technique

---

[3] The concept of profit as the objective of any enterprise or segment of an enterprise is actually quite limited. Profit, as such, can be the indirect or the direct aim, depending upon the thinking of the particular company involved. Profit is residual in nature, a by-product resulting from other direct goals.

selection—a consideration that greatly conditions current information management. As used here, managerial technique applies to both the people as well as to the technological means used. Apparently in the case of managerial techniques applied to personnel the superior approach is not to seek the one best technique, but to use several techniques, selecting for each work activity that technique seemingly most appropriate for the individual conditions. Management by objectives, for example, does not work equally well for all types of jobs and conditions. Under technological means the modern information manager has a myriad of choices. Selection can be made, for example, from systems analyses, office work measurements and office equipment and machines with wide varieties of capabilities, speeds, and costs. Here again the common practice is to use several techniques in keeping with what is thought probably the best suited as judged from the characteristics of the individual work activity with special emphasis given to the number of office employees involved and the extent to which the work is routine and repetitive.

INFORMATION MANAGEMENT ACTIVITIES

The activities included in information management are quite numerous; among them are the following:

1. Determining what information is to be made available, where and to whom.
   a. Develop adequate systems, procedures, and methods.
   b. Apply work simplification to clerical work.
   c. Design information formats utilizing effective office forms, reports, and letters.
   d. Coordinate the work of the office with that of the nonoffice.
2. Deciding the type of processing to be used.
   a. Select and utilize information machines.
   b. Establish integrated data processing (IDP).
   c. Distribute the information properly.
3. Following effective records management.
   a. File records and reports.
   b. Maintain information of permanent value, destroy obsolete material.
   c. Specify amount and place of copying information.
4. Establishing and maintaining an effective office organization.
   a. Utilizing both the formal and the informal organization.
   b. Supplying proper organizational relationships.
   c. Providing organizational continuity and balance.
   d. Arrange the office layout.
   e. Determine effective work environment.

5. Inspire the office personnel to do the best of which they are capable.
   a. Give adequate supervision.
   b. Encourage employee involvement.
   c. Follow effective motivational techniques.
   d. Conduct information developmental programs.
6. Measuring and evaluating the information work.
   a. Establish office standards.
   b. Write office manuals.
   c. Utilize proper time allowances.
   d. Maintain quantity and quality standards for information work.
   e. Keep information costs within acceptable limits.
   f. Prepare and use office budget.

OFFICE JOB OPPORTUNITIES

Brilliant careers await those trained in information management. The increasing importance and the rapid growth in this area emphasizes the need for managers. Currently some 75,000 management members are required annually to fulfill the vacancies and new openings in this dynamic sector of the U.S. economy. And the work is extremely challenging. The opportunity to lead, guide, and inspire employees is ever present. Helping others to help themselves can be a very rewarding endeavor. Also the information manager job is highly interesting not only because it is in a dynamic field, but more importantly because it requires understanding of the work of other departments and working with their managers. This means that the information manager enjoys freedom "to get around" an organization, to be quite familiar with current problems and developments. There are few dull moments in the practicing of information management. Also, the working conditions are pleasant and there are frequent challenges that enrich the possibilities for promotion and advancement. In addition, the major qualifications for this managerial position include analytical ability, stability in dealing with the idiosyncracies and emotions of people, skill in communicating, and practical vision to plan effectively.

A growing number of firms have established an executive position of "vice president of managment services" or "manager—information center" or "administrative services manager" or "information manager" and under it have designated middle managers such as systems manager, data processing manager, archives manager, and office services manager. All of these deal with information requirements and development throughout the entire enterprise and coordinate their efforts into an effective unity of information services. The justification for use of these titles is that they are more descriptive of the current managing of information and better denote the companywide range of activities dealing with information. Simply stated, they are another change in the current evolution taking place in information management. Fresh viewpoints and contributions of information technologists, information administrators, and trained paper-work analysts are reshaping the concept of the information manager's role. They are proving to be an indispensable adjunct to top management and are gaining greater and greater recognition and occupying a vital role in the overall management of the enterprise.

Furthermore, the field of office work offers satisfying and responsible careers for nonmanagers with security and opportunity for advancement. The makeup of an office job varies from one office to another depending upon the type of enterprise, its size, and the office work involved. In a small office, a single employee may perform a number of duties while in a large office, the work tends to be more specialized. Among the typical office jobs are typist, stenographer, correspondent, secretary, cashier, credit clerk, payroll clerk, paymaster, business machine operator, messenger, file clerk, receptionist, mail clerk, order clerk, bookkeeper, accountant, statistical clerk, programmer, and computer clerk. For many of these jobs there are several job categories indicating advanced levels in the particular category. To illustrate, a person may start as a beginner typist, advance to typist II, teletypist, and typist I. Likewise a junior accountant may advance to accountant, cost accountant, or general accountant.

The typical office job requires that its holder be a good teamworker. Ability to see another employee's problem and to lend assistance whenever possible are extremely important. The knack of staying with a task until it is finished, being adaptable as well as tactful, should also be included as highly desirable traits. Advantages are offered by performing office work. It has no geographical limitation because it is an essential component of industry, institutional, and government activity. It provides inside work and regular hours. Promotional opportunities are abundant. The bookkeeper who studies accounting finds the door of opportunity open to a higher and higher paying position. Likewise, the receptionist who learns to type and take shorthand will quickly advance to a more responsible position. On the other hand, office work has its disadvantages. It usually requires working under pressure at times. Reports must be ready for an upcoming meeting or "these letters must go out tonight." In addition, there is an element of confinement—you must adapt to inside "desk work" and little physical activity. However, all things taken into account, office work offers satisfying careers of responsibility. To the qualified person it offers security and advancement under generally favorable working conditions. Most beginning office jobs require at least a high school education. Positions of greater responsibility demand additional education as well as practical experience. As in all success, adequate preparation, plus acquiring knowledge and skill, pay off.

QUESTIONS

1. Discuss the meaning of the statement, "Information is needed to serve as a discipline."
2. Identify each of the following:
   a. Information management.
   b. Compulsory information.
   c. "Information converter."
   d. Basic elements performed on data.
3. Can office work do a service job without being facilitating? Can it be facilitating without doing a service job? Explain.
4. Select three common types of paperwork found in an office with which you are familiar; and, for each type, name the basic elements of data processing required to prepare the paperwork.
5. Relate and briefly discuss six current major challenges of information management.
6. What is meant by the statement, "Office work is a service work"? Of what importance is this in office management?
7. In your own words relate what Figure 1–3 shows.
8. Relate an experience in some phase of office work that illustrates poor controlling. Repeat for poor actuating.
9. Visit an office with which you are familiar and find out its major objectives. What do you deduce from the information obtained?
10. What is meant by involvement being the key word to follow in the managing of people performing information work?
11. What is your opinion regarding the future growth of office work?
12. Discuss the opportunities for jobs in the office.

CASE PROBLEMS

Case 1–1. Solso-Hastings, Inc.

Business has not been good for Solso-Hastings, Inc. and three weeks ago, Allan Marshall, vice president in charge of sales in the New York district was promoted to president of the corporation. His record in New York was outstanding and it was generally believed that Mr. Marshall was the most competent manager the corporation had. Now ten days in his new job and office at the Chicago headquarters, he has found out that (1) net profits of the corporation were $107,000 a month a year ago and for the past month were $61,700, (2) sales have dropped $425,000 during the past year to a current level of $4,600,000 annually, (3) cost of purchased items have increased almost 11 percent during the past six months, and (4) labor costs are incomplete and no definite statement can be made about them. Current reports show favorable public reaction to the corporation's new products, advertising expenditures are up about 6 percent over last year, and accounts receivable reached an all-time high level of $1,043,000, roughly an increase of 8 percent over last year.

From his own personal experience and from conversations with the Chicago vice president of sales and the Los Angeles vice president of sales (via long distance telephone), Mr. Marshall concluded that deliveries are too slow, production promises mean very little for they are not kept, credit records of the corporation maintained by the Chicago central office do not reflect current data, and faulty material is being shipped—the present production quality control is inadequate. Mr. Otto Getzdanner, vice president of production at the Chicago main plant, points out that rush orders have become the rule, not the exception, and are accepted even though production facilities are taxed to capacity, sales personnel do not allow sufficient time to fulfill orders, and the cancellation of a customer's order takes excessively long to reach the factory, frequently being received several days after the order has been shipped.

From several lengthy talks with Mr. Daniel Heckmann, the director of information, Mr. Marshall is informed that the office is insufficiently staffed. Six months ago an order to economize was issued to him by the past president. Since then several office people have left the corporation claiming they secured higher paying jobs for the same work with other employers. No attempt was made to keep them by adjusting salaries or operating budgets. Mr. Heckmann states he has experienced great difficulty in acquiring competent help.

Mr. Marshall believed some long-range planning was needed, but before this could get underway, he asked Mr. Heckmann to take corrective actions immediately to help improve the company's present poor condition. Accordingly, Mr. Heckmann took these measures:

1. Hired an additional five clerks.
2. Wrote a personal note to each office employee stating that both the quality and the quantity of the office work for each employee must be improved.
3. Stated that all office supervisors would become working supervisors in order to locate sources of mistakes in papers being prepared. Any employee caught preparing an incorrect billing or invoice would be given five demerits. A total of 15 demerits means automatic employment termination.
4. Indicated his greater involvement in the credit department to improve the work of credit extensions and collecting past due accounts.

Questions:

1. What is the main problem in this case?
2. What is your opinion regarding the measures taken by Mr. Heckmann?
3. What action do you recommend the company take? Why?

Part II

Planning What Office Work Is to Be Done

Our initial step in accomplishing office work effectively is to identify precisely what office work is required, in what format, and what place, in order to provide the information needed. This is a basic attribute of planning. It requires innovation, time, and thought. Extensive trial and error approaches are examined. Logically, the efforts begin with the design and improvements of systems, advance to procedures, then methods, and finally to the selection of information carrying media including office forms, records, letters, and reports.

The five chapters devoted to this vital area include "System Analysis and Design," "Systems Improvement and Concept of Total Systems," "Office Work Simplification," "Forms and Records," and "Letters and Reports."

Chapter **2**

System Analysis and Design

> *The future that we study and plan for begins today.*
>
> Chester O. Fischer

System is the basic structure of modern information management. The concept and application of a system is essential in understanding how the inclusion and coordination of information needs are acquired. Furthermore, it is the system that makes possible the use of modern technological facilities to process data. System analysis and design is the beginning step in planning what office work is to be done.

System Defined

There is nothing new about the concept of systems. It is as old as the human race. Early in life we become acquainted with the solar system and later discover that we ourselves have digestive, nervous, and circulatory systems. In business, reference is commonly made to the inventory control system, the sales-analysis system, the payroll system, and so forth.

From the information management viewpoint, a system can be looked upon as a vehicle of thought and analysis. It has been called a "think process tool." This identity stresses system as providing the medium of thought and conceptualization.

System includes a group of parts or elements interacting to achieve a particular goal. A system exists within an environment that supplies resources as inputs to the system and that accepts processed resources as outputs from the system. A system exists to achieve something.

27

Figure 2–1 shows a simplified system with its basic environment, its parts, and its interrelationships. From its various environmental factors—employees, costs, customers, vendors and so forth shown in the

FIGURE 2–1
A Simplified System

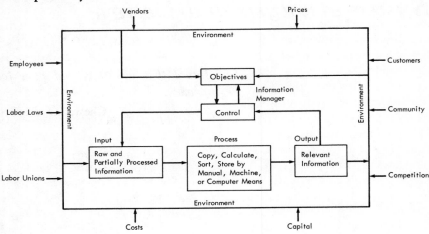

figure, raw information or partially processed information is received. This constitutes input which is processed either manually or by machine resulting in an output which is relevant information for specific needs and used by the firm. It is not only sent back to interested and selected elements of the environment, but also serves as a feedback for control purposes which monitor the system to insure accuracy and reliability of the information.

In many instances, an ordinary activity, commonly viewed as a single activity, is in reality made up of many different and relatively less important activities. Upon close examination we recognize the existence of an orderly relationship of some sort among these various lesser activities making up the entirety. And we discover that the interaction among the lesser actions or parts is necessary so that the entirety or end product performed is in keeping with accomplishing a given goal. Systems-minded people have been viewing problems in this light for many years.

In information management the term, *system,* is commonly used to designate a network of related *procedures* linked together in such a manner as to accomplish a specific goal. In this viewpoint, a system is a network of procedures which are integrated and designed to carry out a major activity. Likewise, a procedure can be considered as *a series of selected clerical steps, usually performed by more than one person, which constitute an established and accepted way of carrying on an entire major phase of office activity.* Office procedures are applied to the handling of such things as incoming orders, accounts payable, purchase orders, making up payrolls, sending out statements, and handling mail. Usually they extend throughout a large portion of the entire office. In turn, a method pertains to an individual's task and a series of methods which are cumulative and integrated make up a procedure. And to repeat, several procedures related and integrated make up a system. Our concern in this chapter is systems—their analysis and design. This includes consideration for procedures, but methods analysis and design is normally treated separately. Hence, we defer discussion of methods, their analysis, design, and improvement until Chapter 4.

To illustrate fully the meaning of system, let us consider an information system followed by an office for the handling of an order received from a customer. In this illustration the efforts of the sales, receiving and shipping, purchasing, and billing departments are included and considered interrelated forming a system. Referring to Figure 2–2, beginning at the left, orders are received from customers by means of salespeople, telephone, or mail. The orders are time stamped and the credit is checked. If credit is not in good standing, a letter is sent to the customer stating the credit situation. If credit is O.K., the items ordered are posted on customer's card and the order is sent to Receiving and Shipping Department where Inventory Control checks inventory to see if adequate stock of required items are on hand to ship the order. If not, a requisition is sent to the Purchasing Department with subsequent steps taken to purchase the items from suppliers with a copy of the purchase order sent to inventory control. For those orders where the inventory count permits shipment, an authorization to ship is sent to order preparation in the receiving and shipping department. Here the order is prepared with copies sent to different destinations as indicated in the figure. Of these copies, one goes to the Billing Department, another copy or packing slip or slips as the case might be—evidence of actual shipment of the order—likewise goes to billing. In addition, the customer's original order is sent to billing. At this point, the customer's original order is checked with the company's order written, and if O.K., the billing copies are made out as indicated by the illustration.

To reiterate, this system for processing customers' orders is really made up of five distinct procedures including the procedure for (1) checking customer's credit, (2) maintaining the physical inventory in the receiving and shipping department, (3) obtaining needed products from vendors, (4) shipping the products purchased to the customer, and (5) issuing billings. The system interrelates and coordinates all the various paperwork activities. It reflects the visualization of how these different types of work tasks are to be handled.

Also, it should be noted that at the bottom of Figure 2–2, is shown

FIGURE 2–2
An Information System for Handling Customer Orders

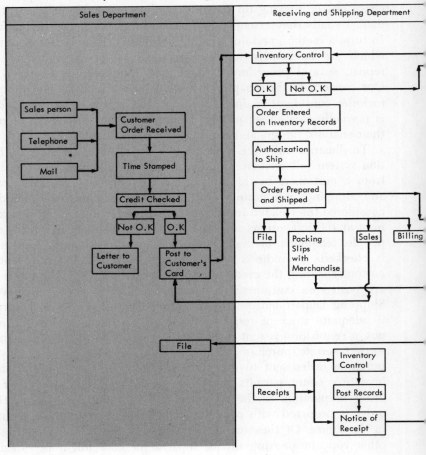

receipts of products by receiving and shipping. Information on these receipts is sent to inventory control and also a notice is sent to purchasing which, after checking, is forwarded to billing for accounts payable purposes.

System Analysis

The detailed examination of a system either to improve an existing one or to design a new system is known as system analysis. The intent is to create a system with the highest practical capability, economy, and efficiency. Manual, limited office mechanization, or full computer means for processing might be utilized depending upon the individual

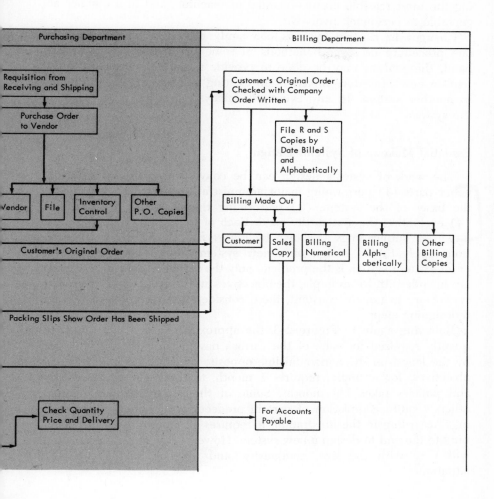

dictates of each case. System analysis comes about for several major reasons: (1) modifications in the information needs require alterations in the present system; (2) technological changes suggest improvements; or (3) a new system is required to fulfill information requirements not supplied by any existent system.

System analysis is extremely challenging. In the case of an existing system, ways must be identified within a relatively short time to improve the system even though those working with the system month after month are unable to suggest how it might be improved. For a new system, the task is equally difficult. What is recommended must be done within the limits established, without needless overlap with other systems, within a predetermined cost that may be very confining, by utilizing the most feasible means—manual or machine, and in a manner acceptable to personnel involved.

Changes in existent systems commonly consist of modifications in one procedure or several methods in some procedures. On the other hand, the analysis may be done to provide a more comprehensive system—a new procedure linked to an existing system, or a system joined to another system. In any event, the analysis precedes the design of the system.

Essential Makeup of Systems Design

The work of systems design can be conveniently divided into four major parts (1) performing major administrative tasks, (2) determining the bases of the system, (3) performing the designing function, and (4) evaluating the system designed. Each of these parts include several important subheadings as shown by Figure 2–3. As indicated, these actions apply to the design of a new system only. When modification of an existent system is the problem, only the activities deemed necessary are included. If, for example, the objectives and constraints of an existent system are to remain constant, these considerations are excluded in the redesigning steps.

Referring again to Figure 2–3, the approximate respective times frequently required for each of the various design activities are indicated by the length of the horizontal line opposite each heading. To establish objectives, for example, requires 1 month, to designate responsibilities and policies takes 1½ months. Some of these activities can overlap, others require completion of certain predecessor activities before starting. According to the illustration, it requires 12 months from the beginning to the end to design a new system. However, the total time required will vary with the size, complexity, and urgency of the particular situation.

Administrative Tasks

Among the first administrative tasks is to establish the objectives. In most instances this is initially performed by a top management group of select members. A simple and general statement is: provide whatever information is required to the recipient in order to fulfill the facilitating and servicing informational needs. This resolves into what information is to be supplied to whom by the system. Further, is the goal also one of reducing present cost, is providing for future growth an important consideration, is more mechanization to be used, and is competition to be equaled or exceeded? At the start of system design, these identifications of objectives are necessarily couched in broad, inclusive, and gen-

FIGURE 2–3
Major Activities in Designing a New System

Activity	Months 0 1 2 3 4 5 6 7 8 9 10 11 12
1. ADMINISTRATIVE TASKS	
a. Establish objectives	▬ (0)
b. Designate responsibilities and policies	▬ (0–1)
c. Define system constraints	▬ (0)
2. BASES OF SYSTEM	
a. Gather facts	▬▬▬ (3–4)
b. Organize facts	▬▬ (4–5)
c. Evaluate facts	▬ (5)
d. Establish system premises	
3. DESIGN OF SYSTEM	
a. Consider various possibilities	▬▬ (5–6)
b. Investigate tradeoffs	▬▬▬ (6–7)
c. Decide on extent of mechanization	▬▬▬ (5–7)
d. Weigh personnel preferences	▬▬ (6)
4. EVALUATE THE SYSTEM	
a. Review overall arrangement	▬ (9)
b. Check company and manager requirements	▬▬ (9–10)
c. Approve proposed system	▬▬ (11)

eral terms. However as the system design progresses, more finite objectives are developed. The exhaustive inquiry for needed information, by whom, when, and in what format uncovers specific goals of information that assist in the creative systems work. But the task of defining objectives must not be compounded. The true objective for an accounts receivable system is to collect money. Net results, costs, and machine availability tend to suffer when statements of objectives become too numerous and too sophisticated.

It is essential that proper designation of those responsible for the system design along with their responsibilities be established early in the program. A growing popular approach is for the top management group to appoint a committee composed of both operating and systems personnel. The former, or operating personnel, provide part-time study participation, assist in defining output requirements, and aid in training operative employees to meet the standards required. The systems personnel conduct the study, evolve the system, and provide the technical support required to maintain the integrity of the informational efforts expended. The committee is guided by and reports to the top management group. Justification for this arrangement is that systems work has become too complex and too important to concentrate it in the hands of one or two persons. Further, a person from each department or representing several departments formally designated to serve as a system liaison makes for system adequacy, acceptance, and affinity.

Constraints of System

Another administrative task is the definition of the proposed system's constraints. Boundaries, even though tentative, must be established to define the scope of the study and possible limits of the system. The boundaries serve to establish the framework within which the system evolved will operate. Any statement of system boundaries depends upon objectives sought and these, in turn, are dependent upon the definition of the proposed system and its content. This definition becomes the initial goal of the system designer. Such requirements can be classified as those which are (1) legal—required by law; (2) operational—required for profitable or serviceable operations; and (3) contractual—required by the customer or outsider to the enterprise.

In some instances, suggestions and specific wishes of top managers are supplied the systems designer. In effect, these serve as constraints for they restrict the scope of certain portions of the proposed system. For example, the chart of Figure 2–4 indicates certain areas for special attention of the designer. Departments are listed along with the respective number of employees. To the right, heading up the several columns are items which might warrant investigation and study. For example, opposite billing, the check mark under organization means that the organization form or the relationship of the billing department to the total organization of the enterprise should be analyzed. A chart like this can be helpful, but admittedly is quite likely to be meager at the initial stage of the system design. In fact, both constraints and objectives are often incomplete at the beginning of system design, but we make assumptions and the best decisions we can, realizing they can be questioned and revised as our design work progresses.

Bases of System

Once the administrative tasks are completed, work can start in determining the bases of the system. For example, to improve an existent

FIGURE 2–4
Chart for Assisting in Determining the Scope of a System

Name of Department	No. of Employees	Objectives	Functions Performed	Controls	Organization	Input	Output	Processing Means
Market Research	9		✓	✓				
Billing	17				✓	✓		✓
Sales	26			✓		✓		
Purchasing	9	✓		✓				✓

system, we would want to know what departments are currently being used, what is the flow of information, how do users evaluate the present information means, and what improvements would they like to see made. An orderly methodology should be followed, otherwise the gathering of data will be chaotic and wasteful. It is possible to playact the part of a piece of paper being processed and trace every step in sequence from origination to its final processing. This is commonly called the "hound-dog" approach. In contrast, the start of getting facts can be made at the final processing stage and subsequently working backwards to the initiation of each document. Or it is sometimes convenient to begin at any point and work forward to the final step or backward to the first step. This is a common approach as exemplified by correcting a bottleneck or backlog in the information flow.

Facts are where you can find them, but care must be exercised in selecting the facts and the sources that are utilized. Experience helps one to be knowledgeable in facts selected, but even lacking experience the planner can proceed to gather many facts which will be helpful. The following fruitful sources are suggested:

1. Organization Charts and Manuals. Organization charts give only sketchy details. However, with organization manuals, they indicate what activities are grouped together, probable authority of the respective members, and the tasks performed. Compiling a list of the tasks performed is especially recommended. From such a list, the identity of the work being done, where it is done, and possible duplications can be ascertained.

2. Systems and Flows of Information. Every pertinent and available file on these subjects can be a source of pertinent information. They reveal the manner of work performance currently and in the past. More important, they indicate the managers' probable preferences. In addition, their general quality regarding accuracy, timeliness, and completeness gives clues as to the status of information handling in the particular enterprise. Usually they also provide valuable information on the paper forms being used; hence, helpful details are supplied.

3. *Observation of Work.*   This source is always used and is reliable. Data collected by this means may be compared with data obtained from other sources for purposes of verification. Effective observation requires the knack of purposive watching and a concentration on meaningful actions. This takes some practice, as most laymen are not skilled in observing effectively.

4. *Study of Accounting Data.*   Valuable material applying to existing cost and other financial controls is obtained from this source. Leads as to what information is considered important, how compiled, and how used are obtained. Sometimes partial, incomplete, or rejected accounting systems are found and for certain types of problems such information proves helpful.

5. *Talks with Managerial and Operative Employees.*   In studying a present system, people who are involved currently in processing the data can be helpful. Conversations with personnel normally should be withheld until after the sources discussed above have been used because such sources assist the system designer in deciding what questions to ask and in being better prepared for the interview—particularly important for noncooperative people. Not all interviews proceed according to plan, however, and the designer may be forced to change a line of questioning or its sequence. Figure 2–5 gives some suggestions that will prove helpful.

6. *Questionnaires to All Affected Personnel.*   Questionnaires are helpful, but they have some limitations. Certain types of data can be obtained by this means which is acceptable when a relatively small amount of information is wanted from a large, dispersed group. On the other hand, effective questionnaires for system design are difficult to design and are probably never inclusive of all the information which it is found subsequently must be obtained. Also, the questionnaire method is slow, the total cost high, due mainly to the need for editing and interpreting the information, and many employees object to filling out questionnaires.

7. *Business Machine Manufacturers.*   While much office work is performed manually, there is some mechanization in most systems even if it is only a typewriter or a device to sort cards. The extent of machine utilization varies from little or nothing to a computer system. Certainly, the manner in which the data will be processed affects the system design. It is therefore imperative that the system designer be familiar with what is available and for what applications specific business machines and equipment are recommended. Business machine manufacturers are an

FIGURE 2–5
Do's and Don't's of Interviewing to Obtain Information for System Design

Do's	Don't's
1. Do make preparation for the interview; be familiar with and have with you organization charts, manuals, position descriptions, flow charts, and the like.	1. Don't interrupt the respondent while answering your question or giving you information.
2. Do radiate a friendly and genuinely helpful interest in the respondent and appreciation for helping you to obtain needed information.	2. Don't let statements not understood go by; terminate the interview only after you have a clear understanding of the issue.
3. Do keep the interview focused on securing data and facts pertinent to the system design.	3. Don't ask questions that can be answered yes or no unless you want an opinion.
4. Do take notes and be a good listener.	4. Don't play the role of a consultant and suggest solutions to problems posed; this is not the purpose of your interview.
5. Do ask questions designed to verify answers secured from this and other sources.	5. Don't argue: if violent differences arise, change the subject area and avoid returning to the controversial area for awhile.
6. Do leave the interview feeling you were the interviewer, not the interviewee.	6. Don't ignore time; be ready to interview at the appointed time and terminate it promptly when the information is obtained or the allotted time expires. Arrange a second interview, if necessary.

effective source for this type of information and they are very cooperative in supplying assistance. Also machine users may be interviewed or observation of their installed units may be conducted. When the machine is quite complicated, the systems designer may seek the help of the specialist in the particular business machine area.

Organize and Evaluate Facts

The data secured from the previous step will be, for the most part, a mass of pieces of information, forms, papers, reports, and ideas. They must be related or classified in order to be used effectively. Precisely how the accumulated information should be organized depends upon the makeup of the particular study. It should be emphasized, however, that at this point we are not trying to design the system; we are simply trying to get the information we have in an orderly and easily understood arrangement.

Graphic representation of data is usually easier to comprehend than that in written form. If the data and facts were not collected in graphic form, it is helpful to convert into this type of format. By this means the interrelationships of data will be revealed, duplicated data can be identified and discarded, and a composite picture of fairly large portions of information is gained. To illustrate, refer to the diagram of Figure 2–6 (pp. 40–41). In this case, the names of the interested parties are across the top. By following the arrow lines, the information work involved in handling bank card credit is depicted. It is helpful to add that also provided is an automated interchange of data and a daily net dollar exchange report for principal and associate institutions. This report shows the net amount due from or owed to each bank.

Facts can be organized in many different ways. One common approach is by *the objectives to which they relate.* Generally this supplies broad classifications. The chief drawback is in identifying the objectives. Furthermore, they are commonly compounded so that this classification does not always give clear and distinct divisions to the information. A favorite means for classifying facts is by *organization.* Information is segregated by who decides what and upon what information a decision is reached. This means associating information—be it in the form of reports, records, or memos—as well as its distribution, to the organization units and their respective personnel. The purpose and use by whom, for each informational segment, serve as the classification. These relations, tied with management organization units, reveal the flow of data, at which level, who decides what issues, and the adequacy of the information structure. Consolidating these types of information into a single picture for the entire enterprise provides a blueprint for designing an inclusive and effective system.

There is also the organizing of facts by *input and output.* This approach is relatively simple and provides meaningful classifications when there are existent systems to be improved. However, to use this basis when there is no precedent from former or present systems, it is necessary to conceive vividly the proposed system and segregate data based on these conceptual notions. Another possibility is classification by the *processing means.* This is advantageous to reveal the current status of the data processing being followed. It is especially helpful in revealing the makeup of the nonautomated processes being utilized and the type of information being obtained. Further, some designers, in certain instances, recommend organizing the facts according to the *major problems or complaints discovered during the collecting stage.* These criteria will separate the information into large classes, but give meaningful related information. Care must be exercised to include only genuine problems and complaints which appear to be of major significance.

After organizing the data, they are evaluated. If possible, quantitative values should be assigned to general statements. When the occurrence is exceptional, the systems person should try to ascertain its frequency or percentage of the total represented. The statement that "certain facts are extremely beneficial" and knowledge of the designer is that they are expensive to provide, suggest an effort to assess the value of the benefit. The system designed must eventually justify itself in terms of benefits so that a cost evaluation of the facts at this stage of the design work is appropriate. By the same reasoning the designer should try to evaluate savings and their effect upon need and convenience.

Generally quantitative evaluation is most helpful in the areas of cost, accuracy, and employee productivity. These possible areas for improvement make for proper consolidation of efforts to obtain desired optimization. Sampling techniques to determine the accuracy of source data and the reliability of reports and records can be followed. Also, some indices of employee productivity should be developed. When these are compared to levels of attainment in similar work elsewhere or to what level appears reasonable, the designer has tangible evidence of how efficient the present information work is.

However, some evaluation must remain the result of judgment and belief. There are nonmeasurable elements about information. No quantitative measure fully takes the intangible and service element of information into account. Also, some facts supply operational information within an organized group while other facts initiate action outside their organized totality, for example, facts which condition the trade or marketing forecasts. Evaluating such facts pose difficulties.

ESTABLISH SYSTEM PREMISES

Actually the previous steps in system design provide excellent clues as to what premises should be established. For example, the objectives of the system suggest certain constraints regarding the breadth of the system. Also, the organized facts supply information on the quality standards and volume of work that have prevailed. It is a simple matter to project these and establish them as the levels upon which the system design will be made. But events of the future may prove far different than the projections so that the system must be modified. It is best, therefore, to keep the system flexible with built-in means for expanding or contracting as the future shows is necessary.

The process used is perhaps the basis of any system. The assumption of the use of existing information machines of a company can condition the system design considerably. And the same effect results from the premise to acquire new machines or even a computer. Their means of doing the work shape the system's makeup, yet these means are subject to radical change, as demonstrated by the introduction of new machines and attachments almost daily on the market. Again, system flexibility is the answer.

FIGURE 2-6
Flow Diagram of Bank Credit Cards

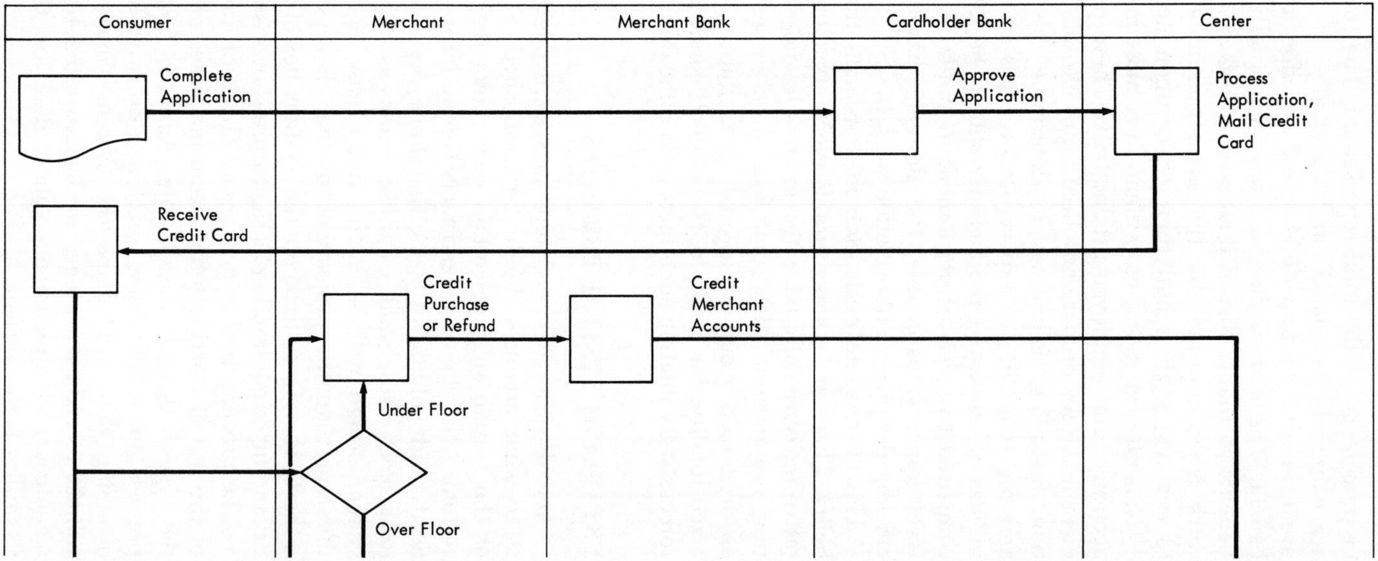

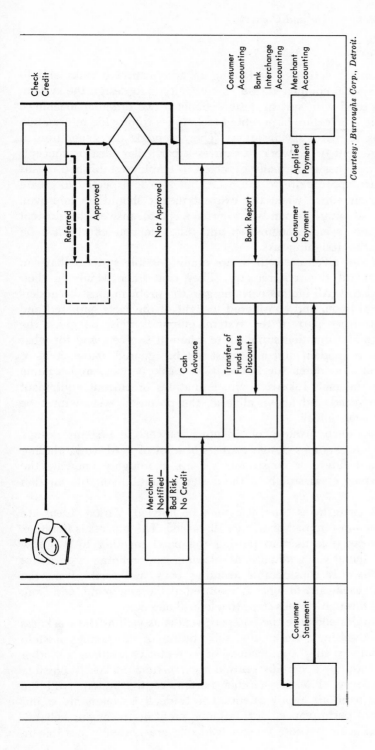

Check Credit

Referred

Approved

Not Approved

Consumer Accounting

Bank Interchange Accounting

Merchant Accounting

Applied Payment

Bank Report

Consumer Payment

Cash Advance

Transfer of Funds Less Discount

Merchant Notified—Bad Risk, No Credit

Consumer Statement

Design of System

With the major activities pertaining to administrative tasks and to bases of the system completed, the next activity is to design the system. Design when used with system design connotes two different meanings. The first is the application of accepted techniques to provide information that conforms to given specifications. The second is the generation of a new arrangement or network to express a particular idea or concept. The systems designer is normally expected to employ established means where they are appropriate to the need, but also is expected to create a new approach either when the existent means should be improved or when the situation demands a new concept to answer the existent problem. In any event, imagination and much mental effort must be committed to the designing task.

Usually in any given case, there are many possible systems that can be designed to fit the requirements. They can differ widely in their suitability and cost. All factors pertaining to the problem must be understood, reflected upon, and considered in light of the facts gathered and evaluated. At every part of the system, emphasis must be given the necessity of the information supplied, to whom it is given, and for what purpose. This is fundamental and must not be ignored. Satisfaction of closing and of due dates for information, peak periods, and volume of work must be met. Likewise, any limitations of current equipment must be recognized and above all else, the proposed system must be practical and economical.

There is no deep mystery of unknown powers in systems design. To a great extent, systems design consists of a lot of hard work, abiding by the "ground rules" or constraints set up, thoroughly knowing the facts, and keeping everlastingly at the designing until a suitable solution is reached.

System designing takes time; it cannot be hurried. Various ideas are tried out, some are retained, many are discarded. The process is iterative. In some respects it is akin to putting the parts together to a jigsaw puzzle. It is tentative, gradually developing, and refining a series of operations. There is considerable working back and forth—from the desirable goal backward to what is required at the beginning, and from the beginning through various steps to a logical outcome.

Tradeoff studies compare the competitiveness as well as the weakness of the system resulting from adding, substituting, or subtracting possible alternatives for existing components of a tentative system. In other words, if by adding a certain portion to a system makes it possible to modify or even eliminate another portion of the system, will the resultant system be an improvement? The tradeoff is commonly evaluated in terms of performance, cost, training, profit improvement, reliability, maintenance, or payout. Several tradeoffs are normally possible in every system design. Indeed, one cannot be certain the most satisfactory system for the stated objectives has been developed until the results from tradeoffs have been ascertained.

A major difficulty in utilizing tradeoffs is to make certain that fundamental problems not their symptoms are being cured by our actions. A careful thinking through of the objectives best orientates what final output is needed. This should be the ultimate criteria in whether a tradeoff is desirable or not. Further, the final selection, no matter what components make up the system, should reflect the systems designer's belief of what combination will prove superior in operating in the particular environment and in keeping with the expressed managerial needs and capabilities. Figure 2–7 lists pertinent questions to answer in order to achieve the most appropriate design.

FIGURE 2–7
Questions to Assist in Designing the Best Possible System

1. Are the stated objectives and requirements satisfied completely by the system?
2. Is every part of the information handled really necessary?
3. Does the system perform more efficiently, more accurately, and more quickly than the previous manner of work performance?
4. If organizational changes are required, are these acceptable, and if some are not, will modification seriously restrict the proposed benefits?
5. At what points are employees' judgments, interpretations, and decision making a part of the system? Are there adequate control mechanisms over employees at these points?
6. Are proposed savings to be gained by reducing personnel? If so, will requisitions for personnel be cancelled, present employees transferred, and normal attrition permitted to take care of the labor surplus?
7. Is any part of the system being accepted on the basis that "it has always been done this way"?
8. Are the inputs and the outputs of data identified as to form, content, method of transmission, time requirements, volume, and peak loads?
9. Are all workplaces well arranged for performing the work?
10. Does the space layout assist in getting the work to flow smoothly?
11. Does the system incorporate adequate feedback and controls?
12. Is the data processing specified regarding type, speed, volume, and other pertinent characteristics?
13. Is the recommended means of data processing completely justified on the basis of clearly stated premises?
14. Are any special purpose requirements included and if so, are they clearly stated and their probable impact upon the system set forth in terms of delivery, delay, maintenance, and cost?

Making Decisions Regarding Mechanization

Decisions must be firmed up regarding what types of business machines and equipment will be used.[1] This is actually a part of the considerations stated previously, but several additional comments are

---

[1] Business information machines are discussed fully in Chapter 7.

in order at this time. How automatic should the processing be is an important question that must be answered. Rarely is closed-loop automaticity a major objective as such. The question is more, to what extent should elements of the system control either the system as a whole or its individual components. The adaptability and flexibility of the machine to fulfill the system's requirement normally merit high priority.

Much office work is performed manually and because of the volume, frequency, cost, managerial wishes, or type of service required, is the most appropriate processing means. The competent system designer will recognize and endorse this means. However, fantastic information machines are available and in many cases their use is the best answer. But to answer in what systems they should be used leads to system design. Also, mention should be made of so-called "bench-mark problems." These arise from the condition of a company having office machines and equipment which dominate and restrict the choice of additional machines and equipment to complement the existing mechanized facilities, even though the additional machines and equipment are better suited to the needs of the proposed system.

The use of copying machines to modify segments of an existing system provides some interesting applications. Where copying by handwriting or typing were once used, the copying work is now commonly done by machine. In some applications, basic information is put on a master and subsequently duplicated as needed onto paper forms designed to direct and control a particular business activity. For example, in purchasing, master sheets for duplicating can be prepared. When an item is to be purchased, its master is withdrawn from the file, and the needed information duplicated on all the purchasing forms. These forms are then processed, and the master is returned to the file for future use. The result is accurate, fast work and much saving in writing time.

An interesting variation of this procedure is used when several of the requisitions to purchase can be assembled for the preparation of one purchase order for one supplier. The requisitions are sent to the purchasing department, where the buyer groups them respectively under the names of the vendors selected. The card for each vendor selected by the buyer is removed from the vendor file and assembled with the requisitions which will make up the purchase order to that vendor. These are placed in a shingled or overlapping position and held in place by a large clip. In addition, variable information form is added, so that the composition of the purchase order can be completed.

The practice is growing in record retrieving of never releasing any document from a file. A wanted document is located, removed from the file, copied, and immediately returned to the file. The copy is sent to the person requesting the document. By this means, the chance of losing the original document is practically nil.

Evaluate the System

This is the last major activity in designing a system. Evaluation of a system is conducted to determine whether the proposed system is satisfactory. Commonly this consists of a careful review of the overall arrangement and a detailed check of its critical areas. Various approaches may be taken, but for our purpose we will confine the discussion to that of assuming the viewpoint of meeting the overall needs of the enterprise and of the managers. From the enterprise viewpoint, the system as conceived should fit in with the long-range plans of the enterprise. The volume of information on which the system is predicated should be ample to meet future requirements. Should work expansion or contraction take place, the future problem areas, as future objectives of the system, should be known; provisions to take care of these changes exist within the system. Further, a determination should be undertaken to assure that this system does not duplicate work performed elsewhere in the enterprise. If it does, the scope of the proposed system might be narrowed, or the possibility of using it as a check upon results, sometimes helpful in financial systems, can be considered. Also, the chances of the proposed system being used in another location, such as an affiliate or branch of the company, may be investigated. If so, the designer might ask if the system is attuned to other environments and whether the system can be transplanted easily. Finally, from the enterprise viewpoint there is the question of whether the system calls for responsibility by members of certain organizational units whose members are unwilling or unable to accept such responsibility. These requirements must be fully explored.

Not all managers manage exactly alike, so the individual managerial informational requirements must be considered and satisfied on an individual basis. This raises the question whether all managers interested in the input and output of the system have been interviewed and their information requirements of the system fully met. Also, agreement to commitments placed on them by the system should be fully understood and accepted. Lastly, if feasible, guarantees should be extended managers assuring accuracy and integrity of the information. Proper measures should be adopted to prevent unauthorized personnel from obtaining the information and to eliminate unauthorized changes being made in it.[2]

IMPLEMENTING THE SYSTEM

After approval of the system design, it is ready for implementation. This may require more time than considered reasonable—commonly

---

[2] The subject of office security controls is discussed in Chapter 25.

10–12 months, but a number of time-consuming activities are involved. Included are the preparing and detailing information about the new system, hiring and training personnel needed, acquiring machines and equipment, installing system and running trial tests, and final conversion to the new system. Commonly a top executive either the president or the vice president of purchasing procures the machines and equipment especially if the purchase is large and for a new item. Assistance by the system personnel is usually called for. Proper specifications are evolved, price, delivery date, guarantees, and installation agreements are negotiated.

Trial tests are the rule and a number of runs should be made to ensure satisfactory operation as indicated by statistical validity. Pilot or test runs make it possible to detect and correct any shortcomings before permanent or large-scale commitments are made. Frequently the approach is to test portions of the system. Testing portions helps to simplify the job and expedite understanding and handling the test. But compatibility of the portions is important. As the system begins to operate, what happens first must satisfy the requirements of those portions that follow.

Modifications may occur as greater insight is obtained from the testing. Some redesign of the system may be in order; usually this is confined to certain areas only. Generally a period is scheduled to permit operating personnel to become acquainted with the new plan of work and to gain the necessary proficiency in performing their assigned tasks. Usually there are some adjustments to be made to satisfy personnel opinions or complaints.

Eventually, after all sources of difficulty have been removed or corrected, the proposed system is put into full operation. Now there is a policing period to insure that what is designed and planned is being utilized properly and is functioning satisfactorily. Usually personnel problems dominate the policing period.

SYSTEM PERSONNEL

Common titles for a system analyst and designer include "systems engineer," "system analyst," and "system administrator." Illustrative of what can be considered the typical basic functions and duties are shown by Figure 2–8.

Most system analysts are employed by a private or a public organization in which the system work is done. They design systems within the organization under the direction of their own manager. In addition, many business machine manufacturers employ analysts to assist in the preparation of the company's sales promotion literature and to aid sales representatives in selling and assisting the customer. Also, analysts are

FIGURE 2–8
A Systems Job Description

Title: System Analyst and Designer   Div: Allen Plant
Dept.: Staff   Job No.: 33

Basic Functions:

Plans, develops, designs, recommends, implements, and coordinates the systems activities within the Allen Plant. Advises vice president in charge of this plant on matters of systems to promote administrative efficiency, reduce clerical costs, and increase employee satisfaction.

Duties:

Within the authority limits authorized by divisional policies, this person has the following duties:
1. Advise and assist the vice president in regard to proposed systems.
2. Develop, recommend, and establish an effective cost and inventory system. This includes development of an effective manner for handling receipts and disbursements, handling vendors' and customers' claims, and taking and reporting physical inventories.
3. Review existing systems periodically in order to introduce improvements and controls to provide better service and lower cost.
4. Develop and maintain a Systems Manual for the division to assure conformity to the pattern and format established by the corporation.
5. Coordinate the office mechanization program with all interested staff and operating personnel.

*   *   *   *   *

10. Keep informed on current developments in the area of systems, appraise their value for the division, and recommend adoption when advisable.

Approved *James C. Elgin*
Authorized *Harry Puterbaugh*
Date *July 2, 197–*

---

employed by management consulting firms to work out system problems for clients and to make recommendations of systems for handling the specific requirements of the client. Those analysts with a management consulting firm face a wide variety of system problems in various kinds of enterprises.

High on the list of desirable qualifications for a system analyst and designer is conceptual ability, along with imagination and objectivity. The analyst must be able to see future possibilities in untried systems and anticipate possible trouble areas. Also, the ability to initiate and "dream practical dreams" are genuine assets. In addition, it is helpful to possess a general yet fundamental grasp of the background activities within which the system is designed and operated. Actually, the analyst should have a keen interest in every aspect of the enterprise's operations and constantly be aware of top managers' present goals and plans for the future, as these usually affect the systems design.

The system person must update periodically his or her knowledge of techniques, tools, and equipment. New and better ways are constantly appearing in these areas. Of special importance is the ability to use logic diagramming, flow charting, and graphs for analysis and display. Definitely advantageous to the system person is an understanding of human nature. The ability to work with top managers, to understand their problems, and to push forward systems efforts despite complaints and disappointments, are of outstanding value. Finally, the art and skill of communication must be developed, for the system person must be able to share ideas, findings, and suggestions clearly and concisely. Communication with people must come easily.

QUESTIONS

1. Relate and discuss briefly the major parts making up the work of systems design.
2. Do you feel that business machine manufacturers are an effective source of information for a system designer? Why?
3. Discuss the importance you attach to systems in information management. Justify your viewpoint.
4. Do you believe it possible to obtain almost any information in order to design an information system? Why?
5. Do you favor quantitative measurement and evaluation of data used in system design? Justify your viewpoint.
6. Explain the meaning and significance of Figure 2–1 in your own words.
7. Name and discuss four common sources of data and information that are used in system designing.
8. Identify each of the following:
    a. Constraints of a system.
    b. Bench-mark problem in system design.
    c. An office procedure.
    d. Hound-dog approach.
9. Discuss the use of tradeoff studies in system design.
10. Relate and discuss the major desirable qualifications for system personnel.
11. Name and discuss briefly three major means for organizing and evaluating factual data in system design.
12. Do you agree with the following statement? "Mechanization is the key consideration in modern system designing. The logical beginning for conceptualizing the information work to be done is either the machine available or what can be made available." Why?

CASE PROBLEMS

Case 2–1. Burris Company

Marie Fennstock has just accepted the job of office manager for a small company recently purchased by Burris Company. The acquired company had sales of $1.2 million last year and expected that figure to be exceeded this year by at least 20 percent. At the present time, there are a total of 31 employees including 11 in the office. They have never had an office manager.

The first day on her new job, Marie was given a cursory review of what records were kept, the papers typed, and a quick inspection of the filed materials. During her first three days, her general impression was that a minimum of information was maintained, the majority of the office employees' time was spent on sales orders—answering the telephone, typing sales orders, checking credit, and handling correspondence in connection with sales subjects. She observed that incoming payments were in the form of checks and she was told that they were held until Tuesday noon of each week and then a weekly deposit was made. Checks were kept in a portable lockbox in the sales manager's office. Also, to pay miscellaneous office expenses as they arose, the general manager or the sales manager used their own funds, later asking verbally for reimbursement. Employee paychecks were made out by an outside service firm specializing in this type of work. When Marie inquired of the general manager why this arrangement was used, she was told it was started when the company was founded and has been continued. The service has been highly satisfactory according to the general manager. However, the office does write checks for other expenses including those for purchases of materials and supplies. Marie found three examples during her second day of work where the invoice was paid by the company before the receipt of goods.

Questions:

1. What recommendations would you give to Marie regarding her new job? Justify your answer.
2. What problems do you anticipate she might encounter in carrying out your recommendations? What action do you recommend she take to minimize these problems? Discuss.

Case 2–2.   Lynch Company

A voucher system is used by the Lynch company to pay all vendor bills. For each expenditure, a voucher is prepared and forwarded to the cashier who makes a record manually of each voucher received thus creating a daily voucher register. This register is made in duplicate, one copy of which is sent to Accounts Payable, the other copy is retained by the cashier. For each expenditure the cashier prepares a check in triplicate, the original copy being sent to the vendor, the second and third copies to Accounts Payable where one copy is filed with the invoice representing a "paid file" of accounts, the other copy is attached to the Accounts Payable voucher register. Any entry on the voucher register not having a copy of the check to show it "paid" represents a payment still due. Also from this posted register, all paid items are distributed to the designated expense account and summarized weekly and monthly.

It is believed that the current bill-paying operations are effective in that they eliminate any need for a creditor's ledger, provide a uniform method of distributing expenditures, and supply a needed check by more than one person on all expenditures made.

Questions:

1. Draw a chart illustrating the voucher system as followed by the company.
2. Does the system followed appear to be satisfactory? Justify your viewpoint.

Case 2–3.   St. Mary Hospital

A cooperative effort by personnel of St. Mary Hospital, representatives of a computer manufacturer, and personnel of a certified public accounting firm has designed and implemented information systems to handle accounts receivable, accounts payable, inventory, and payroll work. Analyses of the various hospital services are also provided. Actually, it can be stated that there are at present four major systems used by St. Mary Hospital including the patient accounting system, the inventory system, the payroll system, and the management reporting system. We are primarily concerned here with the first or patient accounting system.

For each incoming patient the admittance office types identifying data on an admittance form, copies of which go to the business office and the service departments of the hospital. Two copies of the form are retained by the admittance office where one is filed alphabetically, the other numerically. In addition, an identifying plastic wristband showing name, number, and blood type is fastened onto the patient's wrist. From its copies, the admittance office transfers the information into punched cards, likewise the service departments make out service charge tickets depending upon the patient's needs. The information from these tickets is ultimately transferred to punched cards. These media (punched cards) are used to feed the information into a computer from which both (1) a charge master file and (2) a patient master file are updated and stored.

As required, various processed information from the computer in the form of reports is obtained. For example, the following are common: (1) daily summary of charges, (2) patient billing, and (3) census report. Inpatients and outpatients not yet discharged are included in the report covering daily summary of charges. The charges are by different categories and usually detail miscellaneous charges not covered by insurance. The report shows balances due from insurance carrier and patient. It is used by the cashier at the time patients are discharged or as a means of informing the patient about the status of the account.

The patient billing report is produced automatically by the computer every seven days. For every patient in the hospital for 28 days, a balance forward bill is produced and used to bill insurance companies and patients for non-covered portions. Four days after discharge the computer produces the final bill showing what is due from insurance company and patient. At this time, a copy of the account is imprinted on a tubfile card for applying payments or making any adjustments. This file is maintained in the cashier's office, and between this file and the daily summary of charges the cashier has the status of all accounts, both in-house and discharged.

The census report lists each inpatient and outpatient admission, discharges, room transfers, and a midnight count by each hospital unit or wing. Copies of this report are used by personnel in each unit to show percentage of occupancy, patient condition reports, respiration reports, dietary, temperature, and pulse reports.

The hospital revenue from payments for services rendered represents accounts receivable. These are obtained from the charge master file under which are the daily and monthly revenue analysis report and the responsibility report. The former shows each service by inpatient and outpatient revenues. The report is distributed to each revenue producing department for statistical and work measurement purposes. The responsibility report is a tabulation prepared monthly showing for each account the amount and the identity (person or insurance carrier) responsible for the payment of accounts receivable.

Any cash or check payment from patients or insurance carriers is recorded in a receipt card journal with a copy sent to the accounting department. The information is transferred to a punched card form for feeding into the computer. In addition, the systems of accounts payable, inventory, and payroll are handled by the computer. However, different data from that discussed above are required to process information pertaining to these activities.

Questions:

1. Draw the flow chart depicting the relationships of the various information activities dealing with the patient accounting system and accounts receivable of the hospital.
2. Would you describe these two systems as interdependent or dependent? Discuss.
3. What types of information other than that included in this case would you require in the hospital's payroll system? Are these types of information related to that of the patient accounting system? Discuss.

Chapter 3

Systems Improvement and Concept of Total Systems

> *See first that the design is wise and just; that ascertained, pursue it resolutely.*
>
> Shakespeare

Since information and its management are extremely dynamic, it follows that the systems used in it must be updated and kept compatible with the latest requirements and demands of the information handling. Also, as new and better tools become available, it is mandatory that improvements be incorporated. Both the information supplied and the means by which it is made available are eternal candidates for improvement.

We strive to design the best possible systems in keeping with our current knowledge and experience deemed appropriate to the individual case. But we know the systems will require revision at some future date. It is simply a matter of time. With many new ideas popping up, managers' responsibilities and information needs changing, new machines appearing on the market, new applications of existent products being developed, and competitive actions increasing, the answer is to analyze current systems, seek to improve them, or if believed necessary, to develop new systems.

Analysis almost always uncovers possible improvement. The analysis can be viewed as the first step of a cycle. With improvement potential revealed, the next step is to redesign the existent system or start a new one to take advantage of the improvement. Then, or step three, the newly redesigned or designed system, as the case might be, is implemented, followed by step four which is to use the new system and subsequently seek to refine it which leads back to step one, and the cycle is repeated.

Keys to Improvement

In all systems improvement, it is essential to keep in mind that these four simple questions must be answered: (1) who needs the information, (2) what kind of information is needed, (3) in what format and how current should the information be, and (4) within what constraints should the information be provided?

There are a number of different approaches that can be followed to improve systems. However, they all adopt the premise that improvement is obtained by either designing a new system or redesigning an existent system to conform to new objectives, constraints, premises, and facts. Hence, the designing format discussed in the previous chapter can be followed. But it is helpful to point out specific guidelines and selected key considerations which aid in these improvement efforts. Guidelines will be presented first followed by selected key considerations.

Guidelines to Systems Improvement

The following guidelines represent highlights of a long list of proven suggestions for improving systems within an enterprise:

1. Orient the information to a system, not to an isolated problem.
2. Strive to record source information once, thereafter use this source for all recording of that data in all subsequent needed papers, thus avoiding needless repetitive individual recording.
3. Integrate valid procedures into logical systems.
4. Have each piece of paper or record handled as few times as possible, preferably not more than one time per employee involved in the system processing. If this seems unattainable, reanalyze to see what can be done about it.
5. Get each person to ask themselves, "What is the reason why this information is coming to my work station?"
6. Emphasize to each office employee not to pick up a document, form, or paper unless intending to do something with it and don't put it down until something has been done with it.
7. If any managerial or operative employee feels it necessary to see all papers in a department or at a desk, arrange, after review, to put papers in envelopes addressed to whom they should be forwarded.
8. Arrange to inventory all items coming to a selected work station for a 4-week period. Analyze these inputs, decide, and take action deemed appropriate for improvement.
9. When feasible, accumulate information or papers and review several days or a week's work at a time.

✱10. Mark major ideas as you read so you can later refer to them quickly. Marginal notes to yourself are also helpful and save time.

✱11. Train employees to submit a proposed recommended action, along with every statement of a problem or complaint regarding office work processing.

12. Resolve when going over a stack of papers what disposition to make of each piece before going on to the next piece.

✱13. Keep pending papers out of sight in a desk drawer or a file. Concentrate on immediate work about which you can do something.

14. Recognize that systems are not restricted by organizational department boundaries.

✱15. Remember to keep the cost of a system consistent with the values anticipated from it.

The Decision Structure

Going on now to selected key considerations, the first to be discussed is the decision structure. Included in the meaning of this key consideration are the decisions that must be made by each manager, the extent of delegating decision making, and the relationship of information to action taken. We are concentrating upon information supplied by systems for decision making. In essence, to improve information systems is to identify who decides what and strive to supply each decider with better information for decision making.

Following this line of thought, we start at the top management level and work down, identifying the decisions that must be made by each management member. To assist in these efforts, the questions listed in Figure 3–1 can be followed being sure to ask them in the sequence given.

After identifying the types of decisions, work is then directed to supply information specifically helpful for each manager. These efforts, however, are not solely rational. Every decision and its implementation are strongly conditioned by consideration for the human aspects involved and especially by what is the job, authority, responsibility, and relationships with others in the enterprise as seen by each manager. For example, one manager's primary job may be seen as one of processing papers on time. This being true, decisions affecting scheduling are analyzed to reveal what factors are of most importance in meeting schedules. Perhaps controlling overtime and productivity per employee are found to have the maximum impact on achieving schedules. Hence, information on these factors would be supplied this manager who will probably utilize fully such information in meeting responsibilities about schedules.

Some managers want to make all possible decisions themselves while others prefer to delegate portions of their decision making to subordi-

FIGURE 3–1

Questions to Ask to Determine Type of Decision Making Required by Each Management Member

---

1. Specifically, what are your main work objectives?
2. For these work objectives, what are your principal responsibilities?
3. In keeping with these responsibilities, what types of decisions are you called upon to make?
4. What information do you feel you need to reach these decisions from the short-range viewpoint? From the long-range viewpoint? From within the enterprise? From outside the enterprise? From an idealistic viewpoint? From a practical viewpoint?
5. What are the key factors that throttle the work that you are supposed to do?
6. Classify the identified information given in answer to question 4 above into the following groups:
   a. Absolutely essential.
   b. Essential.
   c. Desirable.
   d. Helpful but really not needed.

---

nates. The former is found in a small enterprise where the manager is also the owner. In this instance, detailed information must flow to the top of the organization, since the manager-owner makes all key decisions. In contrast, in larger, more complex enterprises, the top manager allows subordinates to make important decisions and while dealing only with certain types of decision making including objective determination and the measuring of subordinate performance in terms of accomplishments. The manager who delegates decision making, even though reaching certain decisions personally, requires a substantially different type of information system than the manager who decides all major decisions personally.

The relationship of information to the action taken is another facet of the decision structure affecting the amount and type of information provided. The busy manager need not be concerned with those operations running smoothly or keeping within plans. Attention focuses on the exception or the deviates from their respective norm. This concept is expressed by the principle of "management by exception." From the viewpoint of improving an information system, the task may well be that of getting better information about or targeting available information to the exceptional cases—those that require managerial action. This results in shorter, action-geared information that assists the management member to use time most effectively.

The End-Result Concept

Another selected key consideration for systems improvement is the end-result concept. Simply stated, this concept is based on the economic fact that a small proportion of efforts produce a large proportion of results. To illustrate, 20 percent of the salespeople acquire 80 percent of the orders, or 18 percent of the products account for 75 percent of the profits. Commonly referred to as "the 20–80 ratio"—20 percent of efforts produce 80 percent of results, this phenomenon applies to the various areas of activities of an enterprise, areas where $20 of effort will yield $80 of results. It is on these influential areas that the information systems should focus and provide less depth and frequency of information on the numerous and less critical areas. A 5 percent decline in market share, for example, may be far more critical than a 15 percent decline in accounts payable. The challenge is to identify the really important areas and improve the systems to accomplish genuine information effectiveness in these key areas rather than following the traditional approach of spreading the information somewhat uniformly throughout all areas.

Applying the end-result concept to achieve systems improvement offers distinct advantages. Focusing on the really significant areas (always relatively few in number) has great impact on results. In turn, this necessitates considerable thought to decide what issues should be worked on and how much effort directed to each. Areas of critical value thus become known to employees and can be given attention in keeping with their relative worth. Second, deeper insight into major problems is encouraged. To illustrate, costing practices can be modified to reflect more accurately the cost incurred by various activities differing in importance. Thus, dividing a total expenditure by the number of activities to obtain the "average cost," which is questionable and in many cases inaccurate, could be eliminated so that large volume items would not be penalized by carrying an excess of cost which should be borne by certain small volume items. Further, the undercost burdened items lead to underpricing of them and possibly to the proliferation of small production runs and small sales orders. Third, applying the end-result concept to information systems assists in eliminating unnecessary paper work. As managers learn to rely more on information pertaining to essential areas, the preparation of voluminous data dealing with relatively insignificant operations will tend to minimize and hence, lighten the burden placed upon systems.

An interesting modification of the end-result concept is *systems contracting,* a technique for purchasing. Under this approach the traditional materials acquisition-retention cycle undergoes significant changes. Briefly a vendor is selected for a systems contract, the materials to be supplied are carefully identified as to price and specifications, catalogs of materials to be supplied by each vendor are prepared, materials are requisitioned using the catalogs as a guide, requisitions are approved by the purchasing authorization point (PAP), the order is placed with the approved vendor, and a "total payment" method of vouchering is followed whereby one payment check is issued periodically covering all of the completed transactions. A 60 percent improvement in service, better control, and the elimination of much needless purchasing paper work are claimed from utilizing this new system.[1]

Improvement of Information Itself

The next and third key consideration included here is improvement of the information itself that is supplied as a result of the system. To do this requires knowing the various activities and viewing the enterprise in a broad perspective to determine just what information is really essential. Enterprises differ widely in their information needs as reflected by their individual characteristics. For example, some enterprises are highly dependent upon style, others have large inventories subject to potential loss of obsolescence and price fluctuation, while others must exercise tight control to survive in their highly competitive market.

Many managers need to increase their skill in deciding what information they need and how they will use such information when they get it. The information system analyst can aid very materially in this respect, but frequently is not in a position to comprehend or to suggest what specific information should be supplied. A great deal of the more common types of information now used by a manager is designed to meet statutory rather than managerial requirements. Much information describes the past without discriminating between essential and ordinary elements of the enterprise. Frequently lacking is information supplied regularly on adequacy of customer service, productivity, share and rate of growth of market, and competitors' activities—what they are doing, where, and how well. Yet these items would prove helpful to better management.

Some feel that the whole concept of information needs drastic revision. In their opinion much of the present information is incomplete, too late, unreliable, and poorly organized to have maximum value. Facts for today's decisions reach managers next week. Reams of detailed data are supplied, but helpful summaries and relationships are lacking. Distinction between the critical and the immaterial is not indicated. The need is for a complete reorientation of information. A large portion of what we now have is outmoded. In an economy such as ours, where manufacturing techniques, products, and markets change as rapidly as they do, we cannot operate an enterprise on fragmented and historical facts that are basically an extension of the past. The crying need is for improvement of the information itself.

---

[1] See Ralph A. Bolton "Systems Contracting—A New Purchasing Technique," New York: The American Management Association, 1966.

Selection of a Manageable Area

This is the last key consideration included in this discussion. Revamping the information systems of an enterprise may prove too large a job to be handled at one time. At the start, it is usually advisable to choose a manageable area, that is, one which calls for a medium-size staff, average experience in office technology, and not distant geographic communication. If possible, the operations of the selected area should be primarily within itself so that the effect of interactions with other areas is minimized. Ideally the manageable area possesses nearly all of the functions and problems of the entire enterprise and has promise of a fast payout from a high probability of success. It should also represent a viable, growing segment which will most typify the problem of facilitating the managers in the totality of the enterprise.

These specifications are not easy to meet. Frequently, they must be approximated. In some instances, significant assumptions must be made in order to proceed with the system analysis and improvement. But the extent to which these specifications are met enhances the validity and the value of changes suggested for improvement.

Systems Simulation

One technique rapidly gaining favor for redesigning and improving systems is systems simulation which is a technique for determining by means of experiment the effect of varying the variables in the flow of information or material through the processes in a system. In other words, systems simulation permits the trying out of various ideas via the systems route to see what results are obtained. It answers "what if" questions. It is a means of obtaining experience with concepts that are beyond consideration in actual physical testing because of cost, risk, or time involved. The "make believe" work is done either by computer or manual means without trying out the concept in practice. By accumulating and learning from this experience, better systems can be developed or each of several alternative systems can be evaluated.

Systems simulation enables the analyst to analyze not only a system independently, but also the interaction of systems of an enterprise so that the net result of all systems used is the best combination to achieve the stated objectives. Systems integration in keeping with definite goals is accomplished. Activities are expressed in quantitative values, but this is difficult to do for some actions. Quantification is used for as many factors and relationships as possible, thus highlighting the manager's attention to those activities that require managerial judgment.

The medium for simulation is a model which is a precise description, flow-diagram, or mathematical expression that can be manipulated to measure the effect of changing one or several variables in the system. The description may simply state the processes involved and how they

vary and relate to each other, but for manipulability the written statement is usually expressed in the form of a flow-diagram or mathematical
expression. The former indicates the relationships and their logical sequence of operation. The latter can be one or more mathematical formulas or equations. This mathematical model can be developed when there
are sufficient data about the activities and their relationships along with
how and why they vary as they do. The mathematical model adds precision to the technique. It costs less to use a model than the real thing
and it affords a look into the future or the results of putting different
combinations of certain factors together. These actions contribute to
better systems design.

To introduce change in the variables the model is subjected to input
data. This input is processed through and by the relationships built
into the flow-diagram or mathematical expression. After the processing,
the results, or output data, are obtained and subjected to analysis and
evaluation to note the changes obtained from substituting the variables.
When the diagram or mathematical expression is complex and is to
be used many times, it is usually economical to perform the calculations
rapidly by means of a computer. A large number of possible answers
can then be obtained. The answer which best suits the specific needs
of the particular situation can be selected and the system providing
this answer adopted.

Figure 3–2 has been added to visualize the simulation process. The
characteristics of the entity being modeled consist of two types (1)
parameters and (2) variables, which are determined by the person
directing the simulation. The former, or parameters, are defined and
do not change during the process, the latter, or variables are changed
during each simulation. Beginning at left of Figure 3–2, the parameters
and initial variables along with the input data are brought together
and subjected to simulation, S_1, leading to an output, O_1. Then the initial
variables are revised from those used in S_1, or revised variables, RV_1
and used for S_2 which together with the input gives a new output,
O_2. The simulation process is repeated using successive revised variables
to obtain successive outputs.

Systems simulation aids in evaluating new ideas and concepts which
otherwise might remain dormant. Also, the training of personnel is expedited. Further, systems simulation provides a broad and inclusive understanding of systems and their basic nature. Complete analysis is promoted. The cycle from beginning to end, the processes involved, and
the effect of change can be clearly identified. On the other hand, there
are disadvantages of systems simulation. Accurate input data are difficult
to obtain and are frequently underestimated. In addition, there are many
assumptions in applying the technique and, in fact, the quality of these
assumptions conditions greatly the value of the results. It is vital that
all the assumptions made—the constraints, the relationship of one vari-

FIGURE 3–2
Simulation Process of a Model

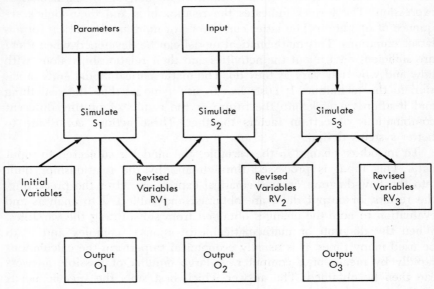

able to another and to a constant—be clearly understood and results viewed in light of these assumptions. Further, it must be remembered that systems simulation is a tool, it permits evaluation of ideas which are the creation of the human mind. It is a technique to solve a problem and the emphasis should be on its problem-solving, i.e., obtaining an improved system. Sometimes the emphasis erroneously is shifted to the effectiveness of the technique itself.

Total Systems—A Logical Development

Attempts to make systems more effective have led logically to extending the systems concept to include all related systems to a totality. Why stop with one or two systems? The relationship of one system to another and to another eventually resolves into one overall inclusive system which it appears would be desirable from the viewpoint of high information service at minimum cost and effort.

Moving from a single system idea to that of several systems as the vehicle of thought informational efforts is a logical development. Historically, early information study focused attention on the task of an individual and how it was performed. Expanding this concept the related tasks of several individuals were considered, resulting in the development of a procedure. Later, related procedures were considered and the concept of a system became accepted. Continuing, from several related systems evolved the idea of a consolidated information system that would effectively provide the required information throughout an entire enterprise.

Slowly but surely, it is being recognized that information is crucially interdependent. What happens in one organizational unit influences what happens in other organizational units. No one bit of information is an island unto itself. It is related to and affects other bits of information. With this fundamental in mind, the natural development was toward a more inclusive and all-encompassing concept about data gathering and processing.

THE TOTAL SYSTEMS CONCEPT

With the total systems concept, a reservoir of information would be available to any management member in the enterprise any time it is needed. The probable impact of any contemplated action in any one segment upon the entire enterprise could be easily and quickly ascertained. Purchasing, marketing, and engineering data could be readily combined with material control, inventory, quality, and production flow information. Research and development progress could be tied in with forecasting; thus where and when to make engineering changes in a product line could be accurately calculated. In brief, complete legal, historical, fiscal, and operational data would be included and interrelated.

A graphic representation indicating the general idea of a total systems concept is shown by Figure 3–3. This is suggestive only and is not intended to be conclusive. Beginning at the top of the figure, top management members, either as individual department heads or as a group, perform basic operations which establish objectives and supply the necessary parameters within which these objectives will be sought. These resulting decisions are forwarded to an Information Service Center which cuts across all organization lines, is centralized, reports to top management members, receives feedback information on actions taken, and regulates information flow. As depicted, the Information Service Center is able to provide top managers with the broad scope of analytical and control data available and in use, plus the information flow related to forecasts, actual performances, feedback, evaluation, and coordination. Thus, effective implementation of information is enhanced and adequate control over it is provided. More specifically, and as shown in the figure, the Information Service Center designs and installs systems, processes data, and supervises information flow. This is done to establish fundamental practices shown on the figure, practices such as stock review, raw materials control, work in process control, product cost reports, and payroll accounting and variance. Feedback is obtained on all these practices by determining for each case the exception to what is wanted

FIGURE 3–3
A Concept of Total Systems for an Enterprise

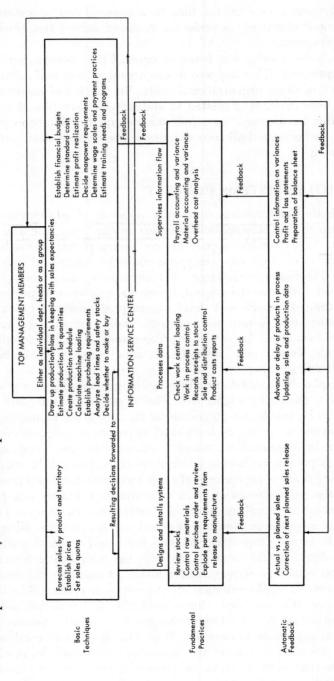

TOP MANAGEMENT MEMBERS

Either as individual dept. heads or as a group

Establish financial budgets
Determine standard costs
Estimate profit realization
Decide manpower requirements
Determine wage scales and payment practices
Estimate training needs and programs

Draw up production plans in keeping with sales expectancies
Estimate production lot quantities
Create production schedule
Calculate machine loading
Establish purchasing requirements
Analyze lead times and safety stocks
Decide whether to make or buy

Resulting decisions forwarded to

INFORMATION SERVICE CENTER

Supervises information flow

Payroll accounting and variance
Material accounting and variance
Overhead cost analysis

Processes data

Check work center loading
Work in process control
Records receipts to stock
Sale and distribution control
Product costs reports

Designs and installs systems

Review stocks
Control raw materials
Control purchase order and review
Explode parts requirements from
release to manufacture

Control information on variances
Profit and loss statements
Preparation of balance sheet

Advance or delay of products in process
Updating sales and production data

Actual vs. planned sales
Correction of next planned sales release

Forecast sales by product and territory
Establish prices
Set sales quotas

Basic
Techniques

Fundamental
Practices

Automatic
Feedback

Feedback
Feedback
Feedback
Feedback
Feedback
Feedback
Feedback

Practice management by exception

(management by exception) and taking the needed corrective action. The automatic feedback is indicated at the bottom of the illustration.

As illustrated, and in most cases, the total systems concept is based on forecasts of requirements over reasonable periods, together with establishment of the optimum manufacturing and selling plans based on the forecast. What is optimum can be from a cost, service, time, or capability viewpoint. Furthermore, implied in the total systems concept are determinations for control limits within which the forecast will remain unchanged, feedbacks of actual requirements compared to the forecasts, and corrective actions either in the form of forecast adjustments or in operations. This is to say that manufacturing and selling efforts are based on the forecasts, not on actual requirements. The latter may vary sufficiently to suggest an adjustment in the forecast, and this is done when the forecast is obviously out of line. But fluctuations within established limits can occur without affecting the forecast.

Observations about Total Systems Concept

The total systems concept is so logical that one wonders why we did not get to it sooner or why it is not universally adopted. Actually the reasons are many. During the initial adoption of office automation there was some tendency to automate the work that had always been done. The existent systems were given a sacred, do-not-alter status. Any new information needs were patched onto the old systems. Reports, records, data of all kinds were seldom culled, and if so, rarely in their entirety. Customarily any inspection was confined to a portion of the entirety. The result was that useless and outmoded information was permitted to exist, even ignored, without purpose and without controls.

Objectives are always important in management, but in discussing the total systems concept, objectives warrant special emphasis. *What constitutes a system, or a total system, is determined by the objectives sought.* In every case, the objectives establish the limits and utilization of the systems making up the total systems concept. In fact, the total systems concept is meaningful to the degree that the objectives are identified. Furthermore, this means that the total systems is not a grandiose composite of all systems to do all things. Rather, it is an integration of systems designed for the purpose of achieving stated objectives. An illustration will clarify this fact.

With reference to an automobile, the question can be asked, "What is an ignition system?" We would answer in terms something like the following: *It is a system actually made up of a combination of several systems designed to make certain activities take place which result in sparks or electric flashes igniting combustible fuel.* Note that identification of the several lesser systems is couched in terms of what the total systems are intended to achieve, or in terms of the objectives. We could go into the details of the lesser systems making up the total ignition system, such as the timing system, the condenser system, the spark plug system, and so forth, but this is irrelevant for the point at hand. Next, suppose the question is asked, "What are the total systems that deliver brake horsepower on the wheels of an automobile?" We would answer, the ignition system, the combustion system, the cooling and ventilating system, and the transmission system. All these systems work together to achieve the objective—deliver brake horsepower on the wheels of an automobile. Suppose we change our objectives to include the potential supplying of transportation to a human being. Since our objectives have changed, we change the inclusion of the systems making up the total systems. Specifically, we would add the system of steering, the system of braking, and a human being, with all the systems that human possesses, behind the steering wheel. Again, if our objectives were to include transporting this human being, we get into additional systems such as a system of roads, traffic lights, highway instructions, and so forth.

The total systems concept expedites managerial planning and controlling. When a particular system is planned as a part of a total system for an enterprise, the system occupies a place compatible to the overall scheme of things and is properly related to the entirely. Likewise, controlling is aided, for every information activity is interrelated with all other information activities of the enterprise. Furthermore, with the total systems concept, it is possible to make decisions that will maximize profits of an enterprise as a whole, minimize costs of the enterprise as a whole, or maximize benefits to the enterprise totality. In addition, information is maintained in a single data stream, a condition which normally insures greater accuracy and a better format of the information. Also special analyses or studies can be provided with minimum effort. And it is not difficult to handle intricate information problems that extend into many facets of the enterprise.

On the other hand, there is a belief by many top managers that total systems are helpful, but not essential and they prefer to direct their efforts to other areas. A plausible explanation for this is the background of the top manager. Relatively few come up through accounting, personnel, or information areas and hence they may have neither a full appreciation of the nature of information problems nor the means to cope with them. It is a common human tendency to practice that about which persons know or think they know the most, either by training or experience. There is also the hidden characteristic of systems improvements. Changes are not easily discerned and the benefits are mainly intangible. The improvement in service or the reduction in cost is frequently neither as meaningful nor as evident as an increase in sales orders or a new production level attained by a factory force. Hence, the total systems idea is more difficult to sell.

Further, some have advanced the thought that the total systems concept is too extensive and too large to use effectively and that, at least for the present, satisfactory results are possible with something less than total systems. There appears to be a good deal of truth in their viewpoint. The question is whether a total systems provides the necessary information more effectively at satisfactory cost, and in a manner acceptable to all employees—both managerial and nonmanagerial.

Developing a total systems for an enterprise poses many hurdles and is far more difficult and elusive than what might at first be suspected. There is unanimity of opinion that within an enterprise a partial total system is superior to several large but noncoordinated systems. As pointed out above, we specify the extensiveness of the coordination by the statement of the objectives. Literally we say that to accomplish these objectives we will use these integrated systems. Hence, what is a partial total systems may provide satisfactory and practical results. Our problem may resolve into that of determining precisely and completely the total objectives of the enterprise. Partial total systems are winning wider and wider acceptance. Inroads are being made as total systems, especially in the military and in government, are being followed. As better techniques for systems are developed and continued, progress in processing equipment takes place, present hurdles to far-reaching and inclusive integrated systems certainly will be surmounted and the total and partial systems concepts will be extensively followed.

TOTAL MANAGEMENT INFORMATION SYSTEM

The ultimate of the total systems concept has been referred to by some as the Total Management Information System(TMIS), which can be defined as a means of providing timely, relevant, and accurate information relative to internal operations and external intelligence to any management member of an organization to aid in decision making or to carry out the assigned work activity. Computer processing is not required for TMIS, but it is difficult to see how in any but a very small company such a system can exist without using a computer. In Figure 3–4, the top portion represents a typical business firm without TMIS. The informational system for each functional unit is confined for the most part to that particular unit. Under this arrangement it is not easy for managers of different functions to know completely what activities and results are taking place in the other functions. The president is the formally designated person who has all the information and has the responsibility to coordinate it. This arrangement makes for barriers in communication and an isolation of departmental units. In contrast with TMIS (lower portion of Figure 3–4) the functional information continues, but it is overlapped and integrated into TMIS so that complete information is available to the top management group

FIGURE 3–4
(top) Business Firm without Total Management Information System (TMIS);
(bottom) Business Firm with Total Management Information System

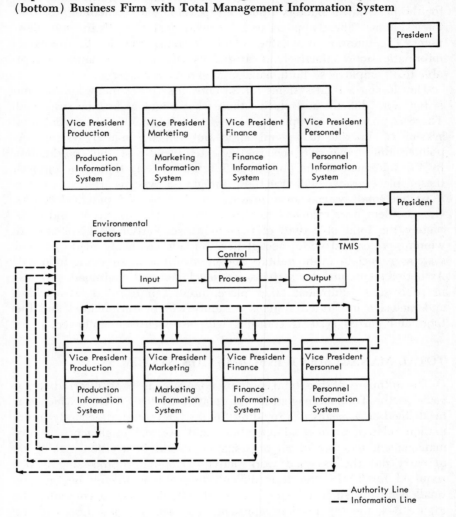

who can better work and make decisions as a team and take into account various conditions possibly lost by the former one-person decision arrangement. Observe that the information flow is shown by single broken lines, whereas the organizational lines of authority are shown by double solid lines. Information availability is increased by TMIS, information that the manager needs—no more, no less—is supplied in an appropriate, accurate, and easily understood format.

Since TMIS is inclusive, it involves information that is needed and related to decision making at different levels and to different functional areas. Also, within an enterprise the decision making is done to achieve ultimately a definite objective. Hence, we can illustrate the concept of TMIS as shown by the top portion of Figure 3–5. The apex of the triangle represents the objective. All decision making is performed to

FIGURE 3–5
A Total Management Information System Concept with Relation to Decision Making Levels

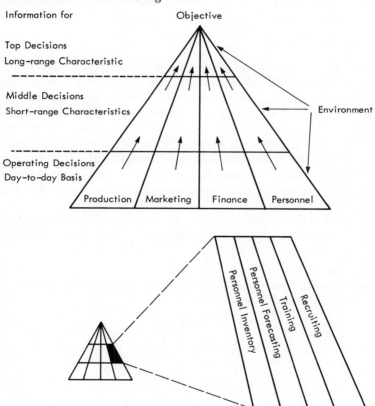

achieve this objective. Represented by the top portion of the triangle is information for long-range decisions such as whether to develop and market a new brand of canned fruit. Below this top level is a located informational needs for short-range decisions which are subordinate to the decisions of the top portion, yet deal with the future but within a more narrowly prescribed scope. Illustrative is information to decide the physical facility or the financial capability requirements to handle a new brand of canned fruit. Finally at the base of the triangle is information for day-to-day operational activities such as payroll data, store

inventories, and preparing accounts payable. With modern data processing facilities, most operational activities are more of a reporting nature
than of a decision making activity.

As the figure indicates, the three levels can be divided functionally
by production, marketing, finance, and personnel. In turn, each of these
functional segments can be divided into subfunctional segments. The
lower portion of Figure 3–5 shows such segments for personnel at the
middle decision level.

TMIS and the Military

Excellent examples of what can be considered total management information systems are found in the U.S. Air Force. They are the Management Control System (MCS) and the Strategic Air Command (SAC).
These are total systems encompassing total operations. If it is believed
they are not truly all-encompassing in their scope, they come very close
to it. They are inclusive in keeping with their stated objectives. Also
worthy of mention is the total logistics system of the U.S. Air Force. It
is worldwide, totally integrated, and covers supply and maintenance.
By its operation, service has been upgraded, yet enormous dollar savings
have been realized.

The other military services have also been active in developing total
management information systems. Both the U.S. Army and the U.S.

FIGURE 3–6
**Diagram Showing Concept of Interrelationship of U.S. Navy and U.S. Marine
Corps Major Information Systems**

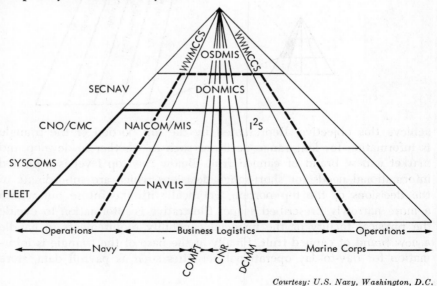

Courtesy: U.S. Navy, Washington, D.C.

Navy have active offices of management information. Figure 3–6 shows the interrelationship of information systems for different command levels and functional areas of responsibilities using the same general schematic plan as used in the previous illustration just discussed. At the top portion of the triangle shown in Figure 3–6, WWMCCS stands for World-Wide Military Command and Control System, and OSDMIS represents Office of the Secretary of Defense Management Information Systems. At the SECNAV (Secretary of Navy) level, DONMICS (Department of Navy Management Information and Control System) interrelates hundreds of information systems in the Navy and Marine Corps. Referring to the figure, below DONMICS at the CNO/CMC level (Chief of Naval Operations/Commandant of the Marine Corps) is NAICOM/MIS and I²S standing for Navy-Integrated Command/Management Information System and Integrated Information System of the Marine Corps. The latter, or I²S, is made up of eleven subsystems as illustrated in Figure 3–7. These subsystems cover the areas of finance, tactical, logistics, and personnel.

FIGURE 3–7
Makeup of Marine Corps Integrated Information System (I²S)

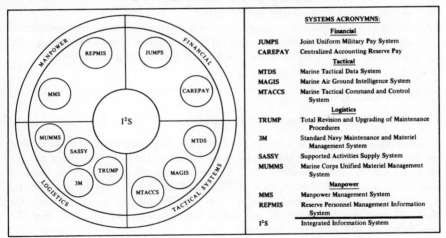

SYSTEMS ACRONYMNS:	
Financial	
JUMPS	Joint Uniform Military Pay System
CAREPAY	Centralized Accounting Reserve Pay
Tactical	
MTDS	Marine Tactical Data System
MAGIS	Marine Air Ground Intelligence System
MTACCS	Marine Tactical Command and Control System
Logistics	
TRUMP	Total Revision and Upgrading of Maintenance Procedures
3M	Standard Navy Maintenance and Materiel Management System
SASSY	Supported Activities Supply System
MUMMS	Marine Corps Unified Materiel Management System
Manpower	
MMS	Manpower Management System
REPMIS	Reserve Personnel Management Information System
I²S	Integrated Information System

QUESTIONS

1. What is meant by the end-result concept in system improvement? Relate an example illustrating the use of this concept.
2. From the guidelines to system improvement given in this chapter, select five guidelines which you feel might be considered of major importance. Give an example demonstrating the use of each guideline selected.
3. In order to improve a system, discuss the need for improvement of the information itself.
4. Discuss the use of the decision structure in improving a system.

5. Suppose the manager for whom a system was being improved was an expert in modern computers. Would this tend to simplify or to complicate the work of the system analyst and designer? Justify your viewpoint.
6. Explain Figure 3–4 in your own words.
7. What is systems simulation, and how is it used to improve systems?
8. Identify each of the following:
    a. A model for systems simulation.
    b. SASSY for the U.S. Navy.
    c. Total systems concept.
    d. Parameters and variables with reference to simulation.
9. As president, you favor a TMIS for your company, but two of your vice presidents feel such a system is unnecessary and will unfavorably affect too many employees. What is your reaction to the views expressed by these two vice presidents? What action, if any, would you take? Why?
10. Select any type of information now used by a business with which you are familiar and suggest ways in which this information might be improved.
11. Referring to Figure 3–6, answer the following:
    a. Is I²S a part of NAVLIS?
    b. Is I²S related with NAVLIS?
    c. What is the meaning of OSDMIS?
    d. Is DONMICS related to OSDMIS?
12. Should a company's management information system be considered divided by functions? By levels of management decision making? By activities using similar office machines? Justify your viewpoints.

CASE PROBLEMS

Case 3–1. Kean Manufacturing Company

Kean Manufacturing Company is in trouble. Slipping sales and dwindling profits make it imperative that changes be made to turn the company around to its former profitable position. Mr. Kenneth Kean, Sr., president, is worried and has just engaged the services of Wilma Allen to help him in determining what to do. At the present time a total of 270 people are employed. Of these 27 are in administration and office management, 40 in sales, and the remainder, or 203, in manufacturing.

Orders from customers are filled from warehouse inventories. Seldom is it necessary to back-order, since the stocks of all items are maintained at an adequate level. Approximately 175 orders are handled daily. There is a slight fluctuation from day to day with Tuesdays and Wednesdays being some 15 percent above the average quantity.

The items on an order are picked from the warehouse shelves and when completed, the order picker makes entries on a Customer's Purchase Record which shows a description of the items purchased, their respective identification numbers, the quantity ordered, and the amount to be shipped. See Exhibit 3–1A. All such records are reviewed for completeness by the supervisor of

EXHIBIT 3–1A

Customer's Dollar Purchases and Returns			
Name ——————————— Sales Clerk——————			
Item	Purchases	Item	Returns

the order pickers. Approved orders are then sent to the Credit Manager for credit approval. If O.K. the total dollar value of the order is calculated and this figure entered on a second form, Customer's Dollar Purchases and Returns. See Figure 3–1B. If credit is not approved, the original order is

EXHIBIT 3–1B

Customer's Purchase Record			
Name ——————————— Sales Clerk ——————			
Item Description	Identification Number	Quantity	Amount to be Shipped

returned to the sales department for handling by the salesclerk. Credit approved orders are forwarded to the sales manager.

Each order received by the sales manager is carefully reviewed. Before forwarding an order for shipment by the shipping department, the customer's record for promotion and local advertising is checked. This information is obtained from individual records, by customer, maintained by a sales clerk in the sales department who posts to The Customer's Promotion and Local Advertising Record. In some instances the sales manager may call the customer long-distance if it is believed the order size is not economical or the quantity and type of merchandise appears either deficient or excessive in view of customer's past sales records. If, as a result of the sales manager's efforts, the order is increased, it is returned to the credit manager for reapproval. For years, it has been mandatory for the sales manager to approve personally all sales orders.

Upon receipt of the order by the shipping department, a shipping order in triplicate is prepared. In this writing the quantities shown on the order are converted to the number of packages for convenience of the shipping clerk in checking the accuracy of the amount being shipped to the amount ordered. Items on the order that cannot be shipped are circled in red ink. As mentioned above, there are relatively few of these items. Upon shipment, the order along with a memo showing shipping charges and date of shipment are stapled and sent to the billing department.

The invoice is now prepared. Price extensions are calculated and the total determined for invoice billing. For product quantities the order quantities, not packs, must be used since prices are in terms of product quantities. Prices are obtained by consulting one of several loose-leaf price catalogues. All orders are doubled-checked before typing. Five copies are made including (1) white original sent to customer, (2) and (3) a white and a blue copy to the sales manager who forwards the blue copy to the salesclerk, (4) a light yellow copy to Accounts Receivable, and (5) a light green copy to the Budgeting Department for sales control purposes.

Questions:

1. Diagram the present means followed for handling customer orders.
2. What suggestions for improvement relative to the sequence followed, records kept, and helpfulness of the information compiled, can you offer? Explain in detail.
3. What specific actions do you suggest that Ms. Allen take? Why?

Case 3–2. Limpert Manufacturing Company

About three years ago a system to provide production cost information by different products or jobs was installed for the manufacturing work of this company. Commonly termed a "cost by job" system, labor time or charge is made against a specific job. Production control makes up in advance a job cost card which identifies the components of a job and accompanies the sequence of the work through the factory. At the top of the card is written (1) the part number, (2) the job number, (3) description, and (4) estimated time. Each employee who works on the job signs his or her company number and name on the card in the space provided, together with time registration at the start and at the finish of the time spent on this job number. For example, an entry may read: "156 G. Lustig 4 May 8:00 8.90 0.90" indicating employee Lustig spent 0.90 hours, or 54 minutes, on job number 156.

In evaluating this present means, Dan Reeves, the assistant factory superintendent, observed that it provides a complete summation of time spent on the job as soon as the job is completed. The total of the times spent is compared to the estimated time. However, a daily posting is not provided since most jobs are in the factory longer than one day. The cost status on a job is not known until it is completed. Further, there is no control over nonproductive time. However, Mr. Reeves feels the company could live with the present arrangement, but if this is done, he suggests the card be modified to provide identification of all the operations to be done and their sequence on the total job. This would make the job card a routing card as well.

Prescott Carr, a systems analyst, suggests a cost by employee per job or per day be used. Under this arrangement, a separate card is used by the employee to register start and stop time on each different job worked. Nonproductive time is registered on a separate card. If the job lasts beyond the close of a working day, a new card is used the following day for registering time. Cards are sorted daily either by (1) labor distribution of employee time or (2) labor distribution to specific jobs. In Mr. Carr's opinion such a system should be adopted since it will supply needed control of labor time in production and can be applied to all types of operations. By using a punched card, the written data can be transferred on the same card to the punched hole median and sorting can be very rapid. Further, if an individual incentive plan is contemplated, the individual payments could be carried on the cards. It is also feasible to include additional helpful information on the card such as standard time, number of pieces made, number scrapped, standard rate, and incentive rate. From the single card, both labor cost of the item and payment due employee are calculated.

Tammy Tambone, assistant director of the accounting department, recommends a perforated daily job ticket be used. As each job is completed, a stub is removed by tearing along a perforated line, and as the work progresses the perforated sections are turned in to the supervisor. Sometimes called a strip ticket or payroll attendance and cost by employee and job system, it provides a continuous flow of time tickets or stubs to the costing department where labor can be distributed against both employee and job. On each ticket or stub are shown the employee's name, number, operation, job number, pieces, time in, time out, and elapsed time. In addition, the heading at the top of the ticket can provide payroll information such as employee name, number, time in, time out for the total working day.

"Eliminate all tickets that are or appear to be timeclock tickets," comments Ray A. Kreitzburg, popular personnel manager of the company. "Employees dislike having to punch in and punch out. Encourage and motivate them to get the work out and you don't need to record how each employee spends every tenth-of-a-minute of the workday."

Questions:

1. Draw a sketch of the ticket suggested by Ms. Tambone.
2. What's your reaction to the suggestions of Mr. Carr? Of Mr. Kreitzburg?
3. Does this case illustrate the interdependence of systems in an enterprise? Discuss.
4. What is your recommendation to Limpert Manufacturing Company?

Case 3–3.   Troast Wholesale Plumbers

The assistant sales manager tells Frank Reinhart, a systems analyst, that, upon receipt, a customer's order is time-stamped and checked for credit. If it is found satisfactory, a "Credit OK" stamp is placed on the order; if not, the customer is written a letter requesting payment on past account or cash for the pending order. Order with credit approval are posted on customers' order cards, which are used for sales analysis work. Orders are then sent to the stockroom for filling and shipping. Subsequently, when merchandise is shipped and billed, the date and amount of shipment are posted on the customer's card. In response to his question of how the sales department knew that the order was shipped, Mr. Reinhart learned that this was by means of a "storeroom packing slip."

He then interviewed Hazel Mead, billing supervisor, who explained that her department receives a "packing slip from 07" which tells them the order is shipped. When they are so informed, this form 07 is checked with the customer's original purchase order and, if accurate, three billing copies are prepared. The first copy is sent to the customer, the second and third copies are filed respectively alphabetically and numerically in the files of the billing department. The original order is returned to sales, where it is filed, and the packing slip is filed chronologically by date billed.

The purchasing department buys upon requisition from the stockroom. The vendors are selected by looking in the vendor card file. Here the cards are arranged by part numbers and names showing the recommended supplier or suppliers. The purchasing agent can either write or telephone for quotations and base the selection of vendor on the answers received or simply select one of the approved vendors. Usually, on orders amounting to less than $100, the vendor is selected based on judgment only. Four copies of a purchase order are made out. Copy No. 1 goes to the vendor; Copy No. 2 goes to inventory control; Copy No. 3 goes to billing for payment, upon receipt of merchandise indicated by a receiving copy slip from the receiving and shipping department; and Copy No. 4 is the copy of purchasing filed by the purchase order number.

George Walker, the assistant manager of the stockroom, was interviewed next by Mr. Reinhart. An inventory card record is maintained for each item. When the amount of stock on hand reaches the replenishing point, an amount calculated for each item, a requisition is sent to purchasing to order a specific amount. Stockroom orders are stamped "PI" when they have been recorded in the daily tally sheet of orders for processing and also in inventory card records to reveal inventory depletion due to forthcoming shipping. PI orders are then picked, checked, packed, and shipped. Receiving and shipping, which is subordinate to the stockroom, makes out four copies of a packing slip 07, one of which is sent to billing; the second is a file copy of receiving and shipping; the third is sent to sales; and the fourth is the packing slip enclosed with the merchandise. Further questioning by Mr. Reinhart revealed that the stockroom receives the original customer's order from sales and that from this original a shop or stockroom order is made out. This latter order form highlights stockroom data, such as best sequence for picking items, location of stock, and approximate unit weights. After carefully checking the stockroom order, the stockroom sends the original customer's order to the billing department, as indicated previously.

Questions:

1. Currently the processing of a customer's order is viewed as four separate operations. Do you agree with this viewpoint? Why?
2. Draw a diagram indicating the processing as described above to substantiate your answer to question 1.
3. Point out and discuss some areas for improvement in the current processing practices being followed.

Chapter 4

Office Work Simplification

> *If there were dreams to sell,*
> *What would you buy?*
>
> Thomas Lovell Beddoes

Continuing our discussion of planning what office work is to be done, we now focus our attention on smaller work segments and different techniques for analysis and improvement. The work segment is a procedure or a method; the technique, work simplification. Our aim remains the same—namely to devise the best possible way of performing the necessary office work as indicated by the minimum requirement of time and effort.

Procedure, Method, Work Simplification

The formal definition of an office procedure was stated in Chapter 2. For convenience it is repeated here. *An office procedure is a series of selected clerical steps, usually performed by more than one person, which constitute an established and accepted way of carrying on an entire major phase of office activity.* In contrast, *a method is the manner of work performance of a task consisting of one or more clerical acts by an individual employee.* To a degree, methods become quite routine under an automated arrangement. Methods planning is probably more important when manual means are followed.

Office work simplification *is common sense organized to eliminate waste of material, equipment, time, energy, and space in the performance of office work.* The possibilities for improvement are limited only by the ability, imagination, and aggressiveness of the analyst. There is no

76

secret formula. Nonprofessionals sometimes erroneously refer to work simplification applied to methods as speedup. Work simplification implies an increase in the rate of work production, not speeding up the movements of the employee. The latter means to hurry *all* the work steps, *both the necessary and the unnecessary ones.* In contrast, by work simplification the rate of work production is improved by *performing only the necessary steps in a normal manner.*

However, office work simplification is applied not only to procedures and methods, but also to office forms, office arrangements, layouts, and equipment and machines. In this chapter we will include considerable material dealing with office procedures because much office work simplification is applied to them. This means that for improving procedures there is not only the approaches included in the previous two chapters, but also the technique of office work simplification.

It is logical to discuss first a system as we have done it, then the procedures making up this system, and finally the methods making up each procedure. In this way the broad activities are established, coordination is enhanced, the feasibility of automation effectively determined, and the end result of the total effort is clearly visualized. In practice, however, the planning of office work is not sharply delineated. Typically the information planner gives some consideration to procedures and methods while designing the system and to methods while designing the procedure. This is taking the bottom-to-top viewpoint and this is usually helpful in connection with the top-down viewpoint. The latter viewpoint, however, is dominant. To reverse this approach by starting with methods, tying them together for the procedure, and tying procedures together for the system is possible, but usually results in coordination difficulties and in excessive work scopes covered by the procedures and the systems.

Guides of Office Work Simplification

Over a period, many lists of guides to office work simplification have been compiled. For our purposes the following five are discussed.

1. Promote "Participation with Know-How" by Every Office Employee by Means of Training in and Encouragement of the Use of Work Simplification. An enthusiastic and strong desire by the operative employee for an improved way of doing the work satisfactorily and an understanding of the reasons for doing it the improved way are cardinal considerations. For the most part, these are won by encouraging employee participation in planning the improvement; for in this way employee interest, self-expression, acceptance, and cooperation are promoted and utilized. A person will usually accept a self-offered proposal.

But participation alone is insufficient. Nothing is more frustrating to employees than to be asked to take part in an activity about which they know little or nothing. This means the know-how must be supplied. Short, effective training programs are in order. Information and examples must be made available to the office employees. Thus, the participation with know-how is supplied.

Most employees dislike being pushed around, not being informed of developments of changes which affect them, and have a fear of what might happen to them as a result of change. Factors such as these cause the employee to desire the *status quo* and to tend to reject a new means of work performance. To overcome this resistance, participation with knowhow is recommended. If employees' enthusiastic participation for eliminating office waste cannot be won, it is almost a certainty that no really significant gains are going to be made. It is also vital to hold frank discussions pointing out the need for improvements to keep the enterprise competitive or to give greater security to the employee. Loss of job may be feared by the employee, but this need not result from work simplification. A policy of retraining and transferring to other jobs can be followed. In many cases, the normal labor turnover will take care of the number of employees needed; those leaving the company are not replaced. But these facts should be explained in simple language to the employees, so that they know what is going on and where they fit into the picture. Actually, the ideas of acquiring a real sense of accomplishment and of getting things done the simple way are strong appeals to many office employees.

2. *Make the Series of Activities Productive and Simple.* The adopted series of work activities should represent the best possible combination for achieving the finished work, taking into account the available facilities and work conditions. Simply stated, justify each activity for its essentiality, and eliminate all the unnecessary ones. As far as possible, those contributing directly to the goal, or so-called productive elements of a procedure, should be maximized; and conversely, the nonproductive elements should be reduced to an absolute minimum. Normally, this provides for the greatest productivity.

3. *Combine Work Activities Wherever Possible to Avoid Recopying.* Frequently found is needless copying of data. In some offices this practice is part of the accepted manner of getting information processed. For example, the salesperson may write an order, the branch office recopy it, the factory recopy certain portions of the order, the billing department recopy on an invoice, and accounts receivable recopy on the proper ledger card. Most of these writing activities can and should be combined into a single operation.

4. *Reduce Distances Traveled to the Shortest Amounts Feasible.* Movement of papers or of people are costly and wasteful; most of

them do not represent purposive effort. Therefore, movements should be closely scrutinized; if not essential, they should be eliminated. When travel is necessary, it is usually better to move the paper than the person. Sometimes, the machine can be brought to the work; or mechanical handling devices, such as conveyors, pneumatic tubes, and gravity feeds to deliver or to take away the papers, can be used. When messengers are employed, perhaps more items per trip are in order. Different arrangements of the office layout might also offer worthwhile improvements.

5. *Arrange Activities to Provide a Smooth Flow from One Clerical Step to Another or a Rhythmic Pattern for an Employee at a Workplace.* Excessive amounts or spurts of unduly heavy work loads tend to discourage the office employee. As a result, the feeling of never "getting on top of the work" or never having a sense of accomplishment plagues the employee. In contrast, the situation of carefully throttling the work in order to keep busy is equally annoying. A steady, constant flow of work is normally desirable.

Delays and hesitations in the work flow should be minimized. Much time and energy are dissipated by tolerating the jumping around from one batch of work to another, then returning to the initial batch. This applies whether automated or manual means are used. It takes time to adjust to the different batches of work, not to mention the lost time in stopping one and starting another. For each employee, a rhythmic pattern of work actions with motions following curved, not straight lines, should be sought.

Applying Office Work Simplification

Four basic steps are followed in applying office work simplification. As shown in Figure 4–1, these steps include: (1) select work to be simplified, (2) obtain all the facts about this work, (3) devise improvement by analyzing these facts and using the questioning approach, and (4) apply the derived improved means.

The first step, select work to be simplified, may designate in the case of procedures a procedure that limits other information work or in which labor requirements appear unduly high. The procedure may be selected on the basis that the number of work activities is too large, the time taken to do the work is excessive, costs are unduly high, or the end result seems unjustifiable. For methods, repetitive tasks are favorites for work simplification. Generally they offer large savings possibilities. Even though the gain on each task performance might be small, the doing of this task over and over again results in sizable cumulative savings. Selecting repetitive tasks does not mean that other tasks do not warrant study. *Any task can be improved with sufficient effort.* Ac-

FIGURE 4–1
Basic Steps of Office Work Simplification

1. Select the Work to Be Simplified

2. Obtain All Facts about This Work

3. Devise Improvements by
   a) Analyzing These Facts and
   b) Using Selected Questions

4. Apply the Derived Improved Means

tually, the job selected and the extent and thoroughness of the study depend upon a number of things, such as the continuity of the work, the amount of processing required, the total cost or number of people engaged in the work, the value connected with the paper handled, and the interest of the operative employee, supervisor, or analyst.

Many feel that five types of office work usually are the best bets for attention including (1) *bottlenecks*—work that backs up everything before it and holds up everything that follows it, (2) *hither and there—*

work involving a considerable amount of rushing around, getting up, looking in file, checking a reference book, and sitting down, (3) *long duration*—work that requires a long time to complete, commonly time extensions are requested, (4) *high make ready and put away*—work necessitating getting out and arranging special papers and facilities, followed by a relatively small amount of processing and then, putting back all the special papers and facilities, and (5) *activity, but little accomplishment*—work being performed with gusto and much fuss by people very busy, but upon investigation it is found very little is actually being accomplished.

Whatever work is selected, it must be defined. This helps to classify the objective and avoids the mistake of attempting to simplify office work without first gaining a clear concept of the work objective. Work definition assists in simplification because all efforts can be concentrated and directed toward this goal.

Obtain All the Facts about This Work

The second step is to find out how the selected work is currently being handled. For example, details of a present procedure are obtained from available record sources, i.e., job descriptions, charts, lists, outlines, and sample forms. Additional information can be obtained from study of the system of which the procedure or the method is a part, talks with members of management, and inspection of the procedure or the method in action, so that the type of work and the equipment used can be observed.

All the facts are needed to devise an effective improvement. To aid in this work, many different types of graphic representations or charts have been developed and are widely used. Each chart has a particular purpose and value, and it is neither necessary nor practical to use every type of chart in a particular study. The major charts for procedure and for method improvements will be discussed in detail later in this chapter.

Devise Improvement

The third step is to devise improvement which is done by analyzing the facts and using the questioning approach. This phase can be described as one of challenging each detail of the present procedure or method. The facts are studied to reveal violations of the basic work simplification guides discussed previously. Correcting these weaknesses provides improvement. Creativity and experience are also helpful in suggesting areas for improvement.

Using the questioning approach is perhaps the most fruitful and widely adopted practice. Every work activity is subjected to questions pertaining to what is done, where, when, by whom, and how. To each of these, the big question of why is added making the first question, for example, what is done and why? and the second question, where should it be done and why? Answers to these questions help relate essentials, reveal unnecessary work, and provide clues for improvement. Figure 4–2 indicates these key questions along with their relationship

FIGURE 4–2

Key Questions, Major Principles, and Resultant Actions Used in Devising the Improvement of an Office Procedure

Key Questions	*Major Principles* *	*Resultant Action*
What and why?	1. Promote "participation with knowhow." 2. Make activities productive and simple.	Eliminate

Where and why?
When and why?
Who and why?
	1. Promote "participation with knowhow."
	3. Combine work activities—avoid
	   recopying.
	4. Reduce distances traveled.
	5. Provide a smooth flow from one step to
	   another.
		Combine } the place
		or } the time
		change } the person

How and why?	1. Promote "participation with knowhow." 2. Make activities productive and simple.	Simplify

* Refer to pages 77–79.

to the major guides of work simplification utilized, and the resultant actions. To illustrate, answer the question "What is being done and why?" following the principles of promote participation with know-how and make activities productive and simple. Point out many unnecessary activities that can be eliminated and do so, for this is the zenith of work simplification. Questions of where and why, when and why, and who and why will suggest combining or changing procedural elements as to place, time, and person, respectively. An improved procedure or method will result. The question "How and why?" emphasizes simplifying the activity.

The sequence of the questioning and subsequent improvement action is logical and practical. Questions should be asked in the sequence shown. If the activity can be eliminated, there is no need to study it further for possible combination or change. Likewise, the "Who and why" question precedes the "How and why" questions because the former might lead to improved labor utilization, and this should be determined before the manner of doing the work is improved.

Additional questions of a more specific nature can also be asked, but it is well to remember that good questions are required to get good answers. The questions should have a purposeful intent and lead to betterment, not just a conglomeration of responses to queries. Suggestions for questions to ask are shown in Figure 4–3.

In the case of improving office methods, it is especially important

FIGURE 4–3
Suggested Questions to Ask for Improving Office Procedures and Office Methods

Questions for procedures improvement:

1. Can the information being given be obtained from another existing source?
2. Can the information be produced in one writing?
3. Is the paper or office form being used of a design that tends to help the progress of the work?
4. Does the information compiled follow a sequence best suited for subsequent processing activities?
5. Would the flow of information be improved by use of: (*a*) an improved office layout? (*b*) a conveyor system? (*c*) messenger service? (*d*) computer and visual terminal units?
6. How is the quality of the office work evaluated?

Questions for methods improvement:

1. Does the work flow to the employee at a fairly constant rate?
2. What special skills seem to be required to perform the tasks satisfactorily?
3. Is a desk necessary, or could the work be done equally as well on a table?
4. Would a specially designed table add to the comfort of the employee and facilitate the use of office machines?
5. Is the working surface of the proper height?
6. Is a machine at reasonable cost available to perform work very similar to that which is being manually handled?

to provide a suitable workplace. This includes pre-positioning papers, cards, and working tools so that they are handy and ready for use as required. For example, devices can be used to hold penciled notes while typing, locating frequently used supplies such as paper clips, stapler, and rubber stamps on a rotor where easy access is possible; and putting reference materials, including books, catalogs, and lists, on convenient racks within easy reach or vision of the operator.

The arrangement of unitizing can also be followed. Under this plan, each operating unit is considered a separate entity and is supplied individually with all the tools and supplies necessary for its work. The required papers, books, supplies, and the like are located on a wall rack or in a floor cabinet near the operator's desk. For the most part, this arrangement brings best results when a large portion of the office consists of widely dispersed and fairly independent units, although it is not limited to this particular type of setup.

Also, it is advisable to utilize the normal and the maximum working areas. The *normal* working area for the right hand on a desk top, for example, is the area determined by swinging the extended right hand

and forearm only across the desk. The pivoting is at the elbow, with the upper arm being relaxed at the side of the body. The arm tends to swing out a little at the outer end of the arc. In a similar manner, the normal working area for the left hand is determined. These two normal areas overlap in front of the employee, and this overlapping area represents the location in which work requiring both hands can be performed most readily.

The *maximum* working areas are the areas determined by swinging the extended hand and entire arm, pivoting at the shoulder. Figure 4–4 shows graphically the normal and maximum working areas with

FIGURE 4–4
Illustration of Normal and of Maximum Working Areas

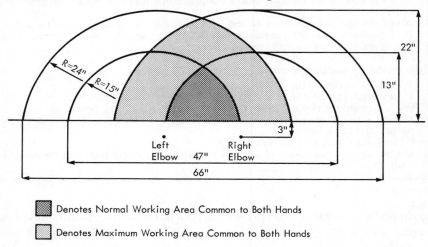

■ Denotes Normal Working Area Common to Both Hands

□ Denotes Maximum Working Area Common to Both Hands

dimensions for an average employee. Paper being worked on should be located within the arcs of the normal working areas common to both hands. Supplies should also be located within the normal and never outside the maximum working areas.

A comfortable workplace implies that the employee's chair, desk, table, or machine is of such dimensions that the work can be accomplished with ease, that is, without excessive physical exertion or strain. When possible, it is usually desirable to have the employee sit part of the time and stand part of the time. Some change is apparently necessary for maximum comfort. The height of the workplace should be such that support is given the underside of the forearm at a point slightly below the elbows. Where the hands are self-supported, the workplace should be of such height that the hands work at a level slightly higher than that of the elbows.

Further, in the case of methods improvement, certain guides can be followed. These have been developed over a long period and represent short cuts which are effective. They are shown in Figure 4–5.

FIGURE 4–5
Guides for Improving Office Methods

1. Do the work by machine, not manually, if possible. Develop the best motion for the operator with the machine being utilized.
2. Use both hands for doing work, avoiding the use of either hand as a holding device. Both hands should begin and complete their motions at the same time, moving simultaneously in opposite and symmetrical directions.
3. Employ a minimum of motions to complete the task. Use hand motions only or, if necessary, hands and eye motions only. Arm, leg, and body motions should be infrequently required.
4. Strive to have high-priced office help do high-priced office work only. Minimize, for example, the private secretary doing strictly typist work.
5. Avoid writing the same information twice.
6. Have source document and end result in the same format, if possible.
7. Use precomputed tables or graphic indicators.
8. Make only the number of copies that are needed and used.

Apply the Derived Improved Means

This fourth and last step is relatively simple to apply providing the employee has participated and understands why and how the new means is to be used. To accomplish procedures and methods improvement there is no adequate substitute for gaining and maintaining wholesome understanding between management and nonmanagement members. The purpose of the improvement should be clearly set forth, and the reasons for its importance in the enterprise made crystal clear to every employee affected by it.

It helps to show examples of what has been accomplished from work simplification in other offices, and to indicate that it is a key in getting the work accomplished effectively, in reducing waste, and in gaining satisfaction from performing the work well and in meeting the challenge that it offers. Everyone dealing with information should realize the importance of improving the way information work is performed. To realize this goal, training can be provided; meetings of department heads and supervisors are common. They can be conducted separately for each group or combined into one group, depending upon the individual circumstances.

COMMON CHARTS OF OFFICE WORK SIMPLIFICATION

The remainder of this chapter will be devoted to work simplification charts. As mentioned above, these charts serve to provide the facts for a work simplification project in a clear and comprehensive manner. Specifically, work simplification charts serve the following purposes: (1) assist in securing, organizing, and visualizing the facts, (2) aid in analyzing and evaluating these facts, (3) help formulate an improved procedure or method and (4) assist in convincing others of the value of the improved means. Unless the chart serves one or more of these purposes, it should not be drawn.

Frequently, more than one chart is used, and the right combination of several charts usually reveals information and clues for work simplification. In total three charts for procedures improvement—process, procedural flow, and movement diagram—and three charts for methods improvement—left- and right-hand chart, production study, and operator-machine activity—will be presented.

Process Chart

One of the most helpful charts in work simplification is the process chart which shows the successive detailed steps in a process. This chart can either be drawn for an entire procedure covering many departments, or it may be confined to a part of a procedure. The steps are indicated by brief statements and symbols arranged vertically in chronological order, with the first step at the top of the sheet. Unfortunately, there is as yet no standardized set of symbols used by analysts. Figure 4–6 shows two sets of symbols that are widely employed. To illustrate, signing a memo constitutes an operation and would be represented by either a large circle or double large circles depending upon the set of symbols followed. Likewise, sending the memo to another office unit is transportation and is shown by a small circle or a small arrow. Filing the memo is represented by an inverted triangle. Checking the memo for errors constitutes inspection and is represented by a square. Many analysts have found that color is helpful in charting work. For example, operations constituting direct processing work and adding value to the product are distinguished by the use of a special color. In contrast, no special color is employed for operations used but not adding value such as operations done for preparatory or cleaning-up purposes. Figure 4–7 shows a simple process chart using popular symbols.

The intended purpose of the process chart and the symbols is to give a clear picture of the office procedure and assist in analyzing and improving it. Any reasonable set of symbols can be used; the best is the set that best assists the analyst's determination to eliminate paper work waste. In addition, it is customary to include on a process chart the time required, the distance covered if movement is involved, and a summary by type of action.

Figure 4–8 illustrates a process chart. It shows the process of stopping an incorrect charge credit in a large department store. It is drawn for

FIGURE 4–6
Symbols for Process Charts

List A	List B	Illustrated by
◯ Operation	◎ Operation – Origin of Record	Writing, Posting, Sorting
— —	⊘ Operation – Adding to Record	Extending a Billing
◯ Transportation	⇨ Travel or Move	Movement of Paper or Walking by Employee
▽ Delay or Storage	D Delay – Avoidable	Paper Awaiting Further Action
— —	▽ File	Placing in File
— —	⚡ Copy Discarded or Destroyed	Terminating Paper
☐ Inspection	☐ Inspection	Verifying But Not Changing Data

the credit form papers. This work is brought about by the following situation. An article of merchandise is purchased by a customer, Mrs. Jane T. Smith, with a charge account. The merchandise is returned, but the clerk incorrectly writes Mrs. Jane F. Smith on the credit memorandum. Later, the customer telephones and informs the adjusting department of the store that the name is not Mrs. Jane F. Smith, but Mrs. Jane T. Smith. Meanwhile, the credit memorandum is in process in either the sales auditing department or the accounts receivable department, both located several floors away from the adjusting department. Hence, a "stop notice" is prepared and a duplicate copy sent to sales auditing or accounts receivable, telling them not to bill the credit memorandum made out to Jane F. Smith. This stop notice, along with the credit memorandum to Jane F. Smith, is returned to the adjustor who handled the telephone call.

The placing of the credit memorandum and stop notice on the desk constitutes step number 1 of the chart illustrated in Figure 4–8 (p. 90). Hence, on line number 1, this action is briefly described in the column to the left. This action is an operation, in that something happens to the papers; hence, it is represented by a large-circle symbol and is indi-

FIGURE 4–7
A Flow Process Chart

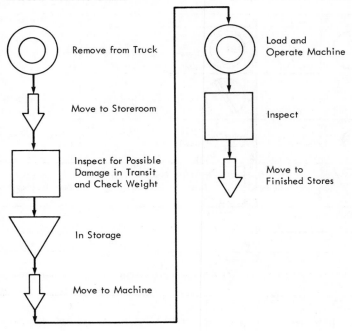

Remove from Truck

Load and
Operate Machine

Move to Storeroom

Inspect

Inspect for Possible
Damage in Transit
and Check Weight

Move to
Finished Stores

In Storage

Move to Machine

cated on the chart by filling in the large circle under "operation" on line number 1. Appropriate notes are made in the column to the right.

Next, the forms are picked up. Hence, on line number 2, this action is expressed and represented by a large circle. In a similar manner, the entire process is described and charted. The totals of each action and of the distances traveled are then determined and recorded in the summary table at the top of the sheet. In this illustration, the figures are:

Operations 17
Transportations 7
Storage 5
Distance traveled . . . . 92 feet

A study of the chart shows that this procedure can be simplified. To do this, the work simplification principles and the questioning attitude, as already discussed, were applied. For example, when step number 3—placed in drawer—is subjected to the question "What is done and why?" it is found to be unproductive and hence can be eliminated. In similar manner, every operation, transportation, storage, and inspection not proved necessary is eliminated; and actions found necessary are combined wherever feasible or changed to provide better accomplishment of the work. Finally, each necessary step is simplified as much as possible.

Figure 4–9 shows an improved procedure over the one shown in Figure 4–8. In the light of what has been written, it is suggested that a careful comparison of these two charts be made in order to gain an insight as to how a procedure can be improved. Under the new procedure, credits are voided with a claim number on them and sent to sales auditing or accounts receivable. The stop notice can be discarded, since its duplicate is already on the claim. The elimination of requests to pull claims out of the central file eliminates steps 7 through 21 of the original procedure. Also, steps 3 through 6 have been eliminated; they were simply delaying actions brought about by the makeup of the original procedure. The improved procedure requires eight less operations, six less transportations, four less storages, and less than 10 percent of the former distance traveled.

Procedure Flow Chart

This type of chart is very effective where multiple-copy forms are used. It depicts graphically the distribution and subsequent steps for each form from physical inception to permanent storage or destruction. Generally, this type of chart is not difficult to construct.

Figure 4–10 shows a procedure flow chart of work performed for handling uniform express receipt-collect shipments. Four separate writings are required for each package. These include a packing slip and duplicate, separate typings for each of two labels, and the copies of the uniform express receipt-collect. As indicated in the chart, the labels are put on the package. One copy of the packing slip is sent to the billing department for filing, the other copy placed in the package. Other operations can be determined from the chart.

A procedure to accomplish the same objective, but with much waste eliminated, is shown in Figure 4–11. As illustrated, a seven-part form is written at one time from the sales order. The writing is checked, and then the copies are sent to the shipping department, where they are distributed and used as indicated on the chart. The total number of operations has been reduced from 30 to 17, a saving of nearly 45 percent. Waste elimination, achieved by planning, has resulted in making activities productive, combining operations, eliminating others, and increasing the accuracy.

Movement Diagram

A movement diagram portrays motion through space. It is drawn on a scaled layout of the office floor plan so that the movement can be measured and viewed in proper relationship with the physical factors. These charts are helpful in spotting backtracking, visualizing the physical

FIGURE 4–8
A Fill-in Type of Process Chart Covering the Work of Stopping
an Incorrect Charge Credit

Courtesy: Marshall Field & Co., Chicago.

FIGURE 4–9
An Improved Procedure over That Shown in Figure 4–8

PAGE.............

MARSHALL FIELD & COMPANY
FLOW PROCESS CHART

JOB *Stopping an incorrect charge credit*

SUBJECT CHARTED *Credit form*

CHARTED BY *Ethel Marable*

DATE *November 19—*

DEPT *Customer's Service* SEC *Adjusting*

SUMMARY			
METHOD	PRES.	PROPD.	SAVG.
NO. OF OPERATIONS		9	8
NO. OF TRANSPORTATIONS		1	6
NO. OF STORAGES		0	4
NO. OF INSPECTIONS			
MAN HOURS OR MINUTES			
DISTANCE TRAVELED		8 ft	89 ft

	DETAILS (PRESENT/PROPOSED) METHOD	OPER.	TRANS.	STORAGE	INSPECT.	DIST. IN FEET	TIME IN MINUTES	WHY? WHAT? WHERE? WHEN? WHO? HOW?	NOTES
1	*Place on desk*	①	○	▽	□				*Credit and duplicate stop attached. Sent from sales auditing or accounts receivable*
2	*Pick up*	①	○	▽	□				
3	*Detach stop notice*	①	○	▽	□				*Stop notice thrown away*
4	*Void credit*	①	○	▽	□				*Writes "Void". Claim number and initials*
5	*Pick up*	①	○	▽	□				
6	*Place in house envelope*	①	○	▽	□				
7	*Pick up*	①	○	▽	□				
8	*Carry to house mailbox*	○	⬤	▽	□	8			
9	*Place in house mailbox*	①	○	▽	□				
10	*Wait for pick up*	①	○	▽	□				

Courtesy: Marshall Field & Co., Chicago.

motion involved, and locating congestion and bottlenecks, so that they can be remedied quickly.

Movement diagrams are of two types: those showing paper movement and those showing employee movement. The entire chart should be of one type or the other. Attempting to follow first one and then the other on the same chart leads to confusion. Figure 4–12 (p. 94) illustrates movement diagrams for paper, showing the movements before and after work simplification. This improvement was gained by changing the office layout.

In many instances, however, the paper is not moved by simply handing it to the person at the adjacent desk or by messenger service; it is carried by the person last working on it to the next successive station. This is part of the procedure. It is therefore apparent that an analysis of employee movement is equally as important as an analysis of paper movement. Charts showing employee movement are especially helpful where the work is nonrepetitive and where the employees operate over a large area. The employee movement chart is similar in appearance to the paper movement chart.

FIGURE 4–10
A Procedure Flow Chart before Work Simplification

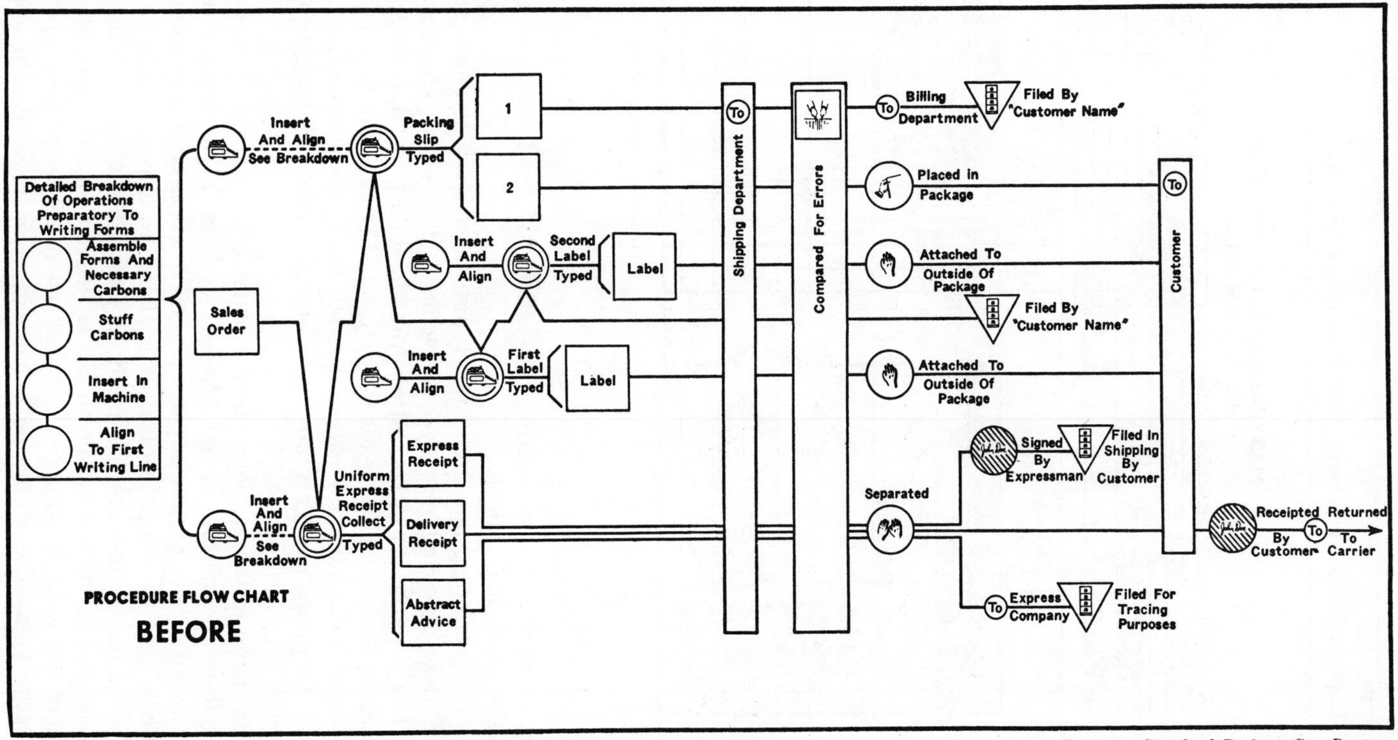

Courtesy: *Standard Register Co., Dayton.*

FIGURE 4–11

The Improved Procedure over That Shown in Figure 4–10, after Work Simplification

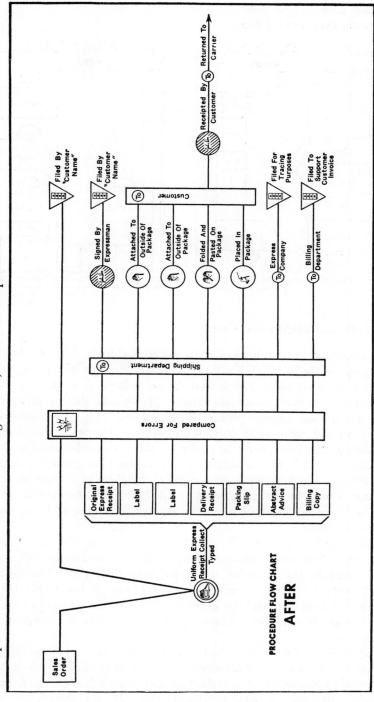

Courtesy: Standard Register Co., Dayton.

FIGURE 4–12
Movement Diagrams for Paper

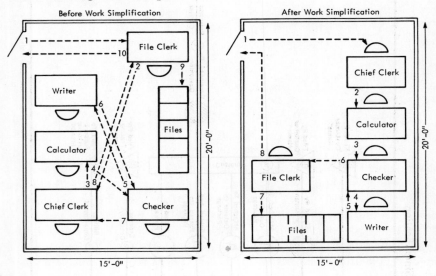

The Left- and Right-Hand Chart

Turning our attention now to methods improvement, the first chart discussed is the left- and right-hand chart. In this chart the detailed motions of each hand are shown. Some believe it is best to observe the actions of both hands to indicate these data on the chart as the work progresses. Others prefer to prepare the chart by following the actions of the right hand only, the actions of the left hand only, then combining the two charts in order to show the relationships existing according to time of execution. Attention must be given to details. A few seconds saved on an action or the elimination of a short movement, perhaps 3 or 4 inches, may seem small; but when the task is repeated over and over again, the cumulative savings in fatigue and time become highly significant.

Six symbols are generally used as illustrated in Figure 4–13. Here again there is no universal agreement on the type and number of symbols to be used in this charting work. Actually this is not too serious as the important concept is to make certain that all the facts about the method are collected and the conceptualizing of the method of the work to be done is complete. The symbols are merely to assist in these endeavors.

Figure 4–14 illustrates a left- and right-hand operation chart for typing, in duplicate, original sales data sent in by field representatives. The workplace layout is sketched at the top of the chart. A number or code system can be used to identify the various materials and equip-

FIGURE 4–13
Symbols Used for Left- and Right-Hand Chart

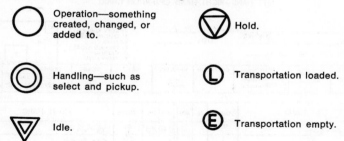

Operation—something created, changed, or added to.

Hold.

Handling—such as select and pickup.

Transportation loaded.

Idle.

Transportation empty.

ment used. Also, provisions for the inclusion of other pertinent data are made at the top of the sheet. Of special interest is the summary information, which shows the total actions by type, along with the distance the hands travel and the time taken to perform the task.

In this case, the task begins with the operator reaching with the right hand to the pile of copy blanks positioned to the right and forward of the typewriter. This action is "transportation empty," since the hand is empty, and is indicated on line number 1 by a small circle with an *E* inside under the symbol column for the right hand. The description "to # 2" is written in the description column on the right. In making this transportation, the hand travels 20 inches; and this is recorded in the distance column, right hand, on line 1. While this is going on, the left hand is idle, so a double triangle is inserted under the symbol column of the left hand and the word "idle" written in the description column on the left.

Next, the right hand grasps a copy blank. This is a handling action and is shown by large double circles on line number 2 under the right hand. "Grasp # 2" is written on the same line in the description column. During this particular operation, the left hand was idle. Since this is the same as the previous entry for the left hand, no new symbol is necessary on the chart,

In a similar manner, each step of the operation is observed and noted on the form. It is important that all details be included and that extreme care be exercised to insure accuracy in this work.

A study of Figure 4–14 shows that the method can be improved. In this figure, it should be observed that the right hand moves first to number 2, the copy blank pile. The analyst will question the necessity and purpose of this action, asking, "What is being done, and why?" The analyst will strive to eliminate this motion and also to get the operator interested and active in this work simplification effort. Participation in simplification is sought.

Also, he will observe that the right hand successively makes six transportations—three empty and three loaded—all to the same general area.

FIGURE 4–14

LEFT HAND—RIGHT HAND OPERATION CHART

Subject_____   Project No._____
Operator_____   Date_____
Location_____

Legend:
1 = ORIGINAL BLANK
2 = COPY BLANK
3 = ORIGINAL DATA
4 = PAPER CLIPS
F = FINISHED WORK
C = CARBON
T = TYPEWRITER

(diagram boxes: F, 1, 4, T, 2, 3, T, C)

CHARTED BY	SHEET 1 OF 1	METHOD BEFORE X AFTER____	OPERATION	HANDLING	IDLE	HOLD	TRANSPORTATION LOADED (10) 131" EMPTY (12) 136"	TIME
HKJ			6	23	4	3		1.25 (x)

(X) NO TYPING

#	LEFT HAND	SYMBOL	IN.	MIN.	MIN.	IN.	SYMBOL	RIGHT HAND	#
1	idle	▽			0.05	20	⊕	to #2	1
2					0.02		◎	grasp #2	2
3					0.05	16	⊕	to top of T	3
4					0.01		◎	release #2	4
5					0.04	9	⊕	to C, carbon paper	5
6					0.02		◎	grasp C.	6
7					0.04	13	⊕	to top of T	7
8					0.01		◎	release C	8
9					0.06	25	⊕	to #1	9
10					0.02		◎	grasp #1	10
11					0.06	25	⊕	to top of T	11
12					0.02		◎	release #1	12
13	grasp #1-C-#2	◎		0.01	0.01		◎	grasp #1-C-#2	13
14	to platen of T	⊕	3	0.03	0.03	3	⊕	to platen of T	14
15	hold	▽			0.02		◎	release #1-C-#2	15
16					0.02	4	⊕	to platen knob	16
17					0.07			twist platen knob	17
18	release #1-C-#2	◎		0.02	0.02		◎	release platen knob	18
19	to keyboard	⊕	6	0.03	0.03	5	⊕	to keyboard	19
20	type	○		—	—		○	type	20
21	to #1-C-#2	⊕	6	0.03	0.03	5	⊕	to T platen knob	21
22	grasp #1-C-#2	◎		0.02	0.02		◎	grasp platen knob	22
23	remove #1-C-#2	○		0.05	0.05		○	twist platen knob	23
24	to top of T	⊕	3	0.03	0.02		◎	release platen knob	24
25	hold	▽			0.03	3	⊕	to top of T	25
26					0.03		◎	grasp C	26
27					0.05	13	⊕	to "C" on desk	27
28	release #1-C-#2	◎			0.02		◎	release C	28
29	to paper clips; #4	⊕	15	0.06	0.05	13	⊕	to top of T	29
30	grasp paper clip	◎		0.02			▽	idle	30
31	to #3, original data	⊕	10	0.04					31
32	grasp #3, original data	◎		0.03					32
33	to top of T	⊕	20	0.05					33
34	release original data card on #1-#2	◎		0.02	0.02		◎	grasp #1-#2	34
35	attach clip	○		0.04			▽	hold #1-#2	35
36	to "F" on desk	⊕	25	0.06			◎	release	36
37	release	◎		0.02			▽	idle	37
38	to T	⊕	25	0.06			▽		38

Are these necessary? Can they be eliminated, combined, or simplified? Can they be made productive? Further, it will be observed that, in the beginning, the right hand is occupied, while the left hand is idle. As already pointed out in Figure 4–5 motion economy results from both hands moving simultaneously in opposite directions. Therefore, arrangements should be made to have both hands moving at the same time, and in opposite directions if possible. By following this minute and careful consideration of each action, the work is simplified and wasted motions are eliminated.

Figure 4–15 shows improvements for accomplishing the same work.

FIGURE 4–15

LEFT HAND—RIGHT HAND OPERATION CHART

Subject _____ Project No. _____
Operator _____ Date _____
Location _____

1. ORIGINAL BLANK
2. COPY BLANK
3. ORIGINAL DATA
4. PAPER CLIPS
F. FINISHED WORK
C. CARBON
T. TYPEWRITER

	F
4	1
3	T	2	C

CHARTED BY	SHEET 1 OF 1	METHOD BEFORE ___ AFTER X	OPERATION 5	HANDLING 17	IDLE 0	HOLD 2	TRANSPORTATIONS LOADED (9) 106"	EMPTY (8) 73"	TIME 0.71
HRJ									

	LEFT HAND	SYMBOL	IN.	MIN.	MIN.	IN.	SYMBOL	RIGHT HAND	
1	grasp #1	◎		0.04	0.04		◎	grasp C and #2	1
2	to top of T	⊖	19	0.02	0.02	16	⊖	to top of T	2
3	grasp C and #2	◎		0.01	0.01		◎	grasp #1	3
4	to platen of T	⊖	3	0.03	0.03	3	⊖	to platen of T	4
5	hold	▽			0.02		◎	release #1–C–#2	5
6					0.02	4	⊖	to platen knob	6
7					0.07		◯	twist platen knob	7
8	release #1–C–#2	◎		0.02	0.02		◎	release platen knob	8
9	to keyboard	⊖	6	0.03	0.03	5	⊖	to keyboard	9
10	type	◯	—	—	—	—	◯	type	10
11	to #4, paper clips	⊖	10	0.04	0.02	6	⊖	to #1–C–#2	11
12	grasp paper clip	◎		0.02	0.01		◎	grasp #1–C–#2	12
13	to #3, original data	⊖	8	0.03	0.02		◯	pull #1–C–#2 from T	13
14	grasp #3, original data	◎		0.03	0.02	2	⊖	to top of T	14
15	to top of T	⊖	18	0.04	0.01		◎	release #1–C–#2	15
16	release on top #1–C–#2	◎		0.02	0.03		◎	grasp c	16
17	grasp #3 and #1–C–#2	◎		0.04	0.05	12	⊖	to "2" on desk	17
18	hold	▽		0.02	0.02		◎	release	18
19					0.03	16	⊖	to left hand	19
20					0.02		◎	grasp clip	20
21					0.04		◯	attach to #3, #1–#2	21
22	to "F" on desk	⊖	25	0.06	0.02		◎	release	22
23	to #1 on desk	⊕	10	0.04	0.03	16	⊕	to "2" on desk	23

The new work layout is sketched at the top of the sheet. Idle time has been eliminated, and simultaneous hand motions have been made a part of the method. The two transportations—empty and loaded—to the copy blanks and the two transportations to the carbon paper have been combined. A comparison study between the two charts will reveal other work simplification accomplishments. The tabular comparison shows:

	Present Method		*Proposed Method*	
Operations.	6		5	
Handling	23		17	
Idle	4		0	
Hold	3		2	
Transportation loaded	10	(131 inches)	9	(106 inches)
Transportation empty	12	(136 inches)	8	(73 inches)
Time	1.25 minutes		0.71 minutes	

Worthwhile savings have been accomplished.

Production Study Chart

The production study chart shows how an employee spends working time and the major functions performed. Either the employee can record activities, or the supervisor or the planner can obtain the data by means of observation. In any event, the employee should be informed of the study and its purpose and told why and how the recordings are made. For meaningful results, the job content should be fairly consistent from day to day, and the observed employee should neither hasten nor retard normal efforts. The data should be collected for several consecutive days, preferably a week, in order to arrive at what would seem to be a normal pattern.

There are several ways in which the information of a production study chart can be recorded. One method consists of using graph paper with sections representing time units throughout the working day. These sections are filled in with colored pencil according to a color-identification key for the various functions performed. Another method consists of simply marking down in tabular form the various types of work done and the time each job is started and finished. The latter is illustrated by Figure 4–16. The usual identification data—employee name, date, and the like—are shown at the top. A series of vertical columns are used for the various functions, with the extreme left column utilized for time and the extreme right for comments. Since the study begins at 9:00 A.M. Monday, the insertion "Mon. 9.00" is written on the first

FIGURE 4–16

Chart Showing How One Employee Spends Her Working Time (data are secured by observing the employee)

PRODUCTION STUDY CHART

Date 3/21   Sheet *1* of *5* Sheets
Study By *EAH*   Employee's Name *Nancy Taussig*
Computations By *EAH*   Division or Unit *Transcription – 32*
Job Title *Transcriber*

TIME	TRAN-SCRIBING	COM-PUTING	FILING	SUPER-VISION Rcvd.	SUPER-VISION GIVEN	TELE-PHONE	HAND-LING MAIL	PERSON-AL TIME	MISC.	COMMENTS
MON. 9:00 / 9:20									✓20	Cleaning typewriter
9:50	✓30									
10:05						✓15				Business Call
10:18	✓13									
10:25				✓7						
10:50									✓25	Rest period & Idle
10:59			✓9							
11:08						✓9				Business Call
11:10			✓2							
11:22						✓12				Personal Call
11:30							✓8			
11:35				✓5						
11:50									✓15	Idle
12:00								✓10		
LUNCH 1:00 / 1:07									✓7	Tardy
1:10				✓3						
1:40	✓30									
1:55								✓15		
3:05	✓70									
3:42									✓37	Rest period & Idle
4:05							✓23			
4:15								✓10		
4:25						✓10				Business Call
4:45			✓20							
4:58									✓13	Idle
5:00									✓2	Cleaning Desk
TOTALS	143	–	31	15	–	46	23	43	119	420
PER CENT	34.1	–	7.4	3.6	–	11.0	5.4	10.1	28.4	100.0%

line under the Time column. The employee is observed cleaning her typewriter, so a check mark(√) is made on the first line under Miscellaneous and "cleaning typewriter" is written under Comments. She finishes this task at 9:20 A.M. and begins transcribing. Hence, "9.20" is written on the first line under Time, and a check mark is made under Transcribing on line 2. She stops transcribing at 10:05 A.M. to telephone. Hence, on line 3, a check mark is made under Telephone, and the entry "10.05" is made in the Time column. In a similar manner, entries are made throughout the entire day.

The calculations for figuring the elapsed time per function can be made as the study progresses or at the completion of all observations. In the illustration, the ordinary 60-minute watch has been used. For the first line, the elapsed time between 9.00 and 9.20 is 20 minutes, which is recorded in the same square as the check mark under Miscellaneous. For the second line, the elapsed time is 9.50 minus 9.20, or 30 minutes. The itemized totals are shown at the bottom of the form along with the percentage figures. For example, the total time spent in transcribing is 143 minutes. This constitutes 34.1 percent of the total day's working time, calculated by dividing the transcribing time, 143 minutes, by the total day's working time, 420 minutes.

These types of data are helpful because they tell what the status of the various types of work are at present and give, per employee, a picture of the overall work pattern which might form the basis for methods improvement, better supervision, and equalization of the work load. They can also be used to supply basic information for the construction of a work distribution chart.[1]

For example, a production study chart may reveal that a typist, with a typing speed of 50 words per minute, spends only 50 percent of work time typing. The remaining 50 percent is spent on other activities, most of which are nonessential, including positioning papers in typewriter, checking work, removing papers from typewriter, separating copies, cleaning typewriter, answering telephone, filing papers, and getting information from the supervisor. In this case, the effective typing production is at a rate of only 25 (50 percent of 50) words per minute. In too many offices, the sole emphasis is upon the speed of the operator. True, this has value, but when the methods improvement efforts reveal only 50 percent of the employee's particular skill being utilized, it is a challenge to the manager to eliminate such waste. The production study chart reveals such situations and assists in correcting them.

Operator-Machine Activity Chart

This last chart to be discussed shows the relation between the operator and the machine. Its use is somewhat limited in office methods, owing to the general nature of most office activities. It is chiefly employed to determine idle machine time and the number of machines which one operator can reasonably handle, thus in effect determining the superior method.

Figure 4–17 shows an operator-machine activity chart. Pertinent data and a sketch of the workplace layout are included at the top. Time is represented by vertical distance on the scale shown in the center

---

[1] See Chapter 13 for discussion of work distribution chart.

FIGURE 4–17
An Operator-Machine Activity Chart

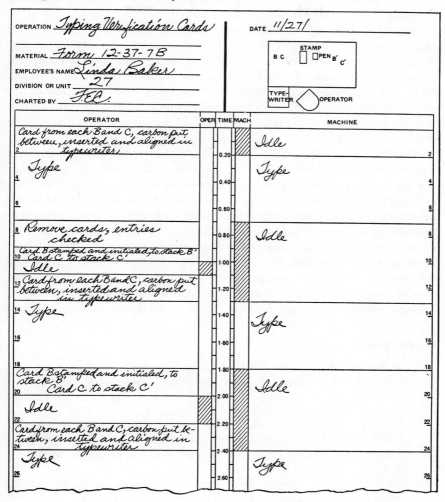

column of the sheet. For example, two scale units represent two minutes, four scale units four minutes, and so forth. The activities of the operator are listed in the left column, those of the machine on the right.

The vertical height of each spacing in these respective columns is determined by the time devoted to the particular activity. For example, in the illustration, the first action by the operator was to take a card from each *B* and *C*, put a carbon between, insert and align in typewriter. This required two tenths (0.2) of a minute, so a horizontal line was drawn two units down from the beginning horizontal line. During this time, the typewriter was idle; hence, a horizontal line was drawn across the right column under Machine, two units from the same beginning line, and "idle" written in the space so formed.

Next, the operator typed. This action continued five tenths (0.5) of a minute, so a horizontal line was drawn across the Operator column five units below the last horizontal line, or in this case opposite the 7 mark on the time scale. The space so formed was marked "type." Since the typewriter action stopped at the same time, a horizontal line was also drawn across the Machine column opposite 7 on the time scale, and the space above was marked "type." In a similar manner, the entire chart was constructed.

This method can be improved easily. Multicopy form sets with interleaved carbon offer one possibility. This would reduce the labor time per unit and increase the operating time of the machine—both contributing to greater efficiency. However, a more significant improvement would be the use of continuous-strip office forms with carbon interleaved, thus permitting the operator to type continuously until a quantity of work is finished. The checking and separating of the forms could subsequently be handled on this quantity. This method would provide a smooth and rhythmic flow of work, permit specialization upon the immediate task, and eliminate unnecessary reaching, as well as excessive finger and arm motions. Elimination of much waste would be achieved.

QUESTIONS

1. Of the four basic steps followed in applying office work simplification which one do you feel is most important. Justify your viewpoint.
2. For each of the following pairs, carefully point out the difference between the two identities: (*a*) Movement diagram and the "Who and Why" question, (*b*) normal working area and maximum working area, (*c*) speedup and motion study, and (*d*) pre-positioning and delay or storage.
3. Describe your understanding of the "questioning approach" in the efforts of devising a work improvement.
4. Discuss the major considerations you would take into account in selecting the office work to be subjected to office work simplification.
5. Referring to Figure 4–5, select one guide from guides No. 2, 3, or 4, and describe an illustration showing the use of your selected guide in improving an office method.
6. Comment fully on the following: "For a given quantity of work, it is entirely possible for methods improvements to reduce employee fatigue in performing that quantity. But methods improvements usually result in increasing the amount of work performed; and as a result, the employee spends the same amount of energy or more than before the improvement. Hence, the employee is quite likely to be just as fatigued under the improved method as before the improvement."

7. Identify each of the following by a simple statement: (a) office work identified as "bottlenecks", (b) participation with know-how, (c) office work simplification, and (d) a "make-ready" operation.
8. Comparing Figure 4–10 with Figure 4–11, point out the improvements made and note what key questions (what and why, and etc.) or other questions were probably asked to develop the improvements.
9. Draw up a tabular listing by including vertically the left- and right-hand chart, the production study chart, and the operator-machine chart. Across the top, list the column headings (1) what data are shown, (2) best means to obtain these data, and (3) use or purpose of chart. Fill in the information for each column as it applies to each chart. What conclusions do you draw from your completed tabular listing?
10. Discuss the production study chart pointing out its makeup, the securing of information for it, and how it can be used to simplify office work.
11. Analyze your motions in typing a letter, or taking notes from a reference book, or sorting and then filing cards in a file. What do you conclude from your study? Discuss.
12. In your opinion will office methods improvement become more or less important in the future? What effect will the increasing use of office automation have upon office methods improvements? Give reasons for your answers.

CASE PROBLEMS

Case 4–1.   Dietrick-Danner Corporation

Supervisor Connie Brown is extremely interested in having an efficient and enthusiastic office work group in her department. She is generally well liked by her members, the general work environment is favorable, and the members have said from time to time that they like their work. However, Connie has closely observed her people especially during the last two weeks and has concluded that a number of them are really working ineffectively in that they are practicing poor work methods.

After talking with several members in private, Connie gained the impression that some instruction in office work simplification by her would be helpful and probably well received. Accordingly it was decided to hold a series of ten ½-hour meetings over a five-week period on company time. Basic principles would be discussed along with the presentation of demonstrations illustrating work improvement of office operations in her department. The entire group appeared to receive the idea very well and favored having such a program. The sessions were lively and much interest was engendered. Many interesting questions were raised and the discussions were timely.

Four weeks after the close of the work simplification program, Connie realized that nothing of a tangible sort of evidence was present from the program indicating that no work improvements were being developed or accomplished as a result of the training sessions. Informal talks with the employees gave indications that they intended to apply work simplification to their respective jobs. After another four weeks passed, the only suggested improvement was from employee Eilene Noyes. It was, in Connie's opinion, not practical and not worthy of pursuing.

The following week, Connie gained approval from the personnel department to tie the work simplification program to the existing and reasonably successful suggestion system in the office. In other words, suggestions for work simplification being submitted by the members of Connie's group would, if accepted, result in a monetary award to the suggestor. The minimum award was $25, the maximum $500 or 10 percent of the estimated savings for the first year resulting from adoption of the improved method. This approach was promoted quite aggressively, but after three months the results were indeed meager. During this period, Eilene Noyes submitted two ideas for work improvement, but neither were thought adequate and upon analysis were found to be totally inadequate from the viewpoint of the required investment in equipment and supplies that the corporation would have to obtain were the method change adopted.

Connie then tried the idea of giving an award for any work simplification suggestion that was subsequently approved. The award was a specially designed trophy to be set on the suggestor's desk as a symbol of interest and contribution in the department's quest for efficient operations and cost reduction. This offer was accepted graciously by the group members, but now some two months later, the only suggestion submitted was one by Eilene Noyes and it was practically worthless. Connie recognized it as a rehash of a previous "improvement" Eilene had submitted.

Questions:

1. As you see it, what is the problem? What probably brought it about?
2. As Connie, how would you handle the relationship with Eilene? Why?
3. What is your recommendation to Connie? Justify your answer.

Case 4–2.   Whittingham Company

In an effort to improve methods and reduce waste, analyses of many paperwork tasks are being conducted. One such analysis is represented by the accompanying process chart. Analyst Arlene Campani shows you the chart and tells you she is certain this work can be improved.

Questions:

1. In your own words describe the work as it is now being performed.
2. Briefly explain the accompanying process chart telling what information it reveals.
3. Draw the process chart for the improved method that you recommend. Indicate and discuss the specific improvements of your revised method.

EXHIBIT 4–2A

Flow Process Chart													Number 1 of 1		

Process Posting 317 Cards	Actions		Summary	
☑ Man or ☐ Material			No.	Time
	O Operations		6	19.40
Chart Begins Card Receipt	⇨ Transportations		7	.35
Chart Ends Card Filed	☐ Inspections		2	5.00
Charted By Arlene Capani Date 1/20	D Delays		1	1.25
	▽ Storages		1	.25
Department Inventory	Distance Travelled (feet)		50	26.25

Details of ☐ Present ☐ Proposed Method	Operation	Transportation	Inspection	Delay	Storage	Distance in Feet	Quantity	Time	Analysis Why? What?	Where?	When?	Who?	How?	Notes
1 Arrange cards by code no.	●	⇨	☐	D	▽			1.00	✓					
2 Check for completeness & errors	O	⇨	■	D	▽			3.00	✓	✓				
3 Walk to telephone	O	➡	☐	D	▽	5		.03						Move phone ?
4 Call cost dept.	●	⇨	☐	D	▽			.20	✓					
5 Wait for information	O	⇨	☐	■	▽			1.25	✓					
6 Write missing data on cards	●	⇨	☐	D	▽			2.50						
7 Go back to desk	O	➡	☐	D	▽	5		.03						Eliminate ?
8 Go to file of books	O	➡	☐	D	▽	5		.03						"
9 Select proper books	●	⇨	☐	D	▽			.70		✓	✓			
10 Return to desk	O	➡	☐	D	▽	5		.03						
11 Enter data in books	●	⇨	☐	D	▽			5.00						
12 Check entries	O	⇨	■	D	▽			2.00						Needed ?
13 Make list of entries – F229	●	⇨	☐	D	▽			4.00	✓		✓			
14 Give sheet to inv. clerk	O	➡	☐	D	▽	12		.10						
15 Return books to file	O	➡	☐	D	▽	13		.10	✓					
16 Go back to desk	O	■	☐	D	▽	5		.03	✓					
17 Put cards in file	O	⇨	☐	D	▼			.25			✓			
18	O	⇨	☐	D	▽									
19	O	⇨	☐	D	▽									
20	O	⇨	☐	D	▽									
21	O	⇨	☐	D	▽									

Case 4–3. Weaver-Grundig Corporation

A great deal of sales promotion material is prepared and mailed by the company's sales service department. One big mailer is a 20-page booklet which is assembled, plastic bound, and inserted into a mailing envelope. Volume on this item now is 1,000 per month and is expected to reach 1,400 per month by the middle of next year.

The time in minutes now for 100 booklets include: assembly 28.5, inspecting 5.0, plastic binding 18.0, inserting in envelope 31.0, stack finished items on dolly 2.0, replenish pages 1.5, and replenish envelopes 1.0. Cost of labor is $2.80 an hour.

Bill McCullough, an office methods analyst, is investigating the present manner of performing the work to see if it can be improved. After study, he estimates that by using a special fixture costing $100, he can save 0.13 minutes per booklet of the assembly. Also, including a simple $125 device for the operation of inserting in the envelope will make possible the performing of this work at a rate of 25.0 minutes per 100 booklets.

Questions:

1. What is the yearly current labor cost for performing this work?
2. How much time per month will be required to do this work with present methods based on the estimated future volume?
3. What is the estimated cost for the future volume under the improved methods suggested by Bill McCullough?
4. Has Bill McCullough exhausted the possibilities to simplify this work? Explain your answer.

Chapter 5

Forms and Records

> *Failure to make a decision will quickly brand a person as unfit for a position of responsibility. Not all of your decisions will be correct . . . but it is better to be right 51 percent of the time and get something done, than it is to get nothing done because you fear to reach a decision.*
>
> H. W. Andrews

Forms and records are necessary to record and to transmit information. They are essential for the existence and utilization of every office system and procedure. No organization can exist for long without forms and records. They have been referred to as management tools since they aid and guide administrative efforts and help coordinate the total work performed. Essential to all processing of data, they have become more prominent and have been given more attention with the increase toward automatic data processing.

The work of studying and improving the role of office forms and records is so important that the term, *forms management,* is sometimes used to identify these efforts. This is an important area of the total office management area. Forms and records reach into every corner of an enterprise; they make contact with every employee, customer, and prospect. In essence, they form a busy network relaying information, issuing instructions and directions, and supplying data for decision making covering every function within an enterprise. It is vital, therefore, that forms and records be properly designed and used to provide a proper flow of required data at reasonable cost consistent with the individually prescribed performance and quality.

FORMS AND RECORDS DEFINED

A simple and satisfactory definition can be stated: *An office form is a printed piece of paper which provides space for entering information*

107

which is to be conveyed to other individuals, departments or enterprises. Common examples include cost tickets, expense accounts, factory orders, requisitions, sales data, purchase orders, invoices, and credit memorandums. *A record is any written data that is made for possible future use.* Records include various papers. Office forms are discussed here, but to a significant degree, what we state about office forms applies equally to records. Further note that letters and reports as common communicative media are discussed separately in Chapter 6.

Forms Design

In designing an office form it is wise to enlist the help of forms-design engineers, for they are trained and experienced in this type of

FIGURE 5–1
Original Form before Redesign

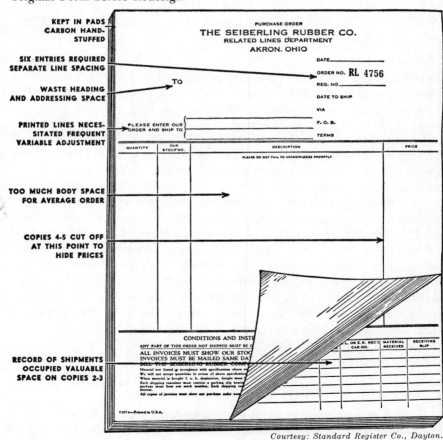

Courtesy: *Standard Register Co., Dayton.*

work. They usually are able to suggest improvements. Most manufacturers of office forms offer the services of design engineers. It is axiomatic
that effective form design aids in processing the data and assists in the
utilization of the information. An excellent illustration, revealed by the
"before and after" comparison, is shown by Figures 5–1 and 5–2. The
opportunities for better design and the improvements accomplished are
noted on these figures. Note the holes along the vertical margins of the
form. These are for pin-feeding which permits the form to advance in
a machine in desired alignment and holds the form in place while entry
is being made. The standard spacing for pin-feed holes is two holes
every inch.

FIGURE 5–2
Form after Redesign

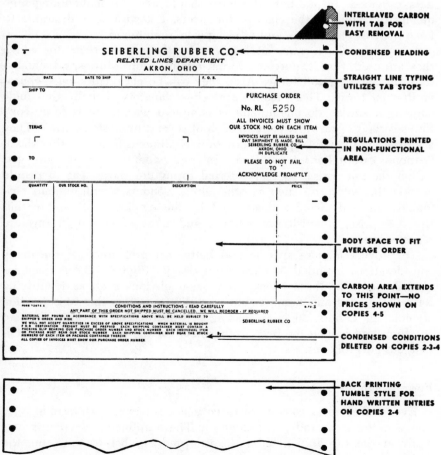

Courtesy: Standard Register Co., Dayton.

The user and the systems analyst frequently have ideas about what the form should be, what information it should convey, and who adds what information where, when, and how. In keeping with the spirit of office work simplification, discussed in the last chapter, the designer of an office form normally questions the necessity for each item. Then the designer determines which items should be grouped, what areas of the form are given to what items, and what are the most convenient sequences for entries. Finally the type of form is decided. More will be discussed about this in the following paragraph.

Usually the best form design is the simple design. It should include the amount and kind of information that is required—no more, no less. The design should also make it easy to enter and to use the information of the form, for it should be thought of as both a recipient of data and a conveyor of data to a receiver who has a definite need for the data provided. In addition, the form should assist in maintaining high quality by reducing the chances for errors. Likewise, it is desirable to keep the cost of the form and of using it to a minimum.

A common classification of forms is by *the main activity* for which they are used, that is, purchase forms, quality control forms, sales analysis forms, and payroll forms. Also, they can be classified *single-copy* or *multi-copy* forms. These names are self-explanatory. Usually the single copy is a source document and is complete within itself. Multi-copy forms serve to provide a copy to each of several interested parties. They are issued in individual packet form or in continuous form. Another classification is *external* or *internal* forms. Internal refers to business transacted within the enterprise; so that external forms are those sent to people outside the enterprise such as other firms, vendors, creditors, and customers. Internal includes those used by the employees of and within the enterprise. Requisitions, reports, and most accounting forms are representative.

To provide a more specific and better comprehension of the many considerations included in office form design, Figure 5–3 has been included. Some of these checks may seem obvious such as identifying form with name and number, but in reality too often this consideration is violated. Others, such as making self-instructing the filling out of the form and having the best arrangement for the data, pose more difficult design problems.

Form Diagnosis

Every office form consists of three major sections: (1) introductory, (2) working area, and (3) conclusion. The introductory section is normally at the top and includes the title and number of the form, the

FIGURE 5–3
Form Design Check List

1. Is the form identified with name and number?
2. Are type faces clear and readable?
3. Are all captions easily understood?
4. Does the information supplied by the form tie in with the stated requirements of the adopted systems, procedures, and methods?
5. If machine-entry, are machine specifications such as maximum size of paper, size of printing characters, and length of line taken into account?
6. Are the supplied space requirements adequate for each individual item?
7. Is fill-in writing reduced to a minimum and is repetitive information printed?
8. Is information grouped logically and, if source document, are data in sequence that they will be transcribed?
9. Are box and columnar arrangements featured?
10. Are vertical and horizontal spacing in conformity with the writing method to be used?
11. Is the need for tabular stops held to a minimum?
12. Are bold types, markings, numbers, shaded areas, and color used to facilitate handling, routing, and checking?
13. Are varying thickness of rulings used to set off sections of the form?
14. Is form self-instructing—are instructions clear, brief, and located either at the top of the form or close to the section to which they apply?
15. Is the routing of the form clearly identified?
16. Is information for filing placed advantageously on the form?
17. Will the form fit standard binders and file folders?
18. Is adequate gripper space included in the form design?
19. Are the proper weight, grade, and color of paper being used?
20. Are the combinations of paper and carbon acceptable for desired carbonization?
21. Are carbonless papers preferable for this form?
22. Are perforations, die-cuts, and narrow plies of paper and of carbon used for positive selection of data on certain copies?
23. Is the form suitable for window envelopes if it is mailed?

routing, the ship to, customer's name and address, and the major instructions on how to fill out the form. Some prefer to locate the instructions at the bottom of the form, but in this location they may not be seen until after at least a part of the form is filled out. The same is true when instructions are put on the reverse side of the sheet. The preference of some designers is to place instructions adjacent to the applicable material. This is effective, but may require an excess of space. In all cases, the instructions should be outlined with a separate paragraph for each statement. To print the instructions in a large single paragraph makes it difficult to read.

The working area, or what is sometimes called the main body, is normally the largest part of the form. Adequate space and proper arrangement are the keys here. The space should provide ample room for all the information needed and be designed to facilitate entries and to reduce errors. Proper use of rulings, columns, data alignment, spacings, and box entries are essential in this section.

The conclusion, at the bottom of the form, includes information relating what happens to the form next. Authorization, signature, and statement of conditions under which data are valid typify the content of this section of the form. Usually the conclusion occupies the smallest space of the three major sections of a form.

It is helpful to consider the designing of office forms in terms of functional considerations and physical considerations. The former deal with factors such as the way the form is used, its purpose, the information supplied on it, and the number of copies required. Physical considerations include the ink, print type, paper, and size.

FUNCTIONAL CONSIDERATIONS

There are seven major functional considerations that merit discussion here, including:

1. Purpose of the Form. The foremost consideration is the job for which the form is to be used. An office form is actually a road map of the work. It shows the flow and sequence to be followed. The form directs employees from the beginning to the end of work. Of course, the overall appearance of an office form is important. However, the primary consideration is the form's utility value. We can state that utility value is first, appearance second, but the ideal answer is to maximize each one in the same form design.

Office forms are used not only because they serve as work guides, but also because their use reduces copying, insures uniformity, gives official sanction to the written work, and implements office mechanization. All or any one of these may be the foremost consideration in any given case. But the major purpose or purposes influence the design that is used.

Usually the purpose is fairly well defined from the system and procedure design. If this is not the case, the usual practice is to follow the form in use and observe precisely the form's normal cycle of operations from point of origin to ultimate disposal. No gaps should be permitted for this is where design inefficiencies frequently exist. Sometimes a sluggish work flow is found among highly skilled personnel. It may be that a procedure is faulty or that personnel hold up the forms or that a poorly designed form is being used. Sufficient observation, questioning, and analyzing of the facts will reveal the apparent cause. The application of work simplification will assist in bringing about the needed correction.

2. Information to Include. Knowing the purpose of the form and observing its application, if now in use, leads to deciding what information should be included in the form. It is difficult to keep such data in mind, so it is best to write it down with the intent being to gather more data than probably will be needed. Actual form design efforts frequently reveal the need for more data than initially anticipated. Help along this line can be secured by answering such questions as those shown in Figure 5–4.

FIGURE 5–4
Suggested Questions to Determine What Information to Include on a Form

1. What information is needed to accomplish the stated purpose?
2. Who uses the form; for what purpose; in what manner; and in what sequence?
3. Specifically what does each involved employee do with the form?
4. How does the form get from one employee to the next employee in the sequence?
5. What suggestions do the present or proposed users of the form offer?
6. Can any of the information be simplified or eliminated?
7. Is the overall size of the form satisfactory?
8. If the form is simplified or eliminated, what problems would result?

3. Adequate Identification. The form name should suggest its purpose. For example, the title "Sales Records" is not complete; "Weekly Sales Records by Territories" is more descriptive. Usually, the identification is in the introductory section. The center or the upper left corner is preferable for the location of the name of the company. Numbering all forms helps identify them and serves as a quick reference. The identification number should be in a convenient location, preferably near the title. In the case of multiple forms, it is usually advisable to number each copy for handy reference. Quick identification can also be gained by using different colors of papers.

4. Sequence of Items. The order should be mainly that of the normal flow of the work, and related items should be grouped. When items are transcribed from one form to another, the items should be arranged in the same sequence on both forms. This means that related items are placed in a sequence which eliminates unnecessary writing motions and makes it easy to transcribe information from one form to another. Search and backtracking are eliminated. The numbering of items makes reference easier and faster. Figure 5–5 shows an effective sequence of items when data from form are transferred to a punched card.

5. General Pattern of the Form. The method of completion is important. If the work is to be done manually, ample writing space is necessary, and horizontal rulings on the form are desirable. A heavier horizontal line about every third line across the form helps the eye to move from left to right. In contrast, if the work is to be done by

FIGURE 5–5
Proper Sequence of Items on Form Expedites Processing

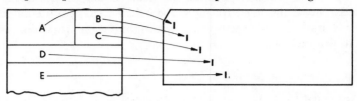

machine, the form should be spaced in accordance with the demands of the machine. The data should be arranged to utilize a tabular alignment, and horizontal lines on the form should be omitted. In general, for hand entries the horizontal spacing should be about eight characters to an inch, vertical spacing not less than four lines per inch. For machine entries, horizontal spacing is one twelfth of an inch per character for elite type, one tenth of an inch for pica, and vertical spacing is one sixth of an inch or multiple thereof. Certain type characters and machines vary from these dimensions and it is best to check the characteristics of the machine to be used.

So-called box captions should be used wherever possible as they assist in both the entry and use of the information, conserve space, give more room for data, and add to the appearance of the form. Figure 5–6 shows effective use of box captions.

FIGURE 5–6
Box Captions Provide Effective Means of
Identification on Items of a Form

TO		FROM	
DATE	CLASS	AREA	

Also the use of check boxes, sometimes termed "boxed style" is effective and should be employed wherever appropriate. Their use saves filling-in time, conserves space, and improves legibility. It is helpful to provide a reference number for each space to be filled in. By this means, tabulation, comparison, and interpretation of data are expedited. Where long sentences are necessary, it is desirable to have them printed in columnar form instead of across the full width of the sheet, as this expedites reading and makes for better appearance. However, when the information to be filled in is lengthy, the boxed style is usually inappropriate; the regular or "open" style is better.

Shading can also be used to advantage. Emphasis is provided by a heavy shaded border around a particular item. Also, shaded areas effectively indicate areas and spaces not to be used. This is especially helpful for somewhat complicated data shown in tabular form.

Even right-end alignment of items is also recommended. This arrangement utilizes the tabular stops of a machine and makes for an easier to read and neater form. It should be followed for all forms—machine and hand entry. This design arrangement is probably the most common of all violations. The correct and incorrect arrangements are:

	Correct	*Incorrect*
	Name:	Name _____
	Address:	Address _____
	S.S. Number:	S.S. Number _____
	Age:	Age _____

If a form is filed, it should include captions to expedite the filing. Normally this should be a part of the introductory section. It is helpful to show the file reference material vertically, if the form is filed on a vertical edge. If frequent filing reference is required, a tab at the top of the form may expedite this retrieving work. Collation of forms within a folder provide clues as to the combining of separate forms into one, with resultant less handling required. Commonly the data on the separate forms are presented differently, but slight design changes overcome these hurdles.

6. Number of Copies. Whether a single or multi-copy form should be used depends mainly upon two considerations: (1) who requires a copy and (2) when the copy is needed. Single copy is used when the original only is required. If needed, copies of the form can be reproduced. Multi-copy forms afford a quick means of supplying copies— usually not more than ten or twelve. Multi-copy forms require only one writing, minimize mistakes, help attain uniformity, improve departmental coordination, and save time. However, it is best to keep the number of copies at a minimum. Only the required number of copies should be made; and extreme prudence and care in this respect is recommended, as excess papers tend to clutter up an office and contribute to inefficiency.

7. Type of Form. There are numerous types or arrangements of office forms. Figure 5–7 shows some interesting examples. In the upper

FIGURE 5–7
Types of Office Forms

RED-I-MAILER

1 PIECE MAILER PRINTED ON CARD STOCK. DESIGNED TO FOLD AND MAIL 1-WAY OR ROUND-TRIP. USES: NOTICES, ADVERTISEMENTS, LETTERS, BILLING, REQUESTS.

DAT-A-CLOSURE

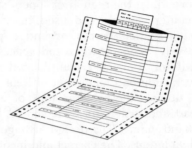

CONTAINS A POCKET TO HOLD DATA, TAPES, PAYMENT, ETC. PRODUCED CONTINUOUS OR AS A UNIT SET. USES: INVOICE, STATEMENT, ORDER, SHIPPING OR SOLICITATION FORMS.

TAB-I-DENT

CONTINUOUS I. D. CARDS ARE USED BY COMPANIES, SCHOOLS AND ORGANIZATIONS. DIE-CUTTING EQUIPMENT CAN ALSO CREATE SECURITY HOLDERS FOR CREDIT CARD MAILINGS.

MULTIPART-CONTINUOUS AND UNIT SETS

FORMS ARE PRODUCED FOR ALL TYPES OF DATA PROCESSING AND HANDWRITTEN APPLICATIONS. AVAILABLE WITH MOD, CONSECUTIVE, MICR AND/OR SECURITY NUMBERING.

PRESSURE SENSITIVE AND GUM STRIP APPLICATIONS

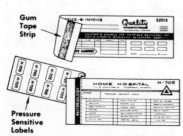

SPECIAL DESIGN PROBLEMS MAY BE SOLVED BY OUR CAPABILITY FOR INCORPORATING PRESSURE SENSITIVE OR GUM STRIPS AND/OR LABELS INTO BUSINESS FORMS.

SHINGLED CONSTRUCTIONS

ANSWERS TO RECORD-KEEPING PROBLEMS WHERE CHECKS, RECEIPTS AND/OR RECAPS MUST BE MADE. INFORMATION IS ENTERED ON ALL FORMS AT ONE WRITING.

Courtesy: Shumate Business Forms Co., Division of Arvey Corp., Lebanon, Ind.

left of this illustration is an effective arrangement for a mailing piece providing for one-way or round trip mailing. A pocket to hold data, tapes, or payment is made a part of and built right in the form and this is a feature of the form type illustrated in the upper right of Figure 5–7. Many forms used in business enterprises are of a continuous design meaning they are joined together to provide a continuous flow of forms through an office machine. See middle portion right of Figure 5–7. On the other hand, many are of a stub type unit design, or a unit set forming a single packet. This type is widely used when the number of stations initiating the form are employed or when the use of the form is intermittent. In addition, some forms arrangements feature shingled construction whereby certain copies contain only selected material (lower right Figure 5–7).

There are also office forms that reflect considerable ingenuity and skill to provide a form meeting the individual needs of the user. To illustrate, in its manufacture by putting a gum tape strip or pressure sensitive spots on the back of a copy of a form, that copy can be affixed easily to a container. The lower left portion of Figure 5–7 shows these types of forms. A close-up of the pressure-sensitive glue spot design is shown by Figure 5–8. Observe that (1) the patches are supplied so that more than one report can be affixed and (2) the ingenious design and manufacturing ability enable the form to carry out its ultimate purpose and function with greatest efficiency.

To provide custom designed office forms meeting rigid specifications requires machines and equipment of a sophisticated sort. Figure 5–9 illustrates such a machine. Note the rolls of paper and of carbon paper to the right being fed through the machine to form the continuous type multi-copy form. Such a machine operates at exceptionally high speed and accuracy. It is also of interest to note that strict environmental control over the manufacturing conditions especially humidity and temperature are necessary in order to ensure that the paper will not stretch or contract during the printing and collating.

PHYSICAL CONSIDERATIONS

The following considerations, although technical in nature, are involved in forms planning:

1. Ink. The ink selected should provide proper contrast to the paper and should give a clear, uniform, and smooth imprint. Certain printing processes require a certain type of ink. Use of more than one color of ink adds to the cost of the form. Special type inks are also used to meet processing machine requirements. For example, magnetic ink containing iron oxide is now common for bank check identification data. Typing or printing with this type of ink makes impressions on the paper

FIGURE 5–8
**Detail of Pressure-Sensitive Glue Spot Design Making It Convenient
to Affix a Report to a Container**

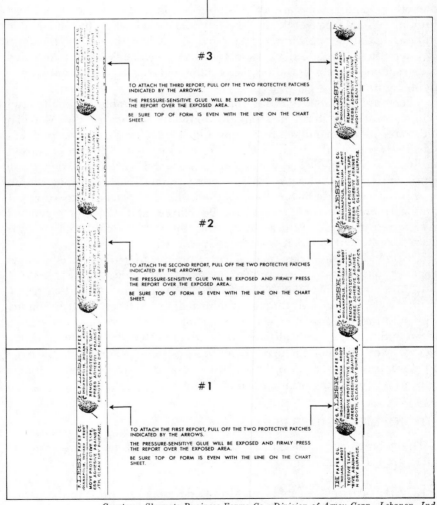

Courtesy: *Shumate Business Forms Co., Division of Arvey Corp., Lebanon, Ind.*

FIGURE 5–9
**Modern Machines Such as This Are Required to Produce Office Forms
to Today's Exacting Requirements**

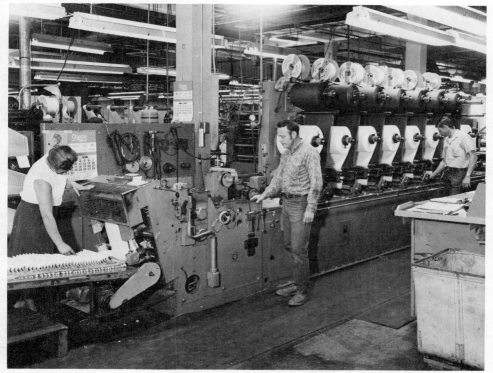

Courtesy: Shumate Business Forms Co., Division of Arvey Corp. Lebanon, Ind.

which can be read by electronic means used to put various counting
and sorting mechanisms into action.[1]

2. Print Type. Readability and distinctiveness should govern the
selection of print type. For any one form, it is best to keep the type
sizes and type styles to a minimum. Items of equal importance should
be printed in the same type throughout the entire form. Normally, italic
and boldface type should be used for emphasis but confined to words
where special stress is required. Again, certain font types may be required if certain machine reading and processing are followed.

3. Paper. The five important physical properties of paper are
weight, grade, grain, color, and size.

a. Weight. Paper is usually sold by weight. Normally, the mill supplies paper in standard sizes according to the different grades and the

---

[1] See Chapter 9, p. 250.

intended purposes for which the paper is to be used. To illustrate, the purposes and corresponding sizes are shown in this table:

Use of Paper	Size
Bonds, ledgers, general writing	17" × 22"
Book papers and offset pages	25" × 38"
Cover stock	20" × 26"
Newsprint	24" × 36"
Bristol board	22½" × 28½"

A ream is the common measurement for quantity of paper and is approximately 500 sheets. For example, bond paper listed as 17" × 22"—20 means that 20 pounds of this grade and size of paper includes approximately 500 sheets. Likewise, bond paper 17" × 22"—13 means that 13 pounds of this grade and size of paper contain approximately 500 sheets. Comparing these two, the latter sheets would be thinner, since, based on the same size and approximate quantity, their weight is less (13 pounds) compared to the former (20 pounds). Frequently the weight is referred to as substance or stock. Thus, 13 pound paper is called substance 13, or 13 pound stock.

The lightest paper which will give satisfactory results should be used. Among the factors which determine the proper weight of paper are number of copies, amount of handling, purpose of the form, how filed—on edge or side, length of time retained, and whether printed on one or two sides. Weights in common usage for several kinds of application are shown in Figure 5–10. For example, for general office use paper of 20 or 16 pound weight is suggested and paper of 9 or 7 pound weight for copies.

FIGURE 5–10
Weight of Paper in Pounds Suggested by Type of Application and Type of Paper

Application / Type Paper	Bond	Ledger	Copy
Letterhead	20		9 or 7
Legal Document	24		9 or 7
Ledger		32 or 28	
General Office Use	20 or 16		9 or 7
Forms-Continuous Type			
Initial Copy	16 or 13		
Other Copies			9 or 7
Forms-Unit Set Type			
Initial Copy	20 or 16		
Other Copies	13 or 9		13 or 9

b. Grade. The grade of paper means the quality and is chiefly based on the kinds of materials used in the manufacturing process. Paper is made from rags, mechanical wood pulp, sulfite wood pulp, soda wood pulp, and sulfate wood pulp, which are used in varying amounts, depending upon the kind of paper. The grade selected for a form depends upon such things as the life of the form, the amount of handling, and the appearance. The following table is helpful.

Life of Form	Grade of Paper
1–5 years	100 percent sulfite
6–12 years	50 percent sulfite and 50 percent rag
Over 12 years	100 percent rag

c. Grain. Like wood, paper has a grain characteristic. The direction of the grain is determined by the alignment of the fibers making up the paper. The expression "with the grain" signifies the longitudinal direction of most fibers. Grain direction is the result of the manufacturing process. The grain of paper determines its rigidity. Some processes require that the grain of the paper run with the length of the printing roll. The grain should be parallel to the typewriter platen, because the paper then rolls around the platen better and there is less tendency for the sheets to slip. Paper folds more easily and quickly when it is parallel with the grain. On the other hand, the graining should run vertically on forms posted by machine or filed on the bottom edge, since in this manner there is less tendency for the forms to buckle and curl.

d. Color. Colored paper for office forms frequently affords an effective medium for securing a strong appeal, a unique identification, and a simple means of facilitating the handling of forms. However, colored paper usually costs more than white.

e. Size. The size of the form is determined by the amount of information, the economical paper size, the size and types of office equipment and machines, and the mechanical requirements. The limitations of the printing process must, of course, be considered in determining the dimensions of a form. Wherever possible forms should be cut from stock sizes of paper. It is advisable to discuss the subject of economical stock sizes with the prospective supplier.

4. Means of Carbonizing Copies. Another important physical consideration is the carbonizing means used. It can be achieved in several ways: (1) inserting carbon by hand, (2) one-use carbon interleaved into the form, (3) carbon in the machine—using a simple "floating carbon" device, and (4) spots of wax carbon applied to the back of the form during the manufacturing process.

Many multi-copy forms provide one-use carbon paper interleaved into position. Another arrangement uses a floating carbon device whereby the forms slip over the carbon sheets which remain in the machine, and these sheets are used many times over until the impressions indicate the need for a carbon change. In yet another method, application of spots of wax carbon, makes it possible to apply the carbon to certain parts of a form, thus permitting only certain portions of the original writing to appear on the copies. Frequently, price information or specification data do not appear on all copies, since this information has little value for the purpose of some copies. A similar result can be achieved in the other carbon methods by shingling the copies or by cutting off certain carbon sheets or portions of them or blacking out, with a solid mass of dots or other marks, that portion of the form which is not to receive an impression. The carbon mark is not visible on the blackened area.

"Carbonless paper" forms are growing in usage. These forms are printed on paper chemically treated on one or both sides. Copies are obtained simultaneously with the original writing, the same as with carbon paper. The labor cost of inserting carbon between sheets, jogging, aligning, straightening, and extracting carbon after writing is eliminated by the use of carbonless paper. In the case of an original and one copy, salary rate of $100 per week, this savings is estimated to be $9.70 per thousand forms. In addition to possible labor savings, carbonless paper is clean and convenient to use.

Optical Character Recognition Forms

With the development of reading machines has come specially designed forms to take full advantage of these mechanical readers. Data from an entire sheet is read in a matter of seconds.[2] Use of so-called OCR (Optical Character Recognition) forms ends the search for a means of eliminating costly and time-consuming data preparation prior to computer processing. *OCR forms serve as a source document for computer input.* Keypunching is eliminated.

Figure 5–11 illustrates several OCR forms. In the top illustration the form is designed for machine-entry of the information. The form printing is in ink that the reader will not pick up except for location registrations to guide the input work into the proper spaces of the form. The entry material is imprinted in OCR type font suitable for the reader. In the bottom illustration the form is a hand-entry form. Note a handwriting guide is included on the form. In OCR, the writing entry is frequently by *manual printing in a distinctive type style* and within specified areas

---

[2] Reading machines are discussed in Chapter 9, pp. 243–46.

FIGURE 5–11
Optical Character Recognition (OCR) Forms

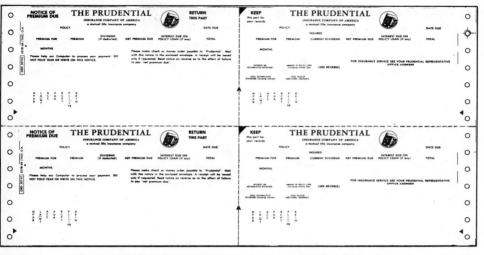

Courtesy: Acme Datagraphic Business Systems, Inc., South Hackensack, N.J.

on the form. Machines are also used, but a special font and sometimes ink are normally required.

An OCR form requires high precision and quality control in order to function properly in the reading machine. Ink too dark, paper too reflective, or the printing matter of the form a fraction out of line can render the form useless, and the information is lost. Except for registration marks and items to be seen by the reading machine, many OCR forms are preprinted in a drop-out blue ink.

Mark Read Forms

Another type of OCR forms is the mark read forms. Here the writing is really a marking or a filling in of a small circle or area. The location of the mark indicates its meaning in accordance with a code established by the form arrangement. Figure 5–12 illustrates a form of this type.

FIGURE 5–12
A Mark Read Type of Office Form

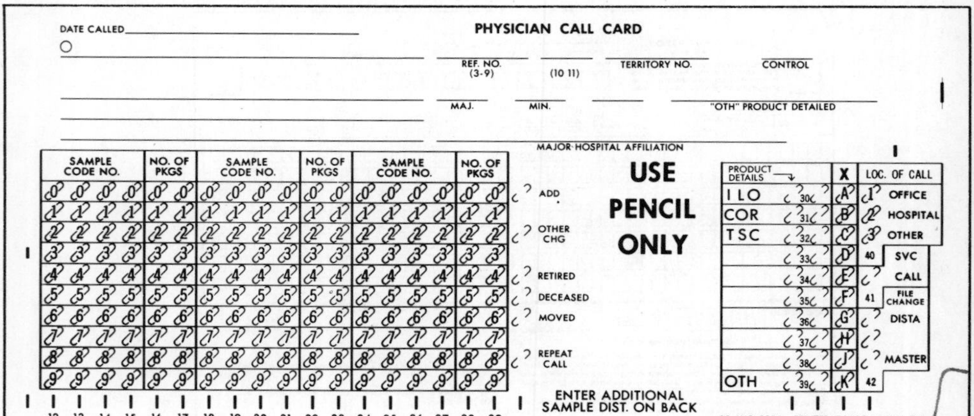
DATE CALLED
PHYSICIAN CALL CARD
REF. NO. (3-9)
(10 11)
TERRITORY NO.
CONTROL
MAJ.
MIN.
"OTH" PRODUCT DETAILED
MAJOR HOSPITAL AFFILIATION
SAMPLE CODE NO.
NO. OF PKGS
ADD
OTHER CHG
RETIRED
DECEASED
MOVED
REPEAT CALL
USE PENCIL ONLY
ENTER ADDITIONAL SAMPLE DIST. ON BACK
PRODUCT DETAILS
X
LOC. OF CALL
ILO
COR
TSC
OTH
OFFICE
HOSPITAL
OTHER
SVC CALL
FILE CHANGE
DISTA
MASTER
12 13 14 15 16 17 18 19 20 21 22 23 24 25 26 27 28 29
09 WC 9016 PRINTED IN U.S.A. JUN 74

Courtesy: Shumate Business Forms Co., Division of Arvey Corp., Lebanon, Ind.

The particular form shown is used for keeping records of what drugs and medicines are distributed as samples to physicians for trial and testing purposes. Manual entry by pencil only is made by filling in the proper areas under the appropriate columns as shown on the form. To illustrate, under the column "Sample Code No." perhaps 1 0 0 would be marked, under "No. of Packages" perhaps 1 2 would be marked. The forms are processed by machine—the pencil marks are sufficient to indicate the information—no punched holes are needed.

Competent design knowledge and precise manufacturing practices are required to produce trouble-free mark read forms. Quality must be controlled at practically each stage of the production and the forms must be in perfect alignment so that they register accurately when being processed. The development of mark read forms depended upon the ability of the forms manufacturer to provide a form that the processing machine can read.

Shingled Paper Strip Forms

Much data can be summarized in a neat and concise arrangement by means of shingled paper strip forms. Figure 5–13 illustrates the use of one type called unit analysis comparative forms. The data are written on the specially designed forms held in place by binder rings through holes at the top of each form. At the close of each period, such as a month, the data for the current month are posted in the left-hand column or strip and the year-to-date figures in the right-hand column; the center of the strip is used for identifying information. By properly positioning the newly completed monthly strip in the binder, comparisons between figures for the current month and those of previous periods are supplied. In the illustration, for example, comparisons are expedited between (1) April this year and previous months of this year and (2) April this year and April last year. If desired, additional data can be included by adding columns to the right. The unit analysis method assists in presenting calculated data in a convenient and usable pattern, in determining trends, measuring the efficiency of the operations, and highlighting the status of different components making up the entire activity.

The same type of arrangement—shingled paper strips with data written on them—can be used for accumulating and summarizing a large amount of accounting data. Since the strips fit into a row of pegs at the top of a board and thus are held in place, the arrangement is referred to as pegboard accounting or summary-strip accounting. Quick summaries and "recaps" can be run off. A movable horizontal bar is used to guide the eye to the proper line across the forms. Distribution analyses of various kinds, including cost, payroll, stock control, and sales, and it can be designed to serve almost every type of business. The boards are made in various sizes, ranging from approximately 20 × 18 inches to 36 × 18 inches. The advantages of the use of peg strips include: Copying of the data is eliminated—the original forms are used to obtain final results; accurate information can be provided; flexibility is permitted, since variations in the number and kind of distributions are

FIGURE 5–13

Comparative and Accumulative Operating and Financial Information Presented in an Effective Arrangement

PERIOD JANUARY THIS YEAR	PERIOD FEBRUARY THIS YEAR	PERIOD MARCH THIS YEAR	PERIOD APRIL LAST YEAR	PERIOD APRIL THIS YEAR	OPERATING REPORT	% OF SALES	TO DATE APRIL THIS YEAR
					SALES		
60,125	62,411	63,147	51,675	57,355	PRODUCT A	55.2	243,038
51,312	61,387	62,298	44,375	55,467	PRODUCT B	44.8	230,464
111,437	123,798	125,445	96,050	112,822	TOTAL	100.0	473,502
					COST OF SALES		
42,086	42,439	43,571	35,643	41,295	PRODUCT A	69.9	169,371
35,462	43,279	43,921	30,234	38,272	PRODUCT B	70.0	160,934
77,528	85,718	87,492	65,877	79,567	TOTAL	70.0	330,305
					GROSS PROFIT		
18,059	19,972	19,576	16,032	16,060	PRODUCT A	30.1	73,667
15,850	18,108	18,377	14,141	17,195	PRODUCT B	30.0	69,530
33,909	38,080	37,953	30,173	33,255	TOTAL	30.0	143,197
					COST OF SALES ADJUSTMENTS		
1,211	657	752	418	455	INVENTORY ADJUSTMENTS		3,076
2,075	1,947	1,846	1,157	1,411	OVER OR UNDER ABSORBED BURDEN		7,279
3,286	2,604	2,598	1,575	1,867	TOTAL	1.9	10,355
30,623	35,476	35,355	28,598	31,388	GROSS PROFIT AFTER ADJ.	28.1	132,842
					GENERAL EXPENSES		
6,317	7,185	7,321	5,732	6,930	ADMINISTRATIVE – SCHEDULE A		27,753
8,245	9,345	8,560	7,048	6,742	SELLING – SCHEDULE B		32,892
3,612	4,762	5,121	3,848	4,637	SHIPPING – SCHEDULE C		18,132
2,098	2,417	2,860	2,461	2,420	BRANCH – SCHEDULE D		9,795
20,272	23,709	23,862	19,089	20,729	TOTAL EXPENSES	18.7	88,572
10,351	11,767	11,493	9,509	10,659	NET PROFIT FROM OPERATIONS	9.4	44,270
					OTHER INCOME		
251	187	252	142	210	INTEREST EARNED		900
516	518	675	567	572	DISCOUNT ON PURCHASES		2,281
122	158	145		112	DIVIDENDS RECEIVED		537
		250			PROFIT ON SALE OF ASSETS		250
218					PROFIT ON SALE OF INVESTMENTS		218
1,107	863	1,322	709	894	TOTAL OTHER INCOME	.9	4,186
					OTHER DEDUCTIONS		
376	112	87	123	75	INTEREST PAID		650
678	458	567	482	420	DISCOUNT ON SALES		2,123
	100				LOSS ON SALE OF ASSETS		100
					LOSS ON SALE OF INVESTMENTS		
1,054	670	654	605	495	TOTAL OTHER DEDUCTIONS	.6	2,873
53	193	668	104	399	NET	.3	1,313
10,404	11,960	12,161	9,613	11,058	NET PROFIT BEFORE TAXES	9.7	45,583
					TAXES		
55	55	55	45	55	CAPITAL STOCK		220
145	152	159	127	121	STATE INCOME		577
3,675	3,742	3,815	2,655	3,420	FEDERAL INCOME		14,652
3,875	3,949	4,029	2,827	3,596	TOTAL TAXES	3.1	15,449
6,529	8,011	8,132	6,786	7,	NET PROFIT FROM ALL SOURCES	6.6	30,134

JUST LIFT UP

Courtesy: Royal-McBee Co., New York.

possible; and the cost is economical—there is a minimum of handling, and the equipment required is simple and inexpensive.

QUESTIONS

1. Define office form and relate the main reasons why office forms are utilized.
2. Select six questions from Figure 5–3 and relate how they would be helpful in office form designing.
3. What is meant by continuous forms? For what type of applications would you recommend them?
4. Enumerate the important considerations to be included in determining the general pattern of a form.
5. Referring to Figures 5–1 and 5–2, point out and discuss four improvements that you deem of special importance in designing a more effective office form.
6. Discuss Figure 5–7 pointing out what meaningful information this illustration shows.
7. Discuss the various means of carbonizing copies of office forms.
8. What is meant by each of the following:
   a. "Foating carbon" device.
   b. Grain of paper.
   c. Mark read form.
   d. Forms management.
9. The sequence of the items on a form is important. Why is this? Illustrate your answer.
10. Relate four different considerations normally included under the physical characteristics of an office form. Discuss the one that in your opinion is probably most important.
11. Discuss in general when you would recommend a shingled type of office form.
12. Discuss the why, what, and where of optical character recognition forms in the accomplishment of office work.

CASE PROBLEMS

Case 5–1. Buckley Corporation

Although the volume of work has held up very well, profits have declined sharply during the past year for Buckley Corporation. Management launched a cost reduction program last month and it covers every segment of the total operations with special emphasis on overhead cost, excess management personnel, and paperwork cost. As a management trainee in the administration office, Marvin Hollis has been assigned the project of analyzing the office forms being used and to evaluate their design and usefulness.

Mr. Hollis first visited and talked with Mr. Muir who heads up the corporation's printing and supplies stores department. It was revealed that all printing orders are personally handled by Mr. Muir and his department stocks all office forms and originates a replacement order for all forms whenever the stock-on-hand reaches a minimum quantity. To procure a new form, any department head can bring a sketch of what she or he wants and request the form be printed. Most of the form designs originate in the systems and procedures department, but not all of them. Mr. Muir offers very little in the way of how costs of forms might be reduced. He remarks, "Forms are needed to run a business these days and I reckon paper doesn't cost any more than other materials. I run a good print shop and you'd pay a lot more for the forms if you were to buy them from the outside."

Subsequently in interviewing various other employees, Mr. Hollis finds he has collected the following notes:

1. Three people suggested a lower grade of paper be used.
2. Some of the forms now used, especially several used in the sales department, do not look "sharp." They lack distinction. Look like simple printed sheets.
3. A favorable mental attitude by the user is not created by many of the forms.
4. The purchasing department seems to be using archaic forms. To illustrate, Exhibit 5–1A shows what is currently being used for purchase requisitions.

EXHIBIT 5–1A

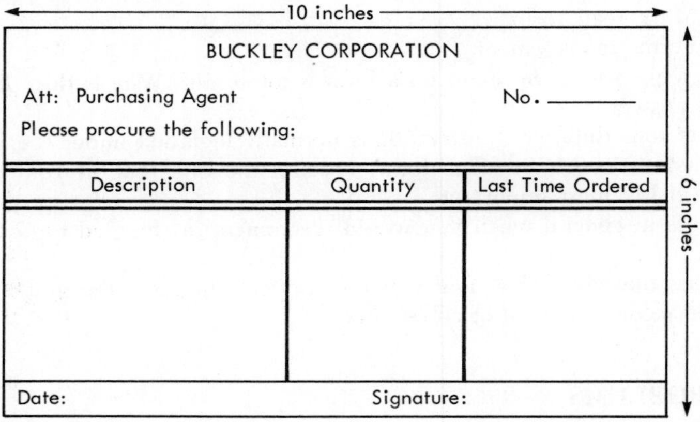

5. With few exceptions, all forms are black ink on white paper.
6. A goodly number of ruled forms are being used, yet practically all the processing means followed by the corporation are mechanized to a considerable degree.
7. About one-half of the employees talked with have asked in some way or other, "Do you really expect to reduce cost by working on an office forms project? What advantages are to be gained by what you are doing?"
8. Seems to be waste in (*a*) not using all the copies, and (*b*) writing in incorrect data, discarding the form, and starting over with a new form. Do employees realize this?

Questions:

1. Comment on the approach and information obtained by Mr. Hollis on his office forms assignment. What alternatives do you feel might have been better? Why?
2. How can the purchase requisition form be improved? Be specific and complete.
3. What action do you recommend Mr. Hollis now take? Why?

Case 5–2. Kessinger Quality Products Company

The assistant office manager has designed a new purchase order and receiving form and asks you what you think of it. You observe the size is 6½ × 10½ inches; total number of copies is six (including original); different colors of paper will be used for each copy; six type styles are used in the composition of the form; and all the printing is in black ink except the company's name, which is in light blue. The column heading for price and the inserts, "total price" and "shipping route," are in red, so that they will stand out. The spacing of lines on the form is five to the inch. In answer to your specific questions, the assistant office manager states an intention to get reactions to the form from various vendors now supplying the company. A good price from the printer can be secured in quantities of 60,000 which is about a two-year supply. A standard typewriter billing machine, pica type, is used for writing purchase orders, and in about 30 percent of those written, two extra copies are needed (seven copies total) and are inserted in the five-copy pack as required.

Questions:

1. Outline your reply to the assistant office manager.
2. Discuss the specific recommendations you would make to the assistant office manager.
3. Explain the probable reasons for the weaknesses, if any, of the proposed form.

Case 5–3. Tiger Company

Many different items of summer clothes for boys and girls are sold by Tiger Company. Sales are made directly to retail stores. Terms vary depending upon the buyer's credit and past experience with the company. In general, relationships with buyers are excellent.

Currently the invoice form being used is shown by the illustration on page 130. Recent study has revealed that this present six-copy form being used can be reduced to a four-copy form. Tiger executives also feel that the format can be improved, although the present form includes all the necessary information.

EXHIBIT 5–3A

Tiger Co.

MANUFACTURERS OF TOUGH, LONG-LASTING
SUMMER APPAREL FOR BOYS AND GIRLS

ORIGINAL INVOICE

No merchandise may be returned for credit without our written consent. All claims for shortages and damages in shipment must be filled out with carrier within 72 hours after delivery. Any claims for errors in filling orders must be made to us within 7 days after receipt of goods.	Shipped		
	Date:	Via:	From:
	Terms:	Invoice Date:	
	Invoice No.	Reference No. Customers Order No:	Customers Account No:

SOLD TO	SHIP TO

Dept./Div. No:	Store No:	No. of Cartons:

Description			Price	
Quantity	Unit	Style and Model	Unit	Extended
Total				

Make check payable to	Total	
TIGER CO. 100 Northbrook Road Halifax, New York 13625	Itemized Additional Charges	
Salesman:	Special Dating:	
Indicate whether complete or partial shipment:	Our Reference No:	GRAND TOTAL

THANK YOU FOR THIS BUSINESS

Questions:

1. Design an improved invoice form which represents a better format than the present one.
2. Point out the specific improvements of your recommended invoice form and indicate why users should favor your suggested changes.

Chapter 6

Letters and Reports

> *Today's put-off objectives reduce tomorrow's achievements.*
>
> Harry F. Banks

Letters and reports are essential information media in that they convey information to people within the information network and are an important means of conducting business and government. In any organized activity, people have a special need to influence and inform others by use of the written word; if they are unable to do so, the activity suffers. And the best laid plans become worthless unless adequate and effective written information is employed to implement the plans as well as to keep designated personnel informed on past, present, and future managerial actions.

The Letter and Report Problem

In the typical enterprise too many letters and reports are written. Replies are written when no reply is required and the habit of preparing certain documents remains long after the original need has ceased. Not only is quantity a problem, but also the quality of the writing. It is common, for example, to recieve a letter which fails to state its purpose and what action or reaction is wanted from its reader. Also the writing style may be difficult to follow and lack strength. Among the common causes of poorly written letters are the use of long sentences, dense subordinate clauses, abstract nouns, and the passive voice for verbs. The emphasis seems to be to avoid writing anything wrong more than to write what is right. Figure 6–1 shows a prize piece of poor writing.

FIGURE 6–1
This Writing Fails to Tell the Employee How to Figure Out the Pay Gain

Date: May 14, 197–
To: All employees
From: Paymaster

Knowing of your interest in how to determine your pay according to the new schedule, we are attaching a chart and advise you as follows:

Locate your present pay on the chart. To find out the range and subrange of your present pay, add the whole number on the same line as your "minimum step of range" to the decimal "range number" (at top of your pay column).

Next, identify the percentage increase for your job class. Add 1.20 to your subrange number for each percent pay increase and two-tenths for each ½ percent pay increase. This total gives you your pay increase which will be included in the next payroll period.

Further, there are many who cling to the practice of individually composing each letter and report instead of using form and guide specimens to assist in handling this work. And handwriting is still found in far more places than would be thought possible. In addition, available machines and equipment like the automatic typewriter, word processing equipment, and copying machine are not extensively used for letters and reports. The conventional typewriter remains the common standby. Discussion of these machines and equipment appear later in this chapter.

A Letter and Report Management Program

To improve letters and reports and to maintain the improvements over the long period, a letter and report management program is recommended. Infrequent writing workshops, memos suggesting improvements, and a statement now and then about "writing better letters and reports" are totally insufficient. Some short-term improvement will result, but the basic problem tends to remain.

The goals of an improvement program need to be identified and made known to correspondence personnel. Included are such things as improved quality, writing for the reader to understand, format to follow, number of copies to be made, training for personnel, reducing cost, and utilizing time-saving machines and equipment. These objectives should be defined in concrete terms. From the very inception of the program, encourage the involvement of all correspondence personnel in the program. Let them know their suggestions are wanted, ask for their ideas regarding the thrust of the efforts for any given period. The delay and confusion from poor letters and reports are so widespread that arousing general interest and participation in the program should not be difficult.

Appoint a director or chairperson who has leadership qualities and is deeply dedicated to the cause of writing improvement. Announce by various well-publicized means the program, its director, its mission, and its full backing by top management. Made clear the responsibility of the director, the unit to which assigned, and the key assistants to the director which should include a qualified management analyst.

The need will be to get facts regarding current writing practices and output, and further to analyze these facts. These data should include the quantity, methods now used, machines and equipment utilized, and samples of output. Ingenuity will be required in these efforts and every person engaged in letter and report writing should be encouraged to assist and cooperate to ensure that complete information is obtained. Employees familiar with the operations are excellent sources. Answers to specific questions are helpful. Figure 6–2 offers suggestions on what might be asked.

FIGURE 6–2
Questions to Ask in Letter and Report Survey

1. Does the letter being written seem to serve a necessary purpose? Explain.
1R. Ditto for reports.
2. From a sampling of incoming mail, about what percentage appears to require an answer by letter?
3. During a four-week period, about how many letters are written?
3R. Ditto for reports substituting "how many report pages."
4. What percentage of letters is handwritten? Dictated to secretary? Dictated to a machine and transcribed?
4R. Ditto for reports.
5. How many electric typewriters are there in the office? Automatic typewriters? Word processing equipment units?
6. How many copies of letters are usually made?
6R. Ditto for reports.
7. To approximately what degree are window envelopes used?
8. Is there opposition to the use of window envelopes? If yes, what are the reasons?
9. During a four-week period, about how many letters are rewritten? What are the major reasons for rewriting?
10. Are form or guide letters used?
10R. Ditto for reports.
11. Is the format, length, writing style, and effectiveness of letters satisfactory? Give details.
11R. Ditto for reports.
12. Does the time taken for letter writing, reviewing, and distributing appear to be reasonable? Elaborate.
12R. Ditto for reports.

The next step is to analyze these facts and *mutually* develop improvements. It is important to emphasize that the improvements are mutually developed. They are not evolved by the expertise of one or two employees. All should have a hand in it so that the improvement program is viewed as their program where their ideas and their participation provide an opportunity to express themselves and gain personal satisfaction from their work. Data from the survey will highlight failures and suggest possible ways of correcting. Writing that can be eliminated, shortening the needed correspondence, reducing the number of copies, following a select distribution, and using mechanized means, represent the more common ways of obtaining improvement.

Finally, the program director should supply feedbacks to top management so that interest and support in the efforts are maintained and evaluation of the program can be made. Likewise reporting to all employees of the gains and benefits should be followed along with awards or recognitions for successful accomplishments.

Letter Quality

From the management viewpoint, two major aspects of letter writing are (1) quality and (2) cost. Quality will be discussed now followed by cost. By quality is meant effectiveness and in good taste. Improving the quality of letter writing requires that the writer has a clear concept of what is to be stated, recognizes the important points, and knows what to emphasize. Further, the writing is kept simple and compact, with use of short words, sentences, and paragraphs. Recommended is the use of active verbs, give answers, then explanations, and let a human, sincere attitude of the writing come to the reader of the letter. Write to express—not impress. Some suggest "talk" to the reader by writing in the same easy rhythm that you use in normal conversation.

To write meaningfully, a writer must have all the facts. To write a sales letter, for example, one must have information on what the product will do, its good points, its price, and the like. If filed material is required, make certain it is made available before the writing starts. Strive to know the subject at hand. In addition, these facts must be related so that the letter can be properly planned. "Think—then write" is an effective guide. Put yourself in the reader's position and focus your thoughts on what you feel the letter should convey. In most instances, a letter is an effort to have its recipient believe and act toward a subject as the writer does. Following this line of thinking, the opening statement of a letter should be designed to get the reader's attention. Following this, develop the reader's interest. Then, lead this interest into a desire and finally cluminate the entire letter with action—to order the service, to accept the adjustment, to pay the bill, or whatever the case might be.

Writing effectively presents a tremendous challenge and it represents a skill that can be developed. It is not an ability with which some are blessed and which others can never hope to achieve. However, too often the challenge of writing is not even recognized, let alone mastered.

To improve our writing the following pertinent guides can be of considerable help.

1. Make the Writing Serve a Known and Definite Purpose.   Know exactly what is to be accomplished by the letter. Settle on one main issue and concentrate on it. Letters pertaining to a single subject are easy to understand, and they expedite filing.

2. Keep the Recipient in Mind.   The aim of a letter stands a much better chance of accomplishment if its text is understood. To expedite this understanding, the needs, wants, and interests of the recipient should be given prime consideration. Put the reader in the center of what is written. Look at the subject from the reader's viewpoint; visualize the reader while writing, and tailor the material and expressions accordingly. For example, compare the use of the "you" viewpoint in "You may have quick service if you'll just telephone ORchard 1-7777," with the far less effective, "We wish to call attention to the fact that we are in the dry-cleaning business and have a 15-year record of excellent service. Our telephone number is ORchard 1-7777."

3. Be Factual and Unbiased.   Accuracy is essential to good writing regardless of the scope, subject, medium, or level for which it is intended. The facts should be relevant to the subject; opinions should be identified as such. Exclude irrelevant details. Include only what is basic to the stated purpose. Remember the writing is being done to inform the reader of the situation or subject as it is. A colorful letter need not be filled with emotional statements.

4. Use Short Familiar Words and Simple Sentences.   Word choice is vital; simple words are bold and clear and usually convey the intended meaning. Employing words in common usage is a good rule to follow. Words having different meanings to different people should be avoided, i.e., "high" salary or "good" job. And simple sentences are an ingredient of clear writing. Some variety in sentence length is desirable, but short sentences are normally preferred. However, too many short sentences make the writing monotonous. Some say that no sentence should exceed 25 words. From the practical viewpoint, however, a sentence should be long enough to convey the thought. Omit involved phrases, weed out the extra words, tabulate lists, and use correct punctuation.

5. Employ Active Verbs.   Present-tense verbs create more interest and convey activity better than past-tense or subjunctive-tense verbs. "He understands" has more vigor than "It is understood by him" or "He should have understood." While some variation is desirable, try to use a good portion of active verbs in your writing.

6. Use Conversational Style.   Letters are communicative media and are more readily understood when written in a style to which we are accustomed. We are familiar with the conversational style and from it quickly grasp the meaning. Ordinarily we do not use exotic words and long sentences with qualifying phrases in our normal speech. Why insist on using these communication blocks in our written work?

7. Establish an Acceptable Mood. When writing use a tone that wins cooperation or puts the reader in a mood to read the letter and give thought to it. Positive expressions help to accomplish this goal. The statement, "We can send you tickets for the November 27 performance," is more effective than, "We cannot send tickets for any performance prior to that of November 27."

Let your writing reflect your own natural self and remember letters are written to human beings, not merely to names. Write naturally and humanly. Stilted, highly formalized statements are taboo. Avoid "whisker" expressions, examples of which, along with improvements, include:

Do not use	Use
I am not in a position	I cannot
My attention has been called	I notice
Enclosed please find	We enclose
Acquaint me with the facts	Tell me
Contents duly noted	I have read
We have reviewed our records	We find
It is our opinion	I believe
At all times	Always

8. Make the Writing Clear. This requires knowing what must be included and in what sequence it should be presented. The writer should express each thought so clearly that the reader is certain to understand it. Normally, the transcriber helps in acquiring clarity by straightening out improper sentence structure and switching words.

Have your writing say exactly what you intend it to say, and mean what the writing says. Keep in mind the adage: "Write so that you cannot possibly be misunderstood."

9. Interpret Findings Adequately. Avoid exaggeration or the inclusion of unqualified interpretations which cannot be reasonably derived from the available information. It is usually best to understate rather than to overstate conclusions. Also, recommendations must be practical and sound.

10. Summarize Briefly and Make Writing Conclusive. Normally, it is best to state the results in a summary statement. Tell the essentials to the reader. Include what action, if any, is desired of the reader and what the writer will do. Be decisive. Avoid double meanings and long, qualified explanations. Strive to set forth the recommendations so clearly and effectively that they will be followed.

Letter Cost

The sum of composing, typing, reviewing, possibly revising, postage, supplies, and machine and equipment cost make up letter cost. These cost contributors are self-evident and can be measured. In addition, there are hidden costs such as the competency level of the writer, complexity of subject, and means of composing. Of all these costs, composing accounts for by far the largest portion.

An analysis of letter cost will reveal that the range extends from about $.30 to more than $75 for a letter. An average cost, using a personnel basis, is approximately $3.59, a form letter costs $.43. The data are shown in Figure 6–3. When the volume is sufficiently large the cost

FIGURE 6–3
Estimated Cost to Write a One-Page Letter of Approximately 200 Words, Original and Three Carbon Copies

	Correspondent (Salary $10,000 yr)		Executive (Salary $20,000 yr)		Corre-spondent or Executive Form Letter
	Dictating to Secretary	Dictating to Machine	Dictating to Secretary	Dictating to Machine	
Planning the letter (minutes) . . .	13	13	13	13	0
Dictating the letter (minutes) . . .	13	8	13	8	0
Transcribing and typing (minutes).	7	9	7	9	4
Checking and signing (minutes) . .	3	3	3	3	2
Total time.	36	33	36	33	6
Average labor cost	$2.29	$2.10	$3.38	$2.77	$0.32
Supplies and office overhead . . .	1.30	.74	1.93	.91	.11
Total Cost.	$3.59	$2.84	$5.31	$3.68	$0.43

is considerably reduced by using an automatic typewriter, duplicating process, or word processing. Obviously, it is important to convert the high cost letter to a format that can be produced at a relatively low cost.

It is usually enlightening to calculate the percentage of office payroll cost represented by letter writing and note if the trend is up or down. Also view this percentage in relation to the total written work being done. Does it appear reasonable? Does it satisfy the purpose for which intended? In what areas can this work be improved? What is being done today to accomplish these improvements?

Efforts resulting in less time for deciding what to say and saying it (composition) reduces letter cost significantly. Since composition is vital, any program designed to reduce it has potential. To illustrate, the use of guide letters, form letters, training sessions in letter composition, and developmental programs to increase cost-mindedness about letter writing offer good cost reduction possibilities.

Cost Reduction—The Writing Time Taken

Not only are guide letters and form letters helpful in reducing composition time, but they are helpful in *cutting down on the writing time taken.* Mutual of New York, a large insurance company, undertook a comprehensive correspondence simplification program and, among other things, drafted a series of "guide letters" for its correspondents. Figure 6–4 shows an example. These letters were meticulously prepared to give customers the answers they wanted in understandable terms and in a

FIGURE 6–4
A Guide Letter Furnished Company Correspondents to Assist Them in Writing More Effectively

```
Example of The "Long" and "Short" of It

                DEATH CLAIM - EXPLAINING AGE ADJUSTMENT
                            Original

        We are enclosing a letter addressed to the payee under
        the above numbered policy, explaining the adjustment
        which we made because of a difference in the Insured's
        age.

        Will you see that we are furnished with the best
        evidence available as to the correct date of birth?  A
        copy made by a notary of a family or public record,
        made at or near the time of birth, of the date of birth
        together with a statement by the notary as to the date
        of publication of the book from which the record is
        obtained, and by whom the record was made and when, is
        the most satisfactory evidence.  Form 3593 covers such
        information.  If no such record is obtainable, an
        affidavit to that effect should be furnished together
        with the best information available with a full
        statement as to its source and why it is believed to
        be correct.

        Please forward the above information to us at your
        earliest convenience.

                                Yours very truly,


                            Revised
                           To Manager

DCA-14   We will gladly make adjustments on this claim, if
         necessary, when correct birthdate is established.   If
         (name) is unable to complete Form 3593, please get an
         affidavit stating why the date is believed correct and
         return with the best evidence available.

         Also, kindly give the enclosed  letter* of explanation.

                             Thank you.

         *  Key No. DCA-15

         Original 160 Words:  Revised 53 Words:  Saving 67 Per cent

           Note:  The Original is a splendid example of a letter
                  that goes to great unnecessary length in stating
                  the obvious.  Notice that the Revised states all
                  that a manager need be told to know how to proceed.
```

friendly, helpful manner. Form letters and paragraphs are useful under conditions where many letters deal with a comparatively limited number of subjects so that the same or similar answers can be given to common requests or inquiries. To illustrate, a form letter may be used for accounts past due. Keyed "Delinquent Collection Letter No. 1," it is sent to all accounts in arrears, with the appropriate name and address added at the top. After a certain amount of time, a "Delinquent Collection Letter No. 2" may be sent to those accounts which remain unpaid.

Form paragraphs, similar in idea to form letters, apply to standardized paragraphs only. Under this practice, letters are composed of form paragraphs plus individual ones. Several variants of a form paragraph are used, thus gaining some diversity. The approved form paragraphs are listed, keyed, and indexed, and are made available to all correspondents.

Form letters and paragraphs are tailored to fit certain conditions and are usually worked over by several correspondents to create the best possible results. Collecting for a period of several weeks a copy of every letter written, sorting these by major subject, selecting the best reply for each subject, modifying as circumstances suggest, and standardizing on these superior replies, constitute one way to develop form letters and paragraphs. They need not be impersonal, and it is not necessary to send the same letter again and again to the same customer. When they are properly handled, there should be no objection to form letters and paragraphs. They provide a uniform operation, conserve time and effort, and reduce correspondence cost. On the other hand, they may not fit a particular case, lack a personal touch, and follow a stilted manner.

Another way to reduce letter cost is to strive for fewer rewrites. Most rewrites stem from the desire to correct typing errors. With corrective paper and liquids available, misspelled words can easily be erased by overstrokes. The errors are flicked away in a few seconds without leaving any tell-tale spots where correction was made. Also, many rewrites occur because of a misunderstanding between the person composing and the person typing the letter. The corrective action here is self-evident.

Further, a telephone call may get the job done as well as or even better than a letter. The telephone is more personal and permits interchange of thoughts—an important aspect for some types of messages. The letter, however, provides a written copy and may be wanted for future reference.

Some believe that using the "reply at bottom" type of letter helps reduce letter cost and should be more widely adopted. In this type of letter, the answer or comment is written in the margin or at the bottom of an incoming letter. A copy is then made and sent to the interested party, the original being retained for the files. While this practice is not suited for all correspondence, it seems satisfactory for many routine inquiries and does save considerable correspondence cost and filing space.

Cost Reduction—The Typing Time Taken

Additional cost saving practices feature *cutting down on the typing time taken.* A letter should convey the necessary information and make a favorable first impression. Information well placed on the page, margins as even as possible, and uniformity of type are universal standbys. Preferably the arrangement followed does not entail requirements that impede typing. Certain arrangements dominate because writers conform; a reader becomes accustomed to look for information in certain locations of the letter. Figure 6–5 shows the format of several different arrange-

FIGURE 6–5
The Respective Forms of Three Different Letters Used in Business

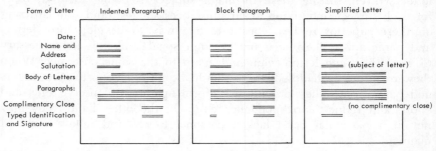

ments including (1) indented paragraphs, (2) block paragraphs, and (3) simplified letter. Slight variations from these three forms of letters are also employed.

The so-called speed letter has won favor and it reduces typing time considerably. Formally defined, a speed letter is a preprinted form designating certain spaces for filling in desired information. Space is provided for listing recipients making up a mailing route and for checking other appropriate information. Commonly, three copies are made. The original is retained by the sender; copies 2 and 3 are sent to the receiver, who writes in a reply, returns copy 2, and retains copy 3. See Figure 6–6.

The "window envelope" is another reducer of typing time. The elimination of addressing and checking envelopes realize a savings of about $.02 per letter, not a large amount, but for a large volume a meaningful amount. However, some people believe that window envelopes are less attractive and dignified than regular envelopes. Certain types of correspondence are probably best handled by regular envelopes. The final decision in this matter rests with the manager.

FIGURE 6–6
A Well-Planned Printed Form to Expedite Written Information Transmission

DEMPSTER CORP. CHICAGO, ILL. SPEED LETTER		DATE	
TO: 1	LOCATION	**INITIALS**	**DATE**
2			
3			
4			
5			

APPROVAL	NOTE AND FORWARD
AS REQUESTED	NOTE AND RETURN
COMMENT	NOTE ENDORS'T OF ACTION TAKEN
FOR YOUR INFORMATION	PER CONVERSATION
INITIAL FOR CLEARANCE	PREPARE REPLY
NECESSARY ACTION	SIGNATURE

MESSAGE

SIGNATURE	TITLE

Another suggestion is: use a "window letter." When a substantial quantity of letters with exact content constitute the mailing, the window letter has definite advantages. A preaddressed card is attached to the back and top of the duplicated letter, so that the name and address appear at the normal location and can be read through a window opening in the letterhead. The card also serves as a business reply card with necessary postage and name and address of the sender on the reverse side. This arrangement is illustrated in Figure 6–7.

Also, a quantity of the same letter can be duplicated with simply "Dear Customer" as the salutation. Name and address is typed on the

FIGURE 6–7

A "Window Letter" Which Features the Use of a Preaddressed Card to Individualize a Form Letter

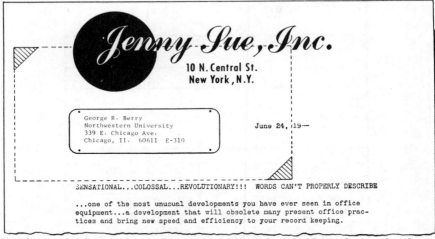

The card, also used as a business reply card, is held in place either by a pocket in the back or by slots into which opposite card corners are inserted (as illustrated). The name and address appear through a window opening in the letter. The mailing can also utilize window envelopes.

envelope or an addressing machine can be used. As an alternative, the name and address can be typed carefully on the duplicated letter and a window envelope used. In this case however, the typing will not match precisely the duplicated part of the letter, but reasonably satisfactory results are possible.

One of the best ways to reduce cost is to have the letter typed, edited, and corrected by the best means possible. When the physical processing of letter writing is studied the contribution toward cost reduction by the use of the automatic typewriter or of word processing is outstanding. These means are discussed later in this chapter.

Reports

Much of the material given above with respect to letters applies equally to reports. There are a few additional comments about reports however, that merit mention here. There is no one best way to arrange the information of a report. In some instances, a standardized format is well established and accepted; but in many cases, the writer is free to choose the makeup. Material should be presented logically. Aids which will help in the reading should be provided—for example, simple statements, sectional headings, summaries at the beginning, and a table of contents. A reader often glances through a report, noting the various headings and reading a sentence here and there. For this reason, it is advisable to make it possible to obtain a "quickie" on what the report is all about and what it includes. This approach will maintain the reader's interest and lead to correct conclusions and proper actions.

Every report should follow a carefully developed general outline. The first step in preparing such an outline is to select the information to be included in the report. This is ordinarily dictated by the purpose of the report, what information is available, or what can be uncovered. Next, the items of information should be classified under headings which normally are grouped as major and minor, or as many groups as judgment suggests.

There are a number of general outlines for reports; the following preferred by many: (1) summary of findings, (2) methodology, (3) detailed results, and (4) appendix. Another outline which is effective and adaptable for many subjects, especially those of a technical nature, includes: (1) summary, (2) objective and scope, (3) equipment used, (4) methodology, (5) data obtained, (6) conclusions, and (7) recommendations. The following has also won favor: (1) introduction and definition of problem, (2) conclusions and recommendations, (3) discussion of procedure and results obtained, and (4) summary. Another is: (1) digest of findings and recommendations, (2) background of study, (3) savings and other benefits to be gained, (4) possible drawbacks, (5) alternatives and why choice of the one recommended, and (6) proposed implementation plan.

It should be observed that in each of these outlines, either the summary, conclusion, or recommendation is included near the beginning of the report. This may seem illogical; but actually it is not. The sequence of items need not be chronologic; however, there should be *some order* in presenting the material. The great majority of report readers want the gist of the findings or the conclusions right away, so it is effective to put this information at the beginning so that the most important information is not missed.

Charts, drawings, pictures, and maps help to convey the meaning to the reader, but they must be carefully selected and employed in "reasonable" amounts for maximum effectiveness. In many cases, the chart or drawing must be explained and significant relations pointed out to the reader, because the exact meaning may not be gained simply by looking at the illustrative material. Pictures are especially helpful in dealing with technical subjects.

The practice of presenting a report "live" rather than in the conventional written form is followed by some companies with great success. The saving of many hours of managers' time and improved communication are claimed for this approach. The short face-to-face meeting with a selected group permits on-the-spot questioning and minimizes the report being neglected because of other matters demanding the manager's time. Visual aids help emphasize the major points. Because both the number of visuals and the time are rigidly limited such as "3 visuals and 5 minutes" to get the message across, the material presented must be carefully prepared and contain only the essence of the material.

Like letters, the cost in the case of reports depends upon many factors. Expense of gathering data and the time of the writer are key costs. Studies show that what appears to be a simple 20-page report may cost upward of $1,500 to prepare. Most executives underestimate what a report costs. Computer-prepared reports also usually mean a considerable expenditure.

A practice commonly used is to inform the recipient of a report what it costs to prepare it and indicate in the future that his unit or department will be charged for this work. If the costs do not justify the use made of the reports, the recipient will request his name to be withdrawn from the distribution list. Discretion and judgment must be exercised in this approach, but it is effective.

The number of copies and their distribution is another consideration that bears close watching in the case of reports. Too often the distribution list includes names of persons who neither need nor read the report. An approach that brings excellent results is to remove the names of nonessential receivers and give no notice of this action. Subsequently, in most instances, the absence of the report is not noticed by the new nonreceiver, complaints or inquiries about the report being rare. Some argue that the cost of copies is low in view of the copying machines available today. This is true, but evades the real issue which is that "surplus" recipients look at the report, become interested in the content which may not be their concern, waste their time on these "foreign" activities, and use filing space to retain the report for some doubtful future reference.

In the case of weekly reports, it may be found that a complete report every week is unnecessary. All that is required is the statement that activities are proceeding according to plans or that they are within acceptable limits. This is called a "tolerance report." If plans are not being fulfilled, the recipient wants to know what is out of line and how best to correct it. Such a report is termed an "exception report." In neither case is it necessary to write a complete report with all the minute details. And, of course, the idea of changing the report to a monthly or quarterly writing merits study.

Dictating Machines

Among the common machines used in letter and report writing is a dictating machine which consists of a recorder unit used by the dictator, and a transcriber unit used by the typist to play back the recorded dictation; or a combination unit featuring both recording and transcribing. The latter is practical when the dictator and transcriber can plan their day for separate periods of dictation and transcription. Most recorders are equipped with a hand microphone for ordinary dictation and a desk microphone for recording over-the-desk conference discussions. By means of a foot-control device, the transcriber is started and stopped as desired in order for the operator to listen and transcribe what has been dictated. Usually a signaling device is included whereby the amount of dictation and places of correction can be indicated. There is usually a backspacer for repeating dictation and voice-control adjustments to regulate speed, volume, and tone. The recording medium is usually a plastic belt, disk, or roll. A plastic belt medium is an endless belt of thin, tough plastic, 3½ inches wide and 12 inches in circumference. It withstands rough handling, accommodates about 15 minutes of dictation, and serves as a permanent, one-time recording medium. As many as five belts, nested one within the other, will fit into a small business envelope and can be mailed for a few cents. Figure 6–8 shows dictating machines.

Different models stress different features. For example, one is completely portably (weight 27 ounces) and operates on either a.c. current or batteries. It fits snugly in the palm of your hand and uses a magnetic tape having 50 minutes of recording time. Precision corrections are possible and connection for remote foot control and earset are provided. Another dictating machine employs "dictate and cut" whereby the roll of magnetic film, serving as the medium, is cut after completion of dictation and written on either to identify or instruct what disposition to make of the material. In some applications, this cut film is attached to a copy of the transcribed material for future reference, if needed. The machine holds enough film for six hours of dictation. Dictated material can be released with only one letter on it; a unit of the dictating medium need not be held until it is fully used.

Advocates for dictating machines include in its advantages that dictation can take place when it is on the dictator's mind; thoughts can be recorded as they occur. The transcriber's presence is not required while the dictation is being recorded, thus saving time. In addition, the dictator can work at any time; it is not necessary to wait for a stenographer. Also, being alone, the dictator can concentrate and think more clearly. Further, the dictating machine makes it feasible to allocate the work fairly among the transcribers.

There is also a machine used by the stenographer for recording dictation. This "shorthand machine" prints letters on a paper tape in accordance with a special code. The machine looks like a miniature typewriter and requires special training for proficient operation.

FIGURE 6–8
Dictating Machines

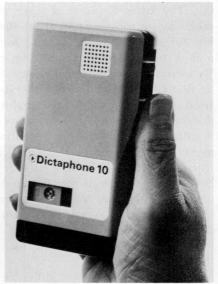

Courtesy: Dictaphone Corp., New York.

Left: Taking up less space than a letter and weighing about eight pounds, this fully automatic dictating machine is recorder-transcriber unit and employs a plastic belt as the medium. Right: A modern, convenient and portable dictating machine handy for many different purposes. Small enough to fit into a shirt pocket, it is big enough to hold thirty minutes of thoughts.

Of course, a dictating machine is not mandatory for writing letters and reports. Preferred by many is the personal basis whereby the dictator talks to a stenographer who manually takes down the statements in shorthand and later transmits these notes. This basis permeates a feeling of mutual understanding of the type of letter or report to be written. For many the written notes employed are easier to comprehend than audible data. Either the dictation or the transcription can take place anywhere—a machine is not required and the cost of it need not be incurred.

Typewriters

The basic machine for letter and report writing is the typewriter. In common use, it speeds the handling of most written work. It should be added, however, that in this day and age many outputs are printed by computers. A convenient classification of office typewriters is manual, electric, and automatic. The first is operated by human energy, i.e., by the depression of a key. While typing, the carriage is moved to the left by action of a spring. In contrast, the electric typewriter is motivated mainly by electricity. Manual energy is still used to touch the keys, but the energy input is about 20 percent of that required for manual machines. Typing can be performed faster and with less fatigue on the electric machine. In addition, the work done is of uniform type impression, and a greater number of copies can be obtained without any increase in manual energy. An electric machine costs more, but if used one-half of the working hours, it will quickly repay the extra cost.

Various styles of type are available so that it is feasible to have regular correspondence in a distinctive type, invoicing of a large type, and personal notes of a script style. In general, almost all typewriters available are equipped with a standard keyboard. Special keyboards or parts of keyboards, such as engineering, mathematical, chemical, or foreign language signs and marks, are available at an additional cost.

Most typewriters on the market today are excellent machines and have many common features including "set" and "clear" tabulators, either of a single- or decimal-key type. Tabulators are very helpful for the rapid movement and alignment of the carriage which is required in reports and other written work that have frequent indentations. Typewriter platens are available in different degrees of hardness. Use of a soft platen is recommended where the number of copies are few and quietness is desired. Conversely, a hard platen is recommended when a large number of copies is required. It causes more noise, however, than does the soft platen.

Automatic Typing Machines

The automatic typing machine has won wide adoption for repetitive typing. It features a standard keyboard and a special mechanism. Masters are typed with copies recorded on paper tape, magnetic cards, or magnetic tape. This work can be done either in the individual office or at the local service office of the machine manufacturer. After proofing, the memory tape or card is inserted into the automatic typewriter mechanism, a task requiring less than a minute. Each tape stores up to 50 paragraphs which can be predated and automatically typed in any desirable sequence. The paper is inserted in the machine in the same manner as in a regular typewriter; and the date, name, and address are typed in by hand. At the touch of a button on the console, the machine takes over and automatically types the letter at a speed of up to 160 words a minute, stopping at the first place where a special fill-in is required.

This is typed in by hand, and then, after another touch of the button, the machine continues typing to the next stop. All paragraphing, spacing, and the like are handled by the machine. If possible, the location of each fill-in should be at the end of a line or paragraph, to provide the required elasticity in space.

An editing feature permits stopping the typing at any point to add or delete desired changes. Automatic typing is then resumed. Also, a letter can be completely precomposed by using say paragraphs No. 2, 7, 9, and 12 obtained by pressing the required button for each paragraph in the desired sequence. As many as 150 average length letters a day can be typed with this machine. Multiple combinations of machines up to four, requiring one operator, can produce approximately 500 letters a day at a very low relative cost. Figure 6–9 illustrates a popular automatic typewriter.

FIGURE 6–9
A Popular Automatic Typewriter—the Model 76 Selector Auto-Typist

Courtesy: American Automatic Typewriter Co., Chicago.

WORD PROCESSING

An exciting development in office technology is word processing. It appears destined to change most of our past thoughts about processing words for writing and the managing of this work. Word processing is a specialized and automated means for producing letters, reports, and lists—in fact, any type of writing at speeds of 150 words per minute. The copy material is received, stored, corrected, and reused with error-proof precision. Word processing includes the improving and speeding up of the office output and providing bigger and better service at reduced cost.

Formally defined *word processing is the combination of people, procedures, and machines that puts ideas into typewritten form.* The machines are sophisticated and capable of production-line performance. Dictation is received and typed by the operator at a rough draft speed. Any typing errors are corected by backspacing and striking over them. Simultaneously the typing is recorded on a magnetic medium or paper tape, put into the machine's storage and then reproduced or "played back" automatically. If revisions are necessary, only the changes need be typed. Material that is already recorded and remains the same, is typed out automatically.

Word processing embodies the idea that words and numbers can be prepared and stored in the machine. Since in office written communication, much material is repetitive, it is feasible to prepare the material ahead and store it for later use. And the ability to easily correct, update, or personalize the material for individual cases add to the desirable features of the system.

The result is that offices using word processing enjoy significant savings of time—some 55 percent less time spent than from previous practice followed. In a large government installation word processing operates 24 hours a day, 7 days a week turning out long, highly technical reports. Estimates are that word processing saves over one-third of the cost per page compared with conventional means. Scientists, researchers, and lawyers are finding that word processing makes possible much less of their time spent on dictating, editing and approving written work so that they can devote more of their efforts to their primary work.

Word Processing—Types of Equipment

Word processing is really a system made up of dictation equipment, typewriters, copiers, and automatic text editing typewriters. There are some 25 manufacturers of word processing systems, each emphasizing exclusive features or special designs to meet particular problems of certain users. Figure 6–10 shows a popular unit consisting of dictating equipment, an automatic input-output typewriter, a console unit containing logic and power supply, and stations. The unit corrects, edits, revises, and duplicates previously typed information automatically without error. The typewriter has a completely automatic format control in the record, playback, left and right margin adjustments, and edit modes. To operate

FIGURE 6–10
Word Processing System

Courtesy: Redactron Corp., Hauppauge, N.Y.

This word processing system, designed to increase office productivity, consists of an automatic Selectric I/O typewriter, a console unit containing logic and power supply, and two magnetic card or tape cassatte stations.

requires just a few hours instruction. No complicated transfer of information is required.

The machine shown in Figure 6–11 stores everything typed on it and lets the operator recall previously typed material. The machine

FIGURE 6–11
A Memory Typewriter

Courtesy: International Business Corp., Franklin Lakes, N.J.

A memory typewriter that has a built-in action file. This unit stores information typed on it and permits recall of this material, selected by the operator, at an error-free speed of 150 words per minute.

has a built-in memory which holds approximately one fully-typed page of material. The playback from the memory is error-free at a speed of 150 words per minute. In addition, in the typewriter is a non-removable continuous magnetic tape loop with a capacity of storing 50 pages of typing. This so-called action file consists of rough drafts, form letters, and material to be updated. The dial on the right of the keyboard operates this file, permits storing and recalling what is typed. Material is retrieved as desired by turning the dial and depressing the proper keys on the machine. When revisions are made, only the changes must be keyboarded. Material already recorded and unchanged types out automatically.

FIGURE 6–12
The Dictaphone Thought Tank

Courtesy: Dictaphone Corp., New York.

Dictated material is stored in the tank shown in the foreground. The flow of material is regulated by the small unit on the desk to the operator's right.

Dictating equipment is available in a variety of styles and types. A number of word processing units employ one type only, others use several or "talk several languages." A popular type is the centralized telephone dictating units which are accessed by means of the regular telephone lines. The dictator simply dials the word processing center and is automatically connected to a recorder and begins to dictate. There is no interruption—if one recorder is occupied, the next one will activate automatically. Another means is the so-called endless-loop or tank central dictating system. The name is illustrative, as a continuous flow magnetic tape is utilized. The endless loop arrangement receives dictation by only one person at a time. There is also what is termed conversational communication, meaning interactive exchange with other information machines such as a computer and other word processing units. In addition, in some cases the word processing unit communicates by different means including Telex/TWX and telephone lines.[1]

To help manage the work load of word processing, a Thought Tank system which monitors all the input and output is available. Under this arrangement all dictation is registered on an Electronic Graph Monitor system which gives pertinent data on how many people are dictating, how long, peak dictation periods, amount of dictation at each typing reservoir station or tank, and so forth. From these data, the typing work can be balanced among the typing personnel and the amount of work completed per typist is counted so that personnel can be evaluated on productivity. The system uses no belts or cassettes. Figure 6–12 shows a Thought Tank in use.

In addition, as discussed earlier in this chapter, there is the more common dictating machine found in many offices. While this machine is economical and convenient, the recorder belts must be taken physically to the typing center, a task requiring time and expense.

Word Processing—Effect on Personnel

In many instances the trend in office job makeups has been toward consolidation and specialization. The traditional secretary's job has lagged behind this trend with the job typically including a number of related and nonrelated tasks. With the development of word processing, many are of the opinion that the secretary's job, training requirements, skills practiced, and position in the organization are changing quite drastically. There is some concensus that the old traditional job of secretary is being divided by word processing into two basic jobs (1) correspondence secretary and (2) administrative secretary. The former performs all work associated with typing including transcribing, proofing, and editing. The title word processing secretary is also used.

---

[1] These means are fully discussed in Chapter 10.

The second, or administrative secretary, performs nontyping tasks such as mail handling, telephoning, and filing. Referred to as administrative support activities, this terminology has won considerable followers. For example, designation of word processing itself is referred to as Word Processing/Administrative Support (WP/AS).

The two types of secretaries are organized into word processing and administrative support organization units, each with its own management structure, but making up a WP/AS department. Figure 6–13 suggests the organization in graphic form.

FIGURE 6–13
A Feasible Organization with Word Processing

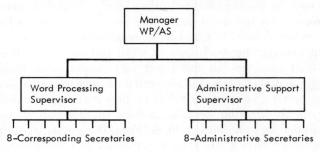

Commonly teams of two or three secretaries work together. This makes possible a backup for the group leader of each team and eases the problem of replacement due to sickness or absence from the work station. In some organization arrangements the work teams are scattered throughout the entire organization—an arrangement suggested by preference for the secretaries being close to the people for whom they are doing most of their work. This arrangement makes for what might be referred to as puddles of word processing units rather than a large centralized word processing pool.

Word processing like every action in office management involves in the ultimate the human element. Some operators of the equipment as well as those appointed administrative secretaries are enthusiastic about their new jobs. They feel it opens up career opportunities and paths higher than supervisor, produces a chance to develop special skills that are in demand, defines the job much better than the previous miscellany of duties performed in the shadow of "the boss." On the other hand, many secretaries are not as satisfied with their new roles as management would like. Complaints include that to them the work is boring and repetitive, too much pressure is exerted to get the work completed on time, there is a lack of being with management personnel, and a loss of prestige and status is suffered. When these unfavorable attitudes and conditions exist, it is imperative that the office manager sees that proper actions are taken to minimize the objectionable situation. Included are to rotate jobs so that each secretary is given more work variety, to express appreciation to employee when appropriate for work well done, to spell out future advancement levels and the basis for achieving them, and to make certain the workload is reasonable and fair as well as understood and agreed to by the secretary. Of course, it helps to take the time and explain thoroughly why word processing is being used and to answer forthrightly any questions the employee may have about it. Planning and using extra sensitivity in dealing with those most affected by the new processing are in order.

However, human relations problems are not confined to the operative level. Some management members may voice opposition or feel a silent resistance to the new arrangement. An executive usually believes a personal secretary is essential and when he loses one, resistance may take place. The reaction is not only rational, but emotional as well. It is a question of losing status and comfort. The feeling is a loss of control over where and how the work will be done which is a basic concern of most management members. The challenge here is to involve the management member in word processing and to assist this manager to understand that it is helpful personally as well as to the entire organization.

Additional Major Considerations

Before closing this chapter there are several additional considerations in the overall managing of letter and report writing that merit discussion. The first is that writing is found in almost every organizational unit—it is not confined to "the office." For example, the assistant sales manager may have the responsibility of writing the monthly sales report; the technician, a research report; and the personnel manager, a report on the company's industrial relations. On the other hand, a large amount of letter writing is performed by correspondents who either have transcribers permanently located in the various departments performing letter writing or have transcribers in a centralized transcribing department or "pool."

Whatever the organizational arrangement, the producing of letters requires coordination among various personnel. For example, the dictator cannot be effective if the file clerk supplies the wrong materials, and the transcriber cannot be efficient if the dictator does that work poorly. The organizational relationship should foster the needed cooperation and coordination among those engaged in letter-writing work. And reliance on effective actuating efforts to improve writing is normally required.

This gives rise to the next major consideration which is to establish the importance of writing and to instill a sense of pride in performing this type of work. A good writer is a valuable member who enjoys prestige and a sense of satisfaction in performing work that is needed and is beneficial to all members of the enterprise. Writing provides the means to desirable ends—to get certain action started, others curtailed, and controversial issues settled.

Regular meetings to discuss the principles of good business writing are helpful. Material written by employees can be evaluated and possible ways for improvement suggested. Frequently it is found that conferences with individual employees are most effective. Samples of the employee's work can be inspected and personalized help given. The belief is growing that a writer needing help has perhaps only two or three weaknesses, not all of them. Intensive corrective work, individually applied, is the best way to correct these faults. But no single training program can guarantee perfect writing. It has been said, one never learns to write, one is always learning to write. Samples to illustrate writing fundamentals and improvements help tremendously.

The fourth consideration in management of writing efforts includes the adoption of standards to measure both quantity and quality of output. Usually the output must be sorted according to type of work, counting the number of each classification that is written during a period of a week or two. This period is suggested in order to obtain a "package of typewritten work"—a requirement brought about by the fact that the work with respect to difficulty of writing varies widely and the work within too small a period may not be repesentative. Quality can be based on freedom from errors, clearness, conciseness, and completeness of the writing. Further, an accounting of such things as the machine assigned to each correspondent, the amount of work turned out by each machine, the extent of machine idleness, and the amount and frequency of repairs can also be employed.

Finally, the use of an office correspondence and report manual should be considered. Such manuals provide the employees with standard practices and instructions in a form that is convenient and easy to use. They help the employees to help themselves and assist in eliminating many needless errors. Manuals are fully discussed in Chapter 25.

QUESTIONS

1. Give five major guides for improving writing and discuss fully one of these guides.
2. Relate your understanding of "the letter and report problem."
3. As an information manager, what measures would you take to make sure that only necessary letters and reports are prepared?

4. In your opinion, what is the best way to get report writers to want to improve their writing?
5. What are some effective ways to reduce letter costs? Discuss in some detail. Repeat the question for report costs.
6. Identify clearly each of the following:
   a. Speed letter.
   b. Simplified letter.
   c. Window letter.
   d. A tolerance report.
7. Assume the list of questions shown in Figure 6–2 must be reduced from its present 12 to eight questions. Which questions would you eliminate? Why?
8. Do you favor the use of the "reply at bottom" type of letter? Why?
9. You have been asked to give a ten-minute talk on "Word Processing" to a group of co-workers or students. Prepare the outline for your talk and briefly elaborate on what you would include under each major segment of your outline.
10. Secure a report written for an executive. Study its contents and determine the main purpose it is intended to serve. Assuming that the purpose is a valid one, explain in what specific ways you feel this report can be improved.
11. Claude Rice, a process engineer, is enthusiastic about having the dictating machine that he was provided three months ago. He uses it to record data and information when they are on his mind and also for ideas that he feels might be helpful in the future. But he finds it extremely difficult to dictate a finished letter or memorandum on the machine. He prefers to write these out manually and make needed corrections and additions. What are your reactions to Mr. Rice's experience and conclusion?
12. Explain how the automatic typewriter is used in writing letters.

CASE PROBLEMS

Case 6–1. Patterson Company

At the present time, Patterson Company uses a magnetic belt system for transcribing dictated material. While no serious problems are being experienced, the workloads are increasing, typists are hard to find, and an average turnaround time of 48 hours is being experienced. Turnaround time is the period between the dictating and the completed typing of the material. At Patterson Company a report dictated on Tuesday morning is typed and checked by Thursday morning. Seven transcribing office units make up 52 transcribing work stations. It is the belief of top management members that the possibilities of using word processing systems should be looked into and accordingly a committee of three was appointed to study the project. The three members included the office manager, the personnel manager, and the controller.

To begin the study, the committee met and after extensive discussion decided some factual information was needed. Accordingly, it was decided that each typist would make an extra copy of everything typed. On this extra copy would be added information by the typist including the method of input used, the number of author revisions, the retypes due to typist error, the type of source material, i.e., rough draft, handwritten, or straight copy, and also the type of document—letter, memo, or report. In addition, a supplemental list for each typist would be maintained. Such a list included typing done on cards, labels, envelopes, and miscellaneous items. These data would be collected for six weeks.

Subsequent study and meetings of the committee were devoted to additional decisions to be made. For example, it was suggested by the controller that work specialization be followed within the proposed word processing units. That is, some typists would specialize on original dictation, others on material employing guide or form paragraphs or letters, while still others would concentrate on special request-composer requests. In this way, argued the controller, skill and familiarity with the work would reach high levels. The personnel manager disagreed. To her, the best arrangement would be to have every typist do everything. This would not only help maintain interest in the work, but it would avoid dependency on a select few for doing a certain type of typing work. A 40-page report might, for example, be worked on by three different typists. The office manager had no strong opinion on the subject of work specialization. "Perhaps the way to handle it is to ask the typists and set it up that way," were her comments.

Further, there was the question of typing priority. Both the personnel manager and the controller favored a policy of "first come first served." This approach, it was pointed out, would ensure equality of treatment and desirable teamwork. Rush jobs would not always be upsetting the orderly and more efficient work flow. But, countered the office manager, if that arrangement is followed, the service element is going to decline. Service in many typing situations is more important than cost. You can't arbitrarily bind yourself to a logical, set schedule. The departments won't stand for it.

The controller believed one goal of switching to word processing is to eliminate all typewriters in the office—all typing would be in the word processing group. The office manager did not agree, pointing out that as a practical matter some typing was certain to remain where it now is. Perhaps 75–80 percent of the typing would be in word processing, but not all of it. Further, she pointed out, that by transferring typing from the present locations, there will be the problem of typing work distribution among the positions that remain in the office departments. Transferring 40 hours of typing a week now spread among seven employees is not simply a matter of eliminating two positions. The problem is far more involved. The personnel manager concurred and said a much more detailed study on this aspect of the proposed change would certainly have to be made.

Finally, the office manager called attention to the need of consolidating the contents of letters and reports as much as possible. Variables will be added to some, paragraphs reworded, some material eliminated, other material consolidated. This alone will be a tremendous task. The personnel manager and the controller agreed, suggesting, however, that much of this could be done by using several key dictators and the present typing personnel.

Questions:

1. In general, are you inclined to agree that the approach of securing a copy of all material typed, classifying it, and analyzing it, is a sound beginning for the project? Why? What alternatives could the company follow? Explain.
2. What is your opinion about following work specialization in the proposed word processing system? Justify your position.
3. What arrangement concerning the handling of rush or emergency typing work do you suggest be followed? Why?
4. Briefly relate what action you recommend the company now take. Justify your viewpoint.

Case 6–2. Dillon Corporation

A fund raising dinner at $100 a plate is scheduled at the largest hotel for the incumbent U.S. senator. President of Dillon Corporation, Mr. Carl M. Dillon, is chairperson of the sponsoring committee. The senator will be the featured speaker and other local elected public officials of the same political party will also appear on the program. At his private club, Mr. Dillon spoke with Mr. Jack Lee, owner of a local prominent manufacturing company urging him to attend. Mr. Dillon pointed out that they hoped to raise considerable money for campaign purposes. Mr. Lee had attended political meetings before with Mr. Dillon. Usually at these dinners, Mr. Lee brought along several of his friends.

The following day Mr. Lee mailed a letter on his own stationery to some 100 of his business executive friends. He selected the names carefully to help ensure a good response. The letter was sent out without Mr. Dillon's knowledge and read as follows:

Dear Friend:

Carl Dillon, who is known and respected by all of us, requests your presence at the forthcoming "Senator's Night" at Hotel Grand, May 24, at 6:30 P.M. You will enjoy an outstanding and informative program and have the opportunity to meet many of our selected public officials.

Carl informs me that the quota and limit is 800 tickets. He is striving to make this "Senator's Night" the best ever. Plan now to attend and enjoy a delightful get-together with friends. Spouses are invited.

Write your check for $100 (each plate) to Senator's Night Committee, Room 504, Butler Building, Megapolis, U.S.A.

Cordially yours,
Jack Lee

cc: Mr. Carl Dillon

One recipient, Mr. Howard Stevens, vice president of the local Chamber of Commerce, destroyed his copy of the letter and telephoned several prominent members of the chamber to inquire if they had received a copy. If so, he informed them what he had done with his copy and urged them to do likewise. He termed the entire affair, "a brazen, unethical, imposition for funds upon local business leaders."

The following day when Mr. Dillon learned of the letter and some of the reaction to it, he immediately got in touch with Mr. Lee who assured him not to worry about it. He would handle the whole affair. Accordingly he issued a second letter in which he stated:

> As a private citizen of our great nation I acted in the best interests of all the people in our community. I do not seek any personal favors. It did not occur to me that my forthright motive might be misinterpreted. If I even thought it might be, I would certainly not have written you.
>
> My invitation, extended honestly and sincerely, is for a very worthy cause. I assure you I have no ulterior motive.
>
> Again I urge you to attend. Won't you come?
> Thank you.

Questions:

1. What is the source of the problem in this case?
2. Why did some recipients feel the Lee letter was "unfortunate?"
3. Evaluate the letters mailed by Mr. Lee. Be specific.
4. What is your recommendation to Mr. Dillon? Why?

Case 6–3. Smeed Company

PRESIDENT: Yes, our year just closing was indeed a good year. Our sales increased and so did our net income. Sales were up nearly $2 million and net income almost $300,000. Here are the data (hands over data shown in the table on page 161). We came out with several new products and I would say the public is receiving them beyond our expectations. I personally attribute this to our realistic appraisal of present and future goals and plans.

NELSON: You emphasize goals?

PRESIDENT: Oh, yes. Very much so. We update our goals every three months to reflect results and new information. All employees right down to the newly hired office clerk are involved in creating and participating in the plans.

NELSON: You must have an excellent sales force.

PRESIDENT: They do a good job and we're always trying to improve. More correctly I would say we have an effective balanced company. Our finance people are pretty astute and I'll stack up our production team against anybody anywhere.

NELSON: What would you say your biggest problem is right now?

PRESIDENT: Inventory. Trying to keep it under proper control is a tremendous task. Habits of buyers are changing constantly and it takes a Solomon to figure out what to do. At the moment we are O.K. on finished goods, but have way too much in raw materials and goods in process.

NELSON: Do your present inventory levels worry you?

PRESIDENT: Well, I'm concerned, but with the present difficulties of getting materials I think we will work out of it all right.

NELSON: How do you view your company's future?

PRESIDENT: The future holds both problems and possibilities. I am confident our company will deal effectively with the problems and I am certain we will take advantage of the possibilities. I am optimistic about the future.

NELSON: Thank you very much. It was nice talking with you.

PRESIDENT: It has been my pleasure.

TABLE 6–3A

	Year just Closed	Previous Year
Cash	$ 485,200	$ 401,837
Inventory		
Finished goods	3,154,013	2,869,380
Raw materials and work in process	1,468,244	621,701
Net sales	15,203,900	13,380,745
Income before taxes	1,750,426	1,220,940
Net income	991,300	702,550
Earnings per share	0.99	0.64

Questions:

1. Do you feel the president is justified in viewing current operations of the company with confidence? Future operations of the company with confidence? Justify your answers.

2. Write a short report about the company using the information obtained from the interview with the president and the data given.

Part III

Planning How the Office Work Will Be Done

After determining with some precision what office work is to be done, the next step is to ascertain how the office work will be done. Our attention is now concentrated on the means. Manual effort or machine power can be used or some combination of the two. The wide selection of different means and the constant new developments in how to perform essential office work have thrust office management into prominence.

The six chapters which constitute this part of the book include "Office Machines and Equipment," "Computers—Managerial Considerations," "Computers—Technical Considerations," "Distribution of Information," "Records Management—Storage and Retrieval," and "Records Management—Stored Information."

Chapter 7

Office Machines and Equipment

An intelligent plan is the first step to success.
Planning is the open road to your destination.

Basil S. Walsh

Having now completed the planning for *what* office work is to be done, we are now ready to develop the planning for *how* or by what means the office work will be done. We can select from a wide spectrum with manual means on the one end and complete or very high mechanization on the other. In between are various combinations of manual and machine means. A considerable amount of office work is accomplished without machines and a great deal with relatively unsophisticated machines and equipment.

Usually the volume, type, and occurrence of the work are decisive in justifying the extent of mechanical means utilized. But there is always some human participation present in all data processing. It is important to remember that not all manual operations are less efficient and more expensive than machine means, and that not all information problems are solved by simply installing sophisticated machines, and that not all enterprises have information requirements that justify highly mechanized information machines. However, in this day and age, some degree of mechanization is usually worthwhile, the extent depends upon the individual requirements.

SELECTION OF OFFICE MACHINES AND EQUIPMENT

Selection of what machine, if any, necessitates having knowledge of available facilities on the market and deciding the best units in keeping

165

with the particular requirements set forth by the planning of the system, procedure, method, and form to be utilized. More specifically, the information manager needs to know the types of machines and equipment available, the characteristics of each, the unit cost of output, the initial outlay, and the maintenance cost.

Although not an easy task, this selection work is one of the most interesting aspects of information management. Excellent machines and equipment have contributed tremendously to the advance and status of information management. And a machine is now available for performing nearly every type of office work and it is surprising to note that many of them were nonexistent ten years ago.

To assist in comprehending what is available, Figure 7–1 relates the more common units with the basic elements of data processing referred to in Chapter 1. For example, as indicated by the check marks, an addressing machine performs recording and sorting. A human being performs all the basic elements of data processing.

It is a common practice to create a committee for purposes of study and recommendations as to which machine should be used along with the reasons why. The information manager is a key person on such a committee. Knowledge about various machines and equipment must be acquired by the committee members, and this is best done by talking with sales representatives of the machine manufacturers, attending schools offered by these manufacturers, reading available literature on the subject, and conferring with executives of companies having the machines in operation. Also, consultants can be retained to give assistance. Their wide and varied experience can save much time and spark the action to move ahead. But participation by company personnel is essential, for it provides them with practical insight as to what is going on and why. Furthermore, familiarity with the proposed processing is gained, and the background needed for successful installation and operation is obtained.

The committee can assist in attaining a desired program of preparation and installation. Employees from various departments such as systems, personnel, and those in which changes will occur can be represented on such a committee. Planning pertaining to the feasibility of the machine and the means for handling changes—especially with reference to personnel—can be handled quite successfully by a committee.

Among the first tasks of the committee is to clarify what the required office work to be done actually is. Although we have covered its essentiality in our initial stages of the planning, it may be advisable to examine it again quite critically to confirm that it is absolutely necessary. It is also important that the individual requirements have high priority; use by others is insufficient grounds for adoption. At the same time, there is a commonness about information processing that makes for a

FIGURE 7–1
Each Office Production Unit Performs Specific Basic Elements of Data Processing

Office Unit Employed	Reading	Writing, Typing, etc.	Recording, Printing	Sorting	Transmitting	Calculating	Comparing	Storing
	Basic Element of Data Processing							
Accounting Machine		✓	✓	✓		✓	✓	
Adding and Calculating Machines		✓	✓			✓		
Addressing Machine			✓	✓				
Computer without Special Attachment			✓	✓	✓	✓	✓	✓
Copying Machine			✓					
Human Being	✓	✓	✓	✓	✓	✓	✓	✓
Micrographic Units			✓				✓	✓
Peripheral Computer Units	✓	✓	✓		✓		✓	✓
Pneumatic Tube					✓			
Punching Machine		✓						
Sorter				✓				
Tabulator			✓		✓	✓	✓	
Telautograph		✓	✓		✓			
Telegraph		✓	✓		✓			
Teletypewriter		✓	✓		✓			
Typewriter		✓	✓					

degree of universality in what general types of machines are used. Determining what information should go to whom is essential. It is vital. If it is omitted, either the wrong machine may be selected or unnecessary information is automated and continued for a long time. Finding out the best way of doing this essential work cannot be overemphasized. The design of the systems, procedures, and methods along with office work simplification aid in answering these requirements. That is why they were discussed in the previous chapters of this book.

As a corollary, the question of the adequacy of present information in terms of service supplied will be considered. When improvements in service are keenly sought, a proposed machine will be evaluated in terms of its probable contribution to this goal.

MAJOR SELECTION FACTORS

Normally the decision on a machine or equipment selection is based upon (1) cost, (2) characteristics of the facility, and (3) employee considerations. All are important, but of the three, cost is usually given the most weight. We will discuss cost first and to do so will divide the presentation into subheadings of productivity, basis of acquisition, and administrative practice.

Cost—Productivity

In most instances acquisition of machines and equipment are made on the basis of increased productivity as expressed by lower unit cost, greater volume, better quality, or expected savings. The factors which determine the machine productivity vary somewhat with the policies of the individual buyer and with the importance attached to each factor. Usually pertinent are (*a*) the current complete price, including installation and delivery; (*b*) if a replacement, the make, model, type, and condition of the replaced unit and its probable current market value; (*c*) the percentage of working time the unit will be used; and (*d*) the investment percentage return to the company taking into account the effect of income taxes and overhead expenses in reducing the gross earnings.

Generally speaking, the greater the capacity, speed, and versatility of the machine the lower the unit cost of work processed. For example, a large computer with high usage rate will do for less than $1 what it would cost $10 to do on a small computer or perhaps $8,000 with an ordinary desk calculator. Volume and type of work are the key factors.

Figure 7–2 shows a quick rule-of-thumb approach to decide whether to purchase a particular piece of office machine or equipment. It is based on timesaving by personnel, as illustrated by a ratio of personnel to machine or equipment. For example, the salary cost per minute for an employee receiving $5,000 a year is approximately 5 cents. The number of thousands of dollars per year is approximately the equivalent number of cents per minute. For a $10,000 office machine, the cost per working day is $4. Hence, $4 divided by 5 cents per minute gives 80 minutes as the time required to be saved each working day by a $5,000 employee to pay for the machine.

FIGURE 7–2
A Quick and Convenient Means of Determining Whether an Office Machine Will Pay for Itself within a Reasonable Period

(1) Salary per Year	(2) Approximate Salary per Minute	(3) Cost per Day for $10,000 Office Machine	(4) Personnel Time Required Daily to Save (in minutes)
$ 5,000	5.0¢	$4.00	80.0
7,500	7.5	4.00	53.4
10,000	10.0	4.00	40.0
12,500	12.5	4.00	32.0
15,000	15.0	4.00	26.6

Note: The approach is based on determining the time required to be saved by the employee who will use the machine.

Column 2 is based on 250 working days a year, 8-hour day, and 83 percent efficiency.

Column 3 is based on 250 working days a year, 10-year life span.

Column 4 is column 3 divided by column 2.

Cost—Basis of Acquisition

Four choices are available to the user of a machine: (1) buy, (2) rent, (3) lease, or (4) use a machine service. The cost differs for each of these conditions. With purchase there is a capital expenditure plus an annual expenditure for operation and maintenance. Rental entails a smaller initial expenditure, with standard expenses for operation. Commonly the rental represents 3 percent of purchase price per month. For a $1,000 machine, the rental would be $30 per month. A lease usually is for a minimum of 75 percent of the useful life of the machine, rates vary, and some provide for purchase for a small percentage of original cost. The terms must abide by the Internal Revenue Service conditional sales regulations. There is also the sales-leaseback arrangement whereby a company purchases the machine, sells it to a lessor who leases it back to the company. By this arrangement the company receives nearly all its fixed assets in the form of immediate cash which, if needed, provides a satisfactory arrangement.

In the case of the federal government, the determination of whether to buy or lease information machines is made on the basis of a *cost advantage point*. This is the point when purchase price plus accrued maintenance equals cumulative rentals for a particular machine. When this point is reached in six years or less, purchase is warranted. Limited research indicates that in the case of computers it usually takes around six years for the investment to be recovered. Low point in recovery is the end of two or three years, due primarily to the effect of start-up costs, changeover, and adjustments.

Information machine service, especially that of a computer, is offered by nearly 200 U.S. companies who are specialists in this area. Some are independent companies, some are banks, others are service bureaus owned or operated by office machine manufacturers. Their charges vary according to the type of machine and the amount of work, but generally charges are considered nominal and in line with the services rendered. The services offered are ideal for excess work loads.

It can be seen that many considerations can enter into the decision on which of the four alternatives should be chosen. The total cost can vary widely. A helpful comparison among the choices is obtained by forecasting the annual total expenses for the most suitable arrangement for each choice. This can be projected over a reasonable number of years. Such data, along with attention to nontangible considerations, assist in arriving at a decision.

Cost—Administrative Practice

Depreciation, trade-in, and maintenance are important administrative factors affecting the cost of an office machine. There is no one answer to the question of how to figure depreciation and when it is economically sound to purchase a machine or to make a trade-in. The planner must refer to the accounting practices followed. Most companies consider office machines and equipment as assets; and over a period, they write them off because of depreciation. The period will depend upon the kind of product. For example, the following are common:

> Desks . . . . 20 years
> Files . . . . 15 "
> Accounting machines . . . . 10 "
> Rugs and carpets . . . . 10 "
> Typewriters . . . . 5 "

The rate used over the period can be calculated by various methods. Straight line and sum-of-digits are common. Also available are special rules, limitations on accelerated depreciation, and special elections. For current information about them, the Internal Revenue Service should be consulted. Some companies follow the practice of charging to expenses any equipment purchase of less than a stated amount, for example, $100; and any equipment purchase over this amount is put into an assets account. Other practices are also followed, but they must be reasonable and within the meaning and intent of income tax laws.

Some general overall guiding policy for trade-ins should be followed, tempered with certain adjustments based upon the individual circumstances. Several considerations influence a trade-in. The availability of the cash and capital resources of the enterprise is always present in any trade-in discussion. Also important is the expected cash savings to be derived from the new unit's use. A trade-in is usually in order if savings will pay for the net outlay within one-fourth the life of the unit or within a rule-of-thumb period of 24 months. Another consideration is the difference between the accrued net depreciation and the expense necessary to keep the unit operating. If the net (present book value minus trade-in) is less than the cost of repair, a trade-in is probably best.

Another cost consideration is expenditure for maintenance. All office machines and equipment require attention periodically in order to keep them in satisfactory condition. Preventive maintenance rather than remedial maintenance, should be stressed. The former seeks to catch trouble before it happens; this is accomplished by scheduling inspections at carefully determined intervals. The latter, or remedial maintenance, deals with trouble after it occurs. Preventive maintenance provides greater employee satisfaction and efficient performance. Maintenance can be handled in any of the following ways: maintenance contracts, individual service calls, company-operated service, and combined leasing-maintenance contracts.

Many manufacturers, or their sales distributors, prefer to service their products in order to insure complete satisfaction; and to this end, they offer maintenance contracts which call for regular inspection, cleaning, adjusting, and oiling. Charges are made on a predetermined basis, and the rates and conditions for special service calls are usually stated. Advocates of this type of maintenance service claim that the regularity of service, the use of genuine parts, the employment of skilled, factory-trained mechanics, and the overall, long-range low cost warrant its use. This means is probably the most popular for offices of all sizes.

Individual service calls are a "when required" type of service. This is sometimes called "no service contract" maintenance. It is of a remedial nature. The age and number of units are the chief factors which influence the choice of this policy. If most of the units are new, it is reasonable to expect that they will not require repair service; likewise, when a large number are in use, it is logical that not all will require maintenance service. However, a service call on an individual basis usually costs more than one under a maintenance contract.

A company-operated service is followed primarily because of considerations of cost, control, or availability of service. Maintenance costs may be lower under this plan, provided there is a sufficient volume to warrant full-time maintenance employees. With a company-operated service, it is possible to exercise close control over the progress of the work, the expenses, and the regularity of inspections. In some instances, available outside services are inconvenient, owing to the remoteness of the office, and in such cases the company-operated plan may be desirable.

When a facility is leased, the leasor usually provides for the maintenance. Terms for such service are included in the lease. Both periodic and on-call maintenance are provided. Also, as a part of the agreement any design improvements in the unit or its attachments are usually supplied as quickly as available.

Cost—Machine Characteristics

Flexibility and capacity are usually given important consideration in machine selection. If the machine being considered can be used effectively for many types of office work, its adoption usually can be viewed favorably. Likewise, the feature of expansion and contraction in order to accommodate varying amounts of paperwork is normally advantageous. In addition, it is imperative that the machine capacity be sufficient to permit efficient operations. The expected output can be judged from experience of actual users, data from the manufacturer, and actual test runs in the office. When feasible, this latter source is recommended, but in any event, it is always advisable to obtain a demonstration of an office machine.

Likewise, the speed of processing may be a contributing factor. Machines do process office work at fantastic speeds, but these rates should not be governing. Speed of processing should be considered in relation to service required. To know that with a given machine, information for a report can be completed in two hours, in contrast to two days under the present setup, is convincing, providing the report is needed and will be used within several hours and will not be ignored or filed away for a week. The challenge here is to get management members to improve their usage of the material made available. Perhaps this starts with more rapid processing to make information available more quickly.

Furthermore, there is the factor of aesthetic values—the appearance of the office resulting from having the latest and finest in office machines and equipment. Aesthetic values are highly subjective and commonly are subdued. Such values have a place, for office machines and equipment are not only a *physical* means of assisting employees to accomplish their work but also serve as a mental stimuli. Supplying the proper unit makes for a positive and cooperative attitude and helps place the employee in the right frame of mind to work efficiently.

Cost—Employee Considerations

In many ways, the installation of office machines and equipment changes the personnel requirements, regarding both the number of employees and the level of their skill; and hence, the problems of transferring, reducing, and training the work force must be considered. The availability of trainable operators commonly is a foremost consideration. Furthermore, when machines are adopted to perform monotonous work, the effect upon personnel is also important, because usually a happier and more satisfied work force is the result.

Employee preference is also of great significance because the human element is vital in determining whether the equipment is properly utilized or operated. A strong bias against a particular unit prevents maximum benefits from being realized, regardless of the suitability of the unit to the work. The highly successful office manager will seldom select a machine for which the employees have expressed a strong dislike. Most office employees will turn out consistently the maximum work of acceptable quality when they are supplied with the equipment and machines *they feel* are the best available.

CLASSIFICATION OF OFFICE MACHINES

To reiterate, planning for data processing necessitates having knowledge of what machines and equipment are available so that the most appropriate unit can be adopted. We will now discuss briefly a few selected types to provide some idea of the range and variation among these units. The list here is limited. Other types of information machines and equipment are included in other chapters under discussion of the specific work or the function that the unit performs. This includes units such as those for word processing units, the typewriter, and the intercommunicating device.

We will organize the discussion around the means and the operation of data processing as shown by the matrix arrangement of Figure 7–3. The means are shown across the top, the operation vertically. That is, the basic operation of any data processing are record, sort, and process. These operations can be done either manually by key-driven machine, by card machine, or by computer. To illustrate, the operation *sort* under the key-driven machine is usually done by hand; the operation *process* under a card machine is performed by a tabulator. Since we have already discussed manual means, let us start with key-driven machines followed by card machines, and the computer.

Key-Driven Machines

Typewriters, accounting machines, adding machines, and desk calculators are representative of key-driven machines which, as the name implies, are operated by depressing keys. There is little processing accomplished which is not directly started by the operator. In the office of today, much processing is done by key-driven machines despite the availability of electronic processing machines and the development of

FIGURE 7–3
Basic Operations of Data Processing by Basic Type of Means

Operations \ Means	Manual	Key-Driven Machine	Card Machine	Computer
Record	Paper and pencil	Hand- or type-written material on paper	Hand- or type-written material into either 80- or 96-column punched card, or notched card	Put material into computer system using Key-driven unit or read material by any of several available means
Sort	By hand with or without rack	By hand with or without rack	By hand or use a sorter	Either by machine direct access or magnetic tape
Process	Metal arithmetic and decisions with help of paper and pencil	Actions by the machine operator and those supplied by the machine	By tabulator	By processor of computer

minicomputers. The reason is the relatively low cost of the key-driven machine and its suitability for low volume work. An example is the nondescriptive accounting machine (numerical keyboard only) used to prepare original ledger, statement and proof-tape journal.

The trend, however, is definitely toward small electronic processors that automate nearly all functions of the processing. The processor is a part of the accounting machine. Yet the keyboard is used to enter certain data and to actuate the machine. Figure 7–4 illustrates the manner in which an accounting machine may be used for processing payroll accounting information. The machine accepts alphabetic and numeric data, performs arithmetic operations by its electronic processor, prints, punches, or stores computer results. Various media can be used for output data. The employee master payroll is retained and updated, including deductions, straight and overtime rates, and current information for governmental reports. Observe that the raw payroll data are sorted and then fed into the machine where such things as the hours worked are indexed and accumulated, verified, and straight and overtime are checked. These data are then run through the same machine with a different program for processing being used, a check with the master file is made, the paycheck is written, and by-products of punched cards and punched tape are made. Subsequently the cards are used to print job order or departmental expense data (shown at upper right) and deduction listings (shown at lower right). The punched tape by-product is used to prepare the payroll registers.

FIGURE 7–4

The Procedure Flow Chart Followed by an Electronic Accounting Machine in Performing Automated Payroll Accounting

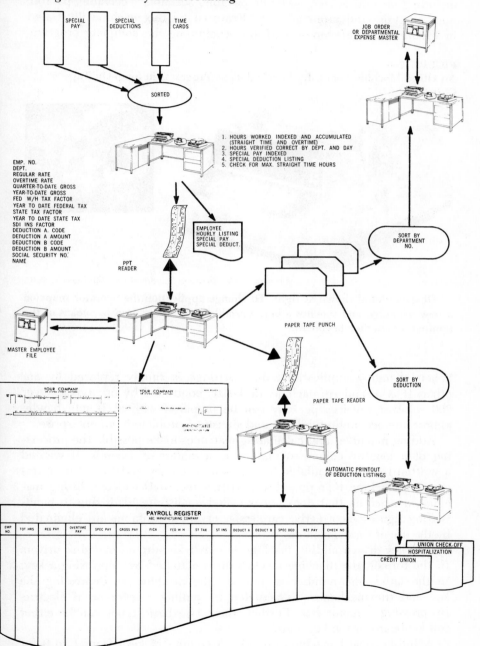

Different features are stressed by many different machines. However, current accounting machines are adaptable for various types of work including general ledger, accounts payable, accounts receivable, payroll, sales analysis, and profit analysis. Featured by the machine illustrated in Figure 7–5 is a snap-on cartridge containing the complete program.

FIGURE 7–5
An Office Machine Featuring Punched Tape Programs in Snap-On Tape Cartridges

Courtesy: Friden Division, The Singer Co., San Leandro, Calif.

Observe detail shown at right. To change application the operator snaps on a new cartridge and touches a key. Variable data are entered by means of the familiar typewriter keyboard.

When changing applications, one cartridge is simply replaced by another. It is a modern machine, desk-size, controlled by one typist. Over 200 sell-cost invoices per day can be prepared with it. It will handle almost any accounting, billing, and statistical problem in an enterprise.

Adding machines and calculating machines make possible the processing of a lengthy column of figures in a matter of seconds. If wanted a written record is available for checking accuracy and for future reference. A machine that provides a written record is called a listing machine, a machine that does not is called nonlisting. Error due to handwriting figures incorrectly, carelessly, or out of column are eliminated by the use of these machines.

The key-driven adding machine is either key-driven or crank driven. In the former, the machine mechanism is actuated by depressing a key; in the latter, the number is put into the machine by depressing the key and the mechanism is actuated by pulling a lever or, if electric, by pressing a motor bar. Further, these two basic types can be either full keyboard or ten-keyboard.

A full-keyboard machine provides a column of keys from 1 to 9 for each digit position. Thus, a five-row machine can handle a number like 628.47. The full keyboard permits high speeds where numbers of four or less digits are involved, because the keys can be depressed simultaneously. A ten-keyboard type has, as the name suggests, ten keys from 0 to 9. Within the machine capacity, all numbers are recorded by means of these ten keys. The number 629.43 would be handled by first pressing the key 6, then 2, and then 9, and so on until the number is completed. The ten-key machine is usually very satisfactory for large numbers. The hand travel is small, since it is confined to ten keys.

Among the latest calculating machines is the electronic unit that displays the results on an illuminated display screen. Featured are simplicity of machine operations, noiseless and automatic accumulator switches for products and multipliers or entries. Units are available for special work such as square root, squaring, and raising to the power.

There is also the popular small calculator that by putting data into the machine by depressing keys and then pressing the function key the answer is given instantly to problems such as those in trigonometry, common and natural logarithms, and exponentials. Most machines in this category can compute the same problems, but some require more key depressions. Figure 7–6 (left) shows a popular model.

The calculator shown by Figure 7–6 (right) is a modern programmable electronic printing calculator. Programs are entered through the keyboard then transferred from memory to a magnetic card which can be used repeatedly. The card is inserted into the slot shown at right

FIGURE 7–6
Calculators

Courtesy: Bowmar, Inc., N.Y.   *Courtesy: Burroughs Corp., Detroit.*

Left: A popular hand-held calculator featuring a five function, 8 digit display, full floating decimal, percent key for automatic mark ups and discounts, and algebraic number entry sequence. **Right:** A modern electronic printing calculator which is programmed either by insertion of magnetic cards into the slot at right top of machine or manually by using the keyboard.

top of the machine. This calculator combines computer-like versatility with the convenience of an office calculator. Referring to Figure 7–7, the sales of a company are shown in lower right portion. These data charted for monthly sales are shown in a solid line, the trend by a

FIGURE 7–7

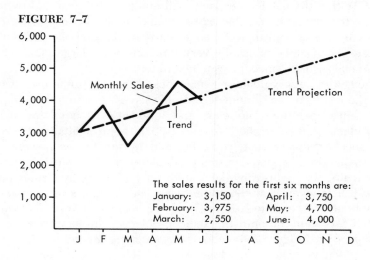

The sales results for the first six months are:

January:	3,150	April:	3,750
February:	3,975	May:	4,700
March:	2,550	June:	4,000

dotted line. If sales continue at the same rate, what will be the sales for the remainder of the year and for the entire year? By inserting the magnetic card program into the machine and keyboarding the input of the sales figures, the calculator automatically projects the data of the sales trend line shown in the chart by a double dotted line. The total sales for the year are projected at $52,101.

Another typical problem for this calculator deals with investment analysis. Suppose machine either A or B is being considered for purchase. The company wants 18 percent return on its machine investment, finance capital costs 10 percent, price of each machine, cash flow (total net cash return generated by the investment), and other pertinent data are known. Again by inserting the proper magnetic card program into the machine, keyboarding the input data, the calculator electronically provides a written record of the calculation showing let us say, machine A will show a 22.31 percent return on investment, while machine B will show 15.62 percent. Accurate data given quickly helps to reach the important investment decision.

PUNCHED-CARD MACHINES

The key physical unit for this type of data processing is a punched card commonly consisting of 80 columns as shown by Figure 7–8. Holes

FIGURE 7–8
The Space on the Punched Card Is Allocated to the Needs of the Particular Study

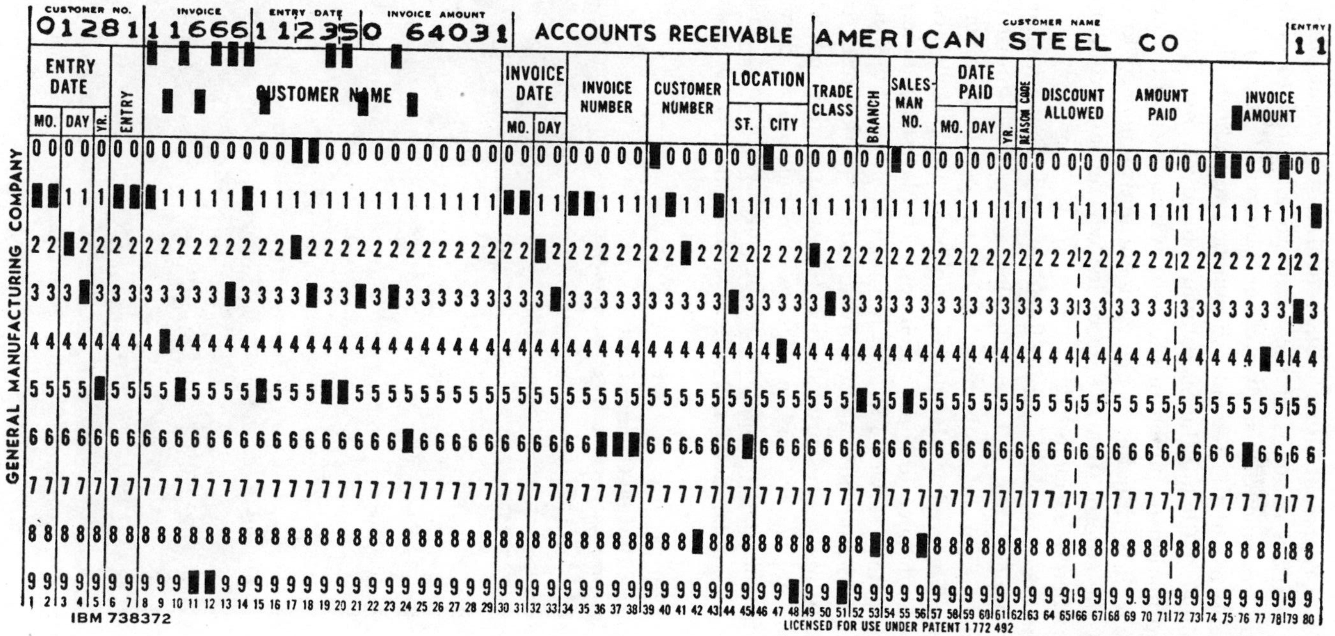

Courtesy: International Business Machines Corp., White Plains, N.Y.

are coded to represent either alphabetical or numerical information. For example, vertical columns of the card are allocated to different items. Information on months is given two columns so that a 1 in the first column and a 1 in the second are punched to indicate 11, or the month of November. Utilizing the 80 columns effectively by carefully deciding what information to punch in the card warrants careful thought. Information which is valuable to management and is needed to conduct the affairs of the enterprise, and data which will reveal pertinent major relationships should be included.

Punched-card machines are still widely used. They provide a relatively low cost, dependable, and versatile means of putting information in such a form that it can be easily handled for any of a number of subsequent operations. The common language supplied by the punched card provides the real significance to these machines.[1] The latest machine models give very satisfactory service for a wide range of applications, including the analyzing and summarizing of statistical data, market research, and sales analyses. In market research studies, for example, the number of respondents who answered "yes" to a given question, broken down according to age, income, and occupation can be quickly obtained. Likewise, sales analyses by units, dollars, territories, and months, or manufacturing

FIGURE 7–9
The IBM 96-Column Card

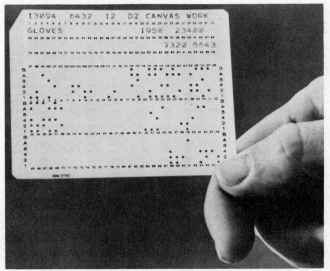

Courtesy: International Business Machines Corp., White Plains, N.Y.

---

[1] The code for punched holes is given in Chapter 8, Fig. 9–12, p. 249.

costs by various types of labor operations, plant locations, departments, or machines can be easily determined.

Smaller in overall size yet containing more data than the 80-column card is the 96-column card shown in Figure 7–9. The upper portion of the card is used for print lines while the lower portion is made up of three tiers used for the punched encoding. The code followed for this card is also indicated. The letter, A, of second print line is coded by a hole in B, A, and 1 of tier 2; the letter, B, by a hole in B, A, and 2.

Basic Punched-Card Machines

There are three basic punched-card machines, including a punching machine a sorter, and a tabulator. They perform respectively the basic processing operations of record, sort, and process mentioned previously in this chapter. A punching machine punches small holes in the card, representing the numerical and alphabetical information desired. The machines have many automatic features, depending upon the model and the manufacture. Figure 7–10 shows a card-punching machine.

The sorter arranges the cards according to any desired classification and in alphabetical or numerical sequence. Cards are passed through the machine; and the punched hole causes a mechanism to operate, resulting in the card being directed into a specific box or pocket of the machine. Sorting at any one time is done according to one vertical column, i.e., a unit number or a letter. For example, by the first run through the sorter the data are sequenced according to the first column on the right, then the second sort rearranges this sequence according to the second column on the right. In like manner, the sorting is continued until the cards are in the sequence desired.

The tabulator prepares printed reports from the data contained on the punched and sorted cards. These machines can print individually or in summary; a great variety of reports is possible. The number of reports that can be printed is almost limitless but depends mainly upon the information to be "read" by the machine, the forms on which the reports are prepared, and the arrangement and rearrangement of the cards. A tabulator—or as it is commonly called when used with a modern office processing system, a card read punch, provides fully buffered card reading and punching capabilities for the system. The machine is illustrated in Figure 7–11.

In addition, there are special punched-card machines for specific operations. Among those most common is an "interpretor" which prints at the top of the card the data represented by the punched holes. This information is sometimes desired for quick identification and reference. A "verifier" can be used to check the accuracy of the holes punched

FIGURE 7–10

A Card-Punching Machine Which Features an Automatic Card Control of Skipping and Duplicating, a Fast Method of Duplication When Desired, and a Design Which Permits Efficient and Rapid Operation

Courtesy: International Business Machines Corp., White Plains, N.Y.

in the cards. Another machine, called a reproducer or "gang punch" punches, on a batch of cards, standardized information such as date and location of customer, which are repetitive and thus avoids punching individually each card. There is also a calculator, or "multiplying punch," which senses, for example, two factors prepunched in the card, computes the product, punches it into the card, and records the factors and the product on a paper.

Variable information such as meter readings, job data, and stores requisitions can be pencil-marked in appropriate spaces on a punched-card area. Then, by means of a machine called an "optical scanning punch," the variable information is read and automatically punched into the card, thus making it ready for processing. With the developments in office automation, many punched cards are now produced simultaneously with the typing of the information on a typewriter equipped with special components.

The most common uses for punched-card machines are (1) correlat-

FIGURE 7–11 ,
A Card Read Punch Machine

Courtesy: International Business Machines Corp., White Plains, N.Y.

ing, analyzing, and summarizing data, such as sales by customer, as illustrated by Figure 7–12; (2) preparing bills or invoices; (3) handling accounts payable; (4) keeping inventory records; (5) preparing payrolls and distributing labor costs; and (6) production control.

Key considerations in the usage of punched cards include preparing

FIGURE 7–12
Samples of the Work Prepared by a Tabulator of Punched Cards

SALES AND GROSS PROFIT BY CUSTOMER							
CUSTOMER			COMMODITY	QUANTITY	UNIT	COST OF GOODS SOLD	SALES AMOUNT
BR.	NO.	CODE	DESCRIPTION				
1 3	6 7		ACE DRUG CO				
1 3	6 7	0 3 0 1	BEAUTY SOAP REGULAR	1 2	D Z	1 9 8 0	2 4 0 0
1 3	6 7	0 3 0 2	BEAUTY SOAP GUEST	1 2	D Z	2 0 4 0	2 5 2 0
1 3	6 7	0 3 0 3	BEAUTY SOAP BATH	1 2	D Z	2 1 6 0	2 7 0 0
1 3	6 7	1 3 1 4	SHAVE SOAP LARGE	2 4	D Z	4 8 0 0	6 9 6 0
1 3	6 7	1 3 5 2	BRUSHLESS CREAM LRG	2 4	D Z	3 1 2 0	4 3 2 0
			[FOR THE PURPOSE OF THIS EXHIBIT, ONLY A FEW COMMODITIES ARE ILLUSTRATED]				
						2 7 5 0 0 *	3 7 5 0 0
1 3	1 0 5		ADAMS DRYGOODS CO				
1 3	1 0 5	0 3 0 1	BEAUTY SOAP REGULAR	2 4	D Z	3 9 6 0	4 8 0 0

Courtesy: International Business Machines Corp., White Plains, N.Y.

the input—the cost and time of getting the raw data punched into the cards, the extent to which correlated or listed information will be helpful, and the value of additional facts gained from being able to interpret the data in a more feasible form. In most instances, punched cards are feasible when the data (1) are fairly repetitious, permitting prepunching for much of the data, and (2) require analysis to show pertinent relationships.

An interesting application using punched cards as a media is the use of a machine, called Source Record Punch, for handling information of material control. The machine requires about 4 square feet of a desk top, it reads simultaneously a typed human readable document and a punched machine-readable document. Merged are three kinds of numeric information (1) constant (alphabetic and numeric)—customer, order, part number (obtained from a prepunched card), (2) semiconstant (numeric only)—date, department, location (obtained from mechanical slides within the machine, and (3) variable (numeric only)—quantity, color, size (obtained from machine keyboard). In essence, the machine gathers all the needed information at the point of origin and in just one operation captures it for input data for machine processing. It can be adopted for many different types of reports and information, fits into the normal workflow, is simple to operate, and the cost is low.

Figure 7–13 shows how the information dealing with purchasing, receiving, inspecting, and stores issuing are tied together. Beginning in the lower left, each purchase request is reviewed against the stock status report (bottom center of illustration). If O.K., the appropriate master item and vendor cards are removed from purchasing files and along with semicontrol and variable information, the four-copy purchasing order is prepared by means of the Source Record Punch. The third copy, or Copy C, of this order serves as a master card for receiving, the functions of which are shown in the upper left portion. Copy E of these receiving documents has a dry gum backing and is pasted to the lead carton to indicate authorized movement and identification. Again one copy, or G, is used to write the necessary three documents for inspection quality as shown in upper right of illustration. In some cases, when the material is moved to stores no master card is sent with the stock since it is unnecessary to identify vendor or purchase order number after it has been inspected. As shown in lower right, stores use punched card to relieve inventory employing a deck of master cards punched with a part number in each card. Stores writes three cards for move ticket, audit card, and data-processing card.

The stock status report is maintained by data-processing cards sent to it, one from each of four functions. The type of information contained in this report is shown by the illustration. Additional reports can be

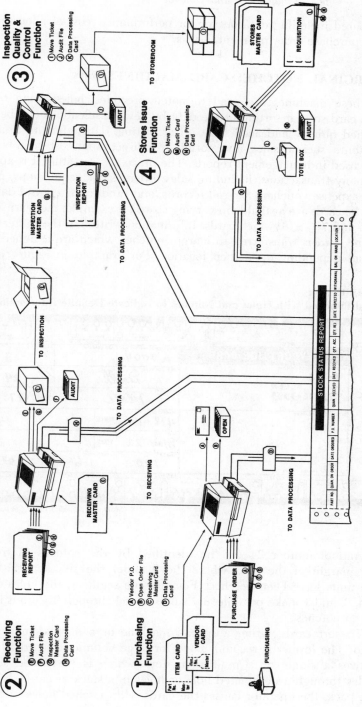

FIGURE 7-13
Basic Flow of Information Providing the Input-Output Data Necessary to Accurate Material Control

Courtesy: Standard Register Co., Dayton.

prepared including data on vendor performance, cost of allocated stock, and purchase order payment checks.

MARGINAL NOTCHED-CARD MACHINES

These machines are used to notch precoded holes *along the edge* of a card so that sorting of the data by key classifications can be accomplished quickly and accurately. After sorting, data referring to a similar attribute, such as sales, inventories, or indirect labor costs, can be totaled and used in management reports. The process is versatile; it is applicable to many transactions, including sales orders, stock requisitions, purchase and expense vouchers, payroll records, and production control data.

The cards are available in varying sizes; for example, there are $2 \times 3\frac{1}{2}$-inch and $7\frac{1}{2} \times 8\frac{1}{2}$-inch cards. Information written in the center position of the card is transferred to margin notches which are assigned definite values depending upon their location. For example, in Figure 7–14, the

FIGURE 7–14
Card Punched with Holes and Notches to Indicate Definite Information

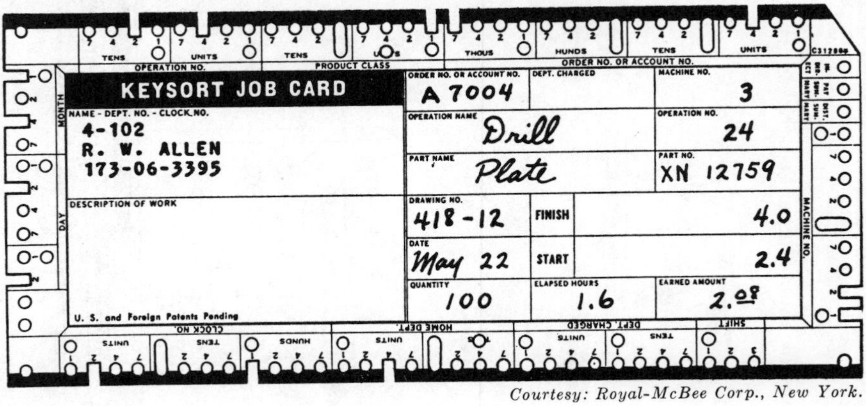

Courtesy: Royal-McBee Corp., New York.

operation number 24 can be identified by the notches in the upper left margin of the card where the 2 under the 10's and the 4 under the units have been notched. For any one segment, the holes of values 7, 4, 2, and 1 make possible any value from 1 through 9. Zero is indicated by no notches.

To sort cards, either a special machine or a manual means can be used. The former is recommended for large volumes of cards. The latter utilizes a single or a multiprong fork which is positioned so that it slides through a designated hole or holes in a stack of cards. By shaking the pack, the operator causes the cards with notched holes at the prong location to fall clear of the other cards. In this way a fast, accurate sort is provided.

MINICOMPUTERS

A dominant trend in office mechanization is the increasing popularity of very small inexpensive computers. These machines do a wide variety of processing work and are suited for most office work, but they are small and their capacity is limited compared with a regular computer system. The minicomputer system is ideal for a user who neither utilizes a large or complicated sequence of operations nor requires the capacity of the regular or large computer system. The most feasible applications range from a relatively simple system for solving mathematical and scientific problems to a system for processing amounts payable, inventory control, financial statements, production scheduling, purchase order preparation and similar kinds of work.

Minicomputers or "minis" are defined in different ways. One simple definition is "a minicomputer is a small inexpensive modern electronic computer." Another states, "A computer of relatively simple logic design whose performance-cost ratios are far below the norms of large, medium, and small computer systems." Some users consider a computer having a *purchase price* of under $30,000 is a minicomputer, others set the top cost at $15,000.

The processing unit of a minicomputer system is a little larger than a typewriter and sits on a desk top. The whole system occupies only a portion of the space in an ordinary clothes closet. Further, it is very easy to operate. Selected units of a minicomputer are illustrated in Figure 7–15.

The minicomputer is a computer in the full meaning of that word; it is not a glorified accounting, addressing, or calculating machine. It has a central processing unit, a main storage for data—commonly 5,000 words are stored, and one or more units to put data into the system and to receive it from the system called input/output (I/O) devices. Depending upon the application these basic components are supplemented with other computer units such as readers, line printers, and plotters (for graphic data) depending upon the user's individual requirements.

Users combine minis instead of using a large computer. For this arrangement, they claim greater flexibility and lower cost. The multi-mini system is normally justified on the following bases. First, a piecemeal approach to the total processing needs is superior because the total needs are not well defined and a step by step implementation of the processing appears plausible. Second, much input data are received during a very short period—typical in many experiments and research,

FIGURE 7–15
Units of a Minicomputer

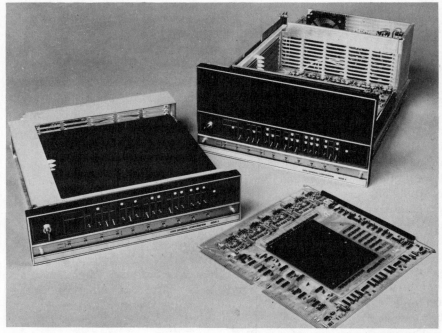

Courtesy: Data General Corp., Southboro, Mass.

Different configurations are employed to customize the total information processing facility including peripherals, interfaces, and the program followed.

and the processing can be delayed, it need not be done immediately. Further, in cases where a backup computer is desirable, for example, where continuous operation is on a first mini, a second mini identical to the first is available to take over if the first for any reason fails.

Frequently minis also serve as terminal units for input or output of a large central computer system. In other words, the mini is used for processing in a limited area and is tied in with the mainstream of central and large computer processing to which the mini receives or gives information pertaining to its limited area. The arrangement or configuration of the mini being a part of and sharing information with the total computer system is referred to as *time-sharing*. The time-sharing computer system shares time with the terminal units, one of which in this example, is a minicomputer. Further, the mini can have terminal units of its own. Modern designs permit up to 32 terminal units.

Using a network of minis usually provides faster on-line, or accessibility to processing, for the reason that the total operation is segmented into well defined components. Difficulty in one segment does not necessarily hamper the entire system. The mini network also gives an inherent modularity in that additional minis can be used to expand the system without extensive adjustments in the remainder units. Some also claim that the multi-minicomputer installation is less expensive than a single large computer, but the type and volume of processing must be taken into account as well as the total time for processing.

Figure 7–16 shows a business minicomputer designed to bring versatil-

FIGURE 7–16
A Modern Design Employing Advanced Concepts to Perform Basic Logic and Arithmetic Functions Is Featured by This Minicomputer

Courtesy: Burroughs Corp., Detroit.

ity to accounting and timely management reporting. This machine features disk memory (stored information in the machine is on a disk), modular electronic design, and advanced micrologic. Above the alphanumeric typewriter keyboard are a number of program keys which are selectively activated to enforce a controlled sequence of operations necessary to prepare the documents. Operator training time is minimum. Input can follow a steady flow regardless of the internal processing and the action of the printing. The input is buffered or held in intermediate storage until the processor can handle it. The machine has the potential for future conversion to an on-line computer. Thus, communication directly with a central computer or a service bureau in order to gain real-time data processing is available. Optional input or output units such as visual terminal units offer further automation and simplification to the information processed.

The whole area of computers is vital in today's office management. Further discussion of this area is warranted and hence, the next two chapters are devoted to this area. Continuing our discussion of office machines, the next category is addressing machines.

ADDRESSING MACHINES

Affixing addresses or other information in applications where the same information is used periodically typifies one of the popular uses for addressing and listing machines. A popular application is in addressing envelopes or advertising literature. The use of these machines is beneficial wherever a small quantity of identical information must be written repeatedly. In addition to mailing lists, the following are typical applications: names of employees along with standardized payroll information, i.e., check number and social security number; addresses on shipping labels and tags; headings on invoices and ledger cards; listing of customers; items ordered; items of storekeeping; lists of tools; tax roll; names and addresses of stockholders; and the list of dividend recipients.

The information is embossed on a plate made of either metal, plastic, or tissue. Metal plates give very long service; they practically never wear out. Plastic plates are lightweight, thin, inexpensive, and easy to emboss. They print clean and make maintenance of the list easy. Plates made of tissue stencils can be prepared on a typewriter equipped with a special platen, last a long time, but should be handled carefully. It is also possible to type or cut a punched tape which, when fed through an automatic machine for making plates, will produce them at a high rate of speed.

Most machines using metal plates permit attachments which add considerably to their value for specific operations. Included are:

1. A Cutoff Device. This permits only part of the plate to print at one time. It is useful where a portion of the information on the plate is printed in the first column of a spread sheet, another part in the second column, a third part in a third column, and so on.

2. A Selector. By its use certain plates pass through the machine without writing. This feature is desirable, for example, when certain plates are wanted for a particular mailing. The sequence of the plates remains unchanged.

3. A Repeater. Duplicate impressions are made from each plate before advancing to the next plate. To illustrate, the name and address might be required on the check stub and on the check, or on the statement and on the envelope. Settings for triplicate impressions are also available.

4.   *A Dating Device.* This enters the date simultaneously with the printing of other data. It is used in connection with statements and letters.

5.   *Tabbing Sockets.* By inserting small metal projections into selected tabs of the plate, selective sorting of the plates is accomplished. The sockets are located along the top edge of the plate and tabs are inserted according to a code.

COPYING MACHINES

During the past decade the most spectacular growth of any office machine has been copying machines. Various copying processes are followed. Figure 7–17 shows basic information helpful in selecting what

FIGURE 7–17
Comparison of Various Copying Processes

Process	Relative Cost of Copied Sheet	Usage	Usually Economical for Number of Copies up to:	Main Type of Material for which Suited*	Speed in Sheets per Minute	Reproductive (R) or Duplicative (D)
Xerography	High	Average	15	T-S-D-P	6	R
Contact.	High	Average	10	T-S-D-P	8	R
Stencil	Low	Wide	5,000	T	200	D
Direct	Medium	Average	300	T	150	D
Offset	Low	Average	10,000	T-S-D-P	150	D
Indirect.	Medium	Limited	300	T	200	D
Multigraph.	Low	Average	10,000	T	150	D
Whiteprint	Medium	Limited	500	T-S-D	8	R
Photocopy	High	Limited	5	T-S-D-P	5	R
Carbon	High	Wide	18	T	5	R
Noncarbon.	High	Limited	4	T	5	R

* Code: T = Typed or Printed, S = Script, D = Drawing, P = Picture.

type copying machine to utilize. Observe that cost, economical number of copies, and the type of material for which each process is best suited are among the major considerations. Brief descriptions of these copying processes follow.

1.   *Xerography* (pronounced zē-rog′-ra-fē). This word stems from the two Greek words meaning "dry printing" and is identified as a dry, fast, electrophotographic copying process. Xerography uses light and static electricity to make copies of anything printed, typed, written,

FIGURE 7–18
Duplicating from Originals

Courtesy: Xerox Corp., Rochester, N.Y.

This XEROX 3600-111 copying machine features an automatic document feeder efficiently speedfeeding stacked originals, a slitter-perforator permitting creation of custom-size forms, and an automatic sorter collating duplicates as fast as they are made.

or drawn. Copies are made on ordinary paper in a matter of seconds. The quality of the copy is excellent. Figure 7–18 shows the popular Xerox model 3600-111, which duplicates practically anything including linework, solids, and halftone photos. Some feel that the xerography principle will be applied to the printing of most books in the future. While tremendous expansion has been achieved, it is not as yet being offered widely for this application.

2. Contact. This means consists of placing a sensitized paper in contact with the material to be copied and inserting it into the machine, which exposes, develops, and fixes the copy sheet. The process is technically known as thermography and means literally a "burning" process. Dark areas, such as typewritten words, absorb more heat than the blank areas. Exposure to infrared light causes the words of the original to burn an image onto the heat-sensitive copy paper. Dry copies are made in a matter of seconds and the process emits no detectable odor. The process is effective wherever carbon is present in the writing, as with pencil or typewriter.

3. Stencil. This is a common means and consists of "typing a stencil," either by typewriter with ribbon removed or nonoperative, by special hand tools (styli), or by a die-impressed operation performed by the manufacturer. The openings thus made in the stencil, i.e., openings caused by the stencil coating being pushed aside and exposing the base fiber, permit ink to pass through so that paper held against the surface receives the image. Even, sharp, and clear strokes on the stencil give the best results. Corrections can be made on the stencil by using a special fluid to reseal the surface and then retyping. It is also possible to block out and remove an area and replace it by attaching a new portion of stencil. The image or printing is usually in a jet-black color, although several other colors are also available. Stencils can be stored for use at a later time.

4. *Direct or Liquid Process.* In this process, the material to be copied is put on a master sheet which has behind it a special carbon layer. The carbon places the image in reverse on the back of the master sheet. Different carbons are used for different colors. The master is placed in a machine, and copies are made directly from it in this manner: The copy sheet is slightly moistened with a special fluid before contacting the back side of the master; and as the copy sheet presses against the master, a very small layer of the carbon is removed and impressed on the copy sheet. Four colors can be reproduced in a single machine operation, and about 300 copies can be made from one master. Master sheets can be stored for reruns.

5. *Offset.* The offset process is subject to many variations. Basically, the principle involved is that the material to be reproduced is (1) prepared on a plate, which is (2) transferred to an intermediate agent, which is (3) printed on the paper. Frequently, the intermediate agent is made of rubber.

One important offset process is photo-offset. The material to be reproduced is photographed, and the negative is transferred to a sensitized plate. This plate is then used in a photo-offset printing unit. Slight variations in this method are commonly termed "planographing" and "offset lithography." Frequently, a xerography process is used for making offset master paper plates.

A well-known process known as "multilith" is based on this offset principle. Either a metal or a paperlike master can be used. The latter is more widely used, since it can be handled like a piece of paper. That is, a regular typewriter plus pencil, pen, ink, brush, or crayon furnished by the supplier are used in preparing the master. Erasures and corrections are handled as with odinary paper, and the paperlike masters can be filed in the office like paper sheets. The process is recommended for quantities over 500 and up to 10,000 copies.

6. *Miscellaneous Processes.* There are many more copying processes—too many to include all of them here. But mention will be made of the remaining six listed in Figure 7–17. The *indirect* process, also known as the gelatin process, consists of putting the material on a master sheet made of special paper; the master sheet is pressed against the gelatin, thus depositing the image on it. Copies are then made by pressing the sheets against the image in the gelatin. *Multigraph* employs either an imprinting or a ribbon process of reproducing. In the former, type, rubber strips, or electrotypes are used. The medium is inked and paper coming in contact with the wet type forms the copy. In the latter, or ribbon process, the duplicating is done through a ribbon similar to that used in standard typing, and the finished work closely resembles original typing. The type used is held in a segment or blanket and consists of up to 70 lines of type. Signature attachments are available, and corrections can easily be made in the type. *Whiteprint* provides a black on white directly from translucent originals. Additions to the master is a feature. The process is flexible and can handle large sizes of paper. Either the copy is given a light coating of a special solution to develop the copy permanently or it is exposed to controlled aqua ammonia vapors. *Photocopy* is one of the oldest copying processes. By photographing a negative, it is possible to make a positive paper print, that is, black lines with white background. Prints can be made in the same size as, or larger or smaller than, the original. *Carbon* exemplified by the use of carbon paper is a widely used means, especially when the information is original and the need does not exceed about 18 copies. For ordinary work where three or four copies suffice, the use of carbon paper is standard practice. *Noncarbon* utilizes carbonless or chemically treated paper. The bottom side of the first sheet is coated with a colorless chemical and the top side of the second sheet with another chemical. Writing on the first sheet reproduces instantly on the second sheet, and similar reaction takes place between the remaining sheets of the pack. Clear copies are obtained, smears and smudges are eliminated, and hands and clothing are not soiled.

It is in order to state here that machines are available to convert any size original up to 12 × 16 inches to the conventional 8½ × 11 inch size. Such a machine is popular for convertng computer hard copy output to the 8½ × 11 inch size.

COMPOSING, COLLATING, AND BINDING MACHINES

Office composing machines are widely used for preparing masters for written material using different type sizes, styles, headings, and the like. These machines bring the versatility of a well-equipped printing shop into the office and are used to prepare type of all sorts for reports, bulletins, booklets, catalogs, price lists, and house organs, where variety in composition is desired.

Figure 7–19 shows an office composing machine. It resembles a typewriter in both appearance and operation. Each type face is on a removable disk which can be quickly inserted into or removed from the machine. Each disk is complete with capital and lower-case letters, numerals, and symbols. Over 600 different sizes and styles of type, ranging from 5½-point newspaper style to 14-point Heavy Gothic type, and including boldface headings and italics, are available. Even margins on both the left and the right, similar to those of regular typeset composi-

FIGURE 7–19
An Office Composing Machine

Courtesy: Addressograph-Multigraph Corp., Cleveland.

Changes from one type to another are accomplished quickly by means of fonts which are inserted into the machine in a few seconds.

tion, are obtained by typing each line twice. To illustrate: line 1 of the copy is typed in the regular manner on the left half of the piece of paper. Then, it is retyped on the right. The machine spaces the second typing so that both margins are even. The procedure is repeated for each line. When completed, the typed material on the right half of the paper constitutes the finished or master copy.

Collating is the assembling of several different sheets of paper to form a report or booklet. To justify a collating machine a rule of thumb is that if 15 work-hours a week are spent on collating by hand, the same work can be done with a collating machine in less than three hours and should be used. Designs vary, but either pigeon holes or stationary and expanding racks are employed. There are also manually operated units where by depressing a foot pedal, one sheet slides off each stack of papers arranged in a double vertical row of pigeon holes. The papers are grasped and gathered together manually.

In many cases, the material is held together by a binding, of which there are many different types. There is side wire stitching, i.e., on the side, and also saddle wire stitching, i.e., through the fold at the back of the booklet. Usually, the latter is preferred, since it enables the sheets to remain flat and open once they are placed in that position. Mechanical fasteners are used extensively, including ring or loose-leaf binders, prong fasteners, or screw-post fasterners. Also the use of wire and of plastic binding machines has won widespread favor. Wire binding is spun or coiled onto the packet of punched paper; plastic binding is fastened onto the paper via punched holes by means of a clasping action. Performed in the office, binding has become more extensive because the machine is inexpensive and simple to operate, and a wide variety of different stock including cards, papers, and charts, such as found with program documentation or different-size papers, photographs, and samples. The binding of paper printouts of computers is being followed by more and more offices.

QUESTIONS

1. Explain Figure 7–1 in your own words.
2. Discuss several advantages in employing a selection committee to study and recommend which office machine to obtain.
3. Discuss the considerations of "cost-machine characteristics" in office machine selection.
4. Identify clearly each of the following:
    a. Cost advantage point.
    b. Direct process of copying.
    c. A tabulator of punched card machines.
    d. Collating of papers.
5. What is a minicomputer and justify its use in a "piece-meal approach" to office automation and its use as a terminal unit in a central computer system.
6. What is a Source Record Punch and how is it used in modern information management?
7. Discuss the advantages of renting office machines rather than buying them. Do you favor renting or buying? Why?
8. Assume an office manager is considering the purchase of an office machine costing $1600 for use by an employee receiving $7000 a year. Explain how Figure 7–2 might assist the office manager to reach a decision regarding the purchase of the calculating machine.
9. What are marginal notched-card machines and for what purposes, in general, are notched cards used?
10. You are contemplating the purchase of seven electric typewriters for a centralized stenographic department. Three different manufacturers' makes are being considered. Basing your decision on the following data, which make of machine would you purchase?

| | Electric Typewriter | | |
	A	B	C
Unit cost	$625	$550	$595
Done business with manufacturer in past.	Yes	No	No
Employees' preference	Third	Second	First
Quality of work done by machine	Satisfactory	Satisfactory	Satisfactory
Aggressiveness and competency of sales representative	Average	Average	Very Satisfactory

Justify your decision.

11. Carefully distinguish between the two entities in each of the following list of pairs:
    a. Key-driven machine and indirect copying process.
    b. A sorter for punched cards and a Vari-Typer.
    c. Marginal notched cards and punched cards.
    d. A listing machine and a gang punch.
12. What arrangement do you favor to provide for the proper maintenance of a new accounting machine in a small office employing nine people? Justify your answer.

CASE PROBLEMS

Case 7–1. DuVall Trucking Company

Starting in 1956, Harry DuVall had three trucks and over the following years through competent management and timely acquisitions, the business has grown tremendously. Today nearly 100 employees, 80 trailers, and 71 power equipment units including line tractors and pickup trucks, and four truck terminals in four different cities are included in the DuVall Trucking Company. Mr. DuVall believes strongly that timely information is a tool that employees must have to work effectively and to contribute to and be a part of the company's success.

A number of papers and records are prepared and used. For example, a daily average of 650 invoices must be prepared and mailed, an accounts receivables listing, payments made, customer's check numbers, and balance due are also prepared and considered important to the company's operation and existence. Further, daily sales reports are prepared showing the individual shippers, consignees, weights, and revenues. Weekly and monthly summaries are prepared from these daily reports.

Each of the four truck terminals prepare their own freight bills for the previous day and forward them to the company's main office by company trucks. Arrival is mandatory by 10 A.M. These data are processed beginning at 10 A.M. sharp and by 1 P.M. the latest revenue report is ready for Mr. DuVall. As a by-product, the freight bill register is prepared. It shows the shipper, consignee, terms of payment, to or from a connecting interline, and amount due any interline. Additional paperwork includes in- and out-bound summaries for each terminal, local cartage revenues by days, and cumulative for the month, quantity of shipments, dollar revenue, and per-ton mile revenue and cost.

Over the past years the company has followed a number of different ways to handle its paperwork. At its beginning, hand-posting was followed, but progress of the company forced a search for supplementary means. A used accounting machine was added, but after several years it became bogged down due to the volume of work. Then too, the company experienced difficulty in keeping an operator for the machine. And when there wasn't any operator for a day or two caused by sickness or a quit, the entire flow of paperwork backed up, causing costly delays and confusion in the office. Next, a card system was brought in, but it proved to be too cumbersome. Furthermore, a few cards would get lost and serious inconveniences were experienced. Three years ago, Mr. DuVall decided to engage the Thrifty Overload Service Bureau, to perform some of the paperwork on its (Bureau) premises. While the service is satisfactory if not excellent, Mr. DuVall doesn't like certain papers about his business being sent out. He greatly prefers to keep them within his own office.

In the opinion of Mr. DuVall the next logical step is to acquire some office machine or machines to handle his office work. He asks you to recommend what he should do. He tells you that he expects the company to keep growing although not at the same rate as during the past. Also he feels it important to emphasize that service is the important concept in his business. "Ours is really a service business. Ideally we'd like to deliver the day after we pick up the merchandise. And we want to know where we stand—I'd say we want to know this every day. Because when we have current information we can make better decisions."

Questions:

1. In general do you feel Mr. DuVall is correct in his evaluation of information needs of his company? Discuss.
2. Based on the limited data available, what machine or machines do you believe probably most worthy of Mr. DuVall's consideration?
3. What recommendation would you give Mr. DuVall? Justify your answer.

Case 7–2.   The Underhill Company

A current problem in the office of the Underhill Company is keeping notes receivable accounts up to date. The majority of these notes are monthly, although some are weekly. Currently, a general ledger and a supplementary ledger in the form of a visible card index are used. When a payment is received, a receipt, in duplicate, is made out; the original is sent to the customer, and the copy is retained by the company for its records. From this copy, payments are posted to the customer or account card, all of which make up the visible card file. When posting, the balances due, discounts earned, and total paid to date are calculated and entered upon the card. Because of the volume and urgency of other work, the posting to the cards is performed about every sixth day and to the general ledger about every three weeks.

Under the present arrangement, it is difficult to be aware of all delinquent accounts immediately. Also, from time to time, serious errors have occurred in the posting of the information to the cards and to the general ledger. Finding such mistakes is a problem in itself, but more serious is rectifying the error with the customer. In addition, during the past three years, there has been a constant growth in the number of accounts, and there is good reason to believe that this growth will continue.

The office manager is considering several actions that might be taken and is of the opinion that an office machine should be used for this work.

Questions:

1. What are the major actions that the office manager should take?
2. Assuming that you agree with the office manager that a machine should be used, what type of office machine would you recommend? Why?
3. Describe in necessary detail how the work would be handled, utilizing the machine recommended in the answer to question No. 2, above.

Case 7–3.   Garner Company

Purchase of an office machine is being considered for work now performed manually. Either machine "A" or machine "B" will process the work satisfactorily, but the cost of the former is $5,850 installed while that of the latter is $5,100 installed. Labor cost to operate machine A will be $3.25 an hour, supplies, $100 a year, power, $9.50 a month. In contrast, for machine B, the labor cost will be $3.00 an hour, supplies, $125 a year, and power, $9.00 a month. Currently, the labor cost is $3.00 an hour for the one employee required who devotes full time to the work, which can be considered 2,000 hours a year (50 weeks × 40 hours a week). Supplies now cost $287 a year.

It is estimated that to accomplish the work, machine A will be used about 70 percent of a normal work year (2,000 hours) or machine B about 50 percent. Practices followed by the company are to charge 7 percent interest on money invested in an office machine, use 10 percent annual allowance for depreciation, and 12 percent annually for taxes and machine maintenance.

Questions:

1. Calculate the total annual costs for the first year using (1) manual, (2) machine A, or (3) machine B.
2. How long will it take for machine A to pay for itself out of savings? Machine B?
3. What is your recommendation for this company? Justify your viewpoint.

Chapter 8

Computers—Managerial
Considerations

*No more important duty can be urged upon those
who are entering the great theatre of life than
simple loyalty to their best convictions.*

Edwin Chapin

Computers have reached the height where the ways in which they can
be used are almost boundless. We live in a computer age. They prepare
and process all types of data for documents, assist engineers in designing,
control manufacturing operations, aid medical doctors, and guide astro-
nauts in orbit. Without the computer we would not have many of our
current conveniences and advancements.

Why Computer Utilization

The driving force behind all this computer progress is for one purpose.
It is to give humans a means to increase our productivity. Computers
do this in many ways but of special interest here is that computers
supply quickly the information needed to facilitate enterprise operations.
They give the information processed and refined to facilitate decision
making and thus serve as a major adjunct to management. Modern managers need considerable data to help them make effective decisions.
In our current rapid movement of events the manager needs updated
data, insights into tremendous amounts of information which in most
cases can be handled only with the help of the computer.

Secondly, computers encourage careful and intelligent planning, organizing, actuating, and controlling. They are a positive force toward better
management. Computers contribute not only in supplying processed
data, but also in monitoring production activities, solving scientific prob-

lems, and helping derive tentative answers to a multitude of involved conditions.

A third major reason for computer utilization is to reduce office costs. With adequate volume, the speed and versatility of the computer reduces paperwork cost, assuming a comparable "before and after" comparison can be made. However, in many instances innovations, changes in data demands, new quality and time constraints negate a valid "before and after" comparison so that proof positive of a lowering of cost is quite difficult to obtain. It is noteworthy to observe that the computer is viable economically, otherwise managers would not use it. Based on an 80-hour workweek operation, many well-managed computer installations will return a savings of approximately 35 percent on the total investment each year.

The search for competent and adequate help plagues the information manager. Ways of getting out the work with a limited number of people have been eagerly sought, or an arrangement requiring employment of only the more competent employees has won favor. Both these conditions are satisfied by the use of a computer. Normally, the capacity of the computerized arrangement is sufficient or can be modified to increase as the work load increases so that it is necessary to add few, if any, people who are difficult to acquire.

There are also several additional reasons for adopting a computer. One is a reduction of errors. The computer tends to integrate data processing, thus minimizing the handling of data by human beings who usually but certainly do not always commit what mistakes are made. Another reason, sometimes not admitted to but having some significance, is the desire for a status symbol which the computer supplies. As computers become commonplace, this status will fade, but having the latest model computer signifies progress, favorably affects public relations, and may supply a competitve edge.

The Computer and Management

The basic issues pertaining to data processsing are the reflection of basic issues of management. Computers enhance the functions of management; they do not replace these functions. The modern computer emphasizes the importance of management. Computers call for better utilization of the managerial mind, better managerial actions, and better managerial accomplishments. Significant improvements in management are possible by use of the computer, but for this to be achieved, managers must know their own requirements to manage effectively, achieve greater clarity of thought, and develop precise plans. It is erroneous to think that depositing a modern computer in the midst of inept management policies, outmoded motivating practices, and an archaic organization will somehow or other cause miracles and tremendous accomplishments to take place.

Properly used, computers increase the power and influence of the human mind, not minimize its importance. Human capabilities are enlarged. Computers provide help never before believed possible or even conceived. Instead of being overburdened with the processing of data, the human mind can be relieved of such mental drudgery and concentrate its efforts and attention to create, to plan, to ponder and reflect about information, and to decide what should be done and whom to inspire. Managerial judgment, insight, coverage, and values are still paramount. Computers should stimulate managers to think, to create, to perform these vital activities which human intelligence can provide.

Computers increase the responsibility of managers. With the assistance given by computers, the human mind can soar to new heights of accomplishment and acquire knowledge and judgment not yet imagined. The computer can show the way to greater progress, but the accomplishment of hoped-for outputs and gains are regulated by the person issuing the instructions to the computer or figuring out how the computer can be utilized to do a job. The potential lies with the manager, not with the computer. In essence, computers are tools to be exploited by managers. The challenge is not to be satisfied with the processing of data as such, but to initiate new and revolutionary applications and concepts which are made possible by the use of computers. This necessitates management thinking of the highest order.

The Computer and the Functions of Management

Let us now look at the computer's effect upon the functions of management and observe briefly in what ways the manager can benefit by the opportunities made available by the computer. We start with:

1. Planning. The computer changes ways of doing things and it has considerable impact upon planning activities. More important is that the scope of planning can be broadened by the use of a computer. More activities can be included, the parameters can be pushed back, and a far more inclusive picture of what makes up the totality of the information work can be included. The entire enterprise is being viewed more and more as a responsive body instead of many clusters of individuals and, to some extent, isolated activities and departments. Further, the influence and the contribution of entities outside the enterprise can be taken into account in the information planning effort. Actually there should be few, if any, restricted areas in the initial development stages of planning when computers are employed. Compromises can always be made later, but beginning with circumscribed areas inevitably means ending with restricted areas. Seldom can the best results be achieved by confining it to predetermined limits of activities or to certain organizational limits. Computer work commonly cuts across conventional lines originally established for nonautomated purposes.

Computers commonly bring about modifications in objectives and adjustments in a number of policies. Computers can open the door to improved management and service opportunities, but to gain them it is necessary and desirable to adjust, delete, and add planning efforts so that these benefits can be won. Commonly more information is obtained on such items as sales, costs, collections, cash flow, and production runs to provide helpful trends or comparisons with current data. Also, greater availability of planning data to and from the lower levels of management is practiced.

The planning should also include the type of decisions for which the computer will be used. It is not only unnecessary, but also unwise to have the computer participate in all decision making. To violate this guide results in a simple decision expanded all out of proportion to its importance. The manager becomes more confused and frustrated. Computers are to assist managers in making better *big* decisions. In addition, periodic reviews of planning and of the computer's contribution to it help uncover hidden opportunities for improvement. The worth of the planning is limited only by the innovation, desire, and effort of the management planner and the computer personnel working together closely and continuously.

2. *Organizing.* For genuine success, the various accomplishments of a computer must be integrated with the operational activities of the company. It is essential that those working directly with the computer have a clear understanding of their relationships with members in other units of the company and that the authority of the computer personnel be clearly defined.

Initially the computer was usually located in the finance department where it is still located in many business organizations. However, as new computer applications have developed, especially in research and in production, there has been some movement toward having the computer occupy a separate organizational unit with the manager in charge reporting directly to the president. More recently with the great growth in the number of minicomputers, there is indication that each organizational and suborganizational unit might well have its own local computer facility, perhaps tied in with the large central computer. This brings up a vital organizational question of whether to have (1) a single large installation to serve the office needs of the various operating units of a big enterprise or (2) a number of smaller facilities, each designed and located to serve the needs of one or several of the company's various operating units. To resolve this issue necessitates consideration for many factors, including the physical size of the enterprise, the total volume of work, the uniformity of work, the top management preference, and the investment required for the machines and equipment.

From the organizational viewpoint, there is also the task of determining clearly the authority and responsibility assigned to those in charge of the computer. Likewise, each subgroup of the computer unit needs to know the particular duties that it is expected to carry out and how it is to work with groups outside the computer unit. It frequently happens that the technician isn't familiar with the manager's needs and, in turn, the manager doesn't understand the technician and is suspicious of the computer because of its far-reaching and revolutionary potential. These divergent viewpoints can be brought together or at least minimized to an appreciable degree. Give the manager basic facts concerning computers and their operation and, likewise, the technician should acquire knowledge of the enterprise and its management. In a sense this is a plea for empathy and, once accomplished, will assist amazingly in acquiring better manager-technician relationships.

3. Actuating. With all the glamour associated with the new computer developments, it is easy to forget that people are still vital to information management and will continue to be so. It requires people to operate and maintain computers, and it requires people to interpret and utilize the information made available to them. Like any other means, the computer means is dependent upon the good will, understanding, and cooperation of the employees. To ignore the personnel considerations is certain to invite disaster.

When a computer system is first introduced, there is the problem of personnel displacement. To cope with this difficulty, it is generally advisable to (1) tell the office automation story as it is developed, so that all employees will know what is going on, (2) terminate the employment of no employee because of the computer—normal attrition commonly takes care of any excess, (3) reduce the salary of no employee because of the computer, and (4) change job content with reassignment and provide retraining. Employees to be affected by the change should be encouraged to participate in designing the change in its beginning stages. Not only are excellent suggestions offered, but by this practice a needed sense of belonging and importance is enjoyed by the employee. High employee participation usually means high employee cooperation.

4. Controlling. Computer utilization is commonly of a multiproject nature, and this fact emphasizes the importance of establishing effective progress-reporting techniques and carefully monitoring them in order to maintain proper control over each project. It is best to keep the reporting simple, yet comprehensive, and to make it easy for either the technical or the nontechnical employee to understand. Keep the emphasis clear, concise, and up-to-date so that the reports reveal how each project is progressing and to what extent established goals are being obtained.

Job completion dates must be realistic and adhered to, otherwise, control efforts become dissipated. Failure to use realistic standards or adequate lead time, or recognize unexpected contingencies represent common causes of establishing controlling goals that cannot be fulfilled. The delay of one project aggravates the entire program because work scheduling, especially in the case of a computer, closely interrelates all projects within the system.

Generally speaking a computer tends to increase relatively the machine cost and decrease the labor cost. In turn, the greater machine expenditure spotlights attention upon questions of depreciation; scheduling and maintaining even work flows, and keeping the mechanical units in top working condition; utilization of records; and format of reports. Commonly a large computer must be operated more than the regular working hours of the office because of the computer's cost factors.

Feasibility of Computer Usage

It is customary to conduct a feasibility study to determine if computer usage is desirable or if a change in present usage should be made. Two major aspects of data processing are involved: (1) the makeup of the paperwork itself, and (2) the processing of the data as such. The first was discussed under planning what office work is to be done, Chapters 2–6 inclusive. It includes the information design of the entire cycle but not to a detailed degree. The second point, processing of the data, includes the selection and actual operation of the machines and computer. Again, it warrants repeating that these two aspects of automation feasibility—the what and how of office work—are interrelated. The experts in each area should work together as a team, with each aware of the other's problems.

What is included in a thorough and sound feasibility study? A number of considerations, including the objectives of the enterprise and the contributions expected of each functional area or organizational unit to the achievement of these objectives. The decision-making activity vested in each management member is clearly stated so that the information needs of each member can be identified. Familiarity with the organization structure assists in answering who officially decides what, who is expected to inform whom, and what information is needed. Generally, it is also helpful to know the relative importance of the various basic functions of the enterprise—manufacturing, marketing, financing, engineering, and personnel—in order to obtain some impression of the probable characteristics of the data to be handled. Also, any future increased work loads and contemplated changes should be taken into account, as well as the existing means of performing the work, no matter how primitive, because such facts can have an important bearing upon the recommendations.

The question to be answered is not whether a computer can be used. It can; the computer is a reality. The issue is: will the resultant costs, time in process, flexibility of usage, and ability to meet future requirements be to the enterprise's best interests and in keeping with the management members' needs and desires? Discretion in emphasing the features of any particular type of computer is suggested; too much attention directed on such things as machine capacities, engineering features, speeds, and peak loads may cloud the essential considerations and purposes which are to process the proper data in order to help somebody do a job better because of the processed data supplied. Discussing too many technical details is chaotic; the average laypeople want to know what the computer will do for them rather than how it does it. Some people must know all the details, but most people who are involved in the "computer age" are neither technicians nor do they want to be. Of course, some technical data are essential and should be provided. But too much regard for how the data are processed can result in too little regard for what kinds of data are being provided. The data processing becomes an end in itself rather than a means to an end.

Social Aspects of Computers

Modern information management encompasses not only economic concepts, but social aspects as well. The computer does have social implications especially in the area of job requirements, individual employee skill, and employment. Without doubt, many irksome, monotonous office tasks are eliminated by the computer system which is performing the laborious and time-consuming office work. Socially, this is desirable and a benefit to workers. Many feel we have entered what might be described as a second Industrial Revolution, which is substituting machines for human beings in performing mental drudgery, just as the first Industrial Revolution substituted machines for carrying out most backbreaking physical drudgery.

Opinions differ with respect to the changes in skill requirements as a result of computer usage. For many new office jobs created by the computer, the skill requirements have increased, yet many relatively low skill jobs remain. Certainly training and the need for proficiency in specific skills are emphasized by information automation. Both the person with no skill and the senior employee, whose total experience consists of performing work requiring little judgment, are hard put to find employment. They are the two classes presenting the majority of troublesome dislocation difficulties.

From the broad sociological viewpoint, change stimulated by computers emphasizes employment modifications which can be viewed as offering either (1) greater opportunities or (2) fewer opportunities. The former stresses the view, "What will computers systems help us do better, or assist us to achieve what has never been achieved?" There are managerial problems, however, in adapting to this greater opportunity. Over a period, much human effort will shift from manual to mental work and from menial to more challenging tasks. Office automation puts at our disposal the means to a materially more abundant life. The belief of fewer work opportunities being available because of office automation highlights a dominant force of fear. It appears to lack long-term justification. Past experience indicates that technological advancements have increased the overall level of employment. New demands have developed, the machines themselves creating a large labor force required for their construction and maintenance. Employees are *displaced*, but not necessarily *replaced*. Examples are available where computers did not cause one person to lose a job; some were transferred, some were retrained, and some were placed in new work. This calls for real managerial ability and, of course, necessitates adjustments on the part of each employee.

ADDITIONAL MANAGERIAL SUGGESTIONS AND CONSIDERATIONS

Many problems of computers must be solved in managers' offices rather than in the laboratories of the designing engineers. Certain general practices by managers usually aid in solving managerial problems relating to computers. Among these practices are:

1. View the computer as a data-processing system, not as a single machine. See it as a means for supplying information to an enterprise, not as a replacement for a single or particular office machine.
2. Learn as much as possible about the various uses of computers. This knowledge will broaden your viewpoint and assist in maximizing utilization of the computer.
3. Have top managers or a top group decide what work should be done with a computer. Do not permit one involved department head to make this decision.
4. Never consider a computer the cure-all for all current information ills. A computer assists in attaining improvements, but employees must improve the system. The computer does what it is told to do.
5. In planning for computer usage, take into consideration the probable needs for the future five to ten years.
6. Always relate computer capability to the specific requirements of the installation being considered. Capacities and special types of

work performed which are not needed by the computer system at hand are superfluous.

7.   With sufficient training, use present personnel for computer operation, as they usually operate a computer very satisfactorily.

8.   Work closely with the computer manufacturer who is anxious to assist and meet every reasonable request.

Converting to a computer system or from a present to a new one can represent a Herculean task and too often is brushed off as a minor consideration. Much work is involved and it is not uncommon to require eight to ten months or more. Conversion difficulties include inaccuracy and lack of uniformity in existing records, missing papers, unexpected deviations of records from a supposed format, errors in reading or in putting information into a computer medium, the maintenance of an adequate work force to accomplish the conversion work, and the accomplishment of the work within reasonable budget limitations.

The conversion process includes what is known as "application in parallel." This means the practice of continuing both the old processing of information and the new way, then comparing the results in order to check the accuracy of the new way. Normally, the work is run in parallel for several complete cycles, or until the new process is completely "debugged." This can be a very frustrating period. Consistent results are obtained; and then, without warning, inconsistencies occur. Finding and correcting the sources of errors frequently pose major tasks.

Computers require nonvarying, disturbance-free electrical power and office space that is regulated as to temperature, dust, and humidity. The layout of the office may have to be changed to place the heavy machine where ample structural support is provided and the flow of information work can most efficiently be handled. Channels under the floor in which to run electrical cables connecting the various units sometimes pose a technical problem, especially when a controlling factor is the maximum lengths of cable specified by the computer manufacturer.

To the newcomer, computers have given rise to its own jargon, comprising a strange terminology unlike anything previously encountered. Words like bit, binary number, access time, real-time, buffer, program, and storage take on special meanings quite different from those previously associated with them.[1] Furthermore, there is some variation and confusion about the meaning of certain basic words. Hence, the same word doesn't always have the same meaning. Obviously, this state of affairs makes for common difficulties and complicates communication among computer and noncomputer personnel.

Computers are arbitrarily classified and a number of more or less common categories exist. In some instances certain design features, special engineering attachments or capacity serve to offer needed distinction.

---

[1] A glossary of computer terms is included in Chapter 9, pp. 238–39.

However, size of the computer, mainly influenced by price, is followed. The designation of large, medium, small, and mini are common and while what size computer is meant by each of these terms is not precise, these designations are widely followed. The classification, large, generally includes computer systems renting for over $30,000 monthly, and with top speeds, almost unlimited memory, special features, and pheripheral equipment. The second group, medium, constitutes those with rental costs averaging between $5,000–$10,000 monthly. They make up the popular computer systems, widely used and perhaps best known of all computers. Most in this group have sophisticated mass memory units and effective input and output devices. The next group, small, represent machines renting for around $1,000–$2,000 per month. These have relatively limited capacity but perform satisfactorily within their limits. The last, or minicomputer, discussed in Chapter 7 represents a relatively small computer of quite limited capability. The minis are growing in use and represent a sizeable segment of the total computer field.

Computer Generations

Let us now direct our attention to a select list of current computer developments. Greater and greater speed, access, and convenience characterize the latest computer models. Already the computer has passed through three technological revolutions, sometimes called "generations." These include: (1) vacuum tubes, 1950–1961, in which speeds were measured in milliseconds (1/1,000 sec.), (2) transistors, 1961–1965, in which speeds were measured in micro-seconds (1/1,000,000 sec.), and (3) integrated circuitry, 1965—, in which speeds are measured in nanoseconds (1/1,000,000,000 sec.). The "fourth generation" is being penetrated and exotic possibilities by using laser beams and other highly advanced scientific discoveries are coming upon us.

We have witnessed a great proliferation of electronic data-processing units. Figure 8–1 illustrates some of the units in varying combinations that are presently included to meet the user's needs. This computer system has "virtual storage" which has accelerated expansion of on-line applications as well as complementing the main memory storage with buffered storage. Ready expansion of the system through the addition of modules of real storage is possible. Further, the overlapping of instruction fetching and execution further enhances performance. In addition, direct access as well as dynamic address translation permit dynamic utilization of the data stored.

Remote Time-Sharing Computer System

Many large computer installations today are communication or data networks consisting of a central computer, referred to as the "main-

FIGURE 8–1
The IBM System/370 Model 168 Offers the Attractive Features of Enormous Storage Giving Unprecedented Flexibility in the Design of Applications, High Input/Output Capability, Metal-Oxide Semiconductor (MOS), Dynamic Address Translation (DAT), and Direct Access

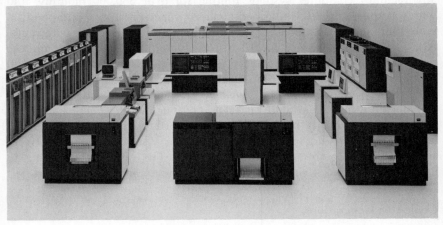

Courtesy: International Business Machines Corp., White Plains, N.Y.

frame," with terminal units such as cathode-ray tube data display units (CRT), input/output terminal units, Teletype terminal, and graphic (chart plotting) data terminal units. See Figure 8–2. In effect the influence of the central computer is spread out to many different kinds of terminal units located in different areas, and supplying or receiving information necessary for the data processing efforts. The time of the

FIGURE 8–2
Various Terminal Units Connected to a Time-Sharing Central Computer (mainframe)

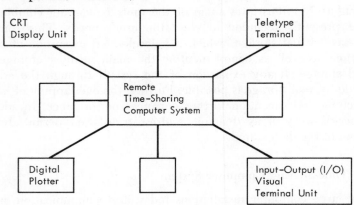

computer is shared, hence, time-sharing means sharing the operation of the computer system so that several users can make use of it. This makes for effective use of the computer. Actually the users queue or wait in line to use the computer, but the computer's operations are so fast that each user has the impression that the computer is solely for that user. The maximum convenience of this on-line arrangement is to have the users remotely located, i.e., not all in one geographic area. This means providing a communication link such as a telephone line between the computer and a device which permits the user to be connected to the computer. It further means that the mainframe is remote, hence the term remote in the name, remote time-sharing computer system. When connected "live," the user has the means to carry out information tasks with the computer in a conversational mode. That is, the user and the computer can react to the inquiries and responses by each other. We will say more about communication links and terminal devices in the following pages.

Technical improvements in the hardware now permit the overlapping of input and output and of the processing activities. Results: a great lessening of computer idle time and fuller utilization of its components. Common now is "multiprogramming," a practice whereby programs are segmented and each portion executed before any complete program is finished. In other words, a program segment need not be finished before another is started. Along with multiprogramming has come "multiprocessing" which refers to the processor and is the use of two or more processors in a complete system having a common jointly addressable memory unit. Further, to make time-sharing practical, the modern computer system allocates small time increments on a rotating or sharing basis to users. To do this a computer timer, or hardware feature, is incorporated in the system. Most common practice is to follow a first-come, first-serve basis or some predetermined priority levels.

Paging, memory protection, and dynamic relocatability should also be mentioned. By paging is meant the segmenting of each user's program into pages, or small portions. These pages are stored in a high-speed secondary storage device. When scheduled for processing, the appropriate page is brought from the secondary to the main memory of the computer. This transferring of pages may require considerable time, and significant improvements in having the required data available to the processor are being gained. It is essential that pages transferred be deposited in the correct location of the main memory. To insure this, the memory protection features of the computer are utilized. Further, the meaning of dynamic relocatability is the capacity to put a page into any vacant location in the main memory, thus eliminating the need for always returning each page to its initial location in the main memory. Again flexibility and speed of the system are featured.

Communication Links

Data communication is technically achieved electronically by employing either wire, cable, or microwave channels which are high frequency radio waves. These media have dimensions or physical properties that control the quantity of communication that can be handled per a unit of time. Important among these physical properties are bandwidth of the electronic channel, transportation loss—a kind of friction, and the amount of force or push conveying the data transmitted.

Communication facilities can be leased for exclusive use, leased for the time used only, or purchased. Leasing involves agreements with existing common carriers such as American Telephone and Telegraph Company and Western Union Telegraph Company. Leasing for exclusive use provides a private communication system. If full use is not made of it, the cost is prohibitive and the better arrangement is to lease on an as-used basis. Under a lease arrangement, certain technical limitations to the transmission quantity transmittable may be present, but usually they are not serious. Finally, a user may purchase a system. This entails a large first cost for installation and continuous maintenance costs, hence, it is practical for very large users only. Since 1965, private parties may apply and receive exclusive use of radio frequencies in the microwave range, a condition widening the alternatives available to a private communication user.

Outstanding improvements have been won in the communication of data. Increased capacity and bandwidths are now being used. Transmission speed in excess of 1.5 million bits per second are specified, and there are developments being used on the threshold of wide application that are unbelievable. Employing space satellites, for example, and lasers in connection with the quantum aspects of light energy are illustrative of progress in the communication field.

Data-Phone

Both the transmitting and the receiving of computer coded data are handled by means of regular or private telephone lines. What makes this possible is Data-Phone which accepts data signals from the computer or other data machines in either punched card, perforated tape, or magnetic tape medium; converts these data into proper tones for telephone transmission; and converts tones to data signals for use by the computer or other machine at the receiving station. There are no intermediate steps.

To utilize the Data-Phone, a user picks up the telephone and dials the service number of the particular receiver wanted. An answer or a dial tone signals connection whether or not computer is ready to receive or read information. If ready, an identification card is inserted into the device attached to the telephone, or the required vocal identification is supplied, thus confirming the user's right to transmit. Then the data in the language of the computer—punched cards, perforated tape, or magnetic tape—are fed into the device; and these data are transmitted at speeds of over 3,000 words a minute directly into the computer. Machines talk to one another, cross-town or cross-country. Payment for each Data-Phone call is made similar to that of an ordinary telephone call.

TERMINAL DEVICES

As already stated, devices connected to the computer by means of communication lines are known as terminal devices. A wide range of new devices is now available. Which device to use depends upon the characteristics of the work to be done with it. For example, small quantities of data sent frequently may suggest a different device from that where large quantities are sent infrequently. The operator's skill and whether a printed copy is needed are further considerations.

In other words, because of developments in terminals, computer systems are now in the unique position to give users meaningful information at the very moment when the information is wanted. The computer maintains a complete master file that can be drawn from by many persons, for many purposes. Information can be pulled out again and again, as required, and it can also be reprocessed in keeping with the requirements for specific uses.

Terminal devices serve as either input or output (or both) devices to the computer. Common input devices, in addition to those shown in Figure 8–2, include Touch-Tone telephones, tape devices, magnetic ink readers, and optical character readers (ORC), all remotely located from the computer. Various types of documents can be handled; the input data may be financial information, time cards, production or sales data, and cash register tapes. Finger-driven or keyboard-oriented devices are still quite popular, yet their input speeds are directly related to the operator's speed which is far below the capacity of the computer.

In contrast, output terminal devices are highly dependent upon the computer characteristics, especially its speed. The availability of a wide variety of output terminals offers much freedom of choice. Popular are the Touch-Tone telephone, line printers, CRT devices of various types, typewriter-like units, TV-screen units, and audio-response or "answerback" devices. There is an output terminal available to meet almost any information need.

Figure 8–3 shows a visual terminal input-output unit. As the data are typed for input, a proof-copy appears on the screen. This is checked

FIGURE 8–3
An Information Display Unit

Courtesy: International Business Machines Corp., White Plains, N.Y.

The Selector Light Pen and program function keys help simplify operator communications. Errors caused by typing can be eliminated and the function keys employed for rapid entry of operator commands.

for accuracy and, if error free, the material is released to the computer by simply pressing a push button. Likewise, for output, the information is flashed on the screen where the operator can read it. If a hard or permanent copy is desired, the device will supply it within seconds.

The Teletype terminal is widely used. One model permits taped information to be transmitted to various terminals at speeds up to five lines per second with a full upper and lower case alphabet. Figure 8–4 shows models of this modern machine which are specifically designed to meet the growing need to interface more rapidly and intimately with process devices or computers. The unit with the screen permits easy checking and correcting. Information typed out on the keyboard appears on the scope and is edited. When a letter, word, or line is erased, the terminal closes the gap automatically.

FIGURE 8–4
The Modern Teletype Machine Gives Comprehensive, Efficient, and
Accurate Data Interchange

Courtesy: Teletype Corp., Skokie, Ill.

The terminal shown on the left is an automatic send-receive terminal. The
unit on the right features a TV-type screen and use of the telephone network.

There are also low-cost, compact input and inquiry display units
which give flexibility to on-line systems design. They permit storing
of data from a computer network and sharing the information on any
of many units employing a $3\frac{1}{2} \times 9\frac{1}{2}$ inch screen or panel. The compact
size and simplicity of operation facilitates installation virtually anywhere.
Among the broad range of applications are finance institutions, hospitals,
hotels and motels, order and customer service departments—where
faster, more convenient, and more personalized service to customers
can be supplied. Figure 8–5 shows the unit in use.

The "answer-back" device has reached the stage where it is no longer
a curiosity. True conversation with the computer is a reality and utilized
where it is believed to be superior for a particular application. To illustrate, a large department store in Chicago now utilizes a computer-
directed credit authorization system that gives a verbal reply to a salesperson's inquiry in less than 30 seconds. All sales-floor telephones in
12 different stores are hooked to the central computer which can handle
10,000 credit approvals daily. However, the computer's capacity is so
large that credit applications use less than 5 percent of its time. Hence,
the computer is used to prepare over 6 million customer statements
a year, write reminder notices to customers, print sales promotion material, and identify probable bad debt accounts. In another example, an
employee in a branch factory in Colorado can obtain information about
inventory from the company's computer in Cincinnati by dialing a telephone number. Seconds later the employee hears a verbal reply to an
inquiry.

FIGURE 8–5
**Terminal Display Unit Which May Communicate with a Central Computer
System over Telephone Lines or It May Be Directly Connected to the
Computer System**

Courtesy: Burroughs Corp., Detroit.

Portable terminals, about the size of a small attache case, enable
an individual to get information by asking questions of the computer
by simply plugging it in the telephone line. Being portable, it can be
carried by salespeople who can obtain needed information directly from
their home office. The possibilities of this portable terminal unit certainly
stimulates the imagination as to possible future changes in our present
mode of doing things.

Another interesting type of terminal unit is the digital plotter. We
know that in a single day a computer can produce thousands of pages
of printed output. But it is also feasible to produce the data in a chart
or graphic form—automatically. This is accomplished by means of a
CALCOMP digital plotter. In some cases, particularly for the larger
computer, the signal instructions are recieved by a medium for subsequent use by the plotter off-line. In other cases, direct coupling can
be followed with a special adapter used to connect the computer output
to a form suitable for driving the plotter. The hookups are shown in

FIGURE 8–6

Hookups and Machines to Obtain Computer Output Data in Graphic Form

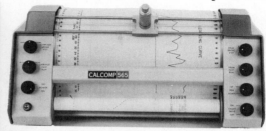

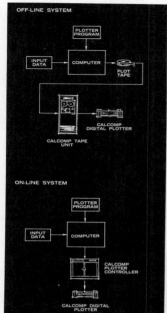

Courtesy: California Computer Products, Inc. Anaheim, Calif.

the left portion of Figure 8–6. In the right bottom portion of this figure is a time-sharing remote plotter working in conjunction with a teletypewriter for two-way communication with a distant computer. The view in the right upper position is a close-up of the plotter. Data for preparation of a learning curve are being plotted. This is a drum-type plotter. The completed chart is removed in a manner similar to that of taking a piece of paper from a roll of wrapping paper. There are also plotters in which fan-fold paper is stored flat in the unit with the plotter moving over this flat horizontal area.

Significant applications include emergency drawings, isometric-piping drawings, economic charting and analysis, critical path drawings, and ray tracing. The list of applications is constantly expanding. It is not necessary to spend long and tedious hours manually plotting data into graphic form. Figure 8–7 illustrates a geologic chart produced automatically by CALCOMP plotter from computer data.

The plotter can also be connected to a cathode ray display terminal, thus expanding the utility of the terminal in scientific application and also making it possible to produce a hard copy of any image on the

FIGURE 8–7
Example of Chart Drawn Automatically from Data in a Computer

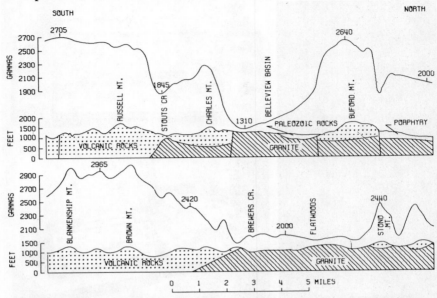

STRUCTURE AND LITHOLOGY FROM AEROMAGNETIC PROFILES OVER THE ST. FRANCOIS MOUNTAINS
Courtesy: California Computer Products, Inc., Anaheim, Calif.

display screen. A button is pressed on the keyboard of the display terminal and the chart or diagram is produced by the plotter.

The plotting is produced by movement of a pen relative to the surface of the paper. Each input impulse causes a very minute step on either the X-axis or the Y-axis. A deflection on the X-axis is produced by motion of the drum, on the Y-axis by motion of the pen carriage. Signals raise and lower the pen as required. Each step can be in any one of the 24 basic step combinations or directions made up of its X and Y values, i.e., the basic step direction for a plotted point can be any of 24 directions within the 360-degree quadrant made up of X and Y values of .01 or .005 inches.

Direct-Dial from Terminal to Computer

Efficient management reporting, faster customer service, and better utilization of a computer are possible by use of a machine which integrates an information network. The concept involves the capturing of data at the point of origin for processing by computer and transmitting these data to the computer center via telephone lines. In essence, the arrangement serves as a two-way data transmission between company field locations and its computer center. In addition, any terminal of the system can send to and receive from other terminals, store and retrieve data, double as an automatic typewriter for writing letters and reports, and serve as an extra desk and typewriter station whenever not in use as a terminal.

Figure 8–8 demonstrates an employee typing a sales order. She is

FIGURE 8–8
The Communitype System Features a Removable Tape Cartridge That Has Extensive Storage Capacity (in Desk Drawer) and a Memory Unit (Right on Desk) for Retrieving Fixed Data Such as Programmed Formats Equivalent to Having 1,000 Punched Cards at Your Fingertips

Courtesy: Communitype Corp., New York.

receiving the phoned-in order from a local salesperson or customer. As information is typed it is recorded on a magnetic tape cartridge shown in the open drawer of the desk. Each cartridge has a capacity of 200,000 characters. At the end of the day, the stored data for all the orders that day are transmitted over the telephone lines to the computer center hundreds or thousands of miles away. There the data are ready for instant input without additional conversion steps. The operator has at her command a memory unit for storing and retrieving information frequently used in an order to expedite her typing of the order. This memory unit is at the right end of the desk in the illustration. The system is also capable of receiving data prepared by the computer center.

INFORMATION UTILITY

A so-called "information utility" giving current information on a selected subject area is also available. To illustrate, there is a law research service having an index of law cases in computer memory. For a nominal fee, lawyers can interrogate the computer by means of a convenient terminal device in their own office and receive an immediate reply of relevant cases. Also, a nationwide credit information system is available covering buyers in over 150 population centers of the U.S. Similarly, the information utility concept is being used by several companies joined together to share time of one large computer the use of which none of the companies can afford separately. This means that each member company has a direct line to the computer, and can send, receive, and process its data when it wants to and from terminals located within its building.

These information utilities are made possible by a computer-terminal units network. Computers can be given questions through keyboard sets, drawings on a TV-like screen, or by voice. The answers come back through print, computer media, on a screen, or by voice. A multistation system allows hundreds of stations across the country or even the world to query a centrally located computer from their desk sets and receive instantaneous replies in a preferred form.

Automated Card Control Terminals

In this age of information automation, we are seeing more and more applications of input from cards conveying data on credit, security, time payment, reorder, production control data, and so forth. This input data must be compared with information stored in a computer for the requested action to take place, that is, grant the credit or ship the merchandise.

Consider the example of accounts receivable. The sales slip is entered on the cash register for store accounting, and customer's credit card and clerk's card are inserted in a Decitron Communication Systems Terminal. See Figure 8–9. The dollar amount and the type of transaction are keyed in the terminal unit machine and the transmit button is

FIGURE 8–9

Diagram of Steps Taken to Verify and Record Instantaneously an Accounts Receivable Transaction and Machine Used for This Purpose

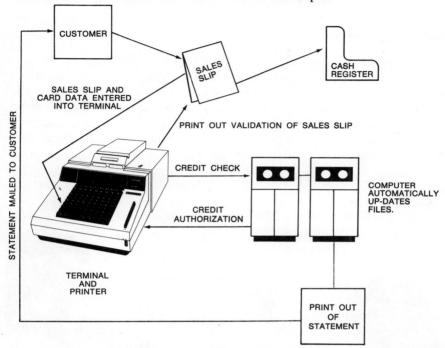

Courtesy: Decitron Communication Systems, Inc., Brooklyn.

pushed. The computer checks credit. If OK, the transaction is recorded and stored in computer for billing. Later the computer prepares the customer's statement.

Point of Sale (POS)

Data collection and dissemination of the retail industry for effective management is included in the Point of Sale (POS) system which brings computer power to the store. Being modular the system can be implemented in numerous ways. For example, any or all of the following activities can be included: receiving, checking, ticketing, and marking; credit authorization; inventory management data entry; managerial data such as stock-turns, markup, and average gross margin, and point of sale data.

FIGURE 8–10
The IBM 3653 Point of Sale (POS) Terminal

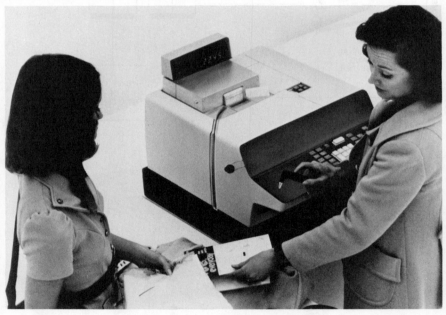

Courtesy: International Business Machines Corp., White Plains, N.Y.

Figure 8–10 illustrates a point of sale terminal which has logic and memory capability. Information on purchases are collected automatically with the optical wand reader shown on the left of the unit. By sweeping over the item, data on the price, merchandise classification and the like are picked up and transmitted to a programmable unit that links the POS transactions, receiving and marking operations, with the central computer from which reports for the retail manager are prepared. At the time of the information input, price data by type of merchandise is registered in the window of the machine and also a listing of the transactions is made. Display terminal units or stations, remote communication units, ticket units, and printers are among the auxiliary units that can be added depending upon the individual needs. The POS system supplies up-to-date information on the store's activities thus enabling the manager to keep fully informed on store operations and to manage effectively.

There is also an automatic checkout system for food stores. As the checker passes items over a line or slot in the counter, a laser light source reads pertinent information on the item which information is coded in keeping with the food industry's universal product code symbols. This information is then transmitted to the computer which relays electronically the item's name and price to a checkout terminal where it is displayed for the customer, listed on a receipt slip, totaled, and tax and change calculated. The system speeds checking out, shortens waiting lines, supplies current management information, and eliminates errors.

COMPUTER GRAPHICS

The area of computer graphics refers to a user communicating with a computer by means of graphic symbols such as lines and curves. In essence, sketching and drawing are added to the input-output of a computer. A cathode ray tube is used. Drawing directly on the scope face of this tube with an electronic stylus pencil permits communication with the computer in a form of graphic symbols. Further, the computer displays graphic information for interpretation by people. Computer graphics offer substantial reduction for the design process. All design work is tentative—an assumed design is determined, stresses are calculated, and the strength and cost properties are ascertained. If not entirely satisfactory or to improve, if satisfactory, a modified design is assumed and the same calculations are made for it. Finally, the so-called best design is evolved. As yet, we have not developed a practical means for having the computer design directly and with finality because designing is creative and we don't know exactly for what we are looking. However, the computer can greatly assist the human designer in a trial-and-error approach.

Given restraints by the sketches on the scope face, the computer can be helpful in determining how this mechanical arrangement will probably perform. Most of the possible design parameters can be analytically determined, designs formulated and tested, and drawings provided. The designer gains increased analysis capability which is more complete in both scope and detail than previously attainable. Hence, favorable results include improved product quality, elimination of prototype developments, and enormous savings of design time. It is believed, for example, that with success in near future developments of computer graphics, the design time for a new automobile might decrease from two years to five months. The use of hard-copy drawings will be minimized. Needed visual information will be obtained from a display terminal tied to the central computer.

NUMERICAL CONTROL

Numerical Control (NC) is a means of operating a factory machine or machines by feeding previously prepared instructions and implementations, expressed by punched or magnetic cards, punched or magnetic tapes, into a mechanism that directs the production facility. A computer can integrate the entire program, a customary arrangement when a large number of machines or an entire production process is included. On the other hand, if only a few machines are involved, the computer is not essential. NC instructions are detailed and include every step required to operate the machine in order to obtain a machined part exactly according to blueprint specifications. The old concept of the operator's "running" the machine is eliminated. Basically there are two fundamental types of numerical controlling: (1) positioning and (2) contouring. The former deals with getting the tool and the material in the desired relationship, after which the tool is advanced either automatically or manually to perform the required work. The second type, or contouring, requires that the path of the tool be controlled continuously. In fact, this type is commonly referred to as the "continuous-path" method. There is constant synchronization of the movement of the tool in several axes. Among the advantages of NC are (1) more machine utilization time, less machine setup time, and lower lead times; (2) elimination of fixtures and templates used as guides in manual means; (3) less inspection and fewer rejects; and (4) feasibility of machining otherwise "impossible" parts.

COMPUTERIZED MANUFACTURING

A vast amount of information is generated during the manufacturing of a product which is of interest to various managerial groups. Included are data on quality control, inventory levels, locations and quantities of raw material, process control parameters, goods in process, finished goods, materials handling, packaging, and shipping. To place all these activities within a data processing system requires ingenious programming and retrieval abilities. To meet the requirements, a network of compact, versatile, and inexpensive minicomputers are used forming a sort of hierarchial system of computers. This approach is proving highly successful in diverse industries such as automotive carburetor production and the process control of photographic film. The hardware configuration, or the amount and arrangement of the type of electronic units needed depend upon the requirements of the individual application. In many instances, one minicomputer has sufficient capacity to handle the entire

FIGURE 8–11
A Computer System Especially Designed to Handle Remote Job Entry, Shop Management, Inventory Control, Process Control, or Numerical Control Data Management in Computerized Manufacturing

Courtesy: Cincinnati Milacron, Lebanon, Ohio.

system. Figure 8–11 shows the units for a highly successful computer-aided manufacturing application.

THINGS TO COME

Experiences of the present point to possible changes of the future. The computer has had and will have profound impact on our society.

Many of our present ways of performing information are destined to fall by the wayside. More and more of our writing and calculating will be done automatically by machines which will operate from sound. Communicative devices will revolutionize further the distribution of information. Networks of computer communication systems will become commonplace.

To take advantage of current and future information technology, managers must carefully examine their information work with the intent of finding out what processing can be improved by using a computer. Today, we have information power that will not be denied. The organization that does not utilize and develop it simply will be passed by.

To reiterate, computer usage stimulates thinking of information work as a whole, not just of a component of it. The larger concept is emphasized. Office automation is geared to volume. It offers numerous benefits, yet difficult decisions are required; deeply entrenched, ineffective and outmoded habits and beliefs must be dispelled. Office automation necessitates high caliber management. And it is well to keep in mind that change is always taking place; the direction and degree of this change in the way information work is accomplished is, and will inevitably be, modified by the computer. The need for more and better information is being accelerated. Properly understood and applied, the computer will assist information managers to employ talents, time, and ideas most effectively in the pursuit of values which are so distinctive and so significant in human progress and betterment.

QUESTIONS

1. Enumerate and discuss briefly the main reasons why computers are used to process business information.
2. What do you believe are and will continue in increasing measure to be the major effects of computer usage upon management planning? Why?
3. What are the major considerations included in an up-to-date feasibility study of office automation for an enterprise? Discuss the one you believe is highly important.
4. Refer to Figure 8–9 and relate how this machine is used in modern information management?
5. Justify the viewpoint that computers increase the responsibility of managers.
6. Are the social aspects of office automation of major concern to the office manager? Elaborate on your answer.
7. Identify each of the following:
   a. Application in parallel.
   b. Data-phone.
   c. Computer generations.
   d. Information utility.

8. Explain Figure 8–6 in your own words relating what a digital plotting system is and the meaning of the diagram at the upper left of this figure.

9. What is your reaction to the following statement: "Eventually and in the not too distant future—possibly by the year 2000, computers will have taken over the work of most managers as we think of managers today. Hence, in the future I envision an important concentration of study known as "Computer Administration." Justify your answer.

10. Describe the meaning of a Point of Sale (POS) system and relate what you believe its future might be.

11. Other than the applications described in this chapter, give examples of computer usage based on your reading or work experience. Discuss.

12. Do you agree with the following statement: "The biggest challenge to successful computer usage is in the technical abilities and capacities to build computers to meet the truly sophisticated requirements of modern information management. Based on the tremendous progress made during the past several decades, it can be stated that we are well on our way toward meeting this challenge quite successfully." Why?

CASE PROBLEMS

Case 8–1.   Hugh Calvin

(*Exchange between Vice President West and Hugh Calvin.*)

WEST: The interchange authorization process is now completed in a few seconds, it formerly required over 30 minutes.

CALVIN: How is that?

WEST: Our new nationwide communication network makes bank charge card use real easy for cardholders, merchants, and member banks. Essentially we have an up-to-date system of data processing that offers both message switching and processing, operating in real time. The member banks are saved many long-distance telephone calls. Also, the cardholders and merchants benefit from little or no delay in completing purchase transactions. We now have uninterrupted 24-hour service, seven days a week.

CALVIN: Do computers do all that?

WEST: Yes, we make inquiry or access the network by means of an on-line computer system using CRT unit (terminal) for inquiry. We actually are using several computers. The System A–72 Computer System performs data collection, concentration, and forwarding. Twice every second they poll the on-line computer and terminals to collect each authorization inquiry or response, and then match the messages. In contrast, the B-5644 computer system logs the time of each authorization inquiry and each response and provides a response-time of 15 seconds for the on-line computer, 25 seconds for the on-line terminals. Actually, these two computer systems operate in tandem.

CALVIN: How many authorization centers do you have?

WEST: Twenty-two right now. Within the next six months, we expect to have 28.

CALVIN: Each center services its immediate surrounding geographic area?

WEST: Yes, you could say that. There are a couple of exceptions, but they are minor.

CALVIN: Let me see if I understand basically how the bank charge card fits into the total picture. Say I make a purchase at store X and present my card for credit. The store takes the card, checks authorization and if O.K., approves the credit sale. X store is paid right away by the bank, usually an amount equal to the purchase price less a small discount. Then the buyer pays the bill figured at the full sales price to the bank upon billing or to the store which remits to the bank. The discount represents the charge for carrying the credit. Is that correct?

WEST: Yes, that is basically how it is handled. There are exceptions and variations, but we don't have to get into them.

CALVIN: What happens when a buyer from center No. 1 holding a bank card issued from that center makes a purchase using his card in area No. 2? Doesn't the buyer get involved in the merchant's dollar "floor limit" and all that?

WEST: No. No. That's the beauty of our system. What you describe is known as an interchange transaction. Formerly, if the purchase exceeded the merchant's "floor limit," the store was required to call, usually by long distance telephone, a local center which, in turn, called the cardholder's center and the two centers exchanged information. Now, this telephoning is unnecessary. All the authorization centers are tied together in a network. We make a charge of 20¢ to handle such a transaction, considerably less cost and time is involved than under the old plan.

CALVIN: How many interchange transaction authorizations do you handle, say, in a month.

WEST: O.K. First, let me distinguish, as we do, between the three types of users of bank cards. Type A users number about 2500 per month. They access directly to the on-line computer system by way of the terminal unit (CRT). This is the type user I was talking about a couple minutes ago. Our Type B user run about 500 to 1000 authorizations per month and hook into the system via a CRT and directly to the System A–72 and B–5644 tandem computer systems.

CALVIN: They don't tie in directly with the on-line system?

WEST: That's right, not directly, but indirectly they can—to the tandems and then to the on-line. Yes.

CALVIN: I see.

WEST: Well, there is also what we term our C users who link their facilities—commonly a telephone, to the CRT unit of the Type A users and it is subsequently handled same as a Type A user.

CALVIN: That's very interesting, Mr. West. Thank you so much.

Questions:

1. Do you favor the use of a bank charge card by consumers? Why?
2. Draw a network sketch showing the relationships of the activities involved when a bank charge card is used.
3. Indicate on one chart the flow of information that takes place when

Type A, B, and C users of bank charge cards are used. Base your answer on the comments of Mr. West.

Case 8–2. Beattie, Edgil, and Thurman, Inc.

The majority of the executive committee members of Beattie, Edgil, and Thurman, Inc., an advertising agency commonly referred to as BET, believe strongly that the agency should acquire a computer. With headquarters in New York City and branch offices in Detroit and Chicago, BET employs 607 people, and its clients number over 75.

Mr. Karl Beck, chairman of the executive committee, reasons that with the amount of paper work they now have, a computer would certainly be advantageous. In his opinion, the number of accounts payable to different TV stations, publishers, and suppliers, as well as the accounts receivable, payroll, cost reports, and research studies presently conducted, make a computer economically feasible. However, several members of the executive committee dissent, pointing out that processing paper work is really not a major problem of the agency and a continuation of "farming out" much of their specialized processing demands, such as research studies, would appear to be the better decision.

After reviewing the various operations in the agency's main office, Alice Noble, representative of a large computer manufacturer, informed Mr. Beck that much of the paper work now being done manually should be automated and that improved systems and procedures should be installed. In her opinion, some of the research work could be put on a computer, but most of this work was special and did not lend itself to computer processing. She offered to make a survey of the agency's work and submit it to Mr. Beck for his consideration. However, Mr. Beck said, he believed such a survey would show the same general conclusion and since the majority of the executive committee agreed, the agency should proceed with the computer acquisition. He added that some agency business demanded his being out of his office a great deal; he was turning the entire project over to Mr. Levinson, the agency's controller.

After several weeks, Mr. Levinson introduced Ms. Noble to the accounts receivable and the accounts payable supervisors, the payroll supervisor, and the assistant director of research and explained her purpose at the agency. To each of these supervisors and their employees a brief letter was given:

This is to advise you that as soon as possible manual handling of work in your unit will be discontinued and a computer will be installed. This move will necessitate some transferring of employees, but rest assured that this will be worked out to the mutual advantage of all concerned.

Signed Harry Levinson
Controller

The accounts receivable supervisor was unfavorable toward the change. She believed it would make the work monotonous and reduce her importance within the company. She spoke with the payroll supervisor, who also was negative about the contemplated change. They are satisfied with processing the work as it is now done.

About five months later, on a Tuesday morning, various units of a computer arrived and were located within the accounts receivable area. On the same morning, the controller held a meeting in his office with two representatives of the computer company and the accounts receivable supervisor at which time each step of the new process was explained. Many questions were asked, and the representatives answered each one of them. The meeting took all morning. After lunch, the controller introduced the representatives to the employees of the accounts receivable department, informed them of the meeting held during the morning, and requested that any questions they might have should be directed to their immediate supervisor, who would either answer the question directly or find out the answer and give it to them. The changeover date was set for three weeks hence; and the names of six employees, with the respective departments to which they were being transferred, were announced.

Two weeks after the changeover date, Mr. Beck, along with Mr. Levinson, visited the accounts receivable department. He spoke with the supervisor, who said: "Well, it is a mess right now. My desk is piled high with work. We're working overtime but not making much headway. We have a manual that appears to give all the details about the operation. It reads O.K., and the representatives are very willing to help in every way possible."

Questions:

1. Evaluate the actions of Mr. Beck.
2. Do you feel that, given a reasonable amount of time, the present difficulties in the accounts receivable department will take care of themselves? Why?
3. Would you expect the same conditions as now exist in accounts receivable to exist in the other units where the computer will first be used? Why?
4. What action, if any, do you suggest Mr. Beck take? The controller? Substantiate your viewpoint.

Case 8–3. The Burton Company

One of the largest department stores in the entire United States, the Burton Company, operates six stores located within a large city and adjacent shopping areas. Studies conducted by the controller, Mr. Lief Huff, show that the company's paper work has been growing at a rate exceeding that of sales. Information efforts dealing with company purchases and inventory are considered satisfactory by Mr. Huff. However, excessive costs exist for handling papers created by store customer relations, the preparing of billings, and the processing of accounts receivable. Currently, for this work the company uses accounting machines purchased some seven years ago.

A customer extended open credit by the company produces a charge plate at the time of making a purchase. This plate is inserted into a small unit on the counter by the sales clerk. The plate imprints the customer's number, name, and address upon the purchase order made out by the clerk in longhand. At the same time, the customer's number is relayed to the central credit department, where a check is made to determine the credit standing. If satisfactory, approval is relayed to the originating small unit, and the sales clerk proceeds with consummation of the sale. In contract, if credit is unsatisfactory, the customer is politely informed by the clerk, who terminates the sale unless cash payment is made on the account or for the current merchandise being purchased. In some instances, it requires five to ten minutes to get the check on credit. Copies of the orders written by the sales clerks are sent to the accounting department where reports and records, including monthly statements to customers, are compiled.

Mr. Huff is thinking of using a computer. The company has approximately 300,000 customers sold on open account. Of the total number of sales transacted, some 22 percent are cash sales. Peak loads occur during the Easter period, late summer before school starts, and the Christmas period. Accounts are divided by stores, with the statements sent out for each store on approximately the same day of each month. During the past five years, the number of accounts has increased an average of 3 percent per year. It is believed that this growth will continue and may even rise to 5 percent per year.

Questions:

1. What approach do you recommend that Mr. Huff follow?, Why?
2. In your opinion, what are some major considerations that will help determine the feasibility of the use of a computer by the company? Discuss.
3. For computer application, give some important general specifications of the computer recommended and discuss the step-by-step procedure of the computer processing that might be followed.

Chapter 9

Computers—Technical
Considerations

> *He who is afraid of a thing gives it power over him.*
>
> Moorish Proverb

The makeup and operation of a computer system involves technical considerations. We will now discuss some of these more important technical aspects. The content of this chapter is minimal for basic computer comprehension.

A computer is actually a group of mechanical and electronic devices connected into a unit or system to process data. Since it is made up of several units, interrelated and operating as a totality, it is more accurately designated as a computer system. It is a tool for solving problems; it takes a bundle of data, processes them according to the necessary string of operations, including any or all ten of the basic elements of data processing discussed in Chapter 1, turns out the answers with fabulous rapidity and without error, and proceeds automatically to the next bundle of data and processes them.

Basic Types of Computers

The basic types of computers are (1) digital, (2) analog, and (3) hybrid digital-analog. Digital computers, or arithmetic machines as they are sometimes described, deal with actual numbers, and their answer is a set of numbers or letters, which can be made as accurate as desired. These computers perform according to a set of instructions. It is a common type of machine for processing business data and represents by far the greatest number of computers in operation today.

An analog computer operates on the basis of using a formula or system to represent that which is being investigated or by duplicating mathematical behavior. It can instantaneously solve a mathematical equation with ten variables. It is actually based on approximations, and both input and output of an analog computer are approximate positions on a continuous scale rather than absolute numbers. Results from the analog computer are never precisely accurate, but they are commonly within $\frac{1}{20}$ of 1 percent, which is entirely satisfactory for most applications. Calculating flows and pressures in pipelines and the position of a moving target are accomplished by an analog computer in only a split second, whereas for the same application the digital computer would calculate enormous quantities of data for an hour or so. Many analog computers are used for research and scientific investigation.

A hybrid digital-analog computer is a combination of the first two, digital and analog, utilized to obtain a computer capable of more work than the two can accomplish working separately. This hybrid type is a more recent development. It has been used advantageously for outer space projects and satellite programs. To date there are relatively few hybrid digital-analog computers in use.

FOUR BASIC CONSIDERATIONS

To simplify this discussion we will organize our thoughts around four basic subject areas. These are:

1. Converting from system to computer programming—includes transferring the planning of the work to be done to a form required for computer programming.
2. Programming for computer processing—constitutes the preparing of the work for computer handling.
3. Coding for computer utilization—puts the work into a form or language that the computer can handle.
4. Anatomy of the computer—deals with the physical make-up of the computer.

The term, *software*, is commonly used to identify the first three areas, and *hardware* to identify the fourth or last area.

1. Converting from System to Computer Programming

The planning of what office work is to be done, discussed in Chapters 2–6 inclusive, provides a blueprint, expressed in written and chart form, of what information is wanted, where, in what format, to whom, and at what time. To carry out these plans poses no new techniques in the case of manually or nonautomated processing. The guides and instructions are studied, and the implementation takes place in accordance with the indicated sequence and relationship of operations.

In contrast, when processing by computer we encounter a different situation. The system requirements must be converted into a form which the computer can handle. Specifically, the relationship is between the system design and the computer programming function which includes the detailing of the work in the form of a package of instructions for a computer to follow.

To get from the system design to the program flow chart, a detailed breakdown of the step-by-step activity requirements of the system are mandatory. Symbols are used in the preparation of the program flow chart. The most widely adopted and recommended symbols and their description are shown in Figure 9–1.

FIGURE 9–1
Program Flow Chart Symbols and Their Descriptions

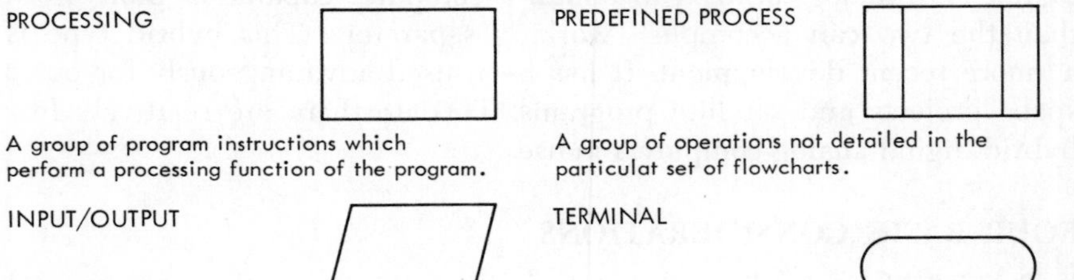

PROCESSING

A group of program instructions which perform a processing function of the program.

PREDEFINED PROCESS

A group of operations not detailed in the particulat set of flowcharts.

INPUT/OUTPUT

Any function of an input/output device (making information available for processing, recording processing information, tape positioning, etc.).

TERMINAL

The beginning, end, or a point of interruption in a program.

DECISION

The decision function used to document points in the program where a branch to alternate paths is possible based upon variable conditions.

CONNECTOR

An entry from, or an exit to, another part of the program flowchart.

FLOW DIRECTION

OFFPAGE CONNECTOR

A connector used instead of the connector symbol to designate entry to or exit from a page.

Courtesy: International Business Machines Corp., White Plains, N.Y.

The computer processes just one tiny step at a time and, if a choice exists, either of two ways must be indicated, such as either "yes" or "no," "stop" or "go" to another operation. When necessary details are missing, the processing by computer is not feasible, and meaningless and incorrect results are obtained.

Figure 9–2 shows a program flow chart constructed from the system design. It deals with the calculation of thermal differential means and variances. Beginning in the upper left, the first step is to test if switch B is on. If yes, indicated by letter Y, the next step is to the right; if no, indicated by letter N, the next step is downward to Test C, to see if switch C is on. The successive steps progress downward in the left column of the figure to the bottom where point A is reached and continue in the column to the right.

From this program flow chart, the block diagram is developed. The start of this is shown by Figure 9–3. Block A is the start and consists of "Test if switch B is on." Moving to the right, block B is the next step, consisting of Test C, which is composed of "Test if switch C is on." Progressing to the right, the next step is indicated in Block C. To the right of each block are two columns for insertion of data needed for conversion to the computer. In block A, for example, in the first column are Y and N standing for yes and no. In the second column and opposite Y is 2L, meaning if the answer is yes, the successive step is 2L; in the same column opposite N is B, meaning if the answer is no, the successive step is B, or block B, shown to the right of block A. The meaning of 2L is a code for a program modification which in this case is "set time switch to transfer setting" as indicated in Figure 9–2, upper left, as the step following a yes answer to the question, "Is switch B on?" By studying Figure 9–2 in conjunction with the block diagram of Figure 9–3, the identity and need for each block of Figure 9–3 is revealed, along with the coded operations which the computer must perform.

In actual practice the systems analyst can stop at the system design and let the computer programmer develop from the system the program flow chart, the block diagram, and the computer program. In contrast, the systems analyst may extend efforts all the way through computer programming, and turn over the complete package to the computer operator. Neither of these extremes is recommended. The best arrangement is an overlap in efforts in the area of reasonable details of the program flow chart. In this way the systems analyst gains an understanding of the programming and the programmer gains an understanding of the system design work. By this approach cooperation is enhanced between the system designer and the programmer, ambiguity of data is minimized, training is facilitated, and interdepartmental flexibility is encouraged.

Figure 9–4 shows a glossary of computer terms which serve as a convenient reference for the special terminology used with computers. Scanning the terms and their meanings will assist in grasping quickly the technical significance of computer operations. Later a more intense review of the glossary may be undertaken.

FIGURE 9–2
A Program Flow Chart

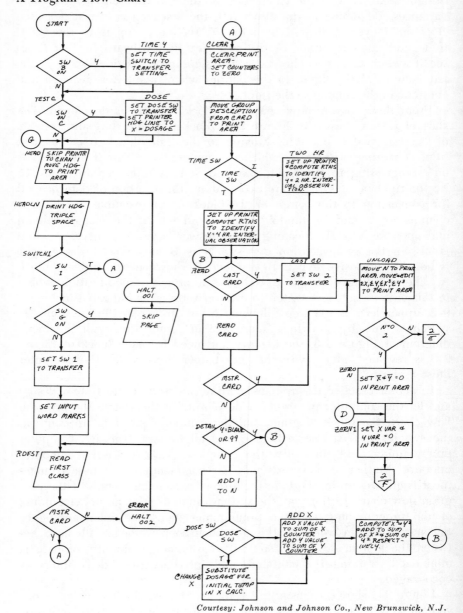

Courtesy: *Johnson and Johnson Co., New Brunswick, N.J.*

FIGURE 9–3

A Block Diagram for Conversion Work to Computer

A — START
TEST IF SWITCH B IS ON
Y 2L / N B

B — TESTC
TEST IF SWITCH C IS ON
Y 2M / N C

C — HEAD
SKIP PRINTER TO CHANNEL 1 AND MOVE HEADING TO PRINTER OUTPUT AREA

D — HEADLN
PRINT HEADING + TRIPLE SPACE

E — SWITCH 1
LOGIC SWITCH 1
I F / T K

(F) TEST IF SWITCH G IS ON
Y 2F / N G

G SET SWITCH 1 TO TRANSFER SETTING

H SET INPUT WORD MARKS

J — RDFST
READ FIRST CARD + TEST IF MASTER CARD
Y K / N 2G

K — CLEAR
CLEAR PRINT AREA + SET COUNTERS TO ZERO MOVE GROUP DESCR. FROM CARD TO PRINTER AREA

L — TIMESW
LOGIC SWITCH TIME
I 2H / T M

M SET UP PRINTER + COMPUTE ROUTINES TO IDENTIFY Y = 4 HOUR INTERVAL OBSERVATION

N — READ
TEST IF LAST CARD READ
Y U / N O

O READ CARD + TEST IF MASTER CARD
Y V / N P

P — DETAIL
TEST IF Y VALUE IS BLANK OR 99
Y N / N Q

(Q) ADD 1 TO N

R — DOSESW
LOGIC SWITCH DOSE
I S / T 2N

S — ADD X
ADD X VALUE TO SUM OF X COUNTER ADD Y VALUE TO TO SUM OF Y COUNTER

T COMPUTE X^2 AND Y^2 AND ADD TO SUM OF X^2 AND SUM OF Y^2 RESPECTIVELY
N

U — LASTCD
SET SWITCH 2 TO TRANSFER SETTING

(V) UNLOAD
MOVE N TO PRINT AREA. MOVE + EDIT ΣX, ΣY, ΣX^2 + ΣY^2 TO PRINT AREA

W TEST IF N = 0
Y 2J / N X

X COMPUTE $\bar{X} = \dfrac{\Sigma X}{N}$ + $\bar{Y} = \dfrac{\Sigma Y}{N}$ + MOVE TO PRINT AREA

Y SUBTRACT 1 FROM N AND TEST IF = 0
Y 2K / N Z

Z COMPUTE X + Y VARIANCES + MOVE TO PRINT AREA
$X_{VAR} = \dfrac{\Sigma X^2 - \dfrac{(\Sigma X)^2}{N}}{N-1}$

(A) PRINT
PRINT LINE + DOUBLE SPACE

B — SWTCH2
LOGIC SWITCH 2
I C / T D

C TEST IF PAGE OVERFLOW
Y 1C / N 1K

D — END JOB
SKIP TWO PAGES AND HALT 000, 999

E SET SWITCHES 1+2 AND DOSE + TIME SWITCHS TO N-TIAL SETTING SET PRINTER HEADING LINE TO X = TEMP.
1A

(F) REPEAT
SKIP PAGE AND HALT 000, 001
1D

G — ERROR
HALT 000, 002
1J

H — TWOHR
SET UP PRINTER + COMPUTE ROUTINES TO IDENTIFY Y = 2 HOUR OBSERVATION
1N

J — ZERON
SET $\bar{X}$ + $\bar{Y}$ = c IN PRINT AREA

K — ZERN 1
SET X_{VAR} + Y_{VAR} = 0 IN PRINT AREA
A

(L) TIME 4
SET TIME SWITCH TO TRANSFER SETTING
1B

M — DOSE
SET DOSE SWITCH TO TRANSFER SETTING + SET PRINTER HEADING LINE TO X = DISAGE
1C

N — CHNGEX
SUBSTITUTE DOSAGE FOR INITIAL TEMPERATURE IN X CALCULATIONS
1S

O (blank)

P (blank)

FIGURE 9–4
Glossary of Common Terms Used in Computer Technology

Access time–time required for computer to move a piece of data or an instruction from a memory unit to a processing unit.

Accumulator–a storage register where results are accumulated.

Active line–a line that is currently available and ready for transmission of data.

Alphameric characters–letters of the alphabet, numerical digits, or symbols used for communicative purposes.

Answerback–a terminal response to remote control signals.

ATS–Administrative Terminal System.

Backup copy–a file or data set retrieval for reference in case original copy is destroyed.

Batch processing–the means by which a number of similar input items are grouped for processing during the same machine run.

Bug–a malfunction or mistake.

Bus–conductor used for transmitting signals.

Cathode ray tube (CRT)–a picture tube used in visual display terminal.

Channel–path along which signals can be sent.

Character–a letter, digit, or symbol used for representation of data.

Checkout–the determination of the correctness of the computer routine, locating errors in it, and correcting them.

Compile–to produce a machine-language routine by translating from ordinary or non-machine program. Concerns programming.

Compiler–a program that compiles, i.e., prepares a machine-language program from a program written in another programming language by making use of the overall logic structure of the program.

Configuration–group of machines, components, and programs constituting a data processing system.

Data bank–a comprehensive collection of organized information used for study and reference.

Data processing–the performance of a systematic sequence of operations performed upon data.

Data transmission–the sending of data from one part of a system to another part.

Decision table–a table of all possibilities to be considered in describing a problem and the actions to be taken. Commonly used in place of flow charts for problems documentation.

Double precision–the using of two computer words to represent a number.

Downtime–interval during which a machine or a piece of equipment is malfunctioning.

Fetch–locating and loading an amount of wanted data from storage.

Hard copy–written or printed copy of input or output data in human visually readable form.

Hardware–the mechanical and electrical devices making up a computer.

Information retrieval–the recovery of specific information from stored data.

Interface–a shared boundary usually applying either to linkage of two devices or to accessibility to stored data by two or more programs.

Interlock–keeping a machine from initiating further operations until the operation in process is completed.

JES–job entry subsystem.

Library–an organized collection of proven and standard routines which can be incorporated into larger routines.

Line printing–the printing of an entire line of characters as a unit.

Linkage–coding in programming that connects two separate routines.

Location–a place in a storage unit where a unit of data or an instruction may be stored.

Loop–a technique of coding in programming whereby a group of instructions is repeated with alterations of some of the instructions and usually with modification of the data being processed.

Macro instruction–instruction in a source language equivalent to a specified sequence of machine instructions.

Mainframe–the central data processing computer.

FIGURE 9–4 (*Continued*)

___

Micro instruction—a basic machine instruction.

Multiplex—to transmit simultaneously two or more messages on a single channel.

Multiprogramming—the concurrent execution of two or more programs by a single computer.

Nanosecond—one-thousand-millionth of a second.

OCR—optical character recognition used by machines for identifying printed characters by means of light-sensitive devices.

Off-line—the operation of input or output devices are not under direct control of the central processing unit.

On demand system—a system for which data are available at time of request.

On-line—the operation of input or output devices are under direct control of the central processing unit.

Openended—refers to a process that can be augmented.

Optical scanner—a device that scans optically and as a result generates a signal.

Parameter—a quantity to which arbitrary values may be assigned for such things as decimal point location, record format, and size.

Parity bit—a binary bit added to an array of bits to make the sum of all the bits always odd or always even.

Parity check—a checking means based on making a total number of "on" or "off" in some grouping of binary digits.

Password—the characters that a computer operator or user must supply to meet security requirements before gaining access to information in the computer system.

Peripheral equipment—any unit of equipment distinct from the central computer group which provides the group with outside communication.

Program—a string of actions proposed to achieve a specific result.

Quiescing—bringing a device or a system to a halt by rejection of new work requests.

Random access—the finding and getting of data in storage is relatively independent of the location of the information most recently obtained.

Real-time output—output data removed at time of need by another system.

Register—a device that holds information while or until it is used.

Roll-out—the recording of the main storage contents into an auxiliary storage.

Sequencing—ordering and performing in a series in accordance with rank or time.

Sneak current—leakage current that gets into telephone circuits from other circuits.

Software—the determining of systems, programming, and coding work required for effective computer data processing.

SVC—supervisor call instruction.

Tape relay—a method of relaying messages between the transmitting and receiving stations when perforated paper tape is used.

Telecommunication—either transmission of telegraph, radio, and TV signals over long distances, or data transmission between a computer system and remotely located devices.

Throughput—volume of processed work accomplished by a computer system over a given period.

Time sharing—participation by multiple users in available computer time by means of terminals.

Turnaround time—interval between submitting a program to a computer and receiving output from that program.

Zerofill—fill in character with the representation of zero.

Zero suppression—elimination of zeros which are nonsignificant in a numeral.

___

2. Programming for Computer Processing

The complete package of instructions for a computer to process specific data is known as a *program*. It is developed by "programming." This work consists of breaking down in most complete detail the operations to be performed by the computer. A programmer performs this work.

By following the programming, the computer progresses by moving from one very tiny element of work to the next in a prescribed sequence. The first operation may be locating specific data in the storage device of the computer, followed by transferring it to the processing device, multiplying these data by a given number, returning it to the storage device along with the separate initial data, and finally outputing the multiplication (processing) result by means of the output device of the computer. Again in some instances the sequential operation can be either of two possibilities, but no more, represented by yes or no, go or no go, on or off, and so forth. When the program designates the answer is yes, for example, the computer follows the element of this designation. In contrast, if the answer is no, the alternate element is followed. This means that minute, detailed, sequential steps in the work to be done must be set forth, and where choices arise, the decision must be one of two alternatives set forth in the program. The computer having the information of the precise element determines if yes or no is to be followed. In this sense computers can be considered to reach simple decisions. The program shown by Figure 9–5 illustrates this concept in a humorous but helpful way. This chart has been drawn to point out clearly the degree or detailed extent to which each step is carried; the common programming chart symbols have not been used.

Since the programmer normally designs and evolves the program in the form of a flow chart listing the precise step-by step action to be taken, it is extremely helpful to have an intimate knowledge of the systems, procedures, and methods being employed. In addition, a complete understanding of the purpose for which the finished data are used appears paramount in programming work. To perceive the detail of programming, consider that it is common for the preparation of customers' invoices to require 1,500 or more steps. Typically, many steps or minute operations covering relatively small amounts of processing to large quantities of data characterize business data processing. The simple recording, recalling, and arithmetic work necessitate much programming. In contrast, for much research and scientific data processing, the work entails relatively small quantities of data processed many, many times. Commonly the processing task is to substitute various values in mathematical formulas in order to determine critical values. Handling such repetitive processing using different numerical values necessitates relatively simple programming. Historically this is a major reason for the computer being used extensively first for scientific work. As the restricting influence of programming was lifted, computer processing for ordinary business data became feasible.

When program or instructions are placed in the storage device of

FIGURE 9-5
This Diagram Illustrates How Programmers Have to Instruct the Electronic System to Work

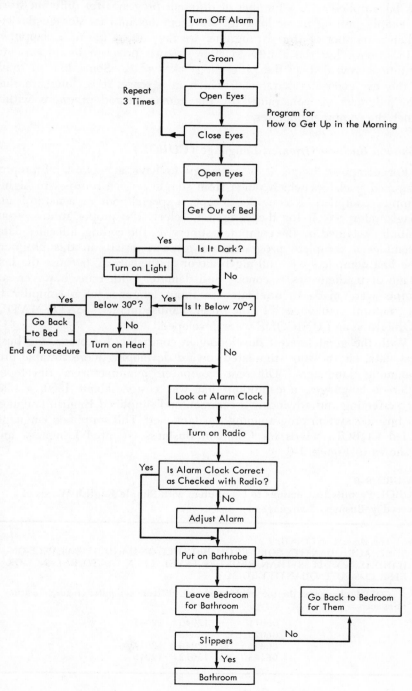

a computer, they are commonly termed *stored programs*. A computer can be supplied with a number of different programs for different work by simply putting in, or loading, the programs into its storage device. When a number of stored programs are thus accessible to a computer, it in essence has the ability to alter its own program in response to conditions revealed as the processing takes place. Some like to think of this as "computer judgment" which in a sense, it is, but note that the "judgment" is constrained by the human-created programs within which the computer operates.

Common Business Oriented Language (COBOL)

For computer usage, it is necessary to have a network of preprogrammed packages which range from simple service routines to highly complex compilers. A compiler accepts a special code or a natural language, interprets it for the computer, selects the proper routine from a library retained by the computer, supervises the coding, allocates data, assembles a complete program, and gives a report on this program. The first compilers were all algebraic or mathematical, because the language of mathematics is concise and definite. With time, however, attempts were made to orientate the input language of a compiler to the natural language of the user. Subsequently MATH-MATIC, FORTRAN, and UNICODE were developed.

With the great interest developing in computers for processing business data, efforts were stimulated toward developing more suitable programming languages. Different computer manufacturers developed different languages, a condition that was costly. About 1960, a plan for perfecting and advancing a common and simplified English language for business system programming was launched. This simplified language, called COBOL, stands for Common Business Oriented Language and is shown in Figure 9–6.

FIGURE 9–6
COBOL Permits Instructions to Computers with Simple English Words of Everyday Business Language

---

This language is COBOL:
SUBTRACT QUANTITY-SOLD FROM BALANCE-ON-HAND. IF BALANCE-ON-HAND IS NOT LESS THAN REORDER-LEVEL THEN GO TO BALANCE-OK ELSE COMPUTE QUANTITY-TO-BUY. . . .

COBOL eliminates the use of detailed and difficult computer language instructions such as:

06011	'	12040	12047
06028	C	12048	
06074	?	12046	12014
06145	S	12012	12010

This advance toward a common computer language suitable for all computers, regardless of their manufacture, is the most significant advance in programming. Once a program is written in COBOL, it need not be rewritten if a switch from one data-processing system to another takes place. Further, the burden of programming is eased. As an indirect result of the COBOL influence, many business-oriented "canned" or subroutine programs have been created for each type of computer. Also, automatic compilers and translators have appeared on the market.

3. Coding the Work for Computer Utilization

The third basic consideration is coding the work for computer utilization. All information is conveyed by symbols. In the English language, there are familiar letters of the alphabet, numbers, and punctuation marks. For everyday correspondence, these symbols are recorded on paper according to a prescribed sequence and grouping. When transported to another person reading and writing English, these symbols convey a particular message.

In the same manner, to communicate with a computer system necessitates that the information be expressed in symbols and in a form that can be read and interpreted by data-processing devices. In the case of the computer, this language has been called "computerese." It is language the machine can understand and act upon, in keeping with the desired processing. People invented computerese to utilize the machines. It represents symbols making up a mutual language to provide communication between people and machines. In other words, every detail which the machine is to follow must be put into language that the machine can handle. This includes the use of special codes and numbers which, put on or into the data-transmitting medium, will cause the machine to perform the operation desired.

There are a number of different media that can be used and their connection with input data and output data, with a computer are shown by Figure 9–7. For input data, the following are most common: (1) typewritten or printed material on paper, (2) punched card, (3) perforated paper tape, (4) magnetic tape and cards, (5) magnetic tape ledger record, and (6) magnetic ink characters. For the output data, the communication media include: (1) print on paper, (2) punched card, (3) perforated paper tape, (4) magnetic tape or card, (5) magnetic tape ledger record, and (6) print on film. Each of these media will now be discussed.

Typewritten or Printed Material on Paper

Data can be transmitted into the computer by a machine that is capable of doing what you are doing right now—reading. All letters

FIGURE 9–7
**Media of Input Data, Processing, and Media of Output Data of a
Computer System**

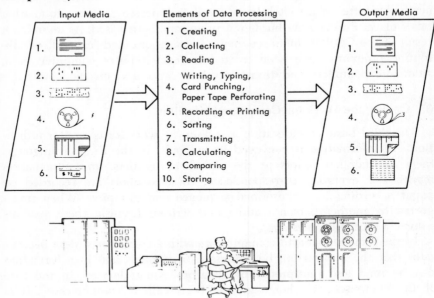

of the alphabet, numeral 0 through 9, standard punctuation, and special symbols are read. Various size documents, even continuous-length fanfold sheets are handled. Up to about 90,000 documents per hour can be read and recorded on the system's own magnetic tape deck. Expressing the speed differently, a reading rate of 370 characters per second or a line-reading speed of about 37 inches per second is attained. The reading speed is attained in part because only that portion of a line that it is instructed to read is read, and time is not wasted scanning blank lines and unwanted data. The font or type style of the information fed into the reader is similar to conventional fonts as illustrated by Figure 9–8.

The machine operates in conjunction with a computer that directs its reading operations, that is, the computer governs the document position, reading, and sorting of the reading machine. Optical-electronic means are followed. Software is available for use with this system either for simple document reading or for editing, proving, sorting, and listing the reading machines output. Actually the machine reads and translates what it reads into computer language. Figure 9–9 shows the machine with the insert in upper left corner highlighting the adjustable loading hopper for feeding documents automatically to the machine.

FIGURE 9–8
Each Character in the Font Has a Distinctive Shape in Order That the Page Reader Performs Accurate Reader Performance

THE PAGE READER READS ONLY UPPER CASE LETTERS AND A TYPEWRITER

USED EXCLUSIVELY FOR PAGE READER DOCUMENTATION NEED HAVE ONLY

AN UPPER CASE FONT. IT IS, HOWEVER, POSSIBLE AND PRACTICAL

TO EQUIP SUCH A TYPEWRITER WITH A LOWER CASE FONT OF SIMILAR

APPEARANCE WHICH ENABLES ITS USE FOR GENERAL BUSINESS PURPOSES

AS WELL AS FOR PAGE READER DOCUMENT PREPARATION.

Courtesy: Control Data Corp., Minneapolis.

Machine readers are also available that read data within a relatively small area of a document in keeping with the processing requirements. It may be an account number, an account to be paid, a name and address, a Zip Code number, or a varying number of lines from a printed listing. If desired, punched cards or perforated tapes are prepared as a part of the system. It is claimed that when three or more operators are continuously employed in reading and punching cards or tapes, the machine reader is to be preferred. Credit invoices, checks, order

FIGURE 9–9
The 915 Page Reader Performs Direct Conversion of Typewritten or Printed Form Information into Computer Language by Optical-Electronic Means

Courtesy: Control Data Corp., Minneapolis.

cards, and bill stubs of public utility companies are among the more common uses. Its main areas of application can be classified under two groups: (1) where the input information consists of a long number of separate units recorded in a great number of places and must be processed quickly and economically, and (2) where the output data of today becomes the input data of tomorrow. To illustrate, if a statement with a stub consisting of printed material only is sent to a customer who subsequently returns payment and the stub, it is feasible to put critical portions of the printed matter of the stub in a form that the machine reader can easily handle when the stub is returned and becomes input data.

Binary Mode

Before proceeding with the discussion of the remaining media, some fundamentals employed in the coding of data should be pointed out. To be processed by the computer, data are converted into electric impulses which follow one another billions of times per minute and magnetize very small areas in the computer enabling the machine to process the data. The data of numbers and letters are represented by two symbols arranged according to a code conveying the information to the computer. The representation of the basic symbols depends upon the medium used and include, for example, a hole in a card or no hole in a card, a magnetic impulse on a tape or no impulse, electric current in one direction or in an opposite direction, and an electric switch either closed or open. In other words, the base is two, just as decimals refer to a base of ten. Tubes or transistors or cores can exist in only two states—"off" or "on," emitting or not, magnetized in one or the other electric charge.

One binary digit is called a *bit*, the contraction for "binary digit." For the decimal digits from 0 through 9, four binary positions are required and represent from left to right the decimal digits, 8, 4, 2, and 1. That is, different values are placed on the four positions and the value represented is the sum of these positions. See Figure 9–10.

The handling of zero in a computer is usually noted as ten, i.e., an eight and a two. In the binary position this avoids registering all blanks for zero, for if we did this it would be difficult to determine whether the register is supposed to be zero or the machine has failed to transfer data.

To express in binary code larger decimal digits and letters of the alphabet additional binary digits would be required. Illustrative is adding to the 1, 2, 4, and 8 columns 16, 32, 64 so that the columns headings would read 64, 32, 16, 8, 4, 2, and 1. Decimal 10 would be binary 1010, and decimal 29 would be binary 11101. Some computers use four binary columns for each decimal digit. To illustrate, the num-

FIGURE 9–10

Illustrating the Four Bit Position and Values to Represent Decimal Numbers (for decimal 5, the "bits" of "4" and "1" are "on," "8" and "2" are "off")

BINARY CODE

DECIMAL	8	4	2	1	TOTAL VALUE (READ ACROSS)
	IS	REPRESENTED		BY	
0	0	0	0	0	0
1	0	0	0	✳	1
2	0	0	✳	0	2
3	0	0	✳	✳	3
4	0	✳	0	0	4
5	0	✳	0	✳	5
6	0	✳	✳	0	6
7	0	✳	✳	✳	7
8	✳	0	0	0	8
9	✳	0	0	✳	9

ber 24 would be shown as 0010–0100. To show 124, we would need another four binary columns. Letters of the alphabet can also be shown binarily; it's a matter of using more bits to show letters.

Returning to the statement made previously that there are only two states—off or on, emitting or not for each position, we can show the decimal numbers and their respective binary numbers as indicated at the top position of Figure 9–11. Examples of addition, subtraction, multiplication, and division are indicated at the bottom of this figure. For example, the decimal $4 + 3 = 7$, expressed binarily is $0100 + 0011 = 0111$.

Codes other than binary are used by some computers including a

FIGURE 9–11

Relationships between Decimal and Binary Codes

Decimal	Binary	Decimal	Binary
1	0001	6	0110
2	0010	7	0111
3	0011	8	1000
4	0100	9	1001
5	0101	10	1010

Examples:

Decimal	Binary
$4 + 3 = 7$	$0100 + 0011 = 0111$
$6 - 2 = 4$	$0110 - 0010 = 0100$
$2 \times 4 = 8$	$0010 \times 0100 = 1000$
$10 \div 2 = 5$	$1010 \div 0010 = 0101$

numerical coding to the base eight, known as octal notation, a seven-bit alphameric, a six-bit numerical, and a biquinary system indicating numbers to the base five. The number system followed is a technical consideration, and assistance in its understanding is offered by the computer manufacturer both before and after machine installation.

Punched Card

The common 80-vertical column punched card is about 7⅜ inches long by 3¼ inches high. In each column are 12 units which read from the top down are: 12, 11, 10, 1, 2, 3, 4, 5, 6, 7, 8, 9. The 12 and 11 zones are frequently called R and X, respectively. Data from original records are put on the cards by means of punched holes; that is, when certain holes are punched in the card, these holes represent definite information. High-speed machines are used for this purpose. It requires four different vertical arrangements to represent all possible letters or numbers. This is clearly illustrated by Figure 9–12.

The 96-column punched card uses a binary code. (Refer to Figure 7–9 again.) The number, 7, for example, is represented by holes in 1, 2, and 4 of tier 1. A punched hole in the card represents yes, no punch indicates no. Information represented or coded by means of the presence or absence in specific and exact locations is read as the card travels through a card-reading mechanism. The reading is automatically converted to an electronic language utilized by the computer in its data processing.

Perforated Paper Tape

Another common medium for the transmission of data into a computer system is perforated paper tape. It is a continuous recording medium and can be used to record long runs of data, being limited only by the capacity of the storage medium into which the data are being placed.

Most perforated paper tape is either of an eight-level or channel code or of a five-level code. A level runs the length of the tape. In any column across the width of the tape, the number of possible punching positions is equivalent to the number of levels of the tape. That is, in the eight-level tape, there are eight possible punching positions; and in the five-level tape, there are five positions.

Figure 9–13 shows the code of an eight-level paper tape. Observe that the lower five levels, identified on the left by 1, 2, 4, and 8, and "check," when used to record numerical characters, are the sum of the position values indicating the value of the character. For example, 3 is expressed by holes in positions 1, 2, and check, while 7 consists of holes in 1, 2, and 4. For alphabetic characters, two additional levels at the top, X and O, are used with the 1, 2, 4, 8, and check levels.

FIGURE 9–12
A Code Used for Punched Holes Which Represent Letter and Figure Data

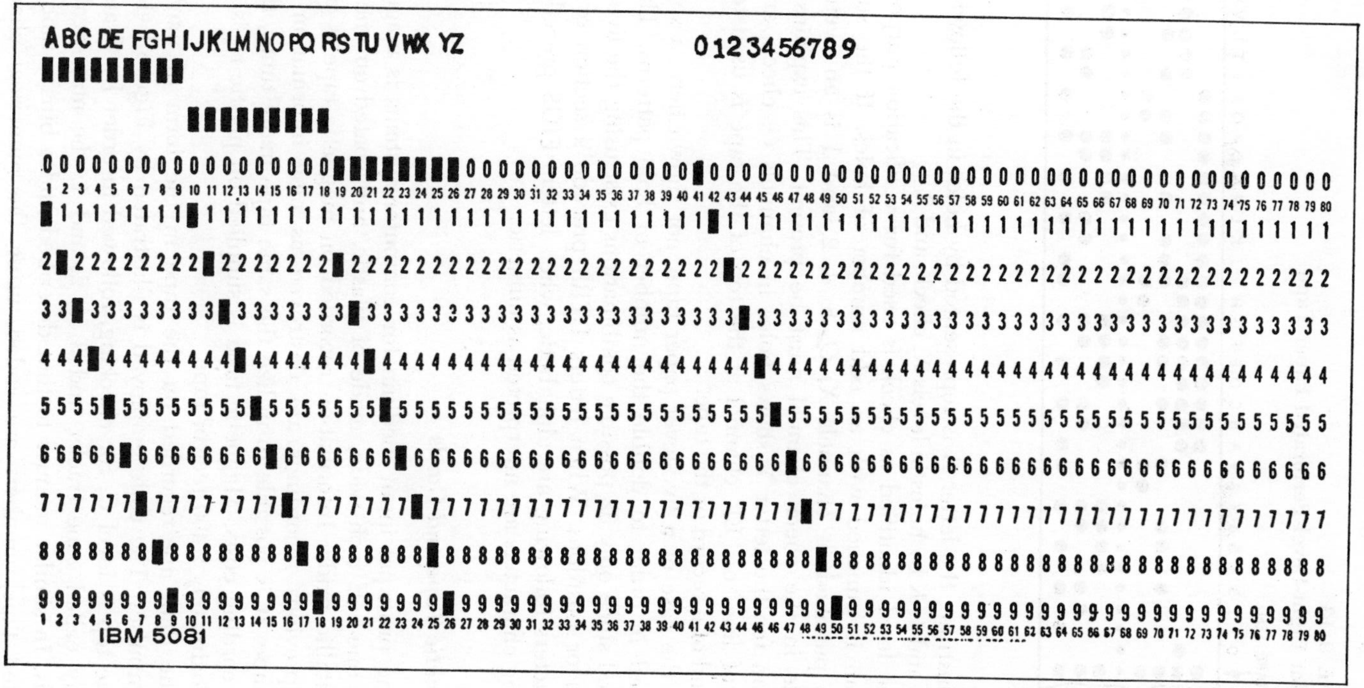

Courtesy: International Business Machines Corp., White Plains, N.Y.

FIGURE 9–13
Code for Eight-Level Perforated Paper Tape

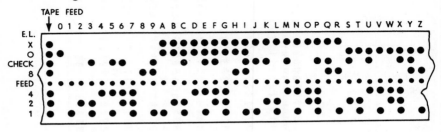

To illustrate, the letter *A* is represented by holes in the following levels: *X*, *O*, and 1; *K* by holes in levels *X*, check, and 2.

The level identified as check is used for verification purposes. Each column is punched with an odd number of holes. If the sum of the holes punched in channels *X*, *O*, 8, 4, 2, and 1 is an even number, a hole in the check channel must be present. This explains why the column for the letter *Y* shows holes in channels *O*, check, and 8. The "end of line" or "El" channel at the top of the tape is used to indicate the end of a record or the tape.

In the case of a five-level paper tape, not shown here, a shift system is used in order to double the number of hole patterns. The shift is needed since only 32 possible combinations exist using the five punching levels or positions. When letters LTRS precede a section of tape, the characters following are alphabetic, when letters FIGS precede, the following characters are interpreted as numeric.

Magnetic Tape and Cards

The principal input medium for computer systems is magnetic tape. It is one-half inch wide, made of plastic, and coated on one side with a metallic oxide. Information recorded on magnetic tape is permanent, but previous recordings are destroyed as new information is put on the tape. It is possible to utilize the same tape many times, thus saving in recording costs. Magnetic tape is supplied on plastic reels containing approximately 2,400 feet of tape.

The data are recorded on the tape in the form of magnetic dots or impulses. The code employed is illustrated by Figure 9–14. Starting at the top is level *C*, for checking, followed in order by *B* and *A*, commonly called zone tracks, and 8, 4, 2, and 1, the numerical tracks or levels. In similar manner to that described under binary mode and perforated tape, numbers are coded, using the numerical channels. The decimal number 3 is coded as binary 2 and 1; and 6 as 4 and 2. The

FIGURE 9–14
Coding of Magnetic Spots on Tape to Transmit Information (this is
the seven-bit alphameric code; translation of the spots is shown at top
of sketch)

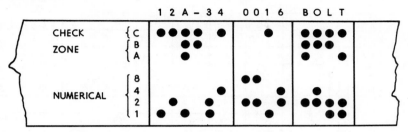

zone tracks are used in combination with the numerical tracks to indicate
letters. In this code, for every column, the total spots add to an even
number. If for a column the total of the spots in the zone and numerical
tracks is an odd number, a spot is added at track *C*.

It is appropriate to state at this point that an electronic system is
not infallible. Therefore, it checks itself to find any error. The impulses
on channel *C*, or check, of the tape are used for this purpose. For
example, every transfer of information from the computer memory units
might be tested on an odd-even basis. If the sum of the group of digits
is an odd number when it is supposed to be even, the machine indicates
the error and stops. This is all done automatically by the machine.

In addition to magnetic tape, there are also magnetic cards or disks
used as a memory medium. These provide a low cost, portable memory
device and vary in capacity depending upon the size of the card or
disk. They are used mainly for actuating peripheral machines to the
computer system or a standalone office machine. By inserting a card
or loading a disk into a machine, the unit is activated. Some cards
have a capacity of about 50 words—enough for a particular program.
The larger disks about 10–12 inches in diameter, have over 3 million
bits of storage capacity and provide a high transfer and reliability rate.
The term, floppy disk, is used in connection with many of these memory
disks since upon insertion in the unit, the disk is clamped at its center
and rotates with some floppiness inside a stationary jacket of the
machine.

Information Interchange

There are strong efforts being made to adopt a permutation code
whereby all coded information could be interchanged between business
machines and computers. To this end the American Standards Association has assisted in developing a standard code which is all-inclusive

FIGURE 9–15

The Standard Code for Information Interchange among Information-Processing and Communications Systems

b7				0	0	0	0	1	1	1	1
b6				0	0	1	1	0	0	1	1
b5				0	1	0	1	0	1	0	1
b4	b3	b2	b1								
0	0	0	0	NULL	DC0	ƀ	0	@	P		
0	0	0	1	SOM	DC1	!	1	A	Q		
0	0	1	0	EOA	DC2	"	2	B	R		
0	0	1	1	EOM	DC3	#	3	C	S		
0	1	0	0	EOT	DC4 (STOP)	$	4	D	T		UN-
0	1	0	1	WRU	ERR	%	5	E	U	U-	AS-
0	1	1	0	RU	SYNC	&	6	F	V	N	SS-
0	1	1	1	BELL	LEM	' (APOS)	7	G	W	A-S	I-G
1	0	0	0	FE0	S0	(	8	H	X	S	N
1	0	0	1	HT/SK	S1	)	9	I	Y	I-G	E-D
1	0	1	0	LF	S2	*	:	J	Z	N	
1	0	1	1	VTAB	S3	+	;	K	[	E-D	
1	1	0	0	FF	S4	(COMMA)	<	L	\		ACK
1	1	0	1	CR	S5	—	=	M	]		Ⓘ
1	1	1	0	SO	S6	.	>	N	↑		ESC
1	1	1	1	SI	S7	/	?	O	←		DEL

Courtesy: American Standards Association, Inc. New York.

It consists of eight columns of 16 characters each. Control characters occupy the first two columns, punctuation the third, numbers the fourth, alphabet the fifth and sixth. The last two columns are unassigned, being reserved for future standardization. This material is reproduced from the American Standard Code for Information Interchange, X3,4—1963, copyright 1963 by ASA, copies of which may be purchased from the American Standards Association at 10 East 40th Street, New York, N.Y., 10016.

and provides room for future standardization programs. Figure 9–15 shows this standard code. Its adoption is voluntary by business machine manufacturers, but no doubt it will gradually and surely be utilized. At the same time, the older codes will continue, due to their existence in present machines and to preferences by certain customers for no change.

Magnetic Tape Ledger Record

This medium consists of magnetic strips imbedded in the margin of either or both sides of a regular hard-copy ledger record. It serves as a dual-purpose record that is readable by machine and by people. Ordinary typing of information is translated into computer language on the magnetic strips of the same ledger record. The strip is capable of storing a large variety of information. Normally, some of the data on the strip is used for positioning purposes prior to an entry being made on the ledger record.

The advantages of this medium are unique. They include unlimited access to external memory and to familiar, hard-copy accounting data. Also, simultaneous access to both electronic and human language is provided, thus eliminating separate searching operations. Instructions to the machine can be stored on the magnetic tape ledger records along with human language instructions on the front side, thus expediting the handling and processing work. Changes in instructions are easy to make. In addition, the stored information on the magnetic tape is introduced into the machine as needed, or on a random access basis, thus permitting greater processing flexibility and more utility of the internal memory of the computer for processing.

Magnetic Ink Characters

Information can be printed with magnetic ink on ordinary paper. This serves as a medium that can be read by either person or machine. This medium is best known for its use in connection with bank checks and deposit slips. For bank checks the magnetic ink character numerals and characters are the same style and size for all checks. The information conveyed by these imprints is utilized in processing the check in its journey back to its maker with the proper bank and individual account being debited or credited. The printing is done with an ink containing iron oxides which are electronically charged and read by magnetic ink character-reading equipment. A special type of design is used in order that the characters can be read visually, and maximum machine readability is provided. The printing type employed is of a style called "Font E-13B," illustrated by Figure 9–16. The characters are located on the bank documents in specific areas, such as definite distances from the bottom and right edge, in order that the machines may perform automatically and not have to search for the data.

As yet, magnetic ink characters have not been extensively adopted for other than bank paperwork. However, many believe that in the future, magnetic ink characters will provide the most reliable and most feasible means yet devised for automating single documents. Current thinking is to use an Encoder, which imprints the proper digits, at each

FIGURE 9–16
Type Font Selected for Magnetic Ink Characters

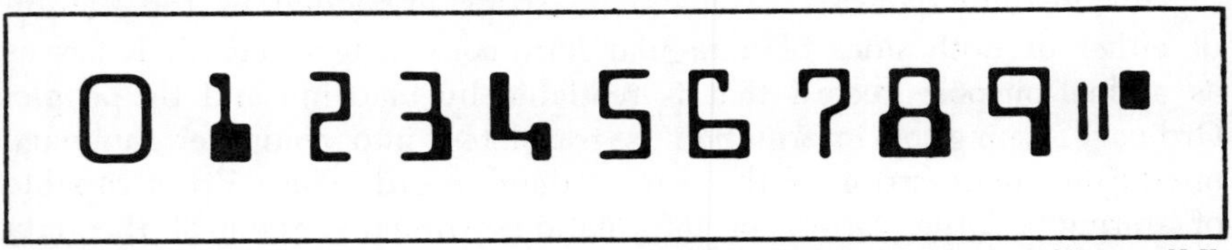

point where a charge form, internal debit or credit, and the like are created. Thus, the documents themselves are made the input data, and the need for other medium such as punch cards or tape is eliminated. The imprinting is such that transit, routing, account number, and amount can be included. Estimates indicate the cost would be only about 25 percent that of other appropriate means.

4. Anatomy of a Computer

The fourth and last basic consideration to be discussed is the anatomy of a computer. The top portion of Figure 9–17 diagrams the essential makeup of a computer; the bottom portion, the general appearance of actual units. Different models will vary somewhat in detail and specific purposes, but the fundamentals outlined here are common to all computers.

For processing, a series of planned operations are applied to the data. Utilizing an *input unit*, the data in a suitable medium are fed into the computer system. They are stored or retained in a *memory unit* which also stores the programmed instructions. When needed, the data are released to a *process unit* which processes the data. The end result of the processing is obtained from the computer by means of an *output unit*. Directing the entire operation is a control section which is regulated by a *console unit*. By its means, the program, or chain of instructions, are given to the system for each new group of data, required data are sent from the memory unit to the process unit, entry of required data by a human operator is made possible, and the processing is started for the next group of data.

In essence, these units are interrelated and make up a totality called a *computer system*. The units include: (1) input-output, (2) memory and storage, (3) processing, and (4) console. Discussion of each in more detail follows.

Input-Output Units

Input units supply data to the computer. As already indicated, they read data from typed or printed paper, punched cards, perforated tape,

FIGURE 9–17
Basic Components of an Electronic Computer

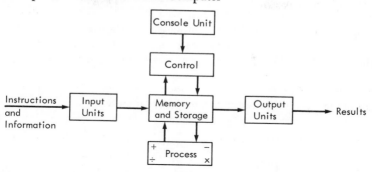

Courtesy: International Business Machines Corp., White Plains, N.Y.

magnetic tape, or magnetic ink characters and make them available to memory and storage units of the computer. Output units covert the processed data from the computer by transferring the "computer language" to a suitable form, such as printed records, punched cards, perforated paper tape, or magnetic tape. In the processing of business data very large quantities of input and of output must be handled. Some output units have a speed equivalent to printing the amount of print on one page of this book in about two seconds.

While this is a terrific rate, it is less than the speed of processing the data by a modern computer. This means that input-output operating speeds commonly limit the total computer operations. Too alleviate this condition, the computer is used to perform other internal operations on available data while the input data are being fed in, or other devices are employed to perform relatively simple handling and transcribing work. A buffer type of device is also utilized to minimize interruption to the computer processing unit. A buffer is actually an auxiliary storage device which receives data at high speed from the input unit or the processor, returns control to the processor, and then either feeds the data at high speeds to the processor or accepts data at high speeds from the processor. One arrangement is shown in Figure 9–18.

FIGURE 9–18
Illustrating the Use of Buffering in Computer Operation

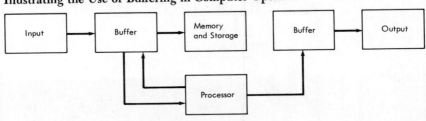

The real challenge is to attain high *throughput* or a maximum of data flow through the computer system. It is not a question solely of maximizing either input or output. In most data processing it is throughput that governs the performance. That is, the quantity of data taken in, processed, and put out as completed results should be maximized for best computer operation.

Memory and Storage Units

These units make up the components of the computer capable of storing information which is subject to recall or reference. Varying in type, size, design, and capacity, the memory and storage units also serve to store programmed instructions and to provide work area for editing. All data to be processed must pass through what is commonly referred to as "main storage." This storage is supplemented by secondary storage units, which are not directly accessible to the processing unit but instead are connected to the processing unit through the main storage. Collectively, the total amount of all the data in storage is referred to as a *data bank.*

Each register, or location, in a memory unit holds one *word.* This may consist of up to 20 digits or letters. A word is the basic measurement of storage capacity. Typically, a computer will have 10,000–15,000 registers, but some large scale machines contain over 4 million registers. Since references are made to memory and storage units during the processing, the accessibility and capacity of these units and their operation in the computer are paramount. Specifically, we are concerned about the time, called *access time,* required to refer to a specific register (location) and obtain the information from it. In addition, the storage capacity of the memory and storage unit is important for we must have enough registers to handle all the information to be processed.

Memory and storage devices in use today are:

1. Magnetic Core. This is illustrated in Figure 9–19. It consists of a series of very tiny cores, or rings of magnetizable material, with

FIGURE 9–19
Magnetic Core Plane as Used in a
Computer

wire passed through the opening in two directions. When an electric current is sent through the wires in one direction the core becomes magnetized with a positive charge; in contrast, when the current is sent through the wire in the opposite direction the core becomes magnetized with a negative charge. Thus, the core stores either a positive or negative value, an on or off condition, which represents a portion of a binary configuration.

Magnetic core offers compact size and relatively low access time. The number of cores in a plane and the number of planes determine the storage capacity. Advances in computer design seem to indicate that, for the magnetic core, future reduction in the cost per storage location is a distinct possibility. Access time now is in excess of 5,000 registers per second.

2. Magnetic Drum. A magnetically coated surface of a cylindrically shaped object is the data-bearing medium of a magnetic drum. The data are coded in the form of the location of magnetic spots or dots on this surface. Figure 9–20 illustrates the magnetic drum means. A magnetic drum is mounted on its axis and is rotated to bring the desired information to a magnetic head that reads the information. More than 1,000 characters can be stored within a square inch of surface and are

FIGURE 9–20
Magnetic Drum Storage

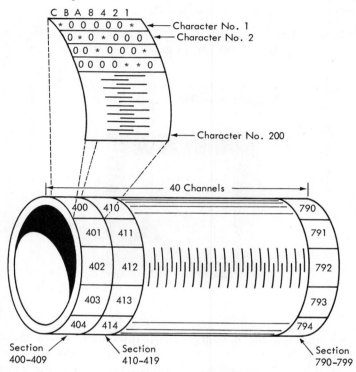

In this illustration there are 200 characters per section. 10 sections per channel, and 40 channels per drum. This makes 80,000 characters per drum.

available at a rate of about 25,000 characters per second. Because of design considerations, the magnetic drum is not used extensively in latest model computers.

3. *Magnetic Disk.* This medium is similar to a phonograph record. The disks are coated on both sides with ferrous oxide recording material and mounted on a vertical shaft. Data are coded and stored as magnetized spots located in concentric tracks. Reading heads mounted on access arms read or write as directed by the computer controlling unit. Storage efficiency is very satisfactory, the access time is excellent especially when several access arms and read-write heads are used. In some designs, the total image is something like a comb of arms interleaved among a number of possible disks; in other designs, the disk is quite

large being some four feet in diameter, thus providng large storage capacity. Figure 9–21 shows disk storage units in a computer system.

FIGURE 9–21
IBM Disk Storage Has Advanced, Direct Access That Aids in Greater Data-Handling Power for Data Base Applications and Batch Processing

Courtesy: International Business Machines Corp., White Plains, N.Y.

4. Data Cell. In this type of memory and storage unit many magnetic film strips are employed. Each strip is about 12 inches long and 2 inches wide. They are grouped into subcells of 10 strips each and, in turn, the subcells make up a data cell. Twenty subcells represent a data cell. Further, ten data cells constitute a cell drive. In other words, there is an orderly arrangement of strips any one of which can be retrieved and information stored on it. Cells may be removed and subsequently replaced with others holding different files. While many data cells are in use, it is not one of the better examples of modern technology in the area of data storage and access. Figure 9–22 shows a data cell unit.

5. Magnetic Tape. This medium can be described as a metallic or plastic ribbon of tape with a magnetic surface. Data for storage are coded and recorded on the tape as spots similar to that of the magnetic drum or disk. Magnetic tape is a common medium for secondary storage. It has too great an access time for wide usage as the medium for main storage.

Processing Units

There is always a central processing unit made up of a control and arithmetic-logical section. The former integrates automatically the operation of the entire computer system in keeping with the program of instructions. This includes controlling the data within the computer such as regulating the input devices, moving data into or out of memory

FIGURE 9–22
A Data Cell Unit

Courtesy: International Business Machines Corp., White Plains, N.Y.

and storage units and between memory and storage units and the arith-metic-logical section, and controlling data entering the output units.

As its name implies, the arithmetic-logical section performs arithmetic and logical operations. These include performing according to algebraic equations and calculus as well as basic processing operations such as reading, sorting, transmitting, comparing, and storing.

Console Controlling Unit

By means of this unit the operator can gain a continual picture of the internal operations of the computer. One can view the console con-trolling unit as actually an integral part of the central processing unit. The operator can start and stop the computer, interrogate for data in memory units, and load data into the computer by means of the console controlling unit. With reference to programming, it is possible to use sense switches to stop processing or to select predetermined program paths. Hence, the flexibility of the program is increased.

There are also cases where not all the program is stored in and accessi-ble to the computer. In such cases, by means of the console controlling unit, programs can be entered directly into the computer step by step as the processing work progresses. Also, the console controlling unit permits tracing a system or a procedure one step at a time and affords high human operator or external control. In some instances, limited data can be entered directly by control buttons on the console. In addition, limited output information may be obtained, thus enabling the console operator to supervise the computer operation.

A magnetic data inscriber console and a tape cartridge reader make it possible to capture information on magnetic tape and then enter it automatically into a computer system. In Figure 9–23 the operator at

FIGURE 9–23
Computer Unit to Enter Information into the System in Order to Update Information to Be Processed

Courtesy: International Business Machines Corp., White Plains, N.Y.

the console types the information, it is recorded on a small tape cartridge which is then placed in the reader (right) which feeds the data into the computer system at nearly 1,000 characters a second. This arrangement is specially helpful where punched chards are not required as a record—usually applications involving continual updating of records already stored in the computer in random order.

QUESTIONS

1. Discuss the work of coding for computer utilization in the use of a computer for business data processing.
2. Is there any significant relationship between systems and electronic data processing? Elaborate on your answer.

3. Explain in some detail the meaning and the designing of programming for computer processing.
4. In each of the following pairs, terms used in computer technology are given. For each pair, point out the difference between the two terms given:

    a. Access time and on-line.

    b. Password and interlock.

    c. Roll out and multiplex.

    d. Throughput and turnaround time.
5. Discuss the purpose and contribution of input-output units in a computer system.
6. Enumerate and give the chief characteristics of three common media for communicating input data for computer processing.
7. *a.* Give the binary number for each of the following: 11, 101, 162, 10001.

    b. Give the regular number for each of the following binary numbers: 1101, 011000110, 100111.

    c. Answer (*a*) above by using four-place binaries for each regular number.
8. For a computer, name the basic components and function of each component.
9. Identify clearly each of the following:

    a. Magnetic tape ledger record.

    b. A program flow chart.

    c. Mainframe.

    d. Nanosecond.
10. Discuss the use of magnetic ink characters in the processing of data.
11. Explain the meaning of Figure 9–15 in your own words.
12. Discuss four different memory devices that are used in computers.

CASE PROBLEMS

Case 9–1.   United-May Laboratories, Inc.

A public announcement was made by Mr. Alex Abramczyk that his company has successfully laboratory tested a new method of printing using heat instead of pressure. A thermal print head brings out letters and numbers in temperature-sensitive paper without impact at speeds up to 375 words a minute. It is believed that this method can be perfected and made commercially feasible for computers.

The print head is a component of an electronic data terminal that handles the information coming in electrical impulses from computers and transmission lines. The unit resembles an electric typewriter in appearance and has storage capacity for a roll of heat-sensitive paper 450 feet long.

Elements are raised on a ceramic base and heated electronically to form letters or numbers. The paper moves over the print head. Tests indicate high speed, reliability, and a clear distinct print image are among the advantages offered by the new method. In addition, the power requirement is low and the process is said to be almost noiseless which is a highly desirable characteristic. Cost is competitive with current methods and could be lower should sufficiently high printing volumes be considered.

Questions:

1. What changes in the computer processing of data do you envision should this new printing process become commercially available? Discuss fully.
2. What technical improvement for a computer would you like to see invented and made commercially feasible? Justify your answer.

Case 9–2.   Kidd Manufacturing Company

When a computer needs data, it goes to a specific address in its storage facilities, reads the data contained in that address, interprets the data read, and does what the instructions say to do. All this is directed by the programming used in operating the computer. In computing the weekly pay for an employee, let us assume that the amount equals the total hours worked multiplied by the employee's wage rate less federal income tax withheld less other deductions. If over 40 hours are worked within the given seven-day period, one and one-half times the wage rate is paid for all time over the 40 hours.

Representing the data required to process the payroll is Exhibit 9–2A show-

EXHIBIT 9–2A

1. Subtract 40 from the figure in 11. If answer is minus or zero, go to address 2. If plus, go to address 3. Go to 3	2. Multiply figure in 11 by figure in 13. Go to 7	3. Multiply figure in 13 by 40; put answer in 16. Go to 4	4. Subtract 40 from figure in 11 and multiply by 1½. Go to 5
5. Multiply answer in 4 by data in 13. Go to 6	6. Add answer for 5 to figure in 16. Go to 7	7. Subtract figure in 14. Go to 8	8. Subtract figure in 15. Go to 9
9. Record answer. Go to 10	10. Store new data in 11, 13, 14, and 15. Go to 1	11. Value of A, total hours worked.	12. Blank
13. Value of B employee wage rate.	14. Value of C federal income tax withheld.	15. Value of D total other deductions.	16. Data from 3.

ing 16 storage addresses. Observe that in a storage box we have information telling (1) where to go to get the needed data, (2) what to do with the data, and (3) where to go to find the next instruction after completing the present one.

Assume for employee No. 333, the data are:

Address 11: 38 hours   (hours worked)
Address 13: $ 4.50   (employee wage rate)
Address 14: $16.20   (federal income tax withheld)
Address 15: $ 8.65   (total other deductions)

Following the instructions beginning with address 1, we get a negative answer (38 minus 40 equals a minus 2). The next operation at address 2, 38 multiplied by $4.50 gives $171 which is calculated by the computer. Address 2 instructs to go to address 7 which tells us to subtract figure in 14, that is, $171 minus $16.20, equals $154.80. Address 7 tells us to go to address 8 which tells us to subtract figure in 15, that is, $154.80 minus $8.65 equals $146.15, and on to address 9 with instructions to record answer.

Questions:

1. Describe the instructions for employee No. 777 who has a wage rate of $7, worked 48 hours, has federal income tax withheld of $58.20, and total other deductions of $9.60.
2. Chart the payroll processing using Figure 9–5 as a guide.
3. Determine the storage addresses for processing the answer to $4X^2 + 8X + 7$. Hint: Develop this expression by a series of elemental steps, starting with X.

Chapter 10

Distribution of Information

> *The life of every man is a diary in which he*
> *means to write the story and writes another, and*
> *his humblest hour is when he compares the*
> *volume as it is with what he hopes to make it.*
>
> James M. Barrie

Included in planning how the office work will be done is determining the distribution of information to people. In other words in this chapter we will be discussing the various means and the management of them by which information is sent from sender to receiver. There exists today many different means. Some are manual, some are mechanized. To provide adequate distributive service it is helpful to follow these guidelines (1) the cost of distribution must be economical in keeping with the volume and urgency of the information, (2) the information must be received in a condition or format usable to the receiver, (3) the information must be transmitted within a time period that enables the information to be considered current from the viewpoint of the receiver's needs, and (4) accuracy in the transmittal of the information is essential.

SELECTING THE MEANS OF DISTRIBUTION

Among the more common means for information distribution are mail, messenger service (either personal or mechanical), telephone, intercommunication systems, telegraphic services, and television. In order to select an appropriate means, it is necessary to know what the real distributive needs of the company are. Various considerations enter into the picture among which the following deserve high priority:

1. The Quantity and Type of Information to Be Provided. Certain means are suited for handling large volumes of information; others are not. Some types of information like art work, blueprints, and drawings can be distributed by certain means only.

2. The Cost of the Distribution Medium. An approximate cost range from the minimum to the maximum, and related to the service provided, is helpful.

3. The Importance of Speed. Certain devices transmit messages in a matter of seconds, others require several days. In many cases, adequate planning commonly reduces much of the need for speed.

4. Is Written or Oral Information Needed? The former tends to be more specific, provides evidence, and helps to lessen misunderstandings. In contrast, the oral is quicker, costs less, and is superior when an exchange of ideas to reach a mutual agreement is desired.

5. The Length or Amount of the Information. Certain media are ideal for lengthy communications, while others are designed for short, terse messages.

6. The Effect of Peak Load Periods. Volumes vary and the capacity of the selected means must satisfy the peak load.

To gain a quick comparison of selected distributive means, Figure 10–1 has been included. This indicates differences for basic considerations

FIGURE 10–1
Comparison of Communication Means on Basic Service Characteristics

| Communication Means | Characteristics | | | |
	Recipient's Presence Required	Contains Illustrations and Drawings	Oral Message	Written Message
Mail.	no	yes	no	yes
Personal messenger	no	yes	yes	yes
Mechanical messenger	no	yes	no	yes
Telephone	yes	no	yes	no
Telex/TWX	yes	no	no	yes
Intercommunication	yes	no	yes	no
Telegraph	no	yes (Wiretax)	no	yes
TELautograph.	yes	yes	no	yes
TV	yes	yes	yes	no

among the several means. Discussion of these characteristics is contained on the following pages.

Mail

It is doubtful that a modern enterprise could exist without mail; it is imperative that some written means of offering the services of the enterprise and of issuing answers to inquiries, statements, and invoices be available. Promptness, accuracy, and reasonable cost are the major requisites of satisfactory mail service.

In addressing mail the Zip Code should always be included because it expedites delivery. Postal authorities offer assistance in providing Zip Codes and a Zip Code directory is available from which the Zip Code for any U.S. address can be obtained. The first digit of the Zip Code designates one of ten national service areas. The second digit identifies the service subdivision, the third digit the post office in that subdivision, the last two digits the post office station from which the mail to that addressee is delivered. Figure 10–2 shows the Zip Code National Areas

FIGURE 10–2
The Zip Code National Areas and Authorized Two-Letter Abbreviations for the Various States

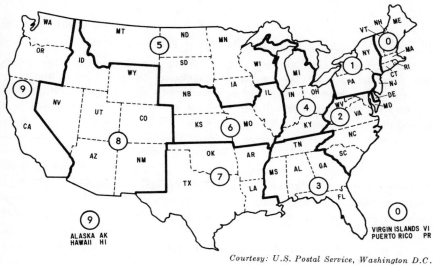

Courtesy: U.S. Postal Service, Washington D.C.

along with authorized two-letter state abbreviations. By using these abbreviations, the city, state, and Zip Code can be written on one line by most addressing machines. There are over 600 major post offices and sectional centers and about 42,000 different Zip Codes. Mass users of second- and third-class mail are required to update and sort their mailings by the full five-digit Zip Code.

Use of proper envelopes also contributes to satisfactory mail service. Standard-sized envelopes are best suited for most purposes. The No. 9 or No. 10 envelope for correspondence is preferable, since only two horizontal folds in the enclosed material are necessary.

The postage-saver envelope permits third-class rates, yet gives the appearance of first-class mail. Also, the two-in-one combination envelope is recommended where a folder or booklet is sent with a letter. With this type of envelope, the letter or other first-class mail is in one compartment, while the folder or other third-class mail is in another compartment. Illustrations of the postage-saver and the two-in-one envelope are shown in Figure 10–3.

FIGURE 10–3
A Postage-Saver Envelope and a Two-in-One Combination Envelope

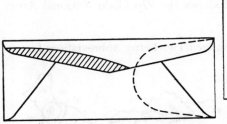 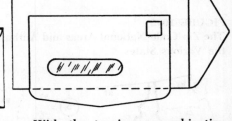

A postage-saver envelope requiring only third-class rate can be top-sealed like a first-class envelope. One end of flap remains unsealed to permit postal inspection.

With the two-in-one combination envelope, first-class mail in one compartment and third-class or fourth-class mail in the other can be mailed as a unit.

Further, to increase returns and lower costs from mail promotions, it is advantageous not to enclose regular stamped envelopes but business reply envelopes. To use them, a no fee permit is required. The postage for such envelopes is of a collect-on-delivery type for which the initial sender pays 10 cents for each reply, based on an 8 cents regular charge plus 2 cents for return privilege. If the return is less than 80 percent of the original mailing, a common result, the use of business reply envelopes results in savings. When regular stamped envelopes are enclosed, the postage for 100 replies is $10; likewise postage on 80 business reply envelopes is $8.

Different types of mail service are available. Familiarity with these various types enables the sender to use the type best suited for the individual needs. Figure 10–4 gives a brief sketch of those services most commonly used. For complete information regarding the various type services and their current rates, a representative of the local post office should be consulted. The standards by which mail is divided into different classes that pay different rates are being reviewed and studied for change in view of the service requirements and the cost of providing these services.

FIGURE 10–4
Selected Types of Mail Service

1. *Airmail.* Use when most expeditious handling is required in dispatch and delivery. This service is advantageous for distances greater than 250 miles.
2. *First-class mail.* For regular correspondence not requiring highest priority. Currently on a space available basis, all first-class mail that can be advanced in delivery is transported by air.
3. *Third-class mail.* Includes material and parcels of 16 ounces or less that qualify for third-class, such as circulars, catalogues, seeds, bulbs, and plants.
4. *Fourth-class mail.* Commonly referred to as parcel post, this service includes printed material and parcels weighing 16 ounces or more that qualify for fourth-class.
5. *Certified mail.* Recommended when proof of delivery is wanted and the material has no monetary value. A record of delivery is provided and the sender can request a receipt when mailing.
6. *Registered mail.* Designed for material that requires security and protection. A return receipt and delivery to the addressee only are provided. Registered mail costs more than certified mail.
7. *Special delivery mail.* Provides that mailed material is given expeditious handling at post office of the addressee.
8. *Special handling mail.* For fourth-class mail which is given first-class priority and handling. Recommended for parcel fourth-class so that it is given first-class treatment in transit.
9. *Insurance.* Liability for insured mail is limited to $200. Its use is justified when replacement cost of item merits the insurance expense.
10. *Military ordinary mail (MOM).* All official Government mail addressed to an APO or FPO address receives airlift from exit point of United States at a cost approximating one-half the airmail rate.

Source: Condensed from *U.S. Postal Guide,* Washington, D.C. Supt. of Documents.

Mail Room Operations

The tasks performed in connection with handling the mail can be conveniently classified into those dealing with *incoming* mail and those dealing with *outgoing* mail. With reference to the former, the following are common and well-defined steps:

1. Receiving and Opening the Mail. Some companies have a representative call for its mail especially for first morning mail which can be distributed by the time the office formally opens. When this is the practice, employees handling incoming mail report for work about one-half hour before the regular opening office hour.

Mail is opened either by hand or by machine, depending upon the volume of mail. For manual means a good standard is 15 pieces per minute. Machines will open as many as 500 letters per minute. In Figure 10–5, the man in the foreground is opening letters by means of a machine. Mail marked "Personal" or addressed to specific individuals is not company mail and may or may not be opened, whichever is the policy of the company. The common practice is not to open it. In some in-

FIGURE 10–5
Handling the Incoming Mail in a Large Bank

Courtesy: First National Bank in Dallas.

stances, mail so addressed is forwarded immediately to the employee's home address.

2. Sorting and Time Stamping. The next step is to remove the contents of the envelopes and, at the same time, sort the mail according to who handles the particular type under question; this might be a department, a division, or an individual. Usually, the name of the person or of the department to whom the letter is addressed determines where it is to be delivered. When this is not given, a quick scanning of the paper is necessary to determine its proper destination. In exceptional cases, the entire contents must be read.

In the case of mail containing money or checks, a listing showing the senders' name and address and the amount enclosed is made out by the mailing department. The cash and checks, along with the listing, are later sent to the cashier department. In other instances, the check is attached to the letter; or in the case of cash, the money is placed in a small envelope and attached to the letter, with appropriate notation. The checks and cash are then delivered to the cashier department.

A letter referring to previous correspondence can either be delivered to the department concerned, which, if necessary, requests the file from the filing department; or it can be sent to the filing department, where the needed file is attached and forwarded to the proper correspondent.

The method used depends chiefly upon the number of such letters received and the system of filing used.

Again referring to Figure 10–5, the man in the background is sorting to the proper compartments in the sorting racks. The general pattern of the various compartments in the rack is similar to that of the mail stations in the office, for in this way the sorted mail can be kept in a logical order for ultimate distribution.

At the time the mail is read and sorted, it is customary to stamp the hour and date received on each piece of correspondence. This provides a timed receipt that can be used as evidence in controversial matters regarding the correspondence. It can also be used for checking the efficiency of mail distribution in the office.

3. Distributing the Mail. This is the final step in the handling of incoming mail and is usually done by messengers, although other means, such as conveyor belts and pneumatic tubes, may be utilized.

For *outgoing* mail, the major steps in mail handling are as follows. Normally, the same employees handle both incoming and outgoing mail.

1. Collecting and Grouping by Destinations. To help in collecting, outgoing mail is usually placed in special desk trays specified as mail stations. Upon receipt at the mail room, the mail is first grouped according to geographical area, then by city, and then by name of addressee. Sorting racks are commonly used for this purpose. All mail of a similar class, and addressed to the same wholesaler, branch, or company, is put together so that it can be mailed as a single piece. Frequently, large Manila envelopes with the address printed or stenciled thereon are used for these large firm mailings. In some instances, each of the outgoing sorting racks contains an addressed envelope which is handy for instant use. Replenishments are made either the first thing in the morning or at regular intervals throughout the day.

2. Inserting, Sealing, and Stamping.. If necessary, the material is folded and inserted by the mail department. When ordinary envelopes are used, the name and address on the material must be checked with that on the envelope. Sealing and stamping can be done either by hand or by machine; the volume of mail should determine the method used. Figure 10–6 shows major equipment in a modern mail room. The machine in the foreground automatically folds, inserts, seals, stamps, and counts the mail.

It is advisable to appoint one mail-room employee as sole custodian of postage. In the case of a manual method, this person should affix the postage to the letters or packages personally or should see the letters or packages it is going on before issuing postage to someone else.

The machine method employs a meter-mail machine that imprints the postage seal either directly on a letter or, in the case of a package,

FIGURE 10–6
Machines Make Sending Mail as Pleasant as Getting It

Courtesy: Friden Division, The Singer Co., San Leandro, Calif.

on an adhesive paper tape which is affixed to the package. At the same
time the postage seal is imprinted, a "meter ad," postmark, and date
are also imprinted. This is illustrated by Figure 10–7. The machines
are offered in an array of capacities and designs; many seal as well
as stamp the envelope.

An important part of this machine is the meter, which is a detachable,

FIGURE 10–7
**Illustrative of Metered-Mail Imprints, Showing
"Meter Ad," Postmark, Date, and Amount of
Postage**

(⅔ actual size)

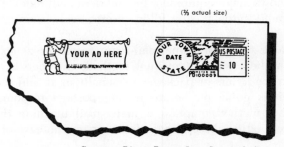

Courtesy: Pitney-Bowes, Inc., Stamford, Conn.

portable unit containing the printing die for the postage and a recording mechanism. In buying postage, the meter is taken to the post office and set for a lump sum which is paid in advance. The set meter is then returned to the place of business and inserted into the machine, from which metered stamps can be printed as and when needed. In essence, *a postage-meter machine is a government-licensed device for affixing postage.* Figure 10–8 illustrates postage-meter machines. Meter

FIGURE 10–8
Postage Meter Machines

Courtesy: Pitney-Bowes, Inc., Stamford, Conn.

On the left is shown the Touchmatic desk-model, 10-key keyboard model; on the right is a fully automatic mail unit for the one-man processing of heavy volume mail.

mail has many advantages, including the following: (1) Time and effort are saved; (2) stamp losses are stopped; (3) accurate accounting of postal expenditures is provided; (4) date of mailing is shown; (5) quicker handling is provided by the originating post office, since no canceling is required; (6) the prestige of the user is increased; and (7) postmark, slogan, and advertising are added.

3. *Mailing the Material.* It is advisable to post mail at regular intervals throughout the day. This practice smooths out the work load, minimizes the usual late afternoon peak, and helps the post office to deliver mail promptly. It is necessary to deliver certain classes of mail to the post office.

Mail Management

To manage all these mail operations requires good management practices. To this end, it is well to begin by examining the mail room operations. The determination of current cost to handle a piece of mail serves as a base to which possible mail handling improvements can be judged. To calculate this cost, first determine total mail handling cost. This can be considered to consist of labor and overhead. Determine the cost for the full time mail employees and to this add an estimate of the cost of employees spending a portion of their time on mail. To calculate mail room overhead cost, multiply the company's total overhead by the fraction of mail room floor space area by the company's total floor space area. As a simplified alternative, the total handling cost can be calculated as total mail room labor cost plus 50 percent for overhead. Now divide this total handling cost by the number of incoming, outgoing, and intracompany pieces of mail. Divide the postage cost by the number of outgoing pieces. Add the handling and postage-per-piece cost to determine the approximate cost to handle a piece of mail. As stated above, this cost figure provides a base figure from which possible improvements in mail can be evaluated.

A big factor in mail management, if not the biggest, is mechanization. Helpful comparisons of manual versus mechanized mailroom operations are indicated by Figure 10–9. For a number of mailroom operations,

FIGURE 10–9
The Rate in Pieces per Minute for Selected Mailroom Operations by Type of Processing Means Followed

	Manual	*Machine*	*High-Speed Machine*
Opening mail	12	45	160
Folding letters	10	60	175
Sealing and stamping letters	10	50	500

a machine can do the work three to four times faster than the manual means. To illustrate, for a medium size company the work of manually folding each bill, inserting into a window envelope, sealing, and stamping formerly required a day. Now the work is completed in slightly over two hours by means of a machine. Or consider the experience of a bank where the outgoing mail was sorted and stamped manually. By adopting available machines, a savings of $3500 per year is being realized.

Another important factor in mail management is the layout of the mailroom. It should be so designed that only necessary motions are required and that proper machines and equipment are utilized and positioned to enable the proper sequence of operations. Too often the mailroom is crowded and the flow of mail is disorderly. Figure 10–10 shows an effective mailroom layout. Separate routing is provided for incoming

FIGURE 10–10
Effective Mail Room Layout

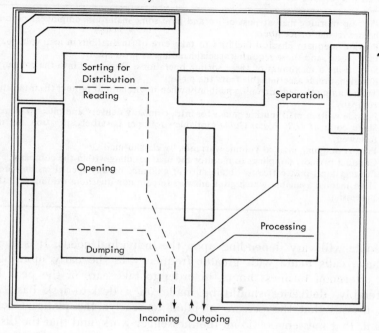

and for outgoing mail, and each is processed in an orderly sequence. Giving adequate attention to what happens to mail when it gets to the mail room can pay big returns. In some cases, 25–30 percent savings are realized by adopting the proper mail room layout for the company's individual needs.

A third and final factor in mail management is to determine and follow certain guidelines. These will vary somewhat with the individual conditions and requirements, but in general those shown in Figure 10–11 will prove beneficial.

Messenger Service—Personal Means

For intracompany delivery of various papers, either a personal or a mechanical messenger service can be used. The selection depends upon such factors as the number and frequency of the papers, the number of delivery points, the distances between these points, the maximum allowable time between these points, and the cost.

The personal means is common. The service should be regular and frequent; calls about every half hour are recommended. However, the

FIGURE 10–11
Mail Management Is Enhanced by Following Guidelines Such as These

1. Pick up morning mail at post office and have some mail room employees process mail before regular office hours.
2. Provide adequate physical facilities to take care of fluctuations in mail volume, size of mail pieces, and those requiring special handling or protection.
3. Sort, using a maximum of three sorting operations. Direct sort into the compartment, if designation is ascertainable from the piece.
4. Time-stamp selected incoming mail only when it will help to protect the interests of the company.
5. Provide written mail routing guides for intra-company delivery and pick-up of mail.
6. Make copy of *U.S. Postal Guide* available so proper postal classification and rate are followed.
7. Presort outgoing mail, as volume warrants, by class of mail.
8. Conduct periodic samplings to monitor the mail handling within the company.
9. Contact local post office to obtain current guidance on any special mailing problems.
10. Have manual available which gives answers to common questions dealing with the mail processing.

schedule will vary depending upon the individual needs. It is common to have calls made with greater frequency in the early morning and late afternoon business hours, in order to take care of the peak loads. Preferably, deliveries should be made on a desk-to-desk basis, since this insures that the person intended to receive the material actually gets it, that messengers do all the messenger work, and that the distribution and collection are accomplished with a minimum of effort and confusion.

A common practice is to include some of the mail personnel in the messenger group. In the opinion of some managers carrying messages provides excellent training for certain new, inexperienced employees. They can quickly learn the names of key employees, location of their work stations, layout of the office and plant, and the work of each organizational unit. Personal messenger service requires close supervision and adherence to these practices:

1. Each route with its designated stations must be defined and the allowable time for one trip must be known. Between trips, rest periods amounting to about 20 percent of the total travel time should be provided.

2. All stations must be visited on each trip.

3. Messengers should confine their efforts to the delivery and pickup of written materials along the prescribed routes. The running of errands should be forbidden.

4. Each messenger has an accordian file and sorts the papers as they are collected so that on each trip deliveries can be made to stations not yet called upon. Papers designated for stations already called upon are delivered on the next trip. The file can be portable or mounted on wheels and pushed from station to station.

5. A designated area or receptacle for "incoming" and another for "outgoing" messages should be used at each station.

6. Control over messenger activities is exercised by having messengers at selected stations either check in with the supervisor or pick up a card and replace it with another of a different color or number. By using different cards each trip, a quick check is provided. To inform of the last collection, leaving a card printed "Last collection has been made" or the messenger saying, "Good night," can be followed.

Messenger Service—Mechanical Means

When the work volume to be distributed is large, fairly constant, and the stations are fixed, the use of mechanical conveyors is recommended. Conveyors can include turns, end of channel stackers, and remotely controlled gates or brush-off stops to deposit at a specific station. It is also possible to transfer materials from one moving channel to another automatically. Figure 10–12 illustrates a conveyor belt being used to transport inquiries within a credit bureau office.

Pneumatic tubes are effective, easy to use, and do not require special skill to operate. Material is carried quickly and accurately to its destina-

FIGURE 10–12
Conveyors Being Effectively Used to Transmit Data in an Office

Courtesy: Data-Veyors Corp., Oakland, Calif.

tion. The initial cost of the tubes is rather high, but the maintenance cost is low. The use of pneumatic tubes is most economical where the volume of work is large. Different-sized tubes and tube carriers are offered. For example, a "4-inch tube carrier" is a popular size and has maximum inside length of 14 inches. Rectangular-shaped carriers are also available for handling bulky items.

Telephone

Verbal distribution of information is entirely satisfactory in many cases and for this purpose the telephone is very effective. Good telephone practices aid in building the good will of any enterprise, save time and energy, and help get work accomplished. Much of the wide usage of the telephone has come about because it provides an inexpensive, convenient, and rapid means of verbally communicating information. But the telephone is also important in transmitting information such as in Data-Phone, already discussed in Chapter 8.

Telephone systems can be classified into three types: (1) the outside telephone with extensions handled through a company switchboard (PBX), (2) the private internal telephone (PAX), and (3) Centrex telephone service. The first provides service for external calls coming into or going out of the office and for internal calls between telephones within the office. However, by using the Dial PBX, outbound calls are dialed directly from every desk, so the telephone attendant can handle incoming calls and perform other work. Figure 10–13 shows a Dial PBX. In the second type, private internal telephone (PAX), "inside" calls do not go through the switchboard. Since, in the typical company, more than one half of the telephoning is internal—between telephones within the company—use of the private internal exchange relieves the regular telephone lines. This clears the way for better service on "outside" calls—those from customers and other important callers. The third type, or Centrex telephone service, features Direct Inward Dialing (DID), that is, all incoming calls, local or long distance, can go directly to the extension, which carries its own number—the usual seven-digit number. Centrex needs no switchboard attendants to handle most calls, insures maximum privacy on every call, saves about one-half minute on each call by dialing directly, and provides itemized telephone billing by individual telephone station. Interoffice calls are handled simply by dialing the last four digits assigned to the extension that is called.

Proper Use of Telephone

Conversing over the telephone places the participants in a relationship whereby they can hear but cannot see each other. The impression must rely entirely on the voice—its tone, clearness, and pleasantness; the selec-

FIGURE 10–13
A Dial PBX Provides an Easy, Part-Time Job for the Attendant

Courtesy: Illinois Bell Telephone Co., Chicago.

tion of words; and the manner of speaking. All of these factors, properly blended, constitute the art of telephoning, which can be acquired.

For the switchboard attendant, a clear, well-modulated voice and the employment of certain phrases and words are assets. To illustrate, it is effective to identify the company immediately by saying "Good morning, American Manufacturing Company." If the caller must be delayed, the attendant should so advise. A caller agreeing to wait should be advised every 30 seconds that the line is still busy. When able to complete the call, "I'll connect you now. Thanks for waiting," is appropriate. When the caller cannot wait, a name and number should be obtained and the call returned.

From the viewpoint of the individual telephone user, it is basic that the telephone be answered immediately and identification supplied, such as "Cost Department, Mr. Allen." If answering for someone else, give that person's name and then yours. Say "Mrs. Brown's office. Mr. Willis speaking." Some incoming calls will have to be transferred and when this occurs the calling party should be so advised. Also, in case it is necessary to leave the line, tell the caller why and for how long—"Excuse me a moment. I must look at our file on this." And on an outgoing call, always introduce yourself promptly to the other person.

There are, of course, technical aspects to the effective use of the telephone. For example, the switchboard attendant must know the correct routing of calls and how best to handle unusual requests, dial numbers, and write messages. On the other hand, the individual user should remember to speak directly into the transmitter, place one hand over the mouthpiece to hear better in a noisy place, move the contact button slowly and evenly to attract the operator's attention, and, to keep the line alive, replace the receiver gently after finishing a conversation.

Auxiliary Telephone Service

It is possible for several executives in different parts of the country to hold a conference by means of a simultaneous telephone hookup known as *conference call service*. The savings in time and trouble from this type of service are obvious. Experience indicates that upward to about 20 persons can hold telephone meetings in a relaxed and trouble free atmosphere. Lack of visual contact is no problem, participants immediately identify who is speaking. If not acquainted with the speaker, each identifies him- or herself the first few times and after several minutes, voice recognition should be automatic. Further, telephone meetings minimize interruptions and diversionary and wasteful discussions. In some instances, the connections are monitored or recorded for possible future reference. When this is done, approval by the parties is necessary. The signal that the call is being recorded is a "beep" tone every 15 seconds.

A perpetual telephone receptionist is afforded by the *automatic answering device*. This unit, about four times the size of a telephone, is linked to the telephone. Incoming calls are answered by a recorded message something like this:

> This is the Avenue Realty Company. Your call is being answered by an automatic answering device. Will you leave your name, telephone number, and message after you hear the "beep" tone? You may leave a half-minute message for me, and I'll call you when I return. Thank you.

After returning to the office, all messages recorded by the unit are audited and the return calls made. The device is especially convenient not only for small, one-person offices and for doctors, but also for large offices during the nonworking hours, thus providing around-the-clock service.

Radio-telephone service provides communication between moving units and any Bell System telephone. It is particularly adaptable for use by trucking, taxicab, and public service companies, and by police and fire departments. For a two-way communication, a mobile unit is called by means of a regular desk telephone. A request is made for the mobile service operator who, by means of radio, signals the driver of the mobile unit. This is done over an approved radio channel. The driver answers the call on the dashboard telephone, and the conversation takes place. In a similar manner, the driver can call the office from the mobile unit. In contrast, the one-way service signals only to the mobile unit. By means of a code, the driver translates the message, such as "Go to Warehouse R immediately."

WATS, or wide-area telephone service. This provides unlimited interstate telephoning within specific areas for a flat monthly rate. It is designed for the customer who makes frequent calls to widely scattered and distant points.

Leased Private Lines. These insure availability of the circuit for the customer who is provided exclusive use between two or more locations for a scheduled period each day. This service is preferred when a large volume is sent regularly to a small number of fixed points.

Dataphone. Machines are able to talk to each other by means of this service. It is very important in the transmission of data in the language of a computer. Dataphone is fully discussed in Chapter 8, page 212.

Management of Telephone Usage

In 1969 the Federal Communications Commission in its *Carterphone* decision ruled it was legal for a user of telephone service to purchase telephone equipment from any vendor. That is, the telephone user has the legal right to buy equipment and connect it to the utilities' lines. Since this ruling, hundreds of companies, called interconnect companies, are now offering a variety of equipment to purchase. Further, the user is now able to secure leased voice or data channels from a number of supplemental common carriers. All this has emphasized more and closer analysis of any acquired telephone equipment and the careful matching of different features to obtain the best economical cost and service. To perform this work properly, the user must identify requirements for service, select the best supplier, and establish control over the system adopted. And, in turn, this means that a manager or a small managerial group should be appointed to see that satisfactory telephone service at an acceptable cost is obtained.

In addition, periodic checkups on the use of the telephone by company personnel are in order. All calls should be handled in the company's prescribed manner. Data can be obtained on the time required to handle calls and on the manner of speech. Concentrate on the promptness in answering the telephone, helpfulness on all calls, and a pleasing telephone personality. Employees should be informed that periodic checkups are made. When necessary, remedial action should be taken without delay.

There is also the challenge of keeping the telephone cost to a minimum consistent with desired service. Of all office expenses, the monthly telephone bill receives relatively little attention. Yet there are many ways provided by the telephone company to keep telephone cost down. To illustrate, Direct Distance Dialing (DDD) carries a lower rate than an operator assisted long-distance call. Also, the rates drop drastically at 5 P.M. If the call is from an east to a west time zone, the person in the called zone may still be at a desk working normal hours. Further, every day from 11 P.M. to 8 A.M., there is a very low one-minute night rate and if the call takes longer, the overtime is billed at a very low rate. Additional helpful suggestions are provided by communicating with the telephone company's special representative who is always glad to be of help.

Another area of telephone usage management, meriting inclusion here, is greater recognition of "telephone power." Telephoning can be very effective in reducing traveling cost. By means of a $5 telephone call as much may be accomplished as a personal face-to-face meeting costing $200. And telephoning can be effective in increasing sales, handling low volume accounts, and contacting delinquent accounts. The telephone is a vital communication means and the management of its usage must include its possible contribution in many decision-making acts.

Intercommunication Systems

Quick verbal communication of information is provided by means of intercommunication systems. Within an enterprise the various individuals or stations are each equipped with a speaking-talking unit. By turning a switch or pushing a button, instant right-of-way is obtained with anyone in the circuit, and conversations can be conducted with great clarity of tone. When privacy is desired, the microphone in the unit can be turned off and a handset substituted.

Many different capacities and features in units are available. It is advisable to consult with the manufacturer or sales representative for specific data regarding individual requirements. The units can be connected in various circuit arrangements, depending upon the needs of the particular enterprise. Figure 10–14 shows models of intercommunication units.

Paging Systems

Important in most companies is the means of locating people through the use of flashing lights, tone bells, and buzzers. These paging devices are usually run by the telephone switchboard operator, or they may be a part of a private internal telephone system or of the intercommunication system. The light or noise outlets are located throughout the office and plant, so that key personnel are free to leave their desks

FIGURE 10–14
Intercommunication Units

Courtesy: Executone, Inc., Long Island City.

Engineered to meet modern requirements, these intercommunication units enable the user to converse conveniently with persons at many other master or staff stations. For the unit on the left most calls will be via amplified voice, but the user has the option of using handset for confidential conversations. The unit on the right features versatility and dependability. "Built-in courtesy" announces incoming calls by tone and signal light.

without fear of missing any calls. By means of a code, such as two long and two short rings for the president, one long and one short ring for the controller, and so on, these people are notified of calls. By calling either the switchboard operator or a designated person, the message is obtained. The system is quite effective, for it is convenient and is a time-saver to all concerned. The latest paging units feature soft sounds in quiet areas and adequately loud sounds in noisy areas.

Telegraph

A well-known means of handling informational communications over relatively long distances is the telegraph. Telegrams secure attention, provide terse businesslike messages, and impel immediate action. They are used for practically all subjects or phrases of business activities and can be sent by any of four main ways: (1) over the counter—giving it to the operator at any branch office; (2) by messenger; (3) by telephone—similar to an ordinary telephone call, charges being made to the telephone account or paid by coins dropped into a public pay telephone; and (4) by mechanical tie lines, such as direct telephone connections which is simply a direct wire between the sender's office and the local telegraph office.

The cost of regular telegraphic communications varies with length of message, distance, and speed of delivery. Domestic messages are classified into (1) telegram, and (2) overnight telegram. The former gives the speediest service, delivery usually being made within an hour or so. The minimum rate applies for 15 words or less; excess words are charged at a low extra word rate. The second type, or overnight telegram, can be sent anytime during the day up to midnight for delivery at destination the following morning. The minimum rate applies for 100 words or less; again, excess words are charged at a low extra word rate. For comparable distances, a 100-word overnight telegram costs less than a fast 15-word telegram. Different rates apply for intrastate and interstate messages.

There is also a *Mailgram* service by Western Union. It is a fast and economical way to reach anyone in continental United States. It is a joint service by Western Union and the U.S. Postal Service. Messages are telegraphic, computer routed by Zip Code to nearest post office of destination. By inputing before 7 P.M., delivery to addressee is assured for next business day. Mailgram is a fast means to reach a single or a thousand persons at a fraction of the cost for either a telegram or a long-distance telephone call.

Cablegrams or services to foreign countries have a different classification and include: (1) ordinary—the standard full-rate service, (2) urgent—priority over all other messages except government messages, (3) deferred—no priority over other types, and (4) night letter—messages permitting overnight delivery.

Code words are sometimes used for telegraphic communications in order to reduce costs or to insure secrecy. For example, the code word "ROEUZ" might mean: "What action shall I take?" Commerical codes are available, or a special code can be created.

Telex/TWX service is the national and international teleprinter network that provides an economical way for companies to communicate with other companies. The speed of the telephone is combined with the accuracy of a letter. Telex/TWX provides direct access to over 500,000 terminals—over 130,000 in United States, Canada, and Mexico, the remainder overseas. Initially, two different services, it is now integrated. Telex and TWX differ primarily in operating speed and code. The teleprinter employed in this service is a machine similar to a typewriter which transmits messages between stations. Basically the keyboard of the machine is standard and when the keys are depressed, electric impulses reproduce the message in typed form on one machine or on many similar machines, the number being determined by the number of connections desired. To send a message, the Telex/TWX subscribers' directory is consulted, the call is placed by number, and the connection is made. The communication is two way; a written conversation can be carried out. The service is especially attractive over long distances. Charges are made on the basis of time and distance, similar to the long-distance telephone with rates being approximately one-half those of the telephone.

In addition, *Datacom* is offered by Western Union and consists of a low-cost bulk digital data transmission service. It employs multiplexing techniques. The service features a wide range of speeds and codes, national coverage, and no long-term contract. The service is available for a minimum of 30 days and there is no installation service charge. *Westar* is a domestic communications satellite system consisting of three satellites—two in orbit and a third when traffic dictates. Each satellite has 12 transponders, each of which has one color TV program, and 1200 one-way voice channels. Westar, put in operation during late 1974 by Western Union, permits relay of information from any point in the United States to any other point or points in the United States. The earth stations are so located to serve major population centers and permit transmission of voice, TV, and data signals with a mix of speeds.

Anything printed or drawn, such as layouts, drawings, or charts, can now be transmitted instantly and accurately by WIREFAX, a special service using telegraph equipment. Actually, WIREFAX is a public facsimile system that transmits in units up to $7\frac{1}{2} \times 9\frac{1}{2}$ inches. Cost depends upon amount and distance. Charges for the initial unit between Chicago and New York are about $5, and each additional unit is about 50 cents.

There are also machines supplying the transmission of printed documents, drawings, and charts. A popular unit, called Desk-Fax, employs facsimile telegraphy which is a fast, accurate, and economical means. The user simply writes or types a message, places it on the drum of the machine, and pushes a button. The rest is automatic. Desk-Fax is illustrated by Figure 10–15.

Machines are also available that convert any written material, chart, or photograph into electrical signals which are sent over telephone lines and reconstructed into an exact facsimile in black and white by a receiving machine. The reproduction is an exact copy of the original. The transmission is rapid, an $8\frac{1}{2} \times 11$-inch page requiring just a few minutes. For example, the Xerox Telecopier automatically receives and transmits by telephone facsimile messages up to as many as seventy-five without an operator in attendance. A copy of anything you put on paper can be sent anywhere in the United States within four minutes. The machine is rented and is popular for copies of legal documents, medical records, rush orders, and design copies. See Figure 10–16.

TELautograph

Another well-known means for transmitting messages is the TELautograph. As the name suggests, it transmits a handwritten message. The writing is electrically reproduced mainly, but not exclusively, over com-

FIGURE 10–15
Desk-Fax Machine for Transmitting High-Quality Facsimiles

Courtesy: Western Union Telegraph Co., New York.

FIGURE 10–16
Facsimile Messages Are Sent and Received Efficiently by the Xerox Telecopier

Courtesy: Xerox Corp., Rochester, N.Y.

paratively short distances. It is popular for communication between main office and receiving room, department and department, and warehouse and main office. In order to send a message, a switch is turned on, and the message is written with a metal stylus on a metal platen. To see what is being written, the sender watches the pen of the instrument writing on a roll of paper. Figure 10–17 illustrates a TELautograph. As

FIGURE 10–17
TELautograph Receiver and Transmitter Instruments Which Handle
Handwritten Messages, Including Special Symbols and Sketches

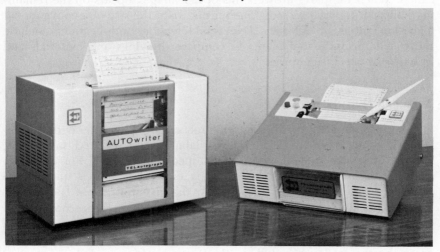

Courtesy: TELautograph Corp., Los Angeles.

the message is written, it is reproduced almost simultaneously at one or a number of connected points.

A TELautograph provides economical and high-speed transmitting and receiving of messages. Handwritten records are furnished and can be attached to such things as inquiries, notices, and shipping instructions. It is possible to carry on a written conversation—messages can be sent and received.

Closed-Circuit Television

Currently application in business is somewhat specialized, but television holds much promise for the future. By means of closed circuits, it is possible to transmit and have instantaneous receipt at many points. Television presents the message visually and in motion—a series of events. However, it does not provide a written record of the information to the recipient.

An interesting application concerns railroad freight car reporting wherein cars move by a TV camera stationed at a strategic point in the freight yard. Pertinent data are viewed on the side of the car and transmitted to a policing and recording center. Floodlights provide proper illumination for both day and night operation.

A television-telephone, enabling the caller to see as well as hear the party at the other end of the line, is available. When the caller lifts the television-telephone, her or his image appears simultaneously on one half of the screen and upon one half of that of the party being called. When the party answers, his or her image appears on the remaining halves of the two screens. The unit is about the size of a conventional television table model set. Television-telephone applications include those in large industrial plants to compare drawings and materials and in banks to check signatures.

Tape and Wire Recorders

For purposes of recording information covering such activities as inventory counts, personnel interviews, laboratory tests, and sales talks, the use of tape and wire recorders is especially effective. For inventory counts, the person taking the count is equipped with a microphone attached to the recorder in the office. As the inventory count is obtained, it is spoken and thus recorded. A typist then plays the recording and types the inventory lists. Intermediate paper work, tally sheets, and the like are eliminated. Likewise, interviews with prospective employees or, in the case of lawyers, talks with clients can be recorded and studied for complete information—a more effective practice than the use of handwritten notes, which often inhibit the speaker. However, when conversations are recorded, approval by both parties is necessary. Tape or wire is used in the operation of the machine. The tape is a narrow, thin, flexible, paperlike material coated on one side with magnetic oxide of iron; when wire is used, it is of a special type.

QUESTIONS

1. Discuss two practices that contribute to effective mail management.
2. State concisely the difference between each of the following:
    a. Certified mail and registered mail.
    b. An automatic answering device for a telephone and "telephone power."
    c. Metered mail and first-class mail.
    d. Wirefax and Datacom.
3. In your opinion is the handling of incoming or of outgoing mail the more difficult to manage? Justify your viewpoint.

4. A number of improvements in modern telephone equipment have expanded the use of this communication medium. Discuss how these improvements contribute to better office work.
5. Discuss the use and management of intercommunication systems in an enterprise.
6. Describe five types of mail service and relate under what conditions you would use each type.
7. Clearly identify and discuss Telex/TWX service in office communication.
8. For what general types of applications would you as an office manager recommend the use of mechanical conveyors for the distribution of office papers? Why?
9. Describe the meaning and use of paging systems.
10. Describe briefly each of the following, pointing out for what type of communication and under what circumstances it is best suited:
   a. Mailgram.
   b. TELautograph.
   c. WATS telephone service.
   d. Personal means of messenger service.
11. Enumerate key considerations in the effective use of the telephone in a modern office.
12. Under what general circumstances would you suggest that an enterprise use (*a*) the telegraph, (*b*) the long-distance telephone (*c*) an airmail letter, (*d*) closed-circuit television, and (*e*) the TELautograph? Give reasons for your answers.

CASE PROBLEMS

Case 10–1. Lane Company

MR. LANE (OFFICE MANAGER): Mrs. Gordon, I have asked you to come to my office so that we can discuss our present telephone service.

MRS. GORDON (SUPERVISOR AND CHIEF OPERATOR): O.K.

LANE: There have been a number of complaints here of late and I'm sure you are aware of the fact that our present telephone service is apparently not what it ought to be.

GORDON: As a matter of fact, I am not aware of any such situation. We get complaints all the time. Some people just want to complain, no matter what. They are never satisfied. Like the other day, late in the . . .

LANE (interrupting): Yesterday Peter Fonville in sales orders told me more and more of our customers are complaining to him about how long they have to wait to get a line into his department.

GORDON: Yeah?

LANE: I've had several out of state people these past few weeks tell me that they have tried to reach me, but could not get through our switchboard. They said they finally made it after the third or fourth attempt.

GORDON: I don't know any long-distance call that did not get their party if they were somewhere in the office or factory area.

LANE: Well, that's what they told me. Also, I feel that several people right in my office and likewise in several units surrounding my office are having trouble in using the telephone.

GORDON: What's their trouble?

LANE: I don't know—the line's busy, they got the wrong party—any of a number of things.

GORDON: You know some of the difficulty may be that they dial or ask for the wrong number or they don't use the proper prefix number. I've explained it a hundred times and so do my operators. And as you know, we have quite a few new people in the office.

LANE: Yes, we do. However, the problem is to improve our service. Our telephone bill is now running around $450–500 a month. It used to be around $200, never over $300. Everything is higher in price—I realize that, but it seems to me that we must take some positive actions about our use of the telephone.

GORDON: Yes, sir, Mr. Lane.

LANE: Well, thank you for coming in. I'm going to give it more thought and I may be coming back to you within the next day or so.

Questions:

1. What is the company's problem as you see it?
2. What major factors have led to the present telephone situation now existent in the company? Discuss.
3. What action do you recommend Mr. Lane take? Why?

Case 10–2. Reba Products Company

General manager Betty Stahl firmly believes in employee initiative, self-discipline, and self-imposed responsibility as the marks of a top-notch office employee. "Give them freedom to operate, permit them to see what's to be done, and help them do it the best way," is her manner of expressing it. For office employees to receive personal telephone calls at the office was all right in the views of Ms. Stahl. Generally, the employees did not abuse the privilege. However, Elmer Willis had frequent long personal telephone conversations. Neither Ms. Stahl nor any of her supervisors had talked to Mr. Willis about it. Ms. Stahl hoped that Elmer Willis' own common sense, or that other office employees, would tell Elmer that he was endangering the telephone privilege for all.

One morning the general manager, in showing the office to a good customer, walked past Elmer's desk and observed him talking quite loudly on the telephone. The gist of the conversation marked it as a personal call. Some time later the general manager, in returning to her office, found Elmer still talking on the telephone. Intrigued by the length of the conversation, she waited until it ended, then told Elmer he talked too long on the telephone and that during working hours the telephone was primarily for business calls. Elmer replied, "Yes, I know that. But that call was not more than five minutes and that's certainly reasonable."

The general manager felt Elmer was flippant about the affair and, checking with the switchboard operator, was informed the call was from a suburban area, was paid for by the caller, and lasted 43 minutes. The general manager called Elmer to her office and gave him the information she had received. Elmer insisted the call was not more than five minutes. He added that the switchboard operator must "have it in for me" to report any greater time. When asked, "What do you consider reasonable time for a telephone call?" Elmer replied, "That's too general a question to answer intelligently. Frankly, I figure the telephone is there to help me. As long as I can do my work satisfactorily and the calls are paid for by the caller, I can't see any useful purpose in your playing Sherlock Holmes." At this the general manager informed Elmer that his employment was terminated and told him to get his paycheck from the cashier.

Questions:

1. What conditions led to this situation?
2. Discuss the practices and controls you advocate for use of the telephone for personal calls in an office.
3. What action do you recommend in this specific case?

Case 10–3. Harold Swink

Several months ago Harold Swink, age 19, was hired as a messenger. He is one of three messengers in a large office located in the center business district of a large eastern city. Harold is proving to be an excellent employee; he is accommodating, reports early every morning to help sort the mail, and radiates a cheerful and pleasant personality. He seems to like his work and appears to be a worthy addition to the office employees.

Harold Swink began to let his hair grow and also acquired long sideburns. Some of the office employees kidded him about his hair, but neither of his fellow messengers approximately the same age as Harold said anything. They wear their hair in a military style and are clean shaven. Several weeks later, Harold Swink began wearing to work clinging pink pants, wide belt, and boots. He also added a necklace with a big medallion. He looked the image of the world of mod.

Many of the employees of the office made comments of a light vein to Harold about his dress. Most were made in a spirit of fun, but several criticized him for wearing such attire. The office manager believed Harold had carried the matter too far. He asked the purchasing agent, father of two teenagers, to have a serious talk with Harold and suggest that he stop wearing the mod clothes to work. Several days later the purchasing agent did so. Harold's response was that what he wore was his own business. His work not his dress should be the basis of judgment. He felt the purchasing agent was of another generation and not tolerant of new ideas.

The purchasing agent reported his experience to the office manager who the next day called Harold to his office and informed him that the accepted customs of the office forbid wearing clothes such as he was wearing. The office manager stated that an employee is expected to abide by the accepted standards of office dress and warned Harold that he must cease wearing such clothes to work or face serious consequences. Harold replied that he saw nothing wrong with what he was wearing. He was simply expressing himself; his clothing was not offensive. Why should he dress like everyone else?

During the following week, Harold Swink continued to wear his mod clothes. At the end of the fifth day, the office manager personally informed him that his employment was terminated effective immediately.

Questions:

1. Was the action taken by the office manager correct? Why?
2. As Harold Swink, what would you do now? Justify your viewpoint.
3. As the office manager, would you have taken any action different than what was taken? Discuss.

Chapter **11**

Records Management—
Storage and Retrieval

Success does not consist in never making blunders,
but in never making the same one the second time.
Henry Wheeler Shaw

Since information is the basis for what is decided and what is done, information storage and information retrieval are daily necessities for any endeavor. We must have the information and be able to retrieve it quickly for effective management to exist. Further, and quite important, is the ability to determine conclusively that required information does not exist in the available storage of information. Likewise, it is important to escape the flood of information that is irrelevant and is not needed.

Each year, greater quantities of information must be stored and retrieved. Problems arise regarding how best to handle the information for quick reference, what arrangement to follow, what policies to adopt, and what equipment to utilize. The office is unique in that it stores many of its "products." This is a necessary part of information service. As we create more records, demand more information, and require more controls, storing and retrieving information has grown in importance. Every record and paper created and processed must have proper disposition. If it does not, or if we permit nonessential information to be stored, we are adding to the problem of achieving efficient records management. Attention will be directed first to recent mechanized means developed for storing and retrieving information followed by the manual or non-mechanized means.

293

Mechanized Means—Computer Storage and Retrieval

As pointed out in Chapter 8, common to many computer applications is an information network capable of storing, retrieving, and printing large quantities of data at high speeds. Computer information retrieval can be thought of as the automation of the intellectual effort of information input to provide quick accessing to voluminous information on any of a multitude of subjects. The future is certain to bring many more specialized libraries in a form that utilizes automated information retrieval. Scientists, business leaders, and governmental officials are especially interested in the retrieval of certain information from a massive bank of data. Such facilities are now in existence and include an automated data center for information in a number of selected subject areas. Many more are destined to be established and grow. Heretofore, much of the money and time spent for decision making and research have gone for searching, scanning, and noting data pertinent to a particular study. Efforts were duplicated, and frequently not all pertinent knowledge was reviewed because of physical limitations. These inadequate methods are being replaced by vastly improved information retrieval.

By no means is the mechanization of information retrieval confined to the computer itself. Other arrangements have emerged and offer exciting possibilities. Before presenting these additional mechanized storing and retrieving means, a discussion of microfilming is included, since it is basic to many of the automated arrangements.

MICROFILMING

Microfilming is a photographic means of retaining information at a reduced size on film. It has been aptly termed, "information miniaturization on film." Microfilm was first employed extensively in banks where it was used in connection with checks. The list of applications grew steadily and its applications are now associated with many types of information. Microfilm is available to the small as well as the large enterprise. There are outside enterprises specializing in microfilming and they will microfilm records either in the client's office or their own. Estimates vary but it is the belief of many practicing information managers that over 95 percent of the financial organizations use microfilm, as do some 70 percent of the public utilities, and over 50 percent of the manufacturers, insurance companies, and governmental agencies.

This broad usage of microfilm has given rise to a micrographic system within a large number of enterprises. In all these, microfilm is the information medium used. The variety of user needs has brought forth a number of microfilm forms. Figure 11–1 shows six common forms including roll or reel, magazine or cartridge, micro-thin jacket, microfiche,

FIGURE 11–1
Common Microfilm Media Forms

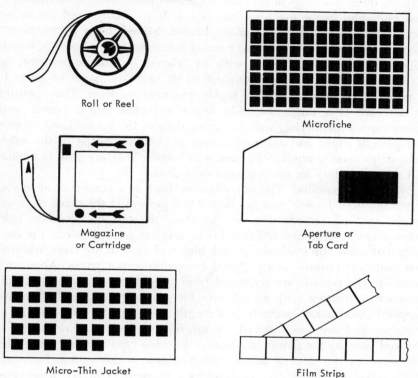

aperture or tab card, and film strips. Which form to use in any given application depends primarily on the type of input, the characteristics of the information stored, and how it is to be used. However, additional factors are important and include the speed and ease of retrieval, the capability of handling the volume of work and supplying hard copies as desired, the frequency of updates or file changes, the security of the material filed, compatability with existing office machines and equipment, and the overall system cost.

The roll or reel resembles a 16-mm. movie film with the pictures in sequence along the roll. The same is true for the magazine or cartridge except in this case the film linage is smaller and the cartridge is more portable. The reel form is commonly used for relatively inactive records while the magazine type is the common choice where automatic retrieval is followed. A micro-thin jacket is about 4 inches by 6 inches and accommodates 16 mm. film in several rows or channels across the jacket. For charts or engineering drawings, a larger or 35-mm. film may be used, which when included in a jacket may require two channels so that perhaps three drawings in one broad channel plus channels of standardized microfilm might make up one jacket. It is usually used for active records frequently updated and duplicated. Microfiche is a transparent sheet of film containing multiple rows of microimages. A 4-inch × 6-inch microfiche may have 7 rows with 14 "views" or frames per row, or a total of 98 frames, the equivalent of 98 ordinary pages of data. It is popular, economical, and a highly practical medium. The aperture or tab card is a single microfilm frame mounted into a punch card which carries identifying and classifying data of the microfilmed subject and permits rapid and accurate access to the information of the card. Film strips usually are 3 to 10 frames in length. They are easy to handle and are satisfactory for small quantities of data.

Why use microfilm? The microfilm medium is a conserver of space. A reel of microfilm will occupy about 2 to 3 percent of the space required by the original records, i.e., two or three drawers of microfilm hold the equivalent of about 100 drawers of original paper records. Or consider that microfilm stacked one inch high will contain the same information that will require nearly 26,000 computer output pages. Also, with microfilm the records are protected from possible wear and tear; a uniform size consistent with an effective filing arrangement and index are supplied; information security is strengthened since the records are in sequence and are easily stored for safekeeping; and the fire hazard is reduced because the film is of a noncombustible type. Further, microfilm can serve as the desired information medium in the system followed. Quite often, the filing can be done as a by-product of the processing work. In addition, the usefulness of records can be extended such as duplicate copies of original information can be made easily or copies of unique and helpful data can be acquired.

Computer Output Microfilm (COM)

Computer Output Microfilm appears to be a logical linking of two technologies—microfilm and the computer. The use of microfilm serves to store and miniaturize information, whereas the computer serves to store and process information. Both have the commonness in that they handle information. By linking them, processed information in a minaturized form becomes a reality. COM is the conversion of computer output information on magnetic tape to microfilm in a readable form at magnetic tape speeds (300 pages a minute). It illustrates a sophisticated mechanical means of storing and retrieving information. The process, sometimes referred to as "micromation," can be briefly described as follows. Data on magnetic tape from the computer are translated into readable text produced on a cathode-ray tube and printed on film. This film is then viewed, as required, at visible inquiry stations or terminals, or used to produce hard copies.

The micromation steps are illustrated by Figure 11–2. Beginning at upper left, data on tape enter the Micromation Printer where the tape-to-

FIGURE 11–2

The Micromation Steps Providing a Distribution Method Handling Output Data at Computer Tape Speeds by Combining the Immediacy of the Cathode-Ray Tube Inquiry Station with the Permanency of Print

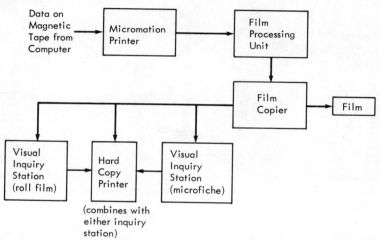

film conversion takes place. Information requiring hours to print on paper is put on film in minutes. Next, the film is developed by a film processing unit which operates at same speed as printer and accepts various film widths. Copies of the film are made by the copier to eliminate multiple print-out-runs and reduce the cost of copies. Either roll film or microfiche can be used. A page per frame can be handled on roll film. On a 4-inch × 6-inch microfiche up to 224 pages of data can be placed. Access to the filmed data is by visual inquiry units or stations as indicated by Figure 11–2. Any small portion of the filmed data can be retrieved quickly—in a matter of seconds.

These visual inquiry units highly magnify the film for easy recognition by the human eye. The equivalent of thousands of pages of information can be viewed quickly and, if desired, a hard copy of any document can be made. This is done by a hard-copy printer which displays and copies the information in full size.

An illustration of the Micromation Printer is shown by Figure 11–3. It moves the output information at computer speeds, gives speedy re-

FIGURE 11–3
The Micromation Printer

Courtesy: Stromberg Datagraphics, Inc. San Diego.

trieval time, and reduces storage space of records. Also, fixed images, such as a photograph, can be merged with the computer information during the print-out run. Many different types of business documents can be produced without expense of preprinted paper forms. Extra copies can be produced without involving the computer.

Other machines offering various features are also available for COM operations. Microimage conversion systems are destined to increase in importance and flexibility. A complete cycle is possible using microfilm and the computer which includes recording data by microfilm (visual form), reading the information into a computer, modifying the data by means of computer techniques, and recording the new data by microfilm (visual form). The applications are many. For example, a large railroad microfilms nearly 600,000 pages of information each month consisting of weekly revenue accounts to daily listings on interchange cars and contents. The COM operation requires only two hours whereas a comparable printout takes 14 hours. Figure 11–4 depicts microfilm output and its possible uses. From the computer tape output, the conversion supplies two microfilm copies, one for active use, the other for archival storage. From the microfilmed information, active references can be made in any of several ways. See left portion of Figure 11–4.

FIGURE 11–4

Possible Steps from Computer Tape Output to Microfilm Output

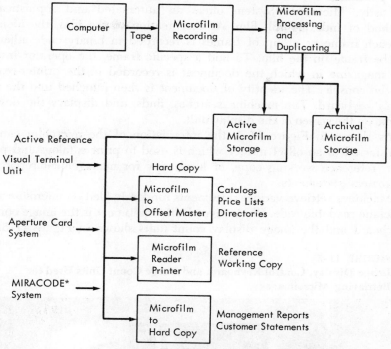

* *MIRACODE is a trade name of Eastman Kodak Co.*

TECHNIQUES OF INDEXING MICROIMAGES

A common method employed for indexing roll or cartridge film is Code-Line which is an address to document location on the roll. Black lines between frames are created at the time the film is created. These lines are changed in a straight progression after about each 20 frames. To locate a frame, reference to an outside index is made in order to obtain the Code-Line number relating to the wanted frame location When advancing the film at high speed in a reading device, the code lines appear as a solid line and are interpreted by means of the scale adjacent to screen to locate the desired frame.

Another method widely used is Image Control. For this an opaque mark is placed on the film under the image. This mark is created during filming. Again, an external index is consulted for the index number to the wanted frame. This number is inserted in a keyboard; the reader logic counts the marks, locates, and displays the document desired.

Referring to Figure 11–4 again, the second type of microform is the aperture or tab card. As already stated, such media are sorted by the key punches in the card in order to locate the card desired.

Lastly, Micracode System offers an automated and sophisticated method of indexing roll film. At the creation of the film, the identity of each frame or group of frames is recorded in binary code adjacent to the frame on the film. To find a specific frame, the operator inserts the magazine in which the document is recorded in the printer-reader on the console. The identity of document is then punched into the system's keyboard. The machine searches, finds, and displays the desired frame on the screen of the display unit.

As shown in Figure 11–4, the information of the microfilm can be transferred to an offset master which is used to print catalogs and price lists, reference working copy, or hard copy for management reports or customers' statements.

Machines retrieve various documents randomly filed on microfilm with machine readable code. Illustrative of this equipment is the image control keyboard and the image display count units shown in Figure 11–5. To

FIGURE 11–5
Image Display, Control Keyboard, and Image Count Units Used for Retrieving Microimages

Courtesy: Eastman Kodak Co., Rochester, N.Y.

locate a document the operator depresses the digit push-buttons which correspond to the microfilm address of the document desired. In a matter of seconds the document image appears on the screen while the keyboard displays the number. Also available is a unit which can be added to produce paper facsimiles of whatever document is retrieved from the information on microfilm.

Managerial Considerations of COM

COM offers advantages including the reduction of (1) the purchasing and bursting of many computer paper forms, (2) the time and effort required to retrieve computer paper outputs, (3) the space needed to store computer paper records, (4) the time and effort to handle physically the computer-generated records, and (5) the cost of reproducing selected computer paper output. These benefits are highly desirable, but before implementing a COM project, it is essential to understand what COM is and the details of its operation. For example, a proper and adequate hook-up with the computer is involved and programs to reorganize the data and prepare them for film output will be necessary. Some knowledge of the available alternative film outputs and the equipment required for each are fundamental. Obtaining some background and understanding of COM are recommended. In this respect, reading several books on the subject might be followed.

Further, among the first questions to be answered are: What material is to be microfilmed? What microfilm medium will be used? What coding or indexing will be practiced? What is the paper-to-microfilm flow and operation? It is a good idea to create a pilot program to determine the viability of the intended program. Equipment selection should be based on that combination that will provide the users with what, where, and when they need information, and at an acceptable cost. Figure 11–6 lists some considerations that have proven helpful to others faced with the task of installing and maintaining a COM project.

FIGURE 11–6
Pertinent Considerations to Cover in Evaluating a Contemplated COM Project

---

1. List the specific benefits anticipated from the adoption of COM.
2. Write a detailed description of the file or records to be converted to a microform.
3. Answer the questions: What will COM do for the file? How will the material be retrieved? How will it be indexed?
4. Draw flow charts showing the document handling, sorting, updating, and recording.
5. Calculate conservatively the savings anticipated.
6. Determine approximate costs that will be entailed.
7. Seek to find out and evaluate any intangible benefits and savings.
8. Encourage participation by others in the planning of the project.
9. Give ample thought to the training and shifting of personnel necessitated by the project.
10. Set target dates for each major phase of the project and publicize them to all interested persons.

USING THE MICROFICHE MEDIUM

The use of microfiche is expanding rapidly for storing and retrieving information because it provides small, easy-to-handle units, and the whole system is economical to install and maintain. Additions and deletions to the total information are expedited by discarding the old fiche and replacing it with a correct new one. Also, additions can be interfiled without difficulty. Duplicates or hard-copy prints can be reproduced at low cost with retention of sharpness and clarity of original material.

The Committee on Scientific and Technical Information (COSTI) specifications state recommended sizes and formats of microfiches to be used, especially when interchange with government fiche is anticipated. Any widely adopted classifying and indexing system can be applied to microfiche. The heading should be well planned so that accurate identification is quickly made. Included are the classification number, document title, source, and other basic information. The pattern followed for storing varies depending upon the type of information, updating requirements, and related factors. Frequently the fiches are arranged in numerical sequence with new fiches added to the end.

Stored microfiche can be retrieved and read by several different means. In one system the microfiches are stored in large quantities in a centralized repository, a popular size of which holds approximately 50,000 microfiches which at 98 frames each is equal to nearly 5 million pages. The repository accommodates intermixed formats, a unique random-access selectivity being used. Desk-top viewing terminals are tied in with the repository. Up to ten terminals, each up to about a mile from the repository, can be used. By means of a control panel, the desired microfiche is selected, positioned, and enlarged on the screen. A six-digit address is entered on the keyboard and this triggers the automatic retrieval and closed TV circuit to the specific location of the storage module. The entire search requires but a few seconds. Hard-copy printers as well as real-time computer interfacing are optional. Available is an electrical lockout which prevents unauthorized viewing of confidential information.

Also available is a manually operated microfiche reader or viewer. It is inexpensive and very simple to operate. The microfiche is placed into a compartment of the unit. By means of a coordinate indexing system, keyed to the microfiche format, getting the correct image location is easy. It is a matter of moving an alphanumeric index pointer horizontally, vertically, or diagonally to the coordinates of the desired image. Magnification can be chosen from 18 times to 42 times. Figure 11–7 shows a popular reader unit.

A completely cut and dried microfiche from the original paper data is made by use of a microfiche recorder and processor. The machine

FIGURE 11–7
An Effective Manually Operated Microfiche Reader

Courtesy: NCR Corp., Dayton.

requires neither chemical handling nor a darkroom, plumbing, additional processors, or extensive training to operate. It is shown by Figure 11–8 (top), along with an interesting illustration (bottom) of the savings in space and the gain in neatness by use of microfiche.

The Ultrafiche Medium

Storing and retrieving work utilizing the microfiche principle has been greatly enhanced by the process, PCMI Microform System, developed by the National Cash Register Company. This process permits tremendous reduction rates to be used in filming the material. The fiche produced by this process is called ultrafiche or ultramicrofiche. To illustrate, over 1,200 printed pages of the Holy Bible are reproduced

FIGURE 11–8
Microfiche Systems

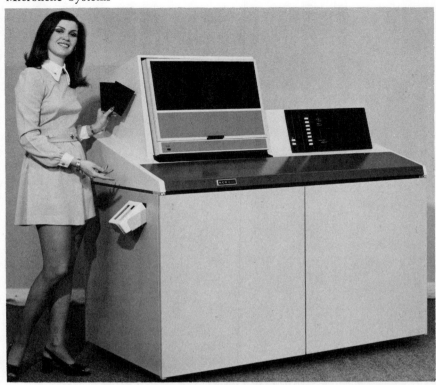

Courtesy: NCR Corp., Dayton.

Top: A Microfiche Recorder and Processor. Bottom: Before and after pictures of records converted to microfiche. The information from nearly 300 legal-size file drawers is now contained in several small cabinets.

on about 2 square inches of film. This means that the pages of a million books can be contained in a stack of film cards about 6 inches high, or the total contents of over 50,000 books could be stored in one drawer of a filing cabinet.

The micro-images are initially made on a special material, photochromic dye. This is erasable by light, thus making it possible to inspect an image and if unsatisfactory erase and redo it. When all images are satisfactory, they are transferred to a photographic plate by contact print.

The PCMI process offers a new dimension to the microfilm industry; it has been called a way of "microfilming microfilm." By it, the storing and retrieving of an enormous quantity of information on microfiche is possible. To illustrate, the entire parts catalog system of a leading automobile manufacturer is available on eight 4-inch by 6-inch ultra-fiches. When projected to the 9-inch × 11-inch screen of a viewer, a clear reproduction of each frame equivalent to the size of a catalog page is provided. Only the ultrafiches and the viewer are required. As stated above, the desired ultrafiche is slipped into the compartment of the viewer and the directional finder moved to view any frame. Effective indexing permits quick finding of desired image. Revisions in material are handled by making a new ultrafiche and discarding the old transparency. Time is saved in retrieving precise information, the cost is very low, and the handling of heavy bulky catalogs is eliminated. See Figure 11–9.

FIGURE 11–9
A Service Man Using Ultrafiche for Retrieving Information of a Parts Catalog. Each Ultrafiche Holds the Equivalent of 3560 Catalog Pages of Information

Courtesy: The NCR Corp., Dayton.

TERMATREX-OPTICAL COINCIDENCE

Another interesting means for handling storing and retrieving work is the use of Termatrex cards and the principle of optical coincidence. In this methodology there is a card for each characteristic and each card has 10,000 positions or coordinates. A coordinate is a location expressed by so many spaces horizontally and vertically on the card. The serial number of an item is represented by the coordinates at which location a hole is drilled through the card. Using a simple example, suppose we want to retrieve information from a large personnel file to identify which personnel have the specific qualifications of administrative experience, radar designing, and electrical engineering background. Termatrex cards marked with these qualifications of administrative experience, radar designing, and electrical engineering background. Termatrex cards marked with these qualifications are superimposed, placed in a Termatrex Reader so that coincidental holes visible as light spots will reveal employees having these characteristics. The left portion of Figure 11–10 shows the information search being made, the right portion,

FIGURE 11–10
An Information Search System Utilizing Optical Coincidence

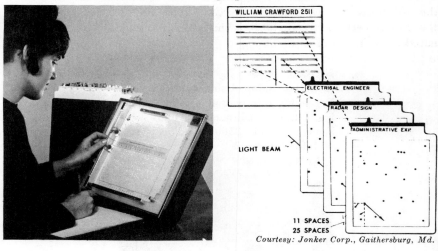

Courtesy: Jonker Corp., Gaithersburg, Md.

the details of the method. The coordinate, 25 spaces vertically and 11 spaces horizontally, designates number 2511, which is employee W. Crawford. If the light spot shows through at this coordinate when the cards for each characteristic are superimposed, it means that W. Crawford has the sought-for qualifications.

MANUAL MEANS—STORAGE AND RETRIEVAL

Under this classification are the more or less typical and traditional "filing systems." The material is stored in a file in accordance with a particular filing arrangement and when material is wanted it is located and removed from the file. Let us discuss the various types of files or filing cabinets first and follow this by the more common filing arrangements that are used. Some of the filing equipment has certain mechanized features such as a motorized file for manual filing. We will start our discussion with this type file.

MOTORIZED FILES

When manual filing means are followed and the work requires access to a large quantity of data, the motorized file is extremely useful. Operated electrically it brings to the seated operator any tray of material in the filing unit at convenient writing height. This means elimination of nonproductive times for walking to storage container, reaching for materials at the top portion of the storage container, and stooping to use the lower portion of the container. Hence, every record is made available at the level where maximum labor efficiency is attainable. This has significance since research indicates that with the nonmotorized file, about 73 percent of the total storing and retrieving costs are for labor. Further, the full space from floor to ceiling is utilized, commonly resulting in nearly doubling the cubic feet for storage per unit of floor space over that of nonmotorized arrangements. Figure 11–11 shows motorized files; the unit on the left handles letter-size documents, that on the right, cards. Also available is a motorized visible card file where the material is filed horizontally with margin exposed to expedite locating the filed card when needed. This type file will be discussed fully later in this chapter.

NONMOTORIZED FILES

In this category are many familiar types. Selected for discussion here are (1) pull-drawer, (2) lateral, (3) reciprocating, (4) rotary, (5) visible—horizontal, and (6) visible—vertical.

1. Pull-Drawer Files. This type is available for various size cards, letters, and legal papers, and in one to six drawers. The one- and two-drawer models are used on a desk or table; the two-drawer is desk height and is usually used beside a desk, providing ready accessibility to papers frequently used. Three-drawer models are used for counter purposes. The five- and six-drawer files provide extra filing capacities

FIGURE 11-11
Motorized Files Providing Effective Work Station with Access to a Large Quantity of Data

Courtesy: Diebold, Inc., Canton, Ohio.

for the floor space occupied. A standard four-drawer file holds about 5,000 sheets of paper, 300 file folders, and 26 file guides.

While the mechanical details differ among manufacturers, most pull-drawer files feature a ball bearing, full progressive sidearm suspension which provides smooth rolling action of the drawer and permits easy opening and closing. Some feature storing the material in suspending folders which transfer the weight from the drawer bottom to two top rails on either side, running the length of the drawer. Suspended folders provide fingertip ease of filing and the folders cannot slump.

2. *Lateral Files.* Proponents of this category stress the ease of getting to the stored material; the fast handling of storing and retrieving work—25 percent more than that of other types; and savings in floor space—about 50 percent compared with a pull-drawer of four drawers using the basis of filing inches per square foot of floor area. See Figure 11-12. Lateral filing cabinets can be divided into four groups: (1) drawer, (2) shelf type, and (3) suspension, and (4) box. For the first, the drawer opens from the side. These units can be equipped to handle either regular or suspension folders. All material can be reached easily. The second, or shelf type, features compartments of filed material exposed for ready accessibility, as shown by left portion of Figure 11-13. Folders can be slid out instead of lifted out, separators within compart-

FIGURE 11–12
Lateral Filing Cabinets, Drawer Style, Are Popular for Use
with a Desk Arrangement and for Areas Where the Depth
Dimension Is Limited, i.e., along the Side of a Corridor

Courtesy: Oxford Filing Supply Co., Inc., Garden City, N.Y.

ments can be supplied if desired, and open file doors serve as work
surfaces. Equipped with heavy-duty retracting springs, the door or panel
opens or closes easily with a slight upward motion by the hand. Exciting
new decorator colors are available to provide zest and flair. Also featured
are adjustable leveling feet to compensate for uneven floor surfaces.
In the third type, or suspension, filed material is contained in special
folders suspended from a pair of rods. The folders, provided with labels
at front edge, are available in many different sizes to accommodate
different sizes and weights to be filed. Figure 11–13 (right) shows the
detail of this file. Modification of the shelf and the suspension types,

FIGURE 11-13
Files

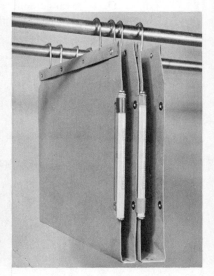

Courtesy: Tab Products Co., Palo Alto.   *Courtesy: Robert P. Gillette Co., Inc.,*
Columbia, S.C.

**Left: Shelf-type steel filing cabinets with retractable doors. Right: Detail
of suspension file construction.**

or so-called open-shelf type is widely used for odd-sized items such
as magnetic reels, paper tapes, art-work, photographs, and line drawings.
The fourth group, or box, consists of top and side open-edged metal
boxes or trays hooked onto the rails of a freestanding metal frame,
which is assembled without nuts, bolts, or screws. The frame is tailored
to fit individual needs and the boxes, into which the material is placed,
hang at a slight angle, creating a stair-step effect to expedite the filing
work. Top- or side-tab folders can be used. Figure 11-14 shows the
detail of this type filing.

3. *Reciprocating Files.* This type permits the operator to remain
seated with necessary machines and tools located within easy reach,
and the file can be moved forward and backward as required. Use
of this type reduces employee fatigue, travel, and waiting time. It also
assists supervision in that all files are at desk-level height and under
full view of the supervisor.

A useful modification of the reciprocating file is the arrangement
whereby files can be moved along tracks, thus utilizing conventional
aisle space for storage space. Figure 11-15 illustrates this idea. Only
one "floating" aisle is used. The units can be moved from side to side

FIGURE 11–14

Detail of the Cutaway Box Permitting Working Folder Corners (the box type is for records not requiring closed storage)

Courtesy: Tab Products Co., Palo Alto, Calif.

to gain access to any one unit. For heavy shelving loads, electrical power can be employed. To operate, a pedal in front of the aisle is stepped on causing the units to open. A safety cord extending between the units is then removed, thus disconnecting the motor to prevent it operating as long as the employee is in the aisle. When ready, the employee walks out of the aisle, replaces the safety cord, and any bay of the arrangement is ready to be moved.

4. Rotary Files. This name applies to filing cabinets either (1) mounted on a platform which revolves or (2) held to the periphery of a wheel which revolves, thus affording a ready and quick locating means at writing height. The first type is designed to expedite work methods. It frequently makes one large set of records quickly available to several employees with work stations around the edge of the common file. See Figure 11–16. The second, or wheel-type unit, provides speedy handling and compactness. Savings up to 75 percent have been estimated. Posting is convenient without removal of the filed material. The range of sizes is from small units about the size of a telephone to large units approximately 36 inches high. The capacity varies, of course, with the size of the wheel; for example, a 21-inch-diameter wheel unit will handle 6000 5 × 8-inch cards. In most cases the filed cards have punched openings at bottom to provide a gripping effect to a retaining rod, but units are available which hold nonpunched cards, folders, photographs, and

FIGURE 11–15
Movable Files Permit Greater Storage and Utilization of Space

Courtesy: Lundia, Myers Industries, Inc., Decatur, Ill.

drawings. Both single- and multiwheel units are offered, as well as a special mechanism for stabilizing the rotation.

5. *Visible Files—Horizontal.* These files, illustrated by Figure 11–17, provide the user, at a glance, visible information in the file. The material in this type is cards that are filed horizontally in a shallow slide or tray in such a manner that the bottom margin of each card is exposed. In this margin are pertinent data concerning the information on the major area of the card. Capacity per tray averages about 80 cards. Each card is fastened in such a way that it can be raised and flipped over its top edge.

In some equipment, the top edge of the card is fastened directly onto the tray; while in other equipment, "pockets" made of strong kraft paper are fastened directly onto the tray and the card is held in place by inserting the bottom edge into a flap made by a U-shaped plastic strip at the bottom of the pocket. The top of the card is held by inserting the corners into slots precut in the pocket.

Effective signaling to denote certain information on the card is one of the outstanding features of this visible arrangement. By sliding differ-

FIGURE 11–16

Six Clerks Have Immediate Access to 60,000 Customer Account Records in This Rotary File

Courtesy: Acme Visible Records, Inc., Crozet, Va.

ent-colored plastic markers along the visible margins, definite dates or quantities, which are signals for specific actions, are brought out in bold relief. By such signals, a whole tray of cards can be scanned and the items requiring immediate attention quickly spotted. Figure 11–18 illustrates a signaling system for accurate follow-up.

6. *Visible Files—Vertical.* With this type, the material is also cards of sizes from about 3 to 20 inches in width and 5 to 12 inches in height. They are similar in appearance to the printed forms for machine- and hand-posting work. One or both of the upper corners of the card are usually cut away to provide diagonal indexing margins; in addition, a horizontal and a vertical margin of the card are used for indexing. An offset arrangement is followed in placing the cards in the file so that the top, diagonal, and side margins of the card are exposed or visible. The card is held in position by means of a notched arrangement at the bottom of the card which fits into a receiving device at the bottom of the file, and the design is such that cards can easily be inserted or removed. Both sides of the card can be used, and signaling devices similar to those already discussed can be employed. Figure 11–19 shows the arrangement of cards in the file. With this equipment, the retrieving

FIGURE   11–17
Visible File Equipment Where Cards Are Filed
Horizontally

Courtesy: Sperry Rand Corp., New York.

The illustration is of a manually operated type.
There are also motorized files of this type.

FIGURE 11–18
An Effective Follow-Up Signaling System

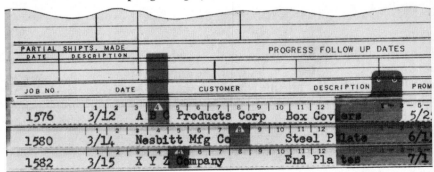

Courtesy: Sperry Rand Corp., New York.

On the top card, the signal over the 4 indicates April, the month in which
follow-up should be made. The signal at the right of the card at the 3 indicates the day of the month on which the follow-up is due.

FIGURE 11–19
The Arrangement of Cards in a File

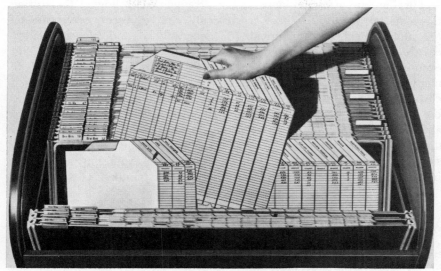

Courtesy: Acme Visible Records, Inc., Crozet, Va.

Groups of cards can be removed and replaced just as easily as one card. This is commonly called an open tub file.

time is minimized, thumbing through cards is eliminated, and exceedingly quick scanning over large numbers of cards is possible—for example, nearly 7,000 cards, 10×5 inches in size, can be accommodated in one file unit.

Visible card storing arrangements are also available in book form. Approximately 2,000 cards can be kept in one binder. The book form affords portability and a posting surface always at desk height. Binders are made to lie perfectly flat when open, to lock against any possible accidental shifting of record sequence, and to lift and guide sheets into proper position when the binder is closed.

In addition to the above five types of files discussed, there are a number of other types—the list is quite long. For example, in one type of card file, the operator presses buttons on a console which causes the wanted material to raise slightly so that quick retrieval is possible. In another type, narrow strips of typed material are filed in a frame. This type of file is helpful for maintaining lists which undergo changes such as names and addresses of customers, prices, rates, directories, reservations, hospital indexes, telephone and switchboard data. The frames are suspended on desk stands or wall brackets. Different colors or marks on the strips can be used for signaling purposes.

ARRANGEMENTS FOR STORED MATERIAL

Turning our attention now to the arrangement followed for storing the material in the file, there are basically four different arrangements: (1) alphabetical, (2) numerical, (3) geographical, and (4) chronological. Modifications and combinations of these are commonly used. For example the alphabetical-numerical plan is often employed, and in many alphabetical files, the material in each subdivision is arranged chronologically, i.e., the latest paper always on top. Likewise, under the geographical plan it is customary to arrange the subdivisions alphabetically. A number of ready-made arrangements are offered by different manufacturers all of whom emphasize provision of ample divisions for the information, allowance for possible expansion, and ample inclusive constraints to cover all information to be handled.

Alphabetical Arrangement

Possibly the most widely used, this arrangement stresses the name or topic as the important item. If the first letter is not sufficient for determinig the proper place of the material, the second and, if necessary, the third and fourth succeeding letters are used. For any given total of names, the probable number which will occur in each subdivision of the alaphabet is known. For example, names beginning with the letters *S, B, M,* and *H,* respectively, are most common; those beginning with *X, Q,* and *U* occur least frequently. For a given quantity of names, there are usually about three times as many names under *B* as under *A,* twenty times as many under *H* as under *I,* and ten times as many under *T* as under *U.* Information of this sort is utilized scientifically in determining filing guide subdivisions, which can be purchased as standard equipment. Sets ranging from 24 to some 2,600 subdivisions are available.

To provide for expansion, sets are available that permit the inserting of additional subdivisions to the original set. For example, a set of 300 subdivisions is converted into one of 400 subdivisions simply by adding an expansion package of 100 subdivisions. None of the original subdivisions are discarded; there is no waste.

The advantages of alphabetical filing are that direct reference is provided, a quick check is offered on misfiled material, and common names are grouped. It is sometimes considered "the natural way to file." Figure 11–20 illustrates an alphabetical storing arrangement for correspondence. From this illustration, the following can be observed:

1. The primary guides, or partitions segregating the material, give the chief breakdowns of the alphabet and are identified by green tabs

FIGURE 11–20
Filing Arrangement under a Modern Alphabetical Correspondence-Filing Plan

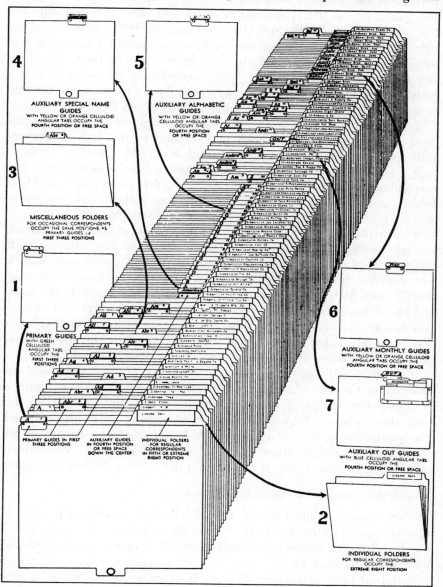

318 *Office Management and Control*

occupying the first three positions which are shown along the top left portion of the guide. Tabs are located by position along the width of the guide. At the left is the first position, and moving to the right are the second, third, fourth, and fifth positions; the fifth position is at the extreme right. In the illustration the tabs are marked with letters and numbers, i.e., $A = 1$, $Abr = 2$, $Ad = 3$, $Ag = 4$, and so forth. The number expedites the filing work. When considering the letter d it is a little difficult to recall that d is between c and e. In contrast, less thought is required to remember that the number 3 is between 2 and 4.

2. Individual folders containing regular correspondence are filed behind their proper primary guide and tabbed in the fifth or extreme right position: "1. Aaron, Carl"; "1. Abbott, A. M."; and so forth.

3. Miscellaneous folders, used for occasional and miscellaneous correspondence, are marked with red tabs in the first three positions. These folders correspond in identification and number with the primary guides and are placed in the back of each primary-guide spacing.

4. Auxiliary guides, tabbed in the fourth or right-center position, are used to simplify and to speed the filing by dividing primary-guide spacings according to individual needs. Auxiliary guides may include (a) common titles and names, such as "American," "Brown," "Smith," and "United States"; (b) alphabetical listings which segregate the material under the common title or name—"American Art Works" or "American Bridge Co.," for example; and (c) monthly listings which separate the material under the common title or name by months—"Baker Bros.—Jan.," "Baker Bros.—Feb.," and "Baker Bros.—March."

5. Out guides are tabbed with blue in the fourth position and are inserted in the file when any folder is taken out. Each out guide is equipped with a holder device for a charge-out card. Entries on this card show when a folder is removed, by whom, and when returned. Out guides are also available in folder form, in which case spaces are ruled on the side in order to record data on removals. The subject of charging material out is discussed fully in the following chapter.

Modifications of Alphabetical Arrangement

Two major modifications of the alphabetical arrangement are (1) subject, and (2) phonetic. In the former the material is arranged according to subject or descriptive feature instead of name. For example, all material pertaining to insurance is put in one main division and all material on taxes in another division. If necessary, subdivisions of each subject are made. For Insurance, the subdivisions might be Accident, Fire, and Group; and the material is usually filed alphabetically under each classification. The choice of subject heading should be inclusive and descriptive of the contents. Any logical grouping based on usage is permissible. Idiomatic terminology should be used. Subject filing places all material of a common descriptive feature together, so that it can be used conveniently.

The second, or phonetic, is based on the pronunciation or sound of the stored identity, usually a name. For example, the name "Bohlin" is pronounced the same but can be spelled "Bowlin," "Bowlyn," and so forth. Under which spelling is such a name to be placed in a file? Poor handwriting and errors in transcribing might add further to the problem. In such bases, the phonetic arrangement is helpful under which all names are coded by use of the "Soundex Code," which is:

Code Numbers	Key Letter Equivalents
1	b, f, p, v
2	c, g, j, k, q, s, x, z
3	d, t
4	l
5	m, n
6	r

The letters *a, e, i, o, u* and *w, h, y* are not coded. In addition, the following practices apply:

1. The initial letter is not coded but is used as a prefix to code a number which always has three digits.
2. The zero is used where there is no key letter equivalent.
3. Doubled key letters are coded as one, that is, *rr* as *r*.
4. A key letter and its equivalent are likewise coded as one, that is, *ck* as *c*.

To illustrate, the name "Bohlin" would be coded B—450; "Bowlin," B—450; and "Bowlyn," B—450. Thus, all names which sound alike, although spelled differently, have an identical filing location and thus can be quickly located. Note that the phonetic modification is of an alphabetic-numeric type. The phonetic arrangement provides these advantages: Ninety percent of all family names are grouped automatically, duplications are detected, unlimited expansion and flexibility are provided, the effect of transcribing errors is minimized, and a uniform and precise indexing method is provided.

Numerical Arrangement

In this arrangement, each item filed has a number, and location of the material is by numerical sequence. This arrangement is popular for such material as bank checks, invoices, engine numbers, and papers pertaining to freight cars. However, it is not confined to prenumbered material. Items such as letters, memorandums, and notices are also filed according to this plan; and in such cases, an auxiliary alphabetical card file is employed to learn the proper filing number. The system of numbers can be basically one of two types: (1) serial—to provide unlimited expansion, or (2) coded—to indicate specific types of items. An illustration of the latter type is given below:

Divisions

100. *General Sales*	200. *Production*	300. *Research*
110. Recap of orders booked	210. Purchasing	310. Consumer studies
120. Recap of sales shipped	220. Payroll	320. Radio ratings
130. Expenditures	230. Budget	330. Television surveys
140. Budget	240. Recap of items completed	340. Readership records
		350. Product testing

The numerical plan offers simple provisions for expansion, some degree of secrecy, ease and speed of operation, and an effective means of identification. Numbers are easy to work with; in fact, most alphabetical arrangements use numbers in addition to letters. Frequently, color is used along with the number to provide quicker identification.

In terminal-digit filing, a variation of the regular numerical arrangement, numbers are used, but they are read from right to left instead of the conventional left to right. Hence, records are filed according to the last digit or, more commonly, the last two digits, then the next two or subdivision thereof. To illustrate:

Numerical	*Terminal Digit by Last-Two Numbers*	*Terminal Digit by Two Last-Two Numbers*
160 79	3 25 41	5 17 41
174 63	5 17 41	3 25 41
325 41	1 74 63	1 74 63
517 41	1 60 79	1 60 79

Why file this way? To eliminate misfiles from misreading six or more digits, as happens in regular numerical filing, and to disperse filing activity—the newest records are not placed at one end of the file, causing congested activity in that part of the file.

Geographical Arrangement

The main divisions for stored material in the geographical arrangement include states, counties, cities, branch-office territories, and salespeople's areas. Usually, the subdivisions are arranged alphabetically; for example, a sales area by cities in alphabetical order, and each city by customers' names in alphabetical order. An effective arrangement of the geographical plan of filing is shown in Figure 11–21.

The geographical arrangement, sometimes called location arrange-

FIGURE 11–21
Geographical Filing

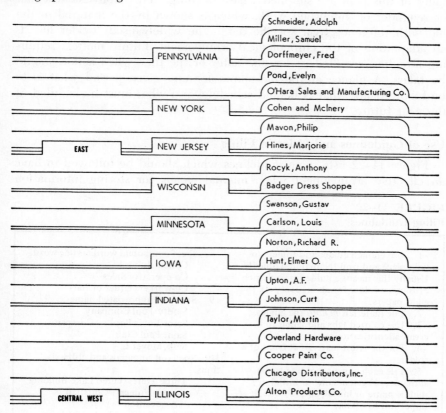

ment, is easy to understand, simple and direct, and can cover the overall work division, particularly that of sales. The files are generally less unwieldy than is frequently the case with the other basic arrangements. Also, several people can work at the files simultaneously—for instance, one in the Philadelphia file for "Cupper Manufacturing Company" and the other in the Los Angeles file for "Cizzla Sales Corporation." In addition, the geographical arrangement makes it comparatively simple to compile mailing lists by states or cities; and the segregation of material for tax, political, or mailing reasons is readily provided.

Chronological Arrangement

Segregating material according to its time sequence is the essence of this arrangement. The main divisions are either months or weeks, with the subdivisions being days. Some correspondence, bills, and pending accounts payable can be handled on a chronological plan. The advantages of this plan are simplicity, ease of filing, and a convenient signal or reminder of unfinished work, which is shown by the material in the file with reference to a specific date. The widely used "tickler file" is an adaptation of the chronological arrangement. Future matters requiring attention are filed under due dates or the time when action should be taken. A glance at the file shows for any given period what is to be followed up, what is behind schedule, and what must be handled in the near future.

Use of Guidelines and Color in Filing

Figure 11–22 lists some guidelines which should be followed to have an effective arrangement when manual means for storing information

FIGURE 11–22
Filing Guidelines

1. Use enough guides and folders to help place and find the material quickly. Usually this means a guide for each inch of filing, a folder for about every six to eight papers.
2. File materials *behind* the guides.
3. Use colored tabs and labels to increase identification.
4. Put the latest material at front of a folder.
5. File each name according to (*a*) surname, (*b*) given name or initial, (*c*) middle name or initial, and (*d*) title, if important to retain.
   Alexander, Charles D. (Dr.)
6. File "nothing before something."
   Carter
   Carter, George
   Carter, George L.
7. File alphabetical material in exact sequence of letters, *A* through *Z*, to the last letter of the last word.
   M & A Stores, Inc.
   Maag, Robert C.
   MacArthur, Thomas P.
   Mack, Henry
   MacTavish, Sam W.

8. Treat compound words as one word.
   Cohen, Julius I.
   Co-operative Sales
   Co-workers Order of Bart
9. Spell out abbreviated names.
   Safety Tool Company
   Saint Louis Poultry Company
   Saint Paul Club
   Salk, Meyer L.
10. Spell out numerals and abbreviations.
    Three Thirty-Three Lake Building
    Young Women's Christian Association
11. When names are identical, file by city; then state; then street address.
    Carson, John M.
      Bangor, Maine
    Carson, John M.
      Springfield, Mass.
12. To save time with alphabetic material, sort by first segregating into four groups, such as A–F, G–L, M–R, and S–Z; then, sort each group according to the first letter. For numeric material, first sort 0–2, 3–5, and 6–9; then sort each group by the first digit.

are followed. In most cases adherence to them will bring the most satisfactory results. However, they are suggestive only; individual circumstances may suggest deviations which work out better.

The use of color to assist in providing instant filing visibility merits additional comment. While color was mentioned in the above descriptions of filing arrangements, it has developed to the degree that quite sophisticated color filing plans can be used. They work well with alphabetical and numerical arrangements. Each file folder has a color combination assigned, there is no longer a need to purchase folders with prenumbered and colored identification that are not needed. The color coding plans available are economical and effective. Faster filing and retrieval, and practically zero misfiles result from their use. A quick glance at the filing shelf reveals any nonmatching color with that of a given filing section and indicates a folder out of place.

Under one system, in the alphabetical arrangement the first two letters of the name or subject is coded by means of two distinctive colors out of a spectrum of ten different colors. Ten colors permit a hundred different combinations when used in groups of two. For the numerical arrangement, the first two, or the last two (terminal-digit filing) digits can be coded. Conversion to the color code is no problem. Either the entire file can be converted at one time or the old files are simply permitted to get old and eventually purged whereas new issues are color-coded and eventually become the entire file. Figure 11–23, left portion, shows a file using color along with numbers as the coding, the right portion shows the simplicity of conversion from noncolorcoded at the top to filed material color coded at the bottom of the open shelf file.

Indexing

An index is a finding tool. It furnishes the key to how the materials are arranged. For any given set of material, a choice is made from several possible indexes. In some cases, the subject is the best index; in others, the name of the customer or the point of destination might be most useful. Consider the following material that could be indexed in one of several different ways as indicated:

Material	*File According to:*
Catalogs	Date, name of company, or name of product
Correspondence	Date, subject, name of company, name of customer, name of seller, point of destination, or point of origin
Invoices	Date, name of customer, or number
Personnel application forms	Name of applicant, or type of work (subject)
Purchase orders	Date, name of vendor, name of product, or number
Tax reports	Date, subject, or name of taxing body

Flexibility is of prime importance in an index so that needed changes can be made simply and quickly. In most manual applications and to a lesser degree in those that are automated, the collection of information

FIGURE 11–23
Color Coding Reduces Misfiles and Filing Time

Courtesy: Tab Products Co., Palo Alto.   *Courtesy: SFI, Inc., El Dorado, Ark.*

keeps growing or changing so that the index must grow and change. Answers to questions such as the following aid in planning the superior index. What is being indexed? Are individual items easily identified and located? Are other indexes already in use and accepted by custom? What form should the index take—a list, on cards, in a manual? It is advisable to avoid the use of synonyms. Information on various types of rentals, such as house, townhouse, apartment, and store should be indexed under the heading, Rentals. If a distinction appears needed, use two headings: Rentals—domestic, Rentals—commercial. The advantage of adopting well-chosen headings is that a logical location is provided to assemble all of the items on a particular subject, and there will be only one place to look.

Cross indexing is used when more than one subject is covered by the material or when several indicators are helpful in finding it. A report dealing with the subjects of market expansion and finances could be filed under the subject of markets, sales, future sales, finances, or costs. Cross indexes provide information as to where to place and to find the report; however, numerous cross references should be avoided in order to simplify the work as much as possible. Cross indexes can be well maintained in a separate card file. A typical card might read:

Wages	*See also* Compensation
	Fringe Benefits
	Job Evaluation
	Salary

That is, information about Wages may be found under all five terms. Some feel that when an alphabetical arrangement is used, the cross-reference index should be by number or code. In contrast, when the numerical arrangement is followed, the cross index should be alphabetical.

Essential in most offices is a *basic classification index* which is a categorical grouping of subjects with apropriate detailed subheadings. In addition, *a relative index* is helpful since it shows, in a dictionary type listing, all possible works and combinations by which the material may be requested. All indexes to stored material should be kept current by making new entries for additional classifications as they occur. Main new sources will be key words, new terminology, or any other means by which material may be requested.

QUESTIONS

1. What is meant by Computer Output Microfilm (COM) or micromation? Discuss its importance and potential in information management.
2. Discuss important considerations in the management of COM.
3. What six forms of microfilm are used as the information medium for storing and retrieving information? Relate under what general conditions each medium is used.
4. Relate your understanding of storing and retrieving information by the PCMI Microform System and include explanation of Figure 11–9 in your answer.
5. Discuss the subject of indexing as an important part of filing.
6. Discuss the various types of lateral files indicating under what conditions you as an information manager would use each type.
7. Identify each of the following, and explain how it is used:
   a. Microfilming.
   b. Terminal-digit file.
   c. Computer information retrieval.
   d. Color coding of filed material.

8. Point out the significant differences as well as the similarities between the Microimage retrieval and the Termatrex-Optical means of storing and retrieving information.

9. As an office manager under what general conditions would you approve the use of motorized files?

10. Discuss briefly the basic four arrangements followed for storing material in a file.

11. For each of the following filing troubles, suggest a feasible solution:
    a. Correspondence papers piled up in miscellaneous folders.
    b. Necessity of fingering many folders before finding the right one.
    c. Need to search through many papers in a folder to find the one wanted of a certain date.
    d. St. Louis correspondence may be found under "St. Louis," "Saint Louis," or "Missouri."
    e. File drawers jammed tight with material.
    f. Too many files in which a needed paper might be found.

12. Explain Figure 11–18 in your own words, using an application of this type filing to illustrate your answer.

CASE PROBLEMS

Case 11–1. Icerman Company

Mr. Jay Fraser joined Icerman Company several months ago as assistant office manager. He has just completed an assignment dealing with the installation of copying machines and the office manager is very pleased with the way it was handled. Now she has requested Jay to study the company's filing system and to see what can be done to improve it.

Jay held several interviews with the filing supervisor, Mrs. Dobey and obtained considerable information on the present filing practices. With her permission, he talked with several of the filing personnel and broadened his knowledge of what was presently being done. Several of the filing employees made good suggestions, in Jay's opinion, but most of the comments were complaints about the old equipment in use, the fact that the drawers stuck, that Mrs. Dobey expected them to accomplish too much work every day, and that their wages were too low.

Jay also talked with the supervisors of other office departments and learned that they received what papers or records they requested from the filing department. In brief, the service is satisfactory. However, several expressed the desire to have material pertaining to their department's activities filed in their own department. This arrangement would be far more convenient and would save a lot of time, they contended. The files are available to all office employees, but it is the exception when an employee other than a filing employee uses the files.

The present filing cabinets are outdated. They are of oak wood, some have broken drawer handles, and are difficult to operate. Forty-eight four-drawer filing cabinets are presently in use. They are filled with material. In response to Jay's inquiry about the use of filing manual, he was told that they did not have one. Some of the material in the file is 10, 11, or even 12 years old. The great majority of the filed material is invoices, purchase orders, correspondence, and reports.

Mrs. Dobey supplied the information that about 3500 incoming letters and 2500 carbon copies of outgoing letters were filed weekly. In addition, other materials filed—invoices, reports, etc. would average about 25 percent of the amount represented by letters.

From several office equipment sales representatives, the following cost information was obtained:

4-drawer filing cabinet, modern steel, letter size	$145.00 each
Open shelf filing unit, letter size, 36-inches long 7 shelves.	89.50 each
File shelves, attached to either drawer cabinet or open shelf	10.00 each
Filing stool	22.00 each
Filing ladder (for open shelf type)	30.00 each
File guides (alphabetical) made of pressboard.	35.00 per thousand
File folders (supreme quality).	45.00 per thousand
Outguides	15.00 per hundred
Cross-reference forms	2.00 per hundred

The universal recommendations by the sales representatives were that:

1. A 36-inch open shelf unit accommodates 30 percent more records than a file drawer (26-inches).
2. Active filed material requires about 100 additional outguides and 1,000 cross-reference forms to be purchased each year.
3. Approximately 5,000 papers is the capacity for one file drawer.
4. File guides number 20 to each file drawer, 25 to each shelf.
5. File folders number 100 to each file drawer, 130 to each shelf. Assume that 20 percent of the current filed material is outdated and will be removed from the file.

Questions:

1. Suitable new containers cost $300 to store the outdated material now in the files. Suggest several ways (in what type containers) to store this material separately from the current active material.
2. Do you recommend the four-drawer filing cabinets or the open shelf filing units be purchased by Icerman Company? Justify your answer.
3. What additional recommendations to the office manager do you feel Mr. Fraser should make? Discuss fully.

Case 11–2. Hennings Construction Company

Custom-built houses in the $27,500–$30,000 price range are constructed by the Hennings Construction Company, which maintains a main office, two construction offices, and an on-the-site sales office. The two construction offices are about 35 miles apart, and the main office is approximately 20 miles from the sales office or either of the construction offices.

The sales office and the construction offices require immediate information on costs, delivery of materials, and dates subcontractors performed work on the houses, and telephone the main office for this type of information. Unfortunately, the desired data are not always available, primarily because the three bookkeepers in the main office are two to four months behind in their work, and each bookkeeper keeps all the pertinent information in his or her desk drawer until the cash receipts and the payments to the subtrades have been posted, or the sales put through the books.

When a call is received from the sales department or from the construction department, the bookkeepers usually cannot get the information requested until the following day—or in some cases, not for several days. This is because, to find the data requested, it is frequently necessary to search through many papers in the desk drawer and six wooden filing cabinets along the wall of the office. Completed records are placed in these filing cabinets. All information pertaining to purchases, for example, is filed alphabetically, no attention being given to date purchases were made.

Under the present state of affairs, canceled checks and monthly bank statements are not reconciled for periods of two to three months. This work is handled by the chief bookkeeper, Betty Dougherty, who guards the canceled check work and permits no one else to perform this work. Some difficulty is experienced in getting the checks written for accounts payable. None of the bookkeepers want to do this check writing because it takes time from their bookkeeping work.

The situation became so bad that Carl Hennings, president of the company, called in Professor Franklin Swope from a nearby university to review the situation and make recommendations regarding what corrective action to take. Professor Swope studied the entire operations and at the end of two days discovered that:

1. The company managers do not believe in overtime work.
2. Office morale is low.
3. Any change to improve the office operation will be welcomed by Carl Hennings.
4. One key area for improvement is to get the processed papers into the files in accordance with an arrangement that will expedite usage of the filed material.
5. Carl Hennings is thinking of firing the entire office force.
6. Carl Hennings has no objections to the company's having two checking accounts—one for general payables, the other for payroll.

Questions:

1. What pertinent recommendations do you feel Professor Swope should make to Mr. Hennings? Be specific.
2. What contributions do you believe improved filing management practices and procedures can contribute to this company? Why?
3. What difficulties do you anticipate in implementing the recommendations you feel Professor Swope should make? How would you overcome these difficulties?

Chapter **12**

Records Management— Stored Information

> *A successful man is one who can can lay a firm foundation with the bricks that others throw at him.*
>
> Sidney Greenberg

In this chapter we emphasize the management of stored office material. Since storing and retrieving information is so vital in every enterprise, it follows that the management of these efforts is of utmost importance. Too frequently, however, these managerial efforts are neglected or let to fend for themselves. Some have termed them the "blind spot of office management" which indicates the challenge of this vital area.

It should be pointed out that the area of records management embodies the creation, maintenance, and disposition of records. It includes the life span of a record and is not synonymous with filing. Our discussion of the last chapter along with this chapter covers the maintenance and disposition of records, but it excludes the records creation which was covered under Part II of this book. Also it may be noted that records include any form of captured information be it in the form of a letter, report, circular, memo, bulletin, microform, or whatever. Paper records represent today's biggest volume and as already noted both mechanized and manual means are used.

MANAGEMENT OF MECHANIZED MEANS

With direct connections to a computer and the use of other sophisticated machines for information storing and retrieving purposes, it seems paramount to have a responsible person head up these activities. Only in this way will specific goals be pursued and needless overlapping of efforts and of records maintained minimized. In addition, legitimate growth or contraction of storing and retrieving activities will be won in keeping with the individual mechanized means being utilized. Further, having an active head over these activities gives recognition to their importance, potential contribution, and proper management.

The mechanized arrangement, because of the machines used, tends to concentrate not only the work physically in a given area, but also to place it under a concentrated or centralized management person or persons. This raises some interesting questions. For example, what control should be exercised over the number of copies? With automated printouts and hard copies readily available, there may be a tendency to provide an excess of such copies. Thus, the retrieval gates might be opened too widely and the office flooded with papers not required. Another problem is the proper maintenance of confidential information. Many machines are equipped with lockout arrangements preventing machine operation to unauthorized personnel. But there remains the question of what information stored in a machine is not confidential and, further, who determines what personnel are authorized. To this can be added, what information should be stored in the first place? The answers, of course, are supplied by competent managers. Again pointing out that the machine is basically an extremely capable tool of management, but not management itself.

In contrast, it should be observed that the centralization effect of mechanization is minimized by the use of many terminal units in the case of computers or of many widely dispersed units in the case of other mechanized arrangements. Further, the rapid transmission of information from one part of an organization to another tends to negate the presence of centralization. Fundamentally, however, the core of the work efforts are performed in a centralized area and it is over these efforts that management is concentrated.

The cost of mechanization should be considered in light of what volume of work and service—speed, accuracy, and convenience—is being supplied. High volume is usually required for sound economic mechanization. In the case of computerized storing and retrieving, the total computer expense is small. If the computer is already available, the managerial information cost is minimal, nevertheless it should be made to reflect reasonably accurate cost data. In an application of microfiche, the cost is about $850 annual rental per viewing unit. Charges for the microfiches vary with the quantity, but are reasonable. Against these costs must be weighed the extra time required to find the information from several manuals, the expense of printing the manual sheets, purchase of binders, and the supplying of fresh copies.

Because of difficulty in establishing, the use of work standards may be ignored in managing storing and retrieving under a mechanized means. This is a mistake. Reasonably accurate standards should be sought and applied. Records of accomplishments should be maintained and expected work outputs mutually agreed upon between the manager and the employees. The need for management is not lessened because the operation is mechanized.

Finally, there is specialized training to provide. Efficiency in operating the machines is aided by adequate instruction in the use of the machines by the personnel. The machine manufacturers commonly supply all the operational information required, but the selection, placement, and instruction of the personnel in performing the work remains the task of the company management.

MANAGEMENT OF MANUAL MEANS

Here again and for the same reasons mentioned above, there should be a management head of storing and retrieving activities. The person should have adequate authority to direct and maintain the activities. The manager may have committees to assist in certain phases of the work and may consult with department heads. But the ultimate responsibility for managing the maintenance and disposition of the records is his or hers alone. One person in charge helps promote needed study and improvements. He or she must, of course, exercise strong leadership, otherwise the efforts are not properly coordinated and directed. To illustrate, locating stored information convenient to those frequently using it may be universally agreed upon. But to implement this recommendation requires decisions as to just where the information will be stored, the number of copies to be retained, and the screening of information to ensure retention of information which has value or a reasonable expectancy of future usefulness.

From the viewpoint of organizing, under nonmechanized means it is common to follow a decentralized basis, which provides accessibility for those needing the information, flexibility in arrangement, and reasonably satisfactory service. But desirable coordination may be lacking. This prompts some to suggest that perhaps an arrangement centralized from the viewpoint of managerial operation and decentralized as to the physical location of files is superior. With centralized management authority, the best of records management knowledge and practices from the overall company viewpoint can be put into use. However, the exact organizational plan depends upon individual requirements and understanding them. The needs are not always the same. The type of material, the work habits of the employees using the files, the normal filing usage, the flow of work, and the frequency of records are several of the more influential considerations. Figure 12–1 lists briefly the important advantages of centralized and of decentralized organizational arrangements.

FIGURE 12–1
Use of the Centralized or of the Decentralized Organizational
Arrangement of Stored Information Has Its Individual Advantages

Centralized advantages:

1. Needless duplication of equipment and records is minimized.
2. Supervision is full-time and usually effective.
3. Employees develop specialized skills and efficiencies.
4. Cost is relatively low.

Decentralized advantages:

1. The confidential aspect of the information can be protected effectively.
2. Records are handy, convenient, and close by to persons using them.
3. Systems best suited for the individual material, its use, and its user can be followed.
4. A total team effort by groups of employees is enhanced.

A major difficulty is better placement of personnel for storing and retrieving work. In too many instances, the attitude prevails that the untrained office employee who cannot be fitted in elsewhere because of lack of skill should be given work pertaining to filing. Entirely overlooked is the fundamental truth that storing and retrieving personnel should possess certain attributes, including a sense of orderliness, accuracy, manual dexterity, quick reading comprehension, and a liking for detail.

To gain the best efforts of personnel the following program is offered. First of all, the records manager must instill a feeling of confidence in the work. Each employee must believe in the work, its importance, and its contribution. It is also necessary to make sure that all requests are clear and complete. Frequently, the file clerk is expected to have an ability to find a piece of paper even though he or she has never seen it and does not know what it was about, who it was from, or when it was written. In addition, a manual supplying information on the procedures and practices to storing and retrieving personnel is also helpful. Data on the type of material stored, the indexing system, and specific duties should be written clearly and made available to anyone whose work is affected by storing and retrieving. Such a manual is extremely beneficial for obtaining better understanding and for training purposes. Further, with the assistance of the employees, the manager should select suitable equipment and create a favorable physical work environment. In addition, an upward adjustment in pay should be seriously considered. All records management is dependent upon the calibre of personnel employed, but this is especially true when the manual means is followed. The work will never be more efficient than the people doing it. Improved pay scales assist in acquiring better skills, lowering turnover, and stimulating improved effort.

Cost is used by many enterprises to keep manual storing and retrieving work within reasonable limits. Some overall cost constraints usually are helpful and should be established. The average expenditure for a typical four-drawer cabinet is about $300 annually. Fifty files, therefore, mean $15,000 annual cost. Cost data on other equipment should be sought. The expenditures for labor and space will vary depending upon the particular location, but cost for equipment is relatively uniform. For this latter, an average cost figure is 40 cents per cubic foot of information stored. However, this may be inappropriate for some types of equipment; the cost of lineal inches of storage space may be better. The number of records is of little value because of the wide variation in type, content, and size of records. Surplus equipment should be transferred to an area where it is required and any purchase of equipment should be reviewed carefully to determine its essentiality.

Labor is by far the most important cost segment when manual means are followed. As shown in Figure 12–2, salaries account for 75 percent of the total cost, while space is the lowest, being only 10 percent.

FIGURE 12–2
Labor Is the Most Important Segment
of Total Cost When the Manual Means
Is Followed

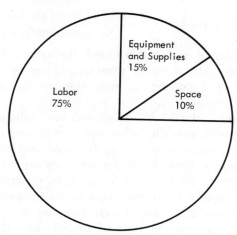

QUANTITATIVE MEASUREMENTS—MANUAL MEANS

Helpful quantitative measurements should and can be derived. To illustrate, the maximum cubic feet of information per employee can be determined and used to assist in the management work. The amount to be permitted depends upon the type of enterprise. In public utilities, for example, an amount of 5 cubic feet of records per employee on payroll is considered satisfactory. For an assembly plant a comparable figure may be only 1 cubic foot of records; whereas in a purchasing department, the amount may be as great as 12 cubic feet, yet qualify as an acceptable amount.

Helpful ratios can also be derived. To illustrate, a "usage" ratio reveals the extent to which the materials stored are being used. The formula is:

$$\text{Usage ratio (in \%)} = \frac{\text{Retrievals} \times 100}{\text{References filed}}$$

For example, if last month, 200 retrievals were made from 20,000 items stored, the usage ratio in percentage would be 200×100 divided by 20,000 or 1 percent. This ratio for stored materials will seldom exceed 5 percent. For active materials, it should run about 15 to 20 percent. Further analysis of usage ratios can be made, taking into account the rate of reference by type of record versus the age of the record. Such studies assist in better controlling of storing and retrieving efforts. Obviously if some stored records are found to never be referred to, they are good candidates for elimination.

Another ratio is the "accuracy" ratio, which is calculated by this formula:

$$\text{Accuracy ratio (in \%)} = \frac{\text{Number of items not found} \times 100}{\text{Number of items found}}$$

For 10 items not found and 10,000 found, the ratio is 0.1 percent. For a rating of excellent, the accuracy ratio should not be greater than 0.5 percent. A value of 3 percent or more signifies that remedial action is required.

Work expectancies should be developed and followed. With these as a guide, along with periodic follow-ups, the manager can determine whether prescribed methods are being followed and whether the level of work is satisfactory. Spot checks for accuracy are advisable. For this purpose a committee can be used in order to generate more interest in the work and enhance an awareness of needed improvements. Expectancies will vary among different enterprises due to a number of variables, chief of which are the type of records and the general work environment. However, to demonstrate what can be done, the following expectancies are shown, based on data from a number of companies:

Manual Task	*Units per Hour*
Sorting letters and filing alphabetically.	180
Filing 5 × 8-inch cards in an alphabetical vertical file.	315
Locating and pulling letters from an alphabetical file.	110
Filing vouchers numerically	700
Marking one-page letters for filing	220

PROCEDURE FOR MANUAL STORING AND RETRIEVING

The chief steps in such a procedure include:

1. Checking Release for Storing. Before any material is stored, it must first be checked to be sure it is released for storing. Material which is still being processed or referred to, or which, because of policy, is not retained by the company, should, of course, not be stored.

A fundamental of storing records is to *file less*. Only records that have future value should be retained. A common condition found wherever poor storing exists is that material is in the files that never should have been put in the file. Also, the habit of having an extra copy filed in case the initial copy is lost adds to the inefficiency. One copy with proper management should provide all the service asked for.

2. Reading and Marking. Reading is done to determine the proper storing classification. A marking to indicate this classification can be shown by underscoring or circling a word or two on the paper or by stamping or writing the proper file data in the upper right corner. A colored pencil usually works very satisfactorily, as the contrast aids future reference. If there is a possibility of storing under several headings, it is helpful to consult the cross-reference index to insure use of the best classification for the material.

3. Sorting. Next, the material is sorted by mark showing the storing classification. Sorting can be performed entirely manually or with the use of a sorting device. In the former, the material is divided into neat piles on a table or desk, each pile being of a different classification. When this method is followed, it is best to sort all material according to major divisions, then each major division by subdivisions, and finally each subdivision as required. For example, for alphabetic material, sort by first segregating into four groups, such as A-F, G-L, M-R, and S-Z; then, sort each group according to the first letter. For numeric material, first sort 0–2, 3–5, and 6–9; then, sort each group by the first digit. Figure 12–3 shows sorting devices being used in a large office. The device consists of dividers properly indexed and hingled, at intervals of about ¼ inch up to 1 inch, to a common base section. Thus, a series of pockets is formed, and each item of the material to be sorted is dropped into the proper pocket. Different sizes are available, ranging from around 30 up to as many as 2,000 divisions or pockets.

4. Storing. Each piece is stored under the proper classification, with the newest addition always on top or at the front of the contents in its respective folder. This acutally amounts to placing the material into its proper place and quickly checking the work as it progresses.

5. Retrieving Information. A definite manner for handling the removal of papers from the container is necessary in order to maintain

FIGURE 12–3
Sorting Waybills in a Large Office (approximately three million waybills per year are sorted in this office)

Courtesy: Erie Railroad, Cleveland.

the file and to know where items are, in the event that several people want the papers at the same time, and also to minimize indiscriminate removals from the files. Records of charged-out materials can be handled in any one of four ways as illustrated by Figure 12–4: (*a*) by substitution card, (*b*) by out folder, (*c*) by out guide, or (*d*) by multiple charge-out form.

When the removed material is a single card or piece of paper, its place in the file can be occupied by a substitution card showing the name of the person to whom the material is issued, along with the date and the initials of the employee issuing the material. Upon return of the material, the entries on the substitution card are lined out, and the card is reused. Out folders are ordinary file folders with one side printed for the recording of data concerning removals from that folder. The out guide is a pressboard guide with tab printed "Out" and a pocket or device to hold a single charge-out slip. It replaces a folder taken from the file and serves both as a record and as a marker for the borrowed material. When the withdrawn material is to be transferred from one user to another, a multiple chargeout form is used. As shown in

FIGURE 12–4

Media Used in Controlling Charge-Outs from Filed Material: (*a*) Substitution Card, (*b*) Out Folder, (*c*) Out Guide, and (*d*) Multiple Charge-Out Form

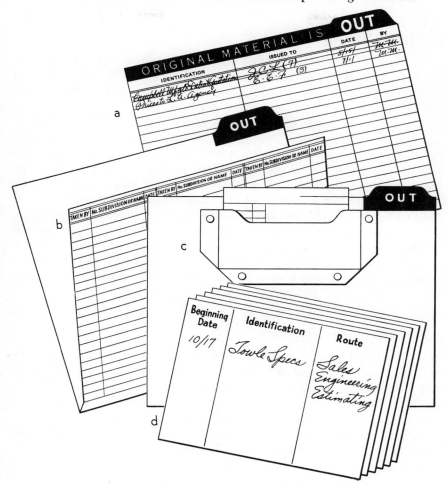

Figure 12–4 the date, identification, and route is attached to the substitution card, out folder, or out guide. A second route of material is written on the multiple forms. One copy of this form copy is filed in a tickler file for follow-up. Other copies are attached to the material so that, as each individual or department using the material finishes with it, a line is drawn through the name or department on the route list; the top copy is returned to the issuing storing and retrieving department; and the remaining copies and material are forwarded to the next

name on the route list. As copies are retrieved, they are attached to the tickler file copy; thus, there is a record of who has the material, without clearance of the material each time through the department.

RECORDS RETENTION

The storing of records cannot continue indefinitely. Containers become filled to capacity and many records stored have outlived their usefulness. Periodic culling of the stored material is required. You cannot file and forget.

The life cycle of all records consists of three stages (1) active use—quick access is important, (2) storage—for possible use, and (3) elimination—no longer of use. Succinctly stated, worthless records should never be stored, records stored should be reviewed periodically to eliminate those that have become useless, and those stored having either permanent or possible future use should be transferred to inexpensive storage areas. These concepts are the essential makeup of records retention, an important part of records management. In other words, as judged by their usefulness, maintenance of records gives way to the disposition of records. Formally stated, *records retention deals with the disposition of records and concerns storing those that must be retained and destroying those that are or become worthless.*

Advantages of Records Retention

A records-retention program can be quite extensive, nearly everyone in an enterprise is affected by it. A great deal of foresight, judgment, and especially a steadfastness of purpose are required. The rewards are high. Better storing .nd retrieving efficiency is gained since inactive material is removed, thus reducing finding time. Space savings are also achieved—throwing out records that have become useless means less space is needed. Also, storing useful but inactive records in an inexpensive storage area means dollar savings. And avoidance from accidental or premature destruction of records is assured. Furthermore, the retained records are better protected and safeguarded. Equipment designed especially for storage can be utilized, and the records are not subject to possible mutilation as a result of frequent handling.

Typically, records retention brings about these results: 26 percent of all stored material is retained as active, 16 percent is placed in inexpensive storage for possible future use, and the balance, 58 percent is eliminated. Think of it. Only one paper in four remains in the office file. The savings in finding time and space are tremendous. The National Records Management Council, Inc., a nonprofit organization, estimates only 5 percent of all records filed are ever referred to after a year and 5 percent of the references made deal with records over five years old. A large public utility reported to be spending nearly $24 million to maintain some 200,000 filing cabinets, adopted a records retention program and trimmed this cost to $17 million and with better service and efficiency. The gains by several other companies are shown by Figure 12–5.

FIGURE 12–5

Typical Disposition of Records by Companies without and Those with Records-Retention Programs

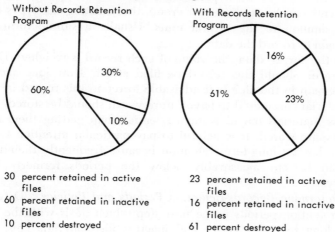

Without Records Retention Program

60% 30% 10%

With Records Retention Program

16% 23% 61%

30 percent retained in active files	23 percent retained in active files
60 percent retained in inactive files	16 percent retained in inactive files
10 percent destroyed	61 percent destroyed

Recommended Program for Records Retention

An orderly and well thought out program should be followed in order to attain the benefits of effective records retention. The following considerations will aid in reducing the amount of useless information retained for retrieval which never occurs.

1. *Appoint a Records Retention Manager.* This person will be in charge of and have the responsibility for the total program. Duties include overseeing the removal of inactive materials from files, establishing an index system for materials placed in inactive storage, supervising the inactive storage activities, obtaining legal clearance for records to be disposed when required, and helping department managers in developing retention policies.

2. *Take Inventory of Records.* The objective of a records retention program is to retain records only as long as they are needed. To this end the first step is to find out what records you have and evaluate them.

The study might begin with a cursory review of the entire enterprise to obtain background and understanding of the current work and to spot what records are used and what ones are filed for satisfactory operation. Following this, a survey is in order to determine (1) what is filed; (2) how much is filed—its size and quantity; (3) where it is filed—including the copies, if any; (4) how often it was used during specific preceding periods; (5) when, if ever, it is permanently removed from file; and (6) what is done with permanently removed material. In some instances, this inventory work is expedited by classifying the material by type or by department. Information applicable to several departments can be studied as a group, thus relating the types of information common to the several units. Usually a simple form is used upon which to record the data.

From the survey data, the value of each record is weighed. Questions decided are: Should this record be filed at all? How long should this record remain in the file? Is it advisable to retain this record in storage? Only material considered to have future worth should be stored. Keeping worthless materials out of storage is easier than getting them removed once they are stored. It is helpful to pay particular attention to records presently having long-term retention because frequently their retention times can be cut measurably below the periods formerly believed necessary.

3. Determine Records-Retention Periods and Policies. Determining records-retention periods is the next step which deals with the problem of how long to retain active and inactive file material. This, in turn, depends primarily upon the usefulness of the material to managers, and the legal requirements. The period of retention differs among companies, but there is a tendency toward the development of standard practices.

What papers to retain and for how long a period can probably best be decided by members most affected by these issues. Usually, the controller, the legal counsel, the tax counsel, and the manager of records retention should be included in this group; they usually are well qualified for such decision making. For the most part, this group sets forth policy instructions on which operating decisions can be based by the manager of records retention.

Papers that are essential to the company's security should be kept. Proof of assets and liabilities is important. Papers giving proof of ownership, property, inventories, machinery, and buildings are included in this category. Insurance is recovered on proof, not guesswork. Records dealing with transactions should be saved. These include receipt of money, proof of payment, proof of expenses or purchases, and payroll. Also, documents providing proof of usage should be retained, for they are vital in matters dealing with research, engineering, and patents.

If the company becomes involved in infringement or other patent-suit claims, certain drawings, properly coded, numbered, and preserved, form the basis for prosecution or defense. Historical data of various types often prove valuable in that they provide trends and statistical analysis helpful in the company's planning efforts. Such data should be retained if there is a reasonable possibility that they will be used in the future or will be referred to for improving decision making by relating the reasons given *why* certain decisions were made in the past with the outcome of such decisions.

Figure 12–6 shows selected retention periods for various records.

FIGURE 12–6

Suggested Schedule for Retention of Various Records in Years

Accounts receivable	10	Insurance—property	8
Agreements with employees	P*	Labor clock records	5
Annual and monthly reports	P	Labor earnings records	P
Articles of incorporation	P	Medical histories	P
Attendance records of employees	7	Minute book of directors meeting	P
Bids	3	Paid bills	8
Cash books	P	Patent records	P
Charge slips	10	Registered mail	5
Checks canceled	10	Requisitions	3
Correspondence—		Sales expenses	6
credit and collection	7	Shipping tickets	6
—purchase	5	Tax bills and statements	P
Delivery receipts	3	Time and motion studies	P
Dividend checks	10	Union labor contracts	P
Financial statements	P	Wage rates	8
General ledger	P		

* P = Permanent

These values represent the consensus of authorities on record storage and reflect current thinking in this area. However, the statute of limitations, which varies for different documents among states, regulatory activities by government agencies, and personal preferences should be considered in the choice. The statute of limitations specifies the length of time a record is alive according to law.

4. Classify the Records. Based on the information obtained from the inventory of records, suggested retention periods, and judgment, records of varying importance can be classified as to their retention. For convenience, they can be divided into four groups:

1. Nonessential. Records so classified should never be stored. Since they have value for a short period only—perhaps a few seconds—retaining them is wasteful. Included are pencil notations, routine inquires, and announcements.

2. Helpful. Records in this group can assist, but only for a very limited time, perhaps four to five weeks. After this period, their usefulness is completed. If filed, they should be placed in a separate drawer or cabinet and destroyed as their helpfulness ceases. An example is general correspondence, most of which has a useful life of not over four weeks.

3. *Important.* These include records containing information of value for relatively long periods—up to five or six years. They should first be stored in the office for handy reference; but ultimately, as they lose their current usefulness, they should be transferred to an inexpensive storage area. How long they remain in the office depends upon the type of record and the retention period established. Many firms keep records such as invoices, accounts receivable, sales records, quotations, and financial statements in active files for one to two years, then transfer to a storage area.

4. *Vital.* As the name implies, these records are paramount. They are retained permanently. They may be transferred to the storage area after a given period of time, but they are never destroyed. Vital records include legal papers of incorporation, titles to ownership, deeds, and reports to stockholders.

5. **Establish Index for Stored Material.** Unless you can find what is stored the storing efforts serve no purpose. The index system adopted should be simple, easily understood by those operating the records retention program, expedite finding the material, and allow for expansion in various areas that may develop over the future years. The records retention manager should assist in developing the index along with the efforts of several selected records retention employees. The information can be kept on small index cards or on sheets in a loose-leaf notebook. It should include subject classification, shelf number, box number or name, and scheduled date for ultimate destruction. It is important that each container be labeled plainly.

6. **Write a Records Retention Manual.** Although this takes some time, it will prove well worthwhile in informing all paperwork personnel about the record retention policies and schedules, when and how material is transferred to inactive status, and how to obtain assistance in retrieving material that is in storage.

7. **Provide a Good Storage Area.** A clean, dry area should be selected to serve as an inexpensive and safe storage area. Proper conditions of temperature, air circulation, and humidity are important. The storage area should be regarded as an attractive work area. The floor must withstand a relatively high weight, as much as 250 pounds per square foot. Location can be either on-site (same as office) or off-site (away from office).

8. **Use Proper Equipment.** Various types of equipment can be used for storing records. Some will work out much better than others. Of

special interest is a specially designed fiberboard drawer file which combines the drawer, shelving, and base, all in one unit. A steel framework carries the entire weight load. The drawer files are interlocking, each drawer locking to the one below and the one above it. The unit "builds its own steel framework as you stack it." As many as 20 drawers can be stacked in one tier. There is no buckling, sagging, or warping. Different sizes are available for punched cards, letter, and legal-size papers. The total space is devoted to drawer units, which results in a compact, efficient use of storage space giving the high storage ratio of 8 to 1, i.e., the cubic feet of records to square feet of floor space. For bulk storage where reference is infrequent, larger containers with the same interlocking feature can be used. Each container is about 15 × 24 inches and holds two boxes, one of which can be used for letter, the other for legal size. Details and illustrations of this storage equipment are shown in Figure 12–7.

9. Schedule Transfers of Records. To implement the records retention program, several moves are necessary including transfer from active to inactive files and from inactive files to a low-cost storage area. In each case the transfer may also lead to a decision for their destruction should the records at that stage be considered worthless. Reference to Figure 12–8 is helpful in discussing the various transfers.

To reiterate, material classified as nonessential should never be filed, but should be destroyed immediately. "Helpful" material is filed in a separate file for the limited period, then destroyed. Material considered important or vital is stored (step 1) and subsequently transferred to the inactive file as a normal practice (step 2). With a four-drawer filing cabinet, the top drawers can be used for current material and the bottom two for inactive material. This arrangement affords convenient reference to inactive material which is necessary from time to time. When the five-drawer file is used, a common arrangement to follow is illustrated by Figure 12–9 (p. 346).

10. Transfer the Material, Destroy Worthless Records. The transferring of material can be done in one of two main ways: (1) the entire unit, or periodically; and (2) the individual, or perpetually. The former requires that all material be transferred at a scheduled time. Usually, an annual basis is used—at the beginning of the calendar year, fiscal year, or busy season. The material remains in the original folders and is moved bodily. New folders are used for the new material in the current file. The individual, or perpetual, means places time limits on individual papers by appropriate marks on the folders. Then, periodically, at intervals of about two or three months—or perpetually, at irregular intervals—the files are screened, and papers found to have been in the file past the allowable limit are transferred to the inactive file. In cases where the transaction is terminated, i.e., a settlement granted

FIGURE 12–7
Storage in Stacking Shells

Courtesy: Bankers Box Record Storage Systems, Franklin Park, Ill.

Storage boxes slide into the stacking shell. These shells are stacked one upon the other forming a unit of interlocking fiberboard drawer files which is compact and sturdy.

or a sale closed, the material is transferred immediately, regardless of date.

From the inactive files all materials are removed periodically and sorted (step 3 of Figure 12–8). The material in these files is now classified as either worthless, important, or vital. Worthless material is destroyed as indicated by step 4A; important material follows either step 4B or 4C; and for the vital information either step 4D or 4E is adopted. This

FIGURE 12-8
A Program of Records Retention

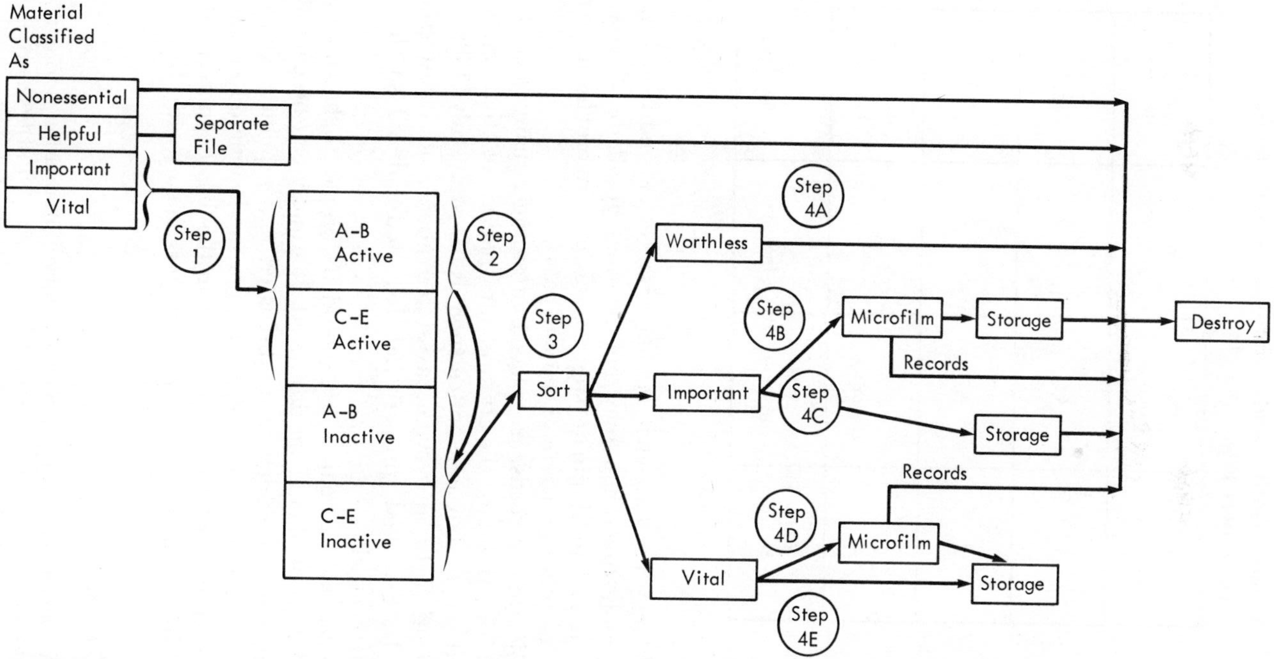

FIGURE 12–9
Arrangement for Active and Inactive Material in
Five-Drawer Files

1 Inactive	3 Inactive	6 Inactive	8 Inactive
1	4	6	9
2	5	7	10
3	4 Inactive	8	9 Inactive
2 Inactive	5 Inactive	7 Inactive	10 Inactive

program may be somewhat modified for certain individual applications. For example, microfilm may not be used at all, or it may be found more practical to eliminate step 3 (sorting), microfilm all records, and use the microfilms for reference in all cases.

At the time records are placed in storage, many records managers suggest determining the future life period of that material. Thus stamped on the box is a notice such as "Destroy July, 1982," or "Retain permanently." In any event, as stated above, all transferred material should be classified, properly labeled, and indexed so that it can be found if needed.

At least once a year, a list should be prepared showing what stored original records should be destroyed. It usually can be compiled readily from data on the index cards discussed under point 5 above. This list is then submitted to the office manager or designated executive for approval and authority to proceed. When this has been granted, the material is destroyed and the list filed permanently for future reference.

QUESTIONS

1. In your opinion will the management of information storing and retrieving become more or less important in the future? Justify your viewpoint.
2. Do you favor a centralized or a decentralized organizational arrangement for information storing and retrieving when manual means are used. Why?

3. If a basic principle of storing and retrieving is to file less, what ways do you suggest that this objective be achieved?
4. Discuss the managerial consideration for organization, cost, standards, and number of copies in storing and retrieving work when mechanized means are used.
5. For how long a period do you suggest each item in the following list of filed material be retained:
   a. Sales prospect lists.
   b. Invoices from suppliers of raw materials.
   c. Real estate deeds.
   d. Payrolls and pay rates.
   e. Application forms from prospective employees.
   f. Quotations to customers.
6. Discuss the proper equipment to be used for storage of records.
7. What conclusions do you draw from Figure 12–5?
8. Do you recommend having a responsible person head up storing and retrieving activities regardless of whether mechanized or manual means for handling the work are followed? Why?
9. Last month, storing and retrieving sorted 5,322 items in preparation for filing, performed 821 successful retrievals, failed to find 40 requested retrievals, and received additional equipment valued at $775. It is estimated that there are a total of 68,000 items in the files. What is the accuracy ratio? The usage ratio? Is any remedial action suggested by your values for either of these ratios? Explain.
10. Describe the meaning of Figure 12–8 in your own words.
11. Write a two-sentence identifying description of each of the following:
    a. Records retention.
    b. Records management.
    c. Multiple charge-out form.
    d. Statute of limitations.
12. An office which has never had a records retention program is now interested in establishing one. Suggest an approach which can be followed to meet this purpose.

CASE PROBLEMS

Case 12–1. GBM Physicians Professional Services

Five physicians, making up GBM Physicians Professional Services, are enjoying very successful practices. The director is Dr. Robert R. Medland who is the overseer of the general operations of the medical unit. A standard schedule of fees is charged and specialization in the practice of medicine is followed by the five doctors, although there is some overlapping. A total of about sixty patients are seen daily except Wednesdays and Sundays. Not all the doctors are in their offices at the same time. Some are mornings only, others afternoons only, some mornings and afternoons. There is also variation by the day of the week.

You have been called in to give recommendations for improving the records now handled for patients' appointments with the doctors. Currently a 8×5 card is maintained for each patient. Entries of appointments and visits are kept on this card. From it, billings are prepared and mailed twice a month, one on the first, the other on the fifteenth of each month. A receptionist-clerk and a nurse-secretary perform all the clerical work. Currently all appointment cards are kept in one large file, a practice established six years ago when the GBM Services was founded. The file has grown quite large due to the increase in the number of cards. Difficulty and delay are experienced in locating active appointment cards. Furthermore, the three available filing cabinets are filled, a fourth cabinet is needed but there is no room for it in the office. The nurse-secretary tells you he talked with clerical personnel at the hospital and it is his understanding that the best thing to do would be to microfilm the appointment cards. You make inquiry as to what the processing is for other records i.e., those covering the sending out for tests, purchases of medicine and supplies, etc., and are told that Dr. Medland wants you to confine your investigations and recommendations to the patients' appointment cards.

Questions:

1. What additional information do you feel is necessary for you to help GBM Services? Discuss.
2. Outline your recommendations to Dr. Medland and include its advantages along with a general description of how you would make your presentation.

Case 12–2.   Quebec-Fortier Services Corporation

Mr. Conrad Boggan, assistant information manager, estimates that 50 file drawers or 75 cubic feet of material are annually placed in records storage. He is not sure, with all the alternatives now available to the corporation, that the best program is being followed. In bringing up the subject with Ms. Michelle Angone, the information manager, an interesting discussion developed during which it was agreed that Mr. Boggan should study further major alternatives to that of the company's present practice.

The first alternative is to microfilm all inactive material removed from the files. A few documents would be stored in their original form, but for purposes here we can consider all material placed in the storage area will be in microfilm. Mr. Boggan talked with a representative from a microfilm service company and was quoted $6.50 per 100-ft. reel which quotation includes total costs, i.e., machine, material, and labor. Approximately 3,500 documents are photographed on a 100-ft. reel and there are 3,000 documents per cubic foot. According to Mr. Boggan, about 140 documents are retrieved yearly from the storage area. The representative indicated that such retrievals with the material on microfilm would cost about $1.25 each. This includes cost of a viewing machine depreciated over a ten-year period.

Mr. Boggan believed the answer might be a sorting of the documents removed from the files into (1) present form storage (2) microfilm and store, and (3) destroy useless material. For this alternative, Ms. Angone secured some cost estimates including ten work-hours of labor at $2.50 an hour, one third of the material microfilmed, and two thirds destroyed. As above, some stored material will not be microfilmed, but it will be a relatively small amount and can be considered microfilmed for purposes of this analysis.

The third alternative is to obtain microfilm records of computer output at time of initial processing using the COM, or computer output microfilm arrangement. These microfilm records would serve as the storage copies for all computer-processed data. There would also be noncomputer processed papers such as customers' orders and correspondence which Mr. Boggan estimates will be 25 file drawers annually, or one half of the present amount now annually removed from the active files. These could be handled as under the first alternative, i.e., microfilmed and to the storage area. Ms. Angone advises that COM cost per year for the computer-processed papers can be estimated at $360. She also noted that the current total cost for retrieving an original record from the storage area is $8.

Questions:

1. Are there other alternatives to the problem of records retention that should be considered? Explain.
2. Make a table by listing the present practice and the three alternatives vertically with cost and other important considerations horizontally. For each alternative fill in the total cost and note the other important considerations.
3. What decision do you recommend be made? Why?

Case 12–3. Martin-Durkee Manufacturing Company

RALPH HESS: Come in, please. You're Mr. Fred Ford, the management consultant?

FRED FORD: Yes. Thank you very much.

HESS: I'll be glad to assist you in every way. I suppose you'd like me to start by discussing what we do here?

FORD: Yes, if you will.

HESS: The engineering design division is divided into three sections: design, administration, and design drafting. I am in charge of the latter. We are responsible for all mechanical drafting work in the designing of new products, improvements in the design of existing products, production drawings relative to the building of prototype products, and products to be built under contract to customers.

FORD: You handle improvements in existing design?

HESS: Yes, sir.

FORD: What does the design section handle?

HESS: They handle the design of new products only. Now, to be able to use the latest commercially offered items as components of design—and this is true for new product design as well, that is, for the design section—it is necessary to have readily available a file of catalogs and design manuals offered by various manufacturers. All these cabinets you see in the room out there are filled with such material. In addition, we have correspondence, blueprints, original drawings, and even samples of various items. Some of these, both papers and samples, are odd sizes and shapes, and are difficult to store; and my guess is that part of what we have out there could be discarded.

FORD: Do the files out there represent all the stored reference material?

HESS: No. There are stacks of stuff in a basement room. The material is stacked up in neat little piles on the floor; each stack is tagged, but it's a mess to find anything down there.

FORD: Do you have need to go to this basement room from time to time?

HESS: Yes, every once in a while. The men resent being sent there to look for something—all except Harvey Pair, who doesn't seem to mind. In fact, I guess you could say he even enjoys it. Gets lost down there for half a day at a time.

FORD: About how frequently do you refer to the files out here in this next room?

HESS: That's hard to say. Sometimes, quite often; at other times, maybe just once or twice a day.

FORD: How is the material arranged in these files?

HESS: It's supposed to be alphabetical by manufacturer's name, that is, for the design manuals. General literature from vendors is kept in a separate tier of cabinets, by vendor's name. Several times a week, an employee from the main office brings current material and files it. But my designers and draftsmen are constantly coming to me and complaining they can't find the material they want, and they insist it was in the files. Sometimes we find it misfiled; sometimes the filer tells us we never did have the material; sometimes, it is lost but turns up later.

FORD: What do you think should be done?

HESS: Well, now. . . . I understand you're the expert, so what I say may not make any sense. But for whatever it is worth, I think there is too much junk in the files—stuff we'll never use. And some way to find what we want would be a big help, too. Why, we've requested new copies of booklets and catalogs from a supplier only to discover before we receive them that we have the same booklets or catalogs in our file. Just could not find them when we wanted them.

Questions:

1. What further information do you feel Mr. Ford should obtain from Mr. Hess?
2. As Mr. Ford, would you hold any other interviews or make any observations within the company? Why?
3. What recommendations would you make to the company's managers? Discuss.

Part IV

Organizing to Determine Who Does What Office Work and under What Environment

We now move to the subject of organizing. Achieving a structure about which employees and facilities can operate effectively, having employees know what parcel of the total office work is theirs to perform, utilizing decision making power properly, attaining good work relationships both within and among work teams, arranging the physical facilities to expedite the work flow, and providing a satisfactory physical work environment are absolute essentials to effective office management. As pointed out in this part of the book, the achievement of organization can be done formally from official decrees or informally by employees on their own finding ways to cooperate and being active in groups arising from their working together.

Five chapters are offered. They include "Formal Office Organizing Basics," "People and Office Organization," "Authority and the Managerial Environment," and two chapters on "Organizing and Physical Environment."

Chapter 13

Formal Office Organizing Basics

Many things which cannot be overcome when they stand together yield themselves up when taken little by little.

Sertorius

Organizing is a fundamental function of office management. It comes into being because the work to be done requires more than one person. A group is required and the various human efforts are coordinated so that both the contribution of the group and of each individual member is effective and in addition, is personally satisfying to the group as well as to each member. Furthermore, organizing brings together all the other basic resources—materials, equipment and machines, systems, capital, and markets—into a desirable and practical format so that the office work can be performed.

That is to say, organizing results in evolving a framework or structure, called an organization that (1) assists people to work together effectively in a group as they work individually and (2) makes feasible the marshalling of the basic resources. Organizing requires answers to questions such as: Who does what information work? Who reports to whom? Who decides what issues? What members are in what work groups? What amounts of what basic resources are used and by whom? What work environment is to be provided?

MAKEUP OF ORGANIZING

From a rational and analytical viewpoint, organizing is concerned with (1) *work*—how to distribute it among employees, (2) *people*—who is going to do what work, (3) *relationships*—what is the relative author-

353

ity and responsibility among the "organizational units" formed by work and employees, and (4) *work environment*—what tools and workplaces will best contribute toward maximum work accomplishments and employees' satisfactions. As already implied, organizing results in an organization structure about which these components are interrelated and centered in order to achieve orderly and desired actions. Stated formally: *Organizing is the allocating of the total work to be done among employees, establishing the relative authority and responsibility of each individual who is placed in charge of each work component, and supplying the proper work environment.*

Our discussion will deal first with *formal organization* which emphasizes rational, economic, preciseness, and work-oriented concepts. In the following chapter, *informal organization* will be included. It modifies formal organization, exists primarily because modern human behavior, judgment, and understanding preclude perfect adaption of a human being to strict formal organization. This condition stems, in part, from changes taking place in individual and social values, in technology, and in research seeking possible improvements.

BENEFITS OF FORMAL ORGANIZING

Organizing enables managers to enlarge their scope or influence; with organizing more can be accomplished than is humanly possible working alone. Activities are placed into manageable units for which the work can be planned effectively, expanded or contracted as required, and adequately controlled. Further, organizing spells out for each manager areas in which decisions and their enforcement are authorized. Teamwork is advanced and at the same time the value of each member's contribution is increased. Further, organizing avoids needless duplication of effort. Confusion and misunderstanding as to who is to do what work is avoided as is also "buck-passing." Also, a satisfactory environment for the work performance is provided. Specific work is assigned and the accountability for its performance is known. Formal communication is expedited and a unity of group effort is encouraged with some freedom of decision making to the individual with reference to his particular work effort.

"The Office"—What and Where?

In the studying of office organizing, it is helpful to begin with consideration of the office organization in relation to the organization of the entire enterprise. This approach places the office in its true perspective, namely that of being a service and a facilitator to the main purposes of an enterprise. In a business enterprise, for example, the work of the office is essential to the functioning of the basic activities—production, sales, finance, and personnel. Although called by different names, these four basic activities are present in almost every organization be it of a hospital, school, or governmental unit. And the office and its organization exist to help fulfill these basic activities, it is not performed apart from them. To illustrate, in an insurance company where typically much paperwork is performed, the basic activities are creating and producing insurance policies, selling them, and handling the matters of financing in connection with them. The paperwork is performed to aid these basic activities.

The questions of what should be the makeup of the office and where it should be located give rise to a number of considerations among which the following are important.

1.   Type and Nature of the Enterprise.   The content and the placement of the office function are affected greatly by the dominance of the production, sales, finance, or personnel activities. If the enterprise is primarily one for production—a large manufacturer, for example, selling its entire output to several large buyers—the office unit probably will be of relatively small importance. However, in a predominantly financial enterprise, the work will be of relatively great importance. Likewise, in a governmental enterprise, the office unit normally occupies a position relatively high in the organizational structure.

2.   Importance Attached to Office Work.   If top managers of an enterprise recognize the work of the office as of relatively high significance, the tendency will probably be to bring it together into one organizational unit and place this unit high in the organizational structure. But if office work is considered minor, although necessary, it probably will be performed by the department needing it and coordinated as completely as possible with the primary activities of the respective department.

3.   Degree of Office Mechanization Used.   In many cases the adoption of office machines has small effect upon the organization structure. However, when machines capable of processing huge quantities of work or of performing work historically handled by several departments are adopted, the result to the organization is to consolidate the work, shrink the department, combine departments, and change the organizational framework. This can most readily be seen in the case of computers and their impact upon office organizing.

4.   Extent of Centralization of Office Functions.   The office work of an enterprise may be concentrated physically and placed in the hands of a single executive who is charged with the management of all office activities in the organization. This arrangement is termed centralization. In contrast, since office work occurs throughout the entire enterprise, from the president's office to the lowest paid clerk, it is possible to have it performed in dispersed locations, under the jurisdiction of the unit in which it arises. In this case decentralization is followed and the office functions are dispersed and are either combined with, or made subordinate to, other nonoffice organizational units.

These two conditions (centralization or decentralization), however, are extreme and actually seldom used. Commonly followed is an intermediate or modified arrangement between these two extremes such as (1) office work is located and performed by major departments, and each department head is fully responsible for the office activities in that department, (2) office work is distributed among all departments, but one person is placed in charge of this office work in order to achieve reasonable coordination, or (3) certain office work is centralized in one unit and placed under one manager, the remaining office work is performed in the unit in which it arises and is supervised by the regular department head of that unit. This latter arrangement is popular and is interpreted in different arrangements, the more common of which are discussed in the following paragraphs.

The Office Services Arrangement

By office services are meant corresponding, report writing, mail and office communicating services, copying, and manually operated filing. In some enterprises these services are included in one organizational unit and placed under the "office services manager." However, all these services are not always centralized, the notable exceptions being corresponding, report writing, and filing. Furthermore, even when all these services are referred to as being centralized, they are only partially so—some of certain services being located in various units throughout the entire organization structure.

The adoption of an "office services" unit arrangement means that the manager in charge of information work has a dual managerial task. First, to manage the services unit; and second, since information work is being performed in various other units in which it arises, to counsel with the executives of these various units and help them accomplish their information work in the best manner. This second task is of paramount importance and in many respects established the true status of the information manager in any organization structure. Actually, it is in essence providing the information management viewpoint to all managers of the enterprise. All use information; hence, help in how to use it effectively constitutes a real service. Figure 13–1, top left illustration, shows graphically the office services arrangement.

The Systems and Procedures Arrangement

As recognition that the use of systems and procedures can increase office efficiency, many companies have established an organization unit

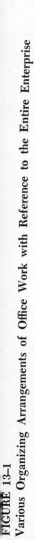

FIGURE 13-1
Various Organizing Arrangements of Office Work with Reference to the Entire Enterprise

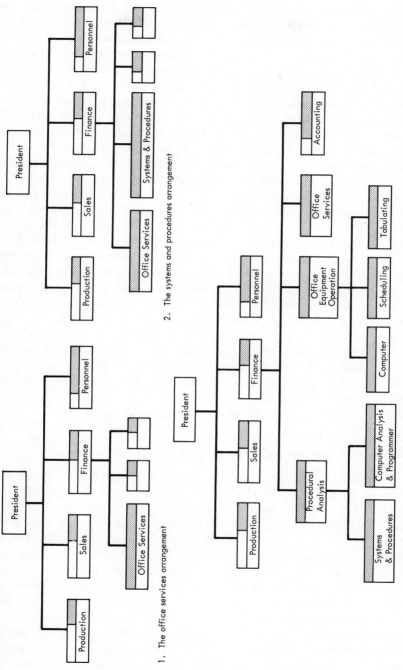

1. The office services arrangement

2. The systems and procedures arrangement

3. The modified systems and procedures arrangement

Shaded areas approximate the relative amount of office work.

to facilitate this particular viewpoint. The exact format, content, and location, of this organizational unit vary considerably from company to company. For our purposes here, it is identified as the "systems and procedures department"; but other common titles are systems department, procedures department, methods department, or business services department. Probably none of these titles identifies completely and clearly the work performed. As shown in the top right illustration of Figure 13–1, this unit is subordinate to the major unit of finance. It is also common to subordinate it to the controller's office. The main reason for favoring the finance vice president or the controller is that one of those executives could move with freedom across organizational lines, is already associated with office machines and systems, and that the work to be done by the computer—notably payroll, accounts payable, and accounts receivable—is already the responsibility of one or the other. Any or all of the following activities may be included in the systems and procedures unit: (1) office systems, procedures, and methods design and implementation—to determine and use the proper office operations, their best sequence, and the manner of performance to get the office work accomplished efficiently; (2) computer analysis and programming to operate the computer; (3) analysis of other office machines and equipment in order to advise what type of machine or equipment should be used for a specific type of office work under the prescribed conditions; (4) office layout and working conditions—to recommend the most effective physical work environment; (5) office standards—to relate useful levels of performance or frames of reference in order to evaluate achievement; and (6) office work simplification—to point out ways to eliminate waste of all kinds and get the office work out more effectively.

The Modified Systems and Procedures Arrangement

As computer usage has increased, some companies have adopted what might be termed a modified systems and procedures arrangement. Here the procedural analysis for systems and computer facilitation is separated from the implementation of the machines. Experience has shown that above certain levels or volumes of activity, the work of computer and other office machine scheduling and usage are best segregated from the design and analysis functions for these machines. The bottom illustration of Figure 13–1 shows this arrangement. Note that the procedural analysis section includes (1) *all* systems and procedures work throughout the company in one unit and (2) the work dealing with computer analysis and programming in another unit. The head of the procedural analysis section coordinates the activities of systems and procedures employees and that of the computer analytical personnel. Also observe that here again the office work activities are under finance. However, this is not

FIGURE 13-2
Corporate Level Organization of Retailing Conglomerate

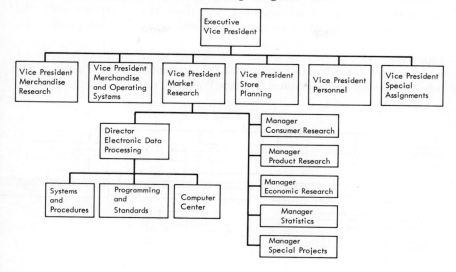

always the case. Illustrated by Figure 13–2 is a large retailer where the director of electronic data processing reports to the vice president of market research who, in turn, reports to the executive vice president. The latter deals with the operations of the corporation's many stores. The functions included under the vice president of market research and of the electronic data-processing director are indicated on the chart.

This company is made up of highly autonomous subsidiary companies the managers of which operate their own respective stores. The only formal relationships that exist between the companies and the corporate level are the presidents of the companies and the corporate president. The corporation exercises financial controls and provides services as requested by the company managements. Over a period of several years the corporate management developed attractive information services including inventory-control methods, accounts payable systems, product-profit analysis, and return on investment programs. All of these are computer processed.

The Administrative Services Organizational Arrangement

Primarily because of the increase in office automation and the strong trend toward computers, further modification in the organization of those supplying information has taken place to better meet current needs. The concept of an "administrative services" organizational unit on par with other major units of an enterprise has developed and is winning favor. This arrangement places most of the information work under a single administrator. The top illustration of Figure 13–3 shows the administrative services arrangement. For illustrative purposes only, the units under administrative services are shown as systems and procedures,

FIGURE 13–3
Two Administrative Services Organizational Arrangements Each of Which Provide Top Recognition and Status to Office Work Efforts

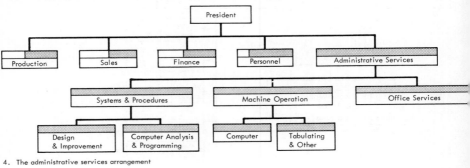

4. The administrative services arrangement

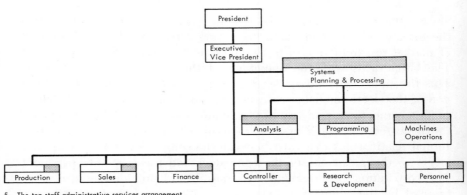

5. The top staff administrative services arrangement

Shaded areas approximate the relative amount of office work.

machine operation, and office services. Observe that the efforts of designing how the work will be accomplished (systems and procedures) is segregated from that of implementation (machine operation). Also, that analyzing and programming essential for computer usage is concentrated in a separate unit from that of the efforts designing the means to be used for the paper work in general. Modern electronic machines make it feasible to handle a large part of the paper work of an enterprise in one organizational unit. However, even under the administrative services arrangement, some office work is performed in other major units, simply because it is easier, more convenient, and of greater service to perform some of the office work in these other units.

The Top Staff Administrative Services Arrangement

The bottom illustration of Figure 13–3 is a simplified form of a large enterprise with an extensive informational services unit and largescale computer processing. Responsibility for all this work is fixed in a department executive reporting directly to the executive vice president. This department serves as a service group to all other departments and permits companywide coordination of all paperwork systems. It identifies informational activities with top management and enhances the enlistment and support of department heads. The informational needs can be determined objectively without predisposition to a particular means or solution. An avowed goal of this arrangement is to improve the quality of information made available to all management members.

WORK AND ITS DIVISION—THE INITIAL BASIS

For organizing to take place, work is divided forming clusters of tasks and later people are assigned to these tasks. The resulting "work division-people assigned" segments provide the nuclei of organization units. We start with work and its division because, in the great majority of cases, this is the superior approach. A manager must coordinate what is being done, not who is doing it. Also the work is relatively permanent, it changes less frequently than the interests and abilities of personnel. Furthermore, to formulate organization units primarily on the basis of personnel often results in unusual combinations of duties that are difficult to manage and for which the securing of replacements is arduous.

The objectives and the nature of the enterprise determine for the most part the work to be done. Using this work as the beginning of organizing efforts minimizes subjective influences, helps to develop clear concepts of what activities must be performed, and minimizes uneconomical overlapping and duplicating of work.

Dividing the work can be accomplished by various means including (1) by function, (2) by process, (3) by customer, (4) by product, (5) by territory, and (6) by project. An organizer can choose any means, and commonly several means are employed in the same organization structure. What best helps to achieve the objective should be used. In a bank, for example, for the top levels, functions or activities may be used; whereas the loan department may be divided by customer— loans to manufacturers of plastics, chemicals, and paper; loans to manufacturers of food processors and package machines; or by product—commerical loans or personal loans. Office work division by territory is common for offices designed to serve sales organizations. The territory divisions constitute the main segments of the sales organizational structure, and the offices serving such organizations are likewise segregated and located throughout the country. Work division by project in office organization has been used to a limited degree. It utilizes the idea of work division being a project or a major and complete program. Assigned to a project is a complete team which is permitted to work on the project assigned until either successful completion or an authorized termination is ordered, at which time the team is disbanded and new projects are activated with newly formed teams believed appropriate for the new work involved. Large research development agencies of government are using project organization with great success. In the future it may become an important segment of office organizing.

The work division obtained by any of these means can be further divided into work subdivisions and, in turn, to sub subdivisions. The extent to which the dividing is carried is guided by considerations for the organization unit to be formed. The desired size of this unit, the quantity and scope of work, the way it is performed, the need for verifying the work of one unit by another, the extent of continuous flow, and the permanency of the work are usually of prime importance. The advantages of specialization are sought, but not at the expense of employee job interest.

All organizing requires some job specialization—no one person can do everything equally well. Complex work is divided into relatively simple components, each accomplished effectively by employees specializing in that single operation or in a group of similar operations. *The question is not whether to have job specialization but to what extent job specialization should be carried.* There are both economic and social limitations to job specialization. The degree and form of job specialization to follow presumably depend upon the type of office work and the individual doing it. The current prevailing belief is that the work division should not be carried to the point where the resultant job is considered monotonous and uninteresting to the one performing the work. To lessen this possible condition, several different arrangements can be followed. They are discussed in Chapter 19.[1]

It must also be noted that the organizational unit being created will be influenced by its manager as well as the employees performing the operative work and their relationships to all other employees in the total organization. Hence, we should keep in mind the type of management member who will take charge of this unit, that is, special attributes, shortcomings, ambitions, accomplishments, and education. If no manager is currently available, we need to decide what qualifications will be sought, and is there a reasonable possibility that such a manager can

---

[1] Pages 513–17.

be hired. Also, adequate thought must be given to evaluating the proposed nonmanagement members of the unit, the capacity and skills required, personnel relationships to be integrated, and the wishes of the contemplated prevailing management member.

The division of work to be done must be carried out to the individual job level. That is, the department functions must be divided ultimately into jobs for each individual. Unless this is done, the formal organizing is incomplete, and the group of people connected with the enterprise may experience difficulty in ascertaining a unity of action.

For an existent organization, data on the current work divisions as well as who performs the different tasks can be surveyed and recorded on a work distribution chart. Basically this is a spread sheet which shows, for a given time period—usually a week—the type of work and the time spent on each job by each employee in the office organization unit under review. A vertical column is used for each employee, along with one to indicate the time spent on each activity. The functions performed are listed in the first column on the left. Information for the chart can be obtained from the supervisor or the employees. Probably more objective data are obtained by observing each employee and recording information on activities, but this approach is expensive. Figure 13–4 shows a work distribution chart.

FIGURE 13–4
Work Distribution Chart

OFFICE FUNCTIONS	TOTAL MAN HOURS	LOIS MILLER Unit Supervisor	MAN HOURS	BETTY HEIDT Stenographer	MAN HOURS	RUTH TORFF Order Clerk	MAN HOURS	EDITH WRIGHT File Clerk	MAN HOURS	SYLVIA GAZEL Telephone Switchboard Operator	MAN HOURS
Correspondence	54	Read and route / Dictation	9 / 10	Takes dictation / Transcribes	10 / 20	Types labels and materials for files	5				
Computing	32	Figures prices	3	Figures prices	2	Figures prices	15	Figures prices	12		
Filing	21					Files correspondence / Finds letters in file	2 / 5	Files correspondence / Finds letters in file / Classifies correspondence	4 / 6 / 4		
Handling mail	26	Opens mail / Time stamps mail	2 / 5	Stamps mail	2	Opens mail	5	Stamps mail	4	Opens mail / Stamps mail	3 / 5
Miscellaneous	67	Answers questions / Answers telephone inquiries / Supervises	8 / 2 / 1	Cleans typewriter / Gets supplies / Arranges advertising stuffing material	1 / 2 / 3	Answers telephone inquiries	8	Errands for postage stamps and supplies / Maintains tickler file for follow-ups	2 / 8	Operates switchboard	32
	200		40		40		40		40		40

Work Division Arrangements

Work divisions for the top levels of an organization structure are usually made on the basis of functions. Divisions for the intermediate levels usually are either by type of product, by customer, or by territory. Common at the lower office organizational levels are work divisions by (1) serial, (2) parallel, or (3) unit assembly. These are illustrated by Figure 13–5 in which the work consists of handling customers' orders made up of three separate operations: (1) credit approval, (2) inventory check, and (3) pricing. The work force is Nancy Brown, Sharon Hewitt, and Virginia Walker.

In the serial arrangement, shown at the top of the figure, the work division is extended to a series of small tasks, each task being performed by a specialist in that particular type of work. Moving progressively from task to task, the work advances until completed. The serial arrangement, or consecutive handling, is the same basic plan as the familiar factory assembly line, commonly found in production plants.

The parallel arrangement, or concurrent handling, shown in the center of Figure 13–5, permits a series of needed and separate tasks to be performed by one individual or a work team. The employee or employees, as the case might be, do not specialize in performing one task but gain proficiency in accomplishing several tasks. Frequently, the tasks are related, but this is not necessary.

The unit assembly arrangement, or simultaneous handling, illustrated at the bottom of Figure 13–5, provides for different employees to perform different work steps upon the same work items at the same time. Specialization is practiced by each employee, but the work sequence is not identical for each item. Coordination of the various tasks is a prime requirement under this arrangement, for the separate tasks usually do not require identical times to perform.

In general, the use of the serial arrangement is recommended when the quantity of work is large, mechanization is employed, and the total work is complex and consists of a series of heterogeneous tasks (i.e.) shifting, for example, from a typewriter to a copying machine to checking to a punched card machine to a typewriter. In contrast, the parallel arrangement can be followed when understanding of the total work is helpful, the "start to finish" performance period must be reduced, competition among employees is desired, duplication of indoctrination efforts, such as reading and checking the document in order to perform the work, are to be eliminated, and some variety in the work is wanted. Finally, the unit assembly arrangement, by permitting work to start at an operation other than the first in the sequence of tasks, provides flexibility in machine utilization and work scheduling, tends to get work completed rapidly, and is commonly used for special rush and emergency work.

JOB ANALYSIS

Job analysis is a formal means of determining the job content. *Job analysis is the process of critically examining the components of a job,*

FIGURE 13–5
Illustrating the Serial, Parallel, and Unit Assembly Arrangements of Work Division

SERIAL
(consecutive
handling)

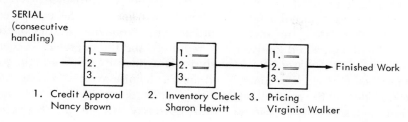

1. Credit Approval   2. Inventory Check   3. Pricing
   Nancy Brown   Sharon Hewitt   Virginia Walker

PARALLEL
(congruent
handling)

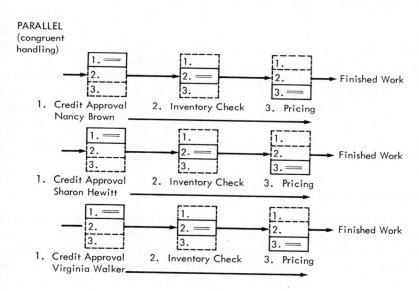

1. Credit Approval   2. Inventory Check   3. Pricing
   Nancy Brown

1. Credit Approval   2. Inventory Check   3. Pricing
   Sharon Hewitt

1. Credit Approval   2. Inventory Check   3. Pricing
   Virginia Walker

UNIT ASSEMBLY
(simultaneous
handling)

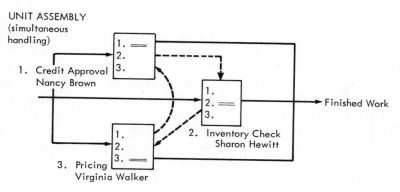

1. Credit Approval
   Nancy Brown

2. Inventory Check
   Sharon Hewitt

3. Pricing
   Virginia Walker

both separately and in relation to the whole, in order to determine all the operations and duties. In short, job analysis deals with facts about jobs and what is required for competent performance. Typical of data included are the forms and materials handled, the equipment and machines used, the methods utilized, the frequency of the operations, the amounts and kinds of skill required, and the degree of concentration needed. By use of job analysis data, identity of a certain job name to certain work becomes fixed, and a definite association between the job title and the content is established.

Job analysis is customarily and quite correctly thought of as an activity logically a part of personnel activities because it is basic in the performance of many personnel department functions. For example, job analysis is the basis for determining the relative worth, compensation-wise, of jobs; it facilitates the formulation of developmental needs, and serves to identify promotions and transfers. These are truly personnel functions in character and are discussed in Part 5 of this book. However, inasmuch as job analysis does identify the job and its content, it is included in this discussion dealing with organizing. As already pointed out, really effective and complete organizing work requires specific work divisions at the individual level. Job analysis helps supply this requirement.

Obtaining Job Analysis Data

In the case of new work or a new organizational unit, the manager doing the organizing must decide the characteristics of the newly created job or jobs. In a going office, however, three methods of securing job analysis data are possible: (1) interview and observation, (2) conferences, and (3) questionnaires. For the first method, the analyst goes to the employee, asks questions about the job, and observes what the content of the job is. While this method is satisfactory for office jobs, it is probably most popular for factory jobs. In the second method, the employees are called into conference and verbally describes their job to the analyst, who records the information. This method usually requires more time than the others, takes employees from their job, and may interfere with the work routine. In the third method, a questionnaire is sent to the employee, who fills in the information. This method is used in cases where the employees can intelligently handle clerical details and are more or less accustomed to paper work. It is commonly used for most office work. The federal government has employed this procedure successfully for over 60 years. Frequently the questionnaires are supplemented with short observations and interviews, especially for the more important jobs.

Whatever method is adopted, it is advisable to secure within practical limits as much information as possible about each job. It is usually better to have too much than too little data. Commonly the data are recorded on a prepared form which serves as a reminder to answer definite questions and thereby secure all the needed facts, so that no part of the job is overlooked. It also expedites recording the data in a standardized manner, thus making it easier to handle and interpret the information. Figure 13–6 shows a portion of a job analysis form.

FIGURE 13–6
Portion of Questionnaire Used for Job Analysis

JOB ANALYSIS

Present title of job _____ Department _____

1. What is the general purpose of this job?
2. What duties are performed in the *usual* course of the work? (Tell from where work is received, what is done with it, and where it is sent.)
3. What duties are performed only at stated intervals? (Give answers by daily, weekly, monthly, etc.)
4. In what organizational unit is this job presently located?
5. Does the job entail supervising other employees? (Explain.)
6. If there are any special training courses essential in order to perform the duties of this job satisfactorily, name them.
7. What past experience is *necessary* for a new employee to have in order to perform the duties of this job?
8. What are the *most* difficult parts of this job?
9. What are the *least* difficult parts of this job?
10. About what proportions of this job require sitting, _____%; standing, _____%; moving about, _____%?
11. What machines or other equipment are operated?
    Regularly:
    Occasionally:

Job Description

The information on the job analysis form actually describes the formal job. When written in a descriptive style, the term "job description" is frequently used. While the format used for writing these descriptions varies, they usually contain a summary of the job, the work performed, and the qualifications generally considered essential. (See Figure 13–7).

Job descriptions are useful in the work of organizing. They give the complete anatomy of the job. Also, they help bring about better understanding within an enterprise because they point out the qualifications required of an employee on the particular job, help in selecting persons best fitted for the requirements of the job, and assist in acquainting the new employee with the job.

Formal job descriptions can be collected and utilized in designing and maintaining a formal organization structure. For maximum utility,

FIGURE 13-7
A Job Description Written in an Effective Form

JOB DESCRIPTION

DATE_____

JOB TITLE__JUNIOR ACCOUNTANT_____GRADE_VI____CODE_____

SUMMARY: Under general direction of Comptroller and immediate
supervision of Accountant, performs general accounting
duties and prepares special reports as assigned.

WORK PERFORMED: Maintains records of cash receipts and/or disbursements,
posts related subsidiary records. Posts various journal
entries and adjustments, maintains record of Supply
Department receipts and prepares minor financial statements.

Handles correspondence, verifies tabulations and reconciles
bank statement. Assists in distributing work to temporary
help, prepares monthly reports and special statements.
Performs related work, such as figuring per capita and
expense ratios. Operates office machines as required.

May supervise work of accounting clerks, typists for
temporary periods, etc. and performs similar duties as
assigned.

QUALIFICATIONS: Normally requires three to five years' training and
experience, including two years' general accounting training plus three years' company accounting experience as
an Accounting Clerk.

Courtesy: J. D. Moore Organization, Ann Arbor, Mich.

the definition should include the duties, authority relationships, and the responsibilities of its occupant. Frequently, this information is included in an organization manual. Getting this information down in black and white helps the organizer to visualize more clearly the division of work and the formal organizational relationships established. Such work also helps to utilize constructive and creative thought in the organizing. Also, the organization manual is helpful for training purposes and provides official answers to organizing questions for the given enterprise.

Current practice tends to use the terms "job description," "job state-ment," and "job title" to identify progressively contracting descriptions of the job. A job statement, usually a simple paragraph, is used to

FIGURE 13-8
Job Statement of Programming Manager

Programming Manager: Reports to director of procedural analysis. Supervises administrative assistant programmer. Is responsible for planning and organizing all programming activities for the computer; maintaining essential records of the programming department; directing, motivating, and evaluating personnel; and participating in the planning of computer usage.

furnish a quick picture of the job. Figure 13-8 shows a job statement. A job title is simply a common name for a job. However, job titles are commonly inadequate to identify a job satisfactorily. For example, the title "secretary" is used to identify jobs of different makeup, as illustrated by the two job statements in Figure 13-9. *The title plus the*

FIGURE 13-9
Job Titles May Be Identical, but the Respective Job Statements May Differ

Secretary: Takes dictation, using shorthand, and transcribes the dictated material into a neat typed format; makes appointments for and reminds executive of them; answers and makes telephone calls; handles personal and important mail; writes routine correspondence on own initiative; maintains executive's files.
Secretary: Takes dictation, using either shorthand or a machine; transcribes dictation from either shorthand notes or a machine; interviews people coming into the office, directing to other employees those who do not warrant seeing the executive; answers and makes telephone calls.

job content are necessary for accurate identification. This is important in office organizing where work division and organizational unit creation must be decided.

CENTRALIZATION AND OFFICE ORGANIZING

Centralization of office functions, mentioned earlier in this chapter, is so important that further discussion of it is merited. Centralization means the physical concentration of office functions with management over them vested in one person. Actually, there are four possible centralization arrangements (1) physical location centralized and management centralized, (2) physical location not centralized and management centralized, (3) physical location not centralized and management not centralized, and (4) physical location centralized and management not centralized. Illustrations of these four possibilities, along with comments for each, are shown in Figure 13-10.

FIGURE 13–10
The Four Possibilities of Centralization

Possibility 2

Physical Location: Centralized
Management: Centralized

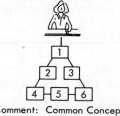

Comment: Common Concept
         of Centralization

Possibility 1

Physical Location: Not Centralized
Management: Centralized

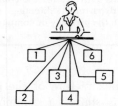

Comment: Common But Sometimes
         Not Fully Comprehended
         as a Type of Centralization

Possibility 3

Physical Location: Not Centralized
Management: Not Centralized

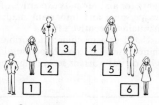

Comment:
         Series of Individual Units.
         Actually No Centralization
         Concept Exists

Possibility 4

Physical Location: Centralized
Management: Not Centralized

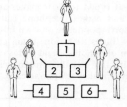

Comment:
         Relatively Rare Concept of
         Centralization – Little Used

Important advantages of office centralization include (1) flexibility is given the organization—work peak loads are easily handled and office machines are utilized more fully, (2) equitable wage schedules are fostered—office output measurement is encouraged, and comparisons of wages for similar work are made more feasible, (3) training of employees is expedited—common developing methods can be followed and new employees added without seriously affecting the operations of the group, (4) methods of office operation can be applied uniformly and quickly, (5) cost of performing office work is decreased—supervisory costs are low and fewer machines are needed, and (6) labor specialization is practiced—employees become highly efficient on work necessitating their highest individual skill and ability.

On the other hand, advocates of office decentralization point out its advantages that (1) employees develop quickly—they become self-directed, confident, and experienced in a variety of tasks and conditions, (2) much office work is confidential and can be handled by those in whom a confidential trust is placed, (3) office management is expedited since the manager most familiar with the use and purpose of the paperwork is near at hand, (4) work is performed with regard for its individual urgency or importance—delays are minimized, (5) nonproductive work is reduced—unnecessary transporting and handling are eliminated, and (6) the work can be performed by those most familiar with its detailed requirements.

Office Organization Dynamics

Organizing is a vibrant, living activity. Change in the organization takes place whether or not it is planned because organizing is what it is. Typically, functions and personnel are added or subtracted, functions are combined or split, values are modified, and new organizational relationships established. Unless organization dynamics is recognized and used constructively, a number of undesirable conditions take place. Among these conditions are activities become disproportionate in their relationship to each other and in their respective value to the enterprise, important activities are neglected, capable persons are confined to mediocre jobs, and authority relationships become blurred.

Many influences bring about organization change. A key contributor is the movement either to or from centralization, a subject discussed above. For purposes here, we will include four major factors:

1. The Continuity of the Organization. When the work flow is steady a relatively stable organization usually results. Under such a condition, the functions remain constant and well defined. In addition, the time element affects organization continuity. An organization structure set up temporarily to accomplish an emergency task is commonly far different from one set up to exist over a long period. Organizations having little continuity are usually very simple. When an organization is created for a temporary objective which later turns out to be permanent, the result is that many changes take place in the organization.

2. The Office Technology Utilized. As already pointed out, the process used often determines the main components of the office structure. With constant research and concentrated efforts for improvement, a better process evolves and, in turn, brings about organization change. In many instances, technology eliminates certain activities and changes others, resulting in the need for different employees or retraining present employees, a shifting of jobs, and new organizational patterns followed.

3. The Relationships Followed. There is an old saying that "decision making tends to cluster around the person willing to accept it." The employee of managerial competence, ambition, and desire for decision making tends to acquire it. Hence, over a period, the decision making opportunities and efforts increase for some individuals; and as a result, organization relationships change, at first in practice, and ultimately formally, in keeping with conditions as they have developed. When the relationships are altered, there is a necessity of change in the organization structure. And observe that an organization change can be caused by a modification of relationships only; a change in functions or in their grouping or in personnel is not necessary.

4. The Personnel Employed. Of all the influences contributing to organization change that of personnel employed is the greatest and most significant. Change due to personnel comes about in different ways one of which is that the manager believes a different organizational arrangement will prove advantageous. Certain types of people tend to work together effectively as a group, while others never seem to reach the level of expected cooperation. The reasons are many; but presumably most important are differences in personalities, capacities, and relationships among the group's members. Also, with time employees change in that they acquire new knowledge, new skills, new interests, and new attitudes. This is inevitable; in fact, it is promoted by managers in management development programs and many efforts of motivation. Actually change is a natural evolutionary process which takes place as a person increases in age, participates in more experiences, and reflects on life and its meaning. No person remains static. In addition, there is the normal attrition of employees leaving due to retirement, better jobs, or desire for a change. All these personnel changes must be taken into account and this means organization dynamics.

Organization Balance

As a result of normal dynamics of organization, an imbalance of the total office organization is quite likely unless definite action is taken to attain organizational balance among the various activities in relation to their real worth and contribution. An office is not all billing, all tabulating, all systems designing, all data processing, or all anything else. It is a proper balance and blending among the many activities believed essential. This is subject to a great many interpretations. Too frequently, however, managers continue to improve what is already relatively effective. Bettering the weak areas would be more helpful from the viewpoint of the entire organization. An important part of the problem is not to place all strong managers of the enterprise in one or a few organizational units. Success begets success. Commonly, strong

managers tends to attract trainees with the grea...
and more proficient managers tend to develop ...
them. There is also a human tendency by manager...
manage well those activities in which they are most i...
perienced. If the office manager "knows" electronic data p...
work will tend to be organized and managed well. On the ...
if she or he knows very little about office personnel research, th...
may be somewhat neglected and not developed to its required i...
importance.

Consider an example of imbalance covering a billing department co...
sisting of four units—posting, typing, filing, and adjusting—shown in
Figure 13–11. The number of employees in each unit is indicated in

FIGURE 13–11
Original Organization of a Billing Department

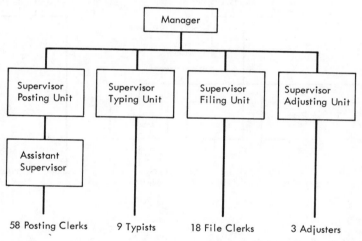

the chart. Analysis and investigation disclosed that nearly 65 percent
of the operative employees are in the posting unit, the supervision is
inadequate, and the efficiency in this unit is quite low. Common complaints include records missing and errors in posting. In the typing unit,
six specialized job positions were found among the nine typists. Each
performed specialized or particular duties. Seniority played an important
role in who was permitted to do certain typing work, a custom that
had evolved over several years. With change in work assignments it
is estimated that six typists can handle the work. In the filing unit, there
was inadequate control. Material is not charged out to the user and
misfiling of records is numerous. As a result excessive search-time to
locate missing records exists. About every week some filing personnel

...test managerial potential,
...good managers under
...s to emphasize and
...terested and ex-
...processing, this
...other hand,
...s activity
...elative

as found that 14 of the 18 filing
en with the company less than
could handle the filing work.
:hanges were discussed with the
s. Suggestions for improvements
discussion a revised organization
re 13–12. The posting unit was

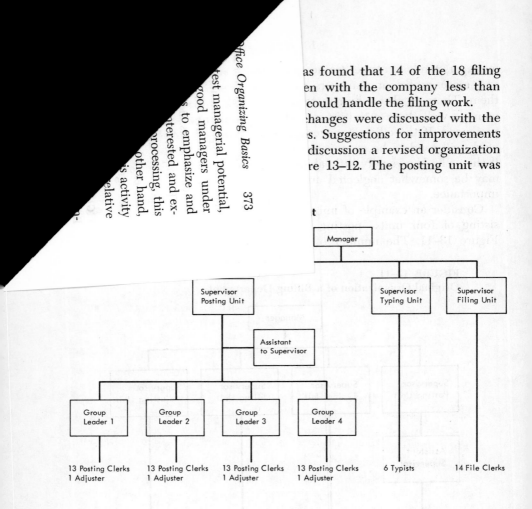

divided into four groups of 13 posting clerks each. These four groups
are more manageable, serve as parallel competitive units, and encourage
improved supervision. The former supervisor of adjusting became the
new supervisor of posting. The former supervisor of posting became
the assistant to the posting supervisor, a position dealing with the
work of establishing work measurement, standards, and a quality program for posting work. The former assistant supervisor of posting was
made one of the group leaders. The other three leaders were selected
from the posting clerks. The former adjusting unit was eliminated and
the three adjusters transferred to posting, one each to each group.

Implementing Organization Change

The astute office manager looks ahead and tries to determine what
future organization changes will probably take place and further, what

changes in the present organization structure should be made. How future data processing will be handled, probable changes in company policy, the future value to be placed on information work, and the type of personnel required are but a few sources which can be used to forecast the probable future organization change. Comparison between present and future requirements reveals the gap that must be filled along with specific actions to gain the transition to the future office organization.

For an existent office organization, improvements can be sought by following this format:

1. Make an Inventory of the Present Organization. It is essential to know the precise identity of the organization structure being reorganized. Guesses in this respect lead to unnecessary trouble and work. The current name of each organizational unit, the exact work performed, the employees performing what work in each unit, and the relationships existing among all the units should be carefully ascertained and put in writing.

2. Write a Description for Each Job. Although it requires much time and detailed effort, preparing a written description of each job is usually extremely helpful. In no other way will the reorganizer fully realize the exact content of the various work segments and how they are related. Preparing written descriptions also greatly assists in securing clues as to what work might better be placed other than where it is in the present organization.

3. Analyze Current Organization and Evaluate Proposed Changes. This step is guided mainly by the objectives of the entire organization and the part that each component is expected to contribute to the goal accomplishment. Knowledge of the people available to perform the various tasks is also essential. This can be gained by researching the personnel records and talking with the supervisors or with the employees themselves. Some means of recording information in a logical order should be followed. Data common to all employees should be obtained so that reasonable comparisons can be made.

From all this information, the proposed organization is gradually evolved. Several different ideas, encompassing different work divisions, people, and relationships, are tentatively drawn up. Subsequently, each arrangement is evaluated, noting what appear to be its strong and its weak points, the probable hurdles involved in putting it into force. Tentative arrangements should be discussed with management and non-management members to be affected in order to gain their appraisals, exchange reactions, and obtain consensus regarding what should be done. Based on the results of this overall investigation, the makeup of the reorganization is decided.

4. *Determine the Phases or Steps to Be Taken from the Present to the Proposed Organization.* In situations where an extremely inefficient organizational structure exists, it may be best to implement the change without delay. However, in many cases, the gradual shifting from the present to the ultimate organization takes place in several phases or steps. Normally, this makes for greater acceptance by the employees. Individual situations may govern the timing of the change. For example, the retirement or resignation of a key employee may signal the most opportune time to adopt change. However, regardless of the

FIGURE 13–13
Phase Charts Are Commonly Used in Reorganization

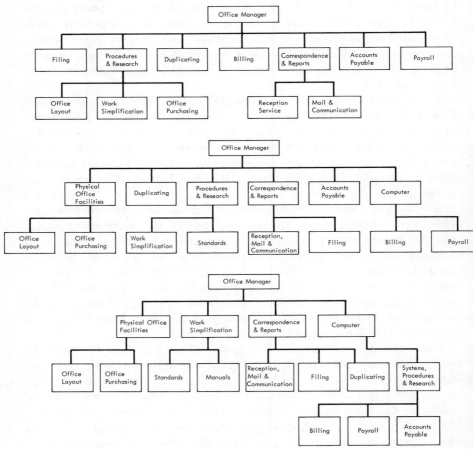

The present organization is illustrated by the top chart. The first phase of changes to be made is shown by the middle chart. Subsequently, the organization of the middle chart is changed to that shown by the bottom phase chart.

reason, in each instance the plan of what is to be done and by whom should be worked out in advance.

Figure 13–13 illustrates the phases of reorganization that might be followed by a company whose present office organization is like that shown by the top diagram. It is desired to reduce the number of managers reporting directly to the office manager, to install a computer, and to consolidate relative functions. The first phase in this reorganization is shown by the middle illustration of Figure 13–13. New top units of physical office facilities and of computer are created. The functions of office layout, office purchasing, filing, billing, and payroll have been relocated. Also an organization unit of standards has been added and units of reception and mail combined. From this initial phase, the second and final phase, shown in bottom illustration of Figure 13–13, consists of adding a unit of manuals and relocating duplicating, procedures and research, accounts payable, and work simplification.

5. Take Necessary Reorganization Action. The last step is to put the reorganization into action. Once it is decided what changes to make and a time schedule established, definite action should be taken. To hesitate or display indecisiveness can hamper the entire reorganization. A positive and fair viewpoint generally assists in getting satisfactory results.

It is important to give the reorganization time to prove itself. Time is required for people to adjust to new assignments, become familiar with new relationships, and utilize new formal channels of communication. All managers should be thoroughly indoctrinated in the reorganization, be able to answer questions concerning it, publicize its advantages, and counsel any employee in need of such help. Successful reorganization plans always include these important follow-up features.

QUESTIONS

1. Explain why organizing enables managers to enlarge their scope of operations.
2. Point out the various means by which the work can be divided for organizational purposes and relate under what general conditions each means is most likely to be used.
3. Do you agree with this statement: "People constitute the essential makeup of an organization. Hence, it is logical as well as advantageous to begin organizing efforts by finding out what people are available and what each of them can do best." Justify your answer.
4. What is the unit assembly arrangement used in organizing and what are its advantages, if any?
5. Discuss the office services arrangement of office organizing efforts.
6. Identify each of the following:
   a. Job description and project organization.
   b. Organizing.

      c. Decentralization.

      d. Phases in reorganization.

7. What are the major influences which bring about organization change? Select one you feel is important and discuss it.

8. Comment fully on this statement: "The old adage of keeping an organization in balance is so much academic nonsense. Activities are never in balance; some are always more important than others. Hence, it is perfectly natural and nothing to worry about to have organizations that are not in balance. It is a natural state of affairs."

9. Many writers and composers have achieved greatness working alone—without an organization at all. Does this demonstrate, in part, that perhaps in management there is a tendency to overemphasize the importance and contribution of organization? Why?

10. Justify your answer to each of the following:

      a. Does centralization give flexibility to an organization structure?

      b. Is work environment an essential component of organizing?

      c. In the typical manufacturing enterprise should a large computer be located under finance?

      d. Is coordination the main purpose of organizing?

11. Enumerate the format of a plan designed to achieve improvements in an existent organization.

12. Do you agree with this statement: "For a given enterprise, personnel changes over a period, but the organization remains fundamentally the same. If more managers kept this basic truth in mind, there would be less organizational problems." Why?

CASE PROBLEMS

Case 13–1.   Harper and Reeves, Inc.

The corporation maintains three offices, one for each of its three separate manufacturing plants in Chicago, Boston, and Oklahoma City. All consolidated reports of the corporation's activities are prepared in the Chicago office, which is considered the main office. Six months ago, new machines were installed in the Chicago office and just ten days ago it was announced that most accounting as well as all statistical tabulating work used primarily for forecasting and sales purposes now performed in Boston and Oklahoma City were to be moved to the Chicago office. The move would start in 30 days and require approximately 40 days to be consummated.

This change gives rise to organizational problems. In the Chicago statistical tabulating unit, for example, there were initially six employees, and the supervisor Paula Isham directed the group informally and kept a close personal touch with all the employees and their work. With rapid increase in sales and a demand for more precise data, Ms. Isham's unit has grown to ten employees during the last 120 days. Now with the centralization of statistical tabulating services in Chicago, Ms. Isham's unit is expected to acquire an additional 12 employees, one of whom is the former supervisor of the Oklahoma City statistical tabulating unit. The office manager is concerned about providing adequate supervision so that the new tab summaries and reports are correctly and promptly prepared and that the old established work is continued satisfactorily in the future as it has been in the past.

Questions:

1. What are some major alternatives open to the corporation?
2. What organizational arrangement do you recommend for the Chicago statistical tabulating unit?
3. Evaluate this recommended organization unit, discussing important advantages as well as disadvantages.

Case 13–2. Orkney Company

Lester Barksdale is supervisor of an office unit made up of employees doing stenographic, typing, and filing work. Many of the employees are young women who work for several years and then leave because they are going to get married, to leave town, to raise a family or become bored with the work. Lester likes to hire employees competent in all types of basic office work so that he can cope with problems arising from emergencies, absenteeism, or quits. In this way he figures he can move his people about to get the needed work out. Some of the employees complain from time to time, but for the most part the arrangement has worked out very satisfactorily.

During the past year, additional employees have joined the department due to the increase in the total workload. Also, several additional types of work have been added to Lester's department. For example, he now has two people operating card punching machines, and an employee handling collating and binding machines. In addition, a copying machine has been added to his unit. He is finding it increasingly difficult to find additional help that can perform effectively any of the tasks in his department. "There are few all-around office persons available," is the way he puts it. Further, the output of the department has not increased in proportion to the additional help hired. And errors in the work appear more frequently than before.

Lester realizes some corrective action is going to be necessary. He is not sure what should be done. One idea he has is to divide the filing group among the other office units giving each unit jurisdiction over the filing material of that respective unit. Informal talks with the supervisors of these units show they favor such an arrangement. However, the present filing personnel tell Lester they prefer to remain with him and ask that he let things as they are. In trying to find out the reason for their preference, Lester is unable to disclose any reasons other than, "It's just the way I feel about it."

Questions:

1. In your opinion, why do the employees in Mr. Barksdale's unit object to his organizational change suggestion?
2. What alternatives are available to Mr. Barksdale?
3. What action, if any, do you recommend Mr. Barksdale should take? Justify your viewpoint.

Case 13–3.   Raut-Wyatt, Inc.

Mark Mattix gave his employer, Raut-Wyatt, Inc., two weeks notice to take the position, vice president in charge of EDP, with the corporation's chief competitor, Arnold Products Company, Mr. Mattix enjoys a reputation for great competency and is a recognized leader in his type of work. With him went considerable knowledge of operations, cost, plans, and problems of Raut-Wyatt, Inc.

Mr. Mattix keeps in touch informally with Sam Neylan, a Raut-Wyatt executive, in charge of programming. They meet about twice a month or whenever Mr. Mattix is in town at a local club where Mr. Mattix has retained his membership. Their meetings may be termed secret, but the fact that they get together is known by the top managers of Raut-Wyatt, Inc.

During the past seven months, two programmers and one computer operator of Raut-Wyatt, Inc. have switched over to Arnold Products Company. They stated they had better offers and left after giving three to four weeks notice. Neither the president or the personnel director of Raut-Wyatt, Inc. have disclosed any tangible evidence that these three former employees were influenced by Mark Mattix to join Arnold Products Company. But the president feels strongly that Mark Mattix is the one behind the changes.

Three weeks ago, Sam Neylan started his vacation. When the vacation ended, he announced his new position as assistant to Mr. Mattix with Arnold Products Company. He was assuming his new job in four weeks. The president of Raut-Wyatt, Inc. was alarmed at the drain of hard-to-get personnel. He resolved to stop it. Summoning Mr. Neylan to his office he stated directly that he did not want to lose him.

PRESIDENT: What do we have to do to keep you?

NEYLAN: Nothing, I am just leaving that's all.

PRESIDENT: Well, why are you planning to leave us?

NEYLAN: I am not planning to leave, I am leaving. I prefer not to discuss the matter.

PRESIDENT: I see. I am sure you know, Mr. Neylan, that we all think very highly of you. Your record with us is outstanding.

NEYLAN: Thank you, sir.

PRESIDENT: Mark's been after you hasn't he?

NEYLAN: I really would prefer not to discuss the matter.

PRESIDENT: Sure he has. You can tell me. We can give you everything he can and more. You think it over, and we'll talk about it again tomorrow.

NEYLAN: As I said, I'd rather not discuss the matter, sir.

Questions:

1.   What factors do you suspect led to the current situation faced by Raut-Wyatt, Inc.?
2.   Comment on the action of Mr. Mattix.
3.   What action do you recommend the president take? Why?

Case 13–4. Roxworthy Company

Edgar Wood, a clerk in computer processing, has developed into a valuable employee. He has contributed a number of suggestions that were adopted for electronic processing of various types of data. Last year he attended night school studying programming and has acquired proficiency in this area. Last week when work was slack in the computer room, Mr. Richard McGill, the supervisor, asked Edgar Wood to help in rearranging the stockroom, marking and indexing the stored items and getting it in better shape. Reluctantly, he abided by Mr. McGill's request. He dislikes stockroom type of work and after four days of it, he had a confidential talk with Mr. McGill voicing the opinion that he was supposed to be given computer processing work only, that's what was stated in his job description. Mr. McGill replied that straightening out the stockroom would indirectly benefit processing. It was work that had to be done. Employees are expected to operate as a team with group efforts coordinated toward given goals. Not satisfied with this explanation, Edgar Wood requested and received permission to discuss the question with Ms. Gail Howell, the office manager, who requested that Mr. McGill attend the meeting.

HOWELL: You have asked to talk with me and I am happy to help you in any way that I can. It is my understanding that the subject is about job descriptions and whether an employee can be required to do work other than what is specifically included in the description. I believe so, because a company has a right to direct its workforce and to make assignments.

WOOD: Job descriptions as I understand them help form a basis for organization. If you discard or change them, the organization is going to suffer. Every employee could be doing everything.

HOWELL: Well, now, let's be reasonable. The descriptions serve as guides only. But all things change, emergencies arise, obviously we must have some flexibility in the organization. The question here deals more with utilization of job descriptions than with its contents.

WOOD: How much longer would you say I'm going to be on clean-up work?

HOWELL: I believe Mr. McGill can answer that better than I.

McGILL: I don't know. There isn't enough programming or other work at the moment to promise you that tomorrow, or the next day, or next week as I see it now.

WOOD: Frankly, I don't like the work I am now doing. From what you say, job descriptions can mean just about what the user wants them to mean.

Questions:

1. What is the problem in this case?
2. Do you feel the situation is being handled properly by the Roxworthy management members? Elaborate on your answers.
3. As Edgar Wood, what action would you now take? Discuss.

Chapter 14

People and Office Organization

> *When we cannot find contentment in ourselves,*
> *it is useless to seek it elsewhere.*
>
> La Rochefoucauld

As stated in the last chapter, organizing logically starts with work division, and the divisions created serve as focal areas for organizational units. In turn, the work within each organizational unit must be accomplished, directly or indirectly, by people. The people aspect of organizing is vital. In fact, it would be difficult to overemphasize the importance of people in organizing.

IMPORTANCE OF PEOPLE IN ORGANIZING

The expression "Organization is people" is trite; nevertheless it stresses the importance of people in the work of organizing. It brings out the basic idea that people constitute the true center about which revolve the organizational concepts of the work to be done, the decision-making relationships, and the work environment. In the final analysis, the organization structure is a tool—it provides the grouping of specific activities and of people for the purpose of applying management. Work is accomplished by people or machines operated by people. Organizing does not accomplish any work objective; it must be implemented with people. Hence, one of the biggest jobs of a manager is to form or maintain an organization which permits the proper placement and the development of employees. Some claim that almost any organization structure will prove satisfactory as long as the right people are operating it.

Organizing helps provide the means for getting effective results

382

through selected people's efforts and these efforts can make or break any organization structure. By means of good organizing we seek to provide the best arrangement and environment in which employees can and will want to perform. Personnel condition performance. This view can be compared to that of writing the story for a motion-picture film. It sets the stage and predetermines what is to take place. How well it takes place, i.e., the quality of the motion picture, depends in great measure upon the actors—the personnel element.

Each employee should be assigned to work that is best suited for the worker. This necessitates considerable knowledge and skill in placement for maximum benefits to all concerned. Let us direct our attention, more specifically, to this task of assigning the right person to the right job. For this purpose, we must first obtain applicants for the work, in the case where none are available, and second, in selecting from these or from the present employees the person to be assigned to the work of a specific organizational unit. This brings up the important subject areas of recruiting, sources of help, and the techniques of personnel selection.

RECRUITING

The recruitment of employees is a permanent activity. Increased emphasis is placed upon this work during peak business periods, but the problem of securing the right employees confronts most offices most of the time. There are always separations because of marriage, illness, voluntary leaves, terminations, and death.

Recruiting has several major aspects. First is knowing the quantity and quality of candidates to seek and where to seek them. People with the required skill, background, attitude, and interest are the target for recruiting efforts. Contacts are also required to obtain the referrals of candidates. Many office managers have found that appropriate recruiting literature is definitely helpful in aiding their recruiting efforts. Also the recruiting practices followed should be reviewed periodically to disclose possibilities for improvement.

Limited data reveal that the number of applicants hired to the number rejected is in the ratio of 1 to 7, and that nearly $400 is spent for each office employee hired. These data suggest that recruiting can be improved. What can be done? As stated in the last chapter, data developed from job analysis such as job descriptions as well as job specifications are most helpful. When the job requirements are vague, the likelihood of finding a satisfactory candidate is considerably lessened. No available source can supply its maximum recruiting assistance when the information supplied is insufficient and not clearly stated. Another improvement possibility is speeding up the selection process. In too many cases, a qualified candidate is lost because of a lack of promptness in dealing with the applicant from the time of application to the time the decision to hire or not to hire is rendered. A third area is developing the reputation of the particular office as being a good place to work. The office possessing this valuable public good will commonly have a satisfactory group from which outstanding candidates can be selected.

Recruiting efforts should include working with a variety of labor sources. The best source usually must be qualified ragarding the type of office job, the geographical location, the prominence of the company, and the skill with which the recruiter uses a particular source. Having several candidates for each job usually helps in obtaining a satisfactory candidate.

Office recruiting is commonly directed to these sources:

1. Persons Recommended by Present Employees. This is usually a very good source, but caution must be exercised to avoid favoritism. Some companies post notices on bulletin boards encouraging employees to recommend friends who might be seeking employment.

2. Former Employees. This group constitutes an excellent source. However, careful screening and selection techniques are required to avoid a "come and go" atmosphere. Frequently, satisfactory part-time employees can be obtained from this source.

3. New Employees. The person just hired usually knows somebody else who is looking for a job. Satisfactory results are usually obtained if candidates are put through the regular selection channels.

4. Employment Agencies. It is well to utilize this source. Some agencies are public, others are private. The former charge no fee; the latter do, and the charge commonly is made to the employer. Agencies have broad contacts and experience; they try to supply likely candidates for vacancies.

5. Schools—Including Vocational Advisory Boards. This is one of the better and larger sources of office employees. Some companies keep in close touch with high schools, business colleges, and universities, and send representatives to talk with students about to graduate. Many schools have placement offices and will cooperate fully with prospective employers. The candidates usually have formal training but limited business experience.

6. Institutions for the Rehabilitation of Handicapped Persons. Frequently, very capable people can be secured from this source.

7. Voluntary Applicants. It is a good practice always to see people who come in looking for a job. Frequently, this source offers excellent personnel, but it cannot be relied upon as the sole source of help.

8. Advertising. Newspaper, radio, and television advertising are effective media for securing a number of candidates. Good coverage is usually obtained; but all respondents will not be fully qualified, and the normal weeding-out process must be used.

Selecting Office Help

Choice of a candidate (new applicant or present employee) for a particular job is normally based on a comparison between (1) what the job requires for successful execution and (2) what the candidate has to offer. For the most part, the better the balance between these two factors, the better the selection work, and the more likely is the attainment of a satisfactory working force. Under job requirements are such attributes as the amount of formal education, knowledge, experience, and physical considerations. Under what the applicant offers are a fund of knowledge, experience, intelligence, physical attributes, and personality. This matching effort, however, must not be thought of as an exacting operation. On the contrary, it is quite flexible. Job requirements should be used as a guide. Frequently, a satisfactory person does not have the *exact* qualifications desired; but with time and experience, may prove satisfactory on the job.

Many feel that employers have the social obligation to hire and train some members from the minority, the older, the handicapped, and the culturally deprived groups. This social consciousness stems from a realization that they are a part of society and want to be in the mainstream of activities with an opportunity to contribute to the general welfare. This viewpoint is augmented by federal and state laws requiring the making of employment opportunities available. to all qualified persons regardless of sex, race, creed, color, national origin, or age (between 40 and 65 years old). Although some of these people do not meet normal hiring requirements, there is increasing emphasis to hire from these groups, some 5 to 10 percent of the total employees in a given category, and train this group by giving them special orientation and instruction so that they will be able to perform at an acceptable level.

The use of vocational requirements facilitates selection. To illustrate, for the job of beginning stenographer, the requirements may include the ability to type at a rate of 55 words per minute on straight copy material for a ten-minute period, with five errors or less; to perform shorthand writing at 100 words per minute; to transcribe notes of unfamiliar material at the rate of 35 words per minute for a ten-minute period, and to produce work of mailable quality; to transcribe from a machine, at the rate of 10 to 12 letters per hour each letter consisting of two to three paragraphs. During the past decade much progress has been made by various associations in getting office managers to request employees who meet definite vocational standards and in getting schools to train students toward these standards.

Tools of Personnel Selection

Among the common tools used for personnel selection are:

1. Application Form. This form provides a means for obtaining in writing the more obvious personnel information, such as identification, education, work history, and activities of the applicant. Sufficient information should be obtained, but superfluous information should be avoided. All questions asked should serve a definite purpose in evaluating the candidate's possible value to the office.

For the higher level jobs, it is often quite helpful to ask several questions designed to gain some insight into the candidate's general attitude toward life and ability to write and to organize material. To illustrate, questions such as the following might be asked: "In narrative form, give us a résumé of your major accomplishments, hopes, and ambition." "Will you tell us about your special qualifications not covered elsewhere in this application?" "What unusual office situations have you encountered, and what did you do about them?"

2. Interviews. The opportunity to meet the applicant and observe verbal ability, appearance, general personality, and attitude are extremely helpful in selection work. The face-to-face meeting with the applicant offers possibilities of information afforded by no other means. The objectives should be to exchange information and to make a favorable impression upon the applicant. Unless these conditions are accomplished, the interview is not wholly satisfactory. The exchange of information is essential to intelligent selection. Creating a good impression establishes a favorable attitude by applicants toward the office, whether they are hired or not. In the opinion of many, the interview is the main selection tool in the employment program.

Figure 14–1 shows interviewing practices that are effective. In addition, it is a sound practice for the interviewer to have a list of items he wishes to cover. The accuracy and quality standards on previous jobs held by the candidate, the supervisory practices liked, and the grades received in school are illustrative of areas to cover that will make for effective interviewing. Rating charts can also be used so that the relative intensities of the important factors are recorded. Use of oral trade questions is recommended. An idea of the candidates's competency is obtained by such questions which deal with names of office machines, office operations, general knowledge of office jobs, and the like. Fourth, an interviewer's guide, designed to help secure essential information, can be used.

3. References. Managers usually like to obtain information on the applicant from previous employers and responsible persons currently acquainted with the applicant. Reference checking is helpful in apprais-

FIGURE 14–1
Follow These Practices for Effective Interviewing

1. Put the applicant and yourself at ease.
2. Explain the duties, responsibilities, chances for promotion, and working conditions of the job. If possible, read or let the candidate read the job description.
3. Encourage the applicant to talk by asking questions that begin with *why, when,* and *how.* Avoid questions that can be answered by a "Yes" or "No."
4. Interrupt the applicant only when what is being said is irrelevant. Start speaking after the applicant has paused for a least ten seconds.
5. Use language appropriate to the educational and experience background of the applicant.
6. Let the applicant ask questions.
7. Grant sufficient time for the interview, but do not prolong it to the extent of useless repetition.
8. Keep interview fresh. Periodically change the questions and the sequence in which they are asked.

ing the candidate's cooperation, dependability, skill, interests, habits and abilities. On the other hand, some believe that references are frequently unreliable claiming that inaccurate evaluations are provided and either excessive praise or excessive criticism is supplied.

Qualifications for reference givers include being fully familiar with the demands of the job, knowing the candidate extremely well, supplying information with absolute honesty, and exercising sound evaluating judgment. These qualifications appear to be filled best by professional people and former employees. Telephone reference inquiries commonly produce better results than mail, possibly because people giving references are usually more willing to speak frankly than to put the same comments in writing. If possible, reference information should be obtained *before* a full interview. Data can be checked, and selected areas for discussion or further probing can be chosen for the interview.

4. Physical Examination. The main purpose of the physical examination is to determine whether the candidate is physically suited to perform the office work required by the job. Testing of the eyes is especially important for office work. Physical examinations help to raise the standard of physical fitness, to increase work output, to lower accident rates, to decrease turnover, and to lessen the amount of absenteeism caused by sickness.

5. Tests. This is the last personnel selection tool to be discussed. Tests are measurements of personnel aspects secured by scientific methods of observing and recording in certain standard situations. The measurements are normally qualitative and are believed to be related to success in performing the work. A test can be viewed as a systematic sampling of human behavior. The scores from tests are an indication of the probability of the candidate's success or failure as determined by possession of the attributes measured and the importance of these attributes in the work accomplishment.

Validity of a test means the relationship between the test score and accepted facts about the attribute measured by the test. To illustrate, the most desirable employees among the present employees should make a high score; the average employees, a lower score, and the least desirable employees, the lowest score. *Reliability* of a test deals with the consistency of the test in yielding similar results when given on different occasions. When a test has been found, through a process of experimentation, to have both validity and reliability, it is commonly referred to as a *standardized* test. A series of numbers indicating performance scores of large numbers of persons who have taken the test are called *norms* of the test. They serve as guides for comparison of scores.

Today, there are a great number of tests designed to measure many different attributes. Actually, there is a test, or so it seems, for every trait that affects human behavior. Comparisons of the contribution, general content, basic implications, names, and main purposes of the intelligence test and the clerical test are given in Figure 14–2.

The National Business Entrance Tests, sponsored jointly by the Administrative Management Society and the United Business Education Association, offer a battery of tests covering machine calculation, stenography, typing, bookkeeping, filing, and business fundamentals. Those who pass these tests are given a card or certificate of proficiency. A 12-hour examination program is utilized for Certified Professional Secretary candidates. The examination, prepared annually, consists of environmental relations in business, business and public policy, economics and management, financial analysis and the mathematics of business, communication and decision making (an in-basket exercise testing basic skills as well as ability to organize, make decisions, and define priorities), and office procedures. Successful candidates are given a CPS certificate and identification card and are permitted to wear the CPS Pin.[1]

Sufficient evidence appears available to show that tests can be valuable in assessing personnel. However, they should not be viewed as perfect tools. Tests help determine what candidates can do, not what they will do. And, for selection purposes, it is usually desirable to make certain that the trait being tested is required for successfully fulfilling the job's requirements. The key question concerns actual performance on the job, not the score on a given test. Also, tests must be cultural-free, that is, they cannot be designed, intended, or used to discriminate because of race, color, religion, sex, or national origin. According to the

---

[1] For further information on the National Business Entrance Tests, write the Administrative Management Society, 1927 Old York Rd., Willow Grove, Pa. 19090; for information on the Certified Professional Secretary tests, write National Secretaries Association, 2440 Pershing Rd., G-10, Kansas City, Mo. 64108.

FIGURE 14–2
Comparison of Various Tests on Significant Factors

Name	Contribution	General Content of Test	Basic Implications	Examples of Standard Tests	Main Purpose of Test
Intelligence and mental alertness tests	Indicates one's adequacy in a number of types of work.	Problems on information and of judgment and reasoning. Questions dealing with contrast or comparison. Memory tasks.	What a person has absorbed is a fair indication of what will or can be absorbed. Differences in background are not taken into consideration. Little indication of how the indicated ability may be applied.	Army Alpha (Original and Several Revisions) Benge Test of General Knowledge The Henmow-Nelson Test of Mental Ability The O'Rourke General Classification Test Otis Self-Administering Test of Mental Ability The Pressy Senior Classification and Verification Psychological Corporation Scott Company Mental Alertness Test	To make preliminary selection To gain an insight to the applicant's ability to understand and to manage ideas.
Trade and clerical tests	Helps to show the degree of achievement possessed by a candidate for this specific type of work.	Questions appraising vocabulary level. Ability to notice details. Problems in simple calculations and arithmetic reasoning Competency in performing clerical work.	Candidate having achievement of certain level and above will probably execute the job requirements most effectively.	Benge's Clerical Test Blackstone Stenographic Proficiency Tests Minnesota Vocational Test for Clerical Workers National Business Entrance Tests O'Rourke's Clerical Aptitude Test Psychological Corporation Shellow's Intelligence Test for Stenographers Thurstone Examination in Clerical Work, Form A	To determine applicant's knowledge of a specific trade or profession. To select candidates having at least a certain minimum of relative ability to perform work in in a particular field.

Civil Rights Act of 1964, tests can be given and the results used providing there is no discrimination as stated above.

MANAGER'S INFLUENCE AND ORGANIZING

Information managers implement their regard for the human element in organizing efforts by recognizing and appreciating the value, as well as the limitations, of employees. This is not a one-shot proposition but a continuing, ever searching effort to keep up to date the placing of each employee on the type of work best suited for that employee and of directing all efforts toward the common goals sought. The mailroom supervisor's behavior, for example, in some degree reflects the human-element values of the office manager's thinking. Likewise, both the job content and the relationships established are presumably what the information manager thinks they ought to be, taking into account what the mailroom supervisor's beliefs and feelings are in this respect. Hence, the statement is sometimes made that an organization structure reflects the shadow of its manager. However, it appears more appropriate to state that an organization structure *reflects the light or understanding* of its manager.

Concentration on a person's strengths pays organizational dividends. A manager holding firm convictions about an employee's abilities to perform the work competently tends to instill confidence in the employee and develops a will to do successful work. At the same time, the manager must realize that not all persons can do all things. To assume otherwise can lead to disaster in organizing. Yet, by proper managerial motivation, leadership, and lifting a person's vision to higher planes, the common person can be stimulated to achieve uncommon things.

At the same time, the office manager who experiences the greatest success in organizing is a realist and accepts people for what they really are. Recognized is the fact that most organizations are the result of many decisions made by many different people and which decisions took into account various considerations, some of which were controversial and contained imponderables. Also recognized is that organizing is actually a "give and take" proposition among persons, and adjustments among persons sometimes with widely different views and behaviors. Essentially, organizing has a compromise characteristic among the persons involved. The chief cohesive force, however, is the criterion to get the work accomplished adequately and maintain a continuity of satisfactory work achievement by satisfied employees.

FORMAL ORGANIZATIONAL DYSFUNCTIONS

Certain characteristics or conditions of the formal organization cause or permit unintended behavior to take place. These characteristics or conditions are called formal dysfunctions. They emit from the formal organization and are a part of it. The behavior resulting from dysfunctions can be desirable or undesirable depending upon the stated objectives. Quite often a dysfunction results in an improvement in efficiency, aids necessary socializing on the job, or assists hidden cultural likes. In such cases the effect of the dysfunction is usually considered advantageous even though it was not planned for and came into being somewhat by chance.

Specification of the type of processing to be followed and the hierarchy of decision makers with the defined limitations on decision making of each are probably the more representative of dysfunctions. By bringing ideas, practices, and personalized efforts to a job, an employee tends to influence to some degree how the work is handled and these contributions may not meet exactly the formal specifications. Yet the work is completed entirely satisfactorily. In the case of decision making, it is extremely difficult and laborious to define each type of formal authority for each type of situation. Some gaps usually exist or unusual or new situations are encountered for which no formal authority is defined. Yet the decision must be reached and the group efforts moved ahead.

It also follows that some dysfunctions bring about behavior that is not in the best interests of the group's unity of effort. Included are lack of fixed responsibility, misinterpretation of the specific duties to be performed, and the unwarranted assumption that available written job instructions are updated and complete.

PEOPLE CONDITION THE FORMAL ORGANIZATION

We will now concentrate our attention on the influence of people upon organization. We begin with this broad statement: *Formal organization is very greatly subjected to and modified by the behavior of the human beings who are members of it.* Many activities are performed in keeping with the prescribed conditions of the formal organization, but there are also many activities that are not—some to a slight degree, others to a significant degree. In most formal organizations are included more than is indicated by the designs of their creators. Cliques among employees develop; some authority relationships grow stronger than intended, others become weaker; communications is carried out through nonofficial channels; and decision making, directly or indirectly, involves far more personnel than the formally assigned management members. That is to state, the prescribed content and order of things become distorted in operational practice, some actions take on unforeseen embellishments, while others, assumed to be present, are lacking.

The attainment of stated objectives supply further evidence of change due to human behavior acting on the individual's interpretation or disagreement or misunderstanding of what the formal objectives are. A stated goal may be given different interpretations by different management members. For example, consider the statement of a company's president who described the purpose of her enterprise as one of supplying high-quality and wanted food products to discriminating buyers; her finance manager described it as realizing an above average amount of profit; the information manager, reporting to the finance manager, interpreted the objective as processing paperwork efficiently and obsoleting certain office practices long followed by the enterprise. These objectives are not necessarily diverse. With mutual explanation and some minor adjustments, they might well be quite compatible. Yet an elaboration of objectives by each would certainly lead to additional differences. Again, we must realize that we are dealing with different people in an organization and they have different behaviors, values, ambitions, and viewpoints. It is with these important properties of organization, over and above those developed logically and rationally, that we are discussing. Many actions are generated that are not prescribed by the rationale of the organization. They are brought about by people's behavior within the organization and they constitute strong influences that must be reckoned with in organization study.

INFORMAL ORGANIZATION

With reference to a given enterprise, the emphasis given to people's behavior, their interrelationships, and their collective efforts upon the formal or prescribed organization can be referred to as conditioning by the informal organization. In other words, the people of an organization through their behavior and actions resulting therefrom, tend to be organized in a somewhat informal manner. An informal organization always exists to some degree whenever group activity is present. It is a normal state of affairs that arises as people associate with one another. Typically, the structure of an informal organization is loose, ill-defined, and spontaneous.

Membership is gained sometimes without real knowledge of it and commonly one person belongs to several informal groups. The exact nature of the relationships among members is unspecified and frequently the precise goals are not spelled out. They usually are more emotional than rational, more social than economic. Let us express it this way: the informal organization conditions the formal organization making it a social as well as an economic entity.

Informal relationships can be quite complex, often difficult to explain, and commonly exert a powerful influence upon job satisfaction and productivity. Power in the informal organization is either given willingly by group members or it is earned. It is neither delegated nor does it follow a chain of command in the sense that these concepts are used in formal organization. Subject to the sentiments of people, it normally is not as stable as formal authority, is of a subjective nature, and typically cuts across organizational lines into various units.

Informal leaders arise for many reasons such as seniority, responsive personality, friendship, work location, and age. Informal groups usually overlap and a member may be the real leader in one, and a subleader or a nonleader in others. The group typically looks to one leader on matters dealing with certain problems and subjects and to another leader for other interest or problem areas. That is, for each area, there usually is one primary leader who stands above all the rest. A significant consideration is the esteem in which each informal leader is held. It should be added that the informal organization is an excellent training ground for future formal leaders to develop, but not necessarily future managers. The reasons are that some informal leaders shun formal responsibility, lack a broad comprehension of the formal job's makeup, or are overcautious.

Figure 14–3 shows a chart of an informal organization. Sometimes

FIGURE 14–3
Informal Interactions of Manager 23 Are Indicated by Dotted Lines A, B, and C; Those of Manager 35 by D, E, and F

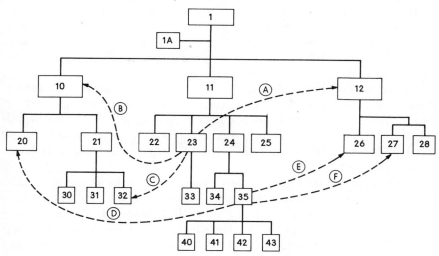

the term *interpersonal chart* is used. It is common to superimpose upon the formal organization chart lines to indicate the interactions of employees based on with whom an employee checks when that person is other than the supervisor, with whom does the employee spend the most time, or with whom does the worker confide and "talk things over." The chart of Figure 14–3 is developed from actions known to management members number 23 and 35. Notice that these contacts are outside formally prescribed communication channels.

Why do informal groups arise and persist? Because they perform functions which the group members want and get due to the informal group's presence. For example, they supply social satisfaction—give members recognition and an opportunity to relate to others. They may look to the informal group gathering to meet friends, exchange experiences, and have coffee with them. These agreeable activities help make work pleasant and something to look forward to. On the other hand, the manager must see to it that the fulfilling of these social satisfactions does not lead members from the objectives of the organization. The informal organization should satisfy and supplement the major goals set forth.

Another contribution of informal organization is the exercise of social control both within and without the group. In other words, the behavior of the members is influenced and regulated by the informal organization. The employee wearing an attire not acceptable to the informal group will be subjected to comments and suggestions that sooner or later will convince the person that the particular attire is not an accepted style in the group. As a result, the person stops wearing it to work. The overall effect is toward conformity as conceived by the informal members. Some management experts point out that this conformity can be carried to undesirable extremes whereby the informal leader may manipulate a group toward selfish or undesirable goals and bring about unnecessary conflict using the group for selfish purposes.

A third major contribution of the informal organization is the continuation of cultural values deemed important by the members. This resolves into maintaining the status quo. Change is viewed as a threat to cultural values. This means that managers contemplating change should understand and take into account the informal groups for they will be a force with which to reckon.

Experienced managers know they cannot abolish the informal organization like they can cancel the formal. Having created the latter, they can do away with it if they so desire. But they did not create the informal and hold no power to abolish it, even though they may so desire. Actually there are important advantages of the informal organization. These are shown in Figure 14–4.

MAJOR FACTORS GIVING RISE TO INFORMAL ORGANIZATION

Earlier in this chapter it was stated that informal organization is a normal state of affairs that arises as people associate with one another.

FIGURE 14–4
Advantages of the Informal Organization

---

1. Improves communication. Informal organization members are without peer in gathering news they want to know and distributing it. The "grapevine" is effective. Also the informal member is commonly a person who will "hear out" a fellow employee with a frustration.
2. Provides satisfactions to the employees. Security, a sense of belonging, and participation in affairs that concern a member are gained by the member.
3. Helps to share the load of the formal organization. With support of the informal group, loose supervision can be followed, and close checks are not required.
4. Makes the formal manager more effective. Plans, decisions, and actions must be mutually known and agreed upon, otherwise the informal group will let the formal manager know about it and not give enthusiastic cooperation.

Let's elaborate on this statement by discussing these pertinent topics: (1) personnel interrelations and values, (2) the group's effect upon the individual, (3) differentials of managers, (4) stability and adjustment, and (5) compromise and control.

Personnel Interrelations and Values

The various and different functions to be performed in an office organization make it possible to match a person of certain likes, capacities, and curiosities with a particular function which requires those particular characteristics. The result is that people with different characteristics are brought together by an entity called an organization. Actions are taken by human beings and some of these actions have little to do with the rationale of the organization. They stem from beliefs, emotions, and reactions of the people within the organization and contribute strong influences that must be reckoned with.

What members of an organization think and don't think, believe and don't believe, do and don't do, affect the tasks to be accomplished and the conditions under which they are or they are not accomplished. The behavior of each group member influences, to some degree, the behavior of the other group members. Personnel interrelations shape most of the decisions and actions taken. That is, within the organization, the behavior of a member is determined not only by motives and personality, but also by the interactions of those motives and personality with those of colleagues. Also exerting some influence are the nature of the work being performed, the rewards, the controls, the formal relationships, and the expectancy of how an employee should behave.

Values affect organizing. They become quite important if the values differ greatly among the members. Many hold the view that the informal organization exists mainly to achieve a practical mode of operation among group members with different values.

What is a value? It can be thought of as the relative esteem or excellence attributed to a belief or preference, and arises from personal choice based on opinions, prejudices, and standards. Values are held and assimulated because they satisfy personal needs and represent what is believed to be really worthwhile and the concept of the desirable. They result from experience, education, reflection, and mores of the culture from which the person is a member.

People have values concerning business, hospitals, concentration of management, size of an office, profits, and work. But values differ among people. For example, some stress economic values such as cost, efficiency, and profit while others stress social values such as improving society—better living and the full life, ameliorating race relations, and preserving national resources.

The Group's Effect upon the Individual

Organization places the individual in a group relationship, and this differs from that of an individual being alone or in an individual-to-individual relationship. Individuals usually act differently when they are alone in comparison to when they are with other individuals. For example, comparing being with a group to that of being alone, the individual tends to produce a larger quantity of physical work, is less inhibited in expressing self, and gives more free-ranging discussion to questions dealing with his or her behavior. There appears to be some commitment, implied or otherwise, by the individual to the behavior and attitude of the peer group. A person joining the employment of an enterprise emphasizing modern information management is likely to become interested in and make contributions to this type of management. The group influence upon the individual is strong and much of this influence comes from the informal organization.

Several generalizations regarding group-individual relationships are helpful. First, change in a group's belief and behavior is easier to accomplish than is change in belief and behavior of individuals separately within the group. For example, a group decision on a debatable subject commonly eases the effectiveness of outside social pressures that might be directed toward an individual taking the same stand as an individual. In brief, the individual is protected by the group within which identity is hidden.

Also, the individual members of a group should participate in the group's decisions if the group is to be truly effective. Ideas and decisions are most readily accepted when the person to whom they are directed has assisted in shaping them. In essence, such behavior tends to support the person's own thoughts and concepts.

Another generalization is that group attitude changes are more likely to be permanent than are individual attitude changes. In part, this arises from the individual's desires to meet the norms of the group. The stronger the group's bonds, the more deeply imbedded are the individual's attitude with the group's standards. From the practical point of view, this means that bringing together affected persons to a joint meeting and trying to establish a group norm among them is superior to meeting each individual singularly and establishing an individual norm for each. The group is quite likely to ignore the individual norms. But observe that group influence creates momentum. Future change within the group is quite probable; permanency of group behavior is not assured. With new external pressures forthcoming shifts are quite likely.

DIFFERENTIALS OF MANAGERS

Managers differ in the way they deal with their colleagues. For example, the manager in one part of an organization may be detail-minded, watch costs very closely, and encourage this type of thinking by subordinates. In contrast, the manager of another unit may give the most attention to developing and maintaining good relationships with co-managers. Further, the controls practiced and the system of rewards followed may differ widely among the various managers within the same formal organization. In other words, the formal behavior of the manager is highly personal and depends in great measure upon personal subjective feelings and co-workers.

Consider the importance given to time. For some management members this is a dominant characteristic—a strong thread in the cloth of managerial actions. Time must be used effectively, schedules met, and time limits placed on all projects. By both custom and environment some managers are far more time-minded than others. The management member faced with the immediate daily problem of processing a large quantity of orders views time and its use in a different light than the systems manager who is researching a new approach which is due three months hence.

There is also a significant managerial differential with respect to goal-orientedness, which differential accounts for a major amount of the different behaviors among managers. This can be a major source of conflict between the information manager and the other managers of an enterprise. Being eager to help, the information manager frequently assumes what information services will best assist the other managers in their work, but the other managers may fail to comprehend what the information services are and in what ways they can be of assistance to the information manager.

STABILITY AND ADJUSTMENT

The almost constant effort to maintain equilibruim for an existent formal organization is another condition giving rise to informal organization. The attempt to spell out organizational concepts in absolute terms, maintain the status quo, and to resist change, will inevitably be opposed by some members who commonly resort to informal organization to alleviate the condition.

Illustrative of efforts to maintain organization stability to an unwarranted degree is the screening of employment applicants in order to select only those believed most likely to adapt to this existing stable status. In fact, indoctrination is commonly undertaken to assist new members to fit into the organization mold. Seniority is a sacred part of the organization, decisions are deeply seeped in precedent, uniformity is viewed as ideal. The attempt is to formalize all organization behavior by prescribing operating procedures which are the accepted relevant human behavior. When achieved, it means that stability is accomplished and predictability is certain.

Most organizations have some element of stability about them. At least, this is true for the short run. In part this stems from the organization's attempt to maintain itself. And this has been the case with many offices. As an organization unit, the office has attempted to maintain itself even while other major units with which it is associated have changed quite drastically. To a significant extent, this condition is due to the beliefs and behavior of the people of the office organization.

Closely related to stability is adjustment. In brief, adjustment identifies the characteristic of an organization unit to exploit a changing environment rather than be exploited by it. For a given organization, an adaptive action functions from the inside out. Adjustment is one way to be adaptive to changing conditions. The information efforts of the office have undergone numerous changes during the last several decades and occupy the position they do today because of successful adjustment to new developments with respect not only to work techniques, but also to human behavior and to work environment. Without question, the outcome from informal organization has played a role in bringing about these adjustments.

An internal structural change is viewed as a threat to the formal organization. In contrast, resolving a difficulty by changing the environment of the organization is not viewed as a threat, but actually a confirmation of the rightness of the existent formal organization. To illustrate, if new employees are performing the office work poorly, we prefer to raise the bases for hiring rather than modify the training and work standards. If the services of an office are not being fully accepted, new ways of supplying the services are more likely to be pursued than going outside the office to the information recipients, finding out what they really want and need, and adjusting the organization accordingly. Here again the presence of the informal organization helps condition the operation of the formal organization to increase the total contribution of organization.

COMPROMISE AND CONTROL

When controversial issues arise, short-term solutions may be followed to keep the organization functioning at least for awhile or until answers of what to do can be determined. Commonly, demands from the informal organization suggest short-term answers. For example, the information manager may find it expedient to settle differences between the computer section and the bookkeeping section on a day-to-day basis making concessions first to one and then to the other. The personal conflicts among several members may continue, but this does not really bother the manager who hopes and believes in a short time the involved members will either quit, retire, ask for a transfer, or be obsoleted by new methods to be inaugurated. Further, a needed replacement in the filing section may be delayed because the replacement and the move are opposed by the informal leader and followers. In time, however, the information manager hopes to resolve the issue, but meanwhile resorts to compromise and control. In other cases, what to decide involves imponderables of long-standing within the organization or the manager does not know which decision will bring the best results and therefore tries to compromise and control since it is easy to apply and causes no friction with the informal organization. Theoretically, however, it seldom is the most efficient approach, but is justified on the basis that it supplies a solution to a complex problem of keeping the organization viable under the current conditions with the people available.

THE NECESSITY OF FORMAL ORGANIZATION

There can be little doubt that informal organization meets important needs of members that the formal organization does not. Formal organization, however, is a basic requirement of management. There must be some well-defined and inclusive foundation by which the efforts of many human beings can be blended together effectively toward a common goal. And the basis should be orderly to avoid needless waste and to operate effectively. You cannot have all members totally independent and actively pursuing goals and performing activities their respective emotions, subjective desires, and personal wishes dictate. This would make for a very difficult situation—something like "all fleas and no dog."

The question arises, "How can the formal and the informal organizations be brought to an acceptable compatible state?" Mutual understanding, adjusting, spotting conflicts, and immediately working toward their resolution are possible avenues. But the approach of striving to relate the organization goals with those of the individual employee seems to offer the greatest practical helpfulness. To the degree that these goals are compatible, the employee attains personal satisfaction in achieving the organization's goal. The personal requirements vary among individuals and, fortunately, the organization requires different kinds of jobs and relationships so that it appears feasible to attain satisfactory combinations of individual needs and jobs. In addition, many managers feel that the answer lies in decreasing the dependency and submissiveness of the employee by providing the employee with greater responsibility and a larger scope of job. The need is for jobs of more challenge to the individual performing them and for the opportunity for the worker to manage job actions. Also required is greater recognition of the fact that organizing provides a facility through which employees join together to support efforts of truly competent leaders, to gain satisfaction of personal needs, and to provide more products and services benefiting others as well as themselves.

To integrate fully the work efforts of the people of the various units into a cooperative and coordinated whole sounds fairly simple, but acquiring it in actual practice is a different story. People are not entirely unpredictable, yet by no means can they be considered the same as material objects. The intricacies of the human mind and human behavior are far more difficult to understand than say the chemical reaction of several compounds.

We must continue to strive for a favorable organizational environment in which people are stimulated and permitted to grow. Environment is among the strongest influences to which an employee is exposed. Every organization provides environmental stimuli that affect its members, and likewise the members affect the organization. Favorable surroundings conducive to the development of a way of life, operating under the arrangement devised by formal organizing, must be provided. Also, this means the existence and operation of a healthy informal organization. In the best of organizing work, there is spirit, and attitude of positiveness, and a strong belief in people and what they can accomplish.

QUESTIONS

1. Discuss in some depth the tools of personnel selection.
2. In your opinion is it better to think of organization in terms of groups of people or as individuals banded together to achieve a common goal? Justify your viewpoint.
3. Carefully identify each of the following:

    a. Recruiting of employees.

    b. Technical proficiency of an organization.

    c. Interpersonal organization.

    d. Formal organization.

4. Many discussions of organizations include the subject of values. What are values and what relationship or influence do they have on organization efforts?

5. Cite an example of a dysfunction arising from formal organization. Do you feel the effect of this dysfunction is good or bad? Why?

6. Discuss in some detail a major beneficial contribution of informal organization.

7. How important are stability and adjustment in organizational activities? Elaborate on your answer.

8. Elaborate on the statement: "Human beings tend to prefer a status quo with internal arrangements and to blame most organizational malfunctioning on outside causes."

9. Explain Figure 14–3 in your own words.

10. What is your understanding of organizational conflicts, and suggest what measures a manager might take to resolve them.

11. In your opinion is formal organization really required in office management? Why? Informal organization? Why?

12. Relate an example from your experience demonstrating that change in the behavior of a group is easier to accomplish than in the behavior of individuals separately within the group.

CASE PROBLEMS

Case 14–1. Doran, Inc.

An opening exists for a draftsman in the engineering and designing department of Doran, Inc., a heavy machinery manufacturer. The corporation has always taken considerable effort to place the person on the job that best suits the applicant. Much attention is given to maintaining good relationships among employees especially those working together within a department. Doran, Inc. has a reputation as a good place to work. Currently there are 17 men in the engineering and designing department.

The personnel department recruits, holds preliminary interviews, and screens applicants for work. Those believed satisfactory are referred to the supervisor of the department where the applicant will work. The final decision on whether to hire is made by the supervisor. For the draftsman opening, the personnel department has referred two candidates to supervisor Bart Osgood.

One candidate is Leonard Baker, age 42, high school graduate, married, two children, just retired from the U.S. Army after 21 years of service, honorable discharge, rank of sergeant. Most of his time in the U.S. Army was spent in engine maintenance work. He studied drafting, engine design, and carpentry from a correspondence school.

The other candidate is Mildred Morse, age 20, single, since graduation from high school has worked as a sales clerk in a local department store. She likes machines, has a brother who is a mechanic and together they have torn down and rebuilt several racers. She says the drafting job is just what she has dreamed of.

During interviews with Mr. Osgood, neither candidate impressed him as highly favorable. However, realizing the labor market is thin, he chose Leonard Baker and advised personnel of his choice.

When Mildred Morse heard of her rejection, she was bitterly disappointed. In her opinion the company is violating the civil rights law which forbids hiring discrimination because of sex, marital status, creed, color, or national origin. Relating her experience to governmental officials, Miss Morse said she knew she could do the work because a friend of her brother works as a draftsman for Doran and she can do the work that he does. Further, while waiting in Mr. Osgood's office for the interview with him, she overheard the conversation between two draftsmen adjacent to the office. The one stated that Bart was talking to a young woman for the drafting job that was open, but he'll never hire her because that would really upset the department. The other one agreed, stating words to the effect that "I hope Bart handles this right. The last thing we want here is a woman. I don't see why he is even talking with her. And I'll never understand why a woman would want to do this kind of work. I'm against it. If a female is hired, heaven forbid, I'll tell you what will happen. She'll get all the easy work and make a silly old fool of Bart."

Questions:

1. Comment on the action taken by Ms. Morse.
2. What effect do you believe the civil rights law may have upon the "people of an organization" in the future? Discuss.
3. What is your recommended action for the company? Why?

Case 14-2.   Tutweiler Plastics, Inc.

Business has been slow for several months and reluctantly it was decided to lay off some 15 percent of the total labor force. An attempt had been made to keep every current employee on the payroll by letting inventory build up, but it was now clear that adjustments were mandatory. The list of those to be laid off was compiled by the assistant personnel manager working with the executives, middle managers, and supervisors throughout the entire corporation. When the final list was completed and given to the personnel manager, he noted that the name of Warren Mobley was included. Mobley had a poor record with the corporation. Employed as a cost clerk, he has shown little development potential and initiative. He has a habit of spending excessive time on menial tasks and has given his supervisor a difficult time on more than one occasion. On the other hand, he seems to get along quite well with his fellow employees especially those in the factory where he goes frequently to investigate the cause of a cost being out of line.

The personnel manager believes that now is a good time to terminate Mobley's employment reasoning that he is going to be laid off and may never return, and it would be a good idea to make certain that he never does return. Calling in Mobley's supervisor and informing him of the proposed action, the supervisor was all for it. "I'll be glad to get rid of him," he said.

That afternoon when the supervisor told Warren his employment was being terminated, Warren reacted, "What do you mean, I'm terminated. For what? What have I done? Nobody told me I did something wrong. Others are getting laid off as I understand it, but they are not getting terminated. Taking my job away without warning or cause, is not fair. There must be some mistake."

The supervisor replied that that's the way it is going to be. Personnel is following out top management's order to trim the workforce. There just isn't enough work.

Near closing time, Warren went to the personnel department and talked with the assistant personnel manager, since the personnel manager had left for the day. Presenting his views to the assistant personnel manager, Warren reiterated his views emphasizing that to terminate a man's employment there must be a cause. "There is," replied the assistant personnel manager. "No work." "But the rest are getting laid off, not fired," continued Warren. "Put me on the layoff list."

Two days later Warren Mobley was given his official termination notice effective immediately.

Questions:

1. Do you agree with the decision and action taken by the corporation? Why?
2. Is the normal reaction of an employee to a lay off that he or she will never return? Discuss.
3. From the viewpoint of a corporation looking upon its human resources as its most vital asset, are you of the opinion that Tutweiler Plastics, Inc. is measuring up to this viewpoint? Elaborate on your answer.

Case 14–3. Gleason Manufacturing Company

Clarence Cross, age 37, an industrial engineer, came to the Gleason Manufacturing Company about two years ago. He was assigned to the industrial engineering department of the manufacturing division. His work record showed him to be a highly competent and qualified man, and the company felt very fortunate in acquiring his services. During the first few months with the company, he handled several projects admirably well; and when the office requested an engineer to assist in some office work measurement, Mr. Cross was given the assignment. Soon he became extremely interested in office work and the possibilities it offered for improvement. He worked diligently and established many standards. However, many of the office employees thought Mr. Cross too aggressive and too much for himself. They did not trust him believing he would eliminate many of their jobs if he could.

Nearly a year ago, the office manager who reports to the vice president of finance quit to move south on account of his wife's health. The dynamic qualities and eagerness of Mr. Cross, together with his competency, suggested to the company's executive vice president that Mr. Cross was the man for the office manager's job. He so advised the vice president of finance who offered the office manager's job to Cross who accepted.

He was elated at the prospect. Within his first two months on the new job, he submitted a new coordinated plan for office operations which would save the company a considerable sum. Reluctantly, the office supervisors approved the plan. Mr. Cross had interviews with the vice president of finance and the vice president of sales. He stressed how his proposal would improve the office work processing and reduce the costs of his department. He also indicated that for too long the office has been considered as a secondary department and should be at a higher level in the company's organization. He hoped to achieve this objevice for his department.

After six months of trying to make headway with the office improvement program, Mr. Cross began to feel he was getting nowhere. His superior, the vice president of finance, kept giving him special work to do, which work Mr. Cross classified as strictly "busy" work and of no real importance. One job was an investigation of the reception service; another, of the trend in the number of items included on a typical order received by the company. Also, at the suggestion of the executive vice president of the company, Mr. Cross visited several large offices using computers and also spent several days each with two different computer manufacturers. Reporting back to the executive vice president on the results of these visits, Mr. Cross felt that the executive vice president had little interest in the visits and would rather not hear about them.

Things continued about the same for the next four months. Mr. Cross kept busy on special assignments which he believed were whims of the company's top executives. He felt that he was achieving nothing. He arranged an interview with his superior and challenged the situation. He received a vague response. Thinking over the situation for several days, Mr. Cross decided to quit and tendered his resignation.

Questions:

1. Should the company accept the resignation of Mr. Cross? Why?
2. What do you think the real problem is in this case? Explain.
3. What action should be taken, and by whom? Discuss.

Chapter 15

Authority and the Managerial Environment

> *I early found that when I worked for myself alone, myself alone worked for me; but when I worked for others also, others worked also for me.*
>
> Benjamin Franklin

In the previous chapters the work division and the people aspects of organization were discussed. The third basic activity of organizing, namely determining relationships among the organizational units, will now be presented. The various organizational units made up of work divisions and people assigned to them must be related, or formally tied together, so that they provide a unified group which can operate effectively. Relating these units leads to the subject of authority.

Authority is the right to act or to exact action by others, within a prescribed area. With the concept of authority is associated the power to make decisions and to see that they are carried out. The compliance aspect of authority is gained by means of persuasion and requests. In a minority of cases, coercion or force is used.

Characteristics of Authority

Authority has definite limitations. First of all, it must, from the management point of view, be used in conformity with the efforts to achieve the accepted goals of the organizational unit. It is not used by an office manager as whims or wishes might suggest. Also, the use of authority is influenced by the people with whom it is being employed. The exacting of certain actions by others must be within their capacity to perform. To illustrate, trying to enforce a decision compelling an inexperienced file clerk to operate a modern bookkeeping machine would be a ridiculous misuse of authority.

In formal organization, the relative position in the organization structure normally indicates the degree of authority. But the amount of decision-making power and ultimate enforcement may be modified by the popularity or acceptance of the one in authority by the person being influenced by that authority. Managerial competence to gain enthusiastic cooperation, to acquire respect, and to inspire may be lacking despite the formal authority established by position in the organization structure. This also means that a person with little or no formal authority established by reason of position in the structure might actually possess extensive authority due to integrity, knowledge, and skill. In punched-card accounting, for example, others may seek suggestions from a certain individual and follow those suggestions. Although the person may not be formally in charge, significant authority is there. In this case, informal relationships are prevailing. Situations of this type are not uncommon. They may be of a temporal nature or may exist for long, continuous periods.

In many office organizational units, situations of an unusual or emergency nature arise from time to time. They may not be provided for in the regular organizational arrangement. In such circumstances, the person assuming the authority has derived it from what is called the "authority of the situation." This usually is temporary and exists until the person normally in charge assumes authority over the unusual event.

The relationship established by authority is either (1) vertical or (2) horizontal. Vertical authority relationships are those between different organization levels and concern the superior-subordinate association. Horizontal authority relationships deal with organizational units within an organizational level and concern the manager-to-manager association within the same organization level.

Lastly, authority is dynamic. Within prescribed limits, its makeup is changed according to the specific conditions and requirements of the group or the individual. It is not always applied in the same way nor to the same degree.

Responsibility

When a management member is given or assumes authority to perform specific work, an obligation to perform the work is created. The acceptance of this obligation is known as responsibility which can be defined as follows. *Responsibility is the obligation for the carrying out of a duty and what one is accountable for in the execution of an assigned task.* That is, responsibility can be viewed as having two parts: (1) the obligation to secure results and (2) the accountability to the one from whom the authority is received. Commonly responsibility takes the form of a list of duties. These are general statements—they do not spell out every detail of what is to be performed.

Being obligated to secure results and being accountable automatically puts a person under pressure and develops the sensitivity to gain satisfactory results. Typically, in a business enterprise the board of directors appoints a president who is expected to manage the business. Obligation to secure results and the president's accountability are well known. In turn, by means of organizing, authority and responsibility are shared with individuals. In fact, this is one of the main purposes of organizing.

Efforts to develop responsibility in management members take many different forms, but an effective practice is to provide the holder of authority and responsibility with a list of questions to improve the exercise of authority and to stimulate enthusiastic acceptance of the responsibility that the authority entails. Figure 15–1 illustrates the type of questions that can be asked.

FIGURE 15–1
Questions to Develop Management Responsibility

1. Do you make a continuing review of excess office processing capacity?
2. What five office work areas require most of your time? Should they?
3. Have you investigated to find out if your instructions are understood?
4. Are you keeping up with the latest developments in office machines that might be used in your organizational unit?
5. Are written procedures brought up to date?
6. Do you receive any useless reports or documents?
7. Do you take an individual interest in each of your subordinates?

AUTHORITY AND RESPONSIBILITY—DEFINITE AND COEQUAL

Both authority and responsibility should be definite and known to all concerned. Defining the authority and the responsibility assists in gaining the needed coordination among the various component efforts. However, this defining does not mean spelling out every detail. Rather, it prescribes in what broad areas managers shall make decisions and for what they are expected to perform and to be accountable for.

Responsibility implies an individual trust, a dependence upon an individual to perform an assigned task promptly and efficiently. When this is definite and fixed, the person realizes the sole responsibility to see that the job is carried out satisfactorily. Defining responsibility tends to develop the individual and to increase reliability. Knowing exactly the task and the activity for which one is being held fully responsible, one strives to overcome common obstacles and to perform the tasks promptly and thoroughly. Human beings like to measure up to the requirements made of them. In addition, when an emergency or critical need arises, the proper person for a specific function can be seen quickly and directly, without waste of time.

Responsibility should be fixed at a level as low in the organization structure as is consistent with the capability of the personnel at that level to assume responsibility—the lower the better. Fixed responsibility tends to increase the individual's feeling of worth, and of doing something that has importance.

The authority of any manager should be coequal with the assigned responsibility and, vice versa, the responsibility coequal with the authority. The association between authority and responsibility is intimate and where one exists so does the other. This relationship is akin to an object and its image in a mirror. If one exists, the other exists also in a coequal status. Authority commensurate with responsibility is needed before responsibility becomes meaningful; and likewise, responsibility without commensurate authority has dubious managerial value.

Span of Authority

In writing of relationships among organizational units, the question arises: How many immediate subordinates can a manger manage effectively? The number is commonly referred to as "span of control" or "span of management." For our purposes here, it is believed the term "span of authority" is appropriate and helpful.

In a given case, there is probably an optimum number of persons who should be immediately subordinate to a manager in order that most satisfactory managerial results are obtained. The number should be large enough to utilize the manager's full time and ability, yet not so large that efforts are diluted over too wide a span. The proper span of authority depends upon many considerations.

The organizational level at which the managerial work is performed appears to be important. At the higher levels, few might report to their immediate superior; while at the lower or operative levels, many might report to one superior. Also, the type of work is important. To illustrate, a supervisor of draftsmen might adequately direct the work of 15 draftsmen, depending upon the particular type of drafting work performed. Generally speaking, a relatively broad span of authority can be used. In addition, adequate consideration must be given to whether all the immediate subunits are of equal size and importance, whether they must be given equal attention by the supervisor, whether the caliber of personnel requires a large or a small amount of supervision; and whether the physical distance between the activities is reasonable. Where the makeup of the work is fairly stable and little communication between units is required, a broad span of authority usually proves satisfactory.

Some time back, a span of from four to eight was preferred. This quantity originated from the military where rapid change in plans and operations may be necessary because of enemy action. However, in civilian organizations, the span should be determined by keeping in mind the considerations mentioned above. The number used may well be four to eight, but it need not necessarily be this amount. The span of authority appears to be increasing in many business enterprises. In some instances, successful operations are reported with spans of 10 to 12 persons at the top levels and with 20 to 25 persons at the lower levels. In the final analysis, the number of subordinates reporting to a manager should be limited to what can be effectively managed.

It is appropriate to point out that span of authority deals with the number of persons reporting to a manager, not the number of persons having access to a manager. The two can be greatly different. Also, span of authority is confined to authority relationships in the formal organization.

Wide spans of authority make for relatively few organizational levels; short spans make for many organizational levels. With wide spans the organizational structure is referred to as a "flat organization," with short spans as a "tall organization." Coordination vertically is relatively easily obtained in the flat organization; and in contrast, it is more difficult in the tall organization because of the depth created by the organizational levels. On the other hand, and because of the same reasons, coordination horizontally within a given organizational unit is relatively easy within a tall organization, but relatively difficult within the flat organization.

The number of organizational relationships increases rapidly as the number of persons supervised increases. Consider manager, M, with two supervisors, A and B. In this case, there are six relationships: M with A, M with B, and A with B, plus the reverse of each, assuming the initiative is taken by the second-named party; i.e., the additional three are A with M, B with M, and B with A. Now, assume that M increases the number of supervisors from two to three, or an increase of 50 percent. What happens? The relationships increase from 6 to 18, or an increase of 200 percent. The third supervisor, C, makes for these additional 12 relationships: M with C, B with C, A with C, M with AB, M with BC, and M with AC, plus the reverse of these six relationships. While not all the relationships are of equal importance, the number should be taken into account when determining the span of authority.

Delegation of Authority

Delegation of authority is the granting or conferring of authority by one manager to another. Usually it is thought of as being from a higher to a lower level, as is commonly the case within business enterprises. However, in some formal organizations of government and some religious groups, delegation of authority is from a lower to a higher level and from one level to another on the same plane. Hence delegation can be downward, upward, or lateral.

By means of delegation an executive widens and deepens an area of formal managerial influence and makes organization meaningful. Without delegation, a manager restricts actions to those that he or she, can perform personally. In fact, formal organizing does not become fully effective until delegation of authority is practiced.

Figure 15–2 illustrates the importance of delegation of authority. At

FIGURE 15–2
Failure to Delegate Authority by Office Executive 3 Tends to Paralyze the Organization Established under Him

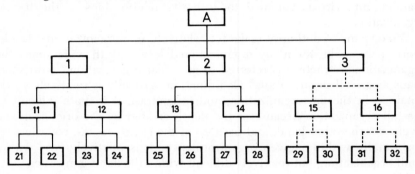

the top of the illustration, office executive A has three assistants, 1, 2, and 3. In turn, assistant 1 has chiefs 11 and 12 reporting to him; likewise, chief 11 has subordinates 21 and 22; and chief 12, subordinates 23 and 24. Persons reporting to assistants 2 and 3 are shown by the illustration. Executive A delegates proper authority to assistants 1, 2, and 3. Of these, 1 and 2, in turn delegate authority to their chiefs; and in turn, these chiefs delegate authority to their subordinates. In contrast, assistant 3 is trying personally to do most of the managerial work of the organizational unit. Very little authority is delegated to either 15 or 16, who can and do delegate very very little authority to 29, 39, 31, or 32. This failure to delegate authority actually paralyzes this portion of the organization under assistant 3. To a great extent, the persons reporting to assistant 3 may just as well not be management members of the organization. There is in reality no formal authority structure below assistant 3.

In delegation, the delegator always retains overall authority for the delegated duties. It is not surrendered or permanently released. He or she does grant the right for others to act officially within the specific areas. Only the authority needed to carry out successfully the assigned functions is or should be delegated. This makes for the tapering concept of authority and simply means that in most organizations the formal authority becomes successively smaller or tapered as successively lower horizontal levels of the structure are considered.

An authority delegator retains in the ultimate all the authority, and likewise retains in the ultimate all responsibility. The person cannot evade a failure of a subordinate by saying it was the fault of the subordinate. The delegator retains the ultimate responsibility and is accountable for what is or is not achieved by that organizational unit.

The Delegation Challenge

In many cases managers do not delegate adequately and in some instances not at all. Asking the manager to delegate seldom brings about the desired practice. A fear exists that if authority is delegated, the right decision may not be made, and the work will not be handled correctly. The nondelegator feels it necessary to keep in close touch with activities and decide most issues. In some instances, failure to realize the amount of authority needed by a subordinate to get the work done properly may exist. In other instances, the manager believes and states that authority has been delegated, but at the same time criticizes and does not permit the delegatee to go ahead with the decision making.

Delegation of authority is not easily acquired. The natural tendency is to do work yourself if you are the one charged with doing it. And if the work is important, there is all the more reason for doing it yourself to make certain that it is done right. These habits develop quite commonly because most persons acquire managerial status after doing nonmanagerial work. The latter type emphasizes doing the work yourself and doing it well; the reward can be promotion to managerial work. But success in managerial work requires getting work achieved by and through others. Failure to realize this fact plus difficulty in making the needed change in thinking, i.e., acquiring the managerial viewpoint, not the direct operative viewpoint, contribute to the lack of delegation by a manager.

Commonly the amount and extent of delegation of authority is arrived at informally by trial and error. The subordinate makes a decision or tries out a certain practice; and if no reprimand results, assumes the management work performed is within his or her province. In many cases, the status of delegation of authority is the result of an infiltration process over a long period of time. Slowly but surely, authority for certain matters has been turned over to the delegatee. Commonly, verbal statements establish the amount of delegation of authority; rarely are written delegations used.

Achieving Adequate Delegation of Authority

The first requirement for adequate delegation to exist is to get the manager to realize the need for it. Managers must recognize that as long as they are limited to doing what they can accomplish personally, they will always be short of time and limited in their achievements. The alternative is to acquire aides, train them, and permit them to do the job, even if their manner of doing it differs from how the manager might have done it. Competent aides are mandatory for group efforts to reach greatest heights. A manager's need is to multiply output. Being a "multiplier manager" pays big dividends. It is nonsense to try to lead the band and play all the instruments too.

Also needed is the establishing of a work climate that encourages delegation. Managers must be made to feel that giving assignments, both structured and unstructured, to their subordinates is the proper thing to do. Both the superior to and the subordinate under the manager approve of such action, interest in the work increases for all, managerial skills are improved, and the organization is strengthened. If the results are short of the expected accomplishment, and they will be from time to time, the deficiency can be charged to the development of managerial skill. Remember that a manager grows most while building subordinates the most.

Furthermore, it is important to establish definite goals and clear policies, for these give guidance to the delegatee and avoid efforts from going too far astray in the fulfillment of the tasks. Work which is routine and which is covered by definite policies should offer little delegation difficulty. Clear and timely communication, complete instructions, and definite job identifications are also helpful. Further, the use of broad controls expedites delegation, for they can supply the desired checks to determine whether the work is being accomplished satisfactorily.

One of the best ways to achieve adequate delegation is to follow the managerial approach of *management by objectives.* Under this approach, the achievement of stated objectives is emphasized. The subordinate participates in determining goals or accomplishments for a given future period along with how the subordinate expects to accomplish them. All this is done within the overall boundaries set forth by the superior. The goals and means are then discussed by the subordinate and the superior, adjusted if necessary, agreed upon, and adopted. The goodness of the work performed is evaluated in terms of what was achieved compared with what was sought, as set forth by the mutually agreed upon objectives. *The management by objectives approach gets the delegation of authority accomplished.* There is, in fact, no delegation problem in management by objectives because the formal authoritarian practice is minimized. In addition, management by objectives is highly motivational.[1]

Meriting inclusion is the statement that belief in delegation is necessary. An office manager must want to make delegation successful, must do everything possible to make it succeed. To this end the manager selects the delegatee carefully, offers counsel but is careful not to give answers, but to help the delegatee find the answers. More specifically the delegator does not just hand the work to the delegatee, sit back, and observe if the delegatee is making good or not. Effective delegating does not just happen. To achieve it takes much effort, time, and persistence.

ORGANIZATION CHARTS

The organizational relations as well as the graphic picture of the total organization is probably best shown by an organization chart. It clearly sets forth the organizational units, the relationships, and the lines of formal authority. Stated briefly: an organization chart is a graphic representation of an organization structure.

To draw an organization chart, use the outline approach. First, list the main functions; next, place those functions which are subordinate to the main functions under the proper main function in the outline list; then, place under each subordinate function the minor functions which properly belong under the respective subordinate function. Thus, a list is developed indicating the relative worth of each function. Transfer this list into a graphic form thereby deriving the tentative organization chart. Now, study the arrangement giving special consideration to the people making up each segment and also to the authority relationships indicated. Make shifts and adjustments where they would appear to bring about overall improvement. Suggestions from others should be encouraged in what modifications to make and why they should be made.

As an alternative, the chart may be prepared by starting with the person of highest authority in the organization structure and working down by determining who reports to this top person and what activities each person handles. This procedure provides the information for the first level of management below the chief executive and is followed for each consecutive layer.

An organization chart helps in visualizing the organization structure; it insures neither good organization nor good management. However, it does compel the organizer to put down in black and white what

---

[1] Management by objectives is discussed fully in Chapter 19.

the structural relationships are and highlights the formal authority locations. This helps clarify organization thinking. Specifically, the main advantages of an organization chart can be listed as follows: (1) a clear, overall concept of the organization is obtained; (2) the main lines of formal authority are brought out in full relief; (3) promotional possibilities are suggested; and (4) the assignment of titles is simplified.

LINE AUTHORITY AND STAFF AUTHORITY

Full comprehension of organizing requires knowledge of the types of authority, their respective characteristics, and when to use what type for which purpose. The two main classifications of authority are (1) line and (2) staff. A manager can have either or both. A manager who has line authority is called a "line manager" and normally exercises direct command over the work of all members in the unit, but with certain exceptions, to be noted later. Characteristically, the authority relation is of a superior-subordinate type, forming "a line" from the top to the bottom of the structure. It is the authority used to accomplish *directly* the major goals of an enterprise and exists at all levels of the organization structure.

As suggested by its name, staff authority is something to lean upon, or to give support. Staff authority exists to support or to aid line authority. Staff authority is normally utilized to contribute *indirectly* to the major goals of an organization. Staff authority flows *to* line authority which flows directly *along* the channel toward objective accomplishment. A manager with staff authority is a staff manager. There are four important types of staff authority including (1) advisory staff, (2) functional staff, (3) service staff, and (4) control staff. While all are staff authority they are dissimilar in important respects, and the common identification of staff is unfortunate. All of these various types of staff authority are in use and are believed necessary. Their specific application depends upon the individual organization. More discussion about the different staffs will be made later in this chapter.

THE LINE ORGANIZATION

The line, or sometimes called scalar, type of organization uses line authority exclusively. Popular in our early industrial development, it is one of the oldest organization forms. Today it is prevalent among proprietors of small businesses and for other enterprises where the number of employees is small.

The line organization is characterized by direct lines of authority from the top executive to the various assistants, and direct from them to the employees at the operative level. Each member is fully responsible for the carrying out or the actual performance of the job to be done.

Throughout the entire structure, each member is in complete charge of all activities within his particular organization segment. Authority and responsibility are greatest at the top, and reduce as successively lower levels of management are considered.

The advantages of the line organization include the following: Authority and responsibility are definitely fixed, and the person who has that authority and responsibility is known to all; the structure is very simple and hence readily understood by all personnel; discipline is easily maintained, since each superior and each subordinate knows what is expected of her and in which areas she is to operate; decisions can be quickly reached, the fact that a single superior who is in complete charge makes for a minimum of delay in decision reaching; and lastly, the line organization offers splendid training opportunities for the development of managerial talent. The line manager is charged with getting things executed, and must be a "doer."

In contrast, the line organization also has its disadvantages. Perhaps most outstanding is that, relatively, specialization of work is not practiced. Particularly is this true at the intermediate and supervisory management levels. Another disadvantage is the difficulty of securing coordination. Each manager is in charge of a unit of the organization, and the tendency is for the head of each unit to develop a rather independent unit and to think only of its activities, without much regard for other necessary functions of the enterprise. In fact, some believe that the line organization probably places too much emphasis on the managers. Another disadvantage is the difficulty of forming organizational units; this is particularly true in cases where the unit is not suggested by the process. Frequently, insufficient opportunity is afforded to modify and to change existing units from the viewpoint of the total organization structure.

THE LINE AND STAFF ORGANIZATION

When staff authority relationships are added to a line organization, the resultant organization is called a line and staff organization which is extensively used. In this type, line managers have line authority to carry out the activities, but their efforts are qualified by staff managers who have authority to carry out their particular work. Both line and staff managers are considered essential, and all are believed needed to accomplish the work effectively. More precisely this means that the line and the staff managers comprise a winning team of managers with varying degrees and types of authority. In the team effort, all are required. None should be thought of as inferior; for if in fact they are, then either they should be replaced or their area of operation should be eliminated.

FIGURE 15–3
A Line and Staff Organization

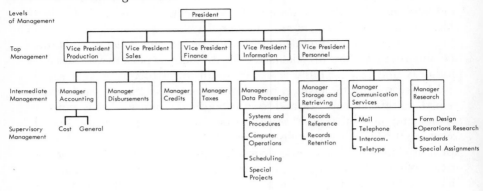

The chart of a line and staff organization is shown in Figure 15–3. Under the vice president of information are the managers of data processing, storing and retrieving, communication services, and research. The organizational units under each of these managers are indicated on the chart. The managers of units without dotted circles around them have line authority, those encircled have staff authority. Likewise, under the vice president of finance are shown the units of line and of staff authority. Note that even though a function is staff, the organization for carrying out that function may be of a line organization type. To illustrate, under the vice president of information, the management of the research unit is staff to the organization as a whole, but the research unit itself is a line organization with the work of forms design, operations research, standards, and special assignments under it. Also observe that a staff unit can exist at various management levels. The chart is intended for illustrative purposes only. Organizational units under the vice president production, vice president sales, and vice president personnel have not been included.

The advantages of the line and staff organization are many. First, the lines of authority are fairly well fixed, good discipline can be attained, decisions can be reached after desirable deliberation, and the principle of specialization can be utilized to the extent of practical limits. Second, coordination can be improved because the line officers are supplied with factual data concerning activities both within and outside their own units. Third, flexibility is provided for the organization structure to expand or contract, as conditions warrant. New activities can be added and old ones discarded without seriously affecting the organization structure. Fourth, proper balance among all the activities, line as well as staff can be maintained. Fifth, more opportunities are afforded to match the desires, capacities, and interests of personnel with the job, since a greater variety of jobs involving different duties, responsibilities, training, and background is required.

In contrast, disadvantages exist in line and staff organizations. These disadvantages tend to center around the relationships existing between the line and staff managers. In the first place, the line manager may tend to ignore the staff manager's counsel, so that the expert information provided is not fully used. Second, the staff manager may tend to ignore the ideas of the line manager simply because specialization and expertness are supposed to be under the jurisdiction of the staff manager. Third, the staff manager may overstep prescribed staff authority and even attempt to take over line authority without authorization. Fourth, a considerable number of staff managers are not convincing in presenting their ideas and decisions and as a result many staff contributions are not fully used. Fifth, decisions and their implementation may be confused by members of the organization with the result that misunderstandings exist and cooperation among the managers is incomplete.

Advisory Staff Authority

The four major types of staff authority will now be discussed more fully. The first is advisory staff authority. According to Webster, staff means "a pole carried in the hand for support." Therefore, staff authority pertains to assistance or support, and much of this assistance takes the form of being advisory. Hence, it is called advisory staff authority. Specifically, a manager with advisory staff authority normally advises, in the assigned specialty, the manager having line authority. Advisory staff is a manager-to-manager relationship and can exist within any organizational level.

FIGURE 15–4

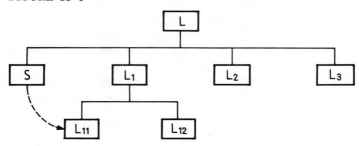

In Figure 15–4, line manager L has four subordinates, S, L_1, L_2, and L_3. The latter three are line managers, while S is an advisory staff manager whose job essentially is to advise L (within S's specialty) so that L can do a better job. The advice of S can be accepted in whole or part and utilized by L in managing the organizational group; or L can reject the advice of S, since L is in direct command of the unit. In some companies, the practice of "compulsory staff service" is followed. This requires a line executive to listen to subordinate staff executives, but the final decision and enforcement rests with the line executive. Also, in some enterprises, the "completed staff work" doctrine is followed. This emphasizes the presentation of complete solutions by the advisory staff to the line managers. Piecemeal recommendations are avoided; and stress is placed on supplying assistance, not placing the line manager in a predicament with questions regarding what should be investigated or what data should be included in a report. Of course, the line and staff people should talk things over, in a constructive way, with each making contributions.

Functional Staff Authority

In information management, the use of functional staff authority is especially common. It concerns specific functions only and is delegated from one manager to another manager who is not related to the former by formally established authority relationships or channels. It can be conferred by a line to a staff manager, or vice versa. To illustrate, in Figure 15–4, line manager L may delegate to her subordinate staff manager, S, the authority for S to issue orders concerning a specific work activity directly to L_{11}, who is a line manager. In this case, the authority possessed by S is functional staff. Actually, L is delegating a qualified amount of line authority for a specific activity to S. The delegated authority is limited to a particular activity and applies only to the authority relationship in this activity between S and L_{11}. Good management practices would include L's informing L_1, L_{11}, and L_{12} that this functional staff authority exists. Functional staff authority expedites efficiency and is convenient. Its use, however, must necessarily be limited; otherwise, established authority relationships are neutralized. Some specialized activities of the office from time to time require a competent office executive to explain and enforce office procedures to nonoffice personnel in order to insure proper handling and good administration. Such situations are solved by the use of functional authority.

Service Staff Authority

When speaking of office organizing, the term "service unit" commonly arises. Its justification is primarily economy and improved work performed or service offered by the unit. Purchasing, mail, telephone, and reception service, and legal counsel are examples of service organizational units. Generally, the head of such a unit possesses service staff authority which actually includes some line authority, as persons are expected to request the service organization unit to perform for them a service included in the service unit's makeup and, furthermore, to be bound by the decisions made by the service unit in its specialty. To illustrate, the manager of billing may not purchase supplies and equipment. This is done by the purchasing unit, and the billing manager abides by the decisions and actions of the purchasing unit.

Service staff authority applies both within and outside of the service unit as it pertains to this specialized service work. In addition, some service organizational units utilize functional authority when delegated, that is, they have jurisdiction over specific work performed by others not normally or formally under the authority of the service unit. In some instances, the service unit's authority is limited to the strictly advisory. The unit recommends and counsels in work regarding its specialty, but the decision as to what to do and its enforcement are not within the province of the service unit.

Control Staff Authority

In many organizations, there are units that perform essential work for achieving the major goals of the enterprise; yet, their work is of a specialty nature and is not supplied on a strictly advisory basis. The contribution is indirect insofar as the chief objectives are concerned; but when necessary enforcement of decisions is present, considerable line authority over the particular function in the enterprise may be present. For example, these conditions frequently exist for an auditing unit, or a procedural analysis organization unit, or one dealing with office standards. Requests by such a unit to line managers to supply certain financial information, to use financial standards supplied, and to abide by prescribed auditing practices are not on a "take it or leave it" basis by the line managers. The requests are essential for required managerial control and when they can be enforced by the auditing unit, such a unit has control staff authority. In a very real sense, it includes aspects of ultimate line authority. Enforcement is usually voluntary because the line managers realize that the specialty offered is important and that, if necessary, compliance with requests can and will be forthcoming.

THE QUESTION OF ORGANIZATION RELATIONSHIP

At this point one might well question why there is so much discussion on line authority and on staff authority along with all the different kinds of staff authority. Does not so much emphasis on authority differentiation confuse rather than clarify organization relationships? They are complex, and no doubt about it, they give rise to difficulties in studying organizing.

Justification of the whole effort is that it is necessary in order that the people can work together willingly and effectively. In essence, it is an important part of trying to identify the formal authority for each member in somewhat precise terms. This preciseness is believed necessary for clear understanding among members, and to supply a stable basic structure upon which various managers can manage. However, we are dealing with people and as already pointed out, they tend through their respective behaviors to modify formal authority arrangements. The influence of the informal organization as well as the modification brought about by such things as the manager's individualized mode of operating, play a significant role in the makeup of the authority actually being used.

Use of Committees

Committees constitute an important part of most organization structures. They can influence the organization's authority relationships as well as serve as a medium which is excellent for shaping and developing decisions, and for contributing to the education of its members. Committees can exist at any organizational level, be of short or of long life, and deal with various subjects. Many are given line authority, that is, they not only discuss and decide issues but also secure compliance of others with the decision. Such a committee is sometimes called a "plural executive." However, probably most committees have advisory staff authority. Their purpose is to discuss and recommend. In some cases, they simply receive information, classify it, and make it available for others to use.

A committee offers several outstanding advantages. First, it permits organization members to take an active part; thus, better cooperation is obtained. Second, it helps to secure coordination. People from different departments have the chance to see the organization's needs as a whole; they have a chance to discuss these problems with other supervisors and employees. Third, the committee is an excellent source of collective advice, ideas, and opinions of top managers. Fourth, the committee offers an excellent medium for educational and training purposes.

In contrast, a disadvantage of the use of a committee is that it divides responsibility. There is no single individual fully responsible. The chairperson commonly neither has the right nor the desire to be decisive especially if the issue is quite controversial and has strong supporters on each side. Second, the committee is weak in carrying out activities. It commonly lacks decisive action and follow-up. Third, most of a committee's decisions are the result of compromise—a "straddle the fence" variety. Usually, the majority rules; and this might tend to bring prejudice, secret agreements, and bargaining, rather than facts only, into the committee's decisions. Fourth, committee meetings usually require a great deal of the members' time. There appears to be little doubt that a sizable amount of this time is wasted and might better be spent by members on their individual tasks.

QUESTIONS

1. Do you favor the use of committees in an office organization structure? Why?
2. In your opinion which poses the more serious problem; a manager deficient in authority or a manager deficient in responsibility? Discuss.
3. Point out the difference between the terms in each of the following pairs:
   a. Span of authority and horizontal authority relationships.
   b. Service staff authority and a flat organization.
   c. Organization chart and authority.
   d. Compulsory staff advice and plural executive.
4. Elaborate on the statement that adequate delegation of authority is emphasized by practicing the approach of management by objectives.
5. Describe a situation illustrating difficulties encountered due to a lack of utilizing the completed staff work doctrine.
6. With reference to a line and staff organization, what are its advantages? Its disadvantages?
7. Enumerate the major reasons why managers do not delegate authority. What inferences do you draw from this state of affairs?
8. Describe an organizational arrangement illustrating the use of service staff authority. Of control staff authority.
9. What is management responsibility and how can it be developed in a management member?
10. Discuss the purpose, use, and limitations in using organization charts in the study of management.
11. Discuss several ways in which the delegation of authority by an office manager can be developed.
12. Based on information from either a recent reading, past experience, observation, or a visit to an office, draw the organization chart for an office. Designate which units are line and which are staff. Also, indicate committees, if any, that exist. Evaluate the organization structure pointing out those features you feel are desirable and also those characteristics you believe are not desirable.

CASE PROBLEMS

Case 15–1. Mathews Company

It is true that Mr. Paynter is a very busy man. The work load is heavy, but based on much organizational study and carefully established work standards, there are ample work divisions and employees in each division. Mr. Paynter reports directly to the vice president of finance, and reporting to

Mr. Paynter are six supervisors, including, respectively, the heads of (1) corresponding, (2) order billing and invoicing, (3) office procedures and methods, (4) mailing, (5) filing and records retention, and (6) office services. Mr. Paynter is known to run a "tight ship." He permits his supervisors to make routine decisions only and frequently there are differences of opinion as to what is a routine decision. He sees to it that he is in on every decision affecting (1) any hiring, promoting, or terminating of an office employee, (2) any office employee's pay adjustment, (3) any change in currently followed procedures or methods, (4) any purchase of office equipment, machines, or supplies, and (5) any contemplated change in office policies. In addition, Mr. Paynter personally directs the office suggestion system, edits and approves changes and modifications in the office manual, and supervises the receptionist two telephone switchboard operators, and the four members of the office janitorial staff working day and night hours.

The president of the company has expressed dissatisfaction with the office to her immediate subordinates, the vice presidents of sales, production, and finance, respectively. She states that she waits an unduly long time for office information, there are many delays in preparing reports, processing customers' orders seems to take longer than it should, and "it takes a month and three summers to get a new idea adopted in the office." She has observed idle office machines during walks through the office. She personally likes Frederick Paynter who is a hard worker, always willing to help, is extremely agreeable, dresses well, and is conscientious about his work. If anything, he appears overly cooperative. With all the office employees, now 83 in number, the president feels the office should be far more effective than it is.

Questions:

1. As you see it, what is the major problem?
2. What action do you recommend the president of Mathews Company take? Why?

Case 15–2.   Vanneman-Biglow Company

CHARLES WILHELM (assistant purchasing agent): You know I really don't understand this "line-staff" concept at all.

FRANCES SNOW (purchasing agent): Line-staff about what?

WILHELM: About organization. Why so much emphasis on who has line authority and who has staff authority?

SNOW: Well, simply because if you are going to have a group of people work together effectively, you must determine who decides what issues and who tells whom what to do.

WILHELM: O.K. O.K. I see that and I go along with it. But this line-staff relationships business confuses rather than clarifies matters. Bert Stanners (expeditor in production control) is confused about what his role is. He has told me he's got well defined responsibility, but not direct authority. And he never really knows what his relationship is with people in the shop or in the office as far as that goes.

SNOW: Perhaps the difficulty is in a clear delineation between those concerned directly with producing and marketing the product or service and those who give expert assistance and advice. Historically, the shift has been slow, but persistently from line to staff. I would say this is probably due to the increase in organizational complexity, the involvement of more difficult issues in business today, and the need for more and more knowledge. At one time the boss felt able to do any job—line or staff—if there were sufficient time. But no more; the boss is more than willing to get the person in who has expertise in the area of difficulty, and prefers to have good people around and work as a member of a team, not as an individual. And, of course, the staff member felt superior and welcomed having a greater piece of the action.

WILHELM: Carl Shenk (factory superintendent) doesn't want me to determine what is required to get a job done. In fact, he told me so just last week.

SNOW: That's right. That's what I'd expect. What Carl Shenk wants from you is to procure wanted supplies and materials at the least cost.

WILHELM: And have them here when he wants them.

SNOW: And have them here when he wants them. Right. You see, Charlie, our job is to provide a special kind of help so that the line person, like Mr. Shenk, and other line persons' efforts are more productive than had we done nothing at all.

WILHELM: Then line people are actually customers of ours.

SNOW: Yes, I think you could say that. We have something to offer and tell the factory line personnel. The difficulty or source of any misunderstanding is the grabbing of authority by staff members and the abdicating of authority by the line members.

WILHELM: I see.

SNOW: There are no unnecessary or second-class management members, or at least there should not be. All are vital-line and staff. If this were not so, we should eliminate those we do not need, be they line or staff.

WILHELM: Yes. Yes. Well, thank you very much, Ms. Snow.

SNOW: All right. That's all right.

Questions:

1. Do you believe Ms. Snow's responses to clarify the "line-staff" concept are helpful and true? Elaborate on your answer.
2. Relate a possible line-staff difficulty that a person in Charles Wilhelm's job might encounter with line factory personnel. Point out how you as an assistant purchasing agent should act in the situation you describe.

Case 15–3. Ruthenburg Enterprise, Inc.

As a manufacturer of components of home appliances, Ruthenburg Enterprise, Inc. has enjoyed remarkable growth since its beginning three years ago. It's success is attributed mainly to excellent research, quality manufacturing, and aggressive and competent marketing. Headquarters are in Cincinnati. The business is headed by a general manager. Currently 373 people are employed in production headed by a production manager who has reporting to him a factory superintendent and a manager of research and development. Reporting to the factory superintendent are ten operating supervisors of various factory units. The additional organizational units include the following:

1. Assistant to the Purchasing Agent. Types the letters of this department and handles the files in this unit. Reports to the purchasing agent and personnel director.

2. Assistant to the Sales Manager. Handles advertising; works with the advertising agency; plans catalogs and brochures, displays, and sales portfolios; corresponds with distributors and customer. Reports directly to sales manager.

3. Billing Clerk. Types the invoices, maintains files of the customers billed. Reports to the information manager.

4. Bookkeeper. Keeps the books, types bills, and also does some filing work. Reports to the controller.

5. Centralized Filing Clerks. Three clerks handle all files not located in the other offices of the corporation. Some 80 percent of the records are maintained by these clerks who report directly to the information manager.

6. Centralized Stenographic Services. Consists of three stenographers who write reports, letters, and other items for members throughout the entire enterprise. They report directly to the information manager.

7. Controller. Directs the work of the accounting, makes up various financial reports, cost analysis, and office employees' payroll; and hires new employees for the office. Immediate superior is the finance manager.

8. Sales Correspondents. Dictate letters on machine and sometimes to a file clerk or typist, makes up shipping schedules and cost estimates. Report directly to the sales manager.

9. Cost Accountant. Makes up factory payroll, assists the controller with cost analysis work and other reports, and does some typing and filing. Reports to the controller.

10. File Clerk and Typist. Alternates between filing and typing, takes shorthand, and is responsible for office supplies. Is under the direct supervision of the sales manager.

11. Finance Manager. Handles all financial matters, makes decisions in the finance area, and reports directly to the general manager.

12. General Manager. Actually the president of the corporation, coordinates the entire operations of the corporation, makes major decisions, and interprets broad policies.

13. Information Manager. Supervises performance of paperwork, forms design, records retention, and general office services. Reports directly to the finance manager.

14. Miscellaneous Office Services Clerk. Handles all clerical matters of a nonroutine nature, prepares certain periodic reports, handles flower fund and campaigns for charitable purposes. Reports to information manager.

15. Order Clerk. Enters incoming orders and is secretary to and reports directly to the sales manager.

16. Purchasing Agent and Personnel Director. Handles all purchasing and is personnel director for factory workers only. Immediate superior is the general manager.

17. *Sales Manager.* Handles contacts with customers, either personal or by mail; travels about 50 percent of the time; and manages the work of the sales department. Reports to the general manager.

18. *Salespersons.* A total of nine salespersons call on prospects and customers, secure orders, take care of customer inquiries by telephone. The sales manager is the immediate superior of all salespersons.

19. *Secretary to the General Manager.* Performs secretarial work for the general manager, which work requires about 35 percent of work time; during the remainder of time, helps the other departments. Reports directly to the general manager.

20. *Switchboard Operator.* Operates the telephone switchboard and does some typing. Reports to the information manager.

Serious consideration is now being given to acquiring a medium-sized used computer. The production manager is extremely interested in having jurisdiction over the computer and cites the work it could accomplish in aiding the research and development now being pursued by the corporation. In contrast, the finance manager claims that if a computer is acquired it should be located organizationwise in his department because there is where it will be used for the greatest number of hours a week and further, would relieve the current heavy workload of the employees of the finance department.

Questions:

1. Draw an organization chart of the company.
2. Evaluate the present office organization, pointing out what may be its strong and weak points.
3. Where do you suggest the forthcoming computer unit be placed from the standpoint of organization? Why?

Case 15–4. Toole-Heedsman Corporation

The operations of the Toole-Heedsman Corporation are worldwide, with plants and offices located in the United States, South America, Europe, Asia, and northern Africa. Mr. Robert M. Fitzgerald, director of systems, procedures, and office machines, has two assistants, one for systems and procedures, and one for office machines. Mr. Fitzgerald finds that he must spend much of his time away from the corporation's main office in New York and quite often it happens that one of his assistants is out of town the same time Mr. Fitzgerald is absent. Under the circumstances, Mr. Fitzgerald has followed the general practice of delegating much work of a semiexecutive nature to his private secretary, Mrs. Irene Best, who has been with the company for seventeen years, the last five with Mr. Fitzgerald and before that, eight years with Mr. Fitzgerald's predecessor.

Officially Mrs. Best has no recognized line authority and issues orders only in the name of Mr. Fitzgerald. It is the opinion of the personnel manager that Mrs. Best is not fitted by training or personality for promotion to any other job in the office. Actually, she has become a fixture in the office, becoming well-nigh indispensable to her superior, Mr. Fitzgerald. She has knowledge of the policies, traditions, and routines of the various departments of the company.

Long experience has made Mrs. Best expert in keeping "in the clear" and in avoiding responsibility, and thus in many instances she is heartily disliked by junior executives who resent her arbitrary assumption of authority but who, nevertheless, are reluctant to register a complaint with their superior or Mr. Fitzgerald because of the recognized dependence of the latter upon Mrs. Best to assume the burden of routine administration.

As a result, Mrs. Best has come to occupy a position of authority out of all proportion to her direct responsibility, and to some exerts an irritating influence detrimental to the morale of many office employees.

Questions:

1. What are the chief weaknesses of the organization situation described above? What advantages?
2. What suggestion would you make to improve the situation?
3. How would you go about getting top managers to accept your suggestions?

Chapter 16

Organizing and Physical Environment

> *There are three ingredients in the good life: learning, earning, and yearning.*
>
> Christopher Morley

As indicated in Chapter 13, organizing includes supplying the proper work environment—the tools and the workplace, so that office efforts can be performed in a manner believed desirable. That is, to the three aspects of organizing—work division, people, and authority relationships—already discussed, will be added the fourth aspect of organizing, namely supplying the proper work environment. In this chapter will be included office location; office furniture, chairs, and desks; and the spatial conditioning factors of office lighting, color, music and sound, and air.

OFFICE LOCATION

Most offices are located in one of the following places: (1) in the factory building, (2) in a separate building adjacent to or near the factory building, or (3) in an office building far removed from any factory building. In the first two cases, the office location depends upon the factory location which is usually determined with reference to factory needs only. However, in the third case, the office can be located in line with its particular needs. Since many location problems arise due to the need for more space, the major alternatives are acquire or build additional space at the present site, or find a new location and either build or rent there. Individual circumstances are paramount, but generally speaking, it is the opinion of many that *it costs less to occupy a new building than to modernize an old one.* Of course, modernization of an old location can be followed. Many considerations enter the picture such as the prestige of the current address, convenience, suitability of remodeled quarters, and the cost of modernization and who pays for it.

Although large metropolitan areas offer many advantages, many enterprises have located their offices in suburban areas. Locations 15 to 20 miles from the downtown area have become commonplace. Manufacturing, publishing, insurance, and research offices are prominent in this movement to suburbia. Major reasons are lower cost, ample room for expansion, excellent labor availability, and a pleasant open work space.

Selected Location Factors

A number of factors can be considered in determining an office location. To illustrate, for banks, population, income per household, penetration by competiting banks, traffic flow, prominence of site, and rate of growth for the area are given top priority. Bank location stresses consumer retail service and is not typical for many office locations, but it points out the usual need of evaluating many factors in any location problem. And this in turn raises the issue of the proper weight to be given each factor. To meet the problem, a chart like that shown in Figure 16–1 can be used. By this means either an existing space can be evaluated or the requirements of a space yet to be constructed are identified.

Eight selection factors are listed on the left, and beneath each factor are statements designed to help identify the intended meaning of the factor. Opposite each factor is a series of numbers indicating the range of points or values which have been assigned to that factor. Also, the points assigned reveal the relative importance of each factor. Those shown are suggestive only. In an actual case, the factors selected and the weights given each one are determined by the evaluator. However, to make comparisons among different possible locations valid, the same chart is used for evaluating the several sites under consideration.

ADAPTABILITY OF THE SPACE

Top priority is accorded adaptability of the space, for that which is selected should permit suitable arrangement for all the desks, chairs, machines, and needs of the personnel. The space should be of adequate size and shape. It is best to avoid odd shaped areas; usually rectangular shapes are best. Occupancy on one floor or level is normally preferred for it is more convenient to travel 100 feet horizontally, than to travel 10 feet vertically, i.e., between floors.

It is advisable to estimate future space requirements and to take

FIGURE 16–1
Chart Used to Determine Office Location Selection

	Excellent	*Good*	*Fair*	*Poor*
1. Adaptability of space	60	45	30	15
Is the space adaptable to the needs of the office? Is there room for expansion?				
2. Building facilities.	60	45	30	15
Are entranceways, wiring arrangements, outlets, ducts, fire protection, and other *fixed* facilities adequate?				
3. The proximity of office building to business factors	44	33	22	11
Is the building near to customers; to transportation facilities; to shopping centers, restaurants, and hotels; and to mail facilities?				
4. The cost involved.	40	30	20	10
Is the rate reasonable and in keeping with competitive prices?				
5. Natural lighting and ventilating provided	28	21	14	7
Is the exposure on the north, east, south, or west? Does it have large glass areas? Do windows face the street or open lots? Are ceilings high?				
6. Characteristics of the building	24	18	12	6
Does the building have a favorable appearance, good name and address that are easy to pronounce and remember, and adequate floor load and ceiling height?				
7. Freedom from dirt and noise	24	18	12	6
Is the general area free from dirt and noise? Is the area itself clean and quiet?				
8. Stability of tenants.	20	15	10	5
Do tenants of the building tend to stay put (are moving and transferring the exception)?				
Maximum total.	300	225	150	75

these estimates into account in considering the space adaptability. The data can be listed vertically showing by columns the identity—private office, computer, filing, and so forth; the number of units, the square feet of floor space required per unit, and the total space requirement per identity and for the total office.

Future requirements mean more than just securing space greater than that needed for current requirements. Consideration must be given to where and how future changes will alter present space provisions. Usually, future considerations are taken care of either by leasing entire floors and subleasing what is not now required or by securing options on adjoining areas. Some office executives feel it is desirable to provide space arrangements to accommodate at least five years of future expectations or the time specified in the lease.

The difference between a site's "rental space" and "usable space" should be noted. Usually, one pays for rental space, which is the area measured between the inside surfaces of the outer boundaries. It includes areas for columns, projections, pilasters, and window arrangements necessary to the building. The usable space is the effective area which can be used for the office and commonly is 80–85 percent of the rental space.

The Building Facilities

A building facility includes any device or feature incorporated in or attached to the building which assists in using the space with convenience and efficiency. It must be fastened to the building, or installation is required to finish the building. Representative are entranceways, elevators, stairways, wiring arrangements, air conditioning, hallways, columnar spacing, janitor closets, water accessibility, noise control features, means of fire protection, and other fixed facilities.

Adequate wiring facilities are a big consideration in building facilities today. Separate runways handle (1) low voltage for telephone and communication systems, and (2) high voltage for normal electrical current. Most older buildings are wired for service far below modern needs especially where machines and lighting demands are high. Either new conduits on the floor surface or a new type of wire replacing the old wire can be used to meet modern requirements. In new buildings the wiring needs are met by using cellular steel subfloors buried in the concrete floor as illustrated in detail by Figure 16–2. This construction provides a network of channels accessible to every part of the total space. A telephone or an electric power connection is never more than 5 feet away. Also, unobstructed underflow ducts for heating and air conditioning as well as channels for main power lines, and telephone cables, are supplied. This is shown by the bottom illustration of Figure 16–2.

Construction and remodeling work is subject to building code requirements, which specify the design and the type of construction that is permitted. Use of certain materials may be forbidden, or stated design principles must be followed for certain structural parts. To reduce the fire hazard, it may be required that all buildings have at least two entranceways. In most building codes some flexibility is provided, certain alternatives and choices being designated. Portions of some building codes have remained the same for a number of years, while others have been modified from time to time. Code requirements are enacted and enforced usually by local government.

Proximity of Office Building to Business Factors

Four important factors should be given careful consideration when the office location decision concerns the location of the building itself.

FIGURE 16–2

Top Left: **Close-Up of Cellular Floor Construction;** *Top Right:* **Components of Telephone Outlet Fitting;** *Bottom:* **Suggested Arrangement for Use of Cellular Floor for Telephone, Power, and Air Needs**

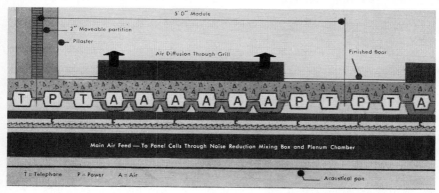

Courtesy: Inland Steel Co., Chicago.

First, the closeness to customers and to others in the same business as yourself. Closeness to customers is generally advantageous. This is a major consideration when personal interviews and associations are frequent, but relatively minor when activities with customers are mainly by telephone or by correspondence. Also, closeness to others in the same line is viewed with favor. This closeness encourages discussions of common problems among occupants, helps simplify the problems of the building manager, and adds to the convenience of customers and clients dealing with occupants of the building. There is, for example, a tendency for offices of financial houses, law firms, real estate firms, insurance agencies, and public utilities to locate in buildings in the financial district. Also, in many cities, specialized buildings to accommodate particular types of business offices are available.

The second factor, transportation facilities, emphasize convenient and low-cost means of getting to and from the building and should be available not only to employees but also to outside representatives, visitors, and delivery and messenger people. Out-of-the-way places, necessitating difficult drives, limited parking, long waits for buses, trains, or taxicabs, are a distinct disadvantage.

The next factor is convenience to retail stores, restaurants, hotels, and motels. The availability of restaurants give employees and customers a selection of handy eating places for noon lunch, or for evening meals when overtime work is necessary. A lack of eating places might necessitate providing a company cafeteria or dining room. Also, nearness to hotels or motels is, in many cases, a distinct advantage in the location of an office.

Last is mail facilities which must be adequate and given consideration in the selection of an office location. Frequent pickups and deliveries, with convenient accessibility to a post office, can contribute very materially to operating efficiency.

The Cost Involved

The cost of office space is of cardinal importance; however, it should always be considered along with the other location factors discussed. The cost of office space is expressed in dollars per square foot per year. To illustrate, assume an office measures 30×40 feet and the rental is $5 per square foot. The cost per year is $30 \times 40 \times \$5$, which equals $6,000, or, on a monthly basis, $6,000 divided by 12 equals $500.

The cost per square foot varies with many factors, such as the size of the city and general business conditions; but in order to gain some idea of the range in rates, a high of around $15 to a low of around 50 cents per square foot can be used. The top figure represents space in the better locations and buildings of the larger cities, while the latter may be converted factory space in a relatively poor location. Included in the square foot cost are services such as air conditioning, running water, wall maintenance, and elevator service. In many respects, the price is subject to negotiation with regard to what is included.[1]

Natural Lighting and Ventilating Provided

Since lighting is very important in an office, the availability of daylight and the building facilities for providing artificial light deserve prime consideration. An area that provides much daylight is normally favorable. Exposures facing the north are generally preferred, as northern light is of a steady and soft type. Eastern exposures are next in preference, followed in order by southern and western exposures. Normally, the outside wall areas should utilize a maximum of glass area and be not less than one fifth of the floor area. Windows extending almost to the ceiling permit a maximum amount of natural light to reach the inner areas of the floor space. Artificial light, however, will also be required

---

[1] See also page 434 for discussion of "Provisions of Lease."

and for this purpose adequate fixtures, electrical outlets, and lighting provisions must either be available or be provided. Agreement on the amount of artificial light to be utilized and the cost of installing and maintaining the necessary fixtures is a further important consideration.

It is imperative that an office be well ventilated. Careful observation should be made of the prospective space area to determine if adequate ventilation is possible. Spaces with few windows, a small number of openings to air ducts, low ceilings, and window openings on inside courts normally do not provide sufficient ventilation. However, with air conditioning, many of these shortcomings can be overcome.

CHARACTERISTICS OF THE BUILDING

In considering a building's characteristics, decisions are made based on such factors as whether the building is modern or old and if its name is in good repute, its name and address are easy to pronounce and remember, it is well known, and offers adequate building services, including elevator service, janitor service, and night protection.

An important technical factor is the allowable floor live load. At least 75 pounds per square foot are needed and a value of 100 pounds is desirable for complete versatility of layout. The floor-to-ceiling heights should be a minimum of 8 feet; however, for large areas, 10–12 feet is more appropriate. Low ceilings create a feeling of congestion and make the office difficult to ventilate; high ceilings make lighting, noise-reducing, and heating efforts difficult. Furthermore, columnar spacing must be considered, for normally the main office partitions are joined to columns. A spacing of 20 x 20 feet or more is acceptable; spans less than 18 feet are normally unsatisfactory. Along the outside walls, a constant dimension of approximately 5 feet, center to center of window sections, or alternating windows and piers, expedites locating partitions and accommodating units of equipment.

Freedom from Dirt and Noise

Certain elements are extremely disturbing to office workers and should be avoided whenever possible. Dirt, smoke, and soot are objectionable, and their presence in an office location and area should be avoided. Street noises are bothersome and interfere with efforts of mental concentration. In addition, the surrounding tenants' types of businesses, with special reference to the amount of traffic and the operations performed, might also be important from the viewpoint of noise.

Stability of the Tenants

Generally it is considered advantageous to locate an office in a building where the tenants are stable. Frequent moves by tenants in and out, and alterations, are undesirable from the viewpoint of solid, substantial enterprises. Real estate companies, law firms, and financial houses are among the most stable. In some cases, their tenure in the same location extends for 25 years and longer. In contrast, manufacturers' agents and advertising agencies tend to move more frequently. However, many of these remain in the same location for 10 or 15 years; and while this is relatively less, it still reflects a strong element of stability.

OWN OR LEASE

Is it better to own or to lease? Like many decisions there are advantages to each course followed. For example, ownership permits the building to be tailor-made for the particular needs of the enterprise. Also, there is prestige for an enterprise in owning its own office building. The name of the enterprise can be used for the building, and the publicity value can be quite high. Further, a relatively safe investment is provided. An office building usually represents a fairly secure equity. In addition, permanency of location is obtained, thus permitting continuity of a desired location, name and address.

In contrast, the main advantages of leasing include freedom of top managers from care and worry in connection with ownership. The problems of building maintenance and repairs are avoided. The lessee retains financial flexibility and does not have large amounts of capital tied up in one relatively long-time investment. The company is free to invest any surplus in the most productive channels. Further, changes in office location can usually be made more freely. The enterprise is not wedded to one location. And for the small enterprise whose requirements are not elaborate, a satisfactory arrangement is supplied.

In the popular "sale and lease back" arrangement, an investor buys a building from a seller and in the same transaction gives the seller a long-term lease on the building. The seller continues to occupy the building, pays rent, and is free of the responsibility of building upkeep and operation. For the seller, the deciding issue to enter into a "sale and lease back" arrangement is financial position, especially that of taxes and desire for liquidity of capital. For the buyer, or investor, the arrangement provides a known income from a known source at an agreeable rate of return. In a variation of this plan, a builder will construct a new office building to the tenant's specifications and lease it to the tenant for a long period.

Provisions of Lease

A lease is a form of contract by which one party conveys real estate to another party for a period of time at a specified compensation. It is in effect for a stated period usually one, three, five, ten, or twenty years. Payments are usually made monthly. A lease can be of a standard form or it can be specially written. If the latter, the contents depend upon the type and value of the real estate involved and the number of subjects upon which the lessor and the lessee believe are advisable. Normally, the lessor provides janitor service, heat, running water, elevator service, window shades, and fire-protection apparatus. The owner usually has the right to change the name and street address of the building; designate all sources for sign painting, ice, towel service, and the like; have pass-keys to the premises; and enter the premises at all reasonable hours for inspection, repairs, and alterations. On the other hand, the lessee usually provides floor coverings, partitions, drapes, awnings, ventilators and fans, and intercommunication units, and normally has the right to remove them (paying the expense) at the expiration of the lease.

It is helpful to have the lease include building services, such as elevator, window washing, and daily cleaning services. Many leases (1) give the lessee the right to sublet or assign the lease, (2) provide for the tenant to pay for increased taxes and labor costs or for some agreed percentage thereof up to a certain stated limit or a stated maximum liability, (3) include a cancellation privilege by the lessee even though if exercised a penalty is incurred, and (4) grant the lessee the right to renew the lease at mutually agreeable terms and price.

Office Furniture

Office furniture makes up a very important part of the office physical environment. It has been termed the vital working tool of the office employee—a very apt description. Furniture adaptable to the needs of its user plays an important role in keeping good people on the job and in controlling costs. Suitable office furniture favorably influences the behavior of employees, economizes on the human exertion required, and reduces the time taken to perform the necessary operations. Since office furniture tends to be used for long periods and represents substantial expenditure, it should be selected with care.

Office Chairs

The office chair, a most important physical facility in an office, is personal to the employee and intimately affects the ease and comfort with which the work is done. Most office work is of a sedentary nature, a fact that further stresses the importance of the office chair. Certain features merit careful consideration. Vinyl upholstering is suitable for chairs in high traffic areas where a strong material with easy cleaning qualities is desired. Fabric upholstery offers cooler seating, a softer appearance and an extremely wide range of colors and patterns from which to choose. Leather provides elegance, comfort, and easy care. The seat cushion should not "bottom out" when occupied, but should provide a firmness that will support adequately. Caster wheels made from relatively hard material are usually best for use on carpeting, while casters of softer material should be used on composition tile and wood flooring. Glides are another consideration. They should protect floors and carpeting and resist corrosion or breaking. Among the many types of office chairs are the familiar straight-back chair, the swivel chair, chairs that tilt, the posture chair, plain or upholstered chairs, wood, plastic, or metal chairs, and chairs with or without armrests. Figure 16–3 shows various types of office chairs of modern and practical designs.

While all are important, the posture chair merits further discussion.

FIGURE 16–3
Contemporary Styled Office Chairs Featuring Rugged Construction, Lasting Beauty, and Comfort

Courtesy: Steelcase, Inc., Grand Rapids, Mich.

It is designed to tailor-fit the occupant and provide maximum seating comfort by means of three adjustments:

1. *The seat height*—so that the feet are comfortably placed on the floor and no undue pressure is present on the underside of the leg just above the knee.
2. *The backrest height*—so that support is provided the small or lumbar region of the back. The swivel joint of the backrest should be approximately one inch higher than the top of the hip bone.
3. *The backrest horizontal position*—so that the occupant can sit way back in the chair in a position that the body weight on the seat is supported by the underside leg muscles.

These adjustments are frequently not proper with the result that incorrect office seating even with posture chairs exists as illustrated by Figure

FIGURE 16–4
Examples of Common Incorrect Seating

Chair Too Low **Steady pressure on spine** **causes great fatigue.**	**Chair Back Too High** **No needed support to** **spine, causing slumping** **and a strain on back and** **shoulder muscles.**

16-4. When a posture chair is not adjusted properly, the advantages of this type chair are lost. What is equally important if not more so, is that the occupant must know how to sit in the posture chair and must sit that way—well back in the chair and using the back rest for needed support for the spine. The proper use of posture chairs improves the appearance of office employees, reduces fatigue, improves morale, and aids in the functioning of important body actions, including breathing, circulation, and elimination.

Office Desks

An office desk provides a work surface, a temporary storage for materials being processed, and a convenient area for selected tools and machines required in accomplishing the work. The trend in desk appearance is toward smooth, streamlined surfaces. Supports touching the floor are recessed in order to conceal them from view, to permit ample toe room when standing near the desk, and to facilitate cleaning the floor. Steel desks are equipped with linoleum or plastic; lighter colors and finishes seem to be preferred. Many wood desks are finished with light stain and bleached colors. Hardware and exposed metal parts are of dull finish to avoid annoying highlights.

The modern desk and its interior are planned to give maximum service to the user. Tailor-made desk drawer arrangements are available to aid work production. As new requirements arise, the drawers can be interchanged and rearranged as desired, they can be "programmed" to simplify and to aid in the kind of work to be done. Figure 16–5 suggests efficient arrangements of materials in desk drawers to meet specific requirements.

The person using the desk is all important. To achieve desk efficiency, these guides are offered: (1) work on one task at a time and finish it before starting another, (2) keep the desk free from excess papers and supplies—have only those items on the desk that are needed, (3) shelve materials that are not urgent, (4) act on important paperwork first, (5) strive to keep the work moving over the desk, and (6) dispose of all mail before going home.

Regarding desk design, a multitude of types are available to serve particular needs. Among the most popular are those for executives, junior executives, stenographers, typists, adding and calculating machine operators, and billing clerks. Desks are available in single- and double-pedestal styles. The pedestal is the support or foundation of the desk, and it contains the drawers or foldaway platform which houses a typewriter or some special machine. The single-pedestal desk is used in cases where a single tier of desk drawers and a smaller-size top are sufficient. Figure 16–6 illustrates two types of desks and pedestal options.

The "conference desk" has an oversized top that overhangs the pedestals at one or both ends and at the back. At meetings, it is possible for five or six people to sit comfortably around a conference desk, since

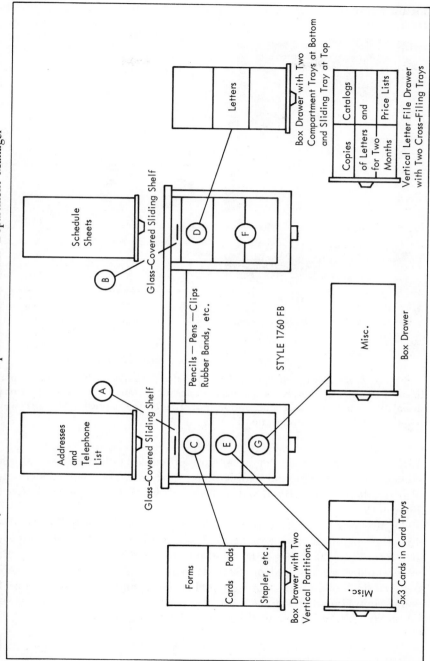

Box Drawer with Two Compartment Trays at Bottom and Sliding Tray at Top

Copies	Catalogs
of Letters	and
— for Two —	
Months	Price Lists

Vertical Letter File Drawer with Two Cross-Filing Trays

Letters

Schedule Sheets

Glass-Covered Sliding Shelf

B

D

F

Pencils — Pens — Clips
Rubber Bands, etc.

STYLE 1760 FB

Misc.

Box Drawer

Addresses and Telephone List

Glass-Covered Sliding Shelf

A

C

E

G

Forms

Cards Pads

Stapler, etc.

Box Drawer with Two Vertical Partitions

Misc.

5x3 Cards in Card Trays

Courtesy: Art Metal Construction Co., Jamestown, N.Y.

FIGURE 16–6
Desk Designs

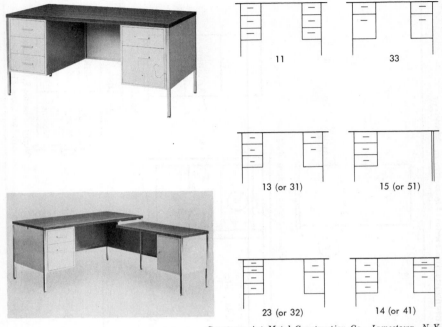

Courtesy: *Art Metal Construction Co., Jamestown, N.Y.*

Upper Left: General-purpose; *Lower Left:* L-shaped with machine platform. (To the right are shown desk pedestal options. The general-purpose desk illustrated has pedestal option no. 13. If the pedestal designs were reversed, it would be option no. 31.)

ample work space and leg room are provided. Other desks featuring contemporary design and emphasizing certain work conveniences are also available. An attractive functional desk of this type is shown in Figure 16–7.

Dimensions of desks vary with the type of desk, the material used, and the manufacturer. Executive desks, usually the largest, range in size from 76 × 36 inches to 60 × 30 inches being the most common. For general office work, sizes from 60 × 34 inches to 42 × 30 inches, but most new clerical office desks are 50 inches wide and 30 inches deep. In some companies certain sizes are specified for certain uses, as for example, the following in a well-known insurance company:

For Employee	*Desk-Top Size*
Department head	78 × 38 inches, triple overhang
Supervisor	60 × 36 inches, front overhang
Staff	55 × 30 inches or special-purpose desk
Clerical	50 × 30 inches

FIGURE 16–7
Functional Modern Design Desk

Courtesy: Herman Miller, Inc., Zeeland, Mich.

Desks are of various heights. The preferred height is 28½ or 29 inches because for the average employee, this height helps maximize the employee's comfort.

Modular Office Furniture

This type of furniture consists of easily and quickly assembled modular components which, when assembled, comprise an effective functional and modern arrangement. Basic units include such "building blocks" as desk tops, desk pedestals, auxiliary tops, end supports, and filing and shelving units. A support or housing for electronic equipment, or a comprehensive desk work area can be supplied by combining the proper components. A number of components are available; they are standard and interchangeable, thus supplying flexibility and many various combinations. One basic design features components suspended and attached from wall panels or partitions to form areas for writing, shelves, and cabinets as indicated in Figure 16–8.

Also specially designed desks, chairs, and storage units allow for a great variety of interchangeable combinations to meet the individual needs of an office and to serve as a basis for expandable office stations where a pleasing appearance and economy are wanted. See Figure 16–9. An interesting modular-type furniture is the Centiform which was initially developed for use in a bank, the intent was to make the customers feel they were with bank personnel who were genuinely friendly and were not inhibited in their communicating by office furniture of standard

FIGURE 16–8
A Modern and Effective Office Space Featuring Work Surfaces, Shelves, Lights and Bins Suspended from Wall Panels, and a Free-Standing Desk— a Design Permitting Flexibility and a Highly Pleasing Appearance

Courtesy: Herman Miller, Inc., Zeeland, Mich.

design. An open, yet closed, effect was sought because customers want to see their banker, but they also want privacy. Figure 16–10 shows the Centiform which offers the facilities of four private offices, yet occupies less floor space than four desks, cabinets, and chairs. Each work station includes a cork board and light fixture, a clothes closet for customer convenience, file drawers, and shelving for storage. Note the traditional desk is replaced with the nonformal conference table and an ample writing area is provided to the back and side of the unit. A variety of arrangements is possible. Figure 16–11 shows an arrangement for seven stations.

OFFICE LIGHTING

The physical environment of an office is also influenced by the major spatial conditioning factors of light, color, music and sound, and air.

FIGURE 16-9
Attractive Modular Office Work Stations Permitting Privacy, Yet Smoothing Out Traffic Patterns and Increasing Efficiency

Courtesy: Haskell of Pittsburgh, Inc., Pittsburgh.

These are taken into account by the manager during organizing efforts—that part dealing with supplying the proper work environment. Quite commonly the services of specialists in these factors are utilized, but the office manager should be familiar with the basic knowledge and practices in each area. We start our discussion with light.

Adequate light is essential to the successful office. Many office tasks require much reading of material that is of small print. Good light of sufficient quantity, diffusion, and brightness, is mandatory.

The quantity of light is expressed in footcandles. *The amount of light one foot distant from a standard candle* is defined as a footcandle. For quick conversion, one watt per square foot of area provides 15 footcandles. Thus, a 100-watt bulb in an area 10 feet by 10 feet provides 15 footcandles of light. Recommended quantities of light are shown in Figure 16-12.

Diffusion of light is required in order for an object to be clearly and easily seen by the human eye. Good light is not absolutely uniform. Delicate contrasts and shadows provide variety and this effect is normal to the eye. In contrast, harsh, strong, contrasting shadows are annoying and should be avoided. Well-diffused light is sometimes referred to as a "soft" light. Proper diffusion of light is obtained by having light in different amounts come from an adequate number of sources and directions. The big challenge is how to add variety but preserve the proper

FIGURE 16–10
The Centiform Arrangement Providing Privacy Yet Promoting an
Environment of Friendliness

Courtesy: Lehigh-Leopold Furniture Co., New York.

lighting for each task and a feeling of lighting unity for an entire large
area. Light must be supplied discreetly. The light need not be monotonous in order to supply the amount required. Certain parts of the
area may need an emphasis of light which can be supplied by a vertical
surface, a planter, a wall, a picture, or even drapes over a window
opening to give a warm sunlight effect.

Brightness is determined by the amount of light reflected from an
object. For light itself to be seen, it must be *associated with surfaces.*
It is the light reflected from the surface that enables a human being
to see. Contrast is necessary. For an object to be seen, it must stand
out from all other things around it. This quality to reflect light is termed
reflectance value and is the ratio of the light a surface reflects divided
by the amount of light it receives. The finish of the surface, its color,
and type of material are major influences regulating the reflectance value.
Recommended reflectances for the office are ceiling, 82–90; wall, 45–55;
desk top, 28–42; and floor, 22–38. These values are higher than normally

FIGURE 16–11
The Centiform Offers a Variety of Arrangements

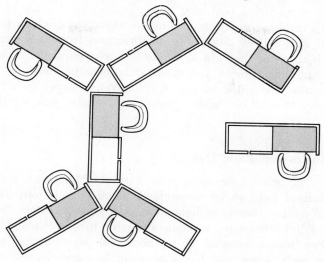

Courtesy: Lehigh-Leopold Furniture Co., New York.

found which means that many office areas are improperly lighted, not because of the fixtures or amount of light supplied, but because the office surfaces do not reflect the light sufficiently for good seeing conditions.

Brightness is also important because it controls contrast, which affects seeing. The human eye sees best when the general areas within its field of vision, such as a desk and its immediate surroundings, are ap-

FIGURE 16–12
Recommended Values of Illumination for Office Work

Type of office or work	Footcandles recommended on working area
Detailed drafting and designing	200
Difficult seeing tasks	150
such as auditing and accounting, business machine operation, transcribing and tabulating, and bookkeeping	
Ordinary seeing tasks	100
such as private office work, general correspondence, and work in conference rooms, active file rooms, and mail rooms	
Casual seeing tasks	30
such as in inactive file rooms, reception rooms, stairways, washrooms and other service areas	

Source: Illuminating Engineering Society, New York.

proximately of the same brightness. An undesirable situation is that in which the light is concentrated on the desk area, and the surroundings are dark, a condition requiring eye adjusting to the bright and dark areas with resultant eye fatigue. For the visual area, which is generally described as about 30 degrees in all directions from the eye, the ratio of the brightness of the light source to its background should not exceed 3 to 1. Lighting fixtures and their arrangements influence this ratio. Needed contrast is aided by use of color. White paper on a black desk top is easy to see, but white paper on a white desk top is difficult to see.

Light Sources and Basic Designs

Sources of office lighting include natural, fluorescent, and filament bulbs. Natural light varies throughout the day and from day to day, and usually other sources of light must be used to maintain the required amount of light. Even so, it seems advisable to have natural light even as a minor source because of its beneficial psychological effects. An employee feels better and has a sense of less confinement when able to look out occasionally and see daylight, observe the weather, and the like.

Fluorescent light is the major source of office light. It closely resembles natural light and provides large amounts of illumination at relatively low operating costs. To illustrate, the light output of a 40-watt fluorescent tube is more than twice that of a 40-watt filament bulb, and further, distributes the light more uniformly.

Filament bulb is still an important source of artificial lighting. Improvements in filament-bulb shape, type of glass, and length of life have been achieved. However, this light source has objectionable characteristics including the yellowish color of this light, the large number of bulbs that are necessary to supply a sufficient quantity of light, and the heat generated from these masses of bulbs.

Sources of light are classified as either (1) general lighting or (2) supplementary lighting. In the former, the entire area is lighted to a prescribed level of illumination. The second consists of illuminating a relatively small area, like a desk top or a portion of an office machine.

The five basic designs of lighting systems are: (1) direct, (2) semidirect, (3) indirect, (4) semi-indirect and (5) general diffuse. Under direct lighting, light from the luminaire is permitted to travel directly to the working surface. This gives a "hard" type of light, and diffusion is not too good. Generally, it is the least preferred type.

Semidirect lighting allows some of the light from the luminaire to travel upward to the ceiling, whence it is reflected downward to the working area. Most of the light, however, travels downward directly to the working area. A semidirect system illuminates the ceiling and lessens the effect of deep shadows.

In the case of indirect lighting, the light travels upward to the ceiling, where it is reflected downward to the working area. This provides a light which is "soft" and relatively free from sharp shadows. For this type, the ceiling should have a high reflectance value. In fact, it is quite possible that the ceiling may be too bright giving rise to some glare and light distraction to the employee.

With semi-indirect lighting, most of the light travels upward to the ceiling and then down to the work area, but some of the light is allowed to travel directly downward. As with indirect lighting, the ceiling is, in effect the main source of light. The direct light helps increase the amount of light on the work area, but consideration must be given to its possible contribution of objectionable shadows and glare.

Under general diffuse lighting, about one half of the light on the working surface comes directly from the lighting unit; the remainder is contributed by reflection from the ceiling and upper wall areas. Commonly a large enclosing globe identifies this type. The globe assists in diffusing the light. Normally, this type should not be used to provide high levels of illumination since the globe may become too bright both for the direct and the reflected light.

Generally speaking, with fluorescent lighting, it is more comfortable to view the fixtures *crosswise,* not lengthwise. Especially is this true in a large office. In a small office, this consideration is relatively unimportant. However, there is one important exception—the use of luminous-sided fixtures with glass or plastic sides. These units should be viewed lengthwise for greatest comfort, regardless of the area size.

Some uniformity or symmetry of the lighting fixtures is usually desirable for better general appearance. The arrangement should bring out the architectural and decorative features that assist in producing a cheerful working environment. Long rows of fixtures may be interrupted or designed with an occasional break, but the foremost considerations are adequate quantity with proper diffusion in a coordinated lighting system. Fixtures can be suspended from the ceiling or recessed into it. The design of having the ceiling completely luminous is also popular. For this purpose, "floating-panel luminaires" can be used. They are economical, easy to install, and create a pleasant atmosphere. Figure 16–13 shows an installation of this design.

Office Lighting as an Investment

Expenditures for proper office lighting represent a sound investment. A well-coordinated lighting system represents about 2 percent of total operating costs of a large office, compared with 0.5 percent normally

FIGURE 16–13
An Office with Ceiling Completely Luminous Supplies Effective Light

Courtesy: Illuminating Engineering Society, New York.

spent for obsolete, inadequate lighting. This increase of 1½ percent is minute when related to all the comfort, greater accuracy, and psychological advantages of proper office lighting. An it is even more so when compared with office productivity where many studies show up to 20 percent gain obtained from providing proper lighting.

Maintenance has a significant bearing on any lighting investment. The practice of replacing bulbs on a regularly scheduled basis is gaining favor. This simplifies maintenance and maintains proper lighting levels. Also needed are periodic cleaning of the luminaires, proper wattage of bulbs, and correct voltage. In one study involving eight locations, the footcandle output was raised from an average of 11.8 to 46.2 footcandles, or an increase of over 350 percent, by cleaning the dirty fixtures, using color of high reflecting value for the walls and keeping them clean, replacing aging bulbs, and supplying the correct voltage.

COLOR CONDITIONING IN THE OFFICE

Color not only beautifies an office but also improves conditions under which office work is performed. It is now well established that color affects the human emotions, senses, and thought processes. For example, color usually has an important influence upon one's blood pressure and disposition to relax. A certain color will impress the minds of some individuals with a particularly favorable feeling or thought; another color will have the opposite effect. Some colors give a lift; others impart a depressed feeling. Some tend to hasten mental action, others to retard it. An interesting illustration is from a New England office where during August the walls were painted blue. The following winter, the employees complained of the office being cold, even though the normal temperature of 70 degrees was maintained. Then, the temperature was raised to 75 degrees, but complaints continued. The blue walls were than redecorated to warm yellow and green. The temperature continued at 75 degrees. Now the employees protested that the office was too warm. A return to the temperature of 70 degrees resulted in the ceasing of the complaints.

Selection of Colors

The general color scheme of an office can follow one of many arrangements, depending upon individual preferences. Color is an excellent medium to express individual preferences. However, a proper color balance is normally wanted, and this means the use of a few colors correctly, not a variety haphazardly. The monochromatic approach is popular. This describes the use of various shades of one color for floors, walls, and draperies, together with one bright accent color. As a beginning point, the desk is selected in a particular color. With this basic color determined, the floor covering is selected to harmonize correctly with the desk. Then, lighter shades of the floor covering can be used for walls and draperies. The accent color can be in the chair or accessories such as pictures, desk pieces, and lamps. Figure 16–14 gives some helpful suggestions.

Additional specific color suggestions include for (1) the general office—having ceilings in white or ivory, walls in soft, cool colors with one or more of the walls in a warm color such as light yellow, (2) the conference room—light and neutral colors with some carefully utilized strong colors, (3) the reception room—neutral colors are usually best, try to avoid severe contrasts, and (4) corridors—use light colors to give more light in the area.

The use of a color wheel can aid in selecting the proper color for an office. Figure 16–15 shows a color wheel. The primary colors are red, yellow, and blue; they are located on the wheel at equally spaced distances. Secondary colors are obtained by mixing adjacent colors on the wheel. For example, red and yellow give orange. Colors directly opposite each other on the wheel are complementary. Green, for example, is

FIGURE 16–14
Suggested Color Guide for an Office

When Desk Is–	Use Carpet of–	Use Walls of–	Use Draperies of–	Use Chair, also Pictures, Desk Accessories, and Lamps of–
Gray	Gray	White	Gray	Red
Gray	Rust brown	Light gray	Rust	Yellow
Walnut or mahogany	Green	Beige	Chartreuse	Dark yellow
Walnut or mahogany	Beige	Light blue	Light blue	Dark yellow
Bleached or blond finish	Light brown	Beige	Beige	Orange
Bleached or blond finish	Charcoal	Gray	Yellow	Coral

the complement of red; blue, of orange. Toward the center of the wheel are the grayer shades which color experts use to minimize the possibility of color violence. The main ways to secure pleasant and harmonious color effects are first, use complementary colors such as red and green, i.e., those colors directly opposite each other on the color wheel; second,

FIGURE 16–15
A Color Wheel, Showing Relationhip of Primary Colors—Red, Yellow, and Blue

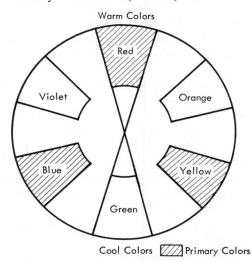

Secondary colors are made by mixing adjacent colors named on the wheel. A combination of all the colors shown produces a neutral gray.

split complementary colors by using the two colors adjacent to the direct complement of the third color. To illustrate, green-blue and green-yellow will be effective when complementing red. Third, select three colors equidistant from each other such as red, yellow, and blue. Such a combination gives a satisfactory color effect.

The relationship between color and lighting is interesting. As stated previously, color has a significant influence upon the lighting of an office. Light colors increase and dark colors decrease the lighting intensity. This is because light colors reflect the light rays, whereas dark colors absorb the light rays. For these reasons, any normally dark area will lighten up when lighter colors are used for the ceilings, walls, and floors. In addition, the use of color influences the apparent proportions of an area. This is due to the reflecting and the contracting light effect brought about by the different colors. Dark colors seem to advance an area, light colors to retreat it. Hence, the dimensional effect of a long narrow room can be changed by the use of a dark color on the end walls and a lighter shade of the same color, or of a harmonizing hue, on the other walls.

MUSIC CONDITIONING AND SOUND CONDITIONING

Music serves as an environmental aid because the physiological and psychological power of music may be used to produce and improve the behavior pattern. Music can make you alert or relaxed, happy or blue. "Music while you work" programs are designed to improve working conditions, relieve mental and visual fatigue, reduce nervous tension, and make the employees feel better in general. Such programs are popular and they are effective.

In general, the types of office work showing the maximum benefits from music are filing, mail room, reception, keypunching, verifying, and typing. Common gains also include a decrease in absenteeism of from 5 to 10 percent, a reduction in clerical errors of 30–35 percent, and a noticeable lessening of nonessential employee conversations.

The music is specifically arranged, orchestrated, and recorded to accomplish a given goal. Distracting and attention-getting music, such as heavy brass effects and solos, is excluded. The music is stimulating and designed to fit the specific office work as well as the temperament of the employees. The music is to be enjoyed subconsciously; the employee doesn't actively listen to it. During the first part of the morning the music may consist of a bright opener followed by moderately bright music, such as several waltzes. Music of maximum stimulus is played during late morning and afternoon. The music is played for specific intervals only because best results are usually obtained from this type of pattern. It is either "piped" from a central sending studio, or a self-contained unit providing the music is installed in the office. The expense is nominal and is paid either on a per diem basis or at a monthly rate per employee.

Sound conditioning ranks high on the list of spatial conditioning factors. A noisy office is seldom an efficient office for its annoying distractions make for difficulty in concentrating, in using the telephone, and in turning out accurate office work. So-called "getting used to noise" is misleading. One may temporarily be unaware of its effects; but over a period, one becomes excessively fatigued and irritable as a result of noise.

The chief characteristics of sound are (1) pitch-frequency of the vibrations, (2) intensity—the energy of the vibrations, (3) quality—the mode or type of vibration, (4) reverberation—the sustaining qualities after the sound has stopped at its source, and (5) the expectancy and acceptance of the individual. Of greatest concern is loudness, which is primarily determined by both intensity and pitch, with emphasis on intensity. To have a relative measurement of the range of sound intensities, a unit of measurement called a "decibel" is used. The decibel scale ranges from 0 to 110. A quiet office will register about 37 decibels, the large stenographic room about 70 decibels, a boiler factory 97 decibels, and thunder 110 decibels.

Office noise can be controlled in a number of ways. An effective means is to locate the office in a quiet space. The top floors of a building or areas not exposed directly to noise sources are recommended. In addition, when practical the sources of office noise can be segregated from the rest of the office. Locate noisy machines in a separate room or in an area off to one side. Also, it helps to place felt pads or rubber cushions under typewriters, calculators, and other types of machines. Soundproofing cabinets are available, they stop noise at the machine. The cabinet resembles a hood and fits the contour and noise output of the particular model of office machine. Furthermore, sound-absorbing materials can be used for office ceilings, walls, and floors. Carpets, for example, eliminate virtually all floor noise. Also, drapes and curtains made of soft fabrics help to absorb noise. Sound travels in waves and is reflected from glazed or nonporous surfaces in the same way that light is reflected. Sound continues to travel in all directions and bounces back and forth until its energy is absorbed, a condition making for a noisy office. Lastly, but by no means least, appeals to employees can be made, stressing consideration for others and the importance of eliminating unnecessary conversations.

AIR CONDITIONING

True air conditioning regulates four basic atmospheric conditions—temperature, circulation, moisture content, and cleanliness. It is possible to control only one or several of these conditions, but such control is more correctly termed partial air conditioning. Either a central or individual units can be used. Varying sizes and capacities are available. Individual units for a small group of offices or for part of a floor area have grown in popularity. Some are designed for a single room and are portable. The cost of air conditioning is reasonable and it is well worth the expenditure because it aids health and comfort, helps to maintain consistent and satisfactory productivity, and reduces cleaning and decorating costs.

Let us look at the four basic atmospheric conditions more closely. First is temperature. It is too high in most offices. This leads to discomfort and drowsiness. Regulators should be installed on heating apparatus so that excessive temperatures are not reached. It is well to become "thermometer-conscious" and to keep the office temperature within reasonable limits, that is, around 72 degrees Fahrenheit, or 22 degrees Centigrade. If air conditioning is used, the recommended temperature range is from 70 to 85 degrees Fahrenheit, depending upon the outside temperature. Too great a differential between outside and air conditioned areas is undesirable.

Lack of proper ventilation can make a person feel sleepy and unduly tired. At 70 degrees Fahrenheit, an adult human body at rest gives off a small amount of heat, which must be carried off by the surrounding air; otherwise, the body becomes unduly heated. The normal ventilation requirement is about 2,000 cubic feet of air per person per hour. Drafts should be avoided. Usually, the best practice is to have the air circulating from a number of outlets so that it is distributed evenly over the entire area. For nonair-conditioned areas, fans and window ventilators help considerably in providing adequate ventilation. The practice of opening windows and airing the office for short, stated periods during midmorning, noon, and midafternoon does much toward expelling stale air and freshening up the office.

Humidity, or the amount of moisture in the air, definitely affects the comfort and efficiency of a human being. At the same temperature, moist air feels hot and dry air feels cool. Excessive dampness may cause physical discomfort of a respiratory nature and induce a heavy, languid feeling. Likewise, excessive dryness or very low humidity frequently induces a feeling of parchedness and nervous irritability. "Relative humidity", the term used to describe the intensity of moisture saturation in the air, should be for the typical office from 40 to 60 percent. When it is below this amount, the office air is too dry; when it is above, the air is too moist.

The last condition, cleanliness, needs no elaboration. Clean records, better operating conditions for machines, lower office maintenance, and working in a clean, pollen-free area are highly desirable.

QUESTIONS

1. Enumerate the major advantages in a company owning its office building. The major disadvantages.
2. Discuss several important aspects or features of office desks with which you feel a competent office manager should be thoroughly familiar.
3. Does the supplying of a posture chair insure that the office employee who occupies it will have good posture while seated? Why?
4. What are some important features to take into account when acquiring chairs for an office?
5. Select two office buildings in the community in which you now live, and make a survey to determine their suitability with respect to (*a*) the characteristics of the building, (*b*) the cost involved, (*c*) the adaptability of the space, and (*d*) freedom from dirt and noise for each of the following prospective tenants:

   a. A sales representative requiring desk space and a room for small samples.
   b. An insurance office requiring a total of about 1,800 square feet, including a reception room, a room about 15 × 25 feet for salespeople, and general office space.
   c. A medical doctor who needs a reception room, an examining room, and, if possible, a small room to one side for records and a library.

   Write your results in a suitable form, using a sentence outline type of presentation.
6. In your own words explain how the chart in Figure 16–1 is used.
7. Mr. Ron Costello has received estimates from different contractors to modernize his general office space. The lighting fixture installer believes productivity will increase some 20 percent due to improved lighting. The air-conditioning people state it is common for their commercial customers to experience 15 percent or greater productive increase due to the comforts offered by air conditioning. The painting contractor states that the newly decorated walls and ceiling will have a favorable effect upon the work done by the employees. He estimates a gain of at least 12 percent. Does this mean that Mr. Costello can expect a productivity increase of 47 percent as a result of his improved lighting, air conditioning, and newly painted general office? Justify your answer.
8. Of the five major factors of physical working conditions in an office, which one do you believe is most important? Justify your answer.
9. Discuss the relationship between color and the lighting of an office. Between sound and music in an office.
10. Define each of the following:
    a. Rental space.
    b. Allowable floor live load.
    c. Monochromatic approach in color selection.
    d. "Soft" light.
11. An office manager heard many favorable comments concerning the adoption of "music while you work" in various offices. Believing this might be desirable in her office, she arranged, through the office supervisors,

to ask her entire office force if they would like to work to music. The response was overwhelmingly in favor of having music. Accordingly, the office manager purchased a wide selection of long-playing records and two record-playing machines—one machine for each of the two main office areas. What benefits or difficulties do you feel might result from the office manager's action. Explain your answer.

12. Select two companies that have moved their offices within the last two years. Find out the reasons for each locating where they did. What conclusions do you draw from your study?

CASE PROBLEMS

Case 16–1. Nikko-Sanwon Chemical Company

This company, an integrated manufacturer of vinyl plastics, produces and sells three major categories of such plastics, including (1) vinyl chloride polymer resins, (2) "PUC" compounds, and (3) calendared vinyl sheeting and polyethylene film. These products are used in a variety of applications such as insulation for wire, flooring, toy components, luggage, and bookbinding.

The sales office of the company is located in the Merchandise Mart, near the Loop in Chicago. In this office, 12 salespeople and 26 clerical personnel are employed. The office is convenient for buyers and is a prestige location where a representative can bring customers and impress them favorably. In addition, "the Mart" is very accessible for employees, who can live in any part of the greater Chicago area and reach the office without trouble.

One of four manufacturing plants of the company is located in the southwest area of the city, some nine miles from the Loop area. Adjacent to this plant is a large warehouse which was constructed two years ago. There is ample space available in the warehouse to house the sales offices, now in the Merchandise Mart. In the opinion of Mr. Tashio Umeda, president of the company, the sales office should be removed to the warehouse. This would reduce overhead and consolidate Chicago operations in one location. However, through Mr. Leonard Griffin, the vice president of sales, Mr. Umeda discovers that many of the salespeople and office personnel do not favor such a move. Some of them have stated that they will quit if the move takes place.

Mr. Umeda strongly feels that the move would be best for the company from the long-range viewpoint. However, he wishes to retain all his present employees if this is possible and suggests that the company (1) reduce the working hours to 7½ hours daily from the present 8 hours, but keep the pay the same; (2) establish a free service to assist employees to find satisfactory housing quarters in the southwest area of the greater Chicago area; and (3) organize car pools, with the company compensating the employees whose cars are used.

Questions:

1. What additional information do you feel appropriate for Mr. Umeda to consider before reaching a decision on whether to move the sales office?

2. Outline the program of action that you recommend Mr. Umeda take. Substantiate your recommendations.

Case 16–2. Heffern Company

At the last meeting of Heffern Company's executives, approval for modernizing the office facilities was granted. Appointment of an interior decorator, Abrail Antoine, was confirmed and she was to work with a newly appointed committee consisting of the office manager, the controller, and the personnel manager. After several weeks, Ms. Antoine submitted a very attractive plan and sketches of the "new office." Difficulty was the estimated cost which was three times what the committee was authorized to spend. Ms. Antoine stressed that the present walnut wood desks should be discarded, and recommended that carpeting be installed to reduce the noise and add to the appearance of the office. It was her contention that unless a properly coordinated job was done, the renovating efforts would look like an unfinished job. "You really can't do anything with those old desks," she explained. "They don't go with anything in the office and they neither are modern nor do they give a progressive impression to the office."

The committee members took her comments quite well, but contended the problem was one of cost. The members are inclined to go ahead with what they can afford with the funds available. The office manager suggested they might consider making a survey of present equipment and limit purchases to what was most in need of replacement. Several suppliers contacted had indicated they had followed such a plan in other offices and would gladly make such a survey free of charge and give an allowance as part payment on the new equipment. The personnel manager, however, objected to this plan, explaining that for an office employee with a new desk and chair to work alongside an employee with an old desk and chair might cause difficulty and some misunderstanding among employees.

The idea was also advanced that either new desks only or new chairs only be purchased. But disagreement over which should be purchased existed among the committee members. One committee member strongly advocated new desks, since these provide the working areas, are in full view, and contribute a great deal toward improving the general appearance of an office. In contrast, it was pointed out that a new comfortable chair probably would mean more to an employee and would result in more favorable comments by the employees.

With all these alternatives, Ms. Antoine disagreed violently. She stated any deviation from installing a completely renovated office from the floor up would be throwing money away. It will never look right, she contended, and the improved working environment will be sacrificed.

About a week later, a committee meeting was called by the personnel manager who announced that Ms. Antoine has resigned from the assignment given her by the Heffern Company. He stated the resignation came as a surprise. He feels that perhaps the project of office modernization should be held in abeyance pending the availability of more money and of time to give adequate thought to the project. However, both the office manager and the controller rejected any delay. They believe a beginning must be made now. In the words of the office manager, "I've been spearheading this project for nearly two years. To delay it now will mean burial of the whole program indefinitely."

Questions:

1. Evaluate the viewpoints of Ms. Antoine. Of the personnel manager. Of the office manager.
2. What additional alternatives are available to the company? Discuss.
3. What action should be taken? Justify your viewpoint.

Case 16–3. Webb Company

Office manager Ivan Burger believes that ventilating, heating, and air conditioning are probably the most important elements which affect office behavioral attitudes. Complaints by employees about the lack of ventilation have been frequent and lately have grown in intensity.

During the last several months as sort of an interesting hobby, Mr. Burger has from time to time noted the office temperature as well as the relative humidity. For nearly 75 percent of his readings, the temperature has been 80 degrees Fahrenheit or more and in about 45 percent of the cases the relative humidity has exceeded 60 percent. Conversations with heating and ventilating suppliers confirm that the office can be made confortable the year round. Quotations for necessary equipment installed range from $18,485 to $27,120. Annual estimates for operating the equipment are from $800 to $1,050.

Mr. Burger feels that the installing of adequate heating, ventilating, and air conditiong would prove to be a good investment. He judges, for example, that office employee productivity would increase at least 10 percent. He bases this increase on a spot review of records of summer absenteeism in his office reportedly caused by weather conditions; his observation of time being wasted during a hot, humid spell; and the slow pace that prevails during uncomfortable days. There is a total of 15 nonmanagerial employees whose average weekly wage is $93.77.

Mr. Burger's superior, Mr. Bert Bleyer, claims that if installation of the equipment is to be justified on the basis of increasing employee productivity, the best decision is to forget the whole proposition. "Ivan, let me tell you something," stated Mr. Bleyer. "You won't get any more work after installing that equipment than you are getting now. They know what is expected of them and on certain days they may have to work a little harder. People adapt to their office environment. On certain days they expend more energy for the same amount of work than on other days. Personally, I would not give too much weight to complaints. If they aren't griping about no air conditioning, they will be complaining about the office machine not working properly, too many telephone call interruptions, or something."

Mr. Burger replied that there certainly were intangibles involved—risks are inherent. In his mind an overruling consideration was whether the company had available money for an expenditure like this. A comfortable place to work could hardly be called a luxury.

To these comments, Mr. Bleyer responded quickly with, "We've got the money. If you decide to go ahead, we can finance it."

Questions:

1. Evaluate the concepts advanced by Mr. Bleyer.
2. Do you feel Mr. Burger is justified in deciding whether to install the heating, ventilating, and air conditioning in the office? Justify your viewpoint.
3. What decision should Mr. Burger make? Why?

Chapter 17

Organizing and Physical Environment (continued)

Progress implies resistance—something to work against.

William Feather

An important part of supplying the proper work environment remains to be discussed—bringing together the various office units and spatial conditioning factors into a coordinated physical arrangement. Commonly referred to as "office space management," it emphasizes effective utilization of space. Included is more than simply locating machines and furniture conveniently. It is this plus facilitating a good flow of work, assisting supervision, adding to the employee's comfort, and providing for future expansion or contraction. Formally stated, office space utilization is *the arrangement of all physical components within the available floor space to provide maximum effectiveness and the coordination of these components into an efficient and attractive unity.*

It is wise to recognize that office space utilization is not all technical. Dimensions, work flows, percentages of effective space, and the like are used, but in addition to these data, the managerial climate, principal likes, and attitudes are taken into account. For example, answers to basic questions such as these are needed: What image or impression should the space convey? Which is most important—cost, prestige, or appearance? Are functions performed or organization status or some other consideration to dictate the location and design of private offices?

FUNDAMENTAL SPACE CONSIDERATIONS

Effective use of office space is a continuous asset. It contributes daily to office efficiency and pleasure by helping to keep operating costs at

459

a minimum and contributing to the work quality, employee satisfaction, and services provided. Space needs change with time, however, and most companies benefit from an examination and reexamination of their present office layouts. There is no "good" or "bad" arrangement, for if a perfect layout existed, most would follow that arrangement. The optimum layout is the one that meets best the individual requirements of its user. This means that the "right" layout changes with time for each company.

Space utilization changes arise mainly when (1) a new or modified system or procedure is adopted, (2) an increase or decrease in either work or personnel is made, (3) a change in organization is made—either adding or taking away from a unit, and (4) complaints from employees are heard about their work areas suggesting elimination of the poor areas that infest the office layout.

It is helpful to observe that most large offices are made up of four separate types of areas, including (1) private offices, (2) general office area, (3) service areas, and (4) storage areas. By keeping these in mind, an overall viewpoint of the layout is maintained, proper balance of the layout is aided, and the essentials for each type of area are included. Also revealed will be the fact that in many offices only about one-half of the total floor area is employed for direct productive purposes.

In order of their increasing difficulty, office layouts are for either new, remodeled, or currently used areas. New areas normally permit the most effective space utilization; completely coordinated space planning is possible. The next group—remodeled areas—sometimes poses difficult-to-solve problems, in that the building facilities are inadequate or the space modernization is incomplete. Finally, the planning of existing areas for space improvement can be both fascinating and frustrating, in that considerable improvement in space utilization can usually be brought about, but certain rigidities prevent a desired level of space efficiency being attained.

Effective office layouts result from unfettered thought. Think first of Utopia—then reduce this to reality for structural cost and people's reasons. Creativity is needed. Break away from what's always been done. Do your own thing. What happens if instead of square and rectangular configurations, triangles and circles are incorporated in the layout? What if most private offices are eliminated or, in contrast, the entire office is made up of private offices? What if completely self-sustaining individual work stations are used rather than group or department units?

In many cases the help of an office layout specialist is engaged. This approach helps assure that a satisfactory office layout will be developed. However, it does not prohibit the office manager or any executive from talking with the layout specialist and contributing to the task of evolving the best office space plans. Some companies have found that a committee works out very well to encourage participation in office layout work.

AMCO–PACT Approach

Most agree that office space utilization should serve not only to get the specific office work accomplished, but also to satisfy personal preferences and human wants. To this end, the *AMCO–PACT* approach is offered; it is illustrated by Figure 17–1. Beginning at the center of the

FIGURE 17–1
The AMCO–PACT Approach to Office Layout
Is Effective

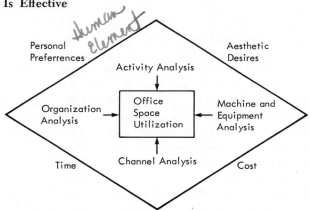

figure, office space utilization is developed from data derived from analysis of *AMCO*—*A*ctivity or the function performed, *M*achine and equipment used, *C*hannel or building service flow facilities required, and *O*rganization giving the number of persons and the respective work types performed.[1] In turn, these AMCO factors are influenced by *PACT* standing for *P*ersonal preferences of the people involved, *A*esthetic desires to be satisfied, *C*ost of the layout, and *T*ime considerations. Let us first discuss AMCO and follow this with some elaboration about PACT.

The *A*ctivity deals with the function or duty to be performed. The analysis of activity is derived from study of the office systems, procedures, and methods prescribed. It represents what action must be taken to perform the work. Frequently, observation and recording of personnel activity are used to supplement the formal data available. The work

---

[1] These four types are from a statement by a prominent authority in office space planning, Mr. William I. Sohl, President, Concept Products, Inc., New York.

and the conditions required to execute it adequately are determined and evaluated. Also, probable needs for five and ten years are forecast. Usually a review and check of operations at each level with a corresponding management member is made. If any special studies seem appropriate they are conducted so that complete activity information is available.

Machine and equipment analysis affects the office layout. Data on these requirements are obtained from the activity analysis discussed above. It helps to work closely with the systems and methods personnel. Also recommended is observation of office practices followed, work station arrangements, reports prepared and used, common office policies followed, and control of traffic. Needed is an inventory of currently used machines and equipment, where they are located, and whether they appear suitable for continued use under either the present or a proposed layout. The need for special equipment warrants careful investigation. All these types of information are necessary to evaluate and take into account the effect of machine and equipment on the layout.

The Channel analysis includes a survey of present building service flow facilities and an evaluation of not only the number, type, and location of units, but also the channel aids themselves including size and location of ducting, floor conduits, and power lines required. Channel data are usually recorded on specially designed sheets to facilitate study. Some include questions to ask, others diagrams to fill in, and still others call for listing specific information. Failure to compile and use such data may result, for example, in telephones having to be changed, power outlets incorrectly located, and unsightly conduits attached to the floors and ceilings.

Organization analysis includes the number of personnel to be housed and for each, the organization level, the organization unit, and the formal authority. Again, to provide for future requirements, projections by organization unit for five years and for ten years are recommended. It is helpful to determine by organization unit the approximate space needed. Space requirements result not only from people on the payroll but also, and more important, from machine and furniture requirements of each member. By tying together data from the machine and equipment analysis and the organization analysis, the following recommended data for each employee can be obtained: name, functional title, machines and size of each, units of furniture and size of each, and other or miscellaneous area requirements. These can be the heads of columns for a spread sheet. Projections for future periods can be included in the extreme right columns, if desired. Incidentally, such data will show the specific makeup of personnel accounting for the anticipated greater space requirements. From these sheets detailed space needs are easily obtained. Incidentally, at this stage, a quick and helpful comparison should now be made. Calculate the square feet of usable space and compare it with the square feet of space needed. This will reveal whether there is too little, too much, or enough space. If there is too little, some rigorous adjustments must be made at once. If there is too much, the surplus should be either utilized for additional purposes, screened off in readiness for future expansion, or rented. Leaving it open and idle may well result in adjacent units spilling into these areas, and after this happens, space control is lessened and an orderly expansion program is ignored.

PACT

The office space utilization conditioned by the analyses of activity, machine and equipment, channel, and organization, is in turn constrained by the four primary forces of *PACT*. As indicated in Figure 17–1, one of these forces is *P*ersonal preferences of the employees—both managerial and nonmanagerial. In the final analysis the office layout will be effective or not, depending upon how well the employee uses and likes the work space environment provided. What's important to the people using the layout is vital and when feasible, should be included in the space arrangement. Layout efforts are not all technical and factual; they are also human and emotional. The personnel element is strong in office layouts that prove most successful.

*A*esthetic desires, or the A in PACT, merit deep consideration. The layout should be pleasing to the eye and in keeping with good taste in design. It should give a highly favorable impression, present a harmonious combinaton of office working tools, and impart an atmosphere in which one would like to be a part. The office layout can be highly utilitarian, yet possess the ultimate in aesthetic desires.

*C*ost is always important. Whether it be people, machines, chairs, desks, tables, files, cabinets, space, aisles, or private offices, all the ingredients of office layout are affected by cost. What is finally decided—what ingredients in what format—is always influenced to some degree by cost. It is the universal regulator.

Lastly, *T*ime affects the layout evolved from data supplied by the AMCO analyses. Certainly a layout intended to be temporary is going to differ considerably from one that is permanent. And the popular office "in-thing" at a given time affects certain characteristics of all office layouts of that same time. In fact, there are styles in office arrangements not unlike styles in car design and house floor plans.

Who Goes Where?

After assembling and relating the information developed from the AMCO–PACT approach, the next task is to determine the general location of the various units within the total usable space. For this purpose, functional flow studies are used. They result in showing the relationship of components and can be illustrated graphically by a block diagram as given in Figure 17–2. Each block identifies the department or unit

FIGURE 17–2
Block Diagram Showing Relationship of Components

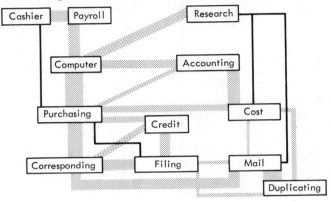

to be included in the layout. The width of the line joining two blocks indicates the quantity of work flow and the physical capacity requirements for communication between these two units.

These efforts show who works with whom and what goes where. Flow is either (1) by papers or (2) by people. We try to minimize the latter, but both must be used. Usually there are key papers about which work of certain units revolve. Tracing the movement of such papers supplies clues as to what units should be related and in what sequence.

An interesting technique for determining the best relationship of components utilizes a computer. First, a block diagram is developed on which are shown the measurements for each flow. Adjustments are then made in relationships in order to find the best arrangement of units contributing to the effectiveness of the totality, as measured by cost or time (some measurable unit) for the various work flows and communication efforts. Input data to the computer start with the total cost of work flow for a given pattern. Then, the change in the total cost brought about by two units exchanging positions is calculated. Subsequently calculations by the computer proceed through all combinations of exchanges among the units. For 20 units or departments, and using paired exchanges, some 190 calculations are required. Hence, by means of a computer, the relationship among components to provide the total minimum cost of work flow can be precisely determined and the framework for an effective layout is supplied.

Significant Layout Concepts

Before describing the actual work incurred in evolving an office layout, it is appropriate to present several concepts about layout that are fundamental as well as helpful in understanding why certain selections are made in layouts. These concepts include (1) the symmetrical-technical approach, (2) the flexible-personnel approach, (3) the administrative substation utilization, and (4) the movable partition and its contribution to office management.

The symmetrical-technical approach is the older, more familiar and most used conceptual plan followed in office arrangement. It is highly engineered and favors gridlike forms where symmetry and uniformity are king. A neat orderly appearance is obtained, and employees are put in comfortable areas reflecting their relative position in the organization hierarchy. The emphasis is upon tradition, efficiency, work, and cost expenditures. The symmetrical-technical office features a pronounced sameness about it.

In contrast, the flexible-personnel approach is the newer and less known approach. It strongly emphasizes some variation in the layout and the avoidance of a monotonous office which commonly creates subtle tensions. Representative of this approach is office landscaping which recognizes and uses workflow, traffic patterns, communication networks, and a minimizing of privacy and privilege. It features a large open landscape rather than enclosed or separated areas. For best results a minimum of 10,000 square feet and neither dimension less than 75 feet are suggested. Column spacing should be 25 feet or more with ceiling height a maximum of 9 feet. Screens and dividers of varying heights replace partitions. Furniture and machines are spaced in functional clusters. Modular office work stations, discussed in Chapter 16, have been used quite effectively in the landscape office. However, this type office is not confined to the use of any particular design of furniture or equipment. The freer, open idea of office landscaping makes for irregularly arranged work stations. Different personnel face different directions, thus personal identity is given to each person. The irregular orientation of work stations permits control by sight lines. This aids supervision. Customarily each sight line is restricted to about 30 feet in order to retain intimacy. Figure 17–3 shows an office landscaping installation.

Administrative Substation Utilization

Gaining wider and wider acceptance in office arrangement is the administrative substation which is a compact work station handling numer-

FIGURE 17–3

An Office Space Arranged in Keeping with the Concept of Office Landscaping

Courtesy: E. I. DuPont de Nemours and Co., Wilmington, Del.

ous information activities closely related but traditionally thought of as separate functions. It may include a secretarial services unit, messenger services, storing and retrieving of certain records, mail room, and copying services. Ideally, substations are joined together with other substations forming a framework linked to a central information center which may have a computer.

Each substation has a supervisor who oversees work input and output of that unit. Frequently this is a private secretary who because of knowledge of company operations can perform this work competently. Supervisors serve as deputies of the information manager of the assistant manager in that they translate requests for information service into working programs. All personnel of the work station are upgraded because they acquire additional skills to perform their varied tasks. Their work is more interesting and challenging.

The concept of an administrative substation evolved from the development of the landscaped office. It can exist, however, in an office layout either as a feature in the flexible-personnel approach or as an important modification of the symmetrical-technical approach. In perspective, it is a workable office layout idea that captures the availability of human skill and ability as well as improved utility of many modern furniture pieces and machines of this present day.

Movable Partitions

For formally dividing the office space as the approved layout requires, movable partitions are widely used. They afford not only great flexibility in office layout but also space control and permit unusual office designs to be followed at feasible cost. Changes in layout can be made overnight or during a weekend. In many instances the cost of erecting movable partitions is only 15 percent of that of immovable tile and plaster walls. Furthermore, eliminated are objectionable inconveniences such as noise, commotion, debris, waiting for plaster and paint to dry, and after partition installation, the cleaning of rugs, draperies, and furniture. In addition, the salvage value is high. The panels can be used over and over again.

Made of metal, wood, or plastic, movable partitions are easily erected or dismantled. Various heights, ranging from the railing to the ceiling, are available. The heights of 36 inches to 84 inches are popular. They provide privacy, yet do not interfere with the ventilating and lighting. Wiring and outlets are contained in the baseboards and joints. The partitions are factory finished and offered in a variety of styles and colors. All are soundproof having insulating material in the core or center. Panels with recesses for bookcases, alcoves for drinking fountains, provisions for door openings, door units, and with or without glass (crystal or obscure) in the top areas are among the many available kinds offered to fit requirements for every type of working space. See Figure 17–4.

PREPARING AN OFFICE LAYOUT

First, obtain a drawing or blueprint of the available area. If it is not available, measure the space and indicate the dimensions on a neatly drawn hand sketch. A convenient scale is $\frac{1}{4}$" = 1', meaning that $\frac{1}{4}$ inch on the drawing is equal to 1 foot of actual floor dimension. The exact location and size should be indicated for windows, building offsets, and door swings, and the location of columns, pipes, electric light outlets and wiring, ducts for telephone wiring, running water facilities, entrances and exits. Frequently, the ability to adapt a suggested layout depends upon the completeness and accuracy of these data. A building offset incorrectly spotted, or the omission of a column, can necessitate alterations in a proposed layout or even rejection.

Next, for the total area, determine locations for main traffic movement. These locations will depend upon such things as the size and shape

FIGURE 17–4
Effective Use of Movable Office Partitions

Courtesy: ADANLOCK-Jamestown Corp., Jamestown, N.Y.

of the space available and the general type of office. Building facilities such as entrances and exits, stairways, elevators, rest rooms, and the like will suggest areas of greatest travel. From this information, the location of the main corridors, storage rooms, reception rooms, and wardrobe rooms in the layout will be suggested.

Third, formulate tentative answers regarding the use of reception room, conference rooms, and private offices. Discussion on the use of these areas is made later in this chapter. For the present, our decision will be based in part on the approach to office layout that we are taking—whether symmetrical-technical or flexible-personnel. In either event, we should approximate the amount of space for these accommodations and include it in our listing of the physical facilities to be provided.

Fourth, study the data from the analyses of the activity, machine and equipment, channel, and organization as pointed out above. Efforts to coordinate the information into an overall picture is not easy, yet it is not especially difficult. We can identify the number of employees and the machines and equipment required for each organization unit. We also have the total size of the area needed for each major unit, and we know, as stated above, the relationship among the units in terms of flow and communication—as shown in the block diagram. Matching the major segments of the space requirements against usable space available sounds like a herculean task and the work does resemble working a jigsaw puzzle. But bit by bit, an adjustment here and there, key areas begin to shape up and the entire layout from the broad viewpoint begins to unfold satisfactorily. Consultation with the leaders of those to occupy the tentative spaces can be followed. Valuable suggestions are received and conflicts, such as several groups wanting the identical space, can be resolved. If not decided before, it is at this stage that the decision whether to use basically a symmetrical or a landscape approach is reached.

We are now ready to work out specific details which begin by making templates to scale of all physical units (or use models) and identifying each. A template is a scaled pattern, made of cardboard or paper, which is used to represent the floor area occupied by a physical unit. The scale of the templates must be the same as that of the drawing showing the available area; as already pointed out, a scale of $\frac{1}{4}'' = 1'$ is convenient. Frequently, the shape of the templates is confined to that of a square or a rectangle; and in most cases, this is satisfactory; but there are instances where the details of cutoff corners, rounded corners, and the like should be included in the templates, as the final arrangement may hinge upon these considerations. A separate template is made for each physical unit considered in the layout. This includes each machine, private office, conference room, reception room, and so forth. For purposes of identification, on each template put the name of the unit and of the basic group by which the unit is to be used. It is also possible to use different colors representing different physical units to help visualize the work.

Instead of templates, small-scale, three-dimensional models of the physical units can be used. These office models are dimensionally accurate and show at a glance the arrangement of the office. Many people can visualize the layout more clearly from scale models than from a technical drawing with which they may be unfamiliar. Complete kits, consisting of several hundred pieces including desks, chairs, files, machines, coat racks, and building columns, are available.

Also available are magnetic templates and magnetic models that can be used along with a steel-covered piece of plywood serving as a base. The magnetic templates or models hold fast to such a base, yet they can be moved to show different layouts. The base can be attached to a wall, thus providing convenient viewing adequate for a group of people.

The templates or models are arranged for each basic group within its respective tentative area. The layout is determined by moving and shifting the templates or models to various positions so as to arrive at an effective arrangement. This phase of layout is a tentative trial-and-error process. It requires considerable time and cannot be rushed. If magnetic templates or models are used, the tentative layout is photographed and copies made so that convenient reference sheets are provided.

Next, the entire tentative layout is reviewed and minor adjustments are made as required. In other words what we believe may be the best arrangement is checked as a totality to see that it is a well-knit arrangement which will meet the particular needs. Attention is directed to the contribution of every major unit. A check is made of the work flow through the entire area and the probable general appearance of the entire layout.

Appropriate markings are added to indicate the major flows of work, the telephone and electric wiring, and the name of the employee to be located at each unit. This information is necessary to gain a complete understanding of the layout. The name of the employee at each work unit is helpful to the office executive in visualizing the arrangement.

Finally, a recheck is conducted with each interested group. The first group to consult, of course, is the top managers. Point out to them where they will be located, what facilities are provided, and the chief considerations determining the recommended layout. Generally, minor changes will be suggested, and they can usually be incorporated. The same approach is followed with each group head. If consultation was practiced as suggested previously, the suggested plans are usually viewed favorably. However, if there are doubts and questions, an explanation of the recommended layout should be made with the reasons carefully pointed out. After all groups have O.K.'d their respective layouts, the entire plan is submitted to the top managers with the statement that this layout has the approval of each group head. Acceptance by the top managers is then usually little more than a formality.

Basic Layout Guides

There have been developed a number of layout guides which when followed help to provide an effective office arrangement. Not all of these can be followed in any one layout. The basic approach followed has significant influence. The list includes:

1. Utilize one large area in preference to an equivalent area of small parcels. The single large area permits better lighting, ventilating, supervising, and communicating.

2. Give major preference to the dominant flows of work and communication needs. Provide for good work flows and avoid backtracking, crisscrossing, and unnecessary movement of papers.

3. Place related departments adjacent, and keep jobs of a similar nature in close relationship.

4. Locate departments which normally have many visitors from the outside near the entrance; or if this is not feasible, make provisions so that this traffic will not disturb other departments.

5. Locate vending machines, fountains, and bulletin boards where they will cause least distraction and congestion.

6. Provide for maximum work loads.

7. Anticipate and provide for future changes.

8. Locate supervisors in such a manner that they can easily observe what goes on in the work area.

9. Have the work come to the employee, not the employee go to the work. Keep employee flow to a minimum.

10. Arrange desks so that ample natural light comes from a little back and over the left shoulder.

11. Avoid private office locations which cut off natural light to the adjacent general office area.

12. Do not have the employee facing a window, too near heat sources, or in line of drafts.

13. For necessary walls, use movable partitions as they are easy to install; part-way partitions with plain or opaque glass permit good light and ventilation.

14. Provide sufficient floor electrical outlets for office machines.

15. Place units making much noise in a soundproof area to avoid disturbance to others.

16.   Put files and frequently used machines near the employees who use them. Abstain from putting all files at dead wall space.

17.   Arrange filing cabinets back to back.

18.   If a corner is required, consider the possibility of providing it with filing cabinets.

19.   If possible, provide lounging areas where employees can relax during rest periods, talk informally, and eat lunch.

20.   Provide convenient and adequate rest-room facilities.

OFFICE SPACE STANDARDS

Studies show that a value of 60 square feet of usable space for each *ordinary clerical employee* is a desirable standard; and when an office layout calls for this amount, the space utilization is considered by some to be highly satisfactory. The value of 60 square feet per ordinary clerical employee is arrived at in this manner:

$$50\text{-inch desk and chair, } 50'' \times 68'' = 23.61 \text{ sq. ft.}$$
$$\text{Aisle per desk, } 18'' \times 68'' = 8.50 \text{ sq. ft.}$$
$$\text{Miscellaneous (files, aisles, etc.)} = 27.89 \text{ sq. ft.}$$
$$\text{Total} = 60.00 \text{ sq. ft.}$$

Some surveys show 75–85 square feet per clerical employee as typical in a fairly large clerical area. However, there is no fact rule for the standard number of square feet per office employee. The amount of space to allow is influenced by many factors including the nature of the work, the available total area, the extent of service areas, the need for privacy, the number and type of equipment and machines, and the shape, exposure, and obstructions within the total space itself. One office with a value of 77 square feet per clerical employee may have an excellent layout, while employees of another office with 77 square feet per clerical employee struggle under cramped office conditions.

Estimates for managerial personnel include:

Top executive...................	400–450 sq. ft.
Intermediate executive..........	275–300 sq. ft.
Supervisory executive...........	110–125 sq. ft.

These data are more valid primarily because there is more uniformity in what machines and furniture an executive or a supervisor is provided. They are helpful as broad estimates.

Over a period, certain prescribed space usages for desks, aisles, and filing cabinets have gained acceptance as representing effective space utilization. Some consider them space standards which in a sense they are, but they should not be viewed as rigid measurements, but rather as the result of reliable practices which assist in providing a satisfactory layout. For the most part they apply only to the symmetrical-technical approach.

Desks. Minimum space suggestions are shown in Figure 17–5. For example, referring to the top illustration, when 50×30-inch desks are

FIGURE 17–5
Minimum Suggested Standards for Back-to-Back Arrangement of Desks under Different Floor Plan Layouts

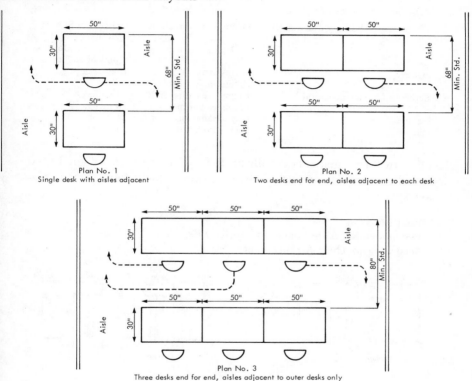

arranged as single units with aisles adjacent, or when they are arranged in pairs, end for end, with aisles adjacent to each desk, the minimum space standard from back to back of desks is about 68 inches. These arrangements provide about a 3-foot strip for the chair and for getting to and from the desk. The bottom illustration of the figure shows space standards for three desks placed end for end. Of the three plans shown in this figure, plan No. 2 requires the smallest area per clerk; in contrast, plan No. 1 requires the most.

Aisles. Main aisles or corridors should be 5–8 feet wide, depending upon the amount of traffic to be handled. A 5-foot aisle can normally accommodate around 850 people in five minutes. Main aisles in an office area should be 4–5 feet wide, and the range of secondary aisles should be from 3 to 4 feet wide. Cross aisles should be provided about every 50 feet.

Filing Cabinets. The spacing of filing cabinets depends upon frequency of use and the type of cabinet.

Material	Type of Cabinet	Position of Filing Cabinets	Aisle Space
Active	Ordinary pull drawer	Facing same direction	Drawer depth plus 24 inches
"	" "	Facing each other	Two drawer depths plus 36 inches
Inactive	" "	Facing same direction	Drawer depth
"	" "	Facing each other	" "
Active	Side or lateral	Facing same direction	24 inches
"	"	Facing each other	30 inches
Inactive	"	Facing same direction	24 inches
Inactive	"	Facing each other	24 inches

The first two arrangements are illustrated by Figure 17–6. When a quantity of filing cabinets are used, always arrange them facing each other, to save space.

FIGURE 17–6
Recommended Aisle Spaces for Active Files According to Their Arrangement

 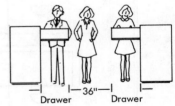

Drawer |—24"—| |—36"—| Drawer
          Drawer

The Private Office

Decisions regarding the use of a private office should be made only after ample consideration has been given to the individual circumstances. A private office should be employed when its use is dictated by facts and unbiased judgment. It should never be provided simply because it has always been provided for a particular job or because requests and sometimes pressure have been brought to bear.

On the favorable side is the need for prestige. It is for this reason that most top management members, department heads, and professional people are supplied with private offices. This helps add weight, influence, and respect to these groups in the eyes of other employees and of visitors to the office.

Also, in support of the private office is the provision of a suitable space for work requiring high concentration. It is contended that creative work, such as writing advertising copy and preparing difficult reports, usually justifies a private office. Likewise, employees doing intricate analysis, original planning, close mental work, and work requiring exclusive attention with a minimum of distraction merit a private office.

Finally, the providing of proper accommodations for confidential work, significant in research, planning, and consolidating recapitulations of important statistics is offered. Also, conversations during personnel-selection interviews are of a confidential sort and should be conducted in a private office. But note that a conference room can be used for this purpose. It is not difficult to overemphasize the importance of confidential work. Hence, extreme care should be exercised in determining whether this consideration actually warrants a private office. Figure 17–7 shows a suggested private office layout making excellent use of space.

FIGURE 17–7
A Private Office Providing for a Desk, Three Chairs, Files, and Books within 81 Square Feet of Space

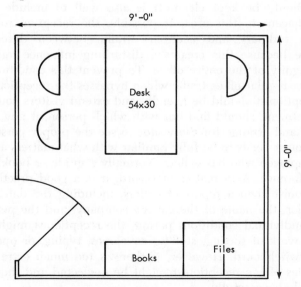

On the other hand, arguments against the use of private offices include first, they interfere with supervisor effectiveness. The closeness of the supervisor to the employees, familiarity with problems as they arise, and being at the heart of all happenings in the unit can be lost when the supervisor is segregated by a private office. It is helpful to be close at hand to give instructions, check performance, and provide encouragement.

Furthermore, private offices complicate the heating, ventilating, and lighting of these areas as well as of adjoining areas. Individual segments of space, set off from the large area, require special arrangements to supply these services, all of which mean additional materials and labor.

Also, the relatively high cost of the private office is a paramount objection. By their use, space utilization is reduced to 35 to 50 percent of that of the open-area arrangement. And the buying, erecting, maintaining, and, in case of alteration, moving of partitions entail expenditures which cumulatively amount to quite sizable figures.

Reception Room

The reception room and the receptionist create the initial impression of the enterprise upon the visitor, and initial impressions are often lasting ones. The reception room should be inviting. Displays of the company's products or services are very effective and assist in building good will. Keeping the room clean is basic. Chairs should be kept in a straight line, with newspapers and magazines arranged neatly on a table, and ash trays should be kept clean. It is also well to include cloakroom facilities adjacent to this area. If possible, the reception room should not handle ordinary and necessary traffic between different areas in the office because this creates a disturbing influence and distracts from the dignity of the entire office. To prevent this condition, provide a passage for regular office traffic which bypasses the reception room.

The receptionist should be friendly and extend visitors courteous and prompt treatment, should find out with which person, if any, the visitor should talk and arrange for the visitor to see the proper person quickly. The receptionist needs to be fully familiar with what matters are handled by each employee who has callers. Normally a guide or booklet is available for reference. As a matter of record, it is a good practice to have the receptionist keep a report of callers, including the date, the name of each caller, the name of the caller's company, and the person called on. When individual conditions permit, the receptionist might also perform office work of sorting, stuffing envelopes, typing, or operating the telephone switchboard. However, if there is too much extra work, the regular duties of the receptionist might be neglected and the supervisor should watch this carefully.

Computer Room

Computer space requirements are demanding and include quality and reliability of electrical power, supply of water and raw air for air conditioning, satisfaction of insurance (especially fire) requirements, accessibility, and ample space for storage of input and output materials and for expansion and future development. Line-to-line voltage tolerance usually must be maintained plus or minus 8 percent of the normal rated voltage measured at the receptacle when the computer system is operating. Also the illumination of the computer room should be somewhat equalized over the machine area as frequently personnel must work behind the various machines. Most computers generate a considerable amount of heat and to maintain good operating conditions, year-round air conditioning is required. It is for this reason that large quantities of water and raw air are necessary. Many managers recommend a cooling system separate from that of the building. Computer systems are connected by cables of limited length and this requires accessibility and working positions which define the work area. In addition, large quantities of cards, tapes, disks, paper printouts, and microform records require a convenient and large area for storage and quick retrieval. The computer room houses a center of vital information. Many records flow into it, many flow out of it. And the computer personnel usually must work closely with other personnel. All of these considerations help to determine the location of the computer room.

Conference Room

For meetings in privacy, a conference room is highly recommended. Most private offices are not suited for the handling of meetings. With a conference room, the participants can be arranged more satisfactorily, a greater number can usually be accommodated and each one can have a convenient place to write or to take notes. Furthermore, the meeting is placed on a businesslike basis, with a minimum of interference and distractions. The conference room should be located conveniently where traffic in and out of the room will be least disturbing to the other office employees. Figure 17–8 shows dimensions of a well-planned conference room layout.

Wardrobe Facilities

Wardrobe facilities can be provided either by having separate rooms—locker or cloakrooms—or by placing wardrobe racks in the office areas. If the former plan is used, provision should include separate rooms for men and women. When racks are used, they can be located throughout the office areas. Units are available which provide storage for coats, hats, overshoes, umbrellas, and the like for as many as three persons per square foot of floor area, i.e., a unit of 6 square feet (3 feet × 2 feet) will accommodate 18 persons.

FIGURE 17–8
Layout of Conference Room for Ten People

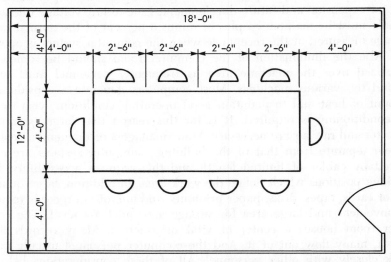

The table is 4 × 10 feet. For each two additional people to be accommodated, add 2 feet 6 inches to table length and to room length.

MOVING THE OFFICE

Change in the office layout may necessitate a move. When this condition arises it is advisable to follow certain practices. When the layout is finalized, tell personnel the information they will want to know, such as the general decor to be used, where they will be located in the new layout, the approximate time of the move, and outstanding features of the new arrangements. Number each item in the new layout. Then tag and number all furniture, equipment, and machines to designate their exact location in the new layout. For large moves a code of different colors and letter prefixes is effective, i.e., red (second floor), C (cost department), yellow (third floor), L (library), and so forth.

It is recommended that a moving committee be appointed. Usually a top executive becomes chairperson with all department heads as members. Each of the latter selects two assistants and the three serve as a departmental subcommittee. They get things in their department ready for the move. On the day of moving they serve as deputies helping to coordinate the move, direct traffic, check to see that items are placed in correct locations in their areas, and answer questions.

Drawing up a check sheet of "things to be done" in connection with the move helps direct efforts to the many tasks that are to be taken care of. Representative of such a list is that shown by Figure 17–9.

FIGURE 17–9
Checklist in Preparation for M-Day (Moving Day)

Arrangements for:
1. Building directory—show new locations.
2. Cleaning all furniture, carpets, rugs, and draperies, if not replaced.
3. Moving company.
4. Stationary—purchase new letterheads, envelopes, and other printed matter.
5. Telephone—request service well in advance.
6. Teletype—request service well in advance.
7. Utilities—request service well in advance.

Follow-up on delivery of new furniture and machines:
1. Accessories.
2. Chairs.
3. Desks.
4. Machines.

Notify:
1. Customers and suppliers.
2. Government—Internal Revenue Service, Social Security, State Unemployed.
3. Insurance companies.
4. Local post office.
5. Publishers of periodicals.
6. Western Union.

Sell obsolete furniture.

It is best to schedule the move over a weekend or vacation period, allowing a maximum of 60 continuous hours (Friday 6:00 P.M.—Monday 6:00 A.M.) and arranging for an adequate number of trucks and crews. It is also preferable to move one section of the office at a time. Attempts to move two or three sections at the same time can result in a serious tie-up. Items to be placed in remote and farthest areas should be moved first, after which should come those located adjacent to the entranceway. The movers, electricians and carpenters, and other personnel should be informed of the schedule.

QUESTIONS

1. Enumerate the four major separate types of areas that make up most large offices.
2. Explain Figure 17–1 in your own words.
3. Identify each of the following:
   a. Scale of ¼″ = 1′ for an office layout drawing.
   b. The symmetrical technical approach.
   c. Office space management.
   d. Movable partitions.
4. What are some office space standards that you would use in making an office layout?

5. Discuss briefly what is meant by the organization analysis as applied to office space planning.
6. What information does Figure 17–2 convey and how is this information used in office space management?
7. Approximately how much office space would you allot to each of the following:
   a. Two desks end for end (50 × 30-inch desk), aisle adjacent, chair for each desk.
   b. Private office for a supervisory executive.
   c. General office space for eight clerks.
   d. A main aisle running the long distance of an office area 20 feet by 28 feet.
8. Discuss the meaning and use of administrative substations in an office layout.
9. What are the minimum dimensions you would recommend for a conference room to accommodate 20 persons? Justify your answer.
10. Describe the layout of an office with which you are familiar, and point out several ways in which you feel it might be improved. Give reasons for your suggested changes.
11. Give some realistic suggestions for an office manager to utilize when planning the office move.
12. What are the major features of office landscaping?

CASE PROBLEMS

Case 17–1. Quinn Company

A portion of the proposed office layout in this company's new building is shown by the accompanying drawing. The overall area is 105 feet by 45 feet, housing four senior offices, space for private secretaries, a general office area, and a reception room. The area for three private secretaries is located along the "executive row" with one dimension along the outside wall to permit use of daylight. As indicated on the drawing, each work station for a private secretary is equipped with an L-shaped desk, a desk chair, credenza, extra chair, and a total of six filing cabinets. Based on previous studies, it was found that the private secretaries' work loads were such that one can handle both the president's and the vice president's work, while a private secretary is needed for the executive vice president as well as one for the controller. The general office area is of a landscape type.

Questions:

1. Study the proposed layout. Enumerate and discuss possible improvements.
2. Quinn managers are not sure that they like the landscape of the general office area. Offer a conventional office layout for this area by drawing up what arrangement you suggest along a conventional design. Does your conventional arrangement accommodate more or less office work stations compared to the landscape layout?
3. What recommendations would you make to the Quinn Company managers regarding the proposed original layout? Substantiate your viewpoints.

EXHIBIT 17-1A

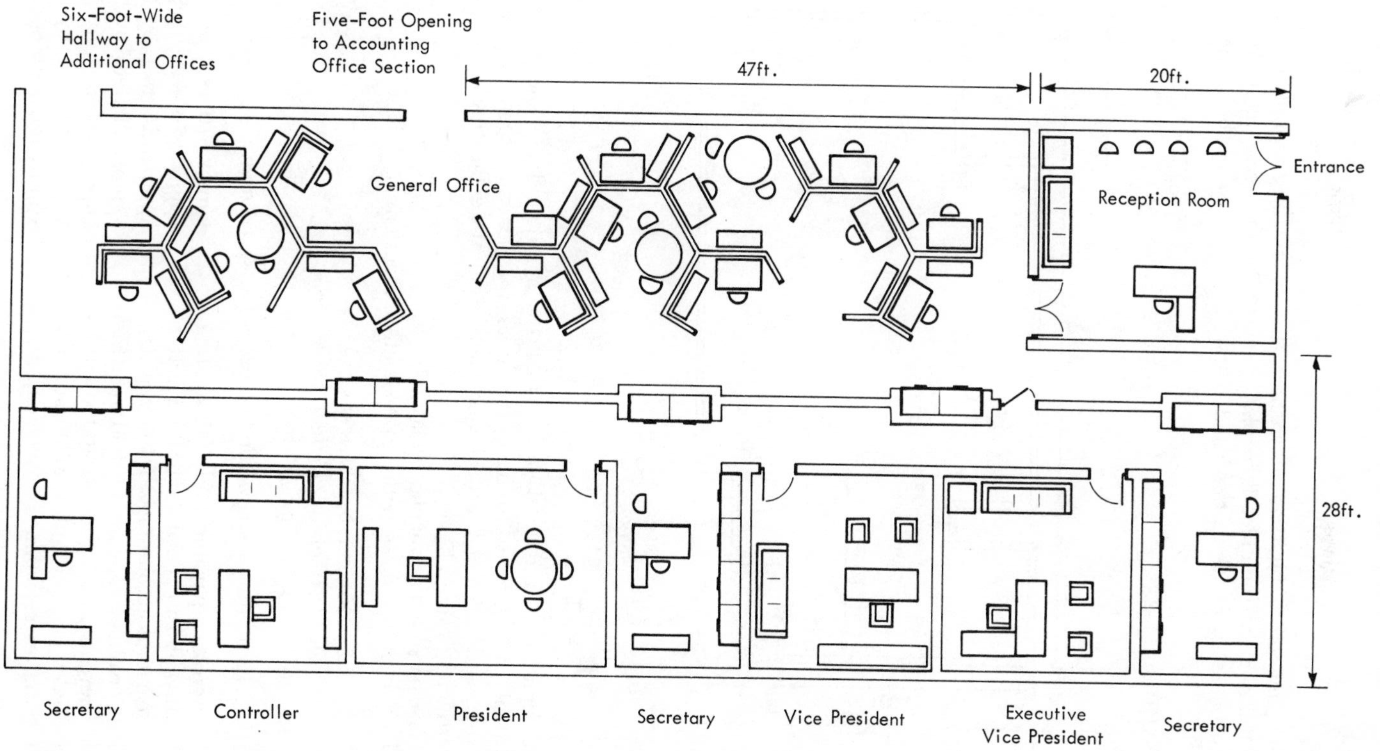

Six-Foot-Wide
Hallway to
Additional Offices

Five-Foot Opening
to Accounting
Office Section

Entrance

28ft.

20ft.

47ft.

Reception Room

General Office

Secretary

Executive
Vice President

Vice President

Secretary

President

Controller

Secretary

Case 17–2.   Fishers, Inc.

The new office building of Fishers, Inc. is nearing completion and the overall outline of the office floor plan is shown by the accompanying drawing. Approximate space needs are listed below. For most areas, both the approxi-

EXHIBIT 17–2A

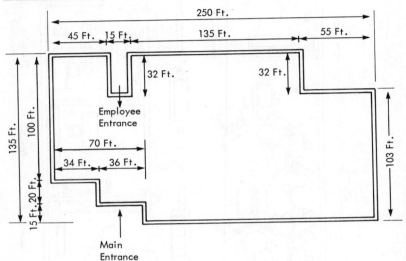

mate dimensions and total square foot space required are shown. It is the desire of management to have the areas for general accounting, accounts payable, and inventory control near each other since the traffic among these departments is quite heavy.

The space requirements are as follows:

5   Executive offices with approximate dimensions as follows:

    (1)   15 feet by 20 feet
    (1)   15 feet by 15 feet
    (3)   15 feet by 10 feet

In addition: space for five executive secretaries.

1	Accounts payable	1,500 sq. ft.	Approx. 70 feet by 22 feet
1	Inventory control	1,800 sq. ft.	Approx. 70 feet by 26 feet
1	General accounting	1,400 sq. ft.	Approx. 25 feet by 55 feet
1	Personnel	800 sq. ft.	Approx. 22 feet by 35 feet
1	Purchasing	400 sq. ft.	Approx. 11 feet by 35 feet
1	Sales	3,000 sq. ft.	Approx. 88 feet by 35 feet
1	Market research	900 sq. ft.	Approx. 28 feet by 32 feet

1	Credit and collections	575 sq. ft.		Approx. 18 feet by 32 feet
1	Mailroom	1,450 sq. ft.		Approx. 45 feet by 32 feet
1	Storage area	800 sq. ft.		Approx. 20 feet by 40 feet
1	Data processing	2,900 sq. ft.		Approx. 52 feet by 55 feet
1	Wardrobe room	700 sq. ft.		Approx. 22 feet by 32 feet
1	Cafeteria	1,200 sq. ft.		Approx. 35 feet by 35 feet
1	Cafeteria storage	400 sq. ft.		Approx. 20 feet by 20 feet
1	Reception room	700 sq. ft.		Approx. 35 feet by 20 feet
1	Large conference room	1,500 sq. ft.		Approx. 45 feet by 35 feet
2	Men's rest rooms	350 sq. ft.	(each)	Approx. 11 feet by 32 feet
2	Women's rest rooms	350 sq. ft.	(each)	Approx. 11 feet by 32 feet

Questions:

1. Prepare an office layout that meets the company's specifications. A scale of 1″ = 10′ is satisfactory.
2. Point out the desirable features of your suggested layout. The undesirable features.
3. Do you feel a different shaped overall floor plan would have been more effective for meeting the company's space requirements? Discuss fully.
4. Assume the sales office requires one private office approximately 11 feet by 22 feet for the sales manager, and six private offices each approximately 11 feet by 11 feet for salesmen. In addition, a desk and chair for sixteen work stations are required, plus a number of 4-drawer filing cabinets. Will the sales area space accommodate these requirements? Draw a suggested detailed drawing of the sales department office layout.

Case 17–3. North American University

Professor Irene D. Matisoff is joining the faculty and is looking forward to her new assignment at North American University. Her work will include not only teaching classes, but also much counseling of students. She will have a secretary three mornings a week to assist her in any clerical work she may have. The secretary will have a work station in Professor Matisoff's office.

Office space is at a premium around the university but the Dean has succeeded in locating a vacant office in a temporary campus building. The office is 12 feet by 10½ feet exclusive of two large closets. There are two windows on the north side of the area, entrance is on the south. Details are shown in Exhibit 17–3A. Professor Matisoff is advised that she can select what furniture she wants from the following: two 58 × 30 desks, two bookshelves 42 × 10, two four-drawer filing cabinets 15 × 28, four desk chairs, three straight back chairs, one 36 × 24 typist desk, one 18 × 18 stand, three table lamps, and one three-drawer filing cabinet 15 × 28.

EXHIBIT 17–3A

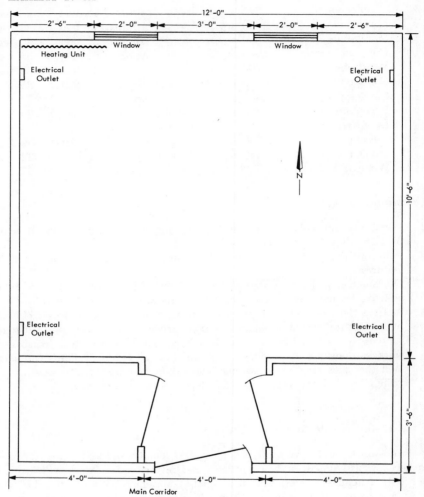

Questions:

1. Develop two office layouts that you recommend for Professor Matisoff's consideration.
2. Point out the advantages and disadvantages of each layout.
3. What is your recommendation to Professor Matisoff? Why?

Part V

Actuating Who Does the Office Work

The office manager of today spends the majority of the day working with people, inspiring them to use their highest attainable work skills and capacities, motivating them to achieve work goals enthusiastically, and satisfying their personal needs from their individual work efforts and accomplishments. Many view actuating as of foremost importance in office management.

Included in this part of the book are six chapters, "Human Resources and Office Management," "Motivating the Office Employee," "Office Supervisory Management," "Developing Office Employees," "Office Salary Administration," and "Additional Considerations in Actuating."

Chapter 18

Human Resources and Office Management

All that is necessary for evil to triumph is for good men to do nothing.

Edmund Burke

People are the most important resource that the office manager utilizes. A study of the possible use of a new system or a new machine that does not take into account the attitudes and expectations of employees can reduce productivity and give rise to serious human problems. Physical resources such as forms and reports, equipment, space and dollars are essential, but they are nothing until the human resource utilizes them to produce a wanted product or service.

From the psychological viewpoint, the behavior of human beings is quite complicated. They are like no other resource. Not only is it complicated, but the human resource is perhaps the most difficult and frustrating to manage because it is not readily predictable. Consider, for example, that the behavior of most people changes from time to time, feelings and emotions enter into what people do, and a multitude of different viewpoints are followed. As a result, some managers tend to concentrate their time on physical and financial assets because they are tangible, remain relatively constant from day to day, and are devoid of emotion. Indeed to manage the human resource may be regarded by them as a chore which interferes with getting the job at hand performed.

However, every office manager should possess an understanding of the factors affecting human behavior or face being unable to cope with the people's problems which must be faced and are ever-present in the manager's daily efforts. When people interact with one another in groups the complexities among their psychological makeups multiply.

Insight into the nature and considerations of human behavior is a must for the manager. It is indeed difficult to conceive of any managerial effort more important or more challenging than utilizing human resources. Never has the understanding and management of human resources demanded a higher degree of competence. Never has the opportunity been greater.

BACKGROUND FUNDAMENTALS

Dramatic changes of economic, political, and social factors reflecting modifications in the values, attitudes, perceptions, and life styles of people are deeply affecting the objectives and the activities of the manager. These changes appear with seemingly increasing intensity and rapidity. And they must be recognized for they are changing assumptions and beliefs about how to manage the human resource.

Office employees of today assume that their jobs will provide more than the satisfaction of their material wants; it will also supply a livable environment, job satisfaction, and a higher quality of life. This view extends to all ages and at all organizational levels. Actions designed to promote the physical, economic, and social well-being of people are numerous including new personnel practices, governmental regulations, and court decisions. Further, consider the fact that employees in the office are rapidly becoming the most highly educated personnel in United States history. It is estimated that by 1985, employees with some college education will outnumber those without a high school education. These employees will expect to have their talents utilized so that they gain self-esteem and self-actualization. Further, the desire to contribute by the well-educated employee is modifying authority relationships from that of dictation by a boss to development of mutually agreed upon objectives, and the manager becoming more of a coordinator and a multiplier of those who are members of the group. Likewise, mushrooming technological change is intensifying this shift. Greater knowledge and skill are required to operate the increasingly sophisticated office machines and equipment. Many unskilled jobs have been eliminated. Yet there are many office jobs that are narrowly specialized and provide only a small sense of involvement or achievement.

With all these changes has emerged a shift in what's important to the employee. Challenge and opportunity are important. Expectations have been sharply stimulated and people are less willing to tolerate work that is not meaningful to them or to wait for opportunity. There is little automatic respect for position or seniority, the emphasis is on ability and accomplishment. And in many cases, first loyalty appears to be to one's self, then to profession or special group identity, and finally to the employer.

In addition to these fundamental changes, it is important to recognize, as a background fundamental, that human resources are heterogeneous. They consist of many different individuals each one of which has a unique personality, a combination of different emotional responses to different stimuli, different values, attitudes, motives, and modes of thought. There are meaningful variations in the abilities and temperaments of people. Their reaction to promises, praise, or criticism, for example, can be quite different. What challenges one man or woman may be frustrating to another. It is these differences that make study of human resources so stimulating. There is nothing more interesting than people.

Another background fundamental, already mentioned above, is that the human being is probably the most complicated organism on earth. To describe a human's behavior by means of a few simple cliches is ridiculous and such a thought should be quickly abandoned. Humanity cannot be squashed into a few sayings or summaries. There is too much to be distilled to so little. Yet we should continue the quest for any valid generalization about people and their behavior. They should, however, be considered tentative, open for further study, and qualified by the realization that the subject is complex and difficult to analyze.

In addition, it appears basic that the office manager's tolerance level must be raised and maintained at a relatively high level. Difference and dissent, presented constructively, have long been a cornerstone in the United States' development. Managers must be aware of contemporary economic and social viewpoints. After all, the manager has to get along with all kinds of people; must work with some people who are liked, others who are disliked, as well as tolerate opinions that are despised. But it is helpful to remember that usually the more different types of people you can get along with, the richer and fuller your own life becomes.

It was the Jeffersonian tradition in the United States that promoted the goodness of people and the idea of an individual being capable of almost perfection. This belief lead to great expectations and the high potential of a human being. However, because of various limitations, it is now recognized that some individuals cannot or will not compete. Efforts to spur these low achievers into action have taken numerous and various forms. Some, but not all, of the results have been encouraging, yet the compulsive urge to adjust everyone to a given mold continues. Frequently the assumption is made that the "problem employee" behavior is the external manifestation of a personality crippled by its life experience. To illustrate, the alcoholic drinks because his mother was overprotective; the employee is late because in her early girlhood the importance of punctuality was not impressed upon her. Identifying the cause is important, but this begs the question. It does not help the person with the problem personality. The need is for *professional* assistance to bring about the corrective action. Believing this need is great, amateurs have attempted to provide this help with, for the most part, amateur results. The office manager should remember, however, that most negative behavior patterns of employees are not easily eliminated, the root cause is beyond the employer-employee relationship. But tolerance in viewing the situation, in standing ready to help when needed, and in remembering that most people want work with which they can identify and which they feel is important, will contribute toward mutual understanding of the behavior dilemma.

AN APPROACH TO HUMAN BEHAVIOR STUDY

Any analysis of the reasons people behave as they do, with the intent that such analysis be helpful to the practicing office manager, is fraught with great difficulties. It is not easy to answer questions such as: What do employees seek from their work efforts? How can the different levels of aspirations among employees be accounted for? What induces office job frustration?

The discussion here is greatly simplified in order to cover the most essential concepts and to provide in a basic manner an introduction to an important and interesting field of study. The presentation is neither exhaustive nor complete. First of all, it is important to state that all human behavior has a cause or causes. Fundamentally, human behavior is aimed at the fulfillment of basic wants or needs. In other words, it is purposive. The office clerk works because it is the socially acceptable thing to do, and to buy a new automobile. Behavior is initiated because a stimulus is present. Interaction between a stimulus (light, recognition, fear) and the person's interpretation of that stimulus causes the behavior to take place. A person's perception is conditioned by the circumstances of the event, personality, experience, and background. For example, a smile by "A" may be interpreted as a friendly gesture by "B", but as a sign of conceit or disdain by "C".

Three major influences affect an employee's perception that leads to a behavior or action. They are the employee's (1) assets, (2) values, and (3) wants. Referring to Figure 18–1, left portion, an employee's assets consist of experience, knowledge, skill, availability, attitude, and health. These are the attributes enabling an employee to contribute to a company's needs. Values represent moral and social concepts of importance or as frequently stated, the concept of the desirable. They are derived from interaction with the thoughts of groups such as those in the place of employment, church, school, and home. Later, in this chapter, we will discuss further the value portion of the diagram in Figure 18–1. Going on to employee wants, these are desires or things that to the employee are believed to be indispensable. They are con-

FIGURE 18–1

Process of Behavior Leading to Satisfaction

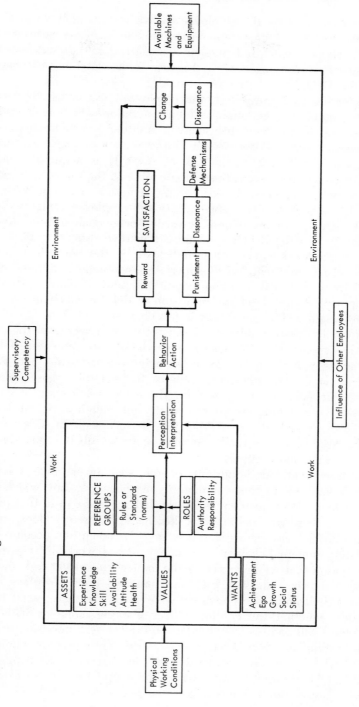

sidered essential by the employee to live the life that he or she wants to live. Employee wants are represented by achievement, ego (self-respect, self-expression, independence, and freedom), growth, social (companionship, belongingness), and status. Again, later in this chapter, discussion of employee wants will be made.

Referring to Figure 18–1, the employee's use of assets, values, and wants condition perception and interpretation which lead to behavior or action. The result of this behavior is either (*a*) favorable—for which a reward is received and satisfaction is gained, or (*b*) unfavorable—for which a punishment (or a lack of reward) is acquired which leads to dissonance—defenses are set up, leading to the use of defense mechanisms such as aggression, regression, resignation or compromise. In turn, this leads back to dissonance where the employee remains dissatisfied until a change in behavior is rewarded or, a change in perception followed by a changed behavior and is rewarded. Affecting all these activities is the work environment indicated by the borderline around the entire chart and identified by supervisory competency, influence of other employees, physical working conditions, and available machines and equipment. More elaborate discussion of defense mechanisms and work environment will be given later in this chapter.

Actually different degrees of satisfaction can accrue to the employee. We are speaking of job satisfaction which is an indicator of how well the assets, values, and wants of the employee are being met. The extent can be viewed as different amounts, for example, those indicated by the employee who (1) does enjoy the work and is doing it enthusiastically, (2) is indifferent to the work, but remains with it because of a dislike of looking for another job, doesn't want to hurt any feelings or be fired, and (3) really doesn't enjoy the job but stays on because of personal responsibilities.

It is evident, but important to note, that an employee's behavior is conditioned by factors common to all behavior, but which differ in amount and influence comparing the behavior of one to that of another. That is, there are *individual* differences in assets, values, and wants of employees and these differences must be taken into account in understanding human behavior and in managerial work. It is primarily for this reason that we keep saying the manager must get to know subordinates—not the names of their children and their birthdays, but what values each employee possesses, what goals are there, what training is needed, whether the employee likes working alone or with a group, prefers detail or broad work, and requires close supervision or considerable autonomy. Answers to such queries help provide understanding as to why employees behave as they do. The understanding, however, will not be complete and it will require updating because human behavior is a dynamic, ongoing process.

Values and Wants

As indicated in Figure 18–1, values are expressed through reference groups of either (1) beliefs or (2) rules or standards. The latter is frequently referred to as norms. Values are discussed in Chapter 14 (p. 395). In addition, values emerge from the reflection of roles, primarily those concerning either authority or responsibility. That is to say, the function, concept, or the impression assumed to be reflected by a person in authority may contribute to an employee's value regarding that entity. For instance, the value attributed by an employee to the presidency of a company may result in part from the employee's mental image or impression of the authority and its use by the person in the president's job. In similar manner roles reflecting responsibility conditions values.

Wants can be classified as to type, for example, innate wants and acquired wants. The former include air, water, food, shelter, periodic rest, and so forth. Innate wants are physiological and their satisfaction is vital to survival. In contrast, acquired wants are dependent upon experience, many are culturally determined. They are learned and vary considerably from one person to another. These acquired wants can be separated into social wants and egoistic wants. Social wants include the desire to be accepted by others, to be wanted, and to belong. When a manager shows by his or her action the disapproval of an employee's work efforts and accomplishments, it normally causes tension and anxiety in the employee. Egoistic wants deal with a person's view of herself. To achieve satisfaction of these wants enhances the person's ego. Representative are self-respect, self-expression, and independence and freedom to do, within legal and socially prescribed limits, whatever the person wants to do. Egoistic wants represent the zenith of human wants and are extremely intense. They normally follow the successful attainment of innate and social wants, are somewhat nebulous, and seldom fully satisfied. Most human beings will always accept more praise, more adulation, and more freedom.

Defense Mechanisms

A person encountering an insurmountable barrier in trying to achieve a wanted satisfaction may adopt a form of behavior known as a defense mechanism. In any given case the type of behavior adopted will depend upon the person's personality, the perception of what the barrier is, and the particular situation. People differ in their reactions to the same barrier, likewise, the frustration tolerance among people varies greatly. A number of different defense mechanisms exist; our discussion here will be limited to those most common.

Aggression can be described as an attack response intended to inflict damage. While it includes physical violence, most examples in the office are of nonviolent forms. Making statements openly against a frustration, and spreading rumors about another whom is disliked are examples of aggression. Sometimes the aggressive action is toward an innocent person or object, a condition brought about by the aggressor not knowing the real source of frustration or thinking it best not to attack the offending party. Aggression is one of the most common forms of defense mechanisms.

Regression includes adopting an immature, childish behavior. The employee given a reprimand or punishment for some behavior may react by pouting, acting like a five-year old, or losing emotional control. These are illustrative of regression. Some believe regression indicates an attempt to return to the comfort and security of childhood where adjustment to other people and things were less critical or seemed to be. It is also evidenced in older employees always talking about the good old days and secretly wishing they could go back several decades and relive their lives. Excessive emphasis on the past when their wants to be considered important and to belong were satisfied is a means of defense against present realities in which they find themselves frustrated and unhappy.

There is also the defense mechanism of giving up. In this case the people lose all hope and cease trying. They may feel that any effort they attempt will encounter a barrier and that it is not possible for them to gain job satisfaction from the present work. They resign to their unsatisfactory work existence. Hence, they avoid the obstacle or situation. This form of defense mechanism is *resignation*.

The fourth defense mechanism to be discussed is *compromise*. Its name indicates its nature, namely one of modifying or altering objectives actually or symbolically in order to relieve the frustration. There are several types of compromise. In one type, called *sublimation*, the person adopts a new objective or behavior commonly on a higher and socially more acceptable level. In another type of compromise, a person defends her ego by claiming she actually did not want that for which she received punishment or about which she is frustrated. She gives false reasons to explain her behavior believing such action will protect her. Commonly, she will offer alibis. In fact, alibing is a common form of this type of defense mechanism called *rationalization*.

Work Environment

Those relatively enduring and distinguishing conditions influencing the behavior of people in a given work situation constitute what is commonly termed *work environment*. It is important because it is related to how employees feel toward managerial practices being used in day to day operations and toward other people, especially management members, of the same organization. As indicated in Figure 18–1, work environment is shown as influencing the entire behavioral process leading to job satisfaction. We cannot state with certainty that work environment causes job satisfaction, but we know that it is closely related to satisfaction and has an effect on the employee's behavior.

For many office employees the competency of the supervisor is the key consideration in work environment. How fairly does the supervisor assign work? Is job pressure to complete work almost constantly present? Are high standards of performance stressed by the supervisor and are they given a sacred status? Is the whole work setting formalized in that job descriptions, work-standards, regulations regarding pay and appraisals of performance established in writing are readily available to the employee so that face to face discussion of such subjects is believed unnecessary. Answers to such questions as these supply an insight into the work environment.

In addition, there is the factor identifying the manner in which the nonmanagement members and management members perceive the general management of the organization. For example, do they believe communication is adequate to satisfy their requirements? Managers and nonmanagers typically want to be in the know especially on matters that affect them. Usually they want open communication, up and down the organization, acknowledgment of their ideas and a reply indicating management's evaluation of suggestions. Also, the risk taken in decision making merits high priority. Who participates in what decision making and who assumes the risk for what decisions are foremost in conditioning the managers and nonmanagers perceptions of practices which are followed in an organization and which contribute so heavily to its work environment. Also, there is interest in the existence and maintenance of teamwork, the manner in which groups work together, how their efforts are directed, modified, and used. Furthermore, their beliefs about the way managers and nonmanagers are promoted and the opportunity for advancement must be considered. This involves organization structure, job definition, and values of management—all of which are vital in conditioning the work environment.

Highly significant are perceptions of one nonmanager concerning the behavior of other nonmanagers and also of managers. Jealousies and rivalries exist to some degree in most offices. Differentiation in pay might be the cause or a belief that the superior thinks more highly of a new employee than of another, and this condition can give rise to rivalry. It may be the established plan of comparing productivity, of one group competing against another. Any feeling by an employee of being mistreated, bypassed, or ignored can cause anxiety and frustration and hence, affect the employee's behavior. The provisions for cooperation among employees in the performance of work and the developmental practices followed are further examples of employer-employee relationships that contribute to the work environment. If one is required to cooperate and work with a fellow employee, whose behavior one dislikes, that requirement from one's viewpoint may lead to an unsatisfactory work environment. In contrast, if special training is given one employee whose co-employees feel has the mental capacity for complete mastering of the new knowledge, the work environment has provided a positive influence upon the employee's efforts.

THEORY X AND THEORY Y

A great deal of the current thinking about the behavior of people in organizations rests on Theory X and Theory Y developed by Douglas McGregor. These two contrasting approaches toward people and their behavior are shown in Figure 18–2.

FIGURE 18–2
Theory X and Theory Y

The chief characteristics of Theory X are:

1. *Most employees of a firm work as little as possible and are by nature resistant to change.* She or he does only what has to be done, and dislikes work.
2. *Most employees must be persuaded, rewarded, punished, and controlled to modify their behavior to fit the needs of the organization.* They are self-centered, indifferent, and passive to the needs of the organization.
3. *Most employees want direction supplied by a formal manager and they want to avoid job responsibilities whenever possible.* Employees require leadership and direction of a recognized manager in authority within the company.

Theory Y includes:

1. *Most employees of the firm do not inherently dislike work.* To fulfill their jobs they expect to expend physical and mental efforts.
2. *Most employees have the capacity for assuming responsibility and the potential for development but management by its action must make them aware of these characteristics.* A committed employee will strive for an objective and exercise self-control in these efforts.
3. *Most employees want to satisfy social, esteem, and self-actualization needs.* The employee wants to use natural intelligence, imagination, and judgment in performing the work in the best way.

In Theory X the dominant belief is that people tend to be lazy and irresponsible, are resistant to change, gullible, and cannot be trusted. With such basic beliefs, a manager will retain authority, make most of the decisions personally, and will establish tight controls to keep employees in line with what he or she wants them to do. In contrast, Theory Y states that people are industrious and imaginative, they want to develop, to work toward organizational goals and to assume responsibility. They are prevented from doing so by the authoritarian organization hierarchy utilized by a Theory X manager.

What is the answer? According to Theory Y, it is to change beliefs and behavior so that a friendly sharing of decision making and a cooperative mode of operation is followed. This will aid people to obtain greater job satisfaction, productivity, and self-development. The role of the manager is then a catalystic coordinator, a team leader, and one who encourages participation, seeks consensus, and assists but does not make decisions for the team. Those having the most knowledge, expertise, and skill lead in the decision making. This is a demanding role calling for complete participation, candor in personal relationships, and much personal freedom by each group member.

Much current thinking is that Theory X and Theory Y represent the two extremes of a management continuum approach. Neither are followed in their pure form, most managers operate somewhere in the in-between area. They may tend to be more X than Y, or the reverse, more Y than X. People and situations vary and management must also vary with them. It seems, however, that a tendency to follow more Theory Y than X is desirable. Efforts to bring out the most constructive behavior of people are definitely worthwhile. Every human action tends to evoke a similar and increasing reaction in the content and terms which it is comprehended. Trust begets trust, and confidence begets greater confidence when they are mutually understood and accepted. Yet it is helpful to remember that human behavior is influenced by a host of highly complex factors including those that are psychological, social, economic, and biological. Some people are lazy, some dislike responsibility, others are industrious, ambitious, and seek responsibility. The majority fall somewhere in between. Managers generally reflect the mores of the culture in which they operate and it is fair to conclude that some managers have long been sensitive to people and their needs. The trend toward people-centered concepts, the contributions of extensive psychological research, and the widespread acceptance of social changes have accelerated the emphasis in management toward Theory Y. Progress is being made and will continue as both management members and nonmanagement members make every effort to understand the role and needs of each other and cooperate in developing new and better ways of achieving common goals.

Decision Making and Human Resources

Decision making filters through and is the common element of the entire management process. There is decision making in planning, in organizing, in actuating, and in controlling. The decision making person or group, as the case may be, is the pivotal point in evaluating the input, determining what course to follow, and monitoring the prescribed actions to attain the objectives. In these efforts, the decisions should reflect not only the potential material benefits, but also the effects of these decisions on the human resources, especially on those who are requested to accept and to implement the decisions.

Decision making is strongly flavored by the human element. First, recognition of the problem is highly people influenced. Next, drawing this problem to the attention of others within the organization is people oriented. Likewise, the seeking of facts, classifying them, formulating alternatives, making the selection and implementing it, heavily involve the human element. With the quantification approaches to decision making, it is true that an exactness and correctness of possible choices and a strategy to reuse in case of disagreement with the choice are provided. But the choice of what quantification technique to follow, and what assumptions to make, must be made by the manager or technician conducting the analysis. Further, those decisions must be made relating to the evaluation of the possible answers provided as well as to their implementation—all of these are related to human beings, to their values, perceptions, and behaviors.

Many objectives are ideals rather than attainable goals. This follows due to the variability of the internal system and the dynamic characteristics of the external environment. And observe that these influences are dynamic, in turn, because of the human resources. In the final analysis, the decision by a person encompasses thoughts, beliefs, ambitions, attitudes, perception, and personality traits. In fact, a person's behavior is the result of mechanisms consciously or unconsciously selected and of complex choice behaviors.

Compromise is a common characteristic of decision making. The theoretically better alternative is blended with another in order to gain acceptability by those who will implement or be affected by the decision. Clearly this common event demonstrates the influence and close relationship of human resources and decision making. They are inseparable. Most of us have witnessed a situation in which the decision was significantly modified due to the lack of cooperation and understanding by those whom the decision affected.

In many instances, the problem requiring a decision is a situation within itself. Some uniqueness exists which necessitates some new consideration of factors or a different factor so that a predetermined answer or style cannot be imposed. This difference can commonly be traced to people differences. Circumstances, constraints, and contributions of people are the vital aspects of decision making.

Productivity and Human Resources

There is no simple relationship between productivity and the behavior of human resources. The principal reason is that human behavior is complex, being conditioned as we have seen by many factors. For example, there is the influence of the job itself, the work group, the supervisor, the total organization, and the work environment—all these upon the personality, action and reaction of the individual.

Productivity can be viewed as output divided by input. The productivity of a group or of an individual is commonly expressed as so many units produced during a given period. It is increased when a greater output results from the same input, when the same output is derived from less input, or when the greater output is gained from less input, without in each instance reducing the quality of the end-product. The inclusive total viewpoint should be taken. For example, increasing the workload of employees usually does not increase productivity. It may create backlogs, adversely affect quality of work, and result in a loss in good relationships and social advances by both the employer and employee.

Genuine productivity gains contribute to service, profitability, social advances, and economic betterment. Spurious schemes to increase productivity can be destructive and self-defeating. The effect of the human resources upon productivity should always be considered for they influence to some degree the final productivity achievement. Interestingly, good productivity is not always highly correlated with what is generally considered favorable human relations. For example, the employees may tend to dislike their jobs and work environment, yet their productivity may be reasonably high. Situations of this type may be found where the work is machine-paced, the work flow is smooth from work station to work station, and fair work standards are rigidly adhered to. In contrast, it is also possible for the productivity to be poor, yet the employees like their jobs and the work environment. For this seeming discrepancy to exist, the workplace may be pleasant, co-workers extremely friendly, socializing encouraged, and the supervision highly permissive. The employees enjoy coming to work and fraternizing with their friends. But the belief and effort to produce more is minimal and viewed as being of secondary importance.

The point here is that productivity and its improvement is a many splendored thing. The human resources play a most important part in what is and what is not accomplished. But their actions and resultant efforts upon productivity are complex. Currently, there is no single formula such as have this and that done by the employees and the resultant effect will be thus and so upon productivity. While the causality relationship may never be completely and precisely known, present-day research is rapidly adding to our knowledge so that a large portion of the enigma can be eliminated.

GUIDELINES TO FOLLOW

Adequate management of human resources is a major contribution to sound human relations. The following list serves as a review and an aid in knowing and applying guidelines which will help in obtaining sincere and cooperative human relationships:

1. *Habit, emotion, and environment are major factors in explaining a person's behavior.* Concentrate on these factors to discern human relationships and why they exist. Reason is of secondary importance. Most people are rational about some things, but irrational about other things.

2. *Human beings differ, no two are exactly alike.* A human being is an individual entity, never having either the same personality, potential, likes, or capacities as any other individual. This recognition of individual differences means that in dealing with people remember everyone is different from everyone else. It is an error to assume that every normal employee has identical values, wants, and desires, and to the same degree.

3. *A person is influenced by the peer group.* The culture, pressures, and norms of the group are important in understanding a person's behavior. In turn, much of what a person does is through a peer group because it helps satisfy the need for friendship, security, and a sense of belonging. Benefits as well as losses come to the group member that would not be possible were the individual working alone. And, it should be observed, that what the individual of a group does affects that group's behavior.

4. *Agreement is more prevalent with those a person likes.* In dealing with people try to know and to understand their behavior. Being impersonal is the best way to turn them off.

5. *People resent authority being used to push them around.* Any resort to domination in order to get something done, will be resented. Condescending gestures and tongue-lashings lead to inefficiencies primarily because they create emotional upset. Respect for and a belief that the other person is reasonable and fair are basic for good human relationships to exist.

6. *Keep in mind the sacred cows in the other person's memory.* Unless you know the other person extremely well, it is best to refrain from any remarks about other persons or things about which he has a very fixed opinion. Beliefs such as his football team is the best, his report format the most effective, or his city the best governed should not be disturbed. Whether true or not is immaterial. Figure out a way to avoid them. Taking pot shots at someone else's castles-in-the-air is one sure way to endanger smooth human relations.

7. *A person likes to be a part of victory.* Everyone wants to be with a winner. We want a leader in whom we feel confident and who knows what is needed and knows how to achieve it. Little value is placed upon what we obtain easily. We want to try and to win. And with this is the deep feeling that we are entitled to everything, accept-

able to us, that we receive. Appeasement is commonly held in contempt, not only by those giving it, but also by those receiving it.

8. *Proper timing is vital in human relations.* Sudden changes should be avoided. Prepare people for the acceptance of new ideas or modifications in their accustomed way of thinking and doing. And remember the great majority of people resent being pushed. They want time to mull a suggestion over, letting it jell for awhile. Further, there commonly is a best psychological time for the introduction of any new thought. By giving it adequate attention, the help of proper timing can bring about near miracles.

9. *People prefer activities that challenge them.* Most want to grow, to acquire new knowledge and skill. In many this means the opportunity to use their highest abilities and to enjoy a sense of accomplishment from the performance of their jobs. They want to be a part of and contribute to progress.

10. *Fair play is paramount.* Give a person the opportunity to understand thoroughly a controversial situation and that person usually is fair and reasonable in evaluating it. The values and stimuli employed may differ as well as the conclusion from that of another person, but in the processing effort of arriving at an answer, most people try to be honest and fair.

11. *People desire to feel important.* We like to be considered a specific person with meaningful feelings and contributions. Our opinions have validity and while not always accepted we want them to be considered. We prefer to give rather than to receive advice. To be considered a number, or to be ignored completely is a deadly blow to most of us.

12. *People want to be informed.* To be fully informed about whatever concerns us is the viewpoint of the normal human being. If accurate information is not given, the typical employee will strive to be "in the know." Guesses, rumors, and questions will be resorted to. And people tend to think and act in keeping with the extent of their personal identification and interests with those of the organization. These identifications and interests are aided by adequate communication.

QUESTIONS

1. How important do you feel human resources and their management are in office management? Elaborate on your answer.
2. Discuss the influence of an employee's basic values in the actuating efforts of a manager.
3. Give an example from experience that illustrates the successful use of the guideline "proper timing is vital in human relations."
4. Describe the meaning of Figure 18–1 in your own words.

5. Elaborate on the statement that "human resources are heterogenous" and point out its significance to the office manager.

6. What is meant by each of the following:
   a. Social wants.
   b. Theory Y.
   c. Compromise is a common characteristic of all managerial decision making.
   d. Perceptions of an office manager.

7. What is your understanding of work environment and discuss its significance in office management.

8. Discuss the subject "Productivity and Human Resources."

9. Do you agree or disagree with this statement: "How well the assets, values, and wants of an employee are being met by job performance indicates the degree of job satisfaction that is being experienced." Why?

10. In your opinion, is it a normal state of affairs to have difference and dissent among persons working for a common goal? Elaborate on your answer.

11. Enumerate four defense mechanisms used by a human being. Select one of these and briefly discuss it.

12. In this chapter, of the twelve guidelines given for obtaining cooperative human relationships, select the three you believe are probably most important. Justify your answer.

CASE PROBLEMS

Case 18–1.   Kubera Company

Edmund DuBarry is a cost clerk, has been with the company two years, and performs satisfactory work. Several months ago he purchased for his home a stereo set and a quantity of long-play records. Soon after that he developed the habit of humming and whistling at his work. His sounds were somewhat lacking in artfulness, but Mr. DuBarry apparently derived much satisfaction from his efforts for he continued with them off and on throughout the entire day. Other cost clerks working near Mr. DuBarry made no complaints, but to his supervisor, Harvey Olsen, "the sounds" were very disturbing. At first, he had hoped that Mr. DuBarry would "stop the music" after a week or so of such goings on. But the practice persisted.

Finally, Mr. Olsen spoke privately to Mr. DuBarry and requested that he stop his humming and whistling during working hours as they were distracting, in bad taste, and not in keeping with a well-run office. Mr. DuBarry complied and was quiet for several days. Then he again started humming and whistling while on the job. After a couple hours of this, Mr. Olsen walked to Mr. DuBarry's desk and in front of the entire department shouted to Edmund, "Stop it." Mr. DuBarry did. Then after several seconds, Mr. DuBarry stated softly, "None of the people here in the department have complained. All of us are doing our work. The trouble is supervisors don't want to adjust to individual employee differences, but employees are expected to adjust to individual manager differences." Mr. Olsen told Mr. DuBarry to keep quiet and get to work. Mr. DuBarry said nothing.

Questions:

1. Is there a problem here? Discuss.
2. What do you believe would have happened had Mr. Olsen said nothing to Mr. DuBarry?
3. What should Mr. DuBarry do now? Mr. Olsen? Justify your views.

Case 18–2. Wilbur Bodner

Wilbur Bodner left for work in his usual manner Tuesday morning, but on his way, stopped at a filling station to telephone the personnel office of his employer to tell them that he would not be in the office since his wife was ill and he had to take her to the hospital. The assistant personnel manager thanked him for calling and said he would forward the message to Mr. Joseph Callahan who was Mr. Bodner's superior.

About ten o'clock that same morning, Mr. Bodner's wife telephoned him at work. The call was taken by the assistant personnel manager and had to do with a question regarding a deduction from Mr. Bodner's paycheck. Satisfying this inquiry, he asked, "How are you?" to which the answer, "Just fine, in fact, great, never felt better in my life," alerted the assistant personnel manager that something was wrong. About 20 minutes later he called back Mr. Bodner's home telephone number. Mrs. Bodner answered and seemed in good health. Next day, Wednesday, reporting to work, Mr. Bodner found a message on his desk requesting that he see the personnel manager immediately. Entering the personnel manager's office, he was directed to a chair, and requested to be seated. The following conversation ensued:

PERSONNEL MANAGER: Where were you yesterday?

WILBUR: My wife was sick and I took her to the hospital. Had to wait—you know for tests and all that. Took the entire morning and then some. Finally got the good news—all is O.K.—about 2 P.M. Since we didn't have any lunch yet, we ate at the hospital and didn't get home till around 3:30 P.M. or so. I figured the day was shot and no use trying to report at that time.

PERSONNEL MANAGER: Is that right?

WILBUR: Well, I called in about it—just like you're supposed to.

PERSONNEL MANAGER: Yes, we received your call. How come your wife didn't know about your absence? She called about midmorning yesterday and thought you were at work.

WILBUR: My wife called here yesterday?

PERSONNEL MANAGER: That's correct.

WILBUR: That can't be. It can't be.

PERSONNEL MANAGER: Well it is. I'll get her on the phone and you can confirm what I am telling you is correct.

Although embarrassed, Mr. Bodner refused to admit that he was not at the hospital with his wife. He kept steadfastly to his story. Finally after another ten minutes of questions and answers, Wilbur admitted his story was not true. Whereupon the personnel manager told Mr. Bodner his employment was being terminated. Mr. Bodner's record shows he has been with the company six years and during the last two years has received four 3-day suspensions for being absent without a legitimate excuse.

WILBUR: Lose my job because of something like this? That's not fair. Why the discharge?

PERSONNEL MANAGER: It should be obvious, Wilbur. Absence for a false reason. Destroying the integrity of the relationship between you and the company. Your record here plus a deliberate falsehood. There is no future employment here for you.

Questions:

1. What possible motives do you surmise might cause Mr. Bodner to behave the way he did? Discuss.
2. Do you feel the personnel manager handled the situation properly? Why? Discuss.
3. Briefly relate what alternatives are now available to Mr. Bodner. Which one do you feel he should adopt? Why?

Case 18–3.   Oliver and Graham, Inc.

The management of Oliver and Graham, Inc. includes a strong emphasis upon the importance of human resources and for years the corporation has boasted about its employees and their role in the corporation's success. Recently a difference of opinion has arisen between the employees and the management members regarding the location of the vending machines in the factory and the office areas.

Currently the machines are in a variety of locations to make it convenient for the employees to get soft drinks, hot beverages, candy, sandwiches, and cigarettes. Employees are permitted to buy from the machine whenever they want to. There are no restrictions. The profits realized from the vending machine sales are given to the employees' welfare fund.

It is believed now by key management members that the machines are too convenient and, in fact, are a disadvantage in that many employees are spending too much of their time and money at the machines. A recent survey reveals the loss of time is substantial.

It is proposed by management to move all the machines to the lunchroom. Here the employees could sit at tables in comfort. Further, debris, wrappers, empty cans, and the like would not be all over the factory and office. The lunchroom is open only certain hours of the day. Vending sales are projected under the suggested rearrangement to be lower, but to compensate for the projected loss in profits from the machines, the corporation offers to give the welfare fund an amount of $6,000 annually. This amount is considered quite satisfactory by everyone.

However, many, but not all, of the employees object to the proposed change. They claim it is an underhanded method to cut their privileges and to make them more dependent upon the corporation. If work-time losses are excessive, or the working areas are cluttered, the corporation should state its case and take the necessary action against the offenders, not inconvenience the entire workforce.

Corporate managers argue that it is simply putting under control a situation that has gotten out of control. The employees do not have the right to congregate around the machines and enjoy refreshments at all hours of the morning and afternoon. Furthermore, both the factory and office areas will be cleaner.

Questions:

1. Evaluate the arguments voiced by the employees.
2. Enumerate several alternatives that are available to the managers.
3. What action should the corporate managers take? Why?

Case 18–4. Howe Products Company

The supervisor of the card-punching and tabulating department, Jennifer Pierce, went to her superior, office manager Byron Duffel, and inquired if there was danger in letting a company romance continue. She explained that one of the women employees in her department was apparently quite interested in a Mr. Daniel Schloesser, an executive in the systems and procedures department. It probably had been going on for six to eight months and everyone in card punching and tabulating seemed to know about it.

DUFFEL: Who is the woman?

PIERCE: Agnes Cushman.

DUFFEL: She's a very good worker, if it is the one I'm thinking about. She has long black hair, short, rather stocky, big brown eyes?

PIERCE: Yes, that's Agnes.

DUFFEL: Well, this Schloesser man must be 40–45 years old. I would guess Agnes at about 25 years.

PIERCE: I believe the records show she is 28 years of age.

DUFFEL: I don't know too much about Schloesser—whether he's married or has been married.

PIERCE: I've heard very little about him. Nothing about a wife or family of his. Do you think I ought to do anything?

DUFFEL: I guess it's their own private affair.

PIERCE: Yes, I guess it is. Yet, on the other hand, he's coming over and talking to her quite a bit. And she gets far more telephone calls now, but I don't know if they are from Schloesser or not. Some of the other girls are making kidding remarks to Agnes and she doesn't seem to be taking them too well.

Questions:

1. What should Mr. Duffel say to Ms. Pierce? Why?
2. What action, if any, should Ms. Pierce take? Mr. Duffel?
3. In general, what do you feel should be done about company romances? Why?

Chapter 19

Motivating the Office Employee

The greatest service we can perform for others is to help them to help themselves.

Horace Mann

Most employees will respond favorably to help. They want to develop, to perform greater service, to acquire status, and to contribute importantly. This means that in many respects managers are really helpers of employees. Their task is to help their followers do their best. Their challenge is to develop a satisfied and a satisfactory work force. Work is to be accomplished effectively, but this can be done and at the same time make the employees' work life happier and their work more meaningful and satisfying.

INTRODUCTION TO MOTIVATION

Motives imply action to satisfy a need or want. They are what causes and keep a person to perform an activity in order to achieve a desired result, meaningful to the person, and for which there is the promise of reward for attainment of the result. The reward sought is fulfillment of a need or want. We can now offer this definition: *Motivation is the willingness to make the effort to achieve a goal or reward.*

To illustrate, an employee, John Smith, seeks to win the esteem of his superior. This drive by John is a motive. To achieve his goal, John performs outstanding work on his job and it is evident to his superior that John has contributed significantly. The superior rewards John with formal recognition and tells him how important his work efforts are to his co-workers and to the company. John perceives these rewards as satisfying.

506

The urge or drive comes from within the individual, not from someone else in the form of an outside force. Others may suggest goals and actions, but it is up to the individual to accept the idea and have the feeling to be willing to expend the energy to win the goal and, as a result, achieve the reward. This means that successful motivating of the office employee usually requires providing work and a work environment that permits, or better, encourages the employee to act in a manner that the employee believes is satisfactory. For the worker, the manager should create opportunities, remove obstacles, provide guidance, and encourage growth. The initiation of actions, however, rests with the employee.

Motivation is conditioned by the fundamental beliefs that the individual possesses. An employee's belief about office work, for example, is an important consideration in motivating efforts. Does the employee view it as a vital service, a real contribution to co-workers, the company, and to society? If so, there is opportunity for satisfying social, esteem, and even self-realization wants from the work situation. In contrast, if office work is looked upon as a boring, something-to-do activity the chances for obtaining genuine wants satisfaction from performing it are indeed minute. Figure 19–1 lists selected questions to check your everyday attitude toward work.

FIGURE 19–1
An Honest Answer of 'Yes," to Each of These Questions Indicates a Favorable Attitude toward Work

1. Do you offer to take over some of the work when absence of another employee means that someone must help?
2. Do you feel it is a privilege and an opportunity to work for the company and the people with whom you are?
3. Do you seek additional work and responsibility to increase your value to the company?
4. Do you accept discipline realizing it is honest criticism and a necessity for most work?
5. Do you review your own work and try to achieve excellence?
6. Do you find genuine satisfaction in your work?
7. Do you willingly help other employees wherever you can?
8. Do you feel you are being paid fairly for what you do?
9. Do you inspire those around you to sound work attitudes?
10. Do you believe that you have been and will be advanced as rapidly as you really deserve?

Thinking "success" on the job and for the employer are essential. Basic to this attitude is that work is an opportunity to provide a product or service of value to others. But again, each person must acquire this viewpoint personally. No one can give it. And with this personal experience or discovery comes the truth that the secret to successful work lies not only in performing what we like, but also in learning to like what we have to do. A person's work attitude is formed by personal thinking; it results entirely from facilities of which she or he can be master.

Of probably more significance is the employee's self-image. Concentrating thoughts on strengths is favorable to motivation in that this viewpoint assists in setting reachable goals the employee believes accomplishable. Two assumptions are implied here that the employee (1) has solid strengths, often unidentified and unused, and (2) has meaningful personal goals. These conditions exist in the great majority of cases and hence, it follows that if the employee can see something to gain or a want to satisfy from work, the employee will be successful and satisfied throughout his or her work life. In some cases, the employee may be unaware of a liking for a given type of work until a trial is suggested. Subsequently, the employee knows the work and gains proficiency in it, and may well find the work quite satisfying.

Furthermore, the manager should keep in mind that the development of subordinates is a cardinal objective to be gained from motivational efforts. By no means are they carried out solely to increase material productivity. The manager must view sincerely the building of people as a principal responsibility and work at it, otherwise the task will not be accomplished. Assigning employees to special projects or to short tours of duty and observing how they perform these tasks represents an effective approach. Also, promoting as rapidly as abilities permit should be followed. Further, it brings good results to hire outside people whose ideas, initiative, and ambition demonstrate that these qualities are recognized no matter where they are found. In addition, employees with limitations should be identified and kept from becoming obstacles to the advancement of others who are qualified.

Achievement of Motivation

Satisfying a want is the key to motivation achievement. Find out what the employee's want is, make it possible for that want to be satisfied from the work efforts, and reward for accomplishment so that the want is fulfilled. It sounds relatively simple, but it is not. Why? Because employees' wants are not identical for each group or for each member of a group. Furthermore, the wants do not remain constant; they vary from day to day. The reasons for these conditions are numerous and quite complex. They include both employee behavior and the influence of the work environment. These will be discussed in the following pages.

The wants of people were discussed and classified in Chapter 18. A popular classification of wants is that suggested by Maslow who viewed wants as a hierarchy consisting of five levels. Starting at the bottom, the *survival or physiological wants or needs* include the need for adequate food, clothing, shelter, rest, and activity. What constitutes adequacy will differ among people and likewise the degree of motivation to acquire satisfactions of these needs will vary. When these needs are taken care of, they cease to motivate behavior, and new and higher needs emerge. Next in the hierarchy are *safety needs* which include protection from physical danger, economic security, philosophic and orderly explanation of the surroundings in which the person lives. Next is *social needs*. Togetherness, belonging to a group, and acquiring acceptance become major goals. In this stage typical employees want to know that what they are doing is worthwhile and has merit, that they expect, at least in part, to satisfy these needs by having an opportunity to demonstrate their talent, acquire prestige, and gain recognition. The fourth level is *esteem needs,* both self-esteem and the esteem of others. Self-esteem is represented by the desire for competence, achievement, and freedom of thought. Esteem by others includes status, prestige, and reputation. Obviously, the fulfillment of these esteem needs are important behavior determinants. Last, and at the top of the hierarchy of wants are *self-realization needs*. This entails the fulfillment of a person's highest potential, to become everything that one is capable of becoming. Satisfaction of this need can take many different forms such as managing a department, advancing a business theory, writing, or being an excellent swimmer. Fulfillment of capacity is the underlying characteristic of this want. Discussion of several means for motivating will follow, but before doing so, let us consider (1) the levels of aspiration of people and (2) leadership, both of which are vital in the area of motivation.

Levels of Aspiration

A person will strive to achieve in keeping with a personal level of aspiration. By repeatedly reaching a goal and being rewarded, that person is moved to seek continuously higher expectations. In contrast, repeated failures bring about frustration, a change in methods, and a lowering of sights. That is, success begets success, and failure tends to beget failure. This is also in keeping with the basic psychological statement that behavior perceived to be rewarding will tend to be repeated; on the other hand, behavior which ends in punishment or is nonrewarding tends to be terminated.

The friends and associates one has exert an influence upon one's level of aspiration. To gain acceptance and approval of associates, a person shapes her or his behavior to resemble their behavior. For example, a programmer will tend to achieve the same work values as each member of the peer group does. Behavior of close friends has a strong influence in establishing the behavioral pattern of an individual.

A person's level of aspiration is also influenced by the values gained from parents and by experiences witnessed while growing up. If by example and statements a parent demonstrates that a senior systems analyst job represents the zenith of success, there is a tendency for the child to believe this is a standard for work achievement.

Leadership

Vital to motivation is the leadership present in the work environment. People prefer to be with a successful leader. Being a part of victorious accomplishments, following a person who has demonstrated an ability to get things done, and having firsthand experience in observing successful management in action are in and of themselves highly motivating to an employee. Members of a group receive strong stimuli from effective leadership; and in turn, a strong leader acquires that position, in part, because of an ability to motivate members of the group.

What is leadership? It has been defined in a number of different ways; but for our purposes here, we can consider that leadership implies a threefold meaning:

1.   *Skill to Direct—to Show the Way.*   A leader possesses the ability to guide people—to point out the proper means for attainment. This leadership characteristic usually means that the leader is out in front leading, not in back pushing. While not directly applicable, the concept can be illustrated by considering a piece of ordinary wrapping twine. When the front end of the twine is pulled and guided along desired paths, the rest of the piece of twine will follow. In contrast, when the twine is pushed, it follows no predetermined path and flounders in an aimless direction.

2.   *Ability to Win Cooperation and Loyalty.*   A leader is able to get people to act jointly and to work toward a common goal. All efforts of the group are knit together and concentrated into one large force toward the attainment of the objective. This unity of operation is accomplished by strong and enthusiastic feelings, so that each member has a deep sense of obligation to the leader.

3.   *Courage to Carry On until the Assigned Task Is Accomplished.*   A leader is dauntless and ever confident that the task to be done will be completely accomplished, he has implicit faith in the success of chosen actions and gives a feeling of confidence and positiveness to all associates.

People like to be led by a dynamic leader. They like to be led by a person who clearly envisages the goal, who knows how to achieve that goal, and who goes out after it. Once the decision is made as to what the goals are and what people must do to achieve them, leadership at all levels of the organization plays a dominant role in seeing that they are accomplished.

Participation

Knowing the employee's wants and the working environment along with the employee's assets including experience, knowledge and skill et al (discussed in Chapter 18), we are now ready to implement actions designed to motivate the office employee. A multitude of different approaches and conditions can be followed, but among the most of the commonly followed concepts is a common theme. It is *participation*, i.e., permission granted the other member, either manager or nonmanager, to have a part in the activity whether it is planning, decision making, or communicating. Giving employees some voice in matters that affect them is heralded as a key principle to follow in efforts of motivating.

Among the major justifications for practicing participation is that it helps win enthusiastic acceptance of proposed actions. People tend to accept their own ideas and will strive to prove them correct once they are put into effect. Obstacles will be overcome by the suggestor, in part, to demonstrate the wisdom of the suggestion. More than this, it is probably true in most cases that the best answer to a perplexing situation is evolved, that is, best in the sense that it is superior for the particular person or group to follow. Participation tends to tailor make the answer. Further, participation aids in the development of employees. Having them become familiar with the problem and evolve what is the most satisfactory way of handling it provides practical experience in issues of management.

However, participation should be used very carefully. It should be encouraged in those subjects which are within the employee's province or knowledge. He or she should be given ample explanation of the situation or acquire knowledge about it in an acceptable way and made to feel that suggestions and opinions are welcomed. It is extremely frustrating and "demotivating" to request participation by an employee who knows little or nothing about the subject at hand. Furthermore, the management member in charge of the activity should not step away from the duty to manage.

MANAGEMENT BY OBJECTIVES

A number of offices have adopted some form of management by objectives (MBO) whereby every responsible employee confers with a superior and makes specific commitments regarding future results. Specifically, the subordinate works out set objectives, the means for obtaining them, and the yardsticks to be followed in determining progress toward or achievement of the objectives. The superior may assist in this work of goal determination and achievement. In any event, the superior reviews, modifies if necessary, and discusses the program with the subordinate so that a mutually agreeable program is evolved. At periodic intervals, commonly quarterly, the superior and subordinate meet to review the progress toward the objectives and to revise any plans to ensure that the objectives are met. Proponents claim MBO is modern and motivational. Mutually known and determined targets enhance understanding and permit useful concentration of effort, the employee is aware of how accomplishments are evaluated and a close superior-to-subordinate relationship is maintained. In addition, the approach serves as an excellent vehicle for not only implementing, but also for controlling change. The people themselves decide the change or decide its delay. And MBO is motivational in that for the most part subordinates participate in deciding what goals are worthwhile and in the ways they believe are best and under conditions that are to their liking.

It is desirable to provide relatively small, well defined targets and meaningful feedbacks. This often requires ingenuity, but it is especially important where the work is relatively repetitive and of a short time cycle, a characteristic of much office work. Short-time cycle work should be subjected to frequent feedbacks, otherwise nonacceptable variances may be permitted to exist too long before correction is made. Feedback must come while the work is being performed and must enable the employee to make a change immediately in personal behavior.

While the idea behind MBO is readily comprehended, it will not provide the motivational quality desired unless it is planned and installed properly. These requisites should be followed: (1) custom design the MBO to fit the needs and requirements of the particular organization, (2) use a team-oriented modification approach to objectives-setting, and (3) involve all organization units in the program. For greatest success the employee must have some leeway in how work is to be performed. There must be some variable that the worker can influence. When the work content and method are rigid and there is little opportunity to change it, MBO gains fall below expectancy. Also, the individual objectives should be coordinated by clearing them through a central agency. Without compatible objectives, there is a possibility that unhealthy and destructive competition among individuals may cause needless overall management difficulties. An "every man-for-himself" syndrome may prevail. In addition, unless all organizational units of an organization are involved, there is lack of control, difficulty in measuring what is being accomplished, loss of organizational balance, and excessive energy directed to strategic maneuvering.

Some contend that MBO is not motivational until it is linked to a reward system. In other words, people won't set up their own goals and means for accomplishing them, and then strive to accomplish them simply to say that they have done so. This is probably true of many people. They want and expect the recognition, praise, or promotion in return for their achievement. On the other hand, what is motivational to an individual is determined by that individual who may feel satisfied in showing other and self that "I can do it."

MBO certainly gets people involvement and encourages the subordinate to "do his thing," to develop planning and problem solving abilities, to measure accomplishments, to increase responsibility, and to be the best person possible performing the given work and within the given work environment. Further, the management member gets the needed authority to the subordinate automatically. There is no problem of delegation. Accountability by the subordinate is retained and creativity is stimulated. While admittedly not a panacea for all office management problems, MBO is an important aid, and when applied properly can be of great assistance.

OFFICE JOB ENRICHMENT

Managers commonly wonder why their people are not motivated. With good working conditions, high pay, long vacations, and work free from pressure, why aren't they happy with their jobs? At one time the prevalent belief was to assign a special task to perform—to make the employee a specialist. This concept gave way to the belief that more pay was the answer and, in turn, declined in prominence to the idea that keeping busy—having many things to do would reduce dissatisfaction because being fully occupied left no time to think about complaints. Emphasis then drifted to plush offices—new desks, colorful walls, the latest in office gadgets, and piped-in music. Yet office employees were not fully satisfied.

Later, the idea was advanced by Herzberg that motivation was closely related to the job itself. From research, he suggested that thinking be directed to (1) job content and (2) job context. The former concerns the work itself and the employee. It has potential for strong job satisfaction determiners or motivators, such as achievement, advancement, and recognition. In contrast, job context includes the environment in which the job is performed. It includes the supervision, working conditions, and salary. These factors, labeled hygienic or maintenance factors, seldom cause, except for temporary or a short period, positive job satisfaction, but they serve as a base upon which the motivators can be added to improve job performance. In other words, when the job itself is personally unrewarding, no amount of job context or outside peripheral factors to the work itself make up for the person's lack of fulfillment. This theory places emphasis on the work itself and the employees who are the focal point. This gave birth to job enrichment.

Job enrichment is *the modifying of job content so that the person has a wider variety of tasks, increased responsibility, and greater opportunity for recognition of accomplishments.* The source of motivation is the work itself. Job enrichment encompasses an increase in the person's autonomy creating opportunity to achieve the work so that it becomes rewarding and meaningful. Specifically, job enrichment is neither rotating employees through a series of boring tasks nor simply adding a number of different tasks together. Examples of office job enrichment are shown in Figure 19-2.

Gaining Effective Office Job Enrichment

Job enrichment requires that the employees want it. If they don't want enriched jobs, don't try to force the issue; it will end in failure. Adequate explaining of what job enrichment is, how it will affect the employee, and what the new job will be like are requisites for its success. If it is to be a viable force bringing about needed change, there is no substitute for employees' wholehearted support for it. In addition, the requirements of the entire organization should be taken into account and the need for it, from this totality viewpoint, revealed. Promotional efforts in its behalf by a management member who has taken a fancy to it is inadequate justification. Its possible contribution should be viewed as fulfilling a need rather than something imposed upon the organization because it is bringing good results to a competitor. And don't expect an immediate payoff from it. Frequently there is a lag between cause and effect in organizational change. One cannot reasonably expect a reversal of existing modes of operation overnight. It takes time for people to adjust to change, and to forget the "old way." Real gains, if any, are difficult to determine over the short period because often a portion of the initial gains are due to the reaction to the newness or the change itself, and not to the before and after methodologies. Finally, adjustments in dollar expenditures be it in pay, improved quality, greater productivity, or whatever, probably will have to be made. Otherwise, the job enrichment remains an adjunct to and never becomes a part of the existing *modus operandi*. Figure 19-3 shows for selected factors the most favorable and least favorable conditions for implementing job enrichment.

If it appears that job enrichment merits serious consideration a four-step program is recommended. First, get the group members involved. Hold meetings devoted to problem solving. When feasible, mention job enrichment as a possible contributor toward easing the problem or per-

FIGURE 19–2
Examples of Office Job Enrichment

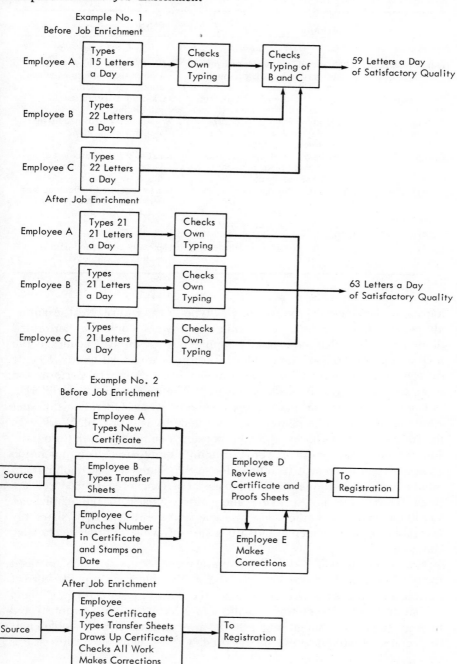

FIGURE 19–3
Conditions Affecting the Implementing of Job Enrichment by Selected Factors

	General Conditions Are	
Factors	*Most Favorable*	*Least Favorable*
Philosophy of management	Believes job should center around the person, not the person around the job.	Believes person should center around the work, not the work around the person.
Leadership	Employee-centered, emphasis on people.	Task-centered, emphasis on production.
Personnel interaction	Work involves tasks by several employees whose efforts must be closely coordinated.	Work is best performed by individual working alone.
Cost	Relatively a small amount of technology (machines and tools) are utilized.	Relatively a large amount of technology (machines and tools) are utilized.
Variety of work	Many parts, tools, and controls involved in the work, and the work pace and physical location can be altered to meet individual requirements.	Work is required to be done by a person working alone or in an isolated location.
Working conditions	Generally considered satisfactory by employees.	Generally considered unsatisfactory by employees.

haps helping to avoid problems of this type in the future. Next, examine all present job make-ups. Determine what work could be performed differently, and what new task groupings are possible. Encourage the help and suggestions of the employees in these analytical efforts. Decide on the enriched jobs. Third, determine what training to perform the proposed enriched jobs will be needed. The requirement of different procedures on different office forms will be common. Operating different office machines and handling unfamiliar records will prevail. Work with the training staff, if you have one, to develop a suitable training program. Job rotation may assist in "cross-training" employees. Too much too soon may cause the switch to flounder so the change to office job enrichment should be gradual—an employee at a time or a procedure at a time. Fourth and last, provide adequate feedback to the employees. Let them know both the good and the bad results so they share the favorable accomplishments and are aware of what improvements they should achieve.

Not everyone will be "for" job enrichment. Some will see no need for it. They will claim, for example, that the problem is simply to correct the excessive absenteeism, not change the entire makeups of jobs. Such a condition calls for getting members to admit there is a problem and to see that job enrichment might be the answer. Mutual trust, confidence, and openmindedness must be restored. Others will claim the cost is too great. The expenditures for modifying the office layout, confusion, and retraining are cited to support their contention. It could be, but get the facts, then decide. Also, the question of interdependency of jobs is raised. Many office jobs are interdependent and a change in one or two can change the whole work flow. In these cases, perhaps several relatively independent jobs can be combined, or the job redesigning efforts scheduled to take place gradually—one or two job aspects at a time.

COMMUNICATION

Top managers like other management members to communicate—to tell them what is going on and what is on their minds. Also, supervisors are eager to hear from the members of their work group. Both the good and the bad news are wanted. And nonmanagers want to know what is going on and to be informed about achievements, problems, or changes especially those that affect them. Communication takes place not only from the bottom up but from the top down which is more common and is essential for managerial direction to exist as well as for decision making and controlling to take place. In other words, downward communication helps provide the implementation for organizational goals, policies, procedures, task direction, and feedback. Upward communication features feedback information and encouragement for the subordinate to express feelings about her or his job and performance, and to share ideas. The normal tendency is to underrate the importance of communication. An aggressive and sincere communicative effort will do wonders toward achieving a cooperative, confident, and enthusiastic working force. An informed employee is usually a satisfied employee.

Most difficulties of communication can be classified under the headings of either telling too little or assuming complete understanding of communication. Both of these habits tend to detract from our communication effectiveness. Managers should take the initiative and supply full information to employees. Dependence upon "word of mouth," or believing that "everybody knows that—it's common information," leads to incomplete and frequently incorrect information. The employee wants to be informed, not coddled. Any information that will help her do a better job ranks high in her preference.

Tell an employee something you want him to understand, and the chances are 12 to 1 he will not fully understand you. Why is this? Because many believe that the act of writing or telling another certain information completely fulfills their job of communicating. However, to communicate effectively requires definite skills and knowledge. Included among these criteria are the following:

1. Communication Is Two Way. One tells, informs, or requests; the other listens, asks, or interprets. Without listenership, the communication just does not exist. As Thoreau put it: "It takes two to speak the truth—one to speak, the other to hear it." Listening is an art and requires effort. For best results, involve the listener as soon as possible. Asking leading questions such as the following are effective: "How do you feel about . . . ?" "Well, what do you think—will it work?" "Now, what other information can I give you?"

2. Think Before You Write or Talk. Some people are so intent on communicating that they start to write or talk before evaluating the situation and organizing their thoughts. As a result, they confuse the reader or listener. Before communicating, it is a good idea to decide: (1) Why do you want to say anything? (2) What do you want to say? (3) What is the objective in saying this? and (4) What do you know about the receiver or listener?

3. Use Effective Words—Focus Words and Mutually Known Words. Focus words help to spot the key points in a communication. The listener or reader is assisted by phrases such as: "Our goal is to . . ." or "To summarize, . . ." These expressions aid in drawing inferences and value judgments. The use of mutually known words is essential. To describe the wage structure as "lucrative" reduces real communication if the receiver does not know the meaning of the word.

4. Practice Empathy. Communication is assisted by the sender placing himself in the position of the receiver and judging the message from the receiver's point of view. This guide helps win acceptance by the receiver and emphasizes his interests, goals, and fears by giving the receiver what he wants to hear or read.

5. Create a Follow-Up. The recipient should be given the feeling that she can return with questions or ask clarification on any part she fails to understand. Offering assistance and closing with expressions such as: "Call me if any questions arise," or "Let's get together again next Monday noon and . . . ," are usually effective in this respect.

Communication Practices and Media

The office manager must understand that communication is not a *privilege,* but an *obligation* to give important information to all members of the office and, in turn, to have them feed back information of value to their respective superiors. However, not everything need be told to everybody; there are limits. Information dealing with security, certain items being reviewed for analysis and decision making, and some areas of labor problems, are not presented to all office employees. When believed advisable, employees should be told they can't be told for explicit reasons. While a restricted communication is not a motivator, it does partially satisfy the desire to know by the offering of a legitimate explanation.

Normally, the formal lines of communication should be employed. These are the same connecting links as "lines of authority," discussed in Chapter 15. Also, as already pointed out, the office grapevine is an effective dispenser of information. It can never be completely eliminated, people and communication being what they are. The wise office manager recognizes this and uses the grapevine as an auxiliary, but is exceedingly careful that accurate, complete, and timely messages are conveyed through the normal channels so that half-truths and incomplete information are not spread by the grapevine.

To make communication effective requires efforts and practices followed honestly and completely. It is recommended that periodic and well planned one-to-one meetings be scheduled between supervisor and subordinate to explore ideas and feelings, to listen to complaints or suggestions, and to discuss the subordinate's efforts in attaining the organization's goals. Also, regularly scheduled meetings among department heads and supervisors help keep lateral communication moving and improves coordination. Likewise, meetings among groups to discuss and exchange beliefs and opinions with regard to pressing problems or proposed changes assist in satisfying the employee's need to feel important and to belong as well as provide involvement in the decision making process. Furthermore, company publications containing articles of interest to the employee such as new products, competition, and company plans are effective.

Actually, a number of communication media are available. The selection depends chiefly upon the type of information and the type of employees to be reached. Figure 19–4 suggests the features and the organizational level for six selected media.

FIGURE 19–4
Media Available for Communication Purposes

Medium	Features	Organizational Level for Which Effective
Conversation	Person-to-person, forthright personal relationship	All organizational levels
Letters	Excellent for statistical data and where permanent record is desired	Top managerial and supervisory levels
Pamphlets and booklets	Suitable for large volume of material	All organizational levels
House organs	Adequate coverage satisfactory for reminders and announcements	All organizational levels
Motion pictures, radio, and television	Dramatize presentation; helpful in training, relating company history, and special achievements	All organizational levels
Speeches	Impressive for special events and celebrations	Top managerial and supervisory levels

TRANSACTIONAL ANALYSIS

Relatively free from jargon, transactional analysis (TA) is an approach to understanding human behavior by means of communication between two or more people. It is based on the analysis of how they interact—studying the transactions—by means of tracing the way a transaction is shaped by the particular ego state of each person. The ego states that determine behavior consist of three patterns (1) parent, (2) adult, and (3) child.

The parent ego state acquired by each of us before the age of five or six, is built on external experiences and feelings impressed upon us when our only alternative was to accept without question. The parent ego is copied from parents and others including grandparents, teachers, and siblings who served as parents while we were growing. This ego state admonishes, nurtures, criticizes, and is prejudicial. It is the ego state that serves as the vehicle for transmitting culture from generation to generation. The adult ego "thinks," deals with factual information logically and without emotion. It emerges as a person is exposed to a variety of experiences and ideas that may challenge the advice and caution of the parent ego. Related to a person's ability to size up reality, the adult ego state has no predetermined feelings and checks out a situation by answering the why, what, when, where, and how questions. The third and last ego state, the child ego, includes all impulses—both the best and the worst—that are characteristic of a child. The behavior is what the person did when a child. Curiosity, rebelliousness, imagina-

FIGURE 19–5
Representative Communication for Each Ego State

Ego State	Verbal Clues	Nonverbal Clues	Representative Statement
Parent	Stupid; don't tell me; absurd; if I were you; as long as you work here.	Tapping foot; snorting; patting a person on the shoulder.	It's awful the way young men wear their hair these days.
Adult	Why; what; when; where; how; I see your point; how do you feel about.	Interested appearance; appropriate response to others.	I recognize that is a possibility.
Child	I want; I'm scared; I got more than you did.	Temper tantrums; whining voice; no answer; it's not my fault; giggling.	I'm so worried about my brother, I can't type.

tion, and self-centeredness are examples. Figure 19–5 shows representative communication for each ego state.

Transactional analysis can be used to achieve better communication and to help motivate people. By identifying the ego state revealed by the other person's communication, one can control personal communication and by means of it, influence the behavior of the other person. One such technique is *stroking* which is expressed by recognition, compliment on appearance, or praise for performance to the other person. Strokes include any signs of recognition or touch. They can be positive or negative. When negative, they make the other person feel badly. Such strokes are called *discounts*. To illustrate, a need for stroking people with an adult ego can be fulfilled by initiating a communication with those people and letting them know that their work is important to the entire office and their good performance is appreciated. To the parent ego, the communication, "Do your work," will bring forth far less loyalty and enthusiasm than the statement, "Is there some way I can help?" In some instances, the child ego is best countered with a strong adult comment. However, sincerity in all communication is a must. Statements not really meant are quickly identified as phonies by their receivers.

The accurate exchange of meaning and intent among human beings is true communication. The difficulty in accomplishing it stems from the fact that people speak, hear, write, read, and understand according to their experiences and their expectations. Feelings and beliefs that accumulate from parental influence and experience and as one grows up are hardened, are altered, and added to by one's thoughts and feelings toward self and others. The result is what is known as a *life position*. There, are four different life positions. They operate for the most part at a largely unconscious level of maturity and are basic to all our behavior. They include (1) I'm O.K.—you're O.K., (2) I'm O.K.—you're not O.K., (3) I'm not O.K.—you're O.K., and (4) I'm not O.K.—you're not O.K. Position No. 1 represents a person free from hang-ups, uses capabilities to the fullest, and accepts and works well with others. Position No. 2 identifies the person who feels self-satisfied, but who disturbs and feels superior to others, who may tend to be offensive to others, pushy, feel others are hostile and opposes efforts to be changed. No. 2 is seldom a good team member. No. 3 occupies a loser's position, is servile, feels inferior, is concerned about approval of others, and does not feel good about personal accomplishments or life. The last, No. 4, is extremely negative, trusts few people, and views life as mostly worthless. It is very difficult to get through to the No. 4 person. Figure 19–6 shows different facets of an employee's behavior related to life position.

SUGGESTION SYSTEMS

A suggestion system is a means by which employees can submit their ideas to a manager and, if these ideas are adopted, receive an award, usually consisting of an amount of cash. Generally, the suggestions con-

FIGURE 19–6
Employee Behavior According to Life Position

Employee Life Position

Employee Behavior	O.K.	Not O.K.	O.K.	Not O.K.	O.K.	Not O.K.	O.K.	Not O.K.
Employee	✓		✓			✓		✓
Other person	✓			✓	✓			✓
1. General attitude toward others is	Equality		Superiority		Inferiority		Despondent	
2. Resolves disagreement by	Clarification and mutual agreement		Other person is at fault		Differences in beliefs showing employee's inadequacy		Involves a third party	
3. Takes action when	Given assignment or by his initiative		Official directives are given		Praised		Threats are made	
4. Accepts delegation of authority	Enthusiastically		After delaying and bargaining		Reluctantly		Unwillingly and trys to beg off	
5. Approach to problem solving is	Self-satisfying and consultation with others		Turns down suggestions of others		Reliance on others		Gives in to problem acceptance	

cern ways to save time, to reduce waste, to improve quality, or to simplify practices and procedures. A suggestion system can be a strong employee motivator because the employees are given the opportunity to say somethings, to feel that the company is "their company," to think of constructive ideas, and to contribute to the progress of the enterprise.

In addition, the economic gains can be quite large. Financial gains accrue to the company as well as to the successful suggester. But these gains should not be stressed to the exclusion of the others mentioned. A suggestion system is more than a mechanism for the buying of useful ideas.

Each and every suggestion should be answered promptly with reasons for decisions reached. Replies can be by individual letters or personal interviews; it is not a good practice to post lists on the bulletin board. Replies to turndowns, i.e., those suggestions receiving no award, must contain the reasons why such action is taken. This practice is recommended because it lets the employee know that the suggestion was evaluated, reveals whether the judging committee understood the idea, and helps the employee become more knowledgeable about what is acceptable, and stimulates further thinking along what might be award-winning ideas. The award must be worthwhile. Many companies have found that $20 is a minimum figure to use with maximum awards being 10 percent of the savings for the first year.

Suggestion systems have a tendency to become dormant; for this reason, they must be continually promoted. Showmanship and publicity stunts can be used to keep the program alive. Successful devices include: attractive suggestion forms; appealing and well-located suggestion boxes bearing the sign "Have you deposited your suggestion here today?"; attention-getting posters; reminders in payroll envelopes; and notices in company papers.

The suggester's identity is unknown to the investigator in most systems. This anonymity is obtained by means of a numbering and coupon arrangement on the suggestion form. The suggester retains a numbered coupon which corresponds to the number of the suggestion. Under this arrangement, impartiality on the part of the investigators is promoted.

Suggestion stimulators can be directed to all employees in order to encourage their participation. Letters and announcements can be used; or a more direct means may be utilized, such as the manager asking: "What can you suggest to save time in the filing department?" Employees then start thinking of ways to improve that department. This practice appears to bring usable results, but it involves a serious disadvantage. It directs attention to fields foreign to the employee. A suggestion system is supposed to enable the employee to take advantage of existing knowledge which has not as yet been used to full advantage. Directing attention to new fields, therefore, might mean a loss of excellent ideas stemming from the employee's intimate on-the-job knowledge.

PERFORMANCE APPRAISAL

A keystone of motivating is that employees want to know what is expected of them and how well they are performing their work. Also, it is motivating to them to know that their employer has an interest in their accomplishments, is willing to give praise when deserved, and is interested to point out shortcomings when existent, so that they can improve themselves.

Performance appraisal can be viewed as an inventory of the most valuable asset of the enterprise—its employees. It is not, however, to be considered an X-ray of the employee. Rather it is an orderly effort designed to improve superior-subordinate relationship and to help the subordinate to self-improvement and progress. The aim is to achieve a two-way understanding between the superior and the subordinate and this includes the mutual understanding of objectives, and developing the means for implementing plans for self-improvement. More specifically the objectives include to (1) improve performance and effectiveness, (2) encourage self-development, (3) provide a record of the progress of new employees or those in training, (4) recognize employee achievements, (5) tell the employee where he stands, (6) assist in developing the superior's critical evaluation of the employee's worth, (7) identify potential for promotion, and (8) guide personnel work in promoting, demoting, or transferring an employee.

Note that salary administration objectives are not included. Current thinking is that separate appraisals should be made for (1) employee development and human relations betterment and (2) salary reviews. Using the same appraisal for both nearly always fail because the salary review will typically dominate the appraising and interviewing so that the proper frame of mind is missing to discuss developmental factors.

Appraisals can be by (1) results, or (2) personal and potential traits. The former zeros in on accomplishments won in keeping with stated goals, the latter, on traits which when performed well lead to desired results. Appraisal by results is an outgrowth of management by objectives (MBO) discussed previously. It places major responsibility on the employee to establish performance goals and appraising progress toward them. That is, establishment of short-term goals by and for the employee. The appraiser's role is to judge the employee based on what was accomplished. In keeping with MBO the appraiser had previously counseled the employee so that the employee gave considerable thinking about the job, carefully assessed abilities and limitations and formulated goals in keeping with limits of the particular case. The results approach has much motivational force and it is successful. However, certain considerations must be taken into account. For the promotion and transfer of personnel, more data are needed than results accomplishment, the job should not be restrictive, and the employee must have achievement tendencies.

Performance appraisal by traits includes rating the employee on a number of predetermined factors. These factors are considered to be directly associated with, as well as indicative of, the employee's performance on the job. They should be carefully selected and include only those factors necessary to give adequate data. Usually, six to eight factors are sufficient, as the use of too many might lead to carelessness in rating, and too few might distort the ratings. Information which is available elsewhere, such as attendance, punctuality, and length-of-service data, should not be included in the performance appraisal form. In each case, however, the factors selected are considered to be applicable to the employee, not to the job requirements.

There are five basic types of performance appraisal plans: (1) employee comparison, (2) person-to-person basis, (3) critical incidents,

(4) check lists, and (5) charts. The first is an elementary form of ranking in which a comparison of the relative performance of employees is determined. Normally, the employees under a given supervisor or in one department are ranked, from the most satisfactory at the top of the list to the least satisfactory at the bottom of the list. The ranking can be by separate traits or on an overall basis.

In the person-to-person type, the employee is rated by comparison to another employee believed to exemplify the highest rating of the particular factor being considered. Sometimes, a rating scale, established by the highest, middle, and lowest exemplary employees, respectively, is used. Thus, on the quality of dependability, for example, employee A is compared with each of the three employees included in the rating scale and is then given a rating. The person-to-person basis is not widely used in offices because it is rather complex and time-consuming. Difficulty is encountered in selecting the employees to use in the rating scale, and wide variations in the characteristics of those selected appear common.

Critical incidents are recordings in a notebook of significant behavior happenings of employees. The events are written daily or weekly by the rater and serve to refresh his or her memory when a formal evaluation is prepared. While the employees may react unfavorably to the use of the "boss's book," it does aid appraising. Care in using this means must be observed. It should also be noted that it is not a rating means as such, but an aid to observe and be alert to influences helpful in appraising.

Check lists consist of a series of statements or questions dealing with the employee's performance. Frequently, the statements have different values or weights which are unknown to the respondent. Questions which can be answered either "Yes" or "No," or by "It applies to this employee" or "It does not apply to this employee," are used. The following illustrates a portion of a check list:

Item	*Scale Value**
1. Works at a slow but steady pace	5
2. Is usually ahead of his work schedule	3
3. Gets along with fellow employees	8
4. Makes few mistakes in work.	10
5. Asks for considerable time off	7
6. Usually thinks of the company first	4

* Not included in form supplied to rater.

Charts are probably the most common type of performance appraisal used in an office. This is because they are easy to use, readily understood, and accepted by both the raters and the ratees. The chart type consists of a list of selected traits, each accompanied by a scale indicating different degrees of the trait. The rater indicates on each scale the extent to which the employee displays that respective trait at work. Figure 19–7 shows a performance appraisal chart. Observe there are seven traits, the top value of some is 20 points, others are 15 points, and still others are 10 points. A maximum possible score is 100, minimum is 7 points.

FIGURE 19–7
A Performance Appraisal Chart

HMH HUNTINGTON MEMORIAL HOSPITAL A Health Care Facility For All Of Huntington County										

(EMPLOYEE PERFORMANCE REVIEW)

Name _____ Department _____ Position _____

Date _____   Probationary   Periodic   Annual   Termination

	OUTSTANDING	ABOVE AVERAGE	AVERAGE	BELOW AVERAGE	UNSATISFACTORY
QUALITY OF WORK	20 19 18	17 16 15 14	13 12 11 10 9 8	7 6 5 4	3 2 1
Accuracy Neatness Thoroughness Economy	Consistently Superior	Sometimes Superior	Consistently Satisfactory	Usually Acceptable	Consistently Unsatisfactory
QUANTITY OF WORK	20 19 18	17 16 15 14	13 12 11 10 9 8	7 6 5 4	3 2 1
Productivity	Consistently Exceeds Requirements	Often Exceeds Requirements	Meets Requirements	Often Below Requirements	Consistently Below Requirements
DEPENDABILITY	15 14	13 12 11	10 9 8 7 6	5 4 3	2 1
Follows instructions Judgment Punctuality & attendance	Consistently Dependable	Dependable Most of Time	Ordinarily Dependable	Not Often Dependable	Consistently Undependable
COOPERATION	15 14	13 12 11	10 9 8 7 6	5 4 3	2 1
With supervisor With fellow employees	Inspires Others	Quick to Volunteer & Assist	Generally Works Well With Others	Seldom Works Well With Others	Does Not Work Well With Others
INITIATIVE	10	9 8	7 6 5	4 3	2 1
Ingenuity Self reliance Planning Ambition	Consistent Self-Starter	Often Keeps Self Occupied	Sometimes Finds Work For Self	Seldom Finds Work Without Supervision	Needs Constant Supervision
SELF IMPROVEMENT	10	9 8	7 6 5	4 3	2 1
Interest Observation Questions Study Continuing Education	Consistently Studious and Interested	Often Inquires and Observes	Fairly Inquisitive and Studious	Seldom Asks Questions	Never Has Any Interest
PERSONALITY/APPEARANCE	10	9 8	7 6 5	4 3	2 1
Grooming Courtesy, Tact Friendliness Expression Integrity	Consistently Inspires Confidence	Well Liked and Respected	Usually Gets Along With Others and Makes Fair Impression	Seldom Attracts Respect from Others	Creates Antagonism

Employee's Signature_____Date_____

Comments_____

Supervisors Signature_____ Date_____

Comments _____

Revviewer's Signature _____ Date _____

Comments _____

Courtesy: Huntington Memorial Hospital, Huntington, Ind.

For each trait, word suggestions are included to clarify the intended meaning of that trait.

The Appraisal Interview

Appraising the performance is followed by discussing it with the employee. The appraisal interview affords an opportunity for a forthright discussion on the employee's performance. It should be carefully planned and designed to (1) tell the employee how what the superior rates the employee's job performance, (2) agree on a program for the employee's development, and (3) promote a close understanding between superior and subordinate. Figure 19–8 gives some questions that can be asked to make the interview more objective and mutually helpful.

FIGURE 19–8

Answers to These Representative Questions Aid in Preparing Adequately for the Appraisal Interview

1. What favorable points do I intend using to compliment the employee?
2. What unfavorable points am I going to use to criticize constructively the employee?
3. What substantiating facts do I have to support my evaluations?
4. What approach or technique am I going to use to win the employee's agreement to suggested corrective measures?
5. What follow-up do I intend to use?

One of the common drawbacks is that the interview becomes personality oriented. It becomes a heart-to-heart talk about the employee, not about accomplishments or goals. And when no specific agenda is followed, the conversation reverts to whatever comes to mind instead of a systematic summarization of just what the employee has accomplished, how development can continue, and what improvements can be made. Also, the employee may not be given full opportunity for self-expression. The best appraisal interview is a mutual and friendly back-and-forth conversation. When it consists primarily of the employee being told what he has been doing right and wrong, the chances are high that the employee does not agree with every statement made.

Administration of Performance Appraisal

Performance appraisal is formally made about twice a year. The supervisor normally is charged with the responsibility of appraising employees. Sometimes, assistance is given by the superior or by a member of the personnel department; and in some instances, several superiors who are in intimate contact with the employee rate her, in order that more than one judgment of her performance will be available. In most cases, the supervisor knows or should know most about the performance of the employee in her division or unit. Actually, no competent supervisor depends upon an appraising form or waits for a given time of the year to appraise her employee. It is a continuous job. Formal and periodic performance appraisal helps codify results and insures that some orderly appraisal is taking place.

Since judgment and subjective factors are so important in performance appraising it is advisable to supply a training program for appraisers in order to help secure intelligent and well-considered appraisals. Training helps to implement the plan properly and constructively. The appraiser must understand the means being employed and the best methods to follow. Also, it is important to provide retraining periodically, so that new developments in performance-appraising work and future plans can be brought to the attention of the appraisers. A retraining program also aids in reviewing the principles of good appraising with each appraiser before each appraisal period.

Employee self-appraisal is another helpful technique. When office employees are fully informed in advance of the purpose, operation, and application of performance appraisal, they make remarkably accurate self-appraisals. There is some tendency, however, for the better employees to underrate themselves, and the problem employees may overrate themselves. Employee self-appraisal helps to give the *how* and *why*

FIGURE 19–9
These Considerations Are of Greatest Significance in Administering a Performance Appraisal Program

1. Top management backing for performance appraisal is essential to its success.
2. Performance appraisal should serve primarily to motivate employees, to inventory personnel, and to improve the working force.
3. The appraisal form should include only those traits that cannot be measured objectively by standard personnel records.
4. Only those traits of greatest importance to an employee's progress should be utilized; usually, eight to ten traits are adequate.
5. To expedite comparisons and the appraising work, rate all employees on one trait, then all on the second trait, and so forth.
6. Normally, and in keeping with statistical probability, of the appraisals for many on a single trait, a few will be low, a few will be high, and the greatest number, perhaps 60 percent, will be average.
7. Each trait should be a single one, not compound; should be defined objectively, not subjectively; and should be in terms of work performed on the job.
8. Appraisals should be based on observations of definite and concrete actions.
9. The employer and appraiser should privately discuss the employee's appraisal.
10. Periodic training and retraining of appraisers are essential for success of a performance appraisal program.

of performance appraisal to the employee. The employee knows what is expected and uncovers areas in which improvements can be made. Self-analysis encourages self-development. Self-appraisals can be recorded on special forms provided for this purpose. They supplement the regular ratings determined by management-designated raters.

Review by a management panel is highly successful in many companies. Funneling all appraisals within an enterprise through one body makes for better control and greater uniformity of ratings. Employees who are qualified for promotions, transfers, training, and salary increases are readily identified. Likewise, those requiring remedial action are identified, and proper measures can be taken. A listing of the major considerations that warrant attention in administering performance appraisals and which listing serves as a review is shown by Figure 19–9.

QUESTIONS

1. What are some fundamental beliefs that an individual should possess in order for motivation to become effective?
2. Referring to Figure 19–1, to which of these questions is your answer "No"? For each such question, what might you do to justify a "Yes" answer?
3. Explain the meaning of Figure 19–2 in your own words.
4. Identify each of the following:
   a. Leadership.
   b. Esteem needs.
   c. Two-way communication.
   d. Critical incidents.
5. Discuss the meaning and influence of employees' levels of aspiration upon their motivation.
6. What is job enrichment and discuss how you as a manager would go about using it in your managerial work.
7. Indicate what medium of communication you would recommend for each of the following, along with your reasons for its use:
   a. Announcing that the company has just purchased another company, the office work of which will be merged into the office of the purchasing company.
   b. Giving employees the data on the company's contribution to the employee's pension fund for the year just ending.
   c. Advising the discontinuance of operations at Plant C in Big Ridge, Michigan.
8. As you see it, what are the five most important considerations in administering a performance appraisal program? Why?
9. Discuss transactional analysis as it applies to the motivation of a person.
10. What area of motivating employees do you feel warrants considerable research over the next five years? What types of additional information would you like discovered?

11. Six months ago, Company XYZ established a suggestion system, which unfortunately has proved to be very ineffective. You are asked to investigate the system and make recommendations for improvements. Describe your approach and what you would do to fulfill this assignment.

12. Do you believe that the management by objectives approach has motivational qualities? Justify your answer.

CASE PROBLEMS

Case 19–1. Morse and Marx, Inc.

Wanda Hutchinson requested a transfer to another department "to get out of the duplicating department" where she has been employed for the last three years. In talking with the company's director of personnel, Ms. Hutchinson stated that she would never get above the job level she was now on because the duplicating department seemed to be a graveyard insofar as advancement was concerned. She indicated that her supervisor, Natalie Walker, appraises her work and she has received small salary increases every six months, the same as all the other employees in the department. Ms. Hutchinson added that all are given increases. The women exchange salary information among themselves. There is a performance appraisal ritual, but it seems to be simply a justification for the pay increase.

The director of personnel assured Ms. Hutchinson she was probably doing satisfactory work and the company was recognizing her work accomplishments. However, he promised to investigate the situation further with Ms. Walker. Subsequently, during an interview, Ms. Walker stated that Wanda Hutchinson was an average worker and did not appear to offer any outstanding value to the company. She was somewhat careless about her personal appearance and suggestions for improvement had brought little change. Ms. Hutchinson was given wage increases because her performance appraisal justified it. Further, help was difficult to get and while Ms. Hutchinson had shortcomings she did come to work regularly and provided a willing pair of hands.

It was well known by the director of personnel that the vice president of finance of the company favored elimination of the present performance appraisal efforts. He suggested replacing it with individual work goals for each employee. How well the accomplishment of this individual work goal was achieved, would determine the employee's rating. In his opinion, the current appraisal program is a source of needless disputes and misunderstandings. The director of personnel encounters differences of opinion about the present performance appraisal, but he doesn't believe it is a major problem. Under the present program, the factors being used include (1) value to the company—future potential developmental power, (2) initiative and adaptability—thinking constructively and ability to meet changing conditions, (3) personal appearance—cleanliness and neatness, and (4) attendance—amount of excessive absenteeism and tardiness.

The supervisor appraises each of his employees once every six months. The appraisal is discussed with the employee. All appraisals are then turned over to the director of personnel where they are reviewed and the recommended action is noted and, if possible, implemented.

Questions:

1. Is there a problem here? Justify your viewpoint.
2. What further action would you take as Ms. Hutchinson? Ms. Walker?
3. What recommendations to the company management do you feel are in order? Why?

Case 19–2. Stivers Company

The employees of Stivers Company voiced through their recognized leaders the suggestion that the company install several bulletin boards throughout the office and factory areas so that better overall communication would be obtained. At first the company turned down the suggestion stating the cost of the boards and of supervising what is posted on them would be prohibitive. At the employees' insistence, however, the company finally agreed and installed four large boards at strategic locations.

At this time it was agreed by the employees and the company that the boards would be restricted in use to the following (1) recreational and social affairs notices, (2) notices of employee meetings, (3) news of employee promotions, (4) lists of new employees, quits, and those retired, (5) important developments within the company—new products, changes in organization, new layouts, and etc., (6) news about any large or unusual sales order received by the company, and (7) periodic forecasts regarding Stivers' future business. In addition, all postings were to be stamped "approved" by the personnel manager before posting.

For several months the arrangement worked out quite well. Items of interest were submitted and routinely they were approved by the personnel manager. Nearly everyone was pleased with the new communication medium and believed the service was being well handled. One morning, however, a news item about a strike in a neighborhood company was given the personnel manager for approval. He returned it without the usual stamp explaining, "I will not approve any item that does not concern Stivers Company or its employees. Actually this material contains language that could be damaging to the company and it also includes some immoral statements and comments that are absolutely unacceptable."

News of the turndown quickly got around the office and factory. In conversations among themselves, questions such as these were asked: Should we go along with being censored? Are not strikes and their related activities—especially a strike right down the street—of interest to both the company and ourselves? Are we not being deprived of our inherent right to express ourselves? Why cooperate with the company when its intent is to use the boards for its own propaganda?

Questions:

1. Was the decision correct to buy and install the bulletin boards and further, draw up the agreement for the use of the boards? Why?

2. Are you inclined to believe the employees are making much ado about nothing? Discuss.
3. In your opinion are the bulletin boards likely to become a trouble spot and a demotivator? Justify your views.
4. What recommendations do you suggest the company follow? Elaborate on your answer.

Case 19–3. Parkman Products Company

Joel Hodges, training director, is conducting a class in communication. The members are employees of the office sales department, credit and collections department, and the shipping department.

HODGES (nearing end of formal presentation): So you see when communicating with others we should control our comments. If we do this effectively we can influence through our behavior the behavior of the person with whom we are communicating. Now, I want to open this meeting for questions. Anybody have any question?

WAYNE AVERY: What you've been talking about applies mainly to talking doesn't it?

HODGES: No, not at all. You were not listening carefully. I made the statement that the basic principles of communication apply to all media, although not to the same degree.

AVERY: I did not get that.

HODGES: It's like I've always contended—most sales people are 90/10 oriented, that is, 90 percent mouths and 10 percent ears.

AVERY (amid chuckles by the audience): Yes, sir.

HODGES: Over here, yes. You have a question and your name again is . . .

MARK CUMMINS: Mark Cummins.

HODGES: Your question is what, Mark?

CUMMINS: It isn't a question. I just wanted to say that before we can communicate and try to solve a problem, like what you were talking about, we must first understand the nature and significance of the problem. The ratio is 10/90, not 90/10. What I mean is we more likely spend 10 percent of the time trying to understand the problem and 90 percent attempting to solve it. The first step in developing the . . .

HODGES (interrupting): Wait a minute. Wait a minute. You are not staying on the subject. It's communication. How to get your thoughts, ideas, and reactions to the other person. How to give effective instructions.

CUMMINS (with forlorn appearance): All right. But it's related to solving problems, isn't it?

HODGES: Certainly. However, I do not want you to think about that now. Concentrate on improving the communication as such. Understand?

CUMMINS: Yes.

HODGES: You again, Avery?

AVERY: Honestly, I don't feel I have trouble telling my people what to do. My problem is figuring out what to do about the problems I got—lack of credit information, one employee doesn't show up for work, conflicts about vacations—you name it. I like my job and I want to make good on it. I'm thinking of changing our whole way of handling incoming orders because there has just got to be a better way.

HODGES (looking down over his rim glasses): Wayne, no doubt you do have problems. I am not interested in discussing them now. As you gain more experience you will be better able to cope with them. Today, we are zeroing in on how communication can help you in your job and in getting along with others. That is the topic for today.

AVERY: Yes, sir. One of these days I'm going to know just what to do, I don't want to mess things up, then I'd be in trouble.

HODGES: That is correct.

Questions:

1. Using transactional analysis, what observations can you make about Mr. Hodges? About Mr. Avery?
2. In general, what ego state do you believe a training director should try to assume? Discuss fully.

Chapter 20

Office Supervisory Management

> *Man is not on earth solely for his own happiness.*
> *He is there to realize great things for humanity.*
>
> Vincent van Gogh

A key figure in office managerial actuating is the supervisor. In most instances supervisory success depends greatly upon the supervisor's attitude toward subordinates, sources of motivation used, and the personal goals that are being pursued. Successful supervisors understand themselves and apply this self-knowledge to interactions with subordinates. Treating people like responsible adults, understanding human needs, and providing a working environment in tune with these human needs are the basis of effective supervisory management. The supervisor is extremely influential in motivating employees, in developing them, and in building teams which carry out specific duties.

In increasing numbers, women are being promoted to office supervisory management. While men and women obviously differ in many respects (vive le difference!), the discussion which follows applies equally to both female and male supervisors.

HUMAN RELATIONS AND THE SUPERVISOR

The daily challenge to most office supervisors lies in gaining complete understanding with the group members regarding what their respective jobs are and what is expected of each one plus making it possible for them to achieve contentment and satisfaction from their work efforts. To gain mutual respect, to have the employee's trust, and to win utmost cooperation without any command or coercion are paramount. Yet the

534

supervisor should not become too friendly or intimate and thus risk the loss of respect and confidence. The amount of friendliness and intimacy is an artistic determination and will differ somewhat for different situations. Always the supervisor must be objective, find out and review both sides of problems or disputes, refrain from jumping to conclusions, and solve the issue fairly without playing favorites. Any promise made to any member of the group should be kept or an explanation to the member's satisfaction should be made, telling why such promise is invalid. Being approachable, listening to work or personal problems, assisting in determining what should be done, and helping, wherever possible, in achieving a favorable solution, are benchmarks of good supervisory behavior.

Impartiality by the supervisor in human relations is extremely important. Characterized as being fair is a cardinal quality to be developed by a supervisor. It can overshadow possible weaknesses. Trying to understand the employee's point of view, giving straight answers to employee's questions, keeping records of work performed by every member, and disciplining, yet still retaining the employee's sincere respect, are indications that a supervisor practices fairness in dealing with group members.

Strong traits of human nature is a craving for recognition, and receiving praise and credit for performing a good work effort. Any recognition or praise, however, must be deserved. Compliments passed out indiscriminately are quickly spotted as worthless by the group members who will view such credit in contempt. Praise must be deserved and when it is deserved, give it without stint. Quiet, judicious praise, or softly spoken appreciation for extraordinary teamwork breathes needed life into the employee.

Some useful guidelines in the area of human relations and the supervisor are indicated in Figure 20–1. This is by no means an exhaustive list, but it can be the beginning of successful practices. Then by observation, feedback, and experience, the list can be expanded so that highly effective and personalized guidelines are developed.

Additional Skills and Knowledge

In addition to being proficient in human relations skill, the office supervisor must have certain other skills and knowledge. These requirements will vary from office to office depending upon the individual conditions.

The additional skills are:

1. Skill in Teaching. A good supervisor is also a good teacher. Skill in teaching is a prime means for making supervision more effective. Generally, an employee is more satisfied, has greater interest, and will be more industrious when informed clearly what work is wanted and

FIGURE 20–1
Human Relations Practices for Supervisors

1. Judge each member of those with whom you work by the individual's good qualities. Work accomplishment is aided by positive attitudes, not by stressing lack of abilities and skills.
2. Realize as a supervisor, to analyze the behavior and needs of your superiors and colleagues or peers before analyzing your subordinates or group members. Direct your attention to those above and on par, then look down.
3. Make every personal contact helpful and constructive. Take the viewpoint that you are trying to assist every member of your group achieve the ultimate of his or her potential.
4. Get your group members to participate in your plans. Modify plans to strengthen them and to uncover and eliminate objections; and adopt the plan that will achieve the predetermined goal most effectively and serve the interests and desires of the group to a maximum. Ask for suggestions, listen to what is offered. You don't have to adopt all suggestions.
5. Eliminate opposition of interests among your group. Find out the common motives. Strive toward group unity and effective teamwork.
6. Act on problems, don't just react to them. It's relatively easy to behave rationally when all is going well. When faced with an unpleasant situation, don't jump to conclusions. Get all sides of the problem, know the facts, think about them, and objectively determine what, if any, supervisory action to take.
7. Know the leaders and important members of each informal group in the organization. Seek their cooperation, but be careful not to destroy any informal group's purpose. Realize the influence of informal groups varies. Use these groups to help achieve departmental goals.
8. Give instructions clearly. Be certain the basic idea is identified and transferred to the recipient of the instruction. Do not take anything for granted. Provide sufficient details.
9. Realize that it is less difficult to introduce change to groups than to individuals. Generally speaking, people feel more secure in groups which not only tend to soften the individual's resistance to change, but also to reduce the individual's responsibility to practically zero.
10. Request and explain, don't demand and assume an employee is adequately familiar with the subject at hand. Be persuasive, not coercive.

is given help in how to perform it. Skill in instructing assists in achieving a well-trained work force.

2. *Skill in Methods Improvement.* Better utilization of resources is the constant aim of progressive managers. Some methods of performing work are inherited, others are hastily thrown together, while still others are copied from similar operations. All can be improved. Skill in analyzing, supplemented by ingenuity, usually results in improved ways of performing work.[1]

The basic knowledge needs are:

1. *Technical Knowledge.* This includes knowledge of systems, procedures, materials, office forms, equipment, and the manner in which results are used. Much of this knowledge might be acquired while one

---

[1] See Chapter 4, Office Work Simplification.

is serving in a nonsupervisory capacity. The supervisor should know enough about the detail work that is done to provide the necessary leadership to those performing the tasks and to plan and control their work so that orderly and reasonable rates of accomplishment are realized.

2. **Knowledge of Responsibilities.** This includes comprehension of the company's policies, rules, and regulations; of the extent of the supervisor's authority and responsibility; and of matters on which the supervisor can make final decisions. An acquaintance with basic information about organization, management, collective bargaining, communication, budgeting, and any area of direct or indirect concern in the particular supervisory job appears to be a minimum requirement.

THE WORK OF THE SUPERVISOR

Actually the supervisor's work, in great measure, consists of *getting work performed properly* by others. Results are what count. And to achieve the results, the help of others is used. Employing the efforts of others is a cardinal consideration of supervision. Many failures in supervision are in getting things done through people. The fault is not always that of the employee, although this is the common explanation. For convenience, a "supervisor" can be defined as *a management member working at an organizational level where personal oversight of tasks assigned to small groups is assumed in order to assure satisfactory performance and to meet the personal needs of the group members.* Usually, a supervisor is thought of as being below the executive level. The supervisor's work is similar to that of the executive, but the scope of the work, the matters on which decisions must be made, and the general overall management work are not as broad in the case of the supervisor as in the case of the executive.

Further, the supervisor is at the critical focal point about which the top managers' wishes are distributed and the operative employees' desires are concentrated. He or she is the point of contact between management members and nonmanagement members. To many employees, the supervisor represents management. And about every plan, decision, and control filter through the supervisory level either going up or going down.

An organization unit is what it is largely because of the supervisor's influence. The accomplishment of satisfactory office production and the establishent of a favorable work climate depend in large measure upon the quality of office supervision. The supervisor is charged with seeing that the work in the unit is performed within a reasonable time, at a reasonable cost, and with satisfied employees. The supervisor is the ultimate regulator of what is accomplished.

More specifically the office supervisor assigns employees definite work, points out certain goals, and gets them to want to perform accurately and do a satisfactory volume of work. In addition, she or he is called upon to review and evaluate the work performance of the employees, and to answer questions concerning the current methods used to accomplish the work. To perform supervisory work various approaches can be used, depending mainly upon the type of employee, the work situation, and the kind of office work.

The work of the supervisor can be classified in a variety of ways. Since the supervisor is a management member, the following outline is logical and helpful.

Under planning, the supervisor has such activities as:

1. Participating in the formulation of objectives for each of the group members.
2. Formulating a clear identity of the work to be done.
3. Knowing and interpreting company policies to the employee.
4. Keeping up with new developments especially those pertaining to office machines and human behavior.
5. Improving current methods being followed.

Organizing efforts by the supervisor include:

1. Delegating work to qualified members.
2. Allocating the work among members of the unit.
3. Placing similar work in the same unit.
4. Establishing proper authority relationships among members of a unit.
5. Keeping employee-work relationships up to date.

The supervisor's managerial actuating efforts deal with:

1. Informing employees of changes.
2. Evaluating the work behavior of each employee.
3. Developing understudies.
4. Securing teamwork and harmony among employees.
5. Meeting the personnel needs and wants.

Controlling encompasses the following work by the supervisor:

1. Following stated practices and procedures.
2. Utilizing standards established for the work.
3. Evaluating work output in terms of cost.
4. Checking accuracy and quantity of work.
5. Minimizing peak work loads.

Selection of Office Supervisor

Selection of office supervisors, can be considered the beginning of effective supervision. The employee having the longest service, the highest production volume, or the longest no-tardiness and no-absenteeism record is not necessarily the best selection for a supervisory job. The work of the supervisor, being managerial, is significantly different from that of the operative employee, being nonmanagerial.

The first step in the selection of office supervisors is to determine the background and characteristics needed for the supervisory jobs. Such information can be used to set the minimum employment qualifications and standards. Preparation of such information should take into account the realities of the specific condition.

The actual task of selection is assisted by the use of any one or all of the following: (1) appraisals of the candidates, (2) written tests, (3) interviews, and (4) evaluation of experience and training. The first, or appraisal of candidates, can take many different forms, including inquiry of the candidate's present superior, talking with those acquainted with the candidate's work performance, and discussing with friends the candidate's activities in clubs and other groups outside the office.

Written tests are increasing in usage, but they probably do not yet qualify as a common means for office supervisory selection. Tests are designed to measure work, personality, and technical factors. They provide a means to screen initially a large number of candidates, and they stress objective evidence instead of someone's opinion and judgment. However, considerable criticism has been leveled against tests in which it is pointed out that they concentrate on selected areas rather than the "entire person," that some candidates are practically certain not to reveal their true ability by written word, and that the candidates answer test questions for a prescribed situation in one way, yet for the same situation perform in a different way under actual working conditions.

As pointed out in Chapter 14, interviewing is perhaps the most common means of selection, and this statement includes supervisory selection. The face-to-face meeting, the opportunity to clarify ambiguous written statements, and the flexibility to shape the interview to the individual case make for the wide use and popularity of the interview method.

Finally, the evaluation of experience and training provides a practical element to the selection method followed. A detailed investigation of the candidate's work history is sometimes undertaken. Thus, elements which might be overlooked in the other selection approaches are brought into the program. Knowledge of the enterprise and technical competence are illustrative of these elements.

Relationships with Superiors and with Peers

Relationships are especially important to the supervisor, whose destiny is controlled largely by other people. Much of what is achieved comes as a result of their approval. We have already pointed out the relationship between supervisor and subordinate. There remains the relationship between supervisor and (1) superiors and (2) peers.

With reference to the first, the supervisor is expected to implement a specific portion of a plan at the operative level. To do this, the supervisor is given instructions, receives specialized assistance from various staff members, attends indoctrination meetings, and communicates with superiors. In these relationships, astute supervisors discover that certain practices assist them appreciably. They find that they must have *a firm belief in the essentiality of supervisory work*. They must realize that their efforts to help manage the office work are fundamental to the success of the enterprise. They should reveal this belief by viewing enthusiastically their opportunity to contribute to the success of the office. Also, with experience it is found that it is wise to *focus appeals to superior's greatest interests*. Normally these are improved service, lower costs of operation, and increased net income. The office supervisor who knows how the unit will help achieve these goals will capture the attention and support of superiors. Actually, with some concentrated thinking, it is not difficult to do this, but some showmanship in presenting the idea is helpful.

Further, the office supervisor learns to *expect some resistance to suggestions and new ideas*. Some top and middle managers favor a sort of "do not disturb things, let them be as they are" attitude. Especially is this true if there are no complaints and things are running quite smoothly. The feeling of "Why take a chance?" may prevail. In addition, it is well to *act in a manner that justifies recognition as a member of management*. Too frequently, recognition of office supervisors as management members is lip service only, the recognition is by decree only. Nothing tangible is done to make supervisors a part of management or to make them feel that they are. To overcome this condition, supervisors can offer, as a group, means for obtaining certain goals of top management by their (the supervisors') efforts. Suggestions along this line are offered by Figure 20–2.

With reference to peers, it is axiomatic that within any given enterprise an office supervisor should have good relationships with the other office supervisors. To achieve this status, most of the points just stated under supervisor-superior relationships apply here. In addition, each supervisor should know where he "fits into the organization picture" of the enterprise. Such information will help to clarify the relationship of any one supervisor. It is also essential that each supervisor knows

FIGURE 20–2
The Supervisor in Management

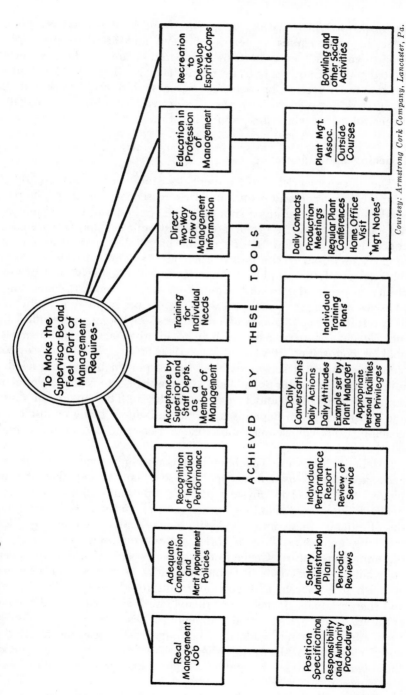

To Make the Supervisor Be and Feel a Part of Management Requires—

Real Management Job

Position Specification
Responsibility and Authority
Procedure

Adequate Compensation and Merit Appointment Policies

Salary Administration Plan
Periodic Reviews

Recognition of Individual Performance

Individual Performance Report
Review of Service

Acceptance by Superior and Staff Depts. as a Member of Management

Daily Conversations
Daily Actions
Daily Attitudes
Example set by Plant Manager
Appropriate Personal Facilities and Privileges

Training for Individual Needs

Individual Training Plans

Direct Two-Way Flow of Management Information

Daily Contacts
Production Meetings
Regular Plant Conferences
Home Office Visit
"Mgt. Notes"

Education in Profession of Management

Plant Mgt. Assoc.
Outside Courses

Recreation to Develop Esprit de Corps

Bowling and other Social Activities

ACHIEVED BY THESE TOOLS

Courtesy: Armstrong Cork Company, Lancaster, Pa.

the work for which she is responsible, from what supervisor or department the work comes to her department, and to what supervisor (or department) she sends it. Close cooperation among these supervisors, related to work flow, should be maintained. Further, practices and decisions found effective by one supervisor should be shared with other supervisors not only to keep them informed, but also to propagate the successful means which are proving helpful.

Coaching and Counseling

The office supervisor has frequent occasion to use coaching and counseling. Information and inspiration are stressed by coaching. The particular data needed for a given situation are supplied and the unique capacities of members of a group are both stimulated and integrated by a coach. Emphasis is on "setting up the plays," but permitting employees to carry them out to the best of their ability. The supervisor must have the respect of the employee, understand how he feels, and possess an ability to use analogies and demonstrations. In contrast, counseling emphasizes leading a person to self-insight and improvement by means of carefully selected questions and suggestions along with skillful listening. To get the person to see how to improve accomplishments is the goal of counseling. It can be viewed as a suggestive and supportive technique to instill self-motivation in the person being counseled. The role of the counselor is to help the employee to self-development to become independent and to build confidence. The amount of direction and assistance given depends upon the individual being counseled. Both coaching and counseling emphasize a person-to-person individualized relationship.

To be able to use coaching and counseling successfully it is first necessary to be sensitive to capabilities, behavior, and likes of the employee. Some excel in physical pursuits, others rank high in mental endeavors. Some are "detailists," other comprehend mainly broad generalities. Find out these individual differences and be guided by them in coaching and counseling. In brief, know your employee. Next, stress the immediate future. Concentrate on the present job. Reach agreement on what is to be done for the next day, next week, or next month at most. It is easy to make commitments for three or four years ahead and then gradually forget about them. Third, stay with specific, concrete examples. Talk about actual happenings. Discuss actual incidents and their effect upon his work and standing. Lastly, use constructive criticism. Tie in with his work and bring out ways which would make for improvement. Stress the potential gains and the feasibility of their achievement.

In this modern age of office management, the supervisor must know how to convince the subordinate to achieve objectives or modify behavior. For this purpose counseling is especially helpful. Hence, some additional comments on counseling are warranted. Think in terms of a helper-receiver relationship in which both parties have values, needs, and feelings that condition their behaviors. To be successful, the supervisor as the helper, must know as much as possible about the employee's values, personality, and feelings. Strive during the early part of the counseling to reach an agreement that (*a*) there is a problem and (*b*) the present receiver's behavior is unacceptable. Then, with the receiver develop a number of possible courses of action. It is important that the receiver understand each course and actively participate in developing and exploring each one. This approach is known as maximizing alternatives.

Now, the receiver has the freedom to select the alternative he or she believes is superior under the circumstances. The helper encourages and aids the receiver in making the choice, but the selection is entirely that of the receiver's doing. This is the key to effective counseling. Permit the receiver to do the deciding. That way she or he identifies with the decision, feels responsible for it, and is more likely to carry out the choice.

To be an effective counselor, follow these helper-receiver relationships:

1. *Listen and try to understand the receiver's point of view.* Part of the help is to let the receiver "talk it out." Encourage the receiver to talk by asking questions such as "What do you think about. . . ." "Do you feel that. . . ." This will bring out values and feelings along with irrelevant details and excuses which can be forgotten. Data affecting present behavior of the receiver are of importance. Also the helper should refrain from excessive talking. An occasional, "I see," "Yes, I follow you," encourages the receiver to continue. Don't give advice, let the possibilities of what to do emerge from the comments of the receiver.

2. *Know what behavior the receiver can change and steer the alternatives to these ears.* To keep the counseling practical, the receiver must be able to make the change decided upon. To leave the receiver with a decision like, "Change to a job paying twice what you are now receiving," is meaningless. It will increase the receiver's frustration and efforts to defend current behavior.

3. *Seek small changes over a period rather than large changes overnight.* People change slowly, don't expect or plan for a sudden reform. As soon as possible after selected events, give the receiver feedbacks. They should be frequent and in small quantities. Following this suggestion makes the counseling on what amounts to a continuous basis, a feature which adds to its effectiveness.

4. *Be alert for signals or opportunities indicating a willingness by*

the receiver to commit himself or herself to change. This is the time, of course, to move the receiver toward implementing the modification. When the receiver has decided what to do to improve his or her behavior and assumes the responsibility for doing it, the counseling task can be called successful.

Effective Time-Use by the Supervisor

Basic to supervisory success is the wise use of time on the job. To this end, the office supervisor can concentrate on essentials—the really important tasks. The best supervisors perform key tasks only and do not let themselves get involved in endless details. Unnecessary work is quickly identified as such and abolished. Also, for most supervisors, the completion of a task once it is started makes for efficient time utilization. Tasks not quite finished are the vexation of many supervisors. Staying with a job until it is finished and not giving in to interruptions are key habits to be followed. In addition, the budgeting of one's time is a time-saver. The time-minded supervisor decides what tasks must be performed, estimates the time for each, and schedules these time periods through the workday. This approach helps utilize time more effectively and establishes goals that are achieved during the day, thus providing a sense of satisfaction. Furthermore, the office supervisor should acquire speed in reading and become more selective in what is read. Few adults receive reading training beyond the elementary school level. Many people read at this pace, which is a serious detriment to their efficiency in time utilization. By practice and accelerated reading courses increases up to 75 percent in reading efficiency can be attained.

With better utilization of time, a proper balance among the various facets of the supervisory work should be attained. An equitable appraisal of all the various supervisory tasks must be made and compared with established levels of satisfactory performance. For example, data on cost, quantity of work achieved, quality of work, number of grievances, number tardy, number absent, and labor turnover rates are helpful. Trends in these data are significant. Also, changes in some factors may help predict future changes in others—frequently before either the difficulty or the favorable accomplishment is revealed by standard operating reports.

The Supervisor's Authority

In a relatively small enterprise, the general manager, who in many cases is also the owner, has supervisory authority over each employee. The general manager makes the decisions that concern job requirements, and keeps the employee informed about changes. With growth of the company and the resultant spreading of the gap between top management and nonmanagement members, it is generally agreed that supervisors must narrow the gap and conduct many of the needed managerial relations with employees.

The size and complexity of the enterprise, as well as the viewpoint toward employees, influence the supervisor's authority. In most offices today, it is not precisely stated what the office supervisor is expected to do. The concept of the supervisor "running the unit," with complete authority to hire, fire, change work sequence, make improvements, and handle operations in any way believed satisfactory, no longer exists. The current state of affairs is a somewhat indefinite arrangement which has evolved over the years and is due, in part, to the very nature of the job—the fact that the work of supervision is so varied, the scope so large, and the activities involved so numerous.

Part of the present status can be said to have been brought about by the use of staff members to assist and to render advice to the supervisor. In some cases, it is believed that the work of office supervising has become so complex that expert help to the supervisor is an absolute necessity. In contrast, others are of the opinion that staff helpers usurp authority and take over activities which constitute the fundamental duties of the supervisor. For example, in many offices, the supervisor does not interview and select new employees, but does have a voice in the final hiring.

Further, the use of management by objectives and of various forms of participation to give members of the group the opportunity to express themselves on matters of mutual interest; the stress on communication, sharing information, and keeping everyone fully informed; and the higher educational level of the typical office group today have modified not only the relationships between the supervisor and the individual members but also the makeup of the supervisory job itself. There commonly exists, however, a difference of opinion between supervisor and the operative employee over the amount of authority the employee has in carrying out duties. Some supervisors complain that the employee won't make decisions, doesn't want responsibility, and keeps coming to the supervisor for answers. On the other hand, some employees claim their supervisor doesn't let them act on their own and keeps them under tight control. Talent and time are dissipated when this controversial issue exists.

To resolve the difficulty it is sometimes feasible to have the supervisor and employee jointly determine the degree of authority the employee has in executing her on his top five or six duties. Representative degrees might include (1) the employee decides and acts independently, (2) the employee acts independently, but is expected to tell the supervisor later what was done, or (3) the employee is required to check with the supervisor for suggestions before acting.

CHECKLIST FOR OFFICE SUPERVISOR

It is helpful for the office supervisor to take stock of himself periodically. Figure 20–3 offers the opportunity to do so. There is no scoring

FIGURE 20–3
Checklist for Supervisor's Self-Appraisal

	Yes	No
1. Do I approach decision making free from preconceived notions and prejudices?		
2. Do I decide and seldom worry about decisions already made?		
3. Do I plan my work so that each member of my group is fully occupied?		
4. Do I have a sense of time-consciousness?		
5. Do I have a reasonable knowledge of what each of the other departments of the enterprise does?		
6. Do I employ periodic meetings or interviews with employees to keep communication channels open to share information and issue instructions?		
7. Do I give time to my members to talk over problems that are bothering them?		
8. Do I listen attentively so that people tend to open up to me?		
9. Do I recognize and reward exceptional contributions?		
10. Do I treat each member of the group as I would like to be treated?		
11. Do I know the best way to motivate each of my key people?		
12. Do my people know where they fall short and what they can do to improve?		
13. Do I set a good example by meeting deadlines, respecting opinions of others, and displaying enthusiasm for the work to be done?		
14. Do I maintain reasonable and fair quality and quantity standards?		
15. Do I take criticism and correction and view them as opportunities to improve?		
16. Do I analyze reverses and see ways to prevent them from recurring?		

system, but an insight into strengths and weaknesses and a spur to improve future performance are provided. The top supervisor can honestly answer, "Yes," to each of the questions.

Supervisory Training

Strictly speaking, any educational activity designed to prepare the candidate for supervisory work or to improve the supervisor in carrying out duties successfully can be termed "supervisory training." The field is quite broad and deals with many, yet related, subjects. Supervisory training is not confined to learning to perform a set of movements more efficiently but includes the development of attitudes, consideration for the viewpoint of others, control of emotions, and the broadening of one's views. Keeping the supervisor fully informed constitutes one of the biggest challenges in supervisory training. Conditions are constantly changing; new developments are taking place; and in most cases, the supervisor is confronted with new personnel, new attitudes, and new problems.

Excellent work in supervisory training is being accomplished by the members of the Training Within Industry Foundation, a nonprofit organization which advocates gaining maximum results from employed people through better supervision. Years of intensive research and many office tryouts with groups of supervisors have helped develop highly successful training programs for supervisors. Among the more important for normal office use are:

1. Job Instruction. The *JI* course consists of five two-hour sessions and is intended to give skill in instructing. It is especially helpful where there is work involving long break-in periods, numerous errors, or difficulty in getting the information work out on time. To illustrate the content, the course consists of four main parts: (*a*) preparing the employee, (*b*) presenting the operation, (*c*) trying out the performance, and (*d*) following up on performance.

2. Job Relations. Known as the *JR* course, this also consists of five two-hour sessions. It helps provide skill in leadership and is recommended where there are too many misunderstandings among employees and complaints are numerous in the human relations area.

3. Job Methods. This *JM* program likewise is five two-hour sessions. It gives skill in improving methods through practice sessions and on-the-job coaching. This program is effective in finding better methods of accomplishing office work.

4. Job Economics Training. Known as the *JET* course, this requires five $1\frac{1}{2}$-hour sessions and presents the basic principles upon which the U.S. economy operates.

5. Discussion Leading. This *DL* course of four three-hour sessions is designed to give skill in getting participation in meetings and in discussing thoroughly matters of common interest.

6. Program Development. The *PD* course is intended for the instruction of one person in a company who has responsibility for designing and conducting training programs in his company or some unit thereof. The normal time required for this course is five days, dispersed among two or three weeks, to permit specific application of program material to the trainee's company.

In addition, the following means of supervisory training are helpful and widely used:

1. Company supervisory schools in which organized classes in problems of supervision are studied.

2. Individual study of the various available materials on the theory and practice of supervisory work.

3. Conferences and seminars that afford discussions with supervisors of other departments, group training, and an opportunity to talk over problems of mutual interest.

4. Dramatized meetings in which supervisors act out their problems, this acting-out to be followed by discussions and comments to bring out possible improvements in the handling of problems.

5. Observation of and talks with employees to gain a better insight into their jobs and their attitudes.

6. Interviews with top management members to gain advice and suggestions regarding what supervisory action might be taken under various circumstances.

7. Involvement in an actual situation, handling the work of supervision with a "learn by doing" technique. Usually, some background data are desirable before using this means of obtaining information.

Securing Effective Supervision

Much material is available concerning how to be an efficient supervisor. Some of it is quite idealistic and contains many platitudes. The subject is broad, but the following ten points are included in order to indicate, in general, the type of activity which is recommended.

1. Practice Participation. Talk things over with the employees and give them an opportunity to suggest what goals are attainable and the best means for accomplishing them. Such a practice makes for a strong group identity and a sense of belonging and recognizes the fact that no one has a monopoly on good ideas. Commitment to goals and the way to accomplish them are emphasized by the management by objectives approach where the employee, subject to the supervisor's approval, establishes goals and the means to be followed in achieving that goal. The emphasis is upon results.[2]

2. Be Aware of the Resources Available to Accomplish the Prescribed Work. This information is found in schedules, budgets, material availability, machines and equipment, human resources, and space allocation. A modern practice is to involve the supervisor in determining the resources available since the supervisor is accountable for their effective use.

3. Know and Enforce Policies and Rules. Policies define the constraints within which the supervisor can operate. They control current

---

[2] Management by objectives is discussed in detail on pages 511–13.

and future activities. In cases where violations of rules are involved, usually nothing is gained by delaying corrective action. In fact, delay might be interpreted as a lack of decisiveness and an inability to cope with the situation.

4. *Find Out the Existing Relationships inside and outside the Immediate Department Being Supervised.* This will reveal a network of organizational relationships. Carefully observe the interactions and coordination of activities that are necessary. Investigate further and try to identify the behavior of persons involved, as well as the functions and the nature of the relationships probably to be used most frequently.

5. *Watch Waste—Material Loss and Time Loss.* Guarding against waste of all types will add significantly to the work output.

6. *Measure Performance to Aid in Getting a Full Day's Work for a Full Day's Pay.* Employees have the right to know what performance standards are expected of them and how such standards are determined. There should be no surprises. Each employee should be able to keep his own score. Satisfactory work outputs are a major ultimate responsibility of every supervisor.

7. *Secure Employees' Opinions Regarding Supervision.* By means of attitude surveys, spot interviews, casual conversations, and discussion groups, find out what is bothering the employees and what "gripes" are developing. Adequate and correct information at the right time and place may avoid much needless trouble.

8. *Develop Capable Assistants.* Good management requires that qualified replacements be available to maintain the supervisory force at a satisfactory number and caliber. Failure to develop an understudy jeopardizes the supervisor's chances for promotion.

9. *Know from Whom Help Is Supplied When Requested or Needed.* Assistance and support from designated superiors, staff personnel, or outsiders are required from time to time and should be utilized. Unfortunately, in many instances these resources are not tapped. The superior does not counsel and the staff personnel are viewed as obstacles that get in the supervisor's way.

10. *Inform Top and Middle Management Members What Supervisory Action Is Taking Place and Why.* This merits attention because supervision is not only vital to the enterprise, but it requires the complete backing by top and middle management members.

QUESTIONS

1. Of the human relations practices for supervisors listed in Figure 20–1, select three you feel especially important and discuss each briefly.
2. Justify your viewpoint toward this quotation: "With more and more

specialists and expert staff people being used in the modern office organizational structure, the importance and status of office supervisors has decreased. They are not as important as formerly. In many cases, they decide virtually nothing, their superiors tell them what to do."

3. What specific skills and knowledge does a supervisor require to work effectively?

4. As you see it, is the office supervisor a key figure in information management? Justify your viewpoint.

5. Make several specific suggestions usually effective for improving the relationship between a supervisor and his superiors.

6. Draw up a program for the recruitment and selection of office supervisors for a large office. Assume candidates will be recruited from both within and outside the enterprise.

7. Identify each of the following:
   a. Supervisor.
   b. Knowledge of responsibilities by an office supervisor.
   c. JR course for supervisory training.
   d. Coaching.

8. Supervisor William Palmer claims for him to make a self-appraisal of his work and his behavior will result in frustration and a decrease in his present effectiveness. "Not so," says supervisor Karen Wilson. Generally speaking with whom are you inclined to agree? Why?

9. What are some planning activities that the typical office supervisor is expected to perform?

10. What is counseling? Relate for what purposes, and how it can be used effectively by an office supervisor.

11. Alice Booth, a very competent accountant, has just been promoted to supervisor of the accounting department in which eleven people are employed. What suggestions can you give Alice to help her succeed in her new job?

12. What means can an office supervisor use in order to make better use of her time?

CASE PROBLEMS

Case 20–1. Hudson Company

Arnold Dahl, a computer operator with Hudson Company for five years, realized from past experience that he probably would be asked to work one or two weekends during the busy season late in November. His son, Don, was captain of the football team of Premier University, located 186 miles from Arnold's home. Arnold wants to be sure to attend the important last and home game of the season to be played the third Saturday of November. Accordingly he used foresight and informed his superior, Mr. Lester Denlinger, that if it came his turn to work overtime the third Saturday in November he'd like to be excused because he wanted to attend the game at Premier U. Mr. Denlinger told him, "O.K. I'm sure we'll manage without you."

Three weeks later during the first part of November, it turned out to be very difficult for Mr. Denlinger to schedule the overtime. The upsurge in work became greater than expected and several employees he had asked to work apparently would not be able to do so. One was having some emergency dental work done, another on the third Saturday was to drive with his wife to a nearby city in order to settle an estate left to his wife by her parents. Two other employees of the total of nine in the computer unit gave excuses as compelling as Arnold's reason for not working overtime. After thinking over the whole problem, Mr. Denlinger decided to wait until Tuesday of the third week in November to see if some of the present difficulties had cleared themselves. Unfortunately, they did not so that Tuesday afternoon he decided to approach Arnold and try to get him to work the upcoming Saturday.

DENLINGER: I promised you next Saturday off, I know. And you know I am a booster for Premier U.'s football team. But I'm in a bind, Arnold, and although I hate to tell you this, you'll have to forget about going to the game on Saturday. It's, I guess you would say, business before pleasure. We've got to get this work out, Arnold. Mr. Traxler (the treasurer) insists and you know he can do our department a lot of good if we cooperate fully.

DAHL: Well, I want to go. My wife and I have been planning and talking about this for weeks. Don expects us and I don't want to let him down. You knew. I spoke to you about it over a month ago. If you must insist on someone to work, why is it me?

DENLINGER: I must have a worker and you are among our best employees. I don't have to tell you this, you already know it. Yes, I did say I thought we could arrange for you to not work next Saturday, but that was before other conditions arose that makes my requesting you to work mandatory.

Arnold went to the football game Saturday. Reporting to work Monday morning, he learned that he was being given a two-day layoff without pay for disobeying his superior.

Questions:

1. As Arnold Dahl what action, if any, would you take?
2. Evaluate the handling of the overtime requirement by supervisor.
3. As you see it, what is the best way to handle a situation such as described by this case? Elaborate on your answer.

Case 20–2. Eaton Company

Charlene Burkhardt is a quiet, very retiring woman who is a clerk in the centralized filing department of Eaton Company. Her supervisor, Hazel Bennett, got her about two years ago from the mail department where Ms. Burkhardt was working as a mail sorter and distributor. The job in filing paid more than the one in the mail department. Ms. Bennett observed Ms. Burkhardt in the mailroom and took a liking to her. At that time Ms. Burkhardt was working for practically starvation wages trying to support herself and

her mother. At the suggestion and encouragement of Ms. Bennett, Ms. Burkhardt since being in filing has attended night school and acquired skill in
typing, shorthand, and secretarial work.

Ms. Bennett is aware that there is an opening for a secretary in the order
writing department. She talked with Lori DiMetro, the assistant supervisor
in order writing about giving Ms. Burkhardt the secretary's job that was
open, since it paid more than the filing job she was now on, she had acquired
the needed skills, and it would be a deserved promotion for her. Ms. DiMetro
agreed that such a move sounded O.K. to her, but pointed out that Ms.
Lynd would be the one to decide.

However, Ms. Lynd, supervisor of order writing, would have no part of
having Ms. Burkhardt joining the order writing department. In her opinion
(Lynd's) the problem is not a shortage of people, but of having the right
kind of people in her department. As she explained it to the office manager,
who mentioned the possibility of transferring Ms. Burkhardt (a suggestion
he received from Ms. Bennett), all that the personnel department sends her
are typists with little or no secretarial skill and experience. Right now, she
related, "I have three typists when I really need only one. As it turned
out, I was given to believe that two people were going to leave and so
I hired another, but the first one decided not to leave and then later the
second one decided to stay, and here I am with three of them."

Further, Ms. Lynd stated to the office manager that Ms. Bennett is always
getting involved in something that isn't any of her business. She delights
in putting something over on you is the way I see it. You will recall, continued
Ms. Lynd, the Buford woman she hired last year was no more qualified
to perform filing work than a monkey. Sure, we can say that help was extremely
difficult to get at that time, but in my opinion you can't rely on her judgment
of what people can and cannot do. Now she is trying to tell me whom
to add to my department. It isn't Ms. Burkhardt. I have nothing against her—
it's just that I don't want her in my department.

Two weeks later, it was announced by Ms. Lynd that Gertrude Schlossman,
a typist of four months in the order writing department was being promoted
to the opening of secretary's job and no further people would be hired for
that department for the foreseeable future.

Questions:

1. What conditions or factors would you say probably contributed to the
   situation described in this case?
2. Comment on the behavior and actions of Ms. Bennett. Of Ms. Lynd.
3. Should the office manager have participated more in this particular state
   of affairs. Elaborate and justify your answer.

Case 20–3. Peerless Products, Inc.

In the accounting department are 14 employees who—Edgar Crawford,
the supervisor, believes—make a very effective team. One employee, Bernard
Oakton, aged 30 years, married, with three children, started a tax service

company last year. He assisted a number of people to prepare their income tax returns and made several hundred dollars extra. As a result of this work, he secured the part-time job of keeping the books for two small businesses. By working several evenings and weekends, he was able to do this work. Although it was confining, he did not mind, as he could use the extra money; and he thought that with some luck, the business might develop into an independent accounting firm of his own.

Oakton has never said anything about this outside work to Edgar Crawford, who nevertheless knows about it through friends and the grapevine. There is no company policy pertaining to such matters, and Crawford has said nothing to Oakton about the outside work. But he has observed that Oakton looks tired, even the first thing in the morning, and for the past six weeks has been absent quite often from his regular job. About two weeks ago, he heard that Oakton had hired a part-time helper to assist him on these outside assignments.

Last week, Oakton was absent for a day and a half. When he reported for work at noon, Edgar Crawford requested that he come to his office and fired him.

BERNARD OAKTON: This is the rawest deal I ever heard of. I wasn't here because my wife is ill. I wanted to explain this to Marcey [the telephone switchboard operator]; but while holding the line, I was cut off.

EDGAR CRAWFORD: Yes? Well I'll tell you something. I do not believe you.

OAKTOWN: Well, now I. . . .

CRAWFORD: You're trying to misrepresent your absence, which is another reason why you deserve to be fired. And if you were cut off on the switchboard, why didn't you call back to offer your explanation? You know as well as I do that company rules require notification from anyone who is not going to report for work on a regular workday.

OAKTOWN: Sure, I know that. But the phone call has nothing to do with it. You're sore because of my outside business.

CRAWFORD: I did not say that.

OAKTOWN: It's what you're thinking, all right. I know. But let me ask you this, Mr. Crawford. You've known about my outside work and never said anything. So what gave you the right to get tough about it all of a sudden and terminate my employment?

Questions:

1. What do you believe Bernard Oakton should do now? Why?
2. What should Edgar Crawford do? Why?
3. Could the circumstances that led to this problem have been eliminated? Explain, showing how and why.

Chapter 21

Developing Office Employees

*If you give a man a fish, he will have a single
meal; if you teach him how to fish, he will eat
all his life.*

Chinese Proverb

The planned development of employees is vital in managerial actuating.
The more an employee is able to do, the more you can motivate him
or her to do. Capability improvement is essential to a person's growth
and is a strong contributor to the fulfillment of personal satisfactions.
Employee development takes place everyday in most enterprises. Employees acquire their development either by means of planned and well-
administered programs or by a hit-or-miss manner which includes learning by mistakes, by trial and error, and by absorption. Since developing
is vital and goes on continually, progressive managers have set up definite
development programs so that proper direction and control can be given
to make the employees more satisfied and their work contribution more
useful to the enterprise.

Objectives of Employee Training

Future plans of the office, anticipated increases in personnel, and
changes in methods are direct and basic sources for determining the
objectives of an employee training program. The specific goals will depend upon the particular needs of the situation. They may include better
creativeness, methods improvement, or human relations. The training
need may be quite specific such as to gain proficiency in the operating
of an electronic office machine and to know and apply satisfactorily
the policies covering the writing of accounts receivables.

Developmental efforts are of two major types (1) job-oriented and (2) self-development. The former help individuals to improve that which they are paid to do; the latter, is directed toward improvement usually on their own time and for the most part to serve their own fulfillment. Both are important not only to the manager in that they assist in accomplishing objectives, but also to the individual because they increase personal satisfaction. The developmental objective of every manager should be to devise a plan which not only will contribute to and make possible an effective and harmonious work force, but also accomplish assigned work goals and provide full opportunity for each individual to develop to maximum potential.

More specifically, each employee should have complete knowledge of what constitutes his job and what its relationship is to other jobs in the organization. This should not be left to chance. Planned efforts in the form of a training program should be utilized to get job content information to each employee. Improved relations are a certainty when the employee understands completely what his job is, the relationship of his work to other work in the department, and, in time, that of his department to the entire organization structure.

Up-to-date knowledge of operating policies and procedures is another important and common objective in office training. Information on personnel practices should be made known to all. Likewise, the general scope of desired public relations and the quality of paper work required are among the types of information which should be a part of every employee's knowledge.

Each member should have knowledge of the best known methods of doing her work. This is fundamental, but typically there are always a few who lack this essential knowledge or do not use it if they do know it. The best methods are needed to attain a satisfactory efficiency in work output.

Also, recognition or advancement should be extended when training is completed satisfactorily. This may take the form of improved status, public recognition, increased earnings, or promotion. An effective practice is to give the graduated trainee added responsibility. This provides recognition, opportunity, and new obligations—the very things that the trainee probably wants the most. It is a mistake for an enterprise to develop an employee and improve or add to her knowledge and skill without subsequently offering her work in which she can use the newly acquired ability, either in the present or at some future date, within or outside the enterprise.

BASIS FOR EFFECTIVE DEVELOPING

The individual being developed is the key figure in all developmental efforts. His personal interest in and capacity for being developed are of prime importance. Economic or social gains may motivate him, but a stimulus must be present. Necessarily, people start from where they are in any training effort, and they are most likely to want to learn when they see what is taught is helpful to them. An indication of the capacity for developing can be gleaned from the use of tests and a study of a candidate's past education, experience, and accomplishment. While not conclusive, such indexes are helpful.

Furthermore, it should be pointed out that for satisfactory developmental achievement, the trainee must be in a receptive mood, emotionally settled, and free from worries, personal troubles, and anxieties. Also, it must be recognized that the trainee must learn for himself; he must subject himself to the learning process. The instructor's role is primarily that of a resource for guidance and stimulation. The main emphasis is on the process of learning rather than on its content.

The differential between what is needed to perform successfully the required work assignments and what the trainee now knows and can perform, constitutes the gap which training seeks to fill. This gap is reduced gradually, because learning is a gradual process. An employee learns bit by bit, not all at once. Knowing the gap to be filled and considering the gradual doses which can be absorbed by the trainee and in what sequence, the formal training operation can be set in motion. Usually, tie-ins or association of new concepts with knowledge or skills already possessed by the trainee proves effective in training work.

There exist today many different schools of thought about the means of developmental efforts. And new proven techniques about training are appearing from time to time and being added to those already available. Certain types of training are superior for certain types of training needs. In other words, the instructors of today have many training tools at their command and an important portion of their job is to select the best training means to be used under given circumstances. In this selection, the objective and the trainee should be foremost in the decision of what form of training to provide.

Some key points in learning include:

1. A person learns favorite subjects best.
2. A person learns by doing; watching or listening is insufficient.
3. A person remembers longer if the *why* of the knowledge is understood.
4. A person tries harder for rewards than to avoid punishments.
5. A person learns fastest when the teaching makes it easier for the learner to learn.
6. A person understands best when the sequence is (*a*) from the known to the unknown, or (*b*) from the simple to the complex.
7. A person follows easiest when the instruction order is prepare, present, and apply.

Psychologic Learning Fundamentals

No two trainees learn the identical material in identical ways or at identical rates. Basically, an individual learns in a way that is uniquely personal. For example, one learns best by means of group discussion, another from a lecture, still another from the reading of a report. This personal way of learning, called a person's "learning style" can be thought of as consisting of three major aspects (1) learning modality, (2) learning tempo, and (3) learning differentiation.

Learning modality concerns interacting with the environment based on the five human senses of seeing, hearing, touching, smelling, and tasting. Of greatest importance in learning is seeing, hearing, and touching referred to respectively as visual, auditory, and kinesthetic means. Trainees attempting to remember aspects of their environment or to think through images are representative of visual learning modality. In contrast, if another person tries to recall what was said, that person reflects auditory modality. And a kinesthetic learner would recall in terms of movements or the contour or consistency of the environment. In most human beings up to about five years of age, the kinesthetic dominates, followed by the visual, and later by the auditory modality. Then at about age 14 years, one of the modalities emerges as dominant, but all three work together so that knowledge gained from the dominant one is supplemented by that gained from the other two.

What does all this mean to the developmental instructor? Assess the learning modality of your learners and select the instructional format which best satisfies the modality requirements. If the majority of trainees are visual types, it should be no surprise when these learners do not participate actively in group discussions. Finding out the learning modality of the group members can make the difference between highly effective developmental efforts and those that are mediocre. If feasible, vary the instruction by utilizing different training means being careful to match the means to the dominate modality of the members. To illustrate, for a group or subgroup that is auditory, schedule panel discussions and buzz sessions. For those who are kinesthetic, lend encouragement to on-the-job demonstrations or role playing.[1] In the event all modalities are present in a class and the instructor does not control the particular assignments, keep the material and means broad and address to all modality preferences so that at least some portion of the material will strike a responsive note, helping to achieve increased work performance and future favorable behavior.

Learning tempo, the second of the aspects included here, deals with the rate of speed in thinking. The bipolar extremes are impulsivity and

---

[1] See page 559 for discussion of the many kinds of available training means.

reflectivity. The tendency to come forth with the first answer or response that occurs typifies the impulsive thinker. In contrast, a willingness to pause and reflect, "to turn it over in the mind" characterizes the reflective thinker. This latter type tends to be analytical in thinking, to ferret out the details and carefully examine each one. The learning tempo is revealed by the problem-solving behavior in a training session. The impulsive trainee may shout an answer to a case problem being discussed while most of the remaining class members are still in the process of searching for pertinent responses. The discussion may be disrupted and the benefits diminished from the case discussion. To combat this condition, the instructor can follow a formal rotation plan for response. Whether a person tends to be impulsive or reflective appears to be independent of intelligence. Excellent answers are given by either type. However, the main point here is that by classifying the learners as one type or another, the trainer will at least alert herself as to why one training means appears to work better with some learners, and another means with other learners.

Learning differentiation also contributes to a person's "learning style" and refers to the continuum extending from the extremes of "field independence" to "field dependence" concepts measuring how an individual perceives his environment. The field independent person perceives elements as discrete or separate and distinct from their background, whereas the perception of the field dependent person is dominated by the background or the overall organization of the field. A field independent person commonly uses intellectualization and isolation as defense measures against stress or conflict situations. He or she may suffer from having too many ideas, tends to be intellectually critical, and is commonly task-oriented. The field independent learner asks "why" questions and is generally superior in answering questions requiring cogitation. In contrast, field dependent persons use many different types of defense mechanisms when confronted with stress and conflict problems, are more adept at interpersonal accommodation, tend to have social facility, to be gregarious, and favor person-oriented jobs. The field dependent person asks questions that are general in nature and do not require much creativity or thinking. Again, adequate consideration for the learning differentiation will aid the instructor to understand better the learners' behavior and how they function, not only as individuals but also as group members.

The three aspects—learning modality, learning tempo, and learning differentiation, greatly condition the learning function. Understanding the individual differences stemming from how learners receive, perceive, think, respond, and justify their answers as a result of the trainee's "learning style" is basic to effective educational instruction and developmental efforts.

Advantages of Training

One who really manages makes use of training to manage. To the management member, training assists in improving planning, organizing, actuating, and controlling. For example, creating effective plans, building a satisfactory organization structure, delegating authority, stimulating employees, and maintaining proper standards of quality are all assisted by effective training.

In addition, the responsibility of supervision is lessened. Training does not eliminate the need for good supervision but it reduces the requirement for detailed and constant supervision. A well-trained office employee is self-reliant, knows what to do, and how to do it. Under such conditions, close supervision is ordinarily not mandatory.

Also, the best available methods of performing the work can be standardized and made available to all employees. High levels of performance become the rule rather than the exception. The advantages of past knowledge and experience can be retained.

Furthermore, well trained office employees will usually show a greater increase in, and a higher quality of, work output than will an untrained group. Employees do a more intelligent job and make fewer mistakes when they possess the know-how, have an understanding of their jobs and of the interdependence of one job and another, and know the *why* of the company's policies and procedures. And it is important to note that morale can be boosted effectively *after* the employee knows what to do.

On the other hand, these advantages are not obtained without a price. Certain difficulties and possible losses are incurred and should be recognized in any training program. First of all, regular office work is likely to be interrupted or delayed by time spent in training. The output of the trainee might be temporarily reduced. Also, training might foster dependence upon others for solutions to challenge which the employee should think through personally. Self-reliance and capacity for new ideas might be stifled. Furthermore, competent training leaders are difficult to obtain. When mediocre instruction is utilized, not only may the results of the training be below what is expected, but they may actually prove harmful.

Types of Office Work Training

Training can be classified in many ways. One useful classification is training for present jobs and training for future jobs. Another is training for any or all of the following: job knowledge, job skills, and attitudes. Still another is training for basic information, for personal development, and for specific production in definite work application. A useful list showing the range and types of training may be outlined as follows:

1. Preemployment Training. This deals with the type and amount of instruction needed by inexperienced employees prior to their entering the office. This training is generally provided by educational institutions outside the enterprise, such as high schools, universities, business colleges, night schools, and correspondence courses. Preemployment training is generally broader and more fundamental than the other types of training. It is intended to provide basic skills. Likewise, it sometimes is of a theoretical nature, in contrast to the practical aspect of the other types; it seeks to provide an intellectual background and to develop the art of thinking and reasoning.

2. Induction Training. The objective of induction training is to provide the new employee with the information necessary for a complete knowledge and understanding of practices and procedures of the enterprise. Included in this aspect of training are welcoming the new employee to the company, explaining the office rules and regulations, informing of employee's benefits, reviewing company's policies and operations, and relating what is expected of every employee. The new office employee's impression of the company is frequently formed during the first several hours at the new job. Introductions should be made to the new employee's department head, fellow employees, and those supervisors with whom he or she will be associated. If it is possible, an introduction to one of the officers is also helpful, as this gives the new employee a feeling of worth and helps to visualize the extent of the company. Experience shows it is a good idea to give new employees some job which they can do without too much instruction and then leave them alone. This gives the new employee a chance to digest some of the new surroundings. Follow this up with contacts about every hour or so throughout the rest of the day. Encourage the new employee to ask questions.

3. On-the-Job Training. This type of training aims to give the employee the necessary skill required for a specific job. The job can be either that of the present or some future assignment. In some cases, the job is of a higher grade than the employee's present one; in other words, the employee is being prepared for promotion. The makeup of on-the-job training takes many different forms, including lectures in specific subjects, practice on new machines, job rotation—including all jobs of a certain group, special assignments of a temporary nature, understudying a junior executive, special courses, reading assignments, and special workshops by professional associations. On-the-job training stresses just that—on the job—but some of the training may be acquired, in part, outside the enterprise. The entire program, however, should be carefully coordinated.

4. Supervisory Training. One of the most important types of training in any office is supervisory training. Training of office supervisors is vital because of their essentiality in management. Special courses in supervisory training have been designed, and many of these are generally considered effective. Discussion of supervisory training is included in the chapter on office supervision (Chapter 20).

Figure 21–1 indicates the type of training which is given to employees

FIGURE 21–1
Types of Training Given to Various Classifications of Employees

Classification of Employee	Type of Training	Training Required
New	Induction	To give information relative to the job and to the policies and practices of the company.
	On-the-job	Specific training in the important details of the employee's job. To help the employee acquire the necessary knowledge and skill.
Seasoned	On-the-job	To instruct in changes in procedures, routines, policies, and new equipment. Also, to prepare for jobs of higher grade (promotion).
Transferred	Induction	To give information relative to new duties and work environment.
	On-the-job	Specific training in the important details of the new job. To help the employee acquire the necessary knowledge and skill.
Supervisor	Supervisory	To give information relative to the theory and practical application of supervisory techniques.

of different classifications or circumstances. For example, the new employee is given induction training and on-the-job training. The former provides information relative to the new job and to the policies and practices of the company; the latter includes specific training to help the trainee acquire necessary skill.

Developing a Training Program

Every training program includes trainees, an instructor, a training period, and training material. We now turn our attention to these areas.

The proper selection of trainees is of major importance if permanent, gainful results are to be obtained. Trainees should be trained for the kind of job they like and are fitted to perform. In this respect, training is closely related to the selection of personnel.

In the case of supervisory training, it is best to include all supervisors and those considered for promotion to such posts. Excluding some employees on the basis that they do not need the training or that they are already doing their work satisfactorily is a poor policy. Even outstanding supervisors profit from well-managed training programs, and their presence assists in many ways the less competent supervisors in attendance.

The instructor is a key figure in an effective training program and contributes immeasurably to its success. Qualified instructors may be obtained from inside or outside the company; however, many office employees are not good instructors. The efficient employee does not necessarily have the ability to teach. Instructors need many qualifications besides knowing how to do the work. A good teacher has the skill to instruct and is tolerant, understanding, and patient. Also important is an appreciation for the value of the training work in relation to the enterprise and an understanding of what the employee goes through in order to acquire the skill and knowledge which the program is designed to achieve.

The length of the training period depends upon the skill to be acquired, the trainee's learning capacity, and the training media used. For example, a simple indoctrination program for clerks may require an hour a day over a period of a week, while a course in computer programming may be given two hours a week for 15 weeks. For many office subjects, the use of effective visual material usually helps to reduce the training time. Some office training directors claim that effective visualization reduces the teaching time by upward of 35 percent. Also, certain means of training such as programmed instruction, which is of a visual nature, is reputed to save up to 70 percent of training time.

To maintain interest and to secure maximum accomplishment, no single session should last longer than two hours. One hour is even better. The best practice is to pay employees for training time if the course relates in any way to their work. Many states have laws or rulings affecting training time; and in addition, certain federal laws are applicable. Controversial issues are likely to appear if the employee does any productive work during the training time, if the training is outside regular working hours, or if the training work is intended to train the employee for a new or additional skill. It is advisable to check federal and prevailing state laws to help determine whether trainee or company time should be used.

There is always the need for training material. A text or some written material is usually desirable as a basis for instruction, review, and reference. For most subjects, a satisfactory book can be selected; but in instances where the course content is of a special nature, it may be well to prepare material for this specific use. A complete outline of the entire course should be made with the main topics included under each meeting or session. When a text is used, the parts to be covered must be clearly indicated; and assignments which require some preparatory time should be made for every meeting. This helps to keep the program on schedule, points the meeting toward definite subjects, and usually assists in the progress and satisfaction of the trainee.

Available Training Means

The means of training to be followed are paramount in every office training program. A number of different means are available. For convenience, we will confine this discussion to the following 12 different means, listed alphabetically: computer assisted instruction, conferences, demonstrations, guided experience, in-basket technique, incident process, job rotation, lectures, problem solving, programmed instruction, reading, role playing, and understudy method. Choice of office training means depends upon many factors, including the objectives of the training, the number of trainees, the preferences of the instructor, the type of material to be covered, the cost, the time allotted, and the wishes of the trainees.

Computer assisted instruction (CAI) features a computerized teaching machine. Instructions, questions, and guidance are stored in the computer and presented to the trainee by means of a typewriterlike communications terminal linked to the computer. A number of trainees can hook into the course at the same time. After giving an identification number to verify trainee and course, the first question is written out by the computer on a continuous paper form of the terminal unit. In a course on statistics, for example, the first question might be, "How is the arithmetic average calculated? Type answer." If you answer, "By determining the number in the series appearing most frequently," the computer will answer immediately, "That answer is incorrect. The arithmetical average is not determined by the frequency of a number in the series but by averaging mathematically. Will you answer again?" Prompted by the hint, you now type the answer, "Add the numbers of the series and divide this sum by the quantity of numbers in the series." To this the computer will answer, "Correct," then proceed to the next question. To date, CAI appears to work best in conjunction with a human teacher who can answer questions and conduct periodic seminars. Computer trainees retain more material than conventional trainees and in a test of a statistics course needed only 13 hours to complete what requires 45 hours in an ordinary classroom.

The conference method permits trainees to express themselves orally and to exchange thoughts, and enables the instructor to judge the trainee's understanding of the subject material. The conference method is especially popular in supervisory training. Trainees are encouraged to express themselves freely. A group of about 20 participants is the ideal size for best results from the conference method. Demonstrations provide forceful presentation of how the job is done. This means stresses learning by eye rather than by ear and is especially helpful for jobs where physical skills are vital. The guided experience method utilizes evaluation of the trainee to reveal weaknesses; then, the causes of these weaknesses are decided, and experience to remedy them is planned. Extreme care is taken to select the proper work assignments so that the trainee's shortcomings are ultimately removed. The assignments vary and include such things as writing reports, serving on committees, solving specific problems, performing research work, and working on normal day-to-day tasks. The guided experience method can be considered a highly personalized, informal type of training.

The in-basket technique realistically stimulates actual office conditions. Actually it is in the nature of a business game. From two to about fifteen play the game which ordinarily takes two hours—one hour actual playing time and one hour of discussion among the players following conclusion of the game. Each trainee or player sits at a desk on which there is an "in" and an "out" basket, paper, and pencil. Instructions are given by the instructor indicating, for example, that you have certain helpers and you are leaving on your three-week vacation tomorrow. Identical packets of papers are then placed in the "in" baskets of all players. These papers require your office managerial attention. A typical packet may contain three letters, five memos, a telegram, two reports, and four telephone messages. Each trainee studies the materials and writes what she believes is the most appropriate action, clips the material to the original paper, and places it in his "out" basket. Figure 21–2 shows a representative paper with answer written at the bottom. The in-basket technique is reasonable in cost, highly practical, and can include an almost unlimited number of potential problems and situations.

The incident process emphasizes careful questioning to obtain pertinent facts upon which to reach decisions or solve problems. An incident or problem situation is presented to the group by the discussion leader. The incident is described in several sentences. The leader has all the background facts about the problem, but he gives out additional facts only as participants ask for them. The technique stresses participation, stimulates thinking, develops insight, and promotes teamwork. It is especially effective for problem solving and supervisory training.

Job rotation, sometimes referred to as the "merry-go-round" basis, rotates trainees among different office organizational units, thus providing the trainees with overall knowledge of many operations, the work done by each unit, and the opportunity to participate in the affairs of the various units. This means assists the individual to gain a broad perspective of the total activities of an office. Lectures are effective for initially explaining information to trainees. They should be carefully prepared, reinforced by the use of charts, sketches, and models, and presented by a qualified speaker. The means of problem solving is effective when the problems are well selected and bring out considerations pertinent to the work at hand. In short, solving the problems should

FIGURE 21–2
Typical Paper from an "In-Basket" Training Session (the top portion poses the problem, the bottom portion is the respondent's answer)

June 17, 197–

To: William Danzek

From: Horace Goulet

Subject: Edith Davis

    I understand through informal sources that Edith Davis is dissatisfied with her salary and is looking for another job. To the best of my knowledge she does not have any other job offer at this time. You know, of course, that she is one of the best girls we have had on the job of filing computer data runs and she is extremely capable and efficient in her work. I believe she would be hard to replace especially at her present salary. Within the next few days, I would like to discuss with you a salary increase for Miss Davis even though regular salary reviews are not scheduled at this time.

6/18
Horace

O.K. to get together on this next Thursday at 3. P.m. Please review our entire work history with Edith Davis and find out if present salary is real cause for dissatisfaction. Also check Personnel to see if any likely applicants for this filing job are on file.

W. D.

---

meet specific development needs, such as an ability to analyze and relate given facts, to determine the problem to be solved, to formulate the recommended actions to be taken, and to justify these recommendations.

Programmed instruction is self-instruction and utilizes a systematic method of presenting information to the trainee. Presented one step or frame at a time, the material can be easily understood. The increasing difficulty between two subsequent frames is narrow so that advancement is gradual but continuous and complex material is encountered only by the trainee prepared for it. The trainee advances at her individual pace and learns at the speed most convenient for her. For each frame, she is required to select an answer from several alternatives and checks her answer with the approved reply. Thus immediate feedback is provided. She proceeds only after knowing the correct response to the question of the immediate frame. Programmed instruction provides uniform and consistent instruction and the trainee advances gradually from the simple to the complex aspects of the material. Programmed instruction is effective, for example, in one study it was found that in imparting knowledge for operating an office machine, training time was 31 percent less with the trainees retaining 53 percent more knowledge compared to that obtained with conventional methods. Furthermore, programmed instruction is suited for individual training—a group is not needed, and the instructor can concentrate on special problems of training; she need not spend the majority of her time on routine training work.

Reading as a means of training is enjoying renewed interest. Although less glamorous than most of the other means, it is effective and very economical for getting the trainee to learn, change, and develop. The reading of carefully selected assignments enhance particular skills and knowledges. It can be used by an organization of any size. And it can be coordinated with regular group meetings at which time participants discuss their readings and how they can be applied to their office work efforts.

Role playing narrows the gap between talking about what should be done and actually doing it. For training purposes, the playing out of a typical problem situation can be quite effective. It is especially helpful in situations involving employee relations. The method permits the trainees to participate, to gain an insight into their own behavior, and to look at the problem from many different viewpoints. By means of the understudy method, the trainee works as an assistant or helper to the teacher, thus acquiring familiarity with the work and practices of the teacher, who normally is an employee at the same or higher organizational level as the trainee. Experience with dynamic events and acquaintance with the atmosphere and position in which the trainee will eventually perform are acquired. On major issues, the trainee may be required to submit complete data affecting the issue along with recommendations for action. In this way, thinking is stimulated, and the accepting of responsibility is encouraged. The understudy method is commonly used in supervisory training.

Regarding these various means, a current practice, growing steadily, is to use a variety of training means to add spice to learning. The change of pace keeps trainees motivated and minimizes boredom. Of course, the selected means must fit the particular requirement, but current thinking is to vary the overall pattern of instruction.

Human Obsolescence

With the rapid and fundamental changes taking place in the information area has come a condition known as human obsolescence. Now grown to significant proportion, it is commonly discussed in connection with developmental efforts, the thought being that such efforts offer a possible answer to the obsolescence dilemma. It appears fitting, therefore, that a brief discussion of human obsolescence be included here.

During the past several decades, office jobs have changed drastically, entirely new methods of work performance have been introduced, and brand new types of work have become commonplace. The trend toward more and more change seems destined to continue. With all this dynamics, the office employee finds that she or he can become obsolescent similar to a plumbing fixture, a road, or an automobile. To a person with more than one half of his or her life to live, this can be tragic. Yet, as the more experienced realize, most things have little certainty. The challenge is to minimize this peril of human obsolescence. What can be done?

First, fully and sincerely recognize that all things change—some more than others. To mediate, in part, these inevitable changes, it is necessary to keep flexible and maintain a constant vigilance against solidifying our ways of doing things. Success frequently breeds contentment and a dislike to change, even in the slightest, our current activities.

The fresh viewpoint, however, is necessary even though somewhat repugnant. To acquire this openmindedness takes cultivation. Belief that there is a better way is essential. Further, will the better way overtake us or will we overtake it? New ideas and new ways of doing things never seek us out. They must be pursued. Being a part of training programs and adopting a definite plan for keeping abreast of things force us to search for new concepts and new developments which will affect our jobs and our life. In other words, a specific combat against obsolescence appears necessary in this day and age.

Remember that human obsolescence is not confined to those over 45 years of age. Obsolescence can happen to a person within five years after graduation from a university. Effective measures against this happening must be applied. Participation in developmental programs is a major part of the answer.

Cost of Training

Training costs money. The expenditures can be segregated into tangible and intangible costs. Under tangible training costs are training materials, nonproductive time of trainee, and nonproductive time of employee, instructor, or fee charged, if an outsider. Under the intangible classification are such things as a longer time for the trainee to attain a reasonable level of production, loss of employees seeking better job opportunities, time of experienced employees asked to "show me how to do this" by the trainee, loss due to work spoilage and errors, practicing of poor work methods, and improper work viewpoints and attitudes being permitted to develop and spread.

Training is a necessity in modern management, and reasonable expenditures for it should be made. The amount depends upon the needs and the aims of the office. Unfortunately many of the analyses of training cost are unrealistic in that the data used are incomplete. Commonly a comparison is made between the expenditures for a formal training program to that for "no training." The cost of the latter is assumed to be zero which is invalid. Expenditures exist for training even though there is no formal program. However, attention to training costs is a step in the right direction for costs should be kept under control. Management members should have some idea of what is being accomplished for the expenditures being made. This brings up the question of training effectiveness.

Effectiveness of Training

From the managerial viewpoint, it is an excellent idea to measure the effectiveness of training efforts. The evaluation, however, must be in terms of a particular training problem. This problem may be expressed in the form of questions, such as:

1. Has the training increased production?
2. Has there been a decrease in the number of errors?
3. Has there been a reduction in labor turnover?
4. Has there been a reduction in absenteeism, requests for transfers, and number of grievances?
5. Has the attitude, work environment, and enthusiasm of the office work force improved?

It is usually best to measure effectiveness by departments or by some homogeneous group, for the problems of measurement become quite complex when the entire office is considered. It is advisable to make comparisons between office groups as units. A good procedure is to use as a control one group which is characterized by little or no formal training, by training of a particular type, or by a different method of training. Special care should be exercised to see that the groups compared are reasonably similar with respect to such factors as age, sex, and time of week, month, or year.

Evaluating the results of training is not, however, a simple matter. Many companies make little effort to evaluate training results as such, or they are satisfied with general overall indications of the training's worth. It is difficult to determine what specific factors contribute to employee development.

It is possible to overdo training to the point that the efforts and costs in its behalf exceed the highest estimates of benefits within a reasonable period. Developmental efforts should be carefully managed, not engaged in simply because "it is the thing to do." It is a continuous, not an "off and on," activity. It can start on a small scale and subsequently increase as the benefits become known and the needs and progress of the enterprise dictate.

As stated above, every enterprise trains its employees, formally or informally. If effective efforts are being exerted in training, the attainment of full manpower potential is enhanced and benefits both to the individual and to the enterprise are being won. To these ends, keep these facts in mind: (1) office training is desirable and necessary, (2) office training must be carefully selected to fit the specific need of the enterprise, (3) the questions of *what* training should be conducted, and *when, where,* and *how,* require answering, (4) the needs of the office as shown by job analysis, prevalence of errors, low work output, employees' attitudes, and supervisory effectiveness indicate where training is needed, (5) office training should be preceded by careful selection of trainees, and (6) the training of office supervisors is vital.

IMPROVING OFFICE DEVELOPMENTAL EFFORTS

Mistakes in training office employees are repeated again and again. The resulting damage is avoidable. These gamuts of goofs can be eradicated. High on the list is the failure to probe sufficiently deep to identify what developmental needs are required and to follow this with the determination of an adequate program for meeting them. Stated positively, for needed improvement to take place, sufficient time for identifying and analyzing the needs, then determining the means for meeting them are mandatory. This ties in closely with objectives which come first—what kinds and degrees of human growth are to be brought about. Selection of the tools and means to be followed are second—what means are appropriate to achieve the objectives.

Second, a realistic view at restructuring personality should be taken. Attempts to modify the personality of the trainee to better meet the organization's unique needs are open to question and may even tend to neglect other possible growth areas. True, people problems should have high priority and many current difficulties are personality related. Proper training can assist in raising the effectiveness of dealing with people. But to change a personality to fit a preconceived image is quite another task. Even though personality adjustments may be highly desirable, it would seem that the wiser course is to recognize limitations in this area and turn our attention to those goals where more meaningful results are more probable.

Furthermore, training is not the exclusive job of the staff training personnel. In fact, it is to a great degree, the responsibility of the person with line authority to develop and utilize the human resources of the group and to achieve results for which he or she is directly accountable. Hence, to improve training efforts, we must remember to keep the line management member involved. The trainer assists, but the training becomes genuinely effective when the line manager comprehends, approves, and cooperates in implementing the developmental gains by effective leadership.

Another consideration is that trainers need training. For any given situation, there are superior ways of teaching and these ways should be known and used. Specific knowledges and skills must be supplied the trainers if they are to discharge their duties in the known best manner. Experience reveals that an understanding of training fundamentals can be acquired with a little help, but the need must be recognized and action taken to make it a reality.

QUESTIONS

1. Clearly distinguish between the following two types of developmental efforts: job-oriented and self-development.
2. Discuss the objectives of employee training.
3. What means of training have you personally found to be most effective? How do you justify this means as being the most effective?
4. Do you agree with this statement: "All known training means have an element of artificiality in them. Of necessity they must operate under an assumed arrangement. This leads to the fundamental principle that actual practice—learning by doing—is the superior teaching process. There is no satisfactory substitute for experience which emphasizes application of the employee's knowledge to a particular task at a particular time." Justify the position you take.
5. Which of these key points in learning included in this chapter are emphasized in the training means of the in-basket technique? Role playing? The incident process? Elaborate on your answers.
6. With respect to "the learning tempo," what is its meaning and what is its effect upon developmental efforts for office employees?
7. Discuss programmed instruction as a means of office developing, indicating whether you favor its use, along with your reasons why.
8. Carefully identify each of the following:
    a. A person's learning cycle.
    b. Computer assisted instruction.
    c. Induction training.
    d. Intangible costs of training.
9. While office training may be highly desirable, it also has some disadvantages. Briefly relate several of these disadvantages.
10. Enumerate and discuss two ways to improve office developmental efforts.

11. Discuss the justification for using developmental programs to cope with the problem of human obsolescence.

12. Discuss the subject, Cost of Training, pointing out what are to you the most important considerations.

CASE PROBLEMS

Case 21–1. Ace National Bank

James Depner is assistant manager of the Beaver Branch of Ace National Bank which has three branches as shown by the accompanying organization chart. Today is Monday, September 21. At 7:00 P.M. Jim Depner was telephoned at his home and informed that the manager of the Acorn Branch suffered an injury in an automobile accident and would be unable to work for the rest of the week. Jim is to take over as branch manager of the Acorn Branch for the remainder of the week. Jim has already scheduled an out-of-town business trip starting at 10 A.M. tomorrow morning (Tuesday) and returning the following Thursday morning. He is to make this trip. He is requested to go to the Acorn Branch first thing tomorrow morning and handle matters there that need attention.

EXHIBIT 21–1A

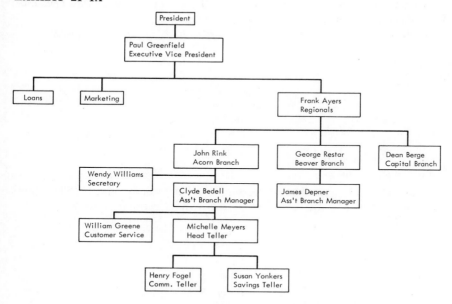

Jim feels this is an excellent opportunity to demonstrate his qualifications for future promotion. Arriving at the Acorn Branch at 8:00 A.M., he has an hour or so to take care of matters. He finds a quantity of material on the manager's desk. The contents of the items are described below.

Referring again to the organization chart, details on the personnel at Acorn Branch include:

Clyde Bedell—Assistant branch manager. Has been with the bank 32 years, not aggressive, opens and closes all types of bank accounts, has a loan limit of $25,000, larger loans must be referred to main bank office.

Wendy Williams—Secretary. Competent in typing and shorthand, age 23, serves as secretary to Mr. Rink, acts as receptionist, helps in safety deposit access when necessary.

William Greene—Customer services. Age 25, has been with bank two years, college graduate major in finance, has no supervisory responsibility, assists Mr. Bedell in opening and closing accounts, not authorized to make loans, but accepts applications for them.

Michelle Meyers—Head teller. Been with bank for 18 years, hard worker, dependable, is responsible for money vault, branch proofing, travelers checks, savings bonds, and money orders. Helps out with regular teller functions and safety deposit access as business requires. Other tellers are supposed to report to her, but do not since she always refers them to talk with Mr. Bedell about any problem they might have.

Henry Fogel—Commercial teller. Age 32, all experience in banking area, been with Ace for three years, responsible for cashing checks and checking deposit accounts.

Susan Yonkers—Savings teller. Handles all transactions on savings accounts along with club payments and installment payments.

Jim Depner found these "in-basket" items early Tuesday morning:

No. 1

Ace National Bank
Acorn Branch
Memo

September 18, 197____

To: Mr. John Rink
From: Susan Yonkers

The older sister of my husband is getting married Saturday and I'd like to get next Friday afternoon, the 25th, off. Is this O.K? I certainly hope so.

❉   ❉   ❉

No. 2

Ace National Bank
Executive Offices

To: John Rink
From: Training and Development

Your Mr. Clyde Bedell has been designated a trainee for our course, "Supervision and Human Relations" consisting of 10 two-hour sessions, 10:00 A.M.–

12:00 noon at the home office, Conference Room 100, beginning September 25. Following each session luncheon will be served in the officers' dining room. As you know selection of trainees is on a limited basis and attendance for all sessions is expected of all those selected.

H. H. Mann
Training Director

❁   ❁   ❁

No. 3

225 Linden Avenue
Campbellsville, N.Y. 12166
September 7, 197___

Dear Mr. Rink:

Since I have had my personal checking account with your bank, I have had nothing but trouble. The balance you show never balances with what I show. Checks bounce when I have adequate funds in my account. How come?

This is getting embarrassing. I expect your bank to straighten things out and send me a letter of apology. Otherwise, I'll take my account elsewhere.

Yours truly,
Cynthia Mueller

❁   ❁   ❁

No. 4

Hoosier Trucking, Inc.
111 Riverside Street
Yonkers, New York

September 16, 197___

Dear Mr. Rink:

It was indeed considerate of you to give me so much of your time regarding our loan application for $75,000. Although I still feel the interest you suggest is too high, I will approve of it and trust that we can settle the loan on that basis.

As you know we had in mind September 25 as the effective date of the loan and I am proceeding with the arrangements I mentioned to you during our talk and on that basis am going ahead with expenditures recommended by our budget committee.

Cordially,
Stephen Hiatt
Executive Vice President

❁   ❁   ❁

No. 5

Ace National Bank
Acorn Branch

September 8, 197___

To: Mr. John Rink
From: Henry Fogel

For five weeks I have covered the drive-in window and now request that I be relieved of this duty. After talking with Mr. Bedell about this, he suggested that I write you about my request—hence this memo. I should add that I am extremely susceptible to colds and the draft from the window is just too much for me. Thank you very much.

✿   ✿   ✿

No. 6

September 21, 197___

Dear Sir:

I am opening a new grocery store next week and a good friend of mine, Mr. Peter DeWitt, has suggested that I bank with you since I am going to be located just 2½ blocks from you. Mr. DeWitt said it was not difficult to arrange for loans from your bank and I expect to see you next week and open up an account.

Sincerely,
Robert Wrenn

✿   ✿   ✿

No. 7

Ace National Bank
Executive Offices

September 21, 197___

To: John Rink
From: Frank Ayers

Your past due loans report has not yet been received. The due date on this was September 15.

Please send it to me without delay.

✿   ✿   ✿

No. 8

Ace National Bank
Capitol Branch

September 18, 197___

To: All Officers
From: Dean Berge

A meeting of all officers on September 30 at 3:00 P.M. in the main conference room will be held to update you on the latest developments and forecasts regarding the money market.
Please make every effort to attend.

*   *   *

No. 9

September 16, 197___

Dear John:

My son, George, has just completed his term of service with the Air Force. He would like to work for a bank and I told him I'd write you and inquire whether you would talk to him. Please let me know when he can come in for an interview.

Sarah sends you her best wishes and asks when you will again be in the old home town. We are all fine and hope you are the same.

Best regards,
Happy Shoup

*   *   *

No. 10

Ace National Bank
Executive Offices

CONFIDENTIAL   CONFIDENTIAL   CONFIDENTIAL

To: John Rink
From: Paul Greenfield

The work record of your assistant, Clyde Bedell, gives us cause for concern regarding his development. There is no growth pattern over the last ten years. And while he is a distant relative of Frank Ayers, we feel we cannot prosper as a bank with any deadwood.

It seems to me that the bank has given Mr. Bedell quite adequate consideration and treatment. Yet he doesn't seem capable to assume greater responsibility.

I am recommending that Mr. Bedell be included in our forthcoming "Supervision and Human Relations" course. If his performance does not improve, I shall be forced to request that you ask him to resign or retire.

Questions:

1. Assuming Jim Depner cannot ask anyone for assistance, record the action you feel he should take on each item including memo, letter, report or interview.
2. What priorities do you suggest Mr. Depner follow? Why?
3. Relate your general impression of the management at Ace National Bank.

Case 21–2. Carrier-Wirth Company

Homer Davis believes that a development program for the 15 office supervisors should be reinstituted at Carrier-Wirth Company. As the newly appointed office manager, he is not impressed with the present office operations in general and feels that regularly scheduled supervisory meetings and training sessions will help, but not answer all of the current shortcomings.

After a recent announcement suggesting the office supervisory development program, Mr. Davis talked informally with each of his office supervisors. Somewhat to his surprise, but not entirely in the case of some supervisors, he found a lack of enthusiasm for his program. However, a few supervisors expressed favorable interest beyond what was expected. Typical of the reactions obtained are:

1. "Yes, I go along with it. Might help. Certainly can't do any harm."
2. "I don't really know. The ones we have had offered good material and I thought were well presented. But for the most part the topics were what we already know. It was the same old stuff all over again."
3. "The past programs have been interesting, but not very practical. There has been nothing I can use directly in my day-to-day work."
4. "Yes, I say have them, but get an outside consultant to handle the sessions. New approach, new ideas, new faces are what we need."
5. "I think I'd get more by taking a course at the local university in an evening class."
6. "Frankly, I feel such meetings are a waste of good time. Nothing is ever settled. Just a bunch of words, and more words."
7. "We never get to the real issues which remain covered and never brought into the open. You know it as well as I do that the old timers won't open up. Each session is a nice friendly get-together. Go ahead and have the sessions but don't expect much from them."

Approval for the development program must be obtained from Clarence E. Tate, president of the company. He must approve the required appropriations and the use of company time during which training sessions have been held in the past. Mr. Davis can keep the appropriations down using company personnel and he has in mind to hold 12 sessions on Tuesdays from 10:50 to 11:50 A.M. which is probably the most convenient time for all the supervisors to get together. Mr. Tate likes to relate all proposed expenditures to forecasted results. He thinks in terms of the company's return on its investment.

Mr. Davis is aware that Mr. John Almen, Jr., the factory manager and close ally of Mr. Tate, is dead set against any development program for factory supervisors. In Mr. Almen's opinion, such meetings are an excellent medium for wasting time, are too theoretical, and raise issues that should not be raised. He advocates having the supervisors work for an effective superintendent of production from whom a supervisor can learn how to be an effective supervisor. In Mr. Almen's opinion there is no substitute for experience for developing a good supervisor.

Questions:

1. What alternatives are available to Mr. Davis?
2. What is your reaction to the viewpoints of Mr. Tate? Mr. Almen, Jr.?
3. What should Mr. Davis do? Why?

Chapter **22**

Office Salary Administration

To know one's ignorance is the best part of knowledge.

Lao-Tse

Compensation is an important area of office management. Salaries provide income for employees and serve as a means by which some of employees' wants can be satisfied. The need for food and shelter, for example, can be satisfied if a person has the money to purchase them. And possession of financial wealth is commonly associated with status and influence. Monetary reward for accomplishing work is therefore a fundamental consideration in office management and helps get work accomplished that otherwise might not be accomplished.

IMPORTANCE OF SALARY ADMINISTRATION

Salaries are important to both the employer and the employee. Some 70–75 percent of total office costs are salaries and hence, represent the largest single cost item. The employer is interested in controlling this cost and commonly resorts to guides such as labor cost per output unit and productivity per employee. Further, the employer seeks to attract and hold competent employees by paying a fair, attractive, and competitive salary. In contrast, the employee views salary as a means for indirectly satisfying certain needs and wants according to personal standards. Also, the typical employee feels he or she should be paid the same salary as others doing the same kind of work in the same office or in offices in the same locality. And most believe a salary differential should be maintained over those doing office work requiring less skill,

578

experience, knowledge, and responsibility. In addition, one desires sufficient salary to support oneself and to contribute to family support, to keep up with the increases in the cost of living, and hopefully to save a certain portion of that income for future contingencies.

There are, in fact, a myriad of influences affecting office salaries. At any given time, some factors are tending to push salaries up while others are having the directly opposite effect. And these respective forces are of varying degrees. For example, important criteria determining salary include the prevailing compensation for a given type of office work, the ability of the employer to pay, the job requirements, the bargaining power of the employer or the employee, and the productivity of the employee. To establish and implement sound policies and methods of compensation is the purpose of office salary administration. It attempts to bring order and sanity to a very complex, dynamic, and vital area. Included in its makeup are job evaluation, salary surveys, salary scales, adjustments in pay, incentive plans, supplementary payments, and other related salary items.

Main Purposes of Office Salary Administration

The question of how much to pay an office employee is especially difficult to answer in this era of spiraling wages, budget constraints, and governmental regulations. Use of a sound, well-planned office salary administration is the best answer. Such a program strives to assist the manager in six important ways:

1. Recruit Persons for Office Jobs. The salary must be sufficient to attract qualified personnel and further, must be competitive with respect to other local employers and major economic trends. The salary level is adjunct to employee recruitment. Pay is an important consideration to the new recruit.

2. Induce and Reward Better Office Performance. Deeply imbedded in the minds of most people is that those who produce more should be paid more. Superior output in quantity or in quality must be rewarded. If an employee produces more and is paid more, the gain is non-inflationary because of the greater productivity. However, there are some who argue that money is not a direct motivator. No salary plan by itself will make people happy. There is, it is contended, a difference between striving harder for more pay and that of gaining satisfaction from performing the work. An employee may diligently apply efforts, receive more salary, but may not be satisfied with the job. Some employees frequently absent themselves from or even quit a job, although the pay is relatively high. On the other hand, employees may enjoy a great deal of satisfaction from their work efforts, but do not strive to produce more even though extra dollars are offered for extra accomplishment. The additional pay is relatively not important to them.

3. *Keep Employees Content, Reduce Complaints, and Minimize Resignations.*   Favoritism and discrimination should never be a part of salary administration. The salary must be fair, satisfactory, and believed adequate by the receiver. Under such conditions a feeling of well-being and contentment is fostered. The employee does not gripe, stir up trouble, or quit. As far as pay is concerned, the employee is satisfied.

4. *Establish a Fair Internal Salary Schedule.*   Different work necessitates different requirements such as education, experience, responsibility, and working conditions in order to perform the work properly. These differences should be taken into account to establish adequate differentials among the various jobs of an office. Relating these differentials into a staircase of grades or levels provides the basis for needed pay differentials among the various jobs. In addition, employees expect their salaries to be equitable to salaries received by co-workers. The "equal pay for equal work" principle is especially pertinent among salaried office jobs.

5. *Conduct Employee Appraisals to Determine Basis for Comparative Pay Adjustments.*   Within any established job level or class, salary differences should be supported by objective appraisals of employees performing the work within that job class. There should be no mysticism surrounding an individual salary adjustment. For the same job level, salary constraints, and performance appraisals, the result should be an identical salary adjustment. A periodic appraisal review enables the employees to know how well they are doing. If below expectancies, the employee can take action to improve performance. When management by objectives is followed, considerable emphasis is placed upon comparable performance within jobs as determined by the results achieved. In any event, an employee appraisal system is needed to help determine how much to pay.

6. *Control Payroll Costs Yet Recognize Productivity Gains and Governmental Regulations.*   In a number of offices careful control is exercised over the distribution of salary rates within a given salary range or level. For example, within a given department only so many junior executives, private secretaries, and typists class I, may be permitted. Likewise, the frequency and size of increases may be regulated. Usually no employee may receive a salary above the top rate of the job level in which the job is included. In addition, governmental regulations affect what is paid. Examples of such regulations include the provisions of the Fair Labor Standards Act of 1938 with amendments which set a minimum wage that is to be paid along with the number of hours worked, and the Equal Pay Act of 1963, reinforced by the Affirmative Action Programs which legislates "equal pay for equal work."

Major Principles of Office Salary Administration

Experience in office salary administration is sufficiently developed so that major principles or guides to follow can be offered. They include:

1. Any office salary administration program should have the backing of top management.

2. The superior program is simple, easily administered, and understood by all office employees.

3. Reasonable openness including the availability of information on pay ranges and median salaries for the various job levels makes for better human relations and confidence in the compensation system itself. The timing and extent of this openness depends on the history of the office and its managerial climate.

4. For effective salary administration, carefully distinguish between jobs and employees. Each job should carry a specific dollar range; a person is assigned to fill a job at a salary within that range.

5. Equal pay should be given for equal work, regardless of who does the work. Note, however, that it is possible within a given salary range, to have employees receiving different salaries within the range.

6. There should be differentials in salary paid for jobs that have different requirements for their satisfactory performance.

7. Recognition of individual differences in ability and achievement in performing a job should be made. This may take place by different means including (a) salary increases within the job range, (b) a sequence of job promotions, or (c) participation in a monetary incentive plan.

8. The salaries paid should be in line with those prevailing in the immediate community office labor market.

THE GUIDELINE METHOD

One of the newer techniques being used for office salary administration is the realistic and fairly simple approach of the guideline method. It emphasizes and reflects the relative job prices as interpreted by the labor market. In the final analysis the price of the position on the market is considered the ruling factor. Job rates change due to the forces of supply and demand and a realistic wage administration takes this into account.

To implement, a guideline wage scale of salary ranges or grades is constructed. This serves as a common scale for all positions to be evaluated. A minimum, midpoint, and maximum are established for each salary grade. Usually this begins with a number of key jobs which are the universal positions easily identified in the marketplace through salary surveys. In essence, this illustrates the direct pricing feature of the method. A relatively large number of these key jobs increase the accuracy of the salary scale. Their selection and comparison are basic to the overall success of the guideline.

Figure 22–1 shows the data for eight salary grades. Usually a spread

FIGURE 22–1
**A Salary Scale for Use with the Guideline Method
of Salary Administration**

Salary Grade	Minimum	Midpoint	Maximum
1	$ 4,080	$ 4,800	$ 5,520
2	4,600	5,500	6,400
3	5,250	6,400	7,550
4	6,150	7,600	9,050
5	7,450	9,300	11,150
6	8,800	11,800	14,800
7	10,800	15,400	20,000
8	12,800	19,700	26,600

of about 30–35 percent exists in the lower grades, and increases gradually to over 100 percent in the higher grades. As indicated in Figure 22–1, the spread for grade 1 is $4080 to $5520, or 15 percent on either side of the midpoint value of $4800. In contrast, the spread for grade 7 is $10,800 to $20,000, or 30 percent on either side of the midpoint value of $15,400. In addition, the differential between midpoints of each successive pair of grades increases as the higher grades are reached. Further, a "salary price" can exist in two or more grades thereby giving needed flexibility. For example, $5,600 can exist in grades 2 and 3.

After data for the key jobs and the guideline scale are established, the evaluation process takes place. The average salary for each key job is matched with the nearest midpoint on the scale. From this can be seen the relationship among key jobs as guided by the salaries being paid in the external market. To this are added and compared the salaries being paid by the company for key jobs that are similar in makeup. If inequities appear within the internal salary schedule, the manager can study such cases and decide which ones, if any, should be adjusted. Likewise, the remaining jobs for which no similar outside comparability exists are evaluated using a ranking or comparing technique, based on the evaluator's judgment and using as a guide the key jobs or other jobs that have already been assigned grades. The finished array of jobs is carefully reviewed both from the entirety viewpoint and from that of salaries for jobs within a department or other organizational unit. Inequities existing can be corrected as a result of this study.

The guideline method gives basic advantages. First, it is inclusive and eliminates the need to have several salary structures to satisfy geographical differentials. And it is objective. Data are based on facts as revealed by what is being paid for different jobs in the marketplace. Not only spotting the inequity, but doing something about it is emphasized by the guideline method. Further, the maintenance cost is low—expensive individual evaluations are kept at a minimum. The entire method is quite simple.

Job Evaluation

Approaches to determine the relative worth of a job start with job evaluation which can be formally defined as follows: *Job evaluation is the determination of the relative value of each individual job in an enterprise and is arrived at by means of a systematic procedure using jobs or selected job factors for comparison or measurement.* There are four main methods of carrying out job evaluation work, including (1) ranking, (2) classification, (3) factor comparison, and (4) point.

1. Ranking Method. The jobs within an enterprise can be arranged according to their relative difficulty. A ranking of the jobs is thus obtained; and in this manner, the relative importance of each one is established. The job at the top of the list has the highest value, and the job at the bottom of the list has the lowest value. The usual procedure is (1) to rank the jobs in an individual department and (2) to combine all departmental rankings into one composite ranking.

Figure 22–2 illustrates the results which might be obtained from this

FIGURE 22–2
Array of Jobs According to Ranking Method

Rank Number	Name of Job	Earnings per Week*
1	Accounting clerk I	$165
2	Purchasing clerk	160
3	Traffic clerk I	155
4	Cashier	150
5	Accounting clerk II	145
6	Traffic clerk II	140
7	Cost clerk	135
8	Tabulating-machine operator	130
9	General bookkeeper	125
10	Correspondent	120
11	Stenographer	115
12	Switchboard operator	110
13	Typist I	105
14	File clerk	100
15	Typist II	95
16	Office messenger	90

* In uniform variation from top to bottom.

method. For example, the job of accounting clerk I was considered of greater value than the job of purchasing clerk, while the job of office messenger was ranked lowest in the office. If the weekly salary of the top job is set at $165 and that of the lowest job at $90, then the rank order of the intermediate jobs, assuming a straight-line or uniform variation, is shown in the last column in the illustration.

2. Classification Method. Under this method, a predetermined number of job classes or groups are established, and the jobs are assigned to these classifications. For example, the job classes, from highest to lowest, might include:

Class A.   Executive
  Office manager
  Office departmental supervisor
Class B.   Skilled
  Purchasing clerk
  Traffic clerk
  Cashier
Class C.   Limited skilled
  Tabulating-machine operator
  Stenographer
  Switchboard operator
Class D.   Unskilled
  File clerk
  Office boy

In this method, the jobs within each grade frequently must be graded further to show more adequately the existing relationships. To do this, the ranking method, previously described, can be employed.

3. Factor Comparison Method. Jobs can also be evaluated according to predetermined factors which have been established as a measure of ranking. Customarily, a key-job comparison scale is established and used for this purpose. Job factors are listed across the top and the dollars per week or salary-rating schedule in the left column. The scale provides the means for applying *salary rates* to job relatives as needed.

Assume four job factors: education, experience, responsibility, and working conditions. On each of these factors, each key job is ranked. Generally, eight to ten jobs are considered key jobs, selected on the basis of the jobs requiring widely different amounts of the job factors being utilized. To illustrate, for the accounting clerk I job, the rating values given for each of the job factors might be:

Education	$ 48.00
Experience.	40.00
Responsibility	58.00
Working conditions	19.00
Total	$165.00

In other words, from the key-job comparison scale, it is possible to determine what portion of the present salary of a job is being paid for each factor.

This scale is the measuring device for evaluating all other jobs in the company. Other jobs are fitted into this scale, with the key-job evaluations being used as guides. To illustrate, consider the job of tabulating-machine operator. The evaluator would first read the job analysis sheet for this job. Then, concentrating attention on the factor of education, the evaluator judges where under the education column the job of tabulating-machine operator seems to fit. The decision might be that this job requires a little more education than a certain key job but less than another key job. Hence, tabulating-machine operator would be evaluated between the two considered key jobs. In similar manner, the job is evaluated according to the other job factors, and the other jobs in the company are evaluated in a similar manner.

4. Point Method. In this method, job factors are selected, and each is assigned a maximum number of points or credits. The selection of job factors is qualified by the following: that each job factor (1) exists in all the jobs to be evaluated, (2) varies in amount in the different jobs to be evaluated, and (3) is mutually exclusive of other job factors. The maximum point value assigned to each factor is determined by its relative importance. This is governed primarily by the judgment and experience of the analyst. Normally, from eight to fourteen factors are used.

Figure 22–3 illustrates 11 job factors selected for use in the evaluation of clerical and supervisory jobs. In this case, the data showing the level and the points of rating, along with pertinent comments for the job of junior accountant, are indicated for each factor. Note that under factor 4, responsibility for loss, the rating level of *B* is valued at 15 points. This value was arrived at by using the guide shown in Figure 22–4. The evaluator believed that the level B definition with a value of 15 points best fitted for this factor the job being evaluated.

Pricing the Job

The ultimate aim of job evaluation is to determine the job price or rate of pay. Jobs of high evaluation should command high rates of pay; in general, the higher the evaluation, the higher the pay. The immediate problem is to determine what the rate of pay should be when the evaluation is a known amount. The job prices to be established must be consistent (1) externally (rates within the enterprise are in line with the rates paid outside the enterprise) and (2) internally (rates within the enterprise are directly associated within the evaluations).

External consistency is accomplished by securing the current wage

FIGURE 22–3
Job Factors, Ratings, and Comments for the Job of Junior Accountant

Code .... Salary Grade ...... **VI** ....
Job Title ...... **JUNIOR ACCOUNTANT** ....

CLERICAL AND SUPERVISORY EVALUATION

	NO.	FACTOR	RATING LEVEL	PTS.	JOB REQUIREMENT
SKILL	1	Essential Knowledge	D	84	Requires a knowledge of advanced accounting methods and procedures and a working knowledge of company financial policies.
	2	Experience and Training	G	73	Normally requires 3 to 5 years' training and experience, including 2 years' accounting training plus 3 years' company experience as an Accounting Clerk.
	3	Analytical Requirements	C	27	Requires analysis of figures and data which vary in content but follow general patterns of application
RESPONSIBILITY	4	Responsibility For Loss	B	15	Requires more than normal care to prevent loss due to miscalculations. However, work is usually checked against totals.
	5	Confidential Information	B	6	Involves preparation and use of limited confidential matters in the Accounting Department.
	6	Contacts Public and Internal	B	28	Involves routine contacts with persons where detailed subject matter must be presented satisfactorily.
	7	Individual Initiative	B	12	Involves initiative in planning details of own work.
EFFORT	8	Mental Effort	C	15	Requires moderate mental effort to solve problems of accounting.
	9	Physical Effort	A	6	Involves light physical effort with intermittent standing and sitting at comfortable intervals.
	10	Work Conditions	A	0	Working conditions are excellent.
	11	Supervisory Requirements	FX	18	Involves immediate leadership over Accounting Clerks and Typists.
	TOTAL POINTS			284	

Courtesy: J. D. Moore Organization, Ann Arbor, Mich.

FIGURE 22-4

Illustrating the Different Levels of Responsibility for Loss and the Number of Points Assigned to Each Level

4. Responsibility for Loss		
Level	LEVEL DEFINITION	Points
A	Nature of work involves negligible opportunity for loss. Normal or reasonable care required and all work is verified or proved by repeating entire operation.	3
B	Nature of work is such that more than normal or reasonable care is required to prevent loss. However, work is checked by proving against totals or some standard rather than by repetition of operation.	15
C	Nature of work involves moderate but constant opportunity for error, limited only by daily or subsequent spot check or examination. Great care should be exercised to prevent loss. Potential serious loss from errors in transcription or computation.	27
D	Good judgment must be exercised regularly to prevent loss. Work is of such nature that complete and correct performance is hard to control, reliance being placed on the individual. Work subject to general supervision and occasional review.	38
E	Work of such a nature that commitments are made which may involve the entire bank. Work is frequently released without any check being made or is checked only by individual doing the work. A high degree of financial responsibility is involved.	50

Courtesy: J. D. Moore Organization, Ann Arbor, Mich.

rates in the area from salary surveys conducted by enterprises specializing in this type of work or from local governmental offices. Sometimes, to supplement available information, a thorough salary survey must be made. It is also well to remember that accurate job descriptions and productivity data add greatly to the usefulness of salary survey results.

Internal consistency is determined by comparing the job evaluations with the rates paid. In some cases, this can be done by a simple compari-

588   *Office Management and Control*

son of columnar data. Very often, however, a graphic representation
helps to visualize this comparison, especially when the point system
of evaluation has been used. Commonly employed is a chart or scatter
diagram in which existent wage rates are plotted on the vertical axis
and evaluations on the horizontal axis. A curve showing consistent relationships between rates and evaluations can then be drawn on the chart.
The deviations of actual rates from this curve can readily be spotted,
and jobs overpaid or underpaid with respect to their evaluation can
be quickly observed.

Figure 22–5 shows by diagram the relationship between wage rates

FIGURE 22–5
**Scatter Diagram Showing Relationship between Wage Rates
and Evaluation Measurements**

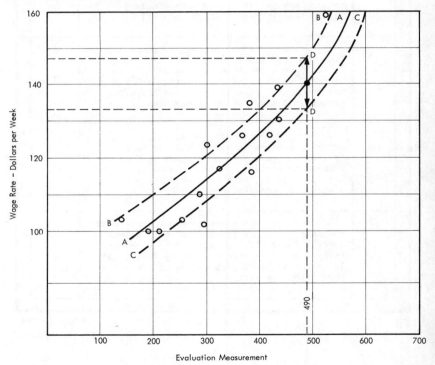

and evaluations. The plotted points are indicated by the small circles.
Curve *AA* has been drawn in and represents what is considered to
be a consistent relationship between rates and evaluations. Curves *BB*
and *CC* have been drawn in for reasons discussed in the paragraphs
that follow.

Job Price Range

From a practical viewpoint, the office manager is interested in more than a job price for each job. What she really wants is (1) *a price range for each job*, not a single price for each job; and (2) *a price range to cover a group of jobs*, not just one job. A price range provides flexibility and makes for a better salary plan. Furthermore, when a group of jobs are within one price range, the entire task of wage determination is simplified.

Referring again to Figure 22–5, a wage range has been indicated by the two curves *BB* and *CC* drawn on the chart. Observe that in the figure the vertical spread between these two curves is a *constant amount*. Some advocate that a *constant percentage* change from the center line be used to establish the outside large lines, a practice which makes the spread greater for higher priced jobs since the percentage is of a larger amount. The job of traffic clerk II, for example, evaluated at 490 points, has a range from $133 to $147 per week, indicated by ordinate *DD* on the chart.

To provide a group of jobs within one price range, it is customary to group jobs into classes so that all jobs in the same class have the same price range. In other words, jobs of the same worth are put into the same class. The number of job classes depends primarily upon the total number of jobs, and the spread between the highest and the lowest job. Usually, a total of six to ten job classes is sufficient in most offices.

To illustrate, with reference to Figure 22–5, the following job classes of perhaps 5 or 6 total job classes might include:

Job Class	Evaluation Points	Dollar Range
I	100–160	$ 90–105
II	161–220	95–115
III	221–280	110–130

Observe that there is a vertical overlap between adjoining job classes, i.e., the top of class I is $105 and the bottom of class II is $95. This provides desirable flexibility in the salary administration program.

ADVANTAGES OF JOB EVALUATION

The point method of job evaluation aids office salary administration for these reasons (1) the method shows the relative value of office jobs within a company, (2) assists in the evaluating of new office jobs, (3) helps obtain a satisfactory wage level for all office jobs within the company, (4) helps to eliminate salary inequalities by putting office jobs having similar requirements in the same salary range, and (5) affords factual data for the settling of salary disputes. It is imperative, however, that the work of determining job content, grades, and price ranges be kept up to date by regular, periodic checkups. The content of many jobs changes in the normal course of events; and this, in turn, frequently changes the relative values of the jobs. Likewise, changes in the general wage levels appear to be the usual rather than the exceptional happenings.

How Well Is the Incumbent Doing Job?

Up to this point the discussion has been confined to what the job price range is or, in other words, what salary range is paid for its performance. We will now consider the equally important concept, how well the incumbent is doing the job. For this purpose, performance appraisal, discussed in Chapter 19, is commonly used. In some programs, performance appraisal tempered with seniority is followed. The justification for this approach is that the employee who has been on the job for a long period tends to perform the work better or at least knows more about how it should be performed. This viewpoint, however, is open to question, but in offices where it is followed, it is usually popular and brings quite satisfactory results.

Bonus arrangements are employed by some companies to demonstrate approval of satisfactory office work accomplishments. Usually the payments of bonuses commemorate special occasions, such as Christmas, a birthday, or an employment anniversary. These payments commonly amount to sizable sums—perhaps an extra month's pay or, in some cases, as much as 20 percent of a year's salary. They are given to share the results of profitable operations, to recognize outstanding service, to continue a traditional custom, or to improve employee morale.

Financial incentive plans are another means of recognizing how well the incumbent is doing. These plans provide for total compensation based to some extent on the amount of work accomplished instead of strictly on the basis of time spent at work. Generally speaking, financial incentive plans are not common in offices, but their use is growing. The more common incentive office work includes transcribing, card punching, order processing, and billing.

FUNDAMENTALS OF OFFICE INCENTIVE PLANS

There are two fundamental concepts in practically all office incentive plans: (1) a base or standard amount of work output and (2) the amount of wage payment which will be given for production below standard, at standard, or above standard. The first concept, the base amount of work output, can be determined by any of the work measurement, time-use techniques discussed in Chapter 26. Customarily, this standard amount of work is expressed as 100 percent. The amount of work which is established as standard is extremely important, for it is commonly, but not always, the point at which the incentive pay begins. The second concept, or pattern of the amount of wage payment, varies with the incentive plan. Most plans guarantee base rates up to standard; a few do not. Some divide the excess above standard equally between employee and employer, while others share the overflow according to various percentages.

The same general type of plan can be used for a group as for a single employee. The group can be used when the nature of the work is such that its segregation among individual employees is very difficult or costly to administer. The group incentive pay is figured first, then divided among the members according to either the individual base wage rates, the number of hours worked by each member, the individual gross base pay, or on some other agreed basis.

Incentive wage plans should be tailor-made to suit the particular work and to achieve the particular objectives desired from the plan. The following guides are helpful:

1. There should be a close relationship between reward (incentive pay) and results (contribution).

2. An incentive based on the individual employee is generally better than one based on a group.

3. The work output should increase as well as the amount of salaries.

4. The base or standard production amounts should be carefully determined—preferably by measured time analyses.

5. The number of temporary standards should be held to a minimum. When standards are temporary, this fact should be known to all concerned.

6. The incentive wage should be neither guaranteed nor limited. In most instances, the base wage should be guaranteed.

7. The standards should be reviewed for possible revision whenever any change is made in the material, machine, or method used.

8. If indirect production employees, such as messengers, receptionists, and telephone operators, are included in the plan, they should be affiliated on some measurable basis, such as the maintenance of an acceptable ratio between the total indirect work-hours to the total direct work-hours, or the total indirect man-hours to total work ouput. This tends to keep the indirect work-hours under control.

FRINGE BENEFITS

Another major area of modern office salary administration is fringe benefits. These include (1) legally required benefits—social security, unemployment, workmen's compensation requirements, (2) pay *away* from the job—paid leaves, vacations, and holidays, (3) pay *on* the job for time off—employee meetings, overtime pay, and shift premium pay, and (4) special benefits—service awards, meal allowances, relocation expenses, group insurance, medical and dental aid, and tuition help. Various estimates point to an average of about 35–40 percent of total base payroll costs constituting expense for fringe benefits. The trend in the amount of fringe benefits has been steadily upward during the last decade.

Many office employees give considerable weight to the fringe benefits included in a job. The dollar "take home" pay is adjusted in view of the fringe benefits received; and many office employees prefer to work for a particular concern where the dollar salaries are average or even low, but the numerous fringe benefits provided make for an attractive total remuneration.

A big need in the fringe benefits area is for employers to explain and publicize their benefit programs. Too frequently complicated mathematical formulas and legal phraseology are communicated in response to simple employee questions. As a rule, employees want to know their benefit position. The wise office manager tells the employee in language that he or she can understand.

QUESTIONS

1. Discuss the importance of salary administration in office management today.
2. Of the eight major principles of office salary administration included in this chapter, which two do you feel are of utmost importance? Why?
3. Would you say that job evaluation is scientific in its determination of the value of a job? Why?
4. Discuss (*a*) what is meant by the guideline method in salary administration, and (*b*) how this method is employed.
5. Explain Figure 22–3 in your own words.
6. Discuss the importance you feel the office employee places upon fringe benefits. Justify your viewpoint.
7. Do you feel that the amount of salary an office employee receives will induce that person to perform better and to behave better, neither of these, or one or the other of these? Justify your answer.
8. Define each of the following:
   a. Salary differentials.
   b. Job evaluation.
   c. Factor comparison method.
   d. Price range for a group of jobs.
9. Which method of job evaluation do you consider the simplest? The most accurate? The easiest for employees to understand? Substantiate your answer.

10. For an office employing 750 employees, can the wage rates be externally, but not internally, consistent? Internally, but not externally, consistent? Elaborate upon your answers.
11. What steps do you feel might be taken to make an office employee more aware of the fringe benefits received?
12. Do you believe we should have more or less office incentive plans in American industries? Why? Is your answer from the viewpoint of a manager or a nonmanager? Does the viewpoint make any difference?

CASE PROBLEMS

Case 22–1. Wiggins Company

The vacation plan practiced for a number of years was that an employee employed during the previous year, defined as the period July 1 through June 30, receives 3 percent of the previous year's pay plus one week of vacation. The agreement worked out very well and it was easily understood by all parties concerned.

On January of this year, Wiggins Company was sold to American General Products, Inc., the effective date of the take-over was established as March 31.

Come June 1, the employees of the now nonexistent Wiggins Company made inquiry regarding their vacation pay. The managers of American General Products, Inc. indicated that employees would be granted vacations in keeping with the following schedule which reflects its vacation practice for the past twelve years:

Employees with service up to 5 years . . . . 1 week paid vacation
Employees with service over 5 and up to 10 years . . . . 2 weeks paid vacation
Employees with service over 10 and up to 20 years. . . . . 3 weeks paid vacation
Employees with service over 20 years . . . . 4 weeks paid vacation

Different reactions to the new vacation and pay plan arose. Several old-timers of Wiggins Company stood to receive more pay under the new arrangement while those with less than 5 years service stood to lose under the new arrangement. About 60 percent of the former Wiggins employees were in the "under 5 years" bracket while approximately 22 percent were in the "over 10 years up to 20 years" and "over 20 years" groups. They heartily accepted the plan of American General Products, Inc. and tried to persuade the younger service employees to accept the plan.

To complicate the situation further, several former Wiggins employees whose jobs were terminated as a result of the merger demanded that the surviving corporation give them a vacation pay equal to 3 percent of their 9-month pay ending March 31. They contended that their jobs were terminated through no fault of theirs and they worked for nine months under the general agreement and practice of getting vacation pay. To these arguments, American General Products, Inc. managers replied no such agreement implied or in writing was ever made with the terminated employees. Further upon investigation, a copy of the agreement they requested and obtained from the Wiggins Company stated the vacation pay was given to those "actively employed for the calendar year", a condition that the terminated employees did not fulfill.

Questions:

1. Which of the two vacation plans do you feel might be the best for a company to follow? Why? For the American General Products, Inc. to follow? Why?
2. How would you resolve the issue with the terminated employees due to the merger? Justify your views.
3. What actions do you recommend the managers of American General Products, Inc. take? Why?

Case 22–2.   Starr Products Company

Orville Drake, information manager, is trying to hire a qualified person for an opening of cost accountant B. He has been seeking such a person for nearly two weeks. To date, the one qualified applicant, Lee Gillis, wants $11,500 a year. He says he will not accept a job for less. Mr. Drake has also interviewed two other accountants who appear qualified, but one wants $13,000 a year, the other $15,000 a year. The credentials of Mr. Gillis are highly satisfactory, his background is good, and during an interview, he impressed Mr. Drake as being desirable to add to the accounting group. Mr. Gillis expressed a desire to join Starr Products Company. In addition to these three candidates, Mr. Drake has interviewed some eight or ten additional people, but none are qualified in Mr. Drake's opinion.

There are currently eight employees in the accounting department including the chief accountant, three general accountants, a cost accountant A, two cost accountants B, and a tax expert. The filling of the present opening for a cost accountant B will make a total of three accountants of that classification. The present salary range for cost accountant B is $775 to $900 a month. Periodically, Mr. Drake checks the company's salary ranges with those paid by other companies in the general area. His last study, conducted six weeks ago, showed his company's salary rates for office jobs are in line with others in the area. The salary range for cost accountant A is $850 to $1100 a month. In Mr. Drake's opinion, none of the three qualified candidates are qualified for the A classification of cost accountant job.

Questions:

1. Name the major alternatives available to Mr. Drake.
2. What action should Mr. Drake take? Why?
3. Discuss the implications of this problem upon the office salary structure of the company.

Case 22–3.   Forsythe Company

Arthur Kadell was being paid $750 a month. He joined the company three and one-half years ago, was promoted to his present job on which he has received two pay increases. Due to the installation of a computer and changes in work content, Arthur Kadell's job will no longer be necessary. His supervisor told him not to worry, that he would be transferred to another job. Meanwhile, he will continue on his present job for approximately the next two months while the changeover is being made.

Some seven weeks later, Mr. Kadell is informed that he will be transferred to another department and job which will pay him $675 a month, and he will retain his full seniority and company benefits. Mr. Kadell protests, claiming he should continue to receive his present rate of pay. He reasons that the company offer gives him a cut in pay through no fault of his own; he has a good work record with the company, and prior to now, nothing has been said about his having to take less pay. He adds, "Had I known this, I would have started looking outside for something else the minute I found out my job was to be eliminated."

Questions:

1. What further action do you feel Arthur Kadell should take? Why?
2. What should the company do? Why?

Chapter 23

Additional Considerations in Actuating

> *Abilities wither under faultfinding, bloom under encouragement.*
>
> Donald L. Laird

There remains a number of other salient areas in the field of managerial actuating to be discussed. Included are: the building of team effectiveness; handling of promotions, absenteeism, and tardiness; working with office unions; maintaining office safety; helping to provide employee economic security; and contributing to employees' recreational activities. This chapter covers these areas. Over a period, most office managers will probably use to some extent most of the practices presented.

BUILDING TEAM EFFECTIVENESS

As pointed out in Chapter 15, organization places the individual in a group relationship. An employee behaves commonly as a group member, not as an isolated, independent individual. As a group member, gains are achieved that would not be possible for the individual working alone. And as we have already seen, the behavior of a group differs from the behavior of an individual. Groups are a reality, the challenge to the manager is to attain effective team efforts from the group. This is essential in modern management. A group with team spirit stands out in bold relief from one struggling with internal wrangling and disharmony.

For teamwork to be effective, two factors must exist (1) shared goals and (2) mutual respect. Conflicting goals among the members of a group prevent genuine teamwork from existing. It is the management member's job to focus the actions and abilities of group members toward a common goal and a desire to cooperate. The second factor, mutual respect, includes a prevalent willingness to trust the skill and expertise of other group members and to become interdependent, not independent. There can and will be differences of opinion and viewpoints, but these can and are resolved when mutual respect is practiced.

The managers' dealings with group members have much influence on the building of a team. They can, for example, recognize and utilize friendship patterns. If A and B want to work together, it is quite likely that their cooperation and respect for each other will be high. Likewise, promoting cooperation among members of the group contributes to teamwork and advances all members on the team. Too much stress on individual effort may give rise to jealousy and misunderstanding among the members. Any favored type of treatment to one individual over another should be avoided, playing favoritism is a certain way to destroy cooperation among the group members. In addition, the management member should stand up for group members, get them proper working conditions, needed machines and equipment, training opportunities and wage increases. Members respond favorably to such leaders and the effect is to formulate an effective team. Also, encouraging participation in decision making about which the members are interested and have knowledge should be followed. Such a practice gives members a sense of belonging and a feeling of importance so that the group really becomes a group that responds to its formal leadership.

Team building programs are recommended and can follow any of a number of programs. However, the first step is to find out what the key issues are, that is, how members view the group's objectives, what adjustments, if any they feel are needed, and their evaluation of each group member as to his or her behavior and contribution. One of several alternatives can be selected to start the program. The management member can interview each member privately seeking to disclose the most pertinent issues. Or a written survey among the members can be conducted with the responses tabulated and classified. In addition, a request from each member to list specific problems as she or he sees them and turn them in by a given date can be followed. This approach also includes a request for a written statement of general impressions for each of the other members in the group—of how the employee sees them as co-workers.

Whatever the approach, the responses are classified and arranged for discussion by the members in a group session. Key questions to answer include: What is each member contributing? In what areas does the member appear to be effective? Ineffective? What can be done to improve contributions? What should the employee cease doing because its effect is negative? The exact procedure followed can vary, but the logical framework for building effective teamwork follows this sequence—determine the issues, analyze team and individual strength and weaknesses, clarify personal goals, coordinate organizational goals with personal goals, and evolve specific recommendations and programs for attaining the goals.

Care must be exercised in handling and discussing these data, especially that given by one member regarding another member. One technique is to prepare a personal inventory for each member from the data. At a group meeting, these personal inventories are posted and the members circulate among them, writing on the appropriate form their suggestions for improving the effectiveness of their co-workers. This approach tends to provide a depersonalized feedback. In addition, it is helpful to request that each member turn in a paper describing personal ambitions and to indicate which ones are, and the ones that are not, being fulfilled by the present work. The effect of all this is to focus on important objectives and behavior as well as to establish a climate in which members can discuss personal issues freely and honestly with the intent of improving their teamwork.

Promotions, Absenteeism, and Tardiness

Promotions are effective motivating actions in that they afford satisfaction to the average individual in his desire to develop, to advance, and to improve his status. Most companies have the policy of promoting from among their present employees whenever possible. This requires keeping a sharp eye open for the discovery of promotable personnel—those people who demonstrate a desire to advance by qualifying for a better and more responsible job. Quite a few managers, however, feel that some of the vacancies for better jobs should be filled by candidates from outside the enterprise. By this means, it is contended, new ideas, new attitudes, and different methods of operation are brought in which tend to foster an active, healthy condition.

The initiative for promotion belongs with the manager. Without prodding, the manager should see that worthy people are promoted. The knowledge of whom to advance is gained through records covering each approved employee's competence, and length of service. Actually, promotion implies two-way action. It calls for action by the managers—to open up avenues along which employees can advance; and it calls for action by employees—to qualify themselves for advancement.

The failure of an employee to report on the job when scheduled to work is one of the difficult personnel problems with which the average office manager must cope. Absenteeism disrupts the smooth flow of work; either the work stops completely, or extra work is forced upon another employee. There is no single cure for absenteeism. It is an individual problem and the correction must suit the particular case. Records revealing who is absent, how long, how often, and why give information on where to concentrate corrective efforts.

Among the means used to reduce absenteeism are pointing out to employees the importance of being on the job, talking with each absentee upon return and thoroughly discussing the cause and explanation offered, checking to see if the right person is on the right job, maintaining a continued health program, allowing a definite number of days off per year, requiring absentees to make up time, and showing some outward thanks and appreciation to those employees who are always on the job. Figure 23–1 offers suggestions to keep absenteeism under control.

FIGURE 23–1

To keep absenteeism under control, the office supervisor should:

1. Let people know that their attendance is important.
2. Keep absence records on an individual basis and let your people know such records are being made.
3. Require absentees who call in sick to report to you personally when they report back to work.
4. Follow special incentive plans—time off, merchandise awards, and so forth to encourage good attendance.
5. Establish a progressive system of discipline measures ranging from a warning to dismissal for excessive absence.
6. Know who the chronic Friday- and Monday-off offenders are and take special steps to curb their practice.
7. Keep your employees up-dated as to how their work performance is.
8. Be accessible to give your group members needed information or advice, upon request.

Tardiness indicates a disrespect for others and a lack of dependability. It is contagious. When one or two continue to come into the office late, the idea gets in the minds of other employees that such behavior has managerial approval. Being early is as much a habit as being late. The hour at which work starts has little influence on the problem. The tendency to procrastinate must be corrected and the importance of keeping time obligations stressed.

An effective motivating means consists of creating a strong employee interest in promptness. Supervisors should set good examples and always be on time themselves. They should also keep reminding the employees about the importance of being on time. In many instances, the employee simply fails to allow sufficient time to get ready for work. Dependence upon hairline transportation connections and failure to allow extra time for travel in traffic jams and under bad weather conditons are common causes. The means of correction here are self-evident.

In many offices, a tardy employee is required to report first to the office manager, where an explanation is given verbally for the tardiness and a form filled out indicating the reason why. The ·idea of going through a "lot of red tape" helps discourage tardiness. The imposition of a penalty, such as making up time lost or doing the least desirable work proves effective. However, before using such a plan, it should meet the approval of the employees, who should agree to "go along with it," or better, to administer the plan. One company uses a unique plan which brings surprisingly good results. An employee's name is selected at random from the payroll list; and promptly at starting time, the employee is called on the telephone. If the employee answers, indicating presence and promptness on the job, a reward of $20 is awarded.

OFFICE TRADE UNIONS

Trade unions for office employees are another important consideration in actuating work. When they exist, managers are required to bargain with the authorized representatives concerning "wages, hours, and other conditions of employment." This includes a broad spectrum of subjects such as wages, benefits, discharge, discipline, and transfer which are incorporated into a mutually agreed upon labor contract. Subsequently, management decisions pertaining to these subject areas may be questioned and an explanation demanded and possibly the decision rescinded due to the union's actions. In essence, the union wants to be consulted and to present its views in matters affecting its members and it has the right to protect and make a grievance regarding any questioned decision or action.

Since the late 1960s there has been an increase in the number of unionized white-collar employees. The Teamsters; Retail, Wholesale, and Department Store Union; Auto Workers; Office and Professional Employees Union; Insurance Workers; and Newspaper Guild are among the most active labor organizations in the white-collar area. Opinions differ regarding what the future trend might be.

The major reasons that appear to encourage office unionism are as follows. First, the office employees' beliefs and feelings about the company such as whether they are treated with respect and with fairness, are vital. Wages are important, but commonly not the real reason. Wages are usually corrected to eliminate inequities. Benefits and job security are more likely to be debatable areas. Second, management members became unaware of what is bothering most office employees. There is insufficient communication whereby the employees can be heard or get their story across. Complaints and beliefs about poor ventilation, for example, or favoritism in assigning overtime or lack of a seniority system are typical of statements about which employees may have strong feelings but to which managers pay little or no attention, taking the position that it is all complaining which will exist as long as someone will listen to it. Third, the belief that office supervisors can and will provide a realistic account of employee opinions regarding their work and its environment. In reality, the supervisor is frequently unable to provide such information. He or she commonly is intimately involved with day-to-day operations and loses objectivity in attempting to evaluate the wants and satisfactions of his or her people. Fourth, the feeling by office employees that they are losing their identity with management, and have less status than formerly is also a contributing factor. Much office work has been de-humanized, more machines and mechanical operations are being utilized.

Collective Bargaining

Collective bargaining concerns the relationships between employers and unions representing the employees. Involved are the organizing of employees to union membership, negotiating, administering, and interpreting of collective agreements covering wages, hours of work, and other conditions of employment. The union serves as the bargaining agent for the employees, the employer is represented by management members. Ordinarily, management initiates action which must, of course, conform with the agreed upon provisions derived by collective bargaining.

The legal framework of collective bargaining is a labor contract which usually follows a pattern such as:

1. Union recognition and extent of bargaining unit.
2. Management rights and security.
3. Union security and status.
4. Strikes and lockouts.
5. Union activities and responsibilities.
6. Wages.
    a. wage structure
    b. job evaluation
    c. bonus and other payments
7. Jobs rights and seniority.
    a. transfers, promotions, layoffs, recalls
    b. seniority regulations
8. Working time and hours.
    a. holidays and vacations
    b. overtime regulations
    c. rest periods
9. Discipline and discharge.
10. Grievance handling.
11. Health and safety.

12. Benefits.
    a. Insurance and pension programs
    b. unemployment benefits

To give some idea of what these items might include, several are briefly discussed as follows.

Union Recognition.   A "recognition of the union" clause points out that the union named in the contract is fully recognized by the employer; frequently, it also states what jobs and what employees are covered by the contract.

Status of Union.   Union status concerns the relationship of members of the union with the company. In general, there are three kinds of union status:

> *1. Union shop.*   Nonunion members may be hired; but after a certain period, they must, as a requirement of employment, become union members.
>
> *2. "Maintenance of membership" shop.*   All employees are not required to join the union, but all present union members must retain membership during the time the contract is in force.
>
> *3. Exclusive bargaining shop.*   The union is recognized as the exclusive bargaining agent for all employees, but no employee is compelled to join it or to remain a member.[1]

Wages.   Clauses on wages frequently include the recognition of job classifications and wage rates for each class. Minimum rates only might be stated. Uniform adjustments, either in amount or in percentage, may be provided; and the effective date of such adjustments may be included.

The following is a typical contractual statement pertaining to wages.

> SECTION 2.   The wage schedules as set forth in this schedule, attached hereto as Exhibit B and made a part hereof, shall apply and be in effect as of July 1, 197–, and shall remain in effect for the life of this agreement.
>
> SECTION 3.   Overtime compensation and deductible time lost shall be computed by dividing the monthly salary by one hundred seventy-three and one third (173⅓) to arrive at an hourly rate to be used for such computations.

Seniority.   While most unions favor the governing of layoffs and re-hires on seniority, they will grant a statement to the effect that seniority shall govern when the employee involved has the ability to do the work under question. Questions arising in connection with seniority are sometimes clarified by the practice of preclassifying employees either by

---

[1] The Labor Management Relations Act of 1947 outlawed in interstate commerce (1) the closed shop—in which the employer agrees to hire only union members, and all employees must continue their good standing in the union during their terms of employment and (2) the preferential shop—in which preference in hiring and in layoff is given union members.

occupation or by departments or divisions. In this way, employees making up a fairly comparable group are associated together.

To illustrate:

> SECTION 3. A reduction in working forces resulting in demotions and layoffs will normally be on a departmental seniority basis except for stenographers and filing clerks, who will be on a company-wide basis.

IMPORTANT LEGAL PROVISIONS

The legal background upon which current management-union cooperation is administered consists of a long list of labor laws, both federal and state. However, for our purpose, the provisions of the Labor Management Relations Act of 1947, commonly referred to as the Taft-Hartley Act, and the Landrum-Griffin Act of 1959 can be considered as making up the current labor legislation. The Landrum-Griffin Act of 1959, among other things, permitted employees to file with the government complaints about the acts of their union leaders. Most of the complaints to date have dealt with questions pertaining to voting by union members in union affairs, and the misuse of the dues by union officers. The Taft-Hartley Act established a National Labor Relations Board (NLRB) with the power to hear testimony, render decisions, and decide the appropriate unit for purposes of collective bargaining. The Board serves mainly in a judiciary capacity.

Three provisions of this law are quite important and pertain to:

1. Unfair Labor Practices. These are prohibited. By an employer they consist of (1) interfering with or restraining employees from forming or joining a labor union, (2) dominating or influencing a labor organization, (3) discriminating in the hiring or in the conditions of employment of any employee because she or he is a member of a union, (4) terminating employment or discriminating against any employee for any charge made or testimony given under this law, and (5) refusing to bargain collectively with representatives of his employees.

Unfair labor practices by unions or their agents include (1) coercing or restraining employees in connection with their joining a union, (2) charging "excessive or discriminatory" union initiation fees (the meaning of "excessive or discriminatory" is determined by the labor board in cases where there is an authorized union shop contract), (3) refusing to bargain collectively with the employer, (4) participating in jurisdictional strikes, and (5) practicing "featherbedding," i.e., making the employer pay for services not performed.

Charges of unfair labor practices on the part of either employer or union are investigated, complaints issued, and prosecution carried on before the National Labor Relations Board by the general counsel, who has exclusive authority to prosecute unfair labor practices. The board decides whether any defendant is guilty of an unfair labor practice. If not guilty, the findings are stated, and an order is issued dismissing the complaint. If guilty, the board states its findings and issues a cease and desist order, prohibiting the continuation of the unfair practice, to be served on the guilty party. For enforcement of its orders, the board has the power to petition the Circuit Court of Appeals with jurisdiction where the unfair labor practice occurred.

2. Strike Controls. A 60 days' notice must be given the other party before the normal termination of a labor contract. If no agreement is reached, the Federal Mediation and Conciliation Service must be notified. Lockouts and strikes are prohibited during the notice period. There is no compulsory arbitration or court injunction right against a legitimate noncritical strike, i.e., one not threatening "national health and safety" or affecting an entire industry. In contrast, threatening lockouts or strikes affecting "national health and safety" or an entire industry can be delayed 80 days by the President of the U.S. who appoints a board of inquiry to determine the facts involved in the dispute. With this board is filed each party's statement which is reviewed and given to the Federal Mediation and Conciliation Service, and the contents are made known to the public. The President may at this time seek a court injunction against the lockout or strike. If issued, there follows a period of 60 days in which to bring about a settlement. If not reached, the National Labor Relations Board holds an election on the last settlement offer, turns the results over to the President who submits a report to Congress, along with recommendations to settle the dispute.

3. Checks on Unions. To file an unfair labor practice charge with the NLRB, the union must previously have filed (1) pertinent union information and (2) noncommunist affidavits by each officer of the union. The former includes name, title, compensation, and allowances for each of the union's three prinicpal officers and for any other union officer or agent whose compensation exceeded $5,000 for the preceding year. Also included in the report are the amount of initiation fees and regular dues; a statement showing the levying of assessments, the disbursement of union funds, and the basis for membership qualification and also for expulsion. All union members have a right to a copy of their union's financial report. The second check, or affidavit, is a sworn written statement signifying that the union officer is not a member or affiliate of the Communist Party and does not believe in, belong to, or support any organization believing in or teaching the overthrow of the United States government.

Additional important provisions of the current labor laws are shown in Figure 23–2. Knowledge of them may prove helpful in a given situation.

FIGURE 23–2
Current Labor Law Provisions Frequently Found Useful

1. An employee or a group of employees can petition that the union's authorization to enter into a union shop contract be withdrawn; such a petition must contain the signatures of 30 percent of the employees represented by the union. However, only one election on union security can be held each year.
2. Where authorized union shop contracts exist, the failure of a member to pay union dues and initiation fee is the only cause for loss of good standing with the union for which an employer can be forced to discharge an employee.
3. The individual employee can present grievances directly to the supervisor, provided the union representative is informed and given an opportunity to be present. Settlement of the grievance can be made if such settlement is not contrary to any terms of the existing union contract.
4. Unions as well as employers can sue and be sued for violations of contract under this act. Judgments against unions must be collected from them, not from the individual employees.
5. Dispute settlement methods include (*a*) bargaining till issue is settled, (*b*) compulsory arbitration whereby parties agree to submit the case to an impartial arbitrator whose findings will be accepted as final, and (*c*) conciliation or mediation in which the dispute is relayed to a third party to help the disputants reach a settlement.

ILLUSTRATIVE CURRENT EVENTS

What is the viewpoint of unions regarding the adoption of job enrichment? Generally, they accept it providing they have been consulted and have been shown that the job enrichment will not reduce the number of employees. They are interested in reducing boredom and in changes that serve the best interests of their employee members. It is best to get the union involved from the beginning concepts of job enrichment. That way they know what is going on and frequently have practical ideas to suggest.

Let's consider a situation in which a management consultant was called in by management to study present paper procedures and paperwork flows to determine whether present practices could be improved. The office manager introduced the consultant to the employees and explained the purpose of the visit. The employees, however, began to take excessive breaks from their work stations and did not fill out accurately their daily production sheets as requested by the consultant. A grievance was filed by the union stating that the labor contract in force was intended to promote "good relations and cooperation" and further, the management's right and security clause in the contract did not include the right to conduct studies regarding office efficiency. The consultant's activities and requests were, the union claimed, in violation of the present agreement. The consultant was called off the job. A number of discussions followed between representatives of management and of the union. Convincing arguments were presented by each side. Finally an agreement was reached. Office efficiency is a primary and reasonable activity of management. Nothing stated in the contract forbids such managerial action. The filling out of production sheets by employees is a minor task requiring less than 10 minutes and does not constitute a substantial interruption to the office work.

Observe that the intent as stated by management was "to study present paper procedures and paperwork flows to determine whether present practices could be improved." Management can do this according to the above decision rendered. However, if these studies suggest changes are in order, something must be changed—motivation of employees, different performance standards, different office layout. The implementing of these changes in any substantial degree gives rise to an entirely different situation which undoubtedly will entail employer-union relationships. The real difficulty in this case is the apparent lack of mutual trust among management members and nonmanagement members as well as a lack of developing good human relations and a work environment which enable employees to gain satisfactions and willingly assist in gaining improvement and progress that is mutually beneficial.

Another case concerns payment of vacation pay to absent employees. Two years ago, company A made such payments. The existing labor contract stated 30 days leave of absence could be counted as time worked for vacation period, the overall stipulation being that 75 percent of the work days scheduled were a requirement for a paid vacation. But this constraint was ignored. Beginning last year, company A sold out to company B who believed that the present vacation practice should be stopped. Immediately after company B managers announced their decision, the union protested. When company B insisted, the union countered with a strike threat. The new management yielded and continued the practice for the remainder of the year. At the beginning of the following year, however, management again brought up the issue. Extended debate ensued; finally, the issue went to arbitration. The verdict: for the union. Justification for the excess benefits beyond what the contract called for was the past practice that had been continued and established by company B and was now expected by its employees. This case again brings out the importance of developing and maintaining mutual respect, good human relations, and modern managerial actuating. Further, precedents are important. Past practices become the accepted mode of operation unless specific statements, mutually agreed to, counteract them or establish new practices to replace the old.

SAFE WORK PLACE

Providing a safe place in which to work is another major activity of actuating. Accidents can and do happen to office employees. Smashed fingers, burns, cuts, and electric shock can afflict the office employee.

And you can break a leg by tripping on an open file drawer, or slipping on highly polished office floors. Cuts and punctures can become infected and cause trouble. Serious, sometimes permanent injuries are suffered by office employees.

All office accidents have two things in common. They result from some human error and they can be prevented. Accident prevention requires much effort and teamwork, but it's worth every bit of it. An injured employee seldom escapes physical pain—sometimes for a very long period. Valuable time may be lost and a shifting of job assignments may be necessary. The hidden costs of accidents are much greater than the measurable direct costs. Such things as the cost of hiring and training new employees, the interference with production, and the loss of goodwill are sizable expenses and equal on the average four times that of direct costs, all of which means that total accident costs are far greater than most people realize. Fortunately much can be done and has been done by means of effective office employee safety programs to keep office accidents at a minimum.

Accident Prevention

Experience and records show that accidents can be reduced; in fact, most can be prevented entirely. Some advocate the so-called triple E program, which consists of engineering, education, and enforcement. That is, the first step is to engineer all equipment and machines with safety guards, cutoff switches, and other devices to make them as safe as is technically possible. Next, education for all employees is provided, to instill work habits and practices for winning high safety achievements. Last, enforcement insures that safety regulations are carried out.

This means that the initiative rests with the manager, but he or she must win the cooperation of the employee to make safety really effective. Aggressive managerial action is required. Merely supplying a safe working place is insufficient. The manager must also see to it that safety measures are recognized and enforced; but what is more important, he or she must accomplish this with enthusiastic approval and encouragement by the nonmanagement members.

Accidents and Attitude

The attitude of the employee toward safety is exceedingly important in accident prevention work. There is a great deal of truth in the saying: "The best safety device in all the world is located an inch or two above the eyebrows." The employee who "thinks safety" and who has developed a safety consciousness "from the ears up" has gone a long way toward preventing accidents.

All efforts designed to keep safety on the employee's mind and to keep accident prevention a live subject in the office will help substantially in the safety program. Although it may seem strange, it is a common occurrence for people to be careless. And accidents can happen to anyone who takes chances. Figure 23–3 illustrates this fundamental.

FIGURE 23–3
Practices Such as Leaning Back in a Chair with Feet on the Desk and Standing on Stools Equipped with Rollers or Wheels Commonly Result in Accidents

Courtesy: National Safety Council, Chicago.

Safety-mindedness requires alert-mindedness. Safety work is a continuous process, requiring constant reminders to the employee to work safely, to avoid taking chances, and to keep safety thoughts foremost. The task is not an easy one, but persistence and steadfastness of purpose will achieve good results.

Each employee should be made thoroughly aware of all the possible dangers on the job. All the details that make for safety should be carefully explained. These efforts can be planned and made a regular part of the job process and the training work. Thus, the correct way of doing the job, which is also the safe way, becomes habitual. And it helps to supply all the necessary provisions for safe working places and equipment. Office floors should be covered with nonslippery material, adequate lighting should be provided, desks and chairs should be free of sharp edges. Furthermore, maintaining an orderly and clean work place contributes to good office safety, because it sets a good example and helps keep the office personnel safety-minded. Stairways should be kept clear of all lose objects, aisles should be marked for traffic lanes, an adequate number of wastebaskets should be furnished, and regular cleanup service should be provided.

Also, employees should be informed of safety fundamentals. This can take various forms, including articles in company papers, talks at meetings, informal suggestions to employees, and movies. In addition, pictures, posters, and cartoon sketches can be used to arouse the employee's interest in safety. It is usually best to have this material specific in nature, telling the employee what to do under particular conditions. It is effective to supplement this type of safety promotion with intensive individual follow-up.

Safety contests are also helpful. They stress the competitive spirit and usually rely upon the employee's desire to excel. An award in the form of a plaque, banner, special pin, or money may be given the individual, group, or department having the best safety record for a given period. A reversal of this technique can also be used, such as giving a booby prize to the unit having the poorest safety record, with the requirement that this "award" be displayed prominently. This approach appeals to the employee's pride and desire to escape any designation which makes him or her look ridiculous. Like all promotional plans, safety contests must be publicized and made acceptable to the employees.

Office Safety Personnel

Department heads are the key personnel in office safety work. In many respects, the success of the entire safety program depends upon the supervisors. It is promoted by the cooperation of the department heads, and they can do more than anyone else toward keeping the employees safety-minded. Furthermore, supervisors can correct unsafe conditions, they can see that safety rules are followed, that first aid is provided in case of accident, and that proper reports are filled out.

Usually there is a recognized head of safety work who may be a member of the personnel department or head a separate department, which includes safety work in the factory and office. The safety director may not spend the entire work day in safety, but generally devotes a certain amount of time regularly to the program.

The use of a safety committee with rotating membership is recommended. A five-member committee, with membership rotating bimonthly, usually works out very well. The system of replacements should be such that not more than two new members are added at any one time, thus insuring that the remaining three members are familiar with the work of the committee. The work of this group is advisory. It submits suggestions for the reduction of accidents within the office. A common responsibility of a safety committee is to make regular safety inspections of the office. A form similar to that shown by Figure 23–4 can be used

FIGURE 23–4
Portion of a Form Designed to Assist in Determining Safety Hazards

OFFICE SAFETY INSPECTION DATA

Carefully inspect the office, and for each question, check whether a hazard exists. If "Yes," briefly note the important details.

QUESTION	DOES HAZARD EXIST? Yes	No	COMMENTS (GIVE LOCATION AND DETAILS.)
1. Are aisles obstructed?			
2. Do pencil sharpeners project over desk or table			
3. Are file drawers kept closed when not in use?			
4. Are machines properly guarded?			
5. Are glass desk tops broken?			
6. Are there any sharp metal projections on any equipment?.			
7. Is electrical wiring concealed?.			
8. Are office accessories insecurely placed?. .			
9. Are papers and waste properly disposed of?			
10. Are facilities for smokers adequate?			
11. Are materials stacked on desks or cabinets?.			
12. Are extension cords used extensively? . . .			
13. Are floors too highly polished?			
14. Is carpeting loose or worn?			

to record the data collected. In addition, the safety committee is usually active in (1) reviewing safety suggestions made by the employees, (2) suggesting additions and changes in safety rules, (3) posting safety materials on the bulletin boards, (4) sponsoring accident prevention contests, and (5) maintaining the first-aid equipment.

OSHAct

The Williams-Steiger Occupational Safety and Health Act (OSHAct) became effective July, 1972 and must be taken seriously. It is a far-reaching and inclusive federal law designed to "assure as far as possible every working man and woman in the nation safe and healthful working conditions. . . ." The enforcement machinery spelled out in the Act is elaborated upon by the Occupational Safety and Health Administration (OSHA) of the U.S. Department of Labor. Among the salient points appropriate for discussion here are who is covered by the Act, what are the standards to be met, who enforces it, how are inspections conducted, what follow-ups are made, and what record-keeping is necessary.

Employers and employees in every state, excepting federal, state, and local government employees are covered. The employee must be provided a safe place of work free from recognized hazards and further must comply with rules, regulations, and standards issued under the Act. Many acceptable safety and health standards have been adopted, but there is also an organization established by the Act to help develop and establish standards believed necessary. For enforcement a three-person commission reviews contested cases of alleged violations, issues orders correcting them and assesses penalties. A number of judges are authorized to hold hearings and give decisions on contested job-safety disputes. Some 100,000 compliance inspections are conducted annually on a regularly scheduled basis or as the result of an employee complaint. The OSHA compliance officer is required to enter the organization unannounced, take a tour, and observe safety and health conditions. If violations are found he can give a citation including a 15-day deadline for correction to the offending employer. A protest by the employer can be made to the Occupational Safety and Health Review Commission who schedules a hearing and issues a final decision in the case. Penalties up to $1,000 for each violation may be assessed. Willful or repeated violations may result in a penalty of up to $10,000 for each such violation. The Act also requires certain record keeping which is discussed below.

Office Safety Records

For high safety to be attained, it is important to know what accidents happened, where, when, the type of injuries incurred, and the conditions which caused them. By studying such data, it is possible to take intelligent corrective action and to know where safety efforts should be stressed.

OSHAct requires three kinds of records covering the data for occupational injuries and illness. The three include (1) a log of such data, (2) a supplementary record, and (3) an annual summary of these in-

jury-illness records. Office forms OSHA-100, -101, and -102 respectively
are to be used for these required reports.

There are two widely used and accepted indexes in safety statistics:
(1) the frequency rate and (2) the severity rate. The former measures
the occurrences of accidents; the latter measures the seriousness of accidents. The frequency rate is calculated by the formula:

$$\text{Frequency rate} = \frac{\text{Number of disabling injuries} \times 1,000,000}{\text{Total number of work-hours worked}}$$

Disabling injuries include death, permanent total disability, permanent
partial disability, and temporary total disability (the injured is unable
to return to his job within 24 hours after the start of the shift during
which he was injured). The formula for calculating the severity rate
is:

$$\text{Severity rate} = \frac{\text{Time charged (in days)} \times 1,000,000}{\text{Total number of work-hours worked}}$$

The time charged for an accident is taken from a table of values to
indicate differentials among various types of accidents. For example,
an accident resulting in death or in permanent disability is charged
at the rate of 6,000 days for each case.

EMPLOYEE ECONOMIC SECURITY

Various arrangements are now available to help provide a measure
of economic security to employees—to satisfy the security want. These
arrangements assist in supplying economic aid in case of sickness or
old age, or at the time of death give some help to dependents of the
deceased. The economic security measures have been brought about
through the efforts of companies and employees and the influence of
state and federal laws, among which are unemployment insurance regulations, workmen's compensation laws, and social security regulations.
The form, purpose, and content of these various plans very considerably
and require special study for complete understanding.

The discussion here will be confined to three arrangements, including:

1. Hospitalization Plans. These plans are a form of insurance which
pays a portion of hospital expenses resulting from all nonoccupational
illnesses or accidents suffered by the employee. Premiums are usually
paid by the employee, although in some instances the company contributes toward the plan. Under a typical plan, costs might be $20 per
month for an unmarried employee for semiprivate accommodations. The
amount of cost varies with such factors as the number of employees
in the plan, their sex and age, and the benefits provided.

2. Pension Plans. These provide regular payments to an employee retired from service. The great majority of large enterprises now have such plans. They make it possible not only to give needed relief and to grant rewards for long service but also to retire older employees, thus permitting the employment of younger persons as replacements. This helps keep the work force alive and vibrant, and the existence of a retirement pension plan makes for high morale and attracts better employees.

The cost of a pension plan can be paid by either the company or the employees, or both. The amount of retirement pay generally provided is about 50 percent of the average rate for the five-year period preceding retirement. The trend is toward a reduction in the waiting period for eligibility and the elimination of high age requirements of participants for pensions. Programs under which the employee contributes are also becoming more common. The plan should be based on a sound actuarial basis. It is usually advisable to employ the services of specialists in this field.

3. Group Insurance Plans. Protection for individual employees as members of a group is provided by group insurance plans. Usually, employees are eligible only after a stipulated period of service and in an amount relative to their earnings. The company or the employees may pay the full cost of the plan, or the cost may be assumed jointly. Employees are usually able to secure protection at a cost below that of individually purchased insurance of the same protection. The exact nature of the policy varies with different plans; the basis of all is straight life insurance coverage, but this frequently is supplemented with other benefits.

EMPLOYEES' RECREATIONAL ACTIVITIES

Recreational activities have actuating influence, but they also help provide a balance between work and play. A well-rounded program of recreational activities is important because it improves employer-employee relations, increases efficiency, and makes for healthy, satisfied employees. Such activities may include the following: archery, baseball, softball, basketball, tennis, horseback riding, golf, bowling, horseshoe pitching, swimming, hiking, band, glee club, photography club and amateur shows.

The participation of management members in recreational activities should consist of a readiness to furnish advice, to offer suggestions, and to lend assistance and support *upon request.* Managers should not attempt to force inclusion of certain activities or to run the program. Any semblance of paternalism should be avoided.

In guiding the development of the program, the following approach is usually helpful:

1. Measure the adequacy of the activity to find out the total number of employees who can participate.
2. Examine each existing activity to see if it is attracting a capacity number of employees.
3. Investigate public and private recreational facilities to determine how and when they can be used.
4. Find out what is included in programs of other companies.
5. Publicize the existence of the activities so that all employees who can and want to participate may do so.

QUESTIONS

1. Your superior feels much can be done to improve the effectiveness of your office department by adopting a team building program. She asks you to draw up and implement such a program. Outline what you would include in this program and how you would put it into effect.
2. As an office manager, outline the general policies and handling of absenteeism that you would follow. Justify your views.
3. What is the meaning of each of the following:
   a. Union shop.
   b. Unfair Labor Practice
   c. Severity rate.
   d. Psychological causes of accidents.
4. Under the present labor laws, what are unfair practices by an employer? By a union or its agents?
5. What are the major reasons that apparently encourage office unionism to exist?
6. Is the work of the office manager changed by the existence of a union in the office? Explain.
7. In a unionized office, should an office employee take work problems to the supervisor, the union steward, or a member of the personnel department? Justify your answer.
8. In company RST, the office employees are nonunion, and the factory employees are members of a union. Recently, as a result of collective bargaining, a 4 percent increase in wages was given factory employees. At the same time, a like increase was given office employees.
   a. Do you feel the office employees are justified in accepting this increase?
   b. How can the managers of the company justify the increase to the office employees?
   c. Should the office employees join the union?
   Give reasons for your answers.
9. Discuss the provisions of the current national labor laws on what is commonly referred to as "checks on unions."

10. Explain the meaning of the statement: "Perhaps the key factor in any office safety program is to develop safety consciousness among all employees."
11. With reference to the Occupational Safety and Health Administration (OSHA) discuss its objective, salient points, and enforcement.
12. As an office manager would you tend to favor or disfavor your employees' having formal recreational activities? Justify your answer.

CASE PROBLEMS

Case 23–1. Hoyt-Baker, Inc.

It was a long-standing company policy that an employee must notify the company in advance, if possible, or before 9:00 A.M. on the day when an absence was required, such as an emergency or sudden illness. Tony Sarbo was absent one Friday and he neither told his supervisor in advance nor did he call in Friday morning. When he reported for work the following Monday morning, he was asked why was he absent on Friday.

TONY: This is the first absence I've had in over a year. I did not come in Friday because of well . . . personal reasons. Frankly, I don't want to tell you what the reason is. And I don't think it is any of your business.

SUPERVISOR: Well, the company is going to insist, Tony. You know they are very strict on absentee matters and you failed to follow the long standing rules on this.

Later, Monday afternoon, Tony received a call to come to the personnel manager's office. Here he was questioned again about his unauthorized absence. Again he refused to disclose his reason. At this, the personnel manager informed him that his refusal was insubordination and for insubordination the penalty could be employment termination. Tony showed his displeasure at this remark in loud and disrespectful language. The personnel manager asked him to be quiet, then Tony started making threatening remarks to the personnel manager.

Upon his arrival for work Tuesday morning (the next day), Tony was given his pay check and termination notice effective immediately. Reason: insubordination. The notice was signed by both Tony's supervisor and the personnel manager.

Tony went right away to the union representative and gave him the complete story of what had taken place. Again he refrained from giving the reason for his absence and the union representative did not ask for it. Subsequently a grievance was filed by the union requesting reinstatement and back pay.

Questions:

1. Is an employer justified in asking for and demanding the reason for an employee being absent? Why?
2. Evaluate the handling of absenteeism by the corporate managers.

3. What recommendations do you feel are in order to give Tony? To give the corporation managers?
4. What decision do you feel should be reached in Tony's case? Justify your views.

Case 23–2. Bellows Company

Not much attention was paid to office safety by the office manager because, in his opinion, there were too many more important things demanding his time. True, there have been very few serious accidents in the office of Bellows Company during the past several years. However, three days ago, an employee in the filing department pulled out the top drawer of a five-drawer file and before he realized it, the entire file cabinet tipped and fell on him. He suffered an arm injury in trying to prevent the file from falling and a broken ankle when his foot was caught under the file. He required hospitalization and latest word is that he will be away from work for at least three weeks.

The office manager deeply regretted this accident happening in his office. He believed some safety measures probably were in order so he wrote a personal letter to each office employee, explaining that an accident had occurred, the company's strong desire to maintain a safe office, and each office employee's responsibility to exercise care to avoid possible accidents in the future. In addition, he urged each office supervisor to cooperate fully in helping to keep the office a safe place in which to work. He also posted several notices on the office bulletin board suggesting, "Be careful. Office accidents do happen. Do not take chances. Help avoid serious injury to yourself." For the most part, these efforts were well received, but some of the employees argued that the office manager was splurging and wanted to look pious in light of the accident that occurred in the filing department.

Yesterday, a fire started in the duplicating division of the company's office. Two employees suffered minor burns in extinguishing the flame, and some damage was done to a desk and to carpeting. An investigation revealed that the cause was carelessness on the part of an employee, who had placed a lighted cigarette on the edge of his desk. The lighted cigarette had fallen into a wastebasket filled with papers, and the fire had started.

Questions:

1. What are your reactions to the handling of the situation by the office manager after the accident in the filing department? Explain.
2. What action do you recommend that the office manager now take? Why?

Case 23–3. Cruse Manufacturing Company

A provision in the current labor contract covering office employees includes:

7.5 Any employee laid off for lack of work shall be considered to remain an active employee with seniority rights, recall rights, and all other fringe benefits of employees with long service.

Gerald Briggs, a production control clerk, returned on March 3 from a three-months layoff for lack of work. At that time, he followed instructions given him and reapplied for hospital insurance by signing a printed statement given him. Briggs did not read the form which stated among other things that there was a 30-day waiting period until the insurance was in effect. In fact, he filled out a number of forms, somewhat like a new employee.

Three weeks after his return, Gerald's wife was injured in a car accident and required surgery. The police record of the accident held Mrs. Briggs responsible. As an employee of Cruse Manufacturing Company, Gerald as well as the hospital assumed his insurance coverage would pay most of the hospital cost. However, within several days he was informed that the insurance company regarded the first 30 days of return following a layoff as a new waiting period. Hence, Gerald and his wife were not covered. Further, the insurance company records showed that Gerald had not kept up the payments while he was not working.

Gerald referred to his employee handbook and found this statement under insurance:

> For a new employee the insurance becomes effective the first day of the calendar month following the completion of 30 days as an employee. For a reinstated employee who re-enrolls for the insurance, the insurance becomes effective on the first day of the calendar month following the date of reinstatement, providing the employee is actually at work. Further, any employee laid off due to work shortage may continue to carry hospital insurance for six months by paying the full cost of the insurance.

Gerald explained his plight to the union which reviewed the case. It was the union's contention that the labor contract clearly indicates that Gerald is entitled to hospital benefits, since he remained an active employee. He was not terminated. Further, the statement he signed upon his recall is a legal insurance application in very fine print which a layman has difficulty in reading and understanding. In addition, his signature was really an enforced signature and should not be held against him.

Questions:

1. Evaluate the merits of the viewpoints taken first by Gerald Briggs. Second, by the union. Third, by the company. What conclusions do you draw from your evaluations?
2. What actions, if any, do you feel the company managers should take? Why?

Part VI

Controlling Those Doing the Office Work

Controlling is basic in office management and normally receives much attention. It is performed to see that what is planned is being accomplished. Applied to either selected segments or to the totality of office efforts, controlling is directed to time-use, accuracy of paperwork, the amount of work and its flow, and the dollars expended.

The five chapters comprising this part of the book are "Office Controlling and Standards," "Typical Office Controls and Manuals," "Controlling Office Time-Use," "Quality and Quantity Controlling," and "Cost and Budgetary Control."

Chapter 24

Office Controlling and Standards

> *Those not looking for happiness are the most*
> *likely to find it, because those who are searching*
> *forget that the surest way to be happy is to seek*
> *happiness for others.*
>
> Martin Luther King, Jr.

As a fundamental function of management, controlling is performed to insure results are acceptable or are in keeping with the planning. Controlling can be viewed as the familiar follow-up either to confirm operations as satisfactory or to reveal deviations that necessitate corrective action. Controlling and planning are intimately related. In fact, it can be stated that a lack of controlling stems from a lack of planning. When plans are fuzzy, the controls are fuzzy because there are no precise directions to which control efforts can be directed and guided.

CONTROLLING IDENTIFIED

The experienced information manager knows that what he or she plans for and hopes to achieve does not always take place. He or she must know what the actual results are if management is to be effective. To this end, the manager receives verbal and written reports regarding accomplishments. But these accomplishments must be appraised by some means to determine if they are satisfactory and if not, to decide what to do to remedy the situation. This leads to the definition of controlling which can be stated as follows: *Controlling is (1) determining what is being accomplished, (2) evaluating it, and (3) if necessary, applying corrective measures.* These three steps are basic and universal in controlling. They exist in every type of control.

Controlling helps a manager see if what has happened was supposed

621

to happen. In a very real sense, controlling requires a commitment to achieve specific objectives. It should not be viewed as merely a stack of reports or various analyses. These are the paraphernalia that confirm or warn the manager whether the intended goals are being gained. Nor should controlling be viewed as a reward or a punishment for past behavior. No one can do anything about the past. Controlling deals with influencing and redirecting future behavior as judged from in hand after-the-fact information. This means, of course, that there is always an inherent time lag in controlling. It may be a second, minute, hour, day, week, or even months from the time an event takes place and something is done about it. Delays are due to the control process itself with it evaluations, decisions, analyses, and approvals. After all, as stated above, controlling is frequently referred to as the *follow-up* function.

The most effective controlling points out areas of high risk and payoffs. The effort is concentrated where the control need is greatest. And alternative controls are worked out so that there is a readily available backup if it is needed. Controls themselves need to be reviewed periodically—no controlling should go unchallenged for too long. Plans change and goals are adjusted. To meet the needs of these dynamics, controls must be updated and kept in step with varying conditions.

Information Is the Guide

Information is fundamental to the control process. And the information should be appropriate for the particular control. Excessive details or voluminous reports normally should be avoided because they burden the manager doing the controlling, cause duplication of efforts, and slow down the whole process. The information must be relevant in terms of what is trying to be done. In many instances it is taken for granted that the information required for performance of managerial duties flows automatically to the job. This is not always true. The manager must innovate, determine what types of information, when, and in what formats will best serve office needs.

Most accounting information tends to flow to the job or can be made to do so without much effort. While vital and extremely useful, such information is incomplete for a manager's controlling as well as planning efforts. For example, it does not reveal information about the future, the adequacy of customer service, and quality. Also, usually not included is discrimination between the critical and noncritical elements of the enterprise highlighting, for example, those elements influencing competitive success.

Both planning and controlling are conditioned by the flow of information—a basic responsibility of the information manager. What managerial action takes place is definitely influenced by the information received by the management member. What he does and does not do, what decisions are made, what plans are drawn up, and what controls are exercised—all depend upon information.

Figure 24–1 illustrates the anatomy of information relative to planning

FIGURE 24–1
Information Anatomy for Planning and Controlling

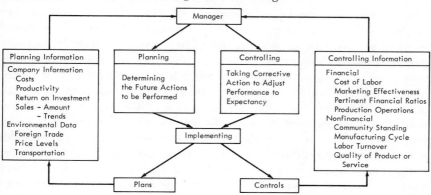

and controlling. From the left, planning information flows to the manager as does also controlling information shown on right of figure. The manager uses these informations respectively for planning and for controlling, which are implemented and result in plans and controls and which, in turn, are fed back respectively to the funds of planning and of controlling information.

Controlling and Human Relations

A controlling effort is good or bad depending upon whether it gets a human being to do better work and with more satisfaction because the controlling was in operation. The people response to controlling is vital. Each step of the controlling process is heavily influenced by the human element. Judgment plays a big part; controlling is not a mechanistic measurement of accomplishment or a comparison of numbers.

Managers in their controlling certainly do not wish to create undesirable effects upon their relationships with their employees. Controls do, however, have the potential for creating pressures which may jeopardize the employer-employee relationships. Managers must be aware of this possibility and refrain from any action that is likely to produce harmful effects. It is helpful to remember that controlling is a means, not an end within itself. How the controls are handled from the human relations viewpoint is of top priority. Are the controls handled in such a way as to help the employees perform their work correctly? Do they encourage a negative attitude, a general disbelief, and undesirable practices? All controls need to be explained in light of their effect not only on formal company activities, but also on the behavior of the employees.

Unfortunately controlling is viewed by some with disdain. This view stems from a multitude of causes such as an employee's opinion of the job, the superior, the lack of opportunities for self-expression, and opinon about the employing company, its products and services. Let us consider first some of the negative views toward controlling followed by some suggestions for making controlling a vibrant, effective activity evoking positive human response. First, the person may feel that the expectancy is too great or too high. Since it is unreasonable, it is meaningless and the control becomes demotivational instead of motivational. Often the difficulty lies in the administering of the expectancy requirement. If too rigidly applied, it will be considered unfair. Some flexibility must be tolerated in all expectancies as well as in the deviations determined from controlling. Further, there is the fear by the employee that once a stated expectancy is reached, it will be replaced by a higher expectancy. There is no stability in the level set and hence, in the employee's opinion, it is unrealistic and simply a coverup to get more and more output from employees.

Second, the means of measurement appears inappropriate. For example, the employee may feel the basis on which the actual and expected costs are figured are improper, may not understand how they are calculated and hence, have a general distrust for the control data. Such conditions, of course, give rise to endless squabbles and destroys confidence and trust between management and nonmanagement members. Salespeople may criticize controls over them because, "They fail to include the effective calls we make, but do not get any orders." They may feel they put forth much effort in these developmental calls which are ignored by the control measurements. Consequently, they criticize the controlling.

Third, group attitudes and pressures may oppose the expectancy and measurements the controls advocate. This opposition is in keeping with the group member's desire to have approval of associates—to satisfy social needs. The worker wants to belong to and be accepted by the group and these wants prevail. She or he stands with the group in opposing alterations in job content or in adjusting standards or expectancies due to what the group believes are insignificant changes and their call for no control modifications.

All these objections are formidable, but they need not prevail. Controlling is essential for consistent achievement. It is simply a fact of life. The challenge is to remove the irritation and replace it with positive attitudes and motivation. Obviously in view of the major reasons for controls being disliked, we could eliminate them, i.e., make the expectancy reasonable and maintain it, adopt measurements mutually believed to be fair and accurate, and so forth. But more specifically what can be done?

Uppermost is to stress the viewpoint that controlling is actually a tool to aid in achieving mutually wanted results. It helps, not hinders in guiding efforts toward goal achievement. Controlling is used to meet the needs of the situation, not to expect employees to perform herculean tasks day in and day out. Point out to the employees the ways in which the controlling followed is designed to help them. Proper controls and their implementation can and should be motivational. Improper controls and implementation give rise to much unrest and resentment. A person gains satisfaction from performing a job proficiently and being informed officially when he or she has done work up to par. Controlling tells the employee what is expected and to be able to meet or exceed this expectancy is satisfying.

Positive response to controlling is also encouraged by our old friend, participation. Genuinely sharing in the controlling program, being a part in determining what the expectancy is, and how it is to be measured contribute to understanding and acceptance. The participative approach works best for controlling when management establishes acceptable premises and contraints, permits ample time for decisions to be reached, and accepts risks inherent in the approach.

Flexibility is a key word in achieving top benefits from controlling. On certain occasions deviations greater than specified will be needed and can be justified. If employees believe the controlling does not give adequate consideration to specific local conditions, the controlling is looked upon as unreasonable and unfair; its contribution is diminished. In some cases, adjustment in the expectancy is automatic, for example, in cost standards which are adjusted in keeping with changes in the cost of material, labor, and overhead.

Fourth, the management member should deal with problems of control in a factual and nonemotional manner. When a person doesn't accomplish what is expected, we tend to react emotionally and place blame. Keep objective. Try to find the real cause of the difficulty uncovered by the controlling. It could be the person, but don't jump to that conclusion. Think in terms of all the actions necessary to accomplish the immediate goal. Stress finding the cause and determining the cure, not identifying a person to blame.

Lastly, strive for employee commitment to the idea that personal aspirations and needs are definitely related to the goals of the employing organization, and that the worker has the capability for performing the work effectively or is currently in the process of gaining that capability. Self-confidence, dedication, and commitment are fundamental. There is also the consideration for communication. Feedback is essential to the individual on what is being accomplished so that he can know whether corrective action is required and, if so, what measures might be taken. It is excellent for the manager to meet at least weekly with each group member to discuss and solve problems arising from the controlling efforts.

MBO and Controlling

It is worth noting that in the management by objectives approach to management, a portion of the controlling resides with the individual performing the direct work. The objectives and the means for accomplishing them determined by the person with the approval and acceptance of that person's superior are subjected to controlling by periodic reviews based on the results achieved. The control is accomplished through self-control by the individuals. Instead of control from above, the emphasis is on control from within. This approach minimizes the effect of the reasons, enumerated above, for a dislike of controlling and the inherent human difficulties arising from this relationship.

In addition, MBO may well contribute to a reduction in an excessive amount of control. To whatever degree this is accomplished, it is a commendable accomplishment. Excessive control normally calls for excessive paperwork—many different multi-copy forms being filled out, detailed reports written, and endless memos and notices of changes. Elimination of this excess is a certainty to be beneficial both to employees and to management.

However, MBO does not alter all controlling. It is supplemental to overall controls such as return on investment and to controls not directly related to specific jobs or an employee's work. Examples of the latter include expenditures for machinery and equipment and company profitability.

COMPUTER INFLUENCE ON CONTROLLING

The computer has made a profound impact on controlling. It has not changed the meaning of controlling as such, but it has modified the means of its implementation considerably. We now have computer based controlling that stores unbelievable amounts of pertinent data, transmits information accurately at incredible speeds, and provides up-to-the-minute feedback in an intelligible format. However, technology alone does not make controlling viable. People decide what input and processing are to be followed as well as what to do with the final controlling information as supplied by the computer. People remain the key factor in computer controlling because they determine what the computer processed data mean and what managerial action should be taken.

To have a useful data base, there must be accurate and timely input. The transmittal of such information and the utilization of the computer to maintain up-dated data, to handle comparisons to prescribed standards, and output the results are of major concern. Present day computers meet these requirements economically and effectively. Commonly there are a number of data entry units on a real-time basis. The output can be any of a number of media, but punched cards are popular and make the feedback of various summary data feasible. The individual requirements must be matched to the particular application. Figure 24–2 shows portions of control reports for a computer production

FIGURE 24–2
Portions of Computer Reports

Production Status

TF7: SML
Time: 1145   Group 2   Status 717

Part	Curr.	Accumulated	Scrap	Rework	Net	Scheduled	Variance
8327117	100	100	4	6	90	500	410
8326940	15	15			15	250	235

Machine No. File Inquiry

TF7: MIR
37 Shift

Part	Time	Machine	Scheduled	Accumulated	Scrap	Rework	Net	Variance
P0833	1400	443B	300	90		2	88	212

status report and a machine number file inquiry. In the former and for the given period, the production scheduled in 100 units (top line), the number of units accumulated is 100, 4 units were scrapped, 6 were reworked, giving a net of 90 units [100 − (4 + 6)]. For the 500 units scheduled to be manufactured, there remain 410 units to be made. For the bottom part of the figure, the data for machine 443B is 300 units of part P0833 are scheduled, of the 90 currently being worked on, 2 were reworked giving a net of 88 units and leaving 212 units yet to be manufactured.

Routine controls whereby the computer is programmed to compare the accomplishment with the standard or expectancy, and if within the allowable deviation spread, do so-and-so, and in contrast, if without the allowable deviation spread, do such-and-such, are readily handled via the computer. However, where *critical* controls are involved, the computer supplies the current feedback data to a person who decides what the data mean and what action, if any, should be taken.

OFFICE WORK MEASUREMENT

Measurement is required to determine what is accomplished and to evaluate it. This means that measurement makes feasible the work of controlling. To measure means to determine quantity. In office management controlling, measurement commonly deals with work. Work measurement concerns accomplishment; it is not concerned with the amount of energy expended, although in many cases this may be in direct proportion to the work output. Office work measurement not only helps managers to control, but it also enables them to distribute work loads fairly, and to evaluate employee performance.

Much of the work in an office can be measured fairly accurately and inexpensively. The extent in any given case will depend upon the particular type of office task performed; but usually from two thirds to three fourths of all work in an office can be measured. It is true that difficulty in measurement is encountered, for example, when the office work is nonrepetitive and irregular, or when it is primarily mental rather than manual. These are impediments, but they are also used as excuses for nonmeasurement far more frequently than is justified.

Measuring Unit

To measure requires a recognizable unit. It should be easy to identify and understand plus possessing uniformity of scope and definition. There are many different units that can be used, the selection depending mainly upon the type of office work. For example, typewritten work can be measured by typing area or sheets, and purchase orders by the number written. Sometimes, the quantity can be determined very easily by means of counting devices on machines; and frequently, the relationship of the weight of paper to the amount of work can be employed. Other examples of work-measuring units in the office are the number of invoices written, the amount of postage (dollar value) used on outgoing mail, the weight of incoming mail handled, the reams of paper used in duplicating work, the number of paychecks prepared, the inches of card stacks filed, and the number of credit investigations made.

In some instances, the selection of a satisfactory unit is extremely difficult; while in other cases, there are several available and acceptable units. In the latter case, for example, typewritten work can be measured in units of (1) pages, (2) standard-length lines, (3) key strokes, (4) square inches of typed material, or (5) disks from which material is transcribed. The choice is guided by the individual characteristics of the work under consideration. No one unit is best under all conditions. For example, the number of pages is satisfactory provided the pages are approximately uniform in the amount of typed material and in difficulty.

Accurate measurement is desirable and should be sought; but in the case of office work, this can be carried to uneconomical extremes. Too precise or too detailed measurements can result in bulky and sometimes cumbersome data which are ineffective in practical application.

Frequently used are modified units to measure office work. For example, the unit of a purchase order may not be satisfactory because all purchase orders are not identical. Some require five lines of typing, others eight lines, some involve calculations, others do not; and for exceptional orders the filling out of special forms is necessary.

To combat these hurdles, modified work measurement units can be employed. One common example of this is to use a "block of orders" instead of a single order as the basic measurement unit. A quantity of 200 orders may make up a block of orders. The content of the individual order may vary considerably, but the content of 200 orders will normally be quite like that of another 200 orders. Thus, a work measurement unit possessing reasonable comparability is provided.

Also, the work measurement can be considered over a period of time, i.e., for 10 or 15 days. During such a period, the average makeup of the modified unit will be fairly constant, that is, comparing one 15-day period with another 15-day period.

Another approach is to employ what can be termed "the core operation." Under this modified work measurement unit, the office work of an entire system or procedure, or any part of it, is expressed by a single unit, considered a core operation. To illustrate, the incoming order might be considered the core. All processing in connection with this order, such as credit investigation, correspondence, billing, and the like, is tied up with the handling of the incoming order. These activities increase as the incoming orders increase, and vice versa. By measuring the core, it is feasible to get a reasonably accurate measurement of all the work. Common core operations include number of policies handled, applications processed, orders received, items on order, units shipped, sheet duplicated, bills sent out, requisitions made, or checks written.

CONTROLLING AND STANDARDS

Returning to our three basic steps of the control process—(1) determining what is being accomplished (2) evaluating it, and (3) if necessary, applying corrective measures,—it is evident that evaluation of accomplishment (2) is essential. To assist in this evaluation, a manager uses standards. They are so important that the balance of this chapter will be devoted to them. Standards are also important for other managerial uses as we will indicate in the following pages, but for the discussion at hand, think of standards in their relationship to controlling and the important role that they play in this fundamental function of management.

First, a clear understanding is needed of what is meant by "standard." *A standard is something established by either custom or authority in order to gauge such things as quality, performance, and service of any factor used in management.* It may be thought of as a basis of reckoning, i.e., a basis of comparison. Most standards represent the best current knowledge of an item or practice formulated and accepted to meet the needs of present conditions.

Specifically, standards do not imply or reflect perfection. A material standard for paper designated by the manager of an office means that paper of these particular specifications is the type desired by the manager and is satisfactory for the specific purpose in mind, taking into account such things as the type of printing press, the price range, and the desired finished product. The standard provides him with a reference by which to evaluate the paper.

Standards not only facilitate controlling, but they are also important to the other fundamental functions of management, including planning, organizing, and actuating. For example, in planning, standards are the essential media for determining what components are required for establishing the sequence of successive operations. In other words, standards provide the common language for carrying out managerial work in areas such as expressing what is to be done, discussing, allocating, and instructing.

Standards apply to all factors of an enterprise. In many offices, the basic types of standards, along with the type of area covered by each, are shown by the following:

Basic Standard	Area
Work:	Measurements of the quantity and the quality of accomplishment
Tools:	Desk, file, machine
Conditions:	Amount of space, equipment layout, lighting, floor covering
Process:	Filing methods, mail distribution, handling of accounts receivable, duplicating process

Under tools, for example, a standard for a machine might designate the specific type, capacity, speed, and possibly the name of the manufacturer. Furthermore, this designated machine would probably be expected to be used for certain work. In this case, the machine standard serves for purposes of controlling.

Means of Expressing Standards

Various means of expressing standards can be used, including the following:

1. Written Specifications. Simply a detailed statement of the requirements that must be followed or that must be met by the factor under consideration.

2. Model. A typical sample, a miniature representation, or an exact representation of a specimen of the factor considered standard.

3. Accepted Rule or Regulation. An established course or guide prescribed by a person in authority.

4. Unwritten Customary Procedure. The habitual usage or generally recognized practice as shown by past experience.

5. Verbal Communication. The conveyance of thoughts and opinions concerning the standard by means of spoken words.

Convenience has tended to associate or group certain of these means with certain factors employed by managers. For example, a standard method is usually expressed by one of three means—a written specification, an unwritten customary procedure, or a verbal communication. In contrast, a standard material might be expressed by any of these means plus a model. Figure 24–3 shows the means most commonly used

FIGURE 24–3
The Means Most Commonly Used to Express Standards According to the Factors of Management

Factor	Written Specification	Model	Accepted Rule or Regulation	Unwritten Customary Procedure	Verbal Communication
Men	X	—	X	X	X
Materials	X	X	—	X	X
Machines	X	X	—	—	—
Methods	X	—	—	X	X
Money	X	—	X	X	—

to express standards according to factors. To illustrate, for machines, the standard is usually expressed by a written specification or by a model.

Change and Standards

Standards are changed primarily for two reasons: (1) to gain improvement and (2) to recognize the interdependence of standards within an enterprise. Experience shows that after a standard has been set, it is common to try to improve it. This is as it should be, for progress in management is dependent in large measure upon improvements in standards. In addition, the setting of a standard seems to place a level below which future standards will not be set.

The interdependence of standards can be comprehended best by considering an illustration. For a given task in an office, assume standards have been set up for the material, machine, and method. These three standards are interdependent and may be called "associated standards." The employee, in order to accomplish the task, must use the standard material in the standard machine and follow the standard method. Figure 24–4 in the second column, illustrates the present standards for the material, machine, and method.

Now, suppose that a change is made in the standard of the material from 12-pound, 8½ × 11-inch paper to 16-pound, 17 × 22-inch paper. In order to handle this new weight and size of paper, it is necessary to change the machine standard from an 11¼-inch to a 19¼-inch-roll typewriter and to change the methods standard from making five copies to four copies and from allowing ½-inch spacing to a 2-inch spacing between vertical columns. These changes in standards and the reasons for making them are shown in concise form in Figure 24–4.

FIGURE 24–4
Illustrating the Interdependence of Associated Standards

Factor	Present Standards	Standards after Changes	Reasons for Changes in Standards
Material	12# white bond paper, size 8½" × 11"	16# white bond paper, size 17" × 22"	New sheet size requested by top management members. Larger sheets necessitate heavier paper.
Machine	11¼"-roll typewriter	19¼"-roll typewriter	Larger roll needed to accommodate new paper size.
Method	Insert paper in machine, make five copies, leave ½" spacing between vertical columns	Insert paper in machine, make four copies, leave 2" spacing between vertical columns	Number of copies reduced from five to four because of heavier paper used. Increased spacing improves appearance of sheet.

In general, a manager should review all standards when any one standard is revised. This is especially important for associated standards, but it also applies for standards of a similar group. All methods standards, for example, should be reviewed whenever a change is made in any one methods standard, because in this way possible sources of improvement and the bettering of all methods standards can be discovered and adopted. To repeat, *standards are not independent, they are interdependent.*

Advantages of Standards

The use of standards in management provides tremendous advantages, including:

1. Aid Managing. The performance of the management is expedited by the use of standards. Identification and measurement of quality, performance, and capacity of the factors used by a manager constitute the supports upon which the managerial functions can be predicated.

2. Provide a Common Basis for Understanding. Standards provide a common terminology, or a common language, between the employee and supervisor or between the buyer and seller. Through the use of standards, it is possible to determine exactly what is being discussed or investigated.

3. Aid in Securing Coordination. Standards serve as focal points around which revolve many problems of management. Managerial coordination depends, in the final analysis, upon the synchronization or interplay of the various standards which are brought together.

4. Reduce Waste. Standards help to determine definite requirements. Losses resulting from obsolete equipment, poor methods, and excess materials are minimized when good standards are employed and enforced.

5. Promote Better Utilization of Employees. Standards help to apply human efforts within carefully defined and known limits. Executives are encouraged to do executive work—not routine work. Likewise, supervisors are impelled to carry out the job of supervising—not perform operative work.

6. Encourage Simplicity. Standards tend to eliminate unusual and complicated practices. The very nature of standards and their interrelatedness tend to encourage the use of simple descriptions and easily understood terms. Also, wide usage encourages understanding of the standard.

7. Act as Stimuli to Research. Standards help to localize areas in which improvements might be made. They serve to help state the problem and to assist the researcher in concentrating on a problem of relatively limited scope.

8. Provide Effective Connecting Links between the Findings of Research and the Application of Research Results. Standards serve as the contact points for the application of research findings. New discoveries are introduced via the standards and the beneficial contributions of research are expedited with a minimum of time and effort.

9. Provide Interchangeability of Part and Machine. Each component may be so specified and accurately determined by the use of standards that it is entirely feasible to use any one of a group of similar components. By the use of standards, all units of product A will be identical within the limits set up by the standards.

10. Make Mass Production Possible. Difficult and complex jobs requiring long and strenuous training periods are reduced by the use of standards to relatively simple tasks, yet at no sacrifice in the total amount of work accomplished.

AMERICAN STANDARDS ASSOCIATION, INC.

For some years the American Standards Association, Inc., and the Administrative Management Society (prior to 1963 known as the National Office Management Association) have worked together in efforts to establish office standards which it is hoped will prove useful to many managers. The American Standards Association does not set standards; it provides the machinery whereby every group concerned in any project has a right to participate in the setting of the standards. The program includes the establishment of office standards for each of the following major groups: office equipment and furniture, paper for office use, office supplies, business machines, personnel, physical and physiological factors, and office forms, records, and procedures. Figure 24–5 shows an office standard for basic sheet sizes and standard stock sizes for bond papers and index bristols. By its use, a reference level for managerial controlling is provided.

OFFICE STANDARDIZATION—MEANING AND IMPLICATION

The wide adoption of a limited number of standards in a particular area can lead to standardization. For example, when a company adopts certain stated standards regarding the type and size of desks it will use, the practice is known as standardization. A degree of uniformity is implied in all standardization. In many instances, standardization deals with an industry, not with just one enterprise. Both the needs and the benefits of standardization are in proportion to the complexity of managing the particular enterprise or industry.

Typically, a number of considerations must be included in standardizing an office item. For desks, the considerations might include size, appearance, utility, comfort, interchangeability, construction, maintenance, depreciation, and initial cost. How much weight to give to each of these factors is primarily a question of judgment, although weights in proportion to the relative costs of the factors might be developed. Standardization can be applied to any number of office areas, such as

FIGURE 24–5
A Written Office Standard

Division 2
Paper

N2.1 - 1955
•
ASA
Reg. U. S. Pat. Off.
X2.2.1 - 1955
*UDC 676.3.001.3:389.172
•

OFFICE STANDARD

Basic Sheet Sizes and Standard Stock Sizes
for Bond Papers and Index Bristols
(An American Standard)

1. Scope

1.1 The scope and purpose of this standard is to list the basic sheet sizes and standard stock sizes of bond papers and index bristols in order to encourage the use of normally available sizes.

2. Definitions

2.1 For purposes of this standard, the terms listed below are defined as follows:

2.1.1 Basic Sheet Size, as defined in the Dictionary of Paper* is a certain sheet size recognized by buyers and sellers as the one upon which its basic weight is figured. Usually, it is also the one which prints, folds, and trims most effectively.

2.1.2 Standard Stock Sheet Sizes are the sizes of paper normally stocked by most paper merchants and most paper mills and from which the sizes commonly used in the office are cut with a minimum of waste.

2.1.3 Bond Paper* is a grade of writing or printing paper originally used where strength, durability, and permanence are essential requirements, as in government bonds and legal documents. Its use has extended into other fields, such as business letterheads and forms, where strength and permanence, though important properties, are not so essential; this accounts for the wide range of quality in this type of paper. These qualities are obtained through the use of rag pulp, bleached chemical wood pulps, and mixtures of these fibers in the manufacturing process. Although bond paper is a typical writing paper, almost all of it is subjected to some form of printing before use. Therefore, it must have good printing qualities which, however, are not as important as writing and erasing qualities, clean-liness, formation, finish, color and freedom from fuzz. It is usually made in basis weights from 13 to 24 pounds (17 in. x 22 in. per 500 sheets).

2.1.4 Index Bristols* are bristols used principally for index records, business and commercial cards. They are a group of cardboards made on the Fourdrinier or cylinder machine of homogeneous stock (such as rag, sulphite, or bleached sulphate pulp) or by pasting together two or more plies of the same kind of paper, and finished and sized for pen and ink work. The usual basis weights are 180, 220, 280, 340, and 440 pounds (25.5 in. x 30.5 in. per 1000 sheets).

*The Dictionary of Paper, published under the auspices and direction of the American Paper and Pulp Association, 122 East 42nd Street, New York, N. Y. (Copyright Second Edition 1951.)

3. Standard Stock Sheet Sizes†

(All Dimensions in Inches)

Bond Papers (Rag Content or Chemical Wood Pulp)	Index Bristols (Rag Content or Chemical Wood Pulp)
17 x 22‡	20½ x 24¾
17 x 28	22½ x 28½
19 x 24	22½ x 35
22 x 34	25½ x 30½‡
24 x 38	
28 x 34	
34 x 44	

† The Standard Stock Sheet Sizes listed in this standard, except for the 22½ x 35 size Index Bristol, are identical with those listed in Simplified Practice Recommendation R22-40 for Paper of the U. S. Department of Commerce.

‡ Basic Size.

NOTE: When the direction of the grain is important, it should be specified.

Courtesy: American Standards Association, Inc., New York; and Administrative Management Society, Willow Grove, Pa.

chairs, files, machines, lighting, forms, procedures, employment qualifications, and training programs.

From an *economic* viewpoint, there is little doubt that office standardization is beneficial. Such economic factors as simplified control, greater quantities of work achieved, advancement of office production techniques, and assistance in managerial decision making are among the virtues generally pointed out.

However, from the *social* viewpoint, there has been much discussion, and differences of opinion exist. Proponents claim that due to standardization the level of both the skilled and the semiskilled employee has been raised; a measurement of performance is provided; the uniformity among similar jobs has widened the market for employee's services; and the employee can develop proficiency in a definite, prescribed area of endeavor. In contrast, those opposed to office standardization claim the employee is deprived of dignity as an employee—valuable skill and enthusiasm for the job are lost; the range within which the employee may exercise a skill is narrowed; the employee is without the overall picture, of which personal efforts are a small part; and the dull and drab work life, with work interest and outlook impeded, can make the employee an undesirable citizen in the community.

QUESTIONS

1. In your opinion, what are the three most important advantages of standards in office management? Point out and discuss your major reasons for selecting these three advantages.
2. Is there any meaningful relationship between office work measurement and office controlling? Discuss.
3. Explain the meaning of Figure 24–1 as you understand it.
4. In your opinion is the management by objectives approach helpful in attaining adequate control? Does it add to or subtract from the amount of controls believed necessary? Elaborate on your answers.
5. Enumerate and discuss briefly four specific actions the office manager can take to help have controlling looked upon with a favorable and positive viewpoint.
6. Do you agree with this statement: "The most helpful controlling points out and concentrates on areas of high risk and payoffs. It always deals with the past, yet it needs to be reviewed periodically and changed if conditions so suggest." Justify your answer.
7. Discuss the extent and importance of standards in the field of office management.
8. Give a brief explanation for each of the following:
    a. Controlling.
    b. Interdependence of standards.
    c. Base line of reference.
    d. Associated standards.

9. Can controlling take place without the use of a standard? Elaborate on your answer.
10. Do you favor office standardization? Cite reasons to support your viewpoint.
11. Can controlling exist without planning? Planning without controlling? Management without controlling? Explain your answers.
12. Discuss the influence of the computer upon controlling. Has this influence been good or bad as you see it? Why?

CASE PROBLEMS

Case 24–1. Tedmont Technical Sales Service

Most office employees of Tedmont Technical Sales Service are on incentive pay. In addition to their base or weekly guaranteed salary, they receive additional pay in keeping with their production of a satisfactory quantity and quality of work.

Currently typing work is not on incentive. Much of this work is provided by typists organized into a typing pool supervised by a group leader. Typists in the pool have little or no opportunity to develop personal loyalties as do the private secretaries, and therefore are not likely to be motivated by such loyalties. Accordingly a financial incentive plan is to be used for the pool and hopefully will provide adequate interest and enthusiasm for good sustained performance. The work of those in the pool includes transcribing letters from dictating machines, typing reports from long-hand or rough-typed materials, and cutting duplicating masters.

It is proposed that time standards will be established for all typing work done in this pool. However, no two tasks will be exactly alike. One task may be a half-page letter, perhaps regular correspondence with several carbon copies and with ordinary vocabulary and more-or-less standard phrases which would be easy typing. The next task may be a report of several pages submitted in long-hand writing, containing technical vocabulary and considerable numerical data which would be difficult to type even for a competent private secretary.

A typing speed of 60 6-letter words (on the average) per minute will be considered acceptable and might well be appropriate for ordinary correspondence. In contrast, for a technical report the speed will be considerably less—perhaps only 20 words per minute.

The belief is that a sophisticated set of work standards could be established which might allow some specified number of minutes per 100 words for simple correspondence typing. Various adjustment factors then could be applied for the nature of the source material, dictation which is easy or difficult to understand, rough-typed copy, long-hand material, and so forth. Other adjustment factors would take into account whether the material is correspondence, technical report, and numerical tabulations. Such a standard could be quite precise and consistently reflect the amount and difficulty of work in each task. But to apply such standards would require an evaluation of each typing task and a check on the quality of the finished work—a most difficult administrative chore.

Hence, the decision has been made to use a single time standard expressed as "minutes per page." To illustrate, the same standard time will be credited to the typist whether a page is filled with numerical tabulations or contains only one or two sentences. After the standard has been established, no further individual task standards need be calculated. Output will be measured by the group leader by merely counting the number of pages of completed work. Quality of output, and maintenance of reasonable amounts of typed material per page, will be controlled by the group leader who occasionally will check random samples of each typist's work. When "defects" in the sample exceed a specified limit the typist's incentive pay will be reduced for the current payroll period. By this simplified approach the program can be administered at a reasonable cost and thus make possible a satisfactory measurement of completed work and the use of incentive so that the typists can enjoy higher earnings as their reward for higher sustained average levels of work output.

Questions:

1. Do you believe the proposed standard for typing will serve adequately for the proposed controlling efforts? Why? Discuss fully.
2. What alternatives are available to the company?
3. Do you favor a financial incentive plan for the typists? Why? Elaborate on your answer.

Case 24–2.   Benton-Donohue Company

For the past several months, Richard E. Schubert, the office manager, has been giving serious consideration to the establishing of standards for posture chairs which his company purchases. Mr. Schubert believes that standards are necessary for three chair classifications—executive, supervisory, and clerical. For each of these groups, a particular model, design, upholstery, and color would be determined and used throughout the entire office.

To substantiate his viewpoint, Mr. Schubert points out that the use of such standards would greatly improve the appearance of the office and save much time in purchasing. Also, chair purchases could be made at better prices for the company. But probably of even greater importance would be the elimination of comparison of chairs by employees of the same general organizational level. For example, one supervisor would not compare his chair to that of another supervisor and feel that he had a better or an inferior chair by comparison. Chair equality would be attained.

The controller suggests that the employees of each office division should be permitted to select the chairs they want. In other words, chair standards should extend within an office division only. Any other standards arrangement would conflict with personnel interests and possibly with the type of work performed. Furthermore, he believes that the company should give its chair business to several suppliers. Competition should be encouraged; otherwise, the company might find itself at the mercy of one supplier.

The president of the company does not see anything wrong with employees of the same organizational level using different chairs, and he asks two questions of the office manager: (1) "How are you going to determine the standards for chairs in our office?" and (2) "What are the tangible savings from adopting the use of chair standards?" As the president sees it, the answer to question one is so involved that the company should not undertake the project. In addition, many employees would question the results and their use regardless of what would be determined. In answer to the second question, it appears that additional expenditures, not savings, would be incurred. Not one, but groups of chairs would probably have to be purchased if chair standards were adopted. Also, the possibility of taking advantage of lower prices on the chair market would be minimized, and further improvements in chair design and manufacture would be discouraged.

Questions:

1. Do you agree with the viewpoint of the controller? Discuss. Of the president? Discuss.
2. What action do you recommend that the office manager take? Why?

Chapter **25**

Typical Office Controls and Manuals

Until you try, you don't know what you can't do.

Henry James

To assist in understanding the meaning and operating of office controls, several selected applications of office controlling will now be discussed. These applications are among the more important and prominent in the office. They will provide a better insight to controlling; they are not intended to be inclusive of all office controls.

Spectrum of Control

Under ideal conditions, controlling would be unnecessary. The means for overcoming obstacles in the way of achievement would be included in the initial plans, every employee would be performing efficiently the work he or she likes best, and good team spirit and individual satisfactions from job performance would prevail. However, in real life there can be and are many changes between what is planned for and what results are obtained. Hence, a number of controls exist and they range from controls applied to the entire organization to those applied to the activities of one employee on one type of work.

We can state that a spectrum of controls exists. Not only is this spectrum *horizontal* in the sense of different coverages by different controls throughout the width of an organization, but the spectrum is also *vertical* among the successively higher echelons of management. Managers in the lowest echelon use certain types of controls, in the next higher echelon, some new controls are added, others are dropped. Given sufficient levels, the controls at the top are wholly different from those at the lowest level.

As a result, there are many different types of control within a given organization. They should be coordinated. Further, it means that different types are needed to provide adequate control. In other words, *a system of controls* makes up controlling in every enterprise. Control in one department or over one activity is incomplete, it is the entirety of the controls that must be taken into account.

There are a number of classifications or types of controls including strategic controls, overall controls, general controls, detailed controls, special controls, functional or activities controls, external controls, and internal controls. Selected for discussion here are overall controls, special controls, functional controls, and internal controls.

Overall Controls

As the name suggests, overall controls cover reasonably large segments of the total office. Basically they can be considered efforts to determine cost-value relationships. Representative of overall control in the office is the audit consisting of a fairly exhaustive review and evaluation of information management using selected attributes as guides. It includes a sort of stock taking of all phases of the office's operations including an examination of systems, procedures, forms, correspondence, physical facilities, quality, service, and the like.

The idea of an audit is not new. It has been the practice of most enterprises to review and evaluate their financial accounts at least annually to be certain of their accuracy and to reveal any weaknesses in controls that may require correcting. "Auditing the books" and a periodic inventory of physical assets are accepted business practices. This sort of stock taking is followed for office operations.

The office audit normally should follow two stages. First is the broad, general survey to provide a reasonable review of current information work and to ferret out any major difficulties. The second stage is a detailed problem-solving study of each area requiring attention as shown by results of the first stage. For example, it may include an analysis and study of the office layout, of the forms being used, or ways to improve the systems now followed.

Audits necessitate the collecting of facts from a variety of sources. To illustrate, production records, work schedules, office organization charts, letters, and office personnel records may be assembled and studied in an audit project. In addition, key personnel at all levels, both supervisors and clerks, may be interviewed to verify information derived from written records. Also, their opinions and suggestions are obtained for possible improvements and changes.

Those performing the audit must decide what data they want along with why such information is wanted. Personal observations of the work being performed may be followed in order to obtain first-hand impressions of the adequacy of the machine, desk, files, as well as the work travel, and work station arrangements. Information may also be obtained on the responsibility and authority of selected employees in particular work groups to ascertain if possible reassignment of duties or reorganization of work groups is advisable, to confirm that no duties overlap or are ignored, and to determine the real need and purpose for many duties.

Commonly a number of questions are formulated, thus probing into a number of possibilities leading to either approval of present activities or recommendations for subsequent improvement. Figure 25–1 shows typical audit questions classified by three major areas.

FIGURE 25–1

ILLUSTRATIONS OF THE TYPE OF QUESTIONS TO ASK UNDER MAJOR AREAS OF INVESTIGATION IN AN OFFICE AUDIT.

Under forms, pertinent questions include:
1. Are similar forms completed elsewhere?
2. Is a definite need served by each present form?
3. Is the information requested on the forms purposeful?
4. Is the information arranged in best sequential order?

For procedures, these questions can be asked:
1. Is the procedure being used by the operating personnel?
2. Is it in written form? Should it be?
3. Is the procedure up to date?
4. Can any part, or all, of the procedure be eliminated?
5. Would elimination cause other work to be added, change policies, or involve organizational change?
6. What effect does present procedures have on employee relations? Customer relations?

For scheduling and work flow, ask these questions:
1. If peak load periods, what causes them? Can work be shifted to level them off?
2. Is work processed immediately upon receipt? Is this desirable?
3. Are there numerous rush jobs? If yes, why?
4. Are certain types of work deferred in processing?
5. Are machines and personnel capacities sufficient for work loads?

Good auditing requires time. The work cannot be rushed as normally much reflective thinking is required to perform the work satisfactorily. Within a reasonable period, however, a report on the findings from the audit should be made so that benefits from it can be enjoyed and its status maintained in the normal conduct of the company's affairs.

Office Security Controls

An expanding and important type of special control deals with providing and maintaining office security of (1) the office building or space and, (2) information from accidental or intentional disclosure to un-authorized persons. Office space security commonly consists of electronic equipment for surveillance of key areas and doors. Cameras and monitors keep a constant watch over loading areas, vehicle ramps, entrances, exits, stairways, and computer operations. For example, critical doors are equipped with alarms. When a door is opened, a signal alerts the operator at the console of the security center. Likewise, any utility failure or irregular use of corridors, elevators and the like are instantly spotted by the security system.

Techniques for information security also include the usual physical means plus computer hardware features and special features about the computer program. While all information is subject to risk, that processed by computer is especially vulnerable to potential security problems primarily because of three reasons. First is the capability of present-day computers to give access to their facilities and stored information to multiple users and for multiple jobs. And the accessiblity is a multitude of data in a fraction of a second. Also, the trend toward the use of more and more information for decision making, for research, and for planning has brought with it demands for the processing and storing of large quantites of data very rapidly. The growth and com-monness of computer data processing has contributed to the problem of maintaining desired security over such data. Third, the increase in the data communication facilities and terminal devices with their inher-ent exposure to risk have also contributed to the problem of providing adequate security.

Many solutions for providing adequate protection are available. Most of them concern safeguards such as to lower the opportunity for manipu-lation by separating responsibilities among personnel, to check carefully the background of everyone hired—try to hire and maintain honest em-ployees, to rotate both programmers and operators from time to time in order to reduce the chances of anyone plundering the system. Also institute the following: computer hardware features of recognition of interrupt, data checking either the base or amount of data processed, full remote programming and testing support, normal need-to-know re-strictions, password verification, and terminal or person identification to access sensitive data with identification verifiable so that user can be held accountable. Figure 25–2 shows relationships between different threats to security and respective countermeasure controls. For example, the threat of copying can be stopped by control of personnel, of oper-ating procedures, of physical access, of threat monitoring, and of terminal access. Part of the latter may be identifying the terminal user by any or all of these means: (1) a memorized password or answers to personalized questions, (2) a prescribed badge, card, or key inserted into the terminal unit, or (3) a vocal statement compared with a stored "vocal-print."

FIGURE 25–2
Security Threats and Respective Countermeasure Controls

Countermeasure Controls

Security Threat	Personnel – Screening and Motivating	Backup Systems and Procedures	Operating Procedures	Hardware Access	Physical Access	Threat Monitoring	Terminal Access
Copying	X		X		X	X	X
Tampering or Modifying Software	X	X	X	X	X	X	X
Misrepresenting or Using Another's Password					X	X	
Fire, Tornado, and Power Failure		X	X				
Theft	X	X	X		X		

The whole area of security is a fascinating subject and challenges the best of creativity minds. It is an area of increasing concern and is destined to occupy a prominent position in the office of the future. Many of the current practices are indeed highly sophisticated. While effectiveness is paramount, the security features must be within reasonable cost limits for the expense of providing it must be less than the cost which would occur as the result of a successful violation of the security.

Office Functional Controls

Among the most widely used office controls are those pertaining to functions such as systems, procedures, policies, physical facilities, forms, reports, telephone, supplies, and service. Usually the functional control most commonly followed is that which influences a large portion of the total office operation. Office forms have this characteristic and represent an important control in the office. Others include reports, telephone calls, and supplies. Each of these will now be discussed.

CONTROLLING OF OFFICE FORMS

In nearly every enterprise, forms have a tendency to continue indefinitely regardless of need. The root of much office inefficiency stems from this situation. In addition, new forms are started whether the information desired is now contained in existent forms or can be secured by a slight modification in these forms. These facts are recognized by many managers who believe operations in their respective enterprises would be greatly improved if proper control over office forms were exercised. Gains to be won from effective controlling of office forms are shown by Figure 25–3.

FIGURE 25–3
Gains from Controlling Office Forms

1. Retention of only forms, copies, and items on form that are necessary.
2. Prevention of unnecessary forms being continued.
3. Improvements to allow for ease of data entry, filing, and reference.
4. Distribution of forms only to those who need them.
5. Production of forms by best means.
6. Expansion of general-purpose forms, a reduction in limited-use forms.
7. Review periodically of forms to insure only needed forms are used.

Studies show that the time spent in using an office form and the effort in getting information recorded, transmitted, and processed—represent by far the greater cost of forms as well as the greater opportunities for improvement. The material considerations—size and weight of paper, and printing cost—are important and must be taken into account, but they are relatively minor. For each dollar spent to purchase forms, about $20 are spent to process the forms. That is, a multiple-copy form costing $75 per thousand involves a processing cost of $1,500. By eliminating unneeded forms, much time, effort, and money can be saved. Office forms controlling is the answer.

Determine What Is Being Accomplished

The first step is to determine the present accomplishment. For this purpose, current information on the various forms now being used, what respective purposes they serve, and specific data on their contents and identification are required. To these ends, the following steps are recommended.

1. Announce to all employees the existence of the forms control unit, and explain its function and its authority. Be specific as to who is the head of it. In many cases, the head may be the office manager. Other members of the unit should include key personnel who are qualified and can give support to the office forms control efforts from different departments of the enterprise.

2. Freeze all forms activity at its *status quo*. Announce that any additions or changes must be taken up and cleared through the forms control unit.

3. Obtain at least two copies of every office form used in the enterprise. Use one copy for a centralized forms control file, the other for purposes of analysis, as described below.

4. Make out a tabulating card for each form indicating its (1) function, (2) numerical designation, and (3) construction features. File these by numerical designation and use as cross-reference with the centralized file. Office forms are employed to assist in any of the following functions: report, request, record, instruct, follow up, authorize, cancel, order, apply, acknowledge, estimate, route, schedule, and claim. Segregating the forms by their major function assists analysis.

5. File each form in the centralized file according to function. This will bring together every form that is similar in nature regardless of its design, its name, or where it is used.

6. Secure a listing of all the office systems and procedures used in the enterprise.

7. Mark all forms in the centralized file according to the system or procedure in which they are used.

The trend in forms procurement has been to consider all forms of one system or procedure at the same time. This approach recognizes the interrelatedness of the forms. Suggestions are made and bids are received for the complete form requirements per system or procedure. This way, better prices and services are obtained.

Evaluation of Present Forms

The second step is to evaluate what is being accomplished. Attention is directed to the determination of how well the present office forms are serving present needs. For this purpose, several different but related activities can be undertaken. Questionnaires sent to those using the forms frequently prove effective. It is helpful for the person in charge of forms control to meet separately with each department head and discuss improvements. These meetings can be followed by group meetings for all department heads in order to decide what improvements can be made in forms that affect more than one department.

It is not uncommon to analyze the existent forms to determine if any can be (1) eliminated, (2) combined with others, or (3) improved. The form's adequacy to meet the work requirements consistent with efficient office management is of foremost importance. Results achieved are sometimes amazing. In the case of one prominent Chicago company, the total number of office forms was reduced from 1,182 to 368.

Figures 25–4 and 25–5 show how forms can be combined to improve office efficiency. Originally, four separate forms—shipping label, invoice, shipping memorandum, and packing slip—were typed separately. Subsequently, the four forms were combined and now require only one typing. In Figure 25–5, a copy has been raised to show the shipping label in the upper left corner, the receiving memorandum in the upper right, and the packing slip below. These are separated by tearing apart at the perforations.

In addition, physical considerations are taken into account—the size of the forms, correctness for filing, cut without waste, and easy folding for enclosure in an envelope. Also, the weight of paper for the original and each carbon, the use of different colors of paper, and their essentiality in the particular form are carefully reviewed. Specifications are checked—the type of ink, punches, and perforations are investigated.

Applying Corrective Measures

The third and final step is *to apply corrective measures, if necessary,* deemed proper and effective. The forms controller or an organization unit usually has the authority to purchase forms and to review and pass on any and all forms if it were concluded that this was the best way to acquire the forms the company should have. The personnel involved in this phase of controlling should have sufficient status so that others will take them seriously. They must work well with others in the company. Suggestions by others should be encouraged and their cooperation won.

Controlling of Reports

To obtain adequate controlling of reports requires an accurate inventory of current reports, evaluation of them by recipients, objective analysis of these evaluations, and determination of the need for each report in relationship to the service it supplies and its cost of preparing, handling, and use. For these purposes, certain steps are taken. The first is to send out a cover letter to the originators of reports explaining the "Reports Controlling Program" and requesting a copy of each report they prepare be attached to a statement giving the title of the report, a list of those receiving a copy of the report, its size, length, frequency, and estimated cost. If desired, a form can be used for the acquiring and recording of these data. Each recipient of the report is requested to evaluate each report he receives with reference to necessity, use, and value of information contained. For this, a covering form letter and a questionnaire are recommended. A report evaluation questionnaire is illustrated by Figure 25–6. The returned questionnaires are tabulated.

FIGURE 25–4
Forms Used by a Clothing Manufacturer; Top to Bottom: Shipping Label,
Invoice, Shipping Memorandum, and Packing Slip

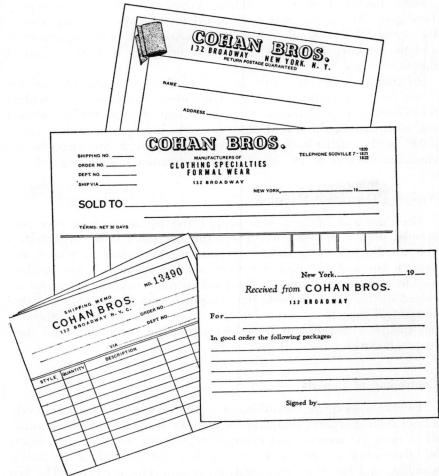

Courtesy: American Sales Book Co., Inc., subsidiary of Moore Corp., Ltd., Niagara, N.Y.

Shown for each report on a spread sheet are the type of information contained, the source of information, and the estimated cost of preparation. Meetings are held with management members and other report recipients to determine the need and possible improvement for each report. Recommendations are evaluated regarding what reports can be eliminated, combined with other reports, improved, or simplified. Subsequently, all approved reports are assigned a report control number which is used along with its title for purposes of identification in the

FIGURE 25–5

A Combination of the Four Forms Shown in Figure 25–4 (now, the same amount of work is accomplished in one typing operation instead of in four)

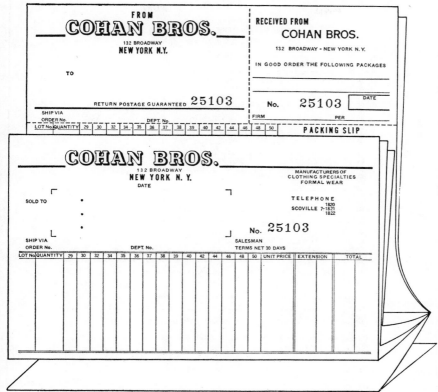

Courtesy: American Sales Book Co., Inc., subsidiary of Moore Corp., Ltd., Niagara, N.Y.

future. Further, a list of reports eliminated is prepared showing the reasons for such action and the estimated savings from their termination.

Like the action taken in a forms control program, some managers recommend that centralization of authority over report writing be established. When this is done it frequently is either the director of correspondence or the head of the systems and procedures department. The purpose is to prevent the spawning of new reports and to require formal approval from a centralized agency before issuing any additions to the reports membership. Thus, controlling of reports is exercised.

TELEPHONE CALL CONTROLLING

Several areas usually attracting the center of attention in telephone call controlling are long-distance calls, personal phone privileges, and

FIGURE 25-6

REPORT EVALUATION QUESTIONNAIRE

To: Location: (Dept.)   Date: .

It is our understanding that you receive a copy of the report indicated
below. Please answer the following question regarding this report and
return to _____ dept. by _____. Thank you.

1. Do you use this report? Yes_____ No_____

    If No, your questionnaire is complete. Please return to us at once.

    If Yes, is report required for:

    a. Making decisions Yes _____ No _____
    b. Checking accuracy Yes _____ No _____
    c. Keeping informed Yes _____ No _____
    d. Other (please write in)_____
    _____

2. Would elimination of this report affect your operations? Yes___No _____
    Comments _____
    _____

3. Would elimination of certain items or portions of this report meet your
    approval? Yes _____ No _____
    Comments_____
    _____

4. If the report in total or in part is necessary, could lessening of its
    frequency be made? Yes_____ No _____

    If Yes, what minimum frequency would be acceptable?_____
    _____

5. Do you retain your copy of this report? Yes_____ No_____

6. About how often do you refer to it after its original use?_____
    _____
    _____

7. Is the report destroyed after its useful life? Yes_____ No_____
    Comments _____

8. Please give any additional comments or suggestions you have regarding
    this report. _____
    _____
    _____

    Your signature _____ Date _____
    Title of Report_____

excess message units. Under the QZ billing for long-distance calls, each
employee who frequently uses long distance is assigned a telephone
number, such as 4Z1-1234. When he places a long-distance call, the
outside operator is dialed directly. He gives her the number he is calling
and his special billing number. Employees infrequently making long-
distance calls use a special number assigned to each department. At
the end of the month, the long-distance expense is itemized by the

telephone company so that a quick and accurate check can be made of who called whom and when. Allocation of telephone expense to departments is made and the supervisor of each unit can review his employees' usage of long distance. This places responsibility for the telephone expense where it belongs. In addition, the company's switchboard operator can concentrate on incoming calls and give better service.

Reducing the number of personal calls by employees on company telephone and time is a fertile field for telephone controlling. It is possible to obtain data on the numbers being called by means of the "Optional Detailed Message Unit Billing" offered by the telephone company. This service must be taken for at least two complete billing periods and supplies a monthly listing of calls for which a charge of two or more message units is made. Study of such data reveals what numbers are dialed frequently and whether they are personal or business numbers. Appropriate action can then be taken.

However, creating the proper psychological climate to use the telephone only when necessary and to minimize personal calls appears to bring about the best mutual results. Getting responsibility placed on the person making the call is essential. Explain that in general the company telephone does not have unlimited "free" calls as provided in many private home installations. Knowing this fact will help to reduce the abuse of excess personal calls. And letting it be known by means of bulletin board notices and supervisors' actions that the personal call privilege must not be abused helps to bring about desired results and satisfactory control in this area.

In large metropolitan areas, calls to outlying areas are charged extra message units, depending on the distance and the length of each call. To minimize this excess cost, an enterprise can have installed "foreign exchange" trunks which enable calls to be made to distant areas at less cost per call. To do so the proper level (a certain number like 8 or 9) must be dialed to get an outside line, depending upon the geographical area or the exchange prefix being called. To assist in making the proper selection, memos can be distributed or stickers located adjacent to the telephone can be used. In some instances a map of the area may be shown with different-colored areas indicating the "dial 8" and "dial 9" locations. Trunk selection errors are thus reduced and savings can be substantial. In one medium-sized company, the excess message units, averaging $450 a month, were reduced subsequently to $235 a month.

OFFICE SUPPLIES CONTROL

Office employees need proper supplies if maximum productivity is to be accomplished. The lack of writing paper, a typewriter ribbon, an order pad, envelopes, or letterheads might cause serious delay in getting important office work finished when required. Also supplies represent an investment of capital approximately $100 worth of supplies on hand for each office employee. Lack of adequate control over office supplies may result in needed items being out of stock, excessive prices paid for certain items, and obsolete material remaining in the stockroom.

One person should be put in charge of supplies control. This person makes and implements the decisions affecting the ordering storage, and issuance of supplies. It is up to this person to know what supplies are being issued, to whom, and evaluating whether such supplies are in order and if not, to take corrective measures. Assistance in fulfilling this responsibility is normally obtained from others. For example, the supplies controller should inform supervisors by means of monthly statements of the costs, kinds, and amounts of office supplies issued to their respective units. The supervisor, in turn, assists in evaluating whether the supplies data "look right."

Supplies should be issued only upon authorized written requisitions, which should be made out, in most cases, by the department head of the unit receiving the supplies. By filing these requisitions, it is convenient to maintain a journal or record by departments of what is issued, when, and to whom. A periodic inspection of such record is helpful to ascertain if consumption of supplies appears to be normal in the light of past requirements and volume of work handled.

The quantity of supplies issued at any one time should be limited to about a two-weeks supply. Large quantities encourage waste; too-small quantities involve excessive requisitions and trips to the stockroom. Packaging supplies in small units tend to economize their use. Further, all issuances might be confined to one day out of the week. If supplies are needed in the interim, a special requisition and approval can be required, a practice which tends to discourage requests for supplies at irregular times. There should be realistic maximum and minimum quantities established for each item, as well as the ordering point. These can be based on judgment guided by past experience. A balanced inventory is sought in keeping with the future probable usage. Usually it is best to buy small quantities at frequent intervals.

Among important physical considerations are that the location of the stockroom be convenient, clean, dry, and enclosed. It should have adjustable shelving and possess a ratio of about 55% storage cubic volume to total cubic volume of the stockroom. The arrangement of supplies should feature (1) placing related items near each other, (2) having heavy items on the lower shelves, light items on the upper shelves, and (3) locating fast turnover items close at hand—near the entrance. All stored items should be indexed by number or code and recorded in a handy reference book to assist in locating any item quickly.

Big savings can be realized by substituting less costly items for certain present items. Also, any reduction in the number of items stored is usually beneficial. And it helps to ascertain if what is now being used is needed and, if so, if it meets requirements. To this end, select at random a requisition for supplies and investigate it thoroughly. Find out how the item is used, who uses it, what the user thinks about it, whether it is the best for the specific use, and whether the price paid for it is reasonable and in line competitively. Answers to these questions either will confirm that adequate controlling of supplies is being done or will uncover areas which require remedial action.

OFFICE MANUALS

What can be considered a part of internal controlling are written general information, instructions, and regulations in the form of an official booklet. Such a medium aids in helping employees to help themselves to know what is expected of them, when, and how. *An office manual is a written record of information and instructions which concern and can be used to guide the employee's efforts in an enterprise.* Actually, it is a guidebook—a source for data believed essential for the highest performance of the job.

An office manual makes instructions definite, provides quick settlements of misunderstandings, shows each employee how the job fits into the total organization, and points out how he or she can contribute to the achievements of office objectives as well as maintain good relationships with other employees. Employee performance and satisfaction are boosted by having this information at the employees' fingertips. Likewise, manuals aid management members significantly. Manuals relieve management members of having to repeat similar information, explanations, or instructions. They not only force decisions on policies and procedures—thoughts about them must be put into writing—but they also provide constancy to them. Employees come and go, but the manual stays. The training of newcomers is enhanced because the manual gives them the information they need in a readily available form. And manuals also serve as effective refreshers for employees who have been on the payroll for some time.

Figure 25–7 lists the basic requirements for success of office manuals. More will be included about these requirements throughout the immediate following pages.

There are some managers who do not advocate the use of manuals. Contending that manuals cost too much, are too much work to prepare, stifle initiative, or won't work, some managers refuse to use them. For certain situations, these objections are no doubt justifiable, but for most enterprises, the use of manuals appears to be beneficial. The great major-

FIGURE 25–7
Basic Requirements for Success of Office Manuals

---

1. Center authority and responsibility for the manual program.
2. Write to the level of the employee who will use the manual.
3. Maintain a distribution list—distribute only those manuals that are needed in each case.
4. Use color to emphasize identity of binder or printing matter.
5. Keep manual simple in arrangement of material and in language used.
6. Adopt adequate indexing and cross-referencing.
7. Use numerous visual aids—charts, illustrations, and cartoons.
8. Keep manuals up to date.
9. Highlight changes and revisions.
10. Audit the material periodically.

---

ity of nonusers of manuals are small companies where the formal communication and mode of operation are considered adequate.

Different offices have need for different manuals. The type is determined by the purpose to be served. Manuals can be written to cover a variety of subjects, including policies, organizational structure of the enterprise, employment, indoctrination, supervision, job instruction, standard work practices, computer data processing, history of the enterprise, and specialized or departmental practices such as in the accounting, corresponding, filing, engineering, purchasing, or sales department. The wide range of subjects suggests different types of manuals among which the most common are a (1) manual of policies, (2) manual of operations, or standard practices manual, or job instruction manual, (3) manual of office rules and regulations, or handbook on employment, (4) historical manual, and (5) multi-purpose manual.

Manual of Policies

A policy is a basic guide to action in that it prescribes the overall boundaries within which activities are to take place. Hence, a manual of policies includes broad managerial intentions or actions likely to take place under certain conditions. To illustrate, promoting employees solely on the basis of merit is a policy. It states the guide and gives boundaries for promoting, but it does not tell who will be promoted. Knowing the policies of an enterprise provides the main framework around which all actions are based. Policies furnish the background for an understanding of why things are done as they are.

It has been said that a policy does not really exist unless it is in writing. To decide each case on its individual merits and to convey this decision verbally is not in keeping with modern management thinking. Proponents of a manual of policies cite these advantages: (1) Written policies require managers to think through their courses of action and to predetermine what actions will be taken under various circumstances; (2) a general program of action for many matters is provided, and only the unusual or exceptional matter requires the attention of the top managers; (3) a framework is provided within which the manager can operate freely; and (4) written policies help to insure equitable treatment to all employees.

On the other hand, there are those who object to having a manual of policies. Among the important points they mention are the following: (1) Policies are extremely difficult to write accurately and completely—the interpretation of words and phrases sometimes leads to serious misunderstandings; (2) written policies make it difficult to keep policies flexible, as is frequently required by changing conditions; and (3) knowledge of policies should be confined to those persons charged with their execution—the top executive, department heads, or supervisors, as the case might be.

Manual of Operations

A manual of operations can serve as a convenient source for information on how the work is to be done. The authorized steps can be listed; and supplementary information, in the form of diagrams, sketches, and charts, can be included in order to clarify the data. The standards and guides to be followed are usually included.

The contents of this type of manual can be directed in one of several directions. First, it can emphasize the performance of *individual tasks and jobs*. Illustrative is the manual which explains how to operate and use a minicomputer. A glossary of terms is sometimes included. Figure 25–8 shows a portion of a page from a correspondence manual which includes assistance in how to write effective letters.

FIGURE 25–8
Portion of a Correspondence Manual

SEC. XI: WORDS, SENTENCES, AND PARAGRAPHING
The choice of the right word is a challenge to the effective writer. Put yourself in the place of the reader and visualize how best to explain what you are trying to say. Develop an adequate vocabulary because choice of words is a matter of having a choice from available word material. Also, be willing to seek the right word and take the effort to do so.
All other things being equal, short words are preferred because they form a letter which is more easily comprehended and can be read quickly. Long words slow the reading and give rise to misunderstanding.
Strive for short sentences mixed with long sentences. Do not use a series of short sentences as they give an appearance of brusqueness. Let the subject and the verb be well identified. Avoid involved or complex sentences.

Second, the manual can be directed toward *departmental practices*. Manuals of this type contain a statement of the duties of each department's members. Divisions are defined, the supervisors listed, and their responsibilities indicated, along with outlines and procedures for operating. An example of this type is shown in Figure 25–9.

FIGURE 25–9
Portion of a Storing and Retrieving Manual

GENERAL INSTRUCTIONS

1. Accuracy is the prime essential in storing and retrieving work; make it your foremost consideration. Speed is important, but it comes after accuracy.
2. Guard against these common mistakes:
   a. Drawers and folders too full.
   b. Papers improperly indexed.
   c. Material in miscellaneous folder not filed alphabetically.
   d. Charge-out system not used.
3. When filing, always pull the folders part way out of the drawer in order to avoid placing papers between folders.
4. All materials are to be stored within the day following its receipt.
5. Most stored material is confidential. Therefore do not discuss the contents of any file with fellow employees or outsiders and never give a stored file to a person whose duties have no relation to the material requested. In case of doubt, see your supervisor.
6. The number of papers taken from the sorter to be worked on at one time should be equal to the quantity you can handle within about 15 minutes of your filing effort.
7. Acquaint yourself with office details other than those in the storing and retrieving department when such knowledge will assist understanding of how materials should be stored.
8. Suggestions for improvement are always welcome. Talk with your supervisor who will authorize the change if your suggested method is simpler and more efficient.

The third area to which a manual of operations may be directed is *general practices in a special field*. This type of manual is becoming more popular, for it furnishes valuable general information which is usable in special lines of work. Its adoption is mainly in large offices, although in certain instances the small office can benefit from manuals of this type. Systems and procedures manuals and those for computer data processing are illustrative. Each of these very considerably in makeup.

Manual of Office Rules and Regulations

Manuals are an excellent medium in which to explain employee benefit plans, including such things as group insurance, hospitalization, and savings facilities. Questions regarding the use of the company library, cafeteria, and recreation club can also be answered. In addition, the prescribed guides for conduct are included and cover such items as sick allowances, the use of rest periods, conduct regarding smoking, solicitation for money in the office, the sale of tickets, hours of employment, holidays, vacations, office etiquette, rest periods, telephone usage, and recreational provisions. A manual of this type can be identified as a handbook on employment. Intriguing titles such as "You and the ABC Company" or "Getting Along at ABC" are effective. Figure 25–10 shows a sample of the type of information included in this kind of manual.

FIGURE 25–10
Page of a Manual Used by a Large National Distributor of General Merchandise

GENERAL OFFICE ROUTINES

Desks—Keep your desk clean. It's a workbench, not a catchall. Never allow a lot of old-fashioned relics to accumulate on it. File everything away in its natural place, and dispose of obsolete matter. (The job of filing is an important one and is not to be neglected or allowed to pile up.)

Avoid having decorations on the desk that might tip and spill, such as flower containers, ink bottles, sponge cups, etc. Keep such things in safer places.

Clear all desks and tables before leaving the building. Any papers or letters of a confidential nature must be put away, never left on the desk top. All lights are to be turned off, fans and ventilators disconnected, and blinds raised. Typewriters should be covered when not being used.

Dusting—Each office is to be thoroughly dusted each morning—during the day too if necessary. No one need resent dusting—it's part of the job.

Pens should be filled, pencils sharpened, and water bottles filled first thing in the morning. See to it that ash trays are kept clean throughout the day. If blotters are used, make sure soiled ones are replaced.

Typewriters should be dusted morning and night, type cleaner applied weekly.

Supplies—If you are responsible for handling supplies for the office, check them regularly and make sure that you are not running low. Keep a list at your desk of supplies that will soon need to be requisitioned (use form 527 for ordering). All requisitions must be authorized by the department head.

Hours—Arrange hours if possible so the office will not be unattended at any time. If it is impossible for someone to be present during lunch hour, do not leave without making arrangements with someone else to take any important calls.

Callers—It is much better to have an understanding with your superior regarding his wishes in the matter of announcing callers, the persons he wishes to see and those he does not, rather than to guess at the proper procedure in each instance.

Keep an accurate, up-to-date list or notebook of telephone numbers and addresses, business as well as personal. Such a list should be readily accessible. Add to it regularly so it will be of value both to you and your superior.

Courtesy: Butler Brothers, Chicago. Reproduced here by special permission.

Historical Manual

Many employers feel that it is important to give employees information regarding the history of the company—its beginning, growth, accomplishments, present management, and current status. This gives the employee an insight into the tradition and thinking behind the enterprise with which he is associated. It probably makes for better understanding, increases morale, and helps the employee to feel that she or he "belongs"—is a part of the company. Giving employees a picture of the whole help them to fit themselves into the total picture. Manuals, of course, are excellent means for conveying this type of information to employees. The story of the enterprise usually can be told on several pages; and quite frequently, it can be a part of a message written by a major officer. Historical information is commonly included as the introductory portion to a manual of office rules and regulations.

Multiple-Purpose Manual

This type of manual represents a combination of any two or all of the types that have been discussed. The company's needs, the size of the enterprise, and the philosophy of the top managers usually determine the makeup. The outline of a multiple-purpose manual might include the following successive topics (1) title, (2) foreword, (3) table of contents, (4) company history, (5) general policies of company, (6) organization, (7) company departments—functions, authorities, and responsibilities, (8) office regulations, (9) office supplies and maintenance, (10) personnel points—hiring, promoting, terminating, sick leave, employee benefits, and social activities, (11) miscellaneous, and (12) index.

Sources for Manual Material

Probably one of the best sources of material for a manual is manuals used by other enterprises. Looking over what has been included in manuals of another company suggests what topics might be covered. The following sources are also recommended (1) minutes of board of directors' meetings, (2) reports of executive conferences, (3) speeches and published articles of executives, (4) bulletins and company circulars, (5) agreements with employees and contracts with unions, (6) grievance records, (7) company magazines or similar publications, and (8) interviews with management members.

Experience shows that, with time, it will be desirable to eliminate certain material and to add other material. The additional material might be secured from the sources mentioned or, because of the unique nature of the information, may be secured from a special source. For example, instructions in the correct use of a new office machine would probably be secured from the manufacture or seller.

Preparation of Manuals

Some orderly process must be followed in the preparation of manuals if they are to be inclusive and to be completed within a reasonable period. The process followed depends a great deal upon the individual in charge of this work. In general, however, it will be helpful to follow a procedure among these lines:

1.   Announce to all members of the enterprise that a manual is to be prepared. Solicit their suggestions and ideas as to what should be included. Appointing a committee of employees often encourages their participation in the preparation of the manual. Special attention should be directed to supervisors, for they are usually rich sources of excellent material.

2.   Draw up a list of all the subjects to be covered by the manual. The purpose of the manual, the cost, and managerial judgment will determine, for the most part, what items are included. Proper subheadings should be made under each main topic, and the list should be arranged according to the contemplated main divisions or sections of the manual. A big time-saver in this respect is to use a separate card for each topic and file behind guides. By this means, material can be classified quickly and the list or outline changed with a minimum of effort.

A logical arrangement of the material is most commonly used, but this sequence is not necessarily the most effective in all cases. Consideration should be given to placing the vital information or that which is most interesting in the beginning, using the last portion of the list for data of less importance.

3.   Write the information under each subject. It is advisable to use headings—major and minor—so that the material is well organized and the reader can follow it easily. Check the source data to help insure accuracy in all writing. Source material can be numbered and indexed, and this means of identification tied in with the writing by means of marginal notes. Keep the prospective reader in mind—write so he or she will want to read the manual and understand what it is intended to mean. A simple, friendly, and sincere style is best. Short words and sentences should be employed. Include charts, cartoons, diagrams, and examples in order to gain greater clarity. These illustrations should be in an inexpensive, rough form until it is decided whether they will be included in the final manual. The amount of detail used in the writing depends upon the importance of the subject.

4.   Prepare a limited number of copies for key executives, supervisors,

employee or union representatives, and several key employees. Have them read the manual and submit criticisms and suggestions. Quite often, better ways of expression are found in this way. Sometimes, subjects can be combined, major items previously overlooked can be added, minor points strengthened, and the entire manual improved.

5. Revise the manual and give it to top management members for approval. Corrections and suggestions from the previous step are incorporated. It is well to include a separate statement to the effect that the entire contents are in agreement with the philosophy of top management members and are acceptable to the employees.

6. Send the approved manuscript to the printer. Details regarding size, paper, and type of binding must also be decided. Generally, it is

FIGURE 25–11
Helpful Suggestions for Preparation of Manuals

PAGE SIZE
  Intended for carrying in pocket, the 6¼ × 4½-inch* is excellent.
  For use as reference on a desk, the 11 × 8½-inch is very satisfactory.
  If printed, the 6 × 9-inch page size is effective. This is the typical book size.
  If typed, the 8½ × 11-inch page size will be preferred by most employees.
  Other popular sizes involving minimum paper waste are 9 × 6-inch, 8½ × 5½-inch, and
    5¼ × 3¾-inch.
WEIGHT OF PAPER
  Determined by the number and size of pages in the manual.
  If under 24 pages, a thick paper can be used.
  For page sizes under 8½ × 5½-inch, use 60 pound paper; for larger size pages, use 70
    pound paper.
ARRANGEMENT OF MATERIAL
  Make headings stand out by generous use of white space around them.
  Place sections most frequently used at front of manual.
  Related sections should be placed close together and interrelated by cross-references.
  Set sections apart by stiff divider page of different-colored paper.
  Either tab sections for ready reference, or use a divider of page size to facilitate a margin
    index.
REMEMBER TO–
  Use color for headings, borders, and drawings to give special emphasis and effect.
  Select type of binding–side or saddle wire stitching, screw post, prong fasteners, ring bin-
    der, wire or plastic edge binding-depending upon usage, cost, and appearance.
  Make the cover attractive by using a clear, brief title and well-selected artwork.
  Include a table of contents and an index so that the reader can quickly find the desired
    topic.

  * For bound manuals, the dimension of the binding side is given first.

well to seek competent advice in these matters. Figure 25–11 offers helpful suggestions.

Distribution of Manuals

It is paramount to provide a copy to everyone concerned with and in need of the information the manual contains. The extent of distribution depends upon the size of the enterprise; in most cases, one copy of the manual should be available for ready reference in at least each department or division. In cases where manuals pertain to specific jobs, copies should be readily available to every employee on such jobs.

To increase the readership of the manual, it is sometimes given to the employee only during an interview. His attention is directed to specific pages, and he is encouraged to read the entire booklet. In some cases, depending upon the type of manual, it is mailed to the employee's home with an accompanying letter. Forewarning that the manual is to be used as the subject for a forthcoming meeting or group discussion is a very effective means of encouraging readership. In addition, sometimes the employee is requested to sign and to return an enclosed card in the manual as evidence of reading the complete booklet; and in other instances, questions are asked on the card to measure the employee's understanding of the manual contents.

Manual Maintenance

The problem of keeping the manual up to date is ever present. In most enterprises, changes are taking place constantly, owing to new work being added or improvements in current work being made. Revisions of and additions to manuals are constantly in process. New pages must replace the old and be distributed to all holders of the manuals. These changes may be covered either by single sheets or by entire supplements. Frequently, amendments are written on colored paper to attract attention to the change. Also, notations made in red ink in the manual will point out those parts which have been changed, omitted, or amended. When many changes cause the manual to be difficult to read and use, it should be rewritten.

All changes in manuals should be cleared through a central control unit so that proper authorization and conformity in results are obtained. If this is not done, needless confusion and misunderstanding will result. The revised sheets should follow the established form of the manual. New material will probably be added every three to six months, together with certain modifications in the old material. When a considerable number of revised sheets are anticipated, a binding suitable for accommodating these changes should be selected.

An old saying is that the three R's of manuals are easy reading, reference, and revision. Much emphasis is placed upon the last R—revision. To aid manual maintenance an excellent practice is to find out what users of the manual think of it. For example, do they believe it is:

1. Readable—effective writing style, good format, and easy-to-read print?

   2.   Illustrated—where needed, and in sufficient detail?

   3.   Practical—titled properly, directions clearly given, adequate coverage of material and effectively indexed?

   4.   Modern—attractive appearance, and up to date in content?

QUESTIONS

1.   Suggest several ways to help in securing adequate security protection and control.
2.   State three benefits derived from the controlling of office forms. Discuss one of these benefits in some detail.
3.   Discuss the evaluation of present office forms as a definite step in the controlling of office forms.
4.   As an office manager, what actions would you take to provide adequate management over office supplies?
5.   Distinguish carefully between the elements in each of the following pairs:
    a.   Controlling and auditing.
    b.   Historical manual and manual of policies.
    c.   An 11 × 8½ manual and an 8½ × 11 manual.
    d.   Managerial controlling and manuals.
6.   List and briefly comment on six basic requirements for success of office manuals.
7.   Discuss controlling of telephone calls in an office.
8.   What are the two stages of office auditing and for what purposes are each conducted?
9.   For each of the following, indicate in what type of office manual you would expect to find the information:
    a.   Practices to be followed in computer data processing.
    b.   Conditions under which books from the company library can be borrowed and taken home.
    c.   The philosophy and working principles followed by Jonathan Rosewell Heinmann, founder of Heinmann and Hertz, Inc.
    d.   General office routines to be followed by all office employees.
10.   Discuss the controlling of reports.
11.   What are some common purposes for which an office manual can be used?
12.   Discuss some important considerations pertaining to the maintenance and updating of office manuals.

CASE PROBLEMS

Case 25–1. Craig Corporation

When Charles Harvey, an assistant bookkeeper with Craig Corporation for nine years, was told by his supervisor that the corporation's percentage of profit was mysteriously off from the previous 6-month period, he offered to assist in reviewing the books and in helping to locate the cause of the discrepancy. Harvey handled the preparation of all corporate checks as well as the clearing of invoices for accounts payable.

Initial routine checkups failed to disclose any source for the loss which is estimated by Earl McMaster, treasurer, at around $75,000. Never had the corporation experienced any loss due to embezzlement or theft before this incident. Mr. McMaster vowed to find the explanation for the loss. Mr. Harvey was under some suspicion since within the past several months he returned from a lavish vacation, had purchased a large new automobile, and was given to bragging about his rather extensive and expensive wardrobe which included several exclusive sport jackets. Such behavior was strange to those who knew Mr. Harvey for the past five to ten years. When casually asked how he could afford to live so well, Mr. Harvey implied that he received a substantial amount of insurance money left to him by a wealthy uncle.

Mr. McMaster hired a private investigator to look into Mr. Harvey's financial affairs, but no evidence of his receiving any insurance money was found. However, a number of his creditors and friends indicated he appeared to be an upright citizen, paid all his bills, was devoted to his wife and three children, and gave the impression of being a competent and reliable employee.

In addition, Mr. McMaster himself started reviewing the corporation's books, but found no discrepancies. Then he announced to all office employees that a complete check on all sales transactions for the entire past year was to start immediately by an outside firm. Sales orders, inventory counts, all checks received and all checks paid would be reviewed. It was to be a complete and thorough search and review—no area would be left uncovered.

Several hours after this announcement, Mr. Harvey went to Mr. McMaster's office and confessed having embezzled "quite a sum of money" over the past four months from the corporation. He did not know the exact amount. When asked how he did this, Mr. Harvey replied, "I prepared one check for the payment of an invoice and would have it signed by either Mr. Crum, Mr. Verley, or Mr. DeLasalle (all authorized officers). Then I would prepare a duplicate check and get it signed by a different authorized officer. I always had the officer sign some ten or twelve checks at a time as this way he did not pay much attention as to whom the checks were made out. I took the second check, made out to a fictitious person, cashed it anywhere I could, and pocketed the proceeds.

McMaster: I just can't believe it. You've been with us for nearly ten years.

Harvey: Yes. I don't know why I did this, Mr. McMaster. Honestly I don't. I'm sorry. At home I have about $3,000 in cash which I'll bring to you tomorrow.

McMaster: Yes. As best I know at the moment, the corporation is short about $87,000.

Questions:

1. What audits or controls should Mr. McMaster follow from now on to ensure that a repeat of embezzlement does not occur? Discuss.

2. What action pertaining to the corporation's operations do you suggest Mr. McMaster take? Why?
3. What action should Mr. McMaster take regarding Mr. Harvey? Justify your views.

Case 25–2. Sherwood State Bank

The managers of Sherwood State Bank, one of the largest in its city, have decided to install automatic cash-dispensing machines at its home office and branches. The machines will be located in the street walls so that customers can withdraw funds (even dollar amounts-no cents) from their accounts 24 hours a day every day of the year. The machines are sturdy and strong enough to resist any physical attack. The money is stored well back and away from the exposed front face of the machine so that the probability of a street robbery of money from the machine is practically zero. The machines at the various locations will form a network connected to the bank's central line control computer which has access to the data processing center and, in turn, to the information on customers' accounts.

According to present plans, to withdraw funds a customer will insert a bank card into an opening, key the amount to be withdrawn, and wait 30 seconds for the money to be vended to him or her. The bank card contains two magnetic stripes readable by the machine. When inserted in the opening, a teleprocessing message is sent to the computer which automatically inspects the customer's account, transmits the information to the cash dispensing machine, and indicates whether the money should be dispensed. If the answer is "yes", meaning there are sufficient funds in the account, the machine automatically dispenses the requested sum and debits the user's bank account. The money capacity of each machine is $4,000 made up of $1, $5, $10, and $20 bills. It is estimated that each machine will be loaded once a day.

Questions:

1. Do you agree with the bank's decision to install the cash dispensing machines? Why?
2. To obtain absolute computer security and avoid any improper vending of funds, do you believe any additional controls are necessary? Discuss fully.
3. What hazards or occurrence of street robberies of cash do you envision? How might these possibilities be eliminated? Elaborate on your answer.

Case 25–3. Clenndenning Company

Ted Woodruff filled out a form for one pad of paper, a box of paper clips, and six large manila envelopes. He deposited this form in the office supplies control basket on the table near the door to the office supplies room. Ted was following the "help yourself" supplies arrangement which had been followed by the company for some time. The filled out forms were collected and reviewed weekly by Craig McKelvey, the assistant office manager, who used the information for reordering supplies reaching a low inventory. Actually, the current system did not work too well. Shortages of items were frequent and Craig McKelvey believed that some employees failed to fill out the required form correctly or, in some cases, not at all. He therefore spent some of his time watching the action around the storeroom to see if he could discover the cause or causes of discrepancies in the supplies. He observed Ted entering the storeroom and emerging ten minutes later with a large wrapped bundle under his arm. Going to his desk, Ted placed the bundle in a desk drawer and resumed his work.

Later, at quitting time Craig observed that Ted removed the bundle from his desk drawer and started down the aisle with other employees leaving for home. Just before passing the doorway leading to the reception room and then to the outside, Ted was stopped by Craig who inquired if the package he had was his own. Ted said that it was. Craig's questions and disclosures resolved that the bundle contained expensive company supplies. After further questioning Ted admitted he was taking the supplies home for use by himself and his family. He added that he frequently did company work at night in his home. Relieved of the bundle, Ted was permitted to go home, but was requested to report to Edward Lasser, the office manager, first thing in the morning.

Next morning Mr. Lasser told Ted his action was strictly against company policy and he was discharged. Ted asked for another chance, pointing out that he had been with the company four years, and other employees took supplies all the time from the storeroom without filling out any form whatever and many of these supplies were taken by the employees to their homes.

Questions:

1. What major conditions have contributed to this situation taking place?
2. Evaluate Ted's behavior. Craig's behavior.
3. Did Mr. Lasser handle the situation correctly? Why?

Case 25–4. Van Debur Corporation

After three days on her new job with Van Debur Corporation, Marilyn Veit, a private secretary for the treasurer of the corporation, had an interview with her superior. She expressed the opinion that the morale of the office employees seemed low, especially of those in the correspondence section. She believed it would help to prepare a manual for them which, among other things, would give information about the corporation's history and the importance of its products as well as definite aids in typing letters and sundry tasks of employees in the section. The treasurer listened attentively to the suggestions, congratulated Marilyn, and authorized her to get together her ideas and some samples of what the proposed manual would be like. He informed the office manager of his decision. The office manager reports to the treasurer.

Marilyn talked with the supervisor of the correspondence section, who offered to assist in every way possible. However, she told Marilyn that a manual would not improve morale. What the employees want is more money, but the corporation will not give it to them. She explained the work to Marilyn and gave her samples of work requested. When Marilyn suggested talking to one or two selected employees of the department, the supervisor countered that this was not advisable, so Marilyn dropped the request. Later, in talking with the treasurer, Marilyn learned that none of the office departments had a manual, that any conversation with office employees should be cleared with their supervisors, and that the corporation very infrequently changed systems in use, the tendency being to stay with established conditions and practices of conducting the work.

Questions:

1. Enumerate the types of information you suggest be included in the proposed manual.
2. Do you believe the proposed manual is appropriate and will be helpful? Discuss.
3. What action do you suggest Marilyn Veit take? Why?

Chapter **26**

Controlling Office Time-Use

> *This time, like all other times, is a very good one,*
> *if we but know what to do with it.*
>
> Ralph Waldo Emerson

The use of time, or time-use, is a major area of office controlling. Using time effectively so that you manage time rather than time managing you is the basic theme. The accomplishing of work is desired *within specific time limits.* The office work is to be completed, but how much time will it require in keeping with fair, reasonable, and adequate time controls. Our discussion starts with the basic importance of time and how it is spent, followed by considerations of the new short work-weeks. We then move on to the subject area of the need and the determination of time standards and of time-use controlling.

Importance of Time

Time is a priceless possession; it cannot be bought, stored, or replenished and to each individual its supply is limited. Yet many of us spend our limited allotment in a way that suggests a belief that in some way our supply of time is limitless. How time is used is an important success factor not only in living a life, but also in objective accomplishment. Some managers keep on top of their job, the work gets done without pressure and seemingly with no oppressive responsibilities. In contrast, other managers experience endless deadlines, constant pressure, and the feeling of frustration that they have more work than they have time for. Yet both groups have identical hours each day, the same number of days in a week, and in a month. Why the difference? Proper use of time which comes about through good planning and especially controlling how time is used, or time-use controlling.

Like all controlling, information is needed on what is being achieved now. Few know how they are spending their time. An effective approach is to keep a "log of time spent" for a period of two weeks. For each five-minute work period, make an entry on what activity that time was spent. Then, classify these data by major tasks and express as a percentages of the total time. You now have a factual background of present time expenditures. By asking questions, try to evaluate these current time expenditures. Are these the types of activities that your time should be devoted to? Where are the excesses? Are activites balanced? Which ones can be cut down or even eliminated? Actually you are comparing achievement to an expectancy or standard of what you feel should be accomplished, and hence, are following the familiar controlling steps.

What matters is what is done with time, not the time itself. You have all the time there is. The challenge is what are you going to do with it. Think in terms of activities in relation to time, not the time itself. Strive to include only activities that are purposive—that lead as directly as possible to goal achievement. This viewpoint will assist in revealing habitual time wasters such as meetings, visiting and visitors, and dreaming, not doing. This is not to say that these activities should be avoided in their entirety. Meetings, for example, serve very useful purposes, but they need to be controlled from the time-use viewpoint. Giving advance notice as to the purpose of the meeting, determining the proper sequence of points to be discussed, and starting promptly and setting a deadline for adjourning, indicate helpful practices to follow.

EFFECTIVE USE OF TIME

Success in effective use of time commonly features several basic concepts. The first is write down the things that must be done during the coming week. Include everything. Number the items and assign them priority. By so doing the mind is relieved of much detail that otherwise would have to be remembered. Of course, long-range planning will also be practiced. But in making the most of time, short one-week periods for controlling purposes are advocated. Second, check off the required activities on your week's list as you accomplish them. Concentrate on one activity at a time. Stay with it until finished or a logical stopping point has been reached. Interruptions are certain to occur, but try to defer them or at least shorten them with a "I'm busy right now. Can we take care of it this afternoon?" Stick tenaciously to the scheduled task even though considerable self-discipline may be required. Third, work one day at a time. Know exactly what is to be done that day and concentrate your thoughts and efforts on it. Don't get side-tracked by thinking unduly about either the past or the future. Let the present day—today—absorb your energies and contribute to good achievement. Remember you are living today—this very moment. Now is when you are or are not accomplishing something. Realize each day is a gift, it may never be offered again. Use it wisely—for definite work accomplishment, but balanced with rest and recreation so that each day is a miniature lifetime, a reflection of time-use at its best.

Work Weektime and Flextime

A number of offices, some very large, have adopted a work-week schedule different from that of the well known 5-day 40 hour week with 2 days off (5/2). Among the more common new time arrangements are the 4-day 40 hour week with 3 days off (4/3); the 3-day 36 hour week with 4 days off (3/4); and the 7-day 70 hour week with 7 days off (7/7). The most popular of these arrangements is the 4/3 week. Companies using it claim employees like it, absenteeism is reduced, productivity shows a slight increase, and it provides an extra day for leisure.

The 3/4 week also has a number of followers. Strongly influenced by the computer operation which economically should be utilized 24 hours a day, six or seven days a week, the 3/4 week provides for around-the-clock operation. Basically four teams are used and in its simplest format, on Monday, Tuesday, and Wednesday team A works 8 A.M. to 8 P.M. and team B from 8 P.M. to 8 A.M. On Thursday, Friday, and Saturday, team C works 8 A.M. to 8 P.M. and team D works 8 P.M. to 8 A.M. The shifts can be rotated or each team can work day shifts for a month or for two weeks and then night shifts for a month or for two weeks. Interesting work patterns have been devised so that by rotation an employee works Saturday night only once in 28 days. Commonly there is a 30-minute shift overlap, that is the hours 8 to 8:30. For vacation allowance, three 12-hour work days are considered the equivalent of 5 vacation days. Replacements needed for vacationing and sick employees are easily taken care of by employees willing to come in for overtime work on their free days.

Do unions favor these shorter work weeks? Some don't, some do. Those that don't, believe that the typical employee gets too tired working successive days of long hours. They prefer not to have over 8-hour work days. In contrast, those favoring the shorter week state that the employees favor it—they have more usable leisure time and suffer no reduction in pay. Some offices with unions have adopted the shorter work week during the summer months only and report good success with it.

Flextime refers to giving employees wide flexibility in choosing their own working hours. Designed originally for office and research laboratories, it has been adopted for many different types of work. Originating in Europe, it is now followed by many organizations in the United States. Flextime is designed to give employees sufficient and convenient time to accommodate their personal wants and thus hopefully to reduce absenteeism and turnover, and to increase productivity and job satisfaction. The hours selected for work must be within the limits to maintain work schedules during peak loads. Commonly referred to as "core time," it is the period during which every employee works—often 10 A.M.–noon and 1–3 P.M. To illustrate, assume regular office hours of 9 A.M.–noon and 1–5 P.M.: Employee A might select to work from 7 A.M.–noon and 1–3 P.M. and leave to keep a physician's appointment. The next day Employee A may work regular hours. Time for lunch at some companies is fixed, at others it is flexible. When the employee is permitted to change working hours from day to day, it is referred to as "gliding time." Further, the "individual working time" plan may be followed. In this plan the employee selects which of several available fixed work schedules he or she prefers for a given future period, commonly one month. An interesting by-product of Flextime is the relieving of traffic jams since few employees pick standard starting and quitting times.

OFFICE TIME STANDARDS

Time is the element which is basic and common to all work. The important questions are: Within what time limits can this amount of work be done? How long should it take? How much time should elapse from the start to the finish?

Time identified with a definite amount of work is known as a "time standard." Formally defined, *time standard is the time required to complete a specified number of work units or a prescribed quantity of work.* Time standards are usually expressed in minutes per piece or 100 pieces, or at a rate of so many pieces per hour. Observe that measurement of work is involved. This identifies the quantity of work as discussed in Chapter 25. We are now assigning time values to a specific number of measurable work units.

The application of time standards is a popular type of controlling. Specifically, time standards help the manager of office work in that:

1. A Basis for Work Distribution Is Provided. Time standards give the office manager the means for determining the number of employees required to get the work out. They afford the establishment of a "fair day's work."

2. The Office Work Can Be Scheduled. Knowledge of the correct amount of time to be allocated to different office tasks expedites the arrangement of the order of work according to a predetermined timetable. By this means, full utilization of all production factors can be more nearly attained. Information on the starting and completing dates for the various tasks can be determined and the office can supply excellent service.

3. *Effectiveness of Department, Division, or Individual Can Be Determined.* The proper and reasonable expectancy for a known working force is provided. Emphasis is directed to "What does the employee accomplish?" not "Is the employee always busy?" Actual productivity compared with standard productivity is determined without any difficulty. Hence, the efficient can be distinguished from the inefficient employee or group and corrective action taken, if needed, to improve the work of the inefficient personnel.

4. *Control over Labor Costs Can Be Exercised.* Time standards make it possible to compare standard against actual labor costs. Control can thus be applied and corrective action taken if costs are out of line. Also, the tendency is to reduce labor cost where good time standards are used.

5. *Human Relations Are Improved.* As stated throughout this book, office employees should know what is expected of them. Basically this provides purpose and helps make the office work more interesting. Generally, the employee will be more satisfied and do better work when he or she knows how much work is supposed to be accomplished within a given time period and further knows the basis upon which the stated work accomplishment is determined. Time standards remove favoritism; they provide needed factual information that aids in treating all employees alike.

Preliminary Essentials

Before attempting to set any office time standard, it is well to observe several key considerations. The first essential is to gain top management support on the need for this type of program. Depending upon the time, place, and situation, this may or may not be a difficult endeavor. Generally this is not a one-meeting session with top managers. Several formal and informal gatherings are common. It must be remembered that problems will arise, some will try to point out the flaws of the proposed program and will bring up the judgment, creativity, and human relations issues discussed previously. Also, care must be exercised to avoid the impression that the program reflects on the management members' ability to manage their departments effectively.

After top management support is assured, personnel to conduct the program should be selected. Mental quickness, ability to grasp details, and skill in human relations are requisites. Experience and education in systems and procedures work and in work measurement are desirable. Normally it is helpful to have some of the analysts taken from the company's personnel and some from outside or from a consulting firm.

Also important is to gather background data including statements on company policies and authority distribution, information on the organization, job descriptions, budget estimates, systems and procedures, and the office layout. Armed with information of this sort, the analysts are in a much better position to gain their acceptance by department heads, their assistants, and the operating employees.

Interviewing with management members supplements the analyst's knowledge of what is being done and the problems involved. The analyst should explain the purpose of the program, major reasons why it is being undertaken, and the general plan of action. Then the analyst should obtain answers to questions pertaining to the department's organization structure; the general flow of work; the work volume, trend, and backlog; overtime requirements; and other pertinent remarks. A friendly, cooperative atmosphere should be created.

At the conclusion of this interview, an informal meeting with all employees of the unit should be held. During this meeting the purpose of the program and what will be expected of each of them are explained. Questions are encouraged and answered.

Subsequently, the work of each employee is carefully identified, and the time standards determined. The analyst should stand ready to discuss any phase of the plan at the manager's or nonmanager's convenience. There must be complete cooperation among analysts, management and nonmanagement personnel because the ultimate success of the program depends upon this cooperation. When mutually agreed upon, implementation of the standards take place. Some adjustments probably will be needed in order to get the program operating smoothly.

The selection of the most appropirate means for determining the time standards is a prime decision. Different means exist and they vary in respect to various criteria as shown in Figure 26–1. For example, the cost of determining the time standard varies from low to high, among the seven means included. These data are relative and serve as a guide only. Individual considerations determine which means to utilize in a specific case. Discussion of these means will now be made.

Subjective Judgment

Time standards set through subjective judgment are sometimes referred to as rule-of-thumb standards. They are based only on the experience and guess of the management member. It is strongly recommended that the manager refrain from the use of such time standards. Even when an accurate guess in establishing the standard has been made,

FIGURE 26–1
Selected Criteria Compared to Seven Means for Determining Time Standards

| | Time Standard Means | | | | | | |
Criteria	Subjective Judgment	Past Performance Records	Work Sampling	Standard Time Data	Stopwatch Study	Standard Data from Stopwatch Study	Report Activity System
1. Cost of determining	Low	Medium	Medium	High	High	High	Medium
2. Time to measure and establish standards	Fast	Fast	Average	Slow	Average	Slow	Average
3. Training and skill required	Low	Low	Low	High	Average	High	Low
4. Relative preciseness	Low	Medium	Medium	High	High	High	Medium
5. Group or individual work application	G or I	G or I	G or I	I	I	I	G or I
6. Assistance in methods improvement	Low	Low	Low	High	Average	High	Average
7. Satisfactory for work variation by volume	Yes	Yes	Yes	No	No	No	Yes
8. Satisfactory for work variation by type of work	Yes	Yes	Yes	No	No	No	Yes
9. Acceptance by employee	High	High	Medium	Medium	Low	Medium	Medium
10. Interruptions to work operations	Low	Low	Medium	Low	Medium	Low	Medium

it is extremely difficult to explain and justify the estimate. Frequently, disagreement over the guess arises and may cause problems.

Past Performance Records

This means consists of recording what is happening. To illustrate, assume billings written as the work measurement unit. The recordings will show accomplishments day by day or week by week as follows: the number of units on hand at the beginning of the period, the number received during the period, the number completed, and the number at the end of the period. These are basic data. The actual performance time standard is derived by dividing the number of total man-hours worked by the number of billings processed. Trends, variations, maximum work loads, and the like can be evolved and subsequently utilized in controlling the work.

Figure 26–2 illustrates the development of a time standard from past

FIGURE 26–2
Data Used to Develop Time Standards from Past Performance Records

| Job Classification | Rank Number | For Month of April, 197– | | Hours Spent on | | |
		Days Worked	Hours Worked	Corre- sponding	Copy- ing	Storing and Retrieving
Supervisor	3	22	462	154	154	154
Assistant Supervisor	2	22	308	154		154
Correspondents	4	20	560	560		
Transcribers	6	20	840	840		
Clerks	5	21	735	147	441	147
Storing and retrieving sorter	1	21	147			147
Storing and retrieving clerks	4	20	560			560
Total time				1,855	595	1,162
Completed work volume				2,610	9,915	4,150
Standard time per work unit				0.71	0.06	0.28

records which have been maintained for purposes other than time control. Also, as will be pointed out, estimates concerning these past records have been used. It has been decided to use a previous month as a base period. Attendance records show how much time was actually worked. The volume of work turned out was obtained from production records maintained by the supervisors. An estimate was made on how each employee divided his time on each type of work. For example, the total time of 735 hours for the five clerks was divided 147, 441,

147 to corresponding, copying, and storing and retrieving respectively. The total time for each work category is divided by the completed work volume to give a standard time per work unit as indicated on the bottom line of the figure.

Time standards derived in this manner are helpful. They identify areas for further investigation and they serve as a reference for future accomplishment. Effective for interoffice comparisons and inexpensive, they give some idea of how much time is being taken and raise the question of whether this appears reasonable. They are also usable in federal offices where watch time study may be prohibited by clauses in appropriation bills. The approach can be refined to apply to smaller identifiable types of work, and accurate counts of both the time spent on each work type and the number of each work units can be achieved. For these purposes it is helpful to follow these steps: (1) determine the basic operation being performed, (2) summarize these operations to know what is performed by the total organization or the portion of it being considered, (3) ascertain the time spent in performing each of the basic operations, (4) keep a count of the work units produced under each operation, (5) relate the time spent and the work count of steps 3 and 4, and (6) utilize the time standard so derived to determine future effectiveness of each of the included organizational units.

As mentioned above, a simple and common technique followed for finding out the amount of time spent on different operations is a log of employee time usually conducted by the employee himself. Each employee keeps a record by minutes of how the work days are spent and gives this information to the superior or analyst who calculates the standards. Normally at least a period of a minimum of two weeks is used to include the effect of cyclical work characteristics. This approach is sometimes referred to as the *time ladder approach,* the name comes from the fact that the data are recorded on survey sheets listing time by minutes in columnar form such as 9:00, 9:01, 9:02, 9:03, and so forth. The employee writes opposite these time values indicating how the time was spent. For example, between 9:00 and 9:20, may be written "reading mail," and between 9:20 and 9:25 "sorting mail."

As already indicated, time standards from past performance have management value. It should be observed, however, that in the final analysis, such standards are really *records of "what is," rather than "what should be."*

Work Sampling

Work sampling is a means employing random observations whereby the ratio of delays and of elements of work to the total process time is determined. It is based on the law of probability. If a comparatively large number of observations are taken at random intervals, the ratio between the observed frequency of a particular activity to the total number of observations taken will approximate the correct percentage of that activity. The technique consists of random but frequent spot checking of the activity of one or more office employees and the recording of the activity at the moment it is observed. From the work sample obtained, the time spent on each type of operation in relation to the total time available is determined.

Figure 26–3 clarifies the manner of establishing office time standards

FIGURE 26–3
Determining Time Standards from Work Sampling Observations

(1)	(2) No. of Observations	(3)	(4)	(5) Work Volume	(6) [(4) ÷ (5)] Unit Time Standard
Type of Work	tions	Percent	Minutes	Volume	Standard
1. Type...............	540	29.8	6,700	5,135	1.31 min.
2. Calculate...........	217	12.0	2,698	5,135	0.53
3. Check	154	8.5	1,911	5,135	0.37
4. File...............	142	7.9	1,777	7,460	0.24
5. Sort	80	4.4	989	7,460	0.13
6. Telephone..........	133	7.4	1,664	514	3.24
7. Misc...............	120	6.6	1,484	–	–
8. Idle...............	105	5.8	1,304	–	–
9. Personal	319	17.6	3,958	–	–
(includes lunch)					
Total...........	1,810	100.0	22,485		

from work sampling. Column 1 shows the different types of work observed and column 2 the observations of each type, making up a total of 1,810 observations. Column 4 reveals that the total work time period over which these observations were made was 22,485 minutes. From official records and counts, we obtain the data of column 5 on work volume for the total work time period. With these basic data, we calculate the remaining data as shown in Figure 26–3. To illustrate, referring to line 1 the calculations for the value under column 3, 540 divided by 1,810, or 29.8 percent; for column 4, 29.8 percent of the total units, 22,485, or 6,700 minutes; for column 6, 6,700 minutes divided by 5,135 units, or 1.31 minutes per unit. The time standards by type of office work are shown in column 6. We have assumed that the total of 22,485 minutes was spent in the same proportion as the observations made.

By work sampling, it is possible to determine effective utilization of time, causes and extent of interference with effective accomplishment, flow of work through an office, and the amount of time devoted to various activities by an employee. The office manager of a large insurance company found, by means of work sampling, that a low utilization of personnel and machines existed in the company's data-processing center. Using these facts as a springboard, the manager, within eight months, by means of control programs, increased machine utilization 17 percent, released 12 rental machines, and won enthusiastic support of supervisors and employees for work sampling as a technique for making jobs less complicated and more productive. Many believe work sampling is one of the most practical and economical means for appraising the time required to perform office work.

Work sampling data can be secured by means of observations by the supervisor. The degree of reliability obtained is increased by increasing the number of observations. The method is economical and measures cyclic effect, a very important concept in most office work. However, it is not practical to take a sampling of too many breakdowns of a job. Work sampling is better suited to broad operations. It is recommended for standards for purposes of cost control, group effectiveness, planning personnel needs, and for taking corrective action. Care must be taken to avoid purposeful behavior by the employee being observed. For example, when the observation starts, the employee may not continue to work at a normal pattern but strive to appear busier and begin moving papers, straightening up the work area, and engaging in similar activities. Such actions decrease the accuracy of the data. To combat this, use the supervisor or a stationary observer throughout the study so that the employee does not know when to exercise purposeful behavior. However, the stationary observer eliminates cost advantages of work sampling and reverts to the all-day study with its relatively high costs. Probably the best ways to eliminate purposeful behavior are (1) to use and train the supervisor as the observer and (2) to explain thoroughly the need and manner of performing the study in order to win the employee's complete cooperation.

Standard Time Data

The data for this means of determining time standards are based upon fundamental motions or muscular movements for which basic time standards have been developed. The time values vary with the nature of the motion and the conditions under which it is made. For example, movement of an arm 4 inches is given a certain time value, turning the wrist has another value, and so forth. Most standard time data are expressed as tables of values. To utilize this material, the standard time data person analyzes each manual operation into the basic motions which are necessary in performing the task. The time for each required basic motion is taken from the table of values and added to determine the time standard for the entire task.

FIGURE 26–4
Data from a Standard Time Study

NO.	ELEMENTAL DESCRIPTION (LEFT HAND)	MOTION ANALYSIS	ELEM. TIME	CUMULATIVE TIME	TIME	ELEM. TIME	MOTION ANALYSIS	ELEMENTAL DESCRIPTION (RIGHT HAND)	NO.
1					.0080	.0080	A20 D	R to sheet	1
2					0080		Ct Gr	1st Gr	2
3					.0103	.0023	F1P	Separate	3
4		Wait	.0119	0119	.0119	.0016	F1	Gr	4
5	R to sheet	A20D	.0080	0199	.0199	.0080	A20D	M sheet to typewriter	5
6	Gr sheet	1/2 F1	.0008	0207	.0207	.0008	Hold		6
7	Approach typewriter roller	A1SD	.0034	0241	.0241	.0034	A1SD	Approach typewriter roller	7
8	A1 (OTS-TD .074")	1-1/2A1SD	.0051	0292	.0249	.0008	1/2 F1	Rl sheet	8
9	GD 5"	1-1/2A1SD 30%.0015		0303	.0303	.0054	A8D	R to roller knob	9
10	IND	A1SD	.0034	0341	.0311	.0008	1/2 F1	Gr roller knob	10
11	INS	A1D	.0026	0367	.0367	.0056	Wait		11
12	Rl paper	1/2 F1	.0008	0375	.0398	.0031	FS180°	Turn roller knob	12
13	R to carriage release	A80	.0054	0429	.0406	.0008	1/2 F1	Rl roller knob	13
14	Gr carriage release	1/2 F1	.0008	0437	.0437	.0031	FS180°	R to roller knob	14
15					.0445	.0008	1/2 F1	Gr roller knob	15
16					.0601	.0156 .0078x2		Repeat elements Nos.12-15	16
17		Wait	.0192	0629	.0629	.0028	FS45°SD	Turn to final line	17
18	Depress carriage release	F1	.0016	0645	.0645	.0016	Hold		18
19	Push carriage to 1st position	VA4SD	.0048	0693	.0693	.0048	VA4SD	Pull carriage to 1st position	19
20	A1 (OTS-TD .100")	1-1/4A1SD	.0043	0736	.0736	.0043	1-1/4A1SD	A1 (OTS-TD .100")	20

OPERATION NAME: Obtain and put an original sheet of paper into typewriter   DEPT. Sales Analysis   SHEET 1 OF 2

TOTAL SELECT TIME: _____ X _____ CONVERSION = _____ HPC   STANDARD PRODUCTION PER HOUR (100 + HPC) _____ EHO

REMARKS:

Courtesy: Wofac Corp., Moorestown,, N.J.

Figure 26–4 shows the standard time values for the elemental motions required to obtain and put an original sheet of paper into a typewriter. On line 4, for example, right hand, the elemental time of 0.0016 of a minute is the time allotted for a motion, *F1*, meaning fingers open 1 inch; and the elemental description is *Gr*, meaning grasp. Similarly, on line 5, the standard time value of 0.0080 of a minute is given *A20D*, arm extended 20 inches to *M*, or move, sheet to typewriter.

Standard time data are predetermined time values for definite basic motion. By their use, time standards can be set before the work is actually performed—especially useful in planning a new or a changed system or procedure. Standard time data are best suited for high-volume, repetitive tasks where manual motions predominate. Even though applicable for reading and mental computations, it is often difficult to convince employees of the data's validity for such work. Three well-known standard time data systems are Work Factor, Methods-Time Measurement, and Office Manning Controls.

STOPWATCH STUDY

The time standard developed from this source applies to specific work done under specific conditions, including the workplace, method, and material. It is not a universal time standard. The work selected for study should be repetitive and of sufficient volume to warrant careful analysis. The proper workplace should be resolved and the work motions economized. There is no point in establishing carefully set time values for work that is performed ineffectively and is soon to be improved. The variable job elements which are affected by changing conditions should be under control. The stopwatch should be one which reads directly in one hundredths (0.01) of a minute. Keeping all values in these units simplifies calculations.

The employee selected for observation should be an above-average type, not because more work is accomplished, but because that employee will probably have the best motions and rhythm in the work. This does not mean that the time standards to be determined will require an above-average worker. Discussion of this point will be given in later paragraphs. Complete cooperation of the employee must be secured. This means, among other things, explaining what is being done, and why, plus answering any questions the employee may have. When ready, take a position a little to one side of and behind the employee. To become familiar with the task, watch the completion of it several times.

The job is divided into components or small motions that can be observed and timed. An illustration of such components for the work of posting material requisition notices on card files is shown by Figure 26–5. The eight components heading up a like number of columns are handprinted across the top of the form.

Next, the time observations are recorded. Under each column appear the letter T for *elapsed* time, and the letter R, for the *reading* of the watch. In the "continuous reading" method the watch is permitted to keep running, the watch reading being noted at the completion of the element and recorded on the form under the R heading of the proper column, and proceeding from left to right, or through the successive eight elements. Subtracting the preceeding from the immediately following cumulative reading gives the value of T, or elapsed time. To illustrate, under column 2, first horizontal line, the value of 9 is obtained by subtracting 12, the previous R, from 21, the immediately following R value.

In the illustration, nine cycles (horizontal lines) or readings were made. Usually this number, a total of about 15 to 20 minutes, is required to derive satisfactory results. It is possible to determine mathematically how many cycles represent a reliable sample. Sometimes interruptions occur as shown on the third line under element 5. It is coded by letter

FIGURE 26–5
Time-Study Data Sheet for an Office Task

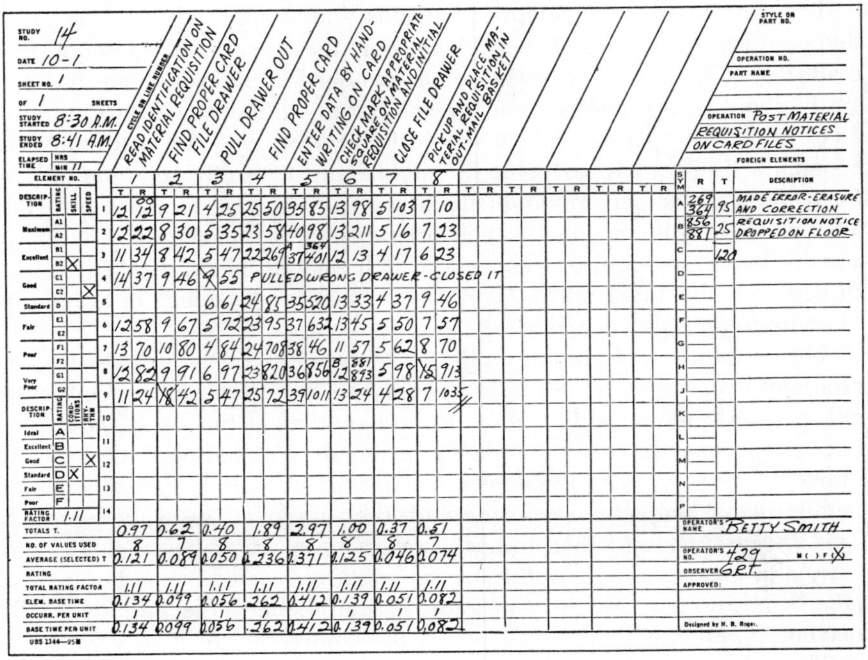

A and is explained under "foreign elements" space on the extreme right of form.

For each element, or vertical column, the average time is calculated. Since we want the time standard for the average employee we adjust this average observed time to the time of the average employee. We do this by "leveling." On the far left, evaluation of the observed employee's skill, effort, working conditions, and consistency are given. These leveling factors give a total level rating factor of 1.11 (determined by consulting a table) which means our observed employee is above the average employee. To convert to the average employee, we multiply our observed time by 1.11, in effect allowing greater time to the average employee upon whom the standard is based. The leveled values per element (bottom line of the figure) are added giving a sum of 1.235. To this is added an allowance for personnel needs, fatigue, and unavoidable delays. Frequently this is 15 to 20 percent. Using 20 percent, the time standard is 1.482 (1.235 plus 20 percent of 1.235). This is in minutes. Expressed as units per hour, the value is 40.5 (60/1.482). Again, keep in mind that this value is the expectancy of the control process. By comparing what is accomplished to this expectancy and making correction for deviation, the process of controlling is carried out.

Standard Data from Stopwatch Study

This means utilizes predetermined or standard data values derived from the data of many actual stopwatch studies from which it is possible to determine the basic allowable times for elements which are common to many tasks. To do this, relationships between time and some meaningful variable, such as distance, size, or weight, are determined. For example, consider the element "pulling out file drawer." From many actual stopwatch studies, the time values for this element are obtained. Some of these values will be for pulling out file drawers a distance of 6 inches, others 10 inches, still others 14 inches, and so on. By mathematical analysis of these data, the relationship between time and distance traveled for the element "pulling out file drawer" can be determined. From this relationship, the amount of time for this element can be predetermined, based on the distance the drawer travels. In similar manner, relationships can be determined for the size of the drawer and the weight of the material in it. The relationships so developed can be expressed as tables of values, as equations, or as graphs.

REPORTING ACTIVITY SYSTEM

Because of varied work load, short job cycles, and changes in work procedures, the more common means for determining time standards (described above) and using them for controlling are sometimes questioned and believed inappropriate for office work. To meet the peculiar conditions of the office, the reporting activity system for office time controlling has been developed and is enjoying increasing favor. In this approach the various job functions in each office department are noted, and improved work methods instituted immediately, if possible. For each function, a reasonable time standard is established using any one of the methods discussed in this chapter. Measurement of the work by major types is then made so that manning tables showing the approximate number of employees required for each type of work can be determined. The supervisor is given these data for the work of the unit. The supervisor's key responsibilities are reiterated in specifics, for example, to regulate the work group in keeping with the work volume being handled, to eliminate idle time, to distribute the work fairly, and to improve human relations by stating reasonable goal expectancies.

A reporting system is applied to provide direct measurement of the work output and to maintain contact between the performance of individual employees and middle management members. A daily report is prepared by each employee showing the volume of work done and the time used. These data are segregated by equally divided intervals during the day, such as two periods in the morning and two periods in the afternoon. This arrangement provides the employee with helpful periodic checkups throughout the day and assists in making the program effective. Figure 26–6 shows the daily individual activity record. Note the activities are identified and, for each, target minutes are supplied. The volume of work completed is recorded four times daily. The overall performance in this case illustrated is 78 percent as shown in lower right of figure. These daily reports are consolidated into weekly reports from which it is easy to spot any improper utilization or coverage, a need for closer supervisory control, reassignment or education of personnel.

EXAMPLES OF OFFICE TIME STANDARDS

The following office time standards have value in connection with various types of office work. They are included here to be helpful in a comparative way only. They were determined for specific work methods and conditions prevailing in a particular office and should be used as guides, not goals.

	Units per Hour
1. Typing:	
Type name and account number on card	180
Type labels from typewritten copy	135
Type ledger cards	105
Type report, double space on 8½ X 11-inch paper, one original and one carbon copy	10
Type address on envelope	85
2. Calculating and checking:	
Compute products of 3-digit number by 3-digit number, using machine	500
Add 20 numbers in a column (each number is 3 digits) by machine	2
Compare columns of figures on tape or report, with columns of figures in like order (number of digits per figure compared equals 5)	4,800
Count items on a tape, or lines on a sheet	9,400
3. Accounting:	
Pull from source, post account to ledger sheet by machine, and replace sheet	130
Make entries in ledger (manual)	40
4. Filing and sorting:	
Sort correspondence papers for filing	480
File correspondence papers in alphabetical file	180
Sort 5 X 3-inch cards alphabetically	300
Locate and pull addressing plates from alphabetical file	420
5. Miscellaneous:	
Hand-fold 8½ X 11-inch sheet with one fold	1,200
Seal ordinary envelope (manual)	450
Assemble three sheets of paper, 8½ X 11 inches, and insert in large 9 X 12-inch envelope	575

FIGURE 26–6
Example of Data Used in the Reporting Activity System

Daily Individual Activity Record

Date: Feb. 17, 197–   *Dept.:* S and R   *Name:* Kim Clements

Activity	Measurement Unit	Target Minutes	Volume Completed				Total Volume	Completed Minutes
			7:45–9:45	10:00–12:00	12:45–2:45	3:00–5:00		
Prepare for sorting	items	1.25	11				11	14.0
Sorting	card	0.07	743	786			1529	107.0
Sorting	paper	0.11	140	70			210	23.0
Placing in file	card	1.15			40	49	89	102.0
Placing in file	paper	1.70			12	10	22	37.0
Handling charge-outs	items	2.90		4			4	12.0
Retrieving	card	2.65						
Retrieving	paper	3.85			5		5	19.0
Misc. clerical allowance	allow.	60.00						60.0
Total minutes completed								374.0
Total minutes worked								480.0
Performance percentage								78.0

PERT

Before closing this chapter a few words about PERT (Program Evaluation Review Technique) are in order. PERT deals with time controlling from the large, overall viewpoint. It is inclusive and an example of several related systems and procedures making up what can be termed a project or a network activity. Multistage industrial operations in connection with the development of certain government defense projects or the construction of several buildings simultaneously by the same contractor may constitute the project.

A chart is usually prepared to visualize better the composite necessary operations for the total project. From the beginning to the end of this network activity, there are typically several paths of work sequence that can be followed. Using the chart as a guide, the time required for the longest sequence of operations is computed; this is known as the "critical path," because it time controls the completion of the entire network. A delay in any task along this path would necessarily delay completion of the entire network. In contrast, delay in any other jobs of the project not included in the critical path could, within limits, be delayed without retarding the whole project. Usually some 85 percent of the individual jobs are found in this category; thus, 15 percent of the jobs are critical in content and sequence to the completion of the entire project within a stated period. In other words, PERT highlights the key or critical jobs or work.

Figure 26–7 shows a portion of a PERT chart which ties separate parts of a large project together. The circles with numbers inside are

FIGURE 26–7
Portion of a PERT Chart

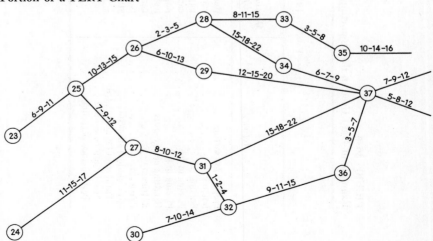

events and represent completion of certain work. The connecting lines are activities and indicate work being done. The time for each activity is shown by the three numbers accompanying each line. For example, the numbers 8–11–15 mean that the first number, 8, is the estimated optimistic time, the second number, 11, the most likely time, and the third number, 15, is the pessimistic time. From these values a weighted average is calculated; this is termed, t_e, or expected time. Various paths or chain of events are now searched for in order to determine possible paths and also the earliest possible and the latest permissible times for each event to be completed. For a complex chart, this work is done by a computer. In our illustration of Figure 26–7 which is a portion of an entire network, considering from event 25 to event 37, we can see that the possible paths are (*a*) 25–26–28–34–37, (*b*) 25–26–29–37, (*c*) 25–27–31–37, or (*d*) 25–27–31–32–36–37. Of these let's assume (*a*) is the longest or requires the most time. This is the critical path between events 25 and 37. Comparing routes (*b*), (*c*), or (*d*) to (*a*) means that (*b*), (*c*), or (*d*) will have extra or slack time in them because they must wait for (*a*) to be completed. Effort is now directed to trading off time now required in (*a*) to either (*b*), (*c*), or (*d*) so that the total completion time can be reduced. If impractical, the work is time controlled very carefully to (*a*) so that the best available schedule is maintained.

Observe that what actions are taken depend upon the situation at each event. To illustrate, we have stated possible actions in terms of routes (*a*), (*b*), (*c*), or (*d*). But route (*a′*), 26–28–34–37, is longer than route (*b′*), 26–29–37, so that there is slack time available for use in (*b′*) when compared to (*a′*). The full solution takes all contingencies into account, for as stated above, the situation at each event is determinant. Also, observe that there is neither a meaningful scale (horizontal or vertical) on a PERT chart nor do the lengths of activity lines have meaning. Values are determined from numerical values only.

QUESTIONS

1. Discuss several suggestions you might give an office manager on the effective use of her or his time.
2. Why should a stopwatch study be made only after the proper workplace has been provided and the motions economized? Are there any exceptions? Explain.
3. Discuss the meaning, advantages, and the conditions under which you as an office manager would approve the use of Flextime.
4. Explain Figure 26–2 in your own words.
5. Identify each of the following:
   a. Critical path.
   b. Time standard.
   c. The 4/3 week.
   d. "Foreign elements" in a stopwatch time study.

6. Explain the following: "Past performance records are actually 'what is,' rather than 'what should be.' "

7. Elaborate on the meaning of the following statement: "You have all the time there is. The challenge is what are you going to do with it."

8. As you see it, does the use of time-use controlling help or hinder the human relationship between a management member and a nonmanagement member? Justify your answer.

9. For what types of office work and under what conditions would you recommend time standards established by standard time data? Discuss.

10. Distinguish carefully between the concepts in each of the following pairs:
    a. Elemental time and time study.
    b. PERT and time ladder approach.
    c. Work sampling and "snap-back" watch readings.
    d. Time standard and leveling factor.

11. Explain Figure 26–3 in your own words.

12. The following data apply to related work. Draw the PERT chart, determine the critical path, and answer how long it will require to complete the entire project.

Activity	Expected Time (Days)	Activity	Expected Time (Days)
A–B	4	F–I	2
A–C	2	I–L	2
A–D	3	I–K	1
B–E	4	J–L	2
C–J	11	J–M	2
D–H	3	K–O	6
H–J	4	L–N	5
E–F	8	M–N	8
E–G	3	N–O	5
G–J	1		

CASE PROBLEMS

Case 26–1. Atwater Manufacturing Company

Office supervisor Jim McCabe is interested in using his time more effectively. For two weeks he has kept a log of his time by 15-minute intervals as indicated by the accompanying data. The code used by McCabe is:

1. Talk with employee about quality or quantity of work
2. Telephone
3. Instruct employee
4. Meeting on scheduling of work
5. Correct mistakes or talking to employees about mistake correcting
6. Counseling
7. Prepare reports
8. Lunch
9. Talk with other supervisors

10. Talk with superiors
11. Study past performance accomplishment data
12. Analyze cost sheets
13. Handle training session
14. Miscellaneous

EXHIBIT 26–1A

	Week 1					Week 2				
Time	M	Tu	W	Th	F	M	Tu	W	Th	F
7:30										
45	1	2	1	14	14	2	2	1	2	14
8:00	9	5	↓	9	2	14	11	9	2	7
15	6	↓	↓	2	5	2	4	5	14	↓
30	2	↓	↓	9	9	2	4	5	9	↓
45	1	4	2	9	9	14	2	2	14	9
9:00	2	2	14	2	8	2	12	6	2	9
15	5	1	10	4	8	6	12	↓	1	2
30	11	↓	↓	↓	2	↓	12	↓	↓	6
45	2	↓	↓	↓	2	↓	9	↓	↓	14
10:00	11	2	↓	6	8	↓	10	2	↓	11
15	9	8	14	6	8	2	6	10	3	14
30	9	↓	↓	1	5	1	↓	↓	↓	↓
45	10	↓	6	↓	5	↓	↓	↓	↓	↓
11:00	10	2	↓	↓	2	↓	9	↓	9	↓
15	9	8	↓	2	12	2	12	14	14	7
30	9	2	↓	2	5	14	12	14	2	7
45	8	8	8	8	8	8	8	8	8	8
12:00	↓	↓	↓	↓	↓	↓	↓	↓	↓	↓
15	↓	↓	↓	↓	↓	↓	↓	↓	↓	↓
30	↓	↓	↓	↓	↓	↓	↓	↓	↓	↓
45	↓	↓	↓	↓	↓	↓	↓	↓	↓	↓
1:00	14	↓	6	1	↓	2	1	↓	↓	↓
15	2	↓	↓	↓	1	10	↓	↓	1	↓
30	4	2	↓	↓	↓	4	↓	14	↓	14
45	12	7	1	6	↓	6	↓	↓	↓	↓
2:00	12	↓	↓	2	↓	7	9	↓	↓	↓
15	2	↓	↓	6	2	↓	9	↓	2	10
30	8	↓	5	6	3	↓	9	2	5	↓
45	14	12	↓	12	↓	↓	12	2	12	↓
3:00	2	12	↓	12	6	↓	12	1	12	↓
15	11	13	14	13	↓	↓	13	↓	13	2
30	↓	↓	2	↓	↓	↓	↓	↓	↓	14
45	↓	↓	14	↓	↓	11	↓	↓	↓	↓
4:00	↓	↓	14	↓	↓	11	↓	14	↓	↓

The position of the code figure indicates the end of the time period. For example, at 7:45, Tuesday, Week 1, the code 2 indicates "telephone" beginning at 7:30 and ending at 7:45.

Questions:

1. Study, consolidate, and analyze these data so that some conclusions can be made regarding what they mean or reveal. What general conclusion do you draw? Discuss.

2. What suggestions do you feel appropriate to make to Jim McCabe?
3. Are you of the opinion that Jim McCabe will have difficulty in following your suggestions? Discuss.

Case 26–2.   Lorne Company

A contact-type duplicating machine is located in the corresponding section of an office where it is convenient to make a duplicate of a letter with handwritten answer on the bottom of the sheet. Use of the machine, however, is for company business by anyone in the office. Both the manager of the credit section of the office and the assistant sales manager of the sales department office, immediately adjacent to the main office, have requested the general manager of Lorne Company to buy each of them a contact duplicating machine. The credit manager states that he uses the duplicating machine very little now because the one in corresponding is being used when he wants to use it. Many times a number of copies were being made and this means too long a wait for him to use the machine. The assistant sales manager points out that the present machine is being cleaned or temporarily out of order too much. She believes it would save her employees much time to have their own duplicating machine.

The general manager asks Michael Miller, the office manager, to look into the situation and give him recommendations as to what to do. Accordingly, Mr. Miller decides to conduct a work sampling study. After some observations and talking with the supervisor of corresponding, he reasons that there are logically eight categories for observation, including (1) machine nonavailable—being used by other than corresponding, (2) machine in use by corresponding for either 1, 2, 3, 4, or 5 or more copies, (3) machine not in use but ready for immediate use, and (4) machine being cleaned or temporarily out of order for any reason. He believes 450–500 observations over a three-week period will provide adequate data. Proceeding with the study, the following data are obtained:

	Observations		
	Week No. 1	*Week No. 2*	*Week No. 3*
Unavailable	22	19	18
Being used for			
1 copy	24	30	41
2 copies	22	26	17
3 copies	3	1	6
4 copies	6	11	6
5 copies or more	5	7	4
Not in use	46	55	57
Being cleaned or temporarily			
out of order	13	13	10

Questions:

1. Complete the table of data by calculating the number of observations (*a*) in each category, (*b*) in each week, and (*c*) in total for the study.
2. Determine the percentage of observations accounted for by each category and the corresponding minutes per workday (480 minutes) for each category.
3. Are the work sampling data complete and conclusive enough to provide the general manager with satisfactory answers? Explain.
4. What recommendation should Mr. Miller make? Why?

Case 26–3.   Evers, Marshall, Rice, and Webster

Mr. Rice, a partner of the law firm of Evers, Marshall, Rice, and Webster, believes very strongly that the present arrangement of having a law secretary assigned to each of the eleven staff attorneys, neither provides the best service for each attorney nor makes the best use of the secretary's time. He decided to do something about it.

His thoughts were that a stenographic pool probably should be adopted, but he knew some of the attorneys were against such an arrangement and probably some of the secretaries, although he wasn't sure what the beliefs were in either group. He decided to secure some data on the present arrangement and so, unknown to anybody in the office, he made frequent observations and recorded the work status of the various secretaries. Collecting data for four weeks, Mr. Rice then analyzed the information and concluded (1) it is difficult to get maximum use of a secretary's skill because the secretary must be available at all times for the supervising attorney, (2) the work fluctuates widely for each secretary—some of the time working is done under great pressure, and some times there is practically nothing to do, and (3) the total present number of eleven secretaries could be reduced to seven under a secretarial pool arrangement with one of the seven being a typist to handle simple copy work requiring no secretarial skill. Under the pool arrangement, Mr. Rice believed each attorney would have adequate secretarial help, the work would be divided fairly among the secretaries, and office costs would be reduced.

At a meeting of the attorneys, Mr. Rice presented his proposal using the data he had collected to substantiate his projected improvements. To his amazement, the attorneys vigorously opposed such a move stating that under his plan the secretary would be unfamiliar with the particular case—its background, deadline dates, and the like. Further, they had grown accustomed to working with one secretary and wished to retain the advantages and rapport of the present arrangement.

Although taken back by their reactions, Mr. Rice still felt that his suggested improvements should in some way take place. Speaking privately to each secretary, he found out that some were for the secretarial pool while others were not. His own secretary suggested that perhaps the installation of a word processing unit might be the answer. A friend of hers, also a legal secretary working in a law office, told her that word processing is used where she works and the results are quite satisfactory. In the other law office she understands the work output of the law secretaries is quite high and they get more money than is paid by Evers, Marshall, Rice, and Webster. "I'm for it if it means more money for me," she added with a grin. "If you want, I'll talk with the other secretaries about it and let you know what they say."

Questions:

1. Comment critically on the actions taken by Mr. Rice.
2. Do you feel Mr. Rice can overcome the objections of the other attorneys? Why?
3. What are your recommendations to Mr. Rice?

Chapter 27

Quality and Quantity Controlling

Beware, as long as you live, of judging [people]
by their outward appearance.

Jean De La Fontaine

An important area of office controlling is that applied to quality of work. Poor quality impedes the essential services of an office. A poorly typed letter, an incorrectly executed office form, an error in extending the cost data, or a misspelled name on a customers' list diminishes the effectiveness of information handling. Some of the work must be done over, some can be "fixed up" by additional expenditure of time and energy, and some is used "as is"—with errors or misstatements undetected, and promising the possibility of subsequent waste.

In reality no office processing is ever completely free of errors. The occurrence will vary depending not only on the particular operation but also on the definition established as to what constitutes an error. What, for example, is an error in letter writing? Is it a misspelled word, incorrect word usage, or an error in grammar? Or does it also include wordiness, inaccuracy of content, vague meaning, and repetition?

Initial Considerations

The first consideration concerning office quality controlling is that it is of major importance. Inadequate quality controlling can result in several types of losses. Paper work errors can cause a wrong decision to be made. Failure to process an inquiry properly might result in the loss of the prospective sale from a very important customer. Or poor quality can jeopardize good will. A customer's payment improperly

691

posted is illustrative. Further, detecting and correcting office errors result in loss of time and money. Frequently, this loss is unnoticed; nevertheless, it is present.

Secondly, making quality is a personal matter. Quality of work in the office is conditioned more by the employee than by any other factor. The employee's attitude toward the job and the desire to do quality work are governing. Discussion of errors with the employee committing them, encouragement for greater accuracy, and suggestions on ways to accomplish improvement are prime courses to follow. Ideally every error found should be reviewed with the employee committing it. As a routine practice, every office employee should be informed on the quality of his or her work and where greater care might be exercised. But positiveness about the program should be stressed. It is vital that the employee accept responsibility for the particular work proposed and likewise know that any improvements in procedures and methods or any other ideas to help attain near perfect quality are welcomed. The effort is to have an army of quality- and reliability-conscious people who are providing the office product or service, not a mass of in-process inspectors and clerks. Of course, some errors result from nonpersonal causes. Included are improper operation of machine, poor alignment of form, short circuit with machine, and so forth. But these are usually quickly spotted by the alert employee and can be corrected before too much improper work is done.

Furthermore, there is the initial consideration to secure information on the present quality being attained. What types and how much quality controlling include the amount of checking presently being followed and the results being obtained. Such data will reveal the adequacy of present quality controls used. To obtain such data, review present systems and procedures and observe what types of checks are performed, how frequent such checks are made, which checks involve a large segment of the total work done, and which work is highly repetitive. These requirements may require many hours of time of management personnel, but it is not always necessary for in many instances. it is feasible for each employee to keep a tally of his or her respective work items reviewed and the errors found over a specified period, perhaps two to four weeks. Figure 27–1 shows a typical example which pertains to order writing. For the week indicated a total of 4.1 percent errors were committed.

Fourth, there is the consideration of balancing the cost of quality controlling to the cost of errors in order to determine if the review is justified. The task of office quality controlling resolves ultimately into a balancing of the time and cost of checking against the benefits realized. As the old saying goes, "The cost of the medicine normally should not be greater than the cost of the disease." The cost becomes excessive

FIGURE 27–1
Tally Sheet for Recording Errors

Department: Order writing	Employee: Polly Myers						
Week Ending: 7/14	Supervisor: Harriet Hermes						
Type of error	*M*	*Tu*	*W*	*Th*	*F*	*Sat*	*Total*
Product name incorrect.	–	–	3	–	–	–	3
Product price incorrect.	–	2	–	1	–	–	3
Wrong extension	–	–	–	1	1	–	2
Incorrect heading	1	–	–	–	–	–	1
Transaction omitted	–	–	–	–	–	–	–
Other	1	–	–	–	–	–	1
Total errors	2	2	3	2	1	–	10
Total units.	48	51	46	50	50	–	245
Percentage of errors	4.2	3.9	6.5	4.0	2.0	–	4.1

usually because the control is either over- or under-adequate, is too time consuming, or is not effective in disclosing the errors and possible causes for them.

APPROACHES TO OFFICE QUALITY CONTROLLING

There are three basic approaches to office quality controlling (1) checking all the work, (2) spot checking the work, and (3) statistical quality control. Checking all the work is commonly called 100 percent inspection whereby each work item—a filled out form, a letter, or a column of figures is gone over to verify the correctness of the work. Some shortcuts in checking all the work are possible, for example, proofing masters only of duplicated material, certain shortcuts for checking calculations, and proofing devices on office machines. For the most part, required is an exact comparison with the original or a general checking for correctness of intended meaning and satisfactory appearance.

When exact comparison is required, it is common for one employee to read from the original while another employee checks the material. A word-for-word comparison is made. The employee reading indicates headings, quotations, and punctuation marks, and spells difficult words. Care must be exercised by the employee checking to catch omissions, misspelled words, and incorrect syllabifications. Along with this, an examination is made to see that the general format, margins, and appearance are correct.

In checking numbers read the columns vertically. Place the original list side by side with the written list, so that the numbers are matched on the same line. This helps to eliminate possible error. The doubling of figures and using the comma division should also be practiced whenever possible. For numbers that repeat, use the expression "two times," "three times," and so forth. To illustrate:

When the number is:	*Say:*				
157	One	fifty-seven			
2,157	Twenty-one	fifty-seven			
2,157	Two	one	fifty-seven		
3,845,157	Three	eight	forty-five	one	fifty-seven
341 ⎫ 341 ⎬ 341 ⎭	Three	forty-one			−three times

Material requiring general checking is carefully read, but a word-for-work comparison is not made. Frequently, general checking work is done by one employee—commonly the one who wrote the material. The meaning of the material must be clear and the general appearance satisfactory. Special attention should be given dates and amounts. In this respect, comparison with the original is recommended.

Spot Checking the Work

In this approach, commonly every third or perhaps fifth document or segment of work is checked. For sample checking a group which is representative of the total is determined statistically and is subsequently checked to determine the quality level of the work being performed. A common arrangement is for the supervisor to select at random a group member and draw a random sample of the work done during the day by this employee. The supervisor checks this work for errors and records the results on a suitable form. As a month or two progresses, several samples of each employee's work are taken. Hence, a basis is obtained for calculating the accuracy of each employee's work. Statistical measurements can be used to determine if the sample size is adequate for valid interpretation. Some managers prefer to sample the work being done for a specific period each day, say 50 minutes, rather than check a specific sample size for a quality review. Figure 27–2 shows an interesting format for a quality report. A separate weekly sheet is maintained for each employe. These are later combined for a departmental report. In the illustration the error categories are identified along with the respective assigned weights for each. Observe that "soiled appearance" is given the highest weight, i.e., is considered the worst typing error. The differences among errors and the trend in a specific category can be quickly observed. It appears that the employee should have help in reducing the number of misspelled words, and the overall quality is too low—a total of 48 error points from only 154 items. An acceptable limit is about 10 percent of the items, that is, about 15 points for 154 items.

FIGURE 27-2
Employee Quality Check

Employee Name: Agnes Lemish   Period: From 7/15-7/19
Department: Typing   Superior: Hazel Burke

Errors	Assigned Weight	Days					Totals	
		M	Tu	W	Th	F	Errors	Points
Capitalization	2	—	1	1	—	—	2	4
Carbon copier illegible	4	—	—	—	—	1	1	4
Erases and smudges.	4	—	—	—	1	—	1	4
Improper divisions	3	—	—	—	—	—	—	—
Misspelled word	3	1	2	1	1	3	8	24
Poor arrangement	3	—	—	—	—	—	—	—
Soiled appearance	5	—	—	—	—	—	—	—
Strikeover	4	2	—	—	1	—	3	12
							15	48
Total items processed . . .		32	30	34	31	27		154

Statistical Quality Control

The third approach for quality controlling is statistical quality control (SQC). For this approach a large number of observations are made, generally over a fairly long period, the exact requirement depending upon the variety and complexity of the work being done. A description of each error, its probable cause, and an estimate of the time required to correct it provide additional information. Study and statistical calculation derived from the data determine the approximate quality level being achieved and also the consistency with which this level seems to be maintained. Basically all the data are used to form a nucleus of establishing statistical quality control which will now be fully discussed.

Basis of Statistical Quality Control

Natural phenomena and their relationships are statistical in character. Repeated productive operations of the same thing will provide a distribution of values. This can be evidenced either by measurement on each of a quantity of similar items or by repeated measurements of the same thing on the same item. This follows because of the inherent characteristics of the measuring method.

The distribution of values can be shown graphically by means of a curve, with the values represented on the horizontal scale and the frequency of the values on the vertical scale. For our purposes here, it can be stated that when the phenomena are natural, sufficiently large, and of random selection, most of the values will cluster in the center around a representative average value, while other values in the group will tend to taper off to the left and to the right of this average. The result is what the statistician calls a normal, or bell-shaped, curve, as shown by the curve *MMM* in Figure 27–3. To illustrate, if the errors of typists are counted, it will be found that most commit, let us say,

FIGURE 27–3

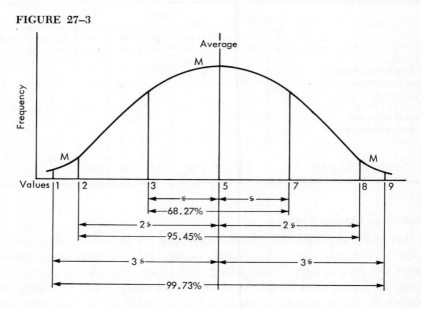

five errors, while a few commit three, and still fewer commit one error. Likewise, to the right (or greater than five errors), there will be some with seven errors, and a few with nine errors.

Based on statistical mathematics and the laws of probability, the statistician can determine the normal dispersion or spread of these data. Commonly, a value known as a standard deviation is calculated. Within a standard deviation to the left and to the right of the average are contained 68.27 percent of the values of the series. Within two standard deviations to the left and to the right are 95.45 percent, and within three standard deviations, 99.73 percent of the values. These concepts are shown in Figure 27–3.

These statistical relationships are utilized in developing effective means to control the quality of work. For a series of data, it is known statistically what variations from the average can be expected on account of the inherent characteristics of the phenomena. Variation within a definable area is inevitable and is *the result of chance*. However, variation outside the definable area can be discovered and subsequently corrected. In other words, statistical quality control reveals when a variation is due to *other than chance*, i.e., when *an assignable cause* is present.

But it does not tell what the cause is. Investigation and analysis are required to find and remove the assignable cause.

Control Chart

A graphic device known as a control chart is constructed and used for plotting data and showing variations from the acceptable goal or standard. The values of the limits placed on the chart are determined statistically. In this work, the statistical concepts of the normal curve, the average or normal quality value, and the limits of variations that are due to chance are determined.

Figure 27–4 illustrates a control chart. This can be thought of as

FIGURE 27–4
A Control Chart

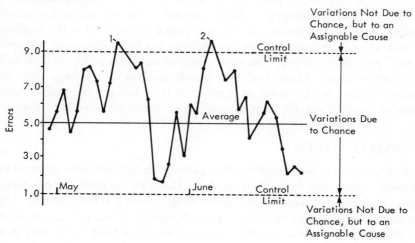

developed from a normal, or bell-shaped, curve placed on its side, so that the area in which variations due to chance occur is represented by a horizontal band. In the illustration, this band is from 1.0 to 9.0 errors which are the limits set by three standard deviations above and three standard deviations below the average. The average or normal expectancy due to the inherent nature of the work is 5.0 errors; however, the quality of the work will vary from 1.0 to 9.0 errors because of chance. It is inevitable and is not assignable to a cause. When the quality measurement goes outside this pattern of variations—for example, as indicated by points 1 and 2—the cause is not chance but an assignable influence which should be discovered and eliminated. It might, for example, be a defective tabulating key mechanism on the typewriter, paper slipping in the machine, or a space bar that is not working properly.

In a control chart, the frequency of plotting the data depends upon the quality and value of the product controlled. Usually, the values are obtained from a sample of the work—that is, a representative number of the total are selected and checked. This may be once every 15 minutes, or perhaps once a day. The value of these selected units is representative statistically of the total being processed.

A different control chart is usually established for each control station. This is done because the work being quality controlled at one station may differ considerably from that at another station.

SQC stresses preventive rather than remedial action. When more than 9.0 errors are found in a batch of work, indicated by point 1 in Figure 27–4, the work is stopped, and the reason for this assignable amount of errors is discovered and corrected before the work is permitted to continue. Thus, processing a large quantity of work and subsequently finding much of it defective is avoided. Usually, the trend of the readings is indicative. For example, the increasing readings climaxing to point 2 in Figure 27–4 point to the occurrence of such a reading as 2 outside the control limits. Many feel that trends leading to readings near the control limits can be used as signals to look for an assignable cause without waiting for the actual reading to exceed the control limits.

QUANTITY CONTROL

Prominent and important in office management is quantity controlling. In most offices the volume of work is likely to be quite large during some periods and, conversely, quite small during other periods. This fluctuation appears to be in the general nature of office work. A study of the demands upon an office over a comparatively long period of time will usually reveal a rhythmic pattern in office activities. For example, it may be found that peak loads are generally experienced on the first day of each week, every Friday, or the last few days of each month.

These conditions require controlling effort to minimize the fluctuation and make the work more manageable. When the peak periods are known fairly well in advance, quite adequate means for handling them can be determined. However, some unbalance is always present. The demands upon an office are continually changing, a condition which makes controlling difficult.

The challenge is to provide adequate office service at reasonable efficiency. Many believe that it is paramount to get the work finished when it is needed. Adequate quantity control can assist tremendously in this respect. But at what cost can this be achieved? Work fluctuation creates a "feast or famine" situation in the factors utilized in processing the work. A manager should have only the number of people and the facilities needed for the expected work volume. For any given period, this brings up questions such as how many people to hire, what machines to employ, and which methods to adopt. On the other hand, the reduction of idle machine and personnel time are paramount; still, lack of sufficient capacity in machine or manpower is of foremost consideration. Reliance cannot be placed on the designation of work as "special" or "urgent." Commonly such a designation is given to all office work and means very little in determining work priority. Furthermore, from the quantity controlling, the information manager likes to designate a completion date for a designated batch of work. Although complicated by work fluctuation, reasonably accurate information on the progress being made, the number of units completed, and the probable finishing time can be supplied by effective quantity control.

Quantity Controlling Efforts

Several fundamentals should be kept in mind when performing quantity controlling. First, it is mandatory that adequate knowledge and information about the things being controlled and which affect quantity of work are available and supplied. Data on personnel, systems and procedures, machines, cost, and due dates must be known. Second, the control efforts should be coordinated, viewing the totality of the work. Quantity control cannot be left to the individual employee. Unbalanced and sporadic work loads are eliminated in part by taking into account the complete and inclusive work requirements for definite periods. Also, the best practice is to have the controlling under the direction of one individual or an organization division designated to handle this function. Third, quantity controlling should be constructive in its ultimate effect. It is an energizing, positive action, not a depressant. The controlling should make it possible for the manager to give more attention to getting the work out, planning efforts, making decisions, improving methods, and reducing costs. Fourth, if possible, express the work in measurable units. We are dealing with amounts of work, and specific measurements of it are basic for the control efforts to have meaning and purpose. Fifth and last, needed are accurate and fast means of communication between the one doing the controlling and the employee doing the actual physical office work. In the smaller office this poses no problem but in the large office where centralized quantity controlling may be used, fast communication service is necessary between the line operators and the controlling unit.

Evaluating what is being accomplished, an essential step in all controlling, takes on special meaning in controlling quantity. The planned sequence of operations for each type of work should be utilized, otherwise the controlling is usually diminished. In many instances, the office system or procedure will supply this information, but details covering a specific job are sometimes also necessary. This is especially true in the case of bottleneck areas. Emphasis should be directed toward getting the specific work accomplished.

Means of Controlling Office Work Fluctuation

The question now arises: "What specifically can the office manager do in order to meet the problems inherent in the fluctuation of the office work volume?" The answer lies in employing either initially, or subsequently as suggested by events as they unfold, one or several major means. Eight possibilities are offered here:

1. Employment of Part-Time Help. This possible solution is self-evident and will not be discussed in detail. In many cases, the use of part-time help is entirely satisfactory. However, the cost of recruiting, hiring, and training part-time employees might be excessive. Flexibility of the work force, however, is gained by the use of part-time people. Service bureaus, discussed below, specialize in supplying skilled office help in the client's office for a specified short-term period.

2. Overtime Work. Although commonly resorted to, this solution to the problem of work fluctuation is not entirely satisfactory. For occasional overloads, it may represent the simplest solution. However, when the amount of work during regular hours is *light* and frequent peak loads are common, the working of overtime is open to serious question as the best way of handling the problem. For one thing, overtime increases unit labor cost considerably. Consider a common case in which an employee works eight hours overtime. These eight hours are paid for at the rate of time and one half. In effect, these overtime hours increase the unit labor cost by 8.33 percent, calculated by dividing 52, the hours paid for, by 48, the hours worked, or 1.0833, an increase of 8.33 percent.

There is also the question of employee fatigue. Over an extended period, there is reasonable question whether the rate of output during the overtime hours will be the same as that during the regular work hours. The rate of production during overtime tends to fall below the normal production rate. Most office managers will concur in the statement that an office employee working an extra two or three hours after a normal eight-hour working day will not produce an extra two-eighths or three-eighths of a normal day's work. The amount will be less—in some instances, considerably less.

Furthermore, legal restrictions must be taken into account. Federal and state laws regulate the type of work and the hours which an employee can work in certain occupations. Where female employees are involved, the regulatory statutes may be of special importance.

3. Forming Mobile Units. In some offices, it is possible to form "flying squadron" units which are moved from area to area to help handle excessive work loads. Normally, the office must be fairly large to utilize this method. However, the same idea is used informally in most small offices by shifting the employees around when and as the work requires. Utilizing mobile units necessitates employees with comprehensive training in a number of different types of office work. Hiring and maintaining such employees present some difficulties, but can be managed satisfactorily.

4. Calling Service Bureaus to Do the Work. Office overloads or work which is of a special nature can be handled by outside enterprises which specialize in this type of work. Most of these enterprises, called service bureaus, are independently owned business firms, but some are units of office machine manufacturers or banks. Service bureaus are located in all major cities throughout the United States; several are nationwide in scope. Some are specialists operating, for example, computer installations only; but many offer complete services in typing, calculating, tabulating, filing, transcribing, duplicating, and direct mailing. In the case of a computer, a user can lease processing time on a central processor and peripheral equipment but commonly supplies the computer program required for the processing work. It is estimated that as of 1975, there were over 1,200 service bureaus in the United States.

Service bureaus offer vast experience and competent, specialized personnel to handle complex jobs. The service is fast. For example, one service bureau completed, for a client, inventory calculations involving 3,500 hours of work within three working days. In view of the service provided, the cost of service bureaus is usually reasonable.

There have been efforts toward the goal of keeping the office workforce to the size needed to handle normal workloads and to use service bureaus to take care of short periodic increases of activity. This approach is commendable, but it will fail if the company doesn't make the best use of any temporary help the bureau provides. To this end the company should (1) spell out and request the temporaries have the precise skills needed to do the work, (2) have machines and equipment ready for the temporaries upon arrival, (3) give careful and complete instructions to the temporaries, and (4) provide proper supervision and control their work output.

It should be observed that these outside service bureaus are useful to the office manager for more than meeting peak loads or emergency problems. They are also helpful when purchase of particular office machines cannot be justified by the office because of its size or the amount or character of the work. Also, a service bureau can be engaged to serve as a laboratory to test the value of a new means of handling office work before the necessary equipment is purchased.

  5. Stress Centralization in Organization. One of the strongest justifications for centralization in office organizing is the more effective handling of peak loads. When the excess work is (1) mainly basic activities such as typing, computing, copying, sorting, and filing and (2) concentrated in different departments at different times, the centralized organizational approach has real merit.

  6. Use of Cycling. Cycling is an arrangement whereby papers are processed throughout a period according to an orderly plan rather than as a group—for example, at the beginning or end of each period. In other words, by means of cycling, the work is spread out evenly throughout the period. The practice of cycling has been used in connection with the mailing of statements and is commonly referred to as cycle billing. The same practice, however, can be applied to other types of office work.

  Cycling has been used for a long time by public utility companies in sending out their bills for service. Meters are read, for example, in a certain section of the city, bills mailed, and payments specified by a certain date. Several days later, other meters in another section of the city are read, bills mailed, and payments requested by a date which is a few days after that of the previous group. In addition, many department stores operate on a cycle-billing basis under which each account is posted once a month, but statements are mailed for a different section of accounts on different days throughout the month. Commonly the accounts are divided into 20 or fewer groups, depending upon such things as the volume of postings, the number of accounts, and the number of trays required to house the accounts.

  7. Maintain Work Backlog. By this means a reservoir of work is utilized in order to level out the peaks and valleys of the office work flow. When certain work can be postponed or moved up, this approach works out quite satisfactorily. The attempt is to make each day an average day.

  An alternate approach is to mix urgent with nonurgent office work. Certain tasks of the office, such as bringing records up to date, replenishing supplies, and putting headings on certain papers, can usually be performed during slack periods. When work having high priority is received, it is processed immediately, the nonurgent work being laid aside for the time being.

  An interesting example of maintaining a work backlog is illustrated by Figure 27–5. Study showed that the work fluctuated in a fairly regular pattern each month, the highest weeks being the first and the second. Before quantity controlling was applied the number of employees varied

FIGURE 27–5

Quantitative Controlling Implemented by Work Backlog Approach

	Week 1	Week 2	Week 3	Week 4
Before Quantitative Controlling				
Items arrived forward	2,740	1,860	1,280	890
Items received	5,228	3,740	4,195	5,075
Total for processing	7,968	5,600	5,475	5,965
Items processed	6,108	4,320	4,585	4,607
Number of employees	10	8	7	7
After Quantitative Controlling				
Items arrived forward	2,740	2,968	1,708	903
Items received	5,228	3,740	4,195	5,075
Total for processing	7,968	6,708	5,903	5,978
Items processed	5,000	5,000	5,000	5,000
Number of employees	8	8	8	8

to meet the work needs. Then a control of backlog was established. Study of past records showed the monthly work volume remained fairly constant throughout the year. The size of the work force was set at eight, using standards. This constant smaller number of employees can handle the work very well. To explain the data, refer to week 1 at the beginning of which 2,740 units awaited to be processed. In addition, 5,228 units were received during this week, making a total for processing of 7,968 units. Since 6,108 were processed during the week, there are 1,860 (7,968 minus 6,108) units held over for the beginning of week 2.

8. Orderly Work Flow through Routing, Scheduling, and Dispatching. This approach consists of establishing specific channels by which the office work is to be accomplished, placing time values on each successive step so arranged, receiving information on progress of work, and issuing authorization for work to proceed from step to step. It emphasizes the controlling of the work quantity and the use of time in work performance. Each of the major components of this approach—routing, scheduling, and dispatching—will be discussed.

ROUTING

Routing is the determining of the route or channel through which the work travels and the sequence of operations required for the completion of the work. For most offices, routing is determined by the system and procedure used. In some instances, the choice of a particular machine or of a certain area may be fixed by the routing process, but this is the exception rather than the rule with most office work. Commonly, a route sheet, showing the sequence of operations, is prepared. In addition, for each operation, the allocated time and the department in which the work is to be performed are indicated.

A practice sometimes followed is to place the office work in a heavy manila envelope with the route sheet attached on the outside. A copy of the sheet is retained by the person or department doing the central control work. In some instances, the form of the route sheet is printed on the envelope to prevent possible loss of the route sheet in the office.

SCHEDULING

Scheduling is the assigning of time values to the work sequence—the determination of when each operation starts and when it should be completed. The extent to which office work can be scheduled depends upon the individual circumstances; but usually, a great deal can be scheduled, including billing, key punching, tabulating, transcribing, check writing, order writing, microfilming and inventory taking.

The common practice in scheduling is to work backward from the time specified for completion. An allowance is made for each operation required by the work; and in this manner a starting time is determined. For example, if the time set for completion of a job is 4:00 P.M., Thursday, June 12, and the work requires 18 hours' time, this means that the work should start 18 work hours before that time and date, or 2:00 P.M., Tuesday, June 10, assuming 8 A.M.–noon and 1 P.M.–5 P.M. work days.

The three common means of scheduling include the use of:

1. Folders. This simple and quite effective informal means provides for a given number of units of work placed in each of a number of folders. These are distributed by the supervisor, who notes to whom each folder is given, the starting time, the machine or workplace used, and the completion time the batch of work in the folder should take. The employee is told the amount of time the work should require. Upon return of the completed work, the time taken is noted, and the process is repeated. The supervisor is the key controlling person under this arrangement and has knowledge of the work on hand, the amount completed, the amount in process, and when it should be finished.

Best results are obtained when the amount of work in each folder is a reasonable amount—probably that requiring an hour or less for completion. Some prefer to call this *short-interval scheduling* and are enthusiastic about the excellent results it brings. It features assigned amounts of work that an employee easily comprehends, frequent and certain follow-up, good time utilization, and adoption of the basic tenet that telling an employee before he starts when you expect a specific job to be completed, usually helps in meeting the schedule.

2. Visible Index Cards. Data required for formal and complete scheduling can be handled on cards. For this purpose visible index cards providing signals for control purposes work out very well. A sepa-rate card is made out for each machine, desk, or workplace. The signals, featured by the visible file, are moved to specific positions along the margin of the card to designate specific scheduled times. Scanning the cards quickly reveals what equipment is available for work and what jobs are currently being worked on.

3. Charts. Another effective means of recording scheduling data is by the use of charts. Devised originally by Henry L. Gantt, the Gantt chart shows work planned and work accomplished on the horizontal scale in relation to each other and also in their relation to time. The vertical scale is used for the item being scheduled such as machines, employees, or orders.

Figure 27–6 shows a Gantt chart representing the scheduling of work

FIGURE 27–6
Gantt Load Chart, Showing Graphically the Degree of Utilization of Machines, Idle Time, and Time Available for Scheduling

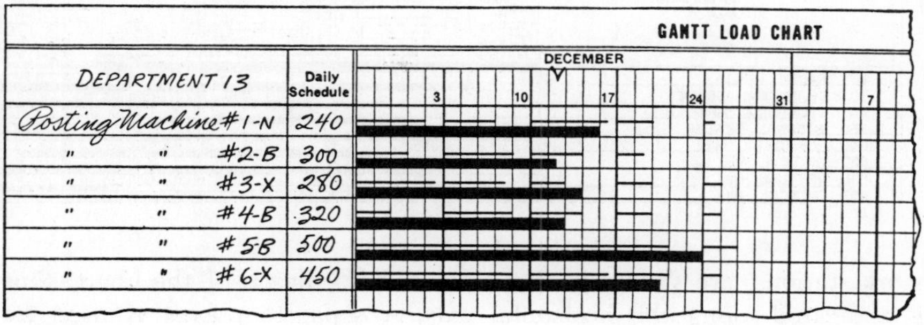

for department 13, in which six posting machines are used. In this figure a main column represents one week, as shown by the date filled in at the right and top of each column, i.e., 3, 10, 17, and so forth. To illustrate, the column with the "3" means the week ending December 3. The five divisions under each main column represent the five working days in the week. The data for each machine are shown in the identified horizontal sections of the chart, i.e., machine No. 1–N by the top hori-zontal section, machine No. 2–B by the second horizontal section, and so forth. For each machine, the work, scheduled by weeks, is indicated by the light line and the total cumulative work scheduled by the heavy line. Thus, for posting machine No. 4–B, work time scheduled for the week ended December 17 is three days, which represents 960 postings (3 x 320); and the total amount of time scheduled for this machine for the six weeks work shown by the chart is twelve days. All this is effective as of the date shown by the V mark on the top of the chart which, in the illustration is December 14. This type of Gantt chart is termed a load chart, since it graphically represents the load assigned to each machine and likewise reveals the idle or available time. Successive additions can be made on the chart by extending the proper lines; a redrawing is not necessary.

Another type of scheduling chart combines the uses of the visible card and the Gantt chart. It has the general appearance of a large, visible card file with the overlapping card pockets hanging vertically. (See Figure 27–7). Scheduled items, such as operations, machines, or

FIGURE 27–7
Visible Card—Gantt Chart Scheduling Chart

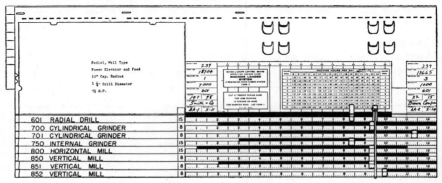

work stations, are shown in the extreme left column of the chart; time is indicated along the horizontal axis. A separate pocket is used for each scheduled item. At the extreme left of each pocket is placed a card which gives frequently used information about the scheduled item, with the identifying data appearing in the visible margin. The remaining portion to the right in each pocket is used to show graphically the scheduled operations and times allotted for the particular item. To do this, two types of cards are used: (1) operation cards and (2) time insert cards. The former are printed card forms on which operational information is written along with scheduled time information shown in the bottom margin of the card. Time insert cards are printed strips of paper placed in the visible margin to show the time scale along the horizontal axis. The strips are folded lengthwise, with the turned-up stub showing the printed scale.

When the operation card is tucked in the visible margin and behind the insert card, only the colored strip of the operation card is visible; and the length of this strip indicates the amount of time required to do the work. The exact placement of the card is determined by the scale of the insert card in the visible margin. Since a colored strip indicates scheduled time, it follows that white space indicates free or un-scheduled time.

DISPATCHING

Dispatching is putting into action and adequately following up the routing and scheduling plans; it represents true controlling and is made up of a signaling to go ahead and a checking to see that action is taking place when and where it is wanted. For office work, dispatching is usually quite simple. It is frequently done informally by the super-visor. An excellent example is the implementation of the short-interval scheduling mentioned earlier. Giving the folder of work to the employee, in effect, gives authorization to proceed with that amount of work and to complete it within a given period. Further, it assumes that by these actions this work is coordinated with the other work of the department. A common practice is to inform the employee that for work completed in less than the allotted time, the time savings (allotted minus actual time) is free time. If, for example, the quota is 30 work items to be completed in 45 minutes and the employee finishes the work in 38 min-utes, there is 7 minutes (45 less 38) free time given the employee. Some managers claim the series of attainable short-term goals is motiva-tional and report great success with it.

When the volume and different kinds of office work warrant, the dispatching can be quite sophisticated. Employees doing only dispatch-ing work may be used advantageously. Quite often, it is desirable to use a central control board which graphically visualizes the dispatching of the many different jobs which are started, moved through the office, and completed.

Different types of control boards exist, including the three-hook, spring-clip, peg-string, and grooved-strip types. The last two are most adaptable to office work. Figure 27–8 shows a peg-string board, which has the controlled items on the left side and such things as time, operations, and departments in separate sections across the top. The board has a series of small holes into which pegs are inserted. For each item in the left column, there are two horizontal rows of holes. The top row is used to indicate the scheduled operations, the bottom for the actual progress. Thus, comparison between the two is easily made.

To show the scheduled operations, a peg with a string attached is inserted in the proper hole corresponding to the operation and time value. The string, which extends from the left of the board to the peg, is always taut, thus giving the impression of a horizontal line. Pegs inserted in the bottom row of holes show the actual progress. For quick reference, an assortment of different pegs, having contrasting colors, shapes, and markings on the top, is employed. A quick glance at the board shows the times for dispatching, what work is behind schedule, and what work is ahead of schedule. A vertical cord representing a specific time and date, frequently a "today line," is used to assist in visualizing these conditions. Each day, for example, the cord is moved to the right a distance equal to one day on the time scale. All data are kept up to date on the board by moving the pegs to the proper positions representing the current condition.

FIGURE 27–8
A Close-Up View of the Peg-String Board

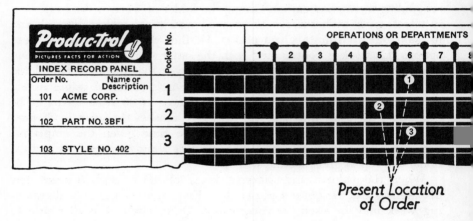

The first line, pocket No. 1, of Figure 27–8 covers order No. 101. The large round peg shows that this order is in department 6. To the right and under July, the small round peg indicates that the order was received July 11. The peg with the string attached to it is shown under July 25, which is the scheduled completion date of the current operation. The "today line" is at July 21. Hence, this order is to be completed in four days. In contrast, order No. 103, in the third pocket, was scheduled for completion on July 16 and is five days behind schedule. This order is in department 6, which should be consulted to determine what can be done to get the order moving. The square pegs to the extreme right of the board indicate the scheduled dates for finishing the orders. Order No. 101, for example, is to be completed August 12.

The other type of office control board, the grooved-strip board, has horizontal cardholder strips for insertion of tickets representing work lots. The extreme left column is used for work-lot numbers, and the remaining columns are headed by department names. Cards are made out for each work lot. As the work progresses, the cards are moved on the board to correspond with the correct department location of the work. In some instances, the time is shown horizontally. When this is done, separate tickets can be made for each operation on each work lot, as well as for the scheduled starting and finishing times indicated on each card. In this manner, the helpfulness of the board is increased by showing the scheduling function.

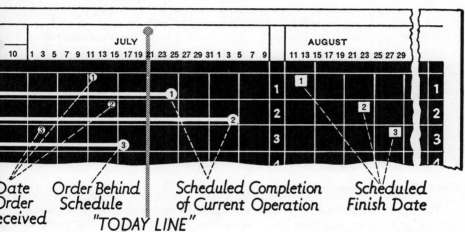

Date Order received | Order Behind Schedule | "TODAY LINE" | Scheduled Completion of Current Operation | Scheduled Finish Date

Courtesy: Wassell Organization, Westport, Conn.

QUESTIONS

1. What is meant by the statement that "quality is a personal matter"? Discuss in full using examples to illustrate your answer.
2. Enumerate three basic fundamentals to keep in mind when performing quantity controlling. Select one of the three you name and discuss it in some detail.
3. What is the specific purpose of quality controlling, and discuss how the results of this effort is used by the effective office manager.
4. Many feel that office work must be 100 percent accurate and free from mistakes. In light of statistical quality control, is this belief reasonable? Should an office manager expect this degree of quality? Discuss.
5. Identify each of the following:
   a. Unassignable cause in statistical quality control.
   b. Peg-string board.
   c. Service bureau.
   d. Gantt chart.

6. Explain Figure 27–2 in your own words pointing out what these data show.
7. What different means can an office manager employ in order to achieve quality control? Discuss.
8. What is meant by dispatching and of what significance is it in office controlling efforts?
9. Discuss the use of spot checking in the work of office quality controlling.
10. As an office manager, would you favor having your employees working overtime to meet fluctuating work requirements? Justify your stand.
11. Indicate what means probably would be used to handle the peak office work load caused by each of the following:
    a. Granting discounts on all bills paid by the tenth of the month following the month in which purchase was made.
    b. Finishing a payroll by Friday morning of each week.
    c. Completing an inventory over a weekend for a large manufacturing company.
    d. Issuing licenses to car owners of a state during the first two months of the year.
12. Explain the meaning of short interval scheduling, indicate where its application is probably most desirable and its relationship with dispatching.

CASE PROBLEMS

Case 27–1. Dommerich Company

The services of Roland Hopkins were engaged to establish statistical quality control (SQC) programs over several operations of the company. The question of SQC had come up for discussion several times during the past several weeks and, while not serious, it was believed the company had operations where effective practices for attaining quality should be followed. Mr. Hopkins was asked to start with the work of machine posting to documents by five operators. Errors in this work resulted in either an over- or an underchange to customers or payments to vendors.

As his first activity, Mr. Hopkins talked with the supervisor and the five operators explaining his mission of establishing an SQC program. He pointed out that this consists of a statistically reliable sample of the work being checked before it is released. The supervisor will be designated to select and check a sample size of work and this is done in a routine manner. The results of these checks alert to an error situation that requires attention and corrective action. He suggested that if they had any questions about what he was doing to ask him about it, and he would try to give them the answer. They agreed to give him their full cooperation.

Next, Mr. Hopkins decided what work categories to check. He reasoned that working with a percentage of errors may not be satisfactory if the errors range from $1 to $100. Hence, he stratified the work which the supervisor assured him could easily be handled by a simple presort and division of the work. The high-value postings represented a small amount of the total.

Accordingly, Mr. Hopkins divided the work into three groups: (*a*) those posting over $50 to be given a 100 percent check, (*b*) those from $25 to $49.99 to be given a spot check, and (*c*) those under $25 to be given SQC.

A test period to determine the error rate in group *c* was then conducted. A total of about 30 random samples daily was taken over a period of six weeks. From a total of 1,080 samples, errors were discovered in 33, making an error rate of 3.05 percent. This rate was considered too high by the company managers. Several ideas to improve the accuracy were tried out over the next month. They included arrangement of the work station, different paper forms, and improved lighting. Mr. Hopkins helped in these efforts, but while these improvements were taking place, Mr. Hopkins spent most of his time on an assignment in the factory. Eventually from daily samples of 30 extending over 40 days, an error rate of 1.65 percent was attained. This was considered acceptable.

Mr. Hopkins then calculated the value at which corrections will be made so that this 1.65 percent error rate is not exceeded. This is the upper control limit (UCL), calculated as follows:

$$\text{UCL} = p + 3\sqrt{\frac{p(1-p)}{n}}$$

where p = error tolerance; n = size of sample

$$\text{UCL} = .0165 + 3\sqrt{\frac{.0165(1 - .0165)}{30}}$$

$$= .0181$$

Since the daily volume of postings under $25 is 265, Mr. Hopkins recommended a daily sampling of 36 postings, adding that the error rate in this sample should remain consistently at or below .0181. When this exists, the statistical probability is that all the work is at or below the 1.65 percent which was decided is satisfactory. Mr. Hopkins recommended setting up a control chart as a visual means to determine whether the work is out of control, i.e., exceeds the UCL.

Questions:

1. What alternatives for controlling quality were available to the company?
2. What is your reaction to the work of Mr. Hopkins?
3. What does the supervisor do if the error rate reaches 2.80 percent?

Case 27–2.   Oakson Company

Shortly before quitting time at 4:45 P.M., supervisor Joseph Ayer noticed four employees of his department, the factory office, getting ready to go home. He called them over to his desk.

Mr. Ayer: You are working overtime tonight—till 8 o'clock at least. (*The employees stared for a moment, then one of them, Walter Brown, spoke.*)

Mr. Brown: Is there something wrong? How come we must work? I don't get it.

Mr. Ayer: There is nothing wrong. We simply have to get caught up in our work. I told you day before yesterday we were working overtime tonight.

Mr. Brown: Well, I can't work tonight. And I don't recall getting any notice about working overtime.

Mr Ayer: I told you while you were standing right where you are right now. And that's all you need.

Mr. Robin (*another employee*): Mr. Ayer, I did not get any memo about overtime tonight.

Mr. Ayer: You don't need a detailed written message delivered to you personally. I told you and that's sufficient.

The men worked past quitting time. About 5:30 p.m. Mr. Ayer told them that he was going down the street for a sandwich and cup of coffee and asked if they wanted to join him. All replied in the negative. When Mr. Ryer returned to the factory office at 6:05 p.m., he found that his four employees had gone for the day.

Questions:

1. Assume you are Mr. Robin and first thing the following morning Mr. Ayer talks with you privately. What explanation or defense for your action would you give? Why?
2. What action do you recommend Mr. Ayer take? Why?

Chapter 28

Cost and Budgetary Control

It is easy to be tolerant when you do not care.

Clement F. Rogers

Managerial success in many cases lies in getting the work completed satisfactorily within a certain cost. Today's information manager requires answers to what things cost, how these costs are figured, and the meaning of the final results in terms of cost. Such data are basic. Hence, the area of cost controlling in information management is of utmost significance.

As used here, cost means the *dollar amount expended for the ownership, use, or service of every component making up and employed in the performance of the work.* Cost is a matter of money outlay for manual or mental work planned, accomplished, or in process of being achieved.

COST AND THE INFORMATION MANAGER

In the opinion of many, cost is the controlling medium. It is the most important and the most common. All other types, such as those for quantity, quality, and time-use are, in the final analysis, expressed in terms of cost. Some contend all control is cost controlling. Cost is a means, not an objective. It helps the manager, especially in the act of controlling, to direct the various activities so that within stated limits the goals will be realized.

Decision making is usually greatly influenced by the consideration of cost information. Whether to install a new procedure, to purchase

713

a new office machine, to perform a new service, or to revise a form design are decided with the aid of cost information. Sometimes, the question is answered almost entirely on the basis of cost. In addition, cost also helps justify a managerial action. Recommendations for a change usually include the cost before and the cost (estimated) after the change is effected. Likewise, if an alteration has been made, the wisdom of this move is frequently confirmed by a "before and after" cost picture. Figure 28–1 illustrates one type of form that can be used.

FIGURE 28–1
A Cost Savings Estimate

COST SAVINGS ESTIMATE

DEPARTMENT NO. ___78___

DATE _9/7/_

DESCRIPTION _Adopt work layout and method described by M-240_

NOTE: ALL COSTS FOR ONE YEAR

COSTS	PRESENT	PROPOSED	SAVINGS
LABOR	$2875	$2130	+$745
MATERIAL	925	800	+ 125
MACHINE TIME	750	1035	- 285
OTHER (WRITE IN)			
TOTAL	$4550	$3965	$585

ACTION _____Recommended and approved on Oct. 3, 196_ by executive_____ _committee, R. C. McGinnis, Chairman._

APPROVED AND PUT INTO EFFECT BY _____CRM._____

An information manager keeps informed of many office practices by means of cost information. Many of the items in reports dealing with accomplishments, and also in ordinary financial statements, are expressed in cost. The number of employees, supplies used; inventory on hand, in process, or finished; charge for floor space occupied; charge for office machine usage; and the like are expressed in dollar values, estimated from cost data.

Cost also serves as an effective medium for coordinating managerial activities. For example, it is helpful in determining the program of action that will achieve the required results, yet maintain the proper balance. The selection and extent of managerial efforts, their timing, and direction can be executed in an orderly manner. Actions predicated on guesses or on hit-and-miss bases are minimized.

Cost information provides the office manager with clues to places where waste can be reduced or eliminated. While curbing waste is a desired result of all controlling, it is especially so in the case of cost. The very nature of cost information focuses attention on what was paid out and what was received. This leads to waste reduction.

Cost-Value Relationships

Examining the purpose and value of each operation and determining how this same purpose might be accomplished at lower cost represent the essential meaning of cost-value relationships as used in information management. It is to a great extent a mental and questioning viewpoint. The purpose of each office activity is identified and what would seem to be an acceptable cost for achieving this purpose is set down. Judgment is used to arrive at this cost as well as knowledge of costs and their relationships applicable to other activities within the enterprise.

Asking certain questions helps in arriving at acceptable data. Significant questions include: Can the activity be eliminated? Does it provide more than is necessary for the basic purpose? Does it seem to cost more than it is worth? What substitute, lower cost methods might give equally satisfactory results? Is excessive quality being maintained?

This balancing of cost against value can be applied to a number of office situations. In each case, the approach is one of comparing mentally what is being done at present cost, quality, and performance to what might be done at another cost, quality, and performance. Comparison is basic to this approach.

Sunk Cost

Another cost concept which the information manager encounters from time to time is sunk cost. Commonly associated with an investment in a machine or facility, sunk cost is an expenditure which is submerged and of a more or less long-term holding which cannot be liquidated into cash at its approximate present net worth to the owner. Usually it is a cost representing a portion of the initial investment that is sacrificed when a substitute or something better is obtained to replace that for which the initial investment was made. To illustrate, suppose purchase of a new office machine is contemplated to replace a present machine and the trade-in allowance for the present machine is very low. The difference between the present value of the present machine and its trade-in allowance represents sunk cost. It must be paid even though the present machine will be discontinued.

Typically, a manager encounters many situations where sunk cost is a factor in cost controlling. It is helpful to recognize them and to realize the responsibility that management has in these situations. In this connection two helpful guides will be offered. First, sunk cost tends to give emphasis to the past which must be considered, but it is the present and future that are vital. For any present situation, even though adverse, the course of action to be selected is usually the one promising the best future results. Second, the presence of a sunk cost in a situation is usually a psychological impediment toward selecting the most objective course of action. The usual desire is to avoid writing off the cost, to backtrack, or to avoid drawing attention to a potentially embarrassing situation. These drawbacks, however, should not be given undue attention.

APPROACHES TO COST REDUCTION

The effective use of cost information leads logically to the maintaining of satisfactory cost levels and, beyond this, to the lowering of these cost levels. Progressive reductions in cost appear to be a normal state of affairs in a progressive economy. The eternal challenge is to achieve better office work at less cost.

To gain significant office reduction, three approaches appear essential: (1) Concentrate on the items offering greatest cost reduction opportunities, (2) develop a cost-consciousness among all employees, and (3) establish an effective cost control program. This three-pronged attack, when efficiently applied, is practically certain to reduce cost levels noticeably.

Items Offering Greatest Cost Reduction Opportunities

Certain items normally offer greater cost reduction possibilities than others. Those representing the big items, the ones on which the most money is now being spent, and those of a cumulative and repetitive nature usually offer the best opportunities for lowering costs. Some research and probing may be required to find this type of information for a particular office.

In most offices, however, the major expense is wages and salaries—employees are the key cost. Office cost segregation under typical conditions usually shows a pattern similar to the following:

Item	Percentage of Total Costs
Office wages and salaries	70%
Supplies, postage, telephone	15
Purchase and maintenance of office equipment and machines, rent, light, and heat	15
Total costs	100%

In other words, nearly three out of every four office dollar costs are for people. Interestingly this pattern has remained about the same during the past several decades, even though office automation is now used extensively. To increase efficiency, this suggests the use of less employees, or the more efficient use of those presently employed. Stressing people as the core of office cost reduction, Fred E. Shelton, Jr., suggests careful examination of four areas: (1) office supervision, (2) habit patterns, (3) servile attitudes, and (4) methods of administration.[1]

For better cost controlling, further segregation of the listed types of office cost should be made. For example, office wages and salaries should be broken down by various types of office work such as office supervisors, stenographers, billing machine operators, punched card operators, general clerks, and so forth. This procedure affords a complete detailed record of office personnel costs in terms of office functions.

COST-CONSCIOUSNESS AMONG EMPLOYEES

Cutting cost is not a job restricted to managers. It is a job in which every employee can and should participate. Interest in costs is fundamental because it is a means contributing to employee security. To reduce costs is a way of keeping an enterprise fit so it can continue to operate successfully and meet its responsibilities.

Cost information can be used to develop a cost-consciousness among employees. A feeling of the importance of cost and its use throughout the entire enterprise must be achieved for cost to have greatest value. Every member on the payroll, from the top executive to the lowest employee, should be made aware of and encouraged to think in terms of cost. When the employees are cost-minded, a basic and broad beginning toward improving operations has been accomplished.

To accomplish this aim, suggestions pointing out possibilities for lowering office expenses are helpful. Figure 28–2 shows this in graphic form and brings out the fact that cost permeates all office activities. Every employee has the opportunity to be cost-minded and to reduce costs. In addition, accurate cost information should be disseminated to all supervisors and employees who are charged with those costs and for which they are responsible. By this means, cost is given important and meaningful status. Employees are quick to recognize this and will seek to use cost as a guide in their everyday tasks.

Some companies have formed a "Holes Committee" whose job is to seek holes through which needless expenditures can leak and to plug up these holes. The committee is made up of representatives from all parts of the office and has the authority to look into any area of the

---

[1] An award winning article by Fred E. Shelton, Jr., "Wanted: Cost Reduction," *Office Executive* (June, 1956), pp. 9–11. Mr. Shelton, now retired, was an executive of the Standard Register Company, Dayton, O.

FIGURE 28-2
Possibilities for the Reduction of Office Costs

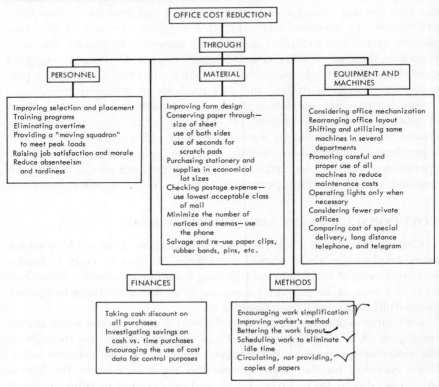

office that appears to be having excess cost difficulties. Areas that have not been reviewed costwise for some time are subject to study. Many such areas are found to be maintaining their personnel power and budget appropriations, but are not contributing adequately and have not been questioned regarding the current essentiality of their operations and contributions to the whole of office endeavors. The Holes Committee uncovers these pockets of inefficiency and comes up with recommendations to correct the situation.

It is difficult to overemphasize the human relations aspect of a office cost reduction program. Complete understanding from top management down as to the primary and detailed objectives of the cost program is a must. And every office employee should be made to feel that he or she is a part of the cost reduction effort and that what is suggested and what actions each employee takes and the suggestions made are not only mutually wanted, but are vital to the program's success. The process of cost reduction should be a pleasant experience to the employees. It must hold no bars for her and it must be an honest program.

If it is a hatchet-type program whereby present employees lose their jobs or is a squeeze-program designed to get more work out of less people, the employees of today will have no part of it.

DETERMINING WHAT IS BEING ACCOMPLISHED COSTWISE

As pointed out throughout these chapters on controlling, three steps make up controlling—determining what is being accomplished, evaluating it, and applying corrective measures, if necessary. These same steps hold true for cost controlling and will now be discussed. In determining what is being accomplished costwise, the obtaining of facts on cost, classifying them by type, and arranging them to expedite quick reference, are fundamental. Sources of cost information include ledgers, cost journals, payroll records, purchases, and records of service charges. Better results are usually secured by concentrating efforts in several selected areas. It is well to take into account these considerations:

1. The Data Should Be Accurate and Timely. Changes to improve the operations are not foreign to the modern office. These changes are sometimes of a major sort and necessitate a new collection of cost data in order to reflect an accurate measurement of current expenditures. Even in the case of minor adjustments, the resultant effect may be sufficiently large to invalidate a considerable portion of previous cost information. Cost data should be closely affiliated and apply to the current situation; otherwise, their value is questionable.

2. The Data Should Apply to Well-Defined Components. Usually, in studying cost data, the most important figures are not the totals but the individual cost figures, covering each component of those which collectively make up the total cost. Sufficient details must be included in all cost information to maximize its managerial value. No single factor tells the whole cost story.

In addition, the "cost per unit" should be used. The unit cost is the important concept. Comparison of a $300 actual cost with a $200 expected cost is not valid. If the work accomplished is 150 units and the expected output was 100 units, the true values become:

$$\text{Actual} = \frac{\$300}{150 \text{ units}} = \$2 \text{ per unit,}$$

$$\text{Expected} = \frac{\$200}{100 \text{ units}} = \$2 \text{ per unit,}$$

which demonstrates that the actual unit cost did not exceed but is equal to the expected cost.

3. The Data Should Be Completely Identified as to (a) General Type and (b) Individual Specifications. A means of classifying cost is essential to effective cost controlling. In fact, the term *cost* in and of itself is practically meaningless. The varieties of cost are almost endless, the different types depending upon the degree and kind of work covered. To facilitate understanding, information concerning "cost of what to whom" is needed.

Several general type identification arrangements will be given. The first, based on the elements of material, labor, and overhead, includes the following:

Element	*Segregation and Meaning*
Material cost:	Direct material cost—expenditures for materials which are or become a part of the product (office forms and letterheads, envelopes, and postage).
	Indirect material cost—expenditures for materials which are not a part of the product but are necessary in the carrying out of the work (typewriter ribbons, erasers).
Labor cost:	Direct labor cost—expenditures for labor attributable to and having a bearing upon the product or service (billing-machine operator, typist).
	Indirect labor cost—expenditures for labor not attributable to or in an unbroken connection with the product or service (methods man, janitor).
Overhead cost:	Expenditures which do not belong exclusively to any part of the material or labor (rent, light, heat, managerial expense, telephone).

The second arrangement utilizing a functional basis consists of total costs made up of:

I. Production costs, under which are:
    A. Production overhead costs
    B. Production direct costs
    C. Office cost consisting of:
        1. Office overhead cost
        2. Prime office costs
            a. Direct office material cost
            b. Direct office labor cost
II. Sales cost, under which are:
    A. Sales overhead cost
    B. Promotion, travel, and advertising cost
    C. Salesmen's compensation cost
        1. Wage payment cost
        2. Commission and bonus cost

These arrangements are illustrative only and are not complete.

Many managers find that apportioning office costs for a specific period to the main office systems and procedures brings very satisfactory results. Specific estimated and actual costs for informational outputs or units of office production can be determined wherever appropriate. Many types of cost analyses are thus possible, such as determination of cost trends and expected office cost incident to various managerial decisions.

Evaluating the Cost Expenditure

To evaluate the cost we need to (1) know what cost is satisfactory and (2) compare this actual cost with the cost deemed satisfactory. For the former, the amount can be determined in several different ways. One is to arrive at the amount from past experience, giving ample consideration to general economic changes and conditions. Another is a judgment or estimate of what is received for a given expenditure. This is in the nature of an educated guess. In addition, standard costs can be employed. This is the preferred means because such standards reflect an analytical and reasonably accurate cost expectancy. A standard cost represents theoretically the cost when the work is done by a standard employee with standard material and under standard conditions. Adjustments to standard cost are made to reflect current conditions; such adjustments are called variances and may be either positive, i.e., added to the standard, or negative, i.e., subtracted from the standard.

The use of standard costs gives rise to several outstanding advantages. Basic references are provided to orientate managerial efforts, strict accountability for deviations from the established standard cost can be placed on those responsible for the deviations, and cost analysis is simplified. In contrast, standard cost usage has its shortcomings. For example, the units of expression are dollars and hence are subject to fluctuating value; personnel must be especially trained for standard cost work so that proper interpretation and use of the standard data are made; and in cases of special work, standard cost data usually cannot be used unless serious adjustments are made. While all these objections are valid, they are not particularly serious. Dollar values tend to remain *relatively* the same even though they do fluctuate in absolute value. It is probably true that some guide to acceptability, although it be found wanting in many respects, is better than none at all. Also, most efforts to guide the performance of work must, of practical necessity, be tempered with judgment.

After we have a fairly firm idea of what cost is satisfactory, we can compare the actual cost to this expectancy and thus determine whether the actual expenditure is acceptable. Cost reports expedite these efforts. For maximum assistance, the report should show the plus or minus deviations from the expectancy for each item and, what is very important, should include sufficient data to establish trends. In many instances, the comparison of actual with expected cost is included under budgetary control, which is discussed later in this chapter.

APPLYING CORRECTIVE MEASURES IF NECESSARY

For the most part, this step includes efforts to reduce expenditures in those cases where actual costs are exceeding the satisfactory cost level. In many cases, the data apply to what has already happened, so that the corrective action is for some future date. However, it is vital to evaluate costs and to seek the reasons for present values. To illustrate, investigation of an increasing trend in office personnel costs may reveal poor selection techniques and high turnover. The remedial action might include a testing program, retraining of interviewers, and specific employee training efforts.

Although costs are detailed in terms of specific office functions, it is necessary to retain the overall viewpoint in deciding the corrective action. A reduction in one expense might increase another, making a total net gain in expenses. For example, centralized office costs may be reduced, but the work has been shifted to branch offices where the costs increase. Other illustrations are reducing the amount of light, resulting in an increase of time required to do the work; and eliminating interoffice telephone service, with the resultant increase in time spent by employees in delivering messages personally.

Another consideration is how to utilize all time and space gain or savings derived from the corrective action. The controlling is ineffective if it permits the former overage to dissipate among other work. For example, consider a six-hour task requiring eight hours to be completed. Through effective cost controlling the eight hours is reduced to the proper six-hour level. But actually the correction is effective only if these two hours saved as a result of the controlling are used to perform other work. Likewise, an additional office machine may save the time of one person out of three; but unless the third person is transferred and put to other work, the net result costwise is not a saving but only a machine added.

What we are saying is that for cost controlling to be effective, it is necessary (1) to check and see that the corrective steps are followed and (2) to know, as a consequence of these revisions, what the new results will be. The first point is achieved through personal means—observation and working with supervisors. For the latter point, some simple type of reporting can be instituted. For these reports to have greatest value, they should be made on a weekly and, in some instances, on a daily basis. It is important to know immediately if costs are getting back into line both for individual and for total costs. Receiving reports at relatively long intervals of time might mean needless continuation of costly practices or receipt of information when it is too late to do anything about it.

Cost controlling is a job that never ends. It varies in intensity with the particular needs of the office and the enterprise, the skill of the personnel assigned to and interested in it, and the beliefs of the top management members. It takes time and is laborious work, but it is well worth the effort. Best results are usually obtained from continuous, not sporadic, efforts.

COST CONTROLLING OF COPYING

Let us now discuss cost controlling in relation to one of the fastest growing areas of the modern office—the use of copying machines. The convenience of having quality copies has modified many former practices followed in office management. With this change and growth has come exploding copying cost with the resultant need for adequate cost controlling of copying. Typical questions include: What is the cost per copy? What minimum number of copies will suffice? What measures should be taken to keep copying cost in line?

To control copying cost it is first necessary to know not only what the cost should be, but also what present cost is being incurred. The common situation is a complete lack of any cost data for this area. Hence, the initial order of business is to set up a system to obtain such information and enlist the active support by employees to the system. Beyond this, the controls utilized should include scheduling of copying to gain better usage of machines from the viewpoint of both time available and type of copying performed. Also included are provision for maintaining security of classified information, the allocation of cost to the organization unit for whom the copying service is being provided, and some flexibility to meet changing needs.

Labor is the highest cost in copying and merits much attention, if copying costs are to be controlled effectively. Human effort cannot be wasted; it should be as productive as possible. In fact, in selecting a copying machine it is wise to give much weight to the determination of how the machine can do the most copying work without costing more in labor. Automatic feeding and continuous operation generally save money because they eiminate labor. Also, basic training in the operation of each copying machine is paramount. Excellent machine instructions given in a step-by-step, easy-to-follow manner and amply illustrated are provided free of charge by most machine manufacturers. In addition, definite copying work goals should be provided. The nature of this work seems to require that a sense of accomplishment be emphasized. Also, the employee's desire to have the manager know what is being achieved must be satisfied. Furthermore, full utilization of employee's time should be stressed. Too little or too much work can result in a dissatisfied employee. Or expecting the work to be accomplished within practically no time at all can dull the employee's enthusiasm.

The copying machine should be under someone's supervision. Overseeing what work is copied, the number of copies, proper use of the machine, and the recording of usage data are helped by having adequate supervision. The practice of issuing to the supervisor billings for the copying machines is effective in keeping copying cost down. If such billing costs appear high to the supervisor who complains about them, guidelines on how to put controls on the copying activity to reduce costs can be given to the supervisor. Included here are controls such as who can operate the machine, what times, number of copies normally permissible, and approval of supervisor before using machine, if necessary.

Present usage and its trend are helpful benchmarks in controlling copying. If there are no data on these, arrange to get some by instituting a "Copying Log" sheet such as illustrated by Figure 28–3. At each

FIGURE 28–3
Copying Log Sheet

Copying Log						
Date	Description of Material	Requested by	Copying Work by	Number of		
				Originals	Copies	Total Copies

machine have the employee who makes a copy, record it on this log. Copying usage data probably will reveal upward spiraling and make one more aware of the exploding costs in this area. Knowing what present copying work is being done, some reasonable projections as to future copying requirements can be drawn, so that proper plans can be made for expansion or contraction as the case might be. While usage data can be interpreted in many different ways, for well managed copying in a privately owned company, there appears to be a useful relationship between dollar sales and dollar copying costs. To illustrate, for a company with sales of $25 million sales, copying costs probably will range between $13,000–$16,000. For a company with $500 million sales, copying costs of from $350,000–$450,000 may be quite satisfactory. The data will vary with the type of business and should not be used as a single copying cost index.

Machine location brings up the question of whether placing a copier near the department having the most need for it is better than establishing several copying stations throughout the office and plant, or having all copiers within a single department location. Usually when the volume is relatively small, but the cost of travel time of an operator is high, it is recommended to locate a small copying machine in each of the several key departments and in each department let the supervisor have jurisdiction over the copier. Other arrangements entail consideration for loss of labor due to travel, work interruptions, and unnecessary corrections which collectively more than offset the cost of the copier. In contrast, advocates of the centralized arrangement point out that better and more complete service is obtained by use of centralized copying. Time loss of highly paid employees is avoided; better utilization and maintenance of machines is feasible; several types of machines can be included yet without costly duplication; and unauthorized use of the machines is minimized. There is a general tendency to utilize copiers on a decentralized basis and duplicators on a centralized basis. A satisfactory practice is to provide on a decentralized basis copying machines to handle immediate needs, but not peak loads or large volume copying jobs and to provide on a centralized basis, backups and facilities for large volume copying. Manufacturers now have made available portable machines mounted on wheels so that it can be moved from place to place to satisfy demands.

The cost per copy will vary depending upon the number of contributing factors taken into account and the accuracy of the data used. One reasonable approach is to use out-of-pocket cost as the common denominator that can be used to compare cost per copy in one organization with that in another. A value of 2¢ per copy for out-of-pocket cost is usually indicative of good control. Values greater are common and reveal that improvement is feasible. An amount of 4¢ a copy means cost controlling is badly needed. It can also be stated that, in general, the cost of copying is on the average approximately twice that of offset duplicating. Hence, whenever possible, the use of duplicating over copying will reduce the cost. Observe, however, that these cost data exclude such considerations as size of runs, convenience, quality of work, and personal preference which might be significant in any given case.

A number of other considerations can be pursued in trying to cut copying cost. Reducing the size of the document copy, copying on both sides of the paper, and using recycled paper, can be mentioned. The speed, capacity, and quality of the copy produced by the machine as well as the freedom from machine repairs should also be considered. Also, whether the machine is leased and payments considered expense or purchased and depreciation allowances taken, will have an effect upon the copying cost incurred. In addition, following a policy of first-come, first-served usually is satisfactory and assists in establishing a known sequence and a desired orderliness which generally makes for a relative low cost. Whenever possible the grouping of copying work that is fairly similar tends to expedite copying and complete it at minimum cost. Finally, some have found the use of meter-key driven devices quite helpful. They restrict the use of certain machines and when in operation register the number of copies run off on them. Others contend that if locks must be put on copying machines, there is a lack of good human relations and a basic security enigma that requires managerial attention.

OFFICE BUDGETING

An important device for implementing controlling, usually associated with cost, is a budget. When a manager speaks of using a budget, he actually has two concepts in mind: the budget and budgetary control. Each of these can be defined formally in the following manner: *A budget is a device consisting of an orderly arrangement of data determined by computed guesses and covering all phases of the enterprise for a definite future period of time.* On the other hand, *budgetary control is the process of using the budget by comparing actual results with the computed guesses in order to correct either the estimates or the causes of the differences.*

The budget and budgetary control are interrelated and must always be considered jointly. A budget without budgetary control is useless from the managerial viewpoint; and budgetary control without a budget is meaningless. Actually, many view and rightly so, a budget as a plan and budgeting as a control. Further, the budgeting or budgetary control is considered as controlling with the budget supplying the expectancy. Hence, budgeting is determining what is being accomplished, comparing it to the expectancy, or budget, and correcting any deviation which is decided is too much out of line.

Budgeting promotes the overall viewpoint, helps reveal strengths and weaknesses in the office organization, and facilitates managerial decision making by providing pertinent data to the manager's fingertips. Budgeting, however, is a managerial tool; it is not management itself. Budgeting is not automatic in its operation. Care in the budget's formulation and wise, meaningful interpretation of the comparisons are required. Budgeting requires time; current ills are not cured overnight. And the data must be updated periodically, a consideration discussed later in this chapter.

All Budgets Concern the Office Manager

A budget can be drawn up for almost any department or division of an enterprise. Frequently, separate budgets are made for sales, production, purchasing, finance, labor, and general expense. These are then combined into one budget, commonly termed the "master budget" or simply the "budget." Subsequently, controlling using each of these budgets follows.

The units are usually in dollars, but physical units, or any other term which is useful and convenient, can be used. Quite often, where physical units are employed, the dollar values are also shown. It is sometimes desirable to include in the budget plan the targets for different levels of activity. Such a budget is called a *step budget;* its value lies in predetermining and thinking through the action to be taken should variations from the estimated goal arise. Actually, the work of preparing a step budget is not difficult. Some items will vary directly with the total volume; others will tend to rise or fall with the operating level, but not in direct proportion to it; others will remain the same regardless of the operating level.

The office manager has an interest in all budgets and budgeting controls used by an enterprise since they reveal projected trends in operations which will probably affect the amount of office work. From the various budget plans, knowledge of changes such as an increase in advertising literature to be mailed, a change in the number of bills payable, the development of new sales markets, a new policy regarding billing practices, and a reduction in the number of purchasing orders can be ascertained and this information utilized to have the office provide its necessary services.

Ordinarily, the office manager is directly active in the preparation of (1) the cash budget and (2) the office expense budget, and in the controlling based upon them. In the case of the cash budget, the extent of office activities affects the cash requirements of the enterprise. The purchase and trade-in of office machines and equipment, the expansion or contraction of any office function in order to keep it in balance with changes elsewhere in the enterprise, or simply action to cut down office expenditures are illustrations of the office's influence on the cash budget.

The office expense budget is the individual budget covering office activities and is one in which the office manager is vitally interested. Typical items include supervision, clerical payroll, stationery, supplies, postage, telephone and telegraph service, reception and messenger service, purchase and maintenance of office machines and equipment, rent, and light.

Figure 28–4 shows a portion of an office expense budgetary control program. In this case entries of actual expenditures have been made

FIGURE 28–4
Office Expense Budgetary Control for the Year 19–

Item	January Estimate	January Actual	February Estimate	February Actual	March Estimate	March Actual
1. Stationary and envelopes. . . .	$ 75	–	–	$ 83	$ 50	
2. Supplies	50	$ 68	$ 35	21	35	
3. Postage	35	35	35	35	35	
4. Telephone and telegraph	185	173	185	186	185	
5. Reception and messenger service	450	440	450	440	500	
6. Magazine and book subscription	18	18	–	–	–	
7. Maintenance of machines and equipment*.	40	53	40	62	40	
8. Purchase of machines and equipment*	440	291	–	165	200	
9. Rent	80	80	80	80	80	
10. Light	22	21	20	21	20	
11. Traveling expenses*.	80	135	80	40	80	
12. Employees' welfare	50	60	50	47	50	
13. Clerical payroll*.	3,750	3,870	3,750	3,920	4,000	
14. Supervision payroll*	1,140	1,140	1,140	1,170	1,300	
15. Miscellaneous (list)	25	–	25	–	25	
Install new electric outlet . .	–	3	–	–	–	
Fix door at north exit	–	–	–	18	–	
Total.	$6,440	$6,387	$5,890	$6,288	$6,600	

* These items must be justified by details on supplementary sheets.
Note: Supplementary sheets are used to show the details of certain items which are selected on the basis of judgment and experience.

for the months of January and February. Expenses for February are nearly $400 in excess of the estimate. A study of the itemized data for this month shows that clerical payroll, machine and equipment purchases, and supervision payroll are the items chiefly responsible for the increase. Further investigation of these expenses should be made.

Preparation of the Budget Plan

Figure 28–5 shows the sequence followed in preparing the budget plan upon which the controlling is based. The total estimated income is determined from expected sales and other sources of income. From this total estimated income are subtracted the expenses of sales, production, purchasing, and general expense. This gives the estimated net in-

FIGURE 28–5
A Normal Sequence of Budget Preparation

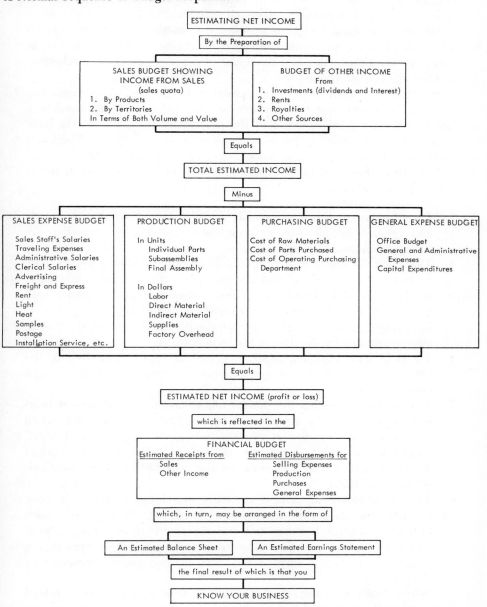

ESTIMATING NET INCOME

By the Preparation of

SALES BUDGET SHOWING
INCOME FROM SALES
(sales quota)
1. By Products
2. By Territories
In Terms of Both Volume and Value

BUDGET OF OTHER INCOME
From
1. Investments (dividends and interest)
2. Rents
3. Royalties
4. Other Sources

Equals

TOTAL ESTIMATED INCOME

Minus

SALES EXPENSE BUDGET

Sales Staff's Salaries
Traveling Expenses
Administrative Salaries
Clerical Salaries
Advertising
Freight and Express
Rent
Light
Heat
Samples
Postage
Installation Service, etc.

PRODUCTION BUDGET

In Units
 Individual Parts
 Subassemblies
 Final Assembly

In Dollars
 Labor
 Direct Material
 Indirect Material
 Supplies
 Factory Overhead

PURCHASING BUDGET

Cost of Raw Materials
Cost of Parts Purchased
Cost of Operating Purchasing
 Department

GENERAL EXPENSE BUDGET

Office Budget
General and Administrative
 Expenses
Capital Expenditures

Equals

ESTIMATED NET INCOME (profit or loss)

which is reflected in the

FINANCIAL BUDGET
Estimated Receipts from
 Sales
 Other Income

Estimated Disbursements for
 Selling Expenses
 Production
 Purchases
 General Expenses

which, in turn, may be arranged in the form of

An Estimated Balance Sheet   An Estimated Earnings Statement

the final result of which is that you

KNOW YOUR BUSINESS

Courtesy: Art Metal Construction Co., Jamestown, N.Y.

The chart shows the coordination of the various individual budgets and the type of information found in each one.

come or loss, which can be reflected in the financial budget, an estimated balance sheet, and an estimated earnings statement. The chart shows some of the details included under each individual budget.

Usually, the sales budget is developed first, since in many cases all other activities are predicated on what the sales expectancy picture is. Using the predicted sales as a basis, the plan for production, purchasing, and the like can be drawn up.

However, in some cases, this approach is reversed. The beginning is made by estimating the approximate income needed to provide a fair return on capital invested in the enterprise; then, one works back to determine the sales required, the production, and so on. There are variations of these two approaches, as well as other methods.

Most procedures for budget making consist of a series of steps somewhat like the following:

1. A conference of top management members is held to discuss trends and general outlook and to formulate broad policies regarding activities throughout the coming year.
2. The basis for the entire program, including sales and net income, or some other entity, is first drawn up by the executive in charge of the particular activity. It is then submitted for discussion and approval to the remaining top management members.
3. Each department head then prepares a budget for his own separate activity, guided by the data in the basic budget.
4. These budgets covering separate departments are submitted to the officer in charge of the budget, generally the controller or the budget officer.
5. A conference between the budget officer and each department head is then held for the purpose of thoroughly discussing and, when necessary, revising the respective individual department budget. Sometimes, a budget committee is used, in which case the budget officer transmits the estimates to the committee along with his recommendations.
6. After a tentative agreement on each individual budget has been reached, the master budget meeting is called. At this time, each individual budget is submitted and discussed. If necessary, adjustments are made, and final approval is obtained. This approval is generally contingent upon a final OK by the general manager or the president.
7. When finally determined, the budget is written up in its approved form, and copies are sent to all persons charged with carrying out a major portion of the plan. In like manner, copies covering specific parts of the master budget are distributed to lesser executives who are responsible for the execution of a particular portion of the plan.

The Period and Revision

The data of budgeting apply to a definite period. Usually this is one year, with breakdowns for quarterly and monthly periods. Two- and five-year periods are also used. If the period is one year, it usually coincides with the calendar year, although if operations are on a fiscal basis, the fiscal year is used.

The budgeting period selected should be long enough to include any seasonal or characteristic variations of "up and down" changes brought about by sales and production cycles. When fiscal income and expenditure are key considerations, the budgeting period should coincide with or fit into the time pattern already existing for other financial controls. And if the budget is to serve as a quarterly check, the time period should include a three-month period. If the purpose is a semiannual check, a six-month period will be used.

A widely adopted practice is to draw up the budget plan during November and December for the following year. Then, the revising and adjusting can follow any of a number of plans.

Under *periodic budgeting* major revisions are made three times a year—in March, June, and September—for the remaining months of the year. For example, in March, adjustments for the period April through December are made. If needed, revisions can be made at other times of the year as well.

Another arrangement is *progressive budgeting,* whereby definite times for major revisions are stated, such revisions covering definite periods following the revision date. For example, assume that revision times are bimonthly or at the end of February, April, June, August, October, and December, and that the period covered is six months. At the end of February, revisions would be made for the following six-month period, March through August; at the end of April, revisions are made for the period May through October; and so on. Revisions made at times other than the definite dates usually apply to the current budget only.

Also, *moving budgeting* can be followed under which a forecast for 12 months is maintained by adding a month as each month is completed. To illustrate, at the completion of October, 1976, a forecast for October, 1977, is added; therefore, the 12-month forecast would cover November, 1976, through October, 1977. Revisions in the forecasts covering the intervening months are made when necessary.

MAKING BUDGETARY CONTROL MORE EFFECTIVE

To recap several helpful considerations, the effectiveness of budgetary control is enhanced by:

1. Participating by All Affected by It. The best budgeting is everybody's budgeting. If it resembles or is thought to resemble the form of an edict from top managers, it becomes a punitive club instead of an effective tool of management. The broad constraints of budgeting are set forth by top managers who are in a position to visualize these needs. To develop and implement the practical means for reaching these goals is the opportunity of management and nonmanagement members who through their cooperation, interest, and suggestions make the budgeting effective and mutually beneficial to both themselves and the company.

2. Setting Specific Targets. Budgeting exists and is intended primarily to help accomplish specific goals within specific expenditures. Think of it in relationship to accomplishment. Budgeting is a tool for specific actions to reach specific goals. Never view it simply as an official means to approve or disapprove stated expenditures.

3. Including Practical Goals and Variances. The best budgeting reflects neither undue optimism nor pessimism. Realize both satisfactory and unsatisfactory results from actions are in the nature of things. View the future favorably but recognize some obstacles to budgeting will probably arise. Sound judgment should filter through all budgetary efforts.

4. Providing for Emergencies. Flexibility is vital in budgeting. The successful meeting of goals usually requires application of reason and intuition at all levels. To help in meeting day-to-day problems easily, budgeting should include possible answers for what to do if so-and-so takes place. Actions commonly change from those anticipated. The work force is increased or decreased, training is altered, layouts rearranged, promotions reduced. Provisions to meet these contingencies are needed. Otherwise the budgeting might well be viewed as an inviolable instrument that instills unsurmountable rigidities into the operations.

5. Looking at Favorable as Well as Unfavorable Variances. The natural tendency is to be most interested in unfavorable variances and to take proper action to correct them. However, it is frequently beneficial to review the favorable variances too. Some may cover activities that can be improved in light of current conditions, while others may be combined with other activities or even eliminated in view of current requirements.

QUESTIONS

1. Name the major approaches to office cost reduction, and discuss briefly the one you feel is most important.
2. Briefly discuss the human relations aspect of an office cost reduction program.

3. Your supervisor believes strongly that present copying costs are too high. You are asked to take any needed actions to reduce these costs. What would you do? Why?

4. State concisely the meaning and give an example of each of the following:
   a. Sunk cost.
   b. "Holes Committee."
   c. Cost-consciousness by employees.
   d. Overhead cost.

5. Do you agree with the following statement: "All cost reduction efforts should be considered from the overall office viewpoint, otherwise a cost reduction in one department may result in a cost increase in another department." Why?

6. From the standpoint of cost, do you recommend having the copying work on a centralized or a decentralized organizational arrangement? Discuss in full.

7. In your opinion, can an office be managed effectively without a budget? Defend your answer.

8. Discuss, evaluating the cost expenditure, giving all the necessary details and relate how this work fits into a cost controlling program.

9. A believes that if an item is in the budget, it is sufficient justification for spending that amount in order to utilize funds advantageously and keep them in balance. In contrast, B claims that, whenever possible, savings on every budget item should be made in order to keep costs at a minimum. With whom do you agree? Give your reasons.

10. Do you agree with the statement: "All budgets concern the office manager"? Explain your answer.

11. Discuss the consideration of providing for emergencies in efforts to make budgeting more effective.

12. As an office manager, what basic arrangement for revising the budget would you follow? Why?

CASE PROBLEMS

Case 28–1. Nelsen-Higham Company

Mr. James X. Mueller, information manager, recently called his employees together to discuss the cost of the work performed by them. In all there were an assistant, 12 managers including 8 supervisors, and 93 nonmanagement members. He criticized no one and stated he believed the overall record for his division was good. He added that Mr. Kiefer (executive vice president) was worried about current cost expenditures by the company and wanted to bring them down. While Mr. Kiefer did not single out any portion of the total operation for cost reduction, he did mention that overhead cost seemed high. From the company viewpoint, expenditures by the information division are included under overhead cost. In Mr. Mueller's opinion, there must be excess cost in the current information activities. He asked the members of his division if they thought they could and if they would like to try to do better than their current efforts.

The group responded strongly in the affirmative. Their interest and comments greatly encouraged Mr. Mueller. Once again he believed he headed one of the best group of employees anywhere. Some pertinent suggestions were made by the group members and the meeting adjourned on a note of optimism. Several days later requests from several supervisors were received by Mr. Mueller for current cost data. They pointed out that it was difficult to tell if improvement was being made when they did not know what costs the company expected or what current expenditures were. Mr. Mueller carried the requests to the cost department where he encountered opposition to releasing cost information such as he requested. It was a strict company policy not to release cost information to unauthorized personnel.

Mr. Mueller saw little possibility in securing the cost data requested. He called a meeting for his supervisors, informed them about the cost information requests, and related his turndown. He said he had some thoughts on what to do now, but would withhold them until the supervisors had a chance to offer their ideas. From this meeting it was decided that the supervisors would estimate the cost wherever feasible. Although an approximation, it would serve the purpose for cost reduction efforts. Records dealing with past performance would be useful. Laborsaving approaches should be sought. Every office employee should be made to feel he is competing with himself to gain cost reduction.

Accordingly each supervisor began to keep records of cost and to accumulate information which he believed helpful in his cost controlling efforts. After several months, Mr. Mueller was greatly encouraged by the progress being made. From the reports of his supervisors at the weekly meetings, the following cost reductions expressed on an annual basis were achieved:

Week	Cost Reduction
1	4.5%
2	3.5
3	3.0
4	3.0
5	2.5
6	1.5
7	3.0
8	1.0
9	1.0

Yesterday, at a management meeting called by Mr. Kiefer, the divisional heads were told that the company's profits had sharply declined during the past two months. To stem this trend, strong cost reduction measures would have to be instituted. The chief offender is overhead cost.

Questions:

1. Appraise the approach used by Mr. Mueller to reduce costs of the information operations.
2. Interpret the results of the cost reduction reported by the supervisors.
3. What action now do you recommend by Mr. Kiefer? By Mr. Mueller?

Case 28–2. O'Reilley Products Company

Stencil-duplicated material has been processed and used in the office of the O'Reilley Products Company for a number of years. Last year, for example, there were duplicated 1,780 memorandums of one page each, 307 reports of six pages each, and 225 reports of eight pages each. For each memorandum, an average of nine copies was made; for the six-page reports, eight copies; and for the eight-page reports, six copies.

Current costs of the company are 20 cents each for a stencil; ink, about $20 a year; labor for typing or operating the duplicator, $2.20 per hour; paper, $1.90 for 500 sheets when purchased in quantity. It requires approximately one minute per line to prepare stencils. The memorandums average 15 lines and the reports are 20 lines to a page. It takes about 8 minutes to put the stencil on the machine, adjust it, and later remove and file it. Speed of the machine is 80 sheets a minute. For hand collating and stapling of reports, a flat rate of 12 cents per report can be used.

Since the present duplicating machine is worn and must be replaced in the near future, the office manager believes that in addition to the stencil method, both the contact and the xerography methods should also be investigated for possible adoption. With this thought in mind, he has compiled cost data as follows. For the contact method, sensitized paper, one of which is needed for each page duplicated, costs 6 cents each, depreciation on the contact machine will be $65 per year, compared to $85 per year for a new stencil machine. Material costs, in addition to sensitized paper sheets, will approximate $30 per year for the contact machine, which it is estimated will produce 150 copies an hour. This includes the work of loading the machine. For xerography, output can be estimated at 350 copies an hour, machine lease cost at $375 a month, and machine supplies at about $0.001 per duplicated sheet. For either the contact or the xerography method, work of adjusting the stencil and removing it from machine is not required.

Questions:

1. Based on cost, which duplicating process should the office manager select? Sustantiate your answer.
2. In addition to cost, what other important factors should be considered by the office manager in arriving at a decision?
3. What should be the decision of the office manager? Why?

Case 28–3. Webber Associates

Being successful during the past with three-day seminars for office work, the managers of Webber Associates now contemplate a two-week or ten-day session program. They are mailing 3,000 announcements at a cost of 20¢ each for the mailing and $500 for preparing and printing these announcements. Each registrant will receive seminar materials estimated to cost the institute $36.50 per enrollee. Meetings will be held at the conveniently located Holiday Inn, which charges $35 a day for a conference room having a capacity of

92. The group will be served lunch each conference day in a special catering room of the hotel, for which a charge of $4 per person, including tips, is made. Also, hot beverages will be supplied at midmorning and again at mid-afternoon in the rear of the conference room. For this service, a charge of $1 per day per enrollee will be made. A total of 14 instructors will be used to cover the various subjects; but only two different instructors for any one day will be scheduled, each handling the group for half a day. Compensation for an instructor for half a day is $125 plus lunch regardless of whether the assigned class is in the morning or in the afternoon.

As a policy, the institute invites ten prominent management members in office work to attend the seminar free of charge. They are extended all the benefits of a regular fee-paying attendee. It intends to follow this same policy with the proposed larger session. Based on past experience, about one half of the invited guests attend. The institute requires a minimum margin of approximately 25 percent of the total income from a seminar. That is, if the total income was $1,000, the institute strives to keep expenses at no more than $750. Registrations from mailings for other seminars have ranged from 1.5 percent to 5.1 percent of the total number of mailings sent out. However, the managers of the institute are at a loss to know whether these response ranges are valid for a seminar such as they are now planning.

Questions:

1. Discuss the major problem facing the institute.
2. Calculate the approximate registration fee that the institute should charge for the office automation seminar.
3. What plan of action do you feel the institute should follow? Why?

Indexes

Case Index

Subject Index

A

Absenteeism, 598–99
  means to reduce, 599
Access time, 238, 256
Accidents; *see also* Safe work place
  attitude of employee toward, 607–9
  frequency rate, 612
  prevention of, 606–7
  severity rate, 612
  triple E program of prevention, 607
Accountability, 406
  by subordinate, 513
Accounting forms, 109
Accounting information, 622
Accounting machines, 173–76
Accounts payable, 176
Accounts receivable, 176
Accumulator, 238
Accuracy ratio, 334
Achievement, 492
Acquired wants, 493
Active information, 8
Active line, 238
Activities control, 641
Activity/little accomplishment work, 81
Actuating function, 14–17, 485 ff.; *see also* Motivation
  computer use in, 204
  decision making in, 497
  supervisors, 538
Adding machines, 173, 176–77
Addressing machines, 190–91
  applications of, 190
  attachments, 190–91

Addressing machines—*Cont.*
  cutoff device, 190
  dating device, 191
  metal plates, 190
  repeater, 190–91
  selector, 190
  tabbing sockets, 191
Administrative management, 4
Administrative Management Society, 388, 634
Administrative secretary, 153–54
Administrative services organizational arrangement, 359–61
  top staff, 360–61
Administrative substation utilization, 465–67
Administrative tasks, 32–34
Administrative Terminal System (ATS), 238
Adult ego state, 520
Advancement, 555; *see also* Promotions
Advertising, 384–85
Advisory staff authority, 417–18
Affirmative Action Programs, 580
Aggression, 492, 494
Air conditioning, 452–53
  circulation, 452–53
  cleanliness, 452–53
  cost, 453
  humidity, 453
  moisture content, 452–53
  temperature, 452–53
Airmail, 269
Aisle space standards, 472–74
Alibis, 494

*This book has been set in 10 and 9 point
Caledonia, leaded 2 points. Part numbers are
24 point Scotch Roman italic and part titles
are 18 point Scotch Roman. Chapter numbers
are 18 and 36 point Scotch Roman and chapter
titles are 18 point Scotch Roman italic. The
size of the type page is 27 × 45½ picas.*